onsensus nd Com- munity	Order and Social Control	Revolution	Prop[e] and t[he] Econo[my]		[P]sychology	[Id]eology [a]nd Religion	History and Social Change
48–52	43–48	64–65	34–35	31–34	27		63–68
77–81 106	108–114	101–114	83–84 100 109–110	90–91 96–100	79–80 82–83		100–101 114
137–138	128–130 136–137	143–145	152–153	130–132	138–140 142–143	119–156	152–155
	171–179	174–175		163–166	166–170 188–192	177–178	186–192
	222–225 228–229	217–218 227–228			202–205	223	
		283–285	238–240 250–265		262–265	254–255 269–270	237–238
303–311 330–339	319–322		297–300		290–303 337–339		
356–357 366–368	368–377	333–334 353–355	368–371	361–368	349–361 374–377	371–374	349–357
	412–413		413–415		401–410		
440–442	440–441 450–451		449–450	435–438 449–452	430–432 438–442 456–459		423–445
	466–470	489–491	483–492	486–492 494–498	478–489		
557–561	537–543 553–557	547–553	517–570	523–557	532–537 543–547	562	517–570
	582–588 592–594		603–604	599–609	590–591 600–601	590	599

POLITICAL THEORY:
Philosophy, Ideology, Science

THE MACMILLAN COMPANY
NEW YORK • CHICAGO
DALLAS • ATLANTA • SAN FRANCISCO
LONDON • MANILA
IN CANADA
BRETT-MACMILLAN LTD.
GALT, ONTARIO

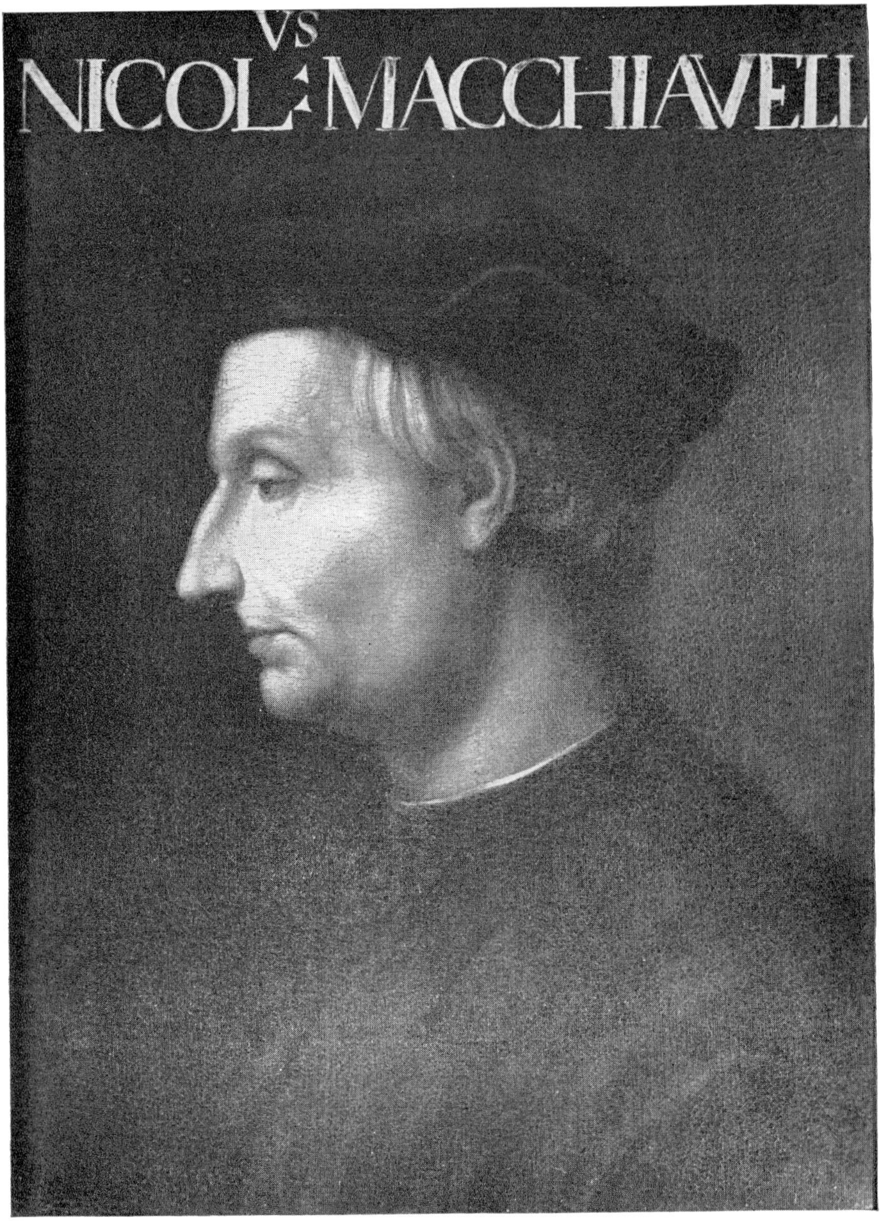
VS
NICOL: MACCHIAVELL

POLITICAL THEORY:

Philosophy, Ideology, Science

ANDREW HACKER

Cornell University

THE MACMILLAN COMPANY

New York

First Printing

Library of Congress catalog card number: 61–5203

The Macmillan Company, New York
Brett-Macmillan Ltd., Galt, Ontario

Printed in the United States of America

To My Father

Preface

For better or for worse, the term "political theory" has two quite distinct meanings for contemporary students of politics. It stands, first of all, for the history of political ideas. Starting with Plato, these ideas are regarded as contributions to an intellectual tradition. They are studied with due regard for the historical circumstances which produced them, and their influence on political practice is a constant matter for speculation. This understanding of political theory is the more traditional of the two, and an honorable tradition of scholarship supports it. The other conception of the theory is newer and, in consequence, less sure of its methods and purposes. Nevertheless, it can be said that this approach calls for the systematic study of political behavior in the modern world. Whereas the older conception has as its subject matter the historical texts and the conditions which surrounded their writing, the more recent approach to theory sees as its subject the actual behavior of men and institutions in our own time. Systematic theory, then, is concerned to create generalizations which describe and explain contemporary political phenomena. By and large it places great importance on the methods of collecting data, for systematic knowledge must be founded on evidence rather than intuition. On the whole, this approach to theory tries to avoid making value judgments or entering into ethical controversies.

As matters stand, there are few bridges between these two conceptions of political theory. The reasons for this are not hard to find. Research in the two fields is generally pursued by scholars of different temperaments and interests. One group is concerned with the development of ideas over an extended period of time; the other is intent on discovering and ordering the facts of contemporary political life. One group defines scholarship as a detailed understanding of the greater and lesser texts of an intellectual tradition; the other sees research in terms of first-hand investigation of the real world and conceptual rigor in the handling of facts. In addition, students of the history of ideas are prone to use the vocabulary they find in the classical writings: General Will, Natural Rights, Sovereignty. Those who are engaged in systematic research, on the other hand, have evolved a language

vii

which draws not only on the words of other social sciences but also the symbols of mathematics: thus one will hear of a Role-Player, a Reference Group, a Correlation Coefficient, and a Chi-Square. And the historical theorists are always prepared to discourse on the philosophical ends which men and societies ought to pursue, whereas their systematic colleagues, as was pointed out, prefer to omit explicit discussion of political goals for fear that this will distort their understanding of the facts.

The differences and the tensions between these two approaches to theory are, in very large measure, based on an ignorance of what the other is trying to do. The historians of ideas tend to see the systematic theorists as undertaking elaborate research projects, and yet it appears to them that the "theories" which emerge are little more than pretentious elaborations of the obvious. At the same time the students of intellectual history are characterized as living in a world of unreality, and their concern with mulling over the ancient writings is seen as pedantry without purpose. Both of these conceptions are wrong, and if they have some small truth in them it is because each school fastens on the more rampant excesses of the other. One of the major aims of this book will be to show the systematic theorists that the historical texts contain just the sort of analysis which is central to their studies. And, coincidentally, it may be demonstrated to the historians of ideas that recent efforts at systematic theory are not unrelated to the propositions discussed in the classical writings. While the intended purpose of this book is to summarize and explain a body of political theory from Plato to Mill, at the same time the hope is held out that a few lines of communication may be extended between two conceptions of the discipline.

Fifteen writers will be considered here, and each one will be given close and detailed attention. These fifteen have been selected on the straightforward ground that, out of the hundreds of authors who have sought to write political theory, their ideas continue to have relevance and significance for our own time. In the intellectual world there is a survival of the fittest, and fitness may here be defined as an understanding of the political life which retains its validity despite the passage of centuries. Furthermore, only the one or two most important works of each of these writers will be discussed. (The only exception to this rule is Marx and Engels, where it is necessary to piece together their political theory from a wide range of sources.) For what is intended is not to cover the whole of a man's philosophy but rather to concentrate on those of his writings which give his political ideas. Were St. Augustine's Confessions or John Locke's Essay Concerning Human Understanding to be introduced, then considerations of space would compel abbreviation of the more frankly political writings. It is not without some regret that works in moral philosophy, such as Aristotle's Ethics or Mill's Utilitarianism, are omitted, for moral and political philosophy stand in direct relation to each other. But in most instances a writer's ideas concerning the

viii

good life are incorporated in his reflections on the good society, and the over-all loss is not as great as might at first be imagined.

To close with John Stuart Mill is not to suggest that there have been no significant contributions to political theory since 1861. At the same time, it is probably wise to err on the side of conservatism and to suggest that it usually takes a full century to discover whether a book and author have the stature which makes for intellectual survival. There is no doubt that there are currently in our midst writers who will one day have the standing of Hobbes, Locke, and Hegel. But it would be premature to pick out any of these theorists now and mark them for eternity; the responsibility for deciding who is to be added to the role of immortals had better wait until the next generation. At the same time, the value of the historical texts lies in the fact that they concentrate their attention on general principles and do not devote much space to the question of specific applications. Locke, for example, talks in a general way of the political role played by private property, but he leaves it to others to elaborate on and apply his ideas. For this reason there will be found in each chapter one or more short discussions showing how these theories may be used for a better understanding of the politics and society we know today. In addition to this, there will be references from time to time to recent writers who have refined or developed the classical principles so they may be applied more specifically to the contemporary world.

There is no substitute, of course, for reading the original texts in their entirety. However, most students of politics do not have the time to sit down with twenty or more weighty volumes, and many are prudent enough to admit that they need help in interpreting what they read. Anyone who sets himself up to explain the writings of one person for the benefit of another stands in an exposed position. The interpreter may claim to be giving no more than a straightforward summary of the original author. Yet his method of selection and emphasis may produce a gross caricature. Indeed, his interpretations may be so distorted that what results is the commentator's own ideas and prejudices, and not those of the writer under consideration. These tendencies are unavoidable, and they are not without some advantages in their own right. However, one or two comments may be made on the approach taken in this book. First, a careful and sympathetic attempt has been made to summarize what each theorist says and, no less important, to discover a rational meaning in his propositions. An effort has been made to present enough in the way of direct quotations so that the original author can be observed speaking for himself in his own language. Second, it is going to be assumed that all of the theorists under discussion are intelligent and sensible men, even if many of them are erratic in their presentation. Therefore, the interpretive remarks will take the form of a sincere attempt to make political sense of what they are saying. The approach will at all times be a sympathetic one, and if apparent inconsistencies or absurdities come to view, the author will be given the benefit of the doubt. There will be no discussion of what other interpreters have said about these writers, as this book is concerned with theories about politics and not theories about theories. This means, finally, that the criticism and evaluation of ideas will in great part be left to the hands of their fellow-theorists. Aristotle, as will be seen, points out Plato's errors; Locke endeavors to answer Hobbes, Burke replies to Rousseau; and Marx and Engels try to convince us where Hegel went wrong. Political theory is a never-ending conversation among theorists. And while the greatest of the debates are never resolved, the criticisms which the writers make of each other are always the most vivid and illuminating. Just as the theorists themselves argue with each other, so is this a book to be argued with. Neither the summaries nor the interpretations offered here make any claim to being the last word. Politics is, after all, the most democratic of sciences. The final judgments concerning political reality and the good life are the responsibility of all who undertake the study of theory.

Acknowledgments. Every student owes a debt to his teachers, and this debt can be acknowledged even if it can never be repaid. At successive stages of my career I have experienced the inspiration and influence of Earl Latham at Amherst College, Wilfrid Harrison and the late G. D. H. Cole at Oxford University, Alpheus T. Mason and William Ebenstein at Princeton University. A number of friends and colleagues have read and criticized portions of this book in manuscript form. My thanks for this help are due to Mario Einaudi, James Lare, J. Roland Pennock, William Riker, H. Mark Roelofs, Clinton Rossiter, David Spitz, and E. L. Wheelwright. I have been fortunate in having three diligent and intelligent typists: Lois Hurlbut, Ruth Cogen, and Joan Scholes. The Social Science Research Center and the Ford Public Affairs Research Committee of Cornell University gave me financial assistance so that two summers could be devoted to work on this book.

A.H.

Contents

xiii

Political Theory:
Philosophy, Ideology, Science

1.
What Is
Political Theory?

THE QUESTION WHICH HEADS THIS PAGE CANNOT RECEIVE A satisfactory answer in an opening chapter. For it is only at the close of a book such as this that a student is ready to speculate on matters of definition and purpose. The best preparation for this task is to give close study to some actual political theories. Only after a wide variety of writers have been observed at work is it possible to formulate an informed judgment on questions of function, method, and style. For this reason, all that will be attempted at this stage will be to set down some rules of thumb on the use of terms and some reflections on the relation between history and political theory.

SCIENCE, PHILOSOPHY, IDEOLOGY

"There are two characters, one or other of which every man who finds anything to say on the subject of law, may be said to take upon him;—that of the expositor, and that of the censor. To the province of the expositor it belongs to explain to us what, as he supposes, the law is: to that of the censor, to observe to us what he thinks it ought to be." So writes Jeremy Bentham in the opening chapter of his *Fragment on Government*.[1] While Bentham has special reasons for confining his remarks to the study of law, what he has to say applies equally well to the study of political theory. In the place of his antediluvian characters, the expositor and the censor, modern usage speaks of the political scientist and the political philosopher. The distinction between these two branches of political theory may be an oversimplification, but it cannot be dispensed with even in an age which is unsympathetic to sharp dichotomies of thought. The theorist whose pursuit is political science is interested in

[1] In *Fragment on Government and Principles of Morals and Legislation* (Oxford: Blackwell, 1948), edited by Wilfrid Harrison, p. 7.

1

describing and explaining the realties of political behavior. He attempts to draw up generalized propositions about the actual relations between states and citizens and about the role of power in society. Not all efforts at description and explanation can lay claim to the status of science, and there is no small controversy concerning what attributes a theory must have if it is to be called scientific. The scope of a theory's subject matter and the research methods employed by the writer will both determine its reception by those who pass judgment on these matters. For the present moment, however, this problem of definition will be left unresolved. It will suffice to say that a theory is an essay in political science if it seems to be the author's intention to offer generalized descriptions or explanations of the behavior of men and political institutions. In later chapters more objective tests will be applied. The theorist whose interest is in writing political philosophy, on the other hand, is concerned with prescribing the goals which citizens, states, and societies ought to pursue. His aim is to generalize about right conduct in the political life and about the legitimate uses of power. Not all prescriptions, to be sure, can lay claim to being truly philosophical. For philosophy in our tradition is a grand enterprise, and the ends prescribed by a philosopher must be broad in conception and wide in application. For the time being, however, questions of definition must be left to later chapters. A theorist may be regarded as engaging in political philosophy if his aim is to suggest rules of behavior which states and citizens ought to follow. How he derives these prescriptions and how they gain an authoritative status will be discussed in specific terms in the pages to follow.

Every political theorist worthy of the name plays a double role. He is part scientist and part philosopher, and he will divide his time between the two pursuits according to his own temperament and interests.[2] Aristotle and Machiavelli, for example, devote most of their energies to creating descriptive theories. Plato and Rousseau, on the other hand, are primarily concerned to provide prescriptions for the rest of us to follow. What is important to bear in mind is that no theorist can make a lasting contribution to human knowledge unless he works in the realms of both science and philosophy. The scientific parts of a theory can only achieve coherence and significance if the writer has a preconceived idea of the goals of political life. There can be no

2 One way of apportioning the emphases has been suggested by Harold D. Lasswell and Abraham Kaplan: "A rough classification of a sample of 300 sentences from each of the following yielded these proportions of political philosophy (demand statements and valuations) to political science (statements of fact and empirical hypotheses): Aristotle's *Politics*, 25 to 75; Rousseau's *Social Contract*, 45 to 55; . . . Machiavelli's *Prince*, by contrast, consisted entirely (in the sample) of statements of political science in the present sense." *Power and Society: A Framework for Political Inquiry* (New Haven: Yale University Press, 1950), p. 118n.

such things as "pure" description or an "objective" political science. The reality which is described is a selective one, and the author's basis for selection is ultimately philosophical. An individual's moral sense always gives shape to his perceptions and governs his interpretation of what he sees. Burke and Bentham, for example, might be confronted with the same political reality, yet each would select his emphasis according to a different light; and the subsequent judgment of each would be in sharp variance to that of the other. Both of these men are political scientists of the first rank, and their stature is not diminished by the fact that they are influenced by philosophical preconceptions. By the same token, the philosophical parts of a theory will be informed by a profound understanding of the facts of political life. The best political philosophers have always been well aware of the existing realities; they have given intense and systematic study to the needs and capabilities of man and society. Even Utopian theorists like Plato and Rousseau realize that their prescriptions set standards impossible for men to follow. The principles which they and their fellow philosophers set down are written only after careful observation of man's experience in the past. Their knowledge of what has occurred throughout history will shape the outlines of what they prescribe for the present and future. There can be no such things, then, as "pure" prescription or an "objective" political philosophy. A philosopher is obliged to demonstrate that he understands what may reasonably be expected of men and societies in their pursuit of political goals. It is left to each reader to ask where the scientific part of a theory stops and the philosophy begins. It is his responsibility, as well, to ascertain how far and at what junctures one influences the other. The theorists themselves are not very helpful on this score. Bentham and Marx, for example, both claim that their writings are untainted by philosophy. The reader should look on such professions with skepticism at all times and endeavor to find the unacknowledged moral assumptions which underlie the theories. They are there.

There is a third variety of political theory which calls for brief comment here. A writer may address himself to his audience, saying something like this: "If this is the end that you want to achieve, then these are the means that you ought to use." Is this kind of proposition scientific or philosophical? It is prescriptive in that it advises on a particular course of conduct. But it is not truly philosophical because the theorist does not suggest the goal to be pursued: the choice of ends is left to the reader, and the theorist only advises on means. This if-then kind of prescription is found, to a greater or less extent, in all theoretical writings, and it may be called "policy science." A policy scientist can only counsel other people on what they ought to do because he has an extensive knowledge of political reality. He is an expert in political behavior, and he is willing to predict which policies are more suitable for obtaining ends that men might want to secure. A policy scientist, for example, might suggest the best ways to prevent revolutions or methods to increase the amount of citizen participation in public affairs. But whether revolutions should be prevented or whether widespread participation are themselves good things are left for others to answer. Policy science, then, is prescriptive only in a technical sense. It is, for the most part, descriptions of how men will behave if you put them in certain hypothetical situations. This question will receive further attention in the chapter on Machiavelli.

"As things are, writers fall into two different classes. Some confine their investigations to the extreme perfection. . . . The rest, addressing themselves rather to an attainable form, still banish from view the general range of existing constitutions, and simply extol . . . one constitution." [3] What Aristotle is saying here is that theorists tend to be either Utopians or ideologues. The former, and Aristotle clearly had Plato in mind at the time, build castles in the air which bear little relation to the needs or capabilities of actual men. The latter group of writers are more down to earth, and they will be considered now. For the chief criticism of the ideologue is that his feet are too firmly planted in his own soil. Is it not strange, Aristotle would ask, that political theorists who live in the United States so frequently seem to end up concluding that the American political system is the best one going? Is it more than coincidence that of all the governmental forms in use throughout the world, the one in our own back yard just happens to be the best? By the same token, there are theorists in many countries who find all the political virtues embodied in the Soviet Union or Communist China. The point, of course, is that in cases like these what is being written is not political theory but rather ideology. Presumably the search for political principles should be carried on independent of national loyalties; presumably the political ends one is seeking to discover can be found in another part of the world no less than one's own. Yet such presumptions can seldom be made. All political theorists are inevitably ideologues, because, like other men, they are creatures of emotion and interest. It is possible, at least for purposes of analysis, to distinguish theory from ideology. A theory, in ideal terms, is dispassionate and disinterested. As science, it will describe political reality without trying to pass judgment on what is being depicted either implicitly or explicitly. As philosophy, it will prescribe rules of conduct which will secure the good life for all of society and not simply for certain individuals or classes. The theorist, in theory, will not himself have a personal interest in the politi-

[3] Aristotle, *Politics* (Oxford: Oxford University Press, 1946), edited and translated by Ernest Barker, pp. 155–156.

cal arrangements of any one country or class or party. Devoid of such an interest, his vision of reality and his image of the good life will not be clouded, nor will his theory be special pleading. Yet scholarly detachment of this order seldom exists, and when it does it is usually unable to make a significant contribution to our political understanding. The intention of ideology is to justify a particular system of power in society. The ideologue is an interested party: his interest may be to defend things as they are or to criticize the status quo in the hope that a new distribution of power will come into being.[4] In the latter case the writer has a vested interest in the future: he will be speaking in the name of revolution or reform, and he has a stake in the political arrangements which may emerge in time to come. Much of what passes for political philosophy, then, is ideology. Rather than disinterested prescription, we have rationalization. Much of what passes for political science is no less ideological. Rather than dispassionate description, we have a distorted picture of reality. The distortion is not so much a matter of outright lies as it is a partial or selective depiction: one ideologue will emphasize a society's positive features, while another will stress its more sordid aspect; one will suggest that a radically different future can only be an improvement, while another will imply that any change from existing arrangements is bound to be either hazardous or harmful. What has been said so far, therefore, can be summarized as follows:

THEORY	IDEOLOGY
Philosophy: A disinterested search for the principles of the good state and the good society.	*"Philosophy":* A rationalization for current or future political and social arrangements.
Science: A disinterested search for knowledge of political and social reality.	*"Science":* A distorted description or explanation of political and social reality.

Not all theorists are aware of the ideology which inheres in their writing, and of those who are not all feel obliged to declare their interests. Theories, furthermore, vary in their ideological content; if Burke and Hegel stand high on such an index, Aristotle and Bentham have a relatively low rating. Yet, despite the rationalizations and distortions which are endemic to political theory, a substantial body of disinterested knowledge has emerged over the years. Each generation produces a theorist who, while blinded and bounded by interests, manages to achieve a broader perspective and to provide generali-

[4] The classic work in the field of ideology is Karl Mannheim's *Ideology and Utopia* (New York: Harcourt, Brace, 1936). Mannheim's usage has been revised here to the extent that the rhetoric of reform, which he calls "Utopia," is now considered as a special branch of ideology.

zations which transcend the immediate conditions of his time. Most writers in the field of political ideas are so blatantly ideological that they are consigned to obscurity within a few years or are only remembered for their antiquarian interest. The pyramid of pamphlets and polemics which they produce may be called "political thought." Anyone with a mind can think about politics, and anyone with a pen can set down his political thoughts. But only a small minority can theorize. Only a few writers have the intelligence and insight to cut through the ideological prisms which distort the perceptions and warp the mind. The men who achieve this intellectual feat may legitimately be called theorists, and they are the ones who will be read long after their time has past.

THE SEARCH FOR SIGNIFICANCE

The historical writers are not nearly as preoccupied with questions of methodology as are contemporary theorists. For them the problem of how to write theory seldom gives pause; they simply go ahead and write it. And if, in framing their generalizations, they often throw scholarly caution to the winds, this is because they are more intent on making their points than they are on adhering to the niceties of method. Machiavelli, for example, says: "It may be said of men in general, that they are ungrateful, voluble, dissemblers, anxious to avoid danger, and covetous of gain." [5] On reading this proposition the first impulse is to protest that it simply is not true. Men may be the things that Machiavelli says they are, but they are also trustworthy, loyal, helpful, friendly, and kind. Yet to say that Machiavelli's characterization of mankind is not the whole truth is protesting too much and too soon. The reader should first of all acknowledge that Machiavelli is no fool, and he knows full well that his description is selective and one-sided. He is aware that men are often trustworthy and loyal, helpful and friendly. If he omits mention of these worthy attributes and chooses to emphasize the more somber ones, then he has a reason for doing so. It is the reader's responsibility to discover why Machiavelli selects this particular emphasis. The answer, at least in part, is that it is his concern to develop a general theory of political behavior. To do this he must uncover and lay stress on the dominant tendencies at work in human relationships. A theory can only make a significant contribution to political understanding if its author is willing to speculate on the major trends. The theorist's main tools, in short, are the depth of his intelligence and the range of his imagination. "Let us begin by laying the facts

[5] Machiavelli, *The Prince*, in *The Prince and the Discourses* (New York: Modern Library, 1940), p. 61.

aside, as they do not affect the issue."[6] When Rousseau comes out with a statement like this, he simply means that too much information can divert our attention from the major issues. Suppose that Machiavelli had taken a more common-sense view and had granted that men are both brave and cowardly, trustworthy and deceitful, good and evil. The trouble with taking account of all the facts is that it admits all the ambiguities. A theory which says that men have equal proportions of good and evil in them is, in the final analysis, no theory at all. Generalizations are always risky, but to be meaningful they must come down on one side or the other.[7] A political theorist has to be committed to a point of view, and this often entails uttering a half-truth or selecting a single tendency for disproportionate emphasis. He must, in sum, have the courage to speculate on the important questions and to put the facts aside when they get in his way.

Some theorists take great pains to convince their readers that the generalizations they develop rise out of systematic treatment of the available data. Aristotle, Machiavelli, Bentham, and Marx and Engels all claim to use scientific methods, and they would like us to believe that their conclusions rest squarely on a rigorous analysis of the facts. These professions ought not to be taken too seriously. Once these writers embark on the study of serious questions they forget about methodological rigor and say whatever it is they really want to say. The real problem, to return to Rousseau, is what role is to be assigned to facts in the writing of theory. The approach taken by modern writers is to say that facts should be treated as *evidence:* they should be gathered and analyzed in such ways that they give convincing and conclusive substantiation to the generalizations they support. If evidence is not available, or if the methods by which it is obtained are subject to dispute, then the theorist should refrain from overstating his case. The traditional approach is far less cautious. The historical writers possess a great deal of factual information, and they are free in their use of it. Burke, for example, gives a statistical analysis of the French budget in 1789, and Tocqueville reports conversations he had concerning the voting rights of American Negroes. Yet these facts are being used as *illustrations:* they are employed as examples and their purpose is to clarify the generalizations which the theorist is intent on

---

[6] Rousseau, *A Discourse on the Origin of Inequality,* in *The Social Contract and Discourses* (London: Everyman, 1913), translated by G. D. H. Cole, p. 161.

[7] Albert Einstein has this to say: "In the field of politics and social science there has grown up a justified distrust of generalizations pushed too far. When thought is too greatly dominated by such generalizations, misinterpretations of specific sequences of cause and effect readily occur, doing injustice to the actual multiplicity of events. Abandonment of generalization, on the other hand, means to relinquish understanding altogether. For that reason I believe one may and must risk generalization so long as one remains aware of its uncertainty." *Out of My Later Years* (New York: Philosophical Library, 1950), p. 252.

making. These data, in other words, do not constitute evidence which has been systematically obtained and on the strength of which a theory will stand or fall. The historical writers would say that the kind of questions with which they are dealing are so subtle and complex that factual verification of the answers is not really possible. For this reason, they are frequently unable to present a convincing case that what they say is true.[8] But this, to their minds, is not a major concern; they are far more interested in saying something which is significant.

If the search for significance rests in large measure on the restless and roaming imagination of the theorist, there is always the danger that his inspirations will get out of hand. Some writers construct Utopias which are so ingeniously devised that virtually every unsolved problem of existing society is—at least on paper—either ameliorated or abolished. Others build logical systems which effortlessly—again on paper—integrate theories of personality, political institutions, and social structure. Many students of politics, on gazing at these majestic edifices, sense that they are too good to be true. Too many complex questions seem to be answered without much of an intellectual struggle; too many variables are assumed capable of being integrated into a few preconceived formulas. It is not hard, in these instances, to detect that some of the key assumptions are faulty. What of Bentham's idea that all men seek pleasure and desire to avoid pain? Or Plato's that just as the individual is divided into a mind and a body, so society is naturally bifurcated into a ruling and a ruled class? Or Marx's that capitalism will decay because of its internal contradictions and be replaced by a communist society? There is always a strong temptation to discard an entire theory because one or more of its major assumptions seems to be patently untrue. This tendency is heightened when the theorist himself suggests that his writings are a seamless web with all parts dependent on all others. Nevertheless, it must be repeated that truth and significance are never the easiest of bedfellows. If important issues are to receive discussion, then standards of logic and even of veracity must be relaxed. Furthermore, it should be pointed out that within the interstices of the grand schemes propounded by the historical writers there

_____

[8] The great divide which Reinhard Bendix sees in sociology is no less a problem for political theory: "It has been observed that methodological rigor can be obtained only at the price of dealing with relatively insignificant problems, whereas the investigation of significant problems suffers from a lack of this rigor. We can obtain agreement on social science propositions, but the content of the propositions makes us question whether this knowledge is worth obtaining. Yet, when we deal with propositions which we feel are worthwhile, we find it almost impossible to 'prove' them. Modern social science reveals a cleavage between propositions which are significant and propositions which command assent, and there is no sign as yet that this condition will be improved." *Social Science and the Distrust of Reason* (Berkeley and Los Angeles: University of California Press, 1951), p. 28.

are many "theories of the middle range" which have value for political understanding even if they are abstracted out of their general systems.[9] Aristotle's theory of social class is an example of a middle-range theory, and it is useful even when dissociated from the rest of Aristotle's framework. The same holds true for St. Thomas' theory of law, Machiavelli's of elites, and Hobbes' of political education. Locke on property, Hegel on nationalism, and Mill on representation are further instances of theories which apply to partial but important segments of the political life. To be sure, each one of these middle-range theories may have deep roots in the writer's larger system, and to sever it from its original context is bound to produce some intellectual damage. Nevertheless, the student of politics cannot always stand on ceremony at this point. He is entitled to secure his education wherever he can, and he should not be reluctant to accept some of a theorist's ideas while at the same time he discards others. The time is not yet at hand when an all-embracing system by a single writer will be found satisfactory in most major respects. The human mind is an instrument of as yet untapped potentialities, and we can be sure that new theorists will emerge to shed light on the areas of darkness which now exist. At the same time, a reading of the historical writers will demonstrate the limits of even outstanding intellects when they grapple with the central questions of political theory. Political science and political philosophy have always been a great debate; theories are ultimately dependent for their acceptance on the minds and hearts of their readers. So long as students are skeptical in temperament and possessed of varying interests there is little point in asking for definitive descriptions or universal prescriptions. The most we can demand is that the significant questions which face man and society be pursued with wisdom and imagination. And this, there can be no mistaking, is what the historical writers have done.

THE HISTORY OF POLITICS
AND THE HISTORY OF IDEAS

It is impossible to read or write political theory without an understanding of history. Knowledge of the present, no matter how pervasive, gives no

[9] What Robert Merton has to say about the study of sociology applies equally well to political theory: "Sociology will advance in the degree that its major concern is with developing theories of the middle range and will be frustrated if attention centers on theory in the large. I believe that our major task today is to develop special theories applicable to limited ranges of data—theories, for example, of class dynamics, of conflicting pressure groups, of the flow of power, and the exercise of interpersonal influence—rather than to seek at once the 'integrated' conceptual structure adequate to derive all these and other theories." *Social Theory and Social Structure* (Glencoe: Free Press, 1957), revised edition, p. 9.

standard for judgment and no perspective for analysis. The institutions and behavior we observe in our brief moment of time are the products of centuries; the principles and precepts we acknowledge are embedded in a long tradition. The historical knowledge which a political theorist stands in need of is not the chronicle of kings and battles. Indeed, discrete personalities and events are among the least of his concerns. Nor should history be regarded as a convenient shelf of examples, one or another of which can be plucked down the better to make a point. The proper study of history must be broad in conception. It need not embrace sweeping "laws" of development, but it should ask questions about the evolution of a society's structure, about the rise of its technology and economic organization, about the growth of its institutions of government. Social classes, productive processes, and political power do not emerge overnight and they cannot be understood if they are examined only in their contemporary setting. The historical writers were all well aware of this fact, and their theories are not snapshots of a single moment in time but rather dynamic portraits of the evolving relationships between man and society.

One illustration may give some clarity to this point. The idea and the fact of political liberty emerged historically in the context of a particular social structure and at a certain stage of economic development. The theory which defines liberty as freedom from political and social restraints was propounded by Locke, Tocqueville, and Mill, and it was given full account by Rousseau, Burke, and Marx and Engels. The demand for political liberty had a definite meaning in this historical epoch, and the behavior of states and citizens can only be understood by referring to the class structure and the economic institutions of that time. The men who wanted to be free had undergone certain experiences and they harbored certain aspirations. There is no small feeling in our own day that this conception of freedom should be preserved and encouraged. If history is paid its due attention, however, the student cannot fail to acknowledge that both society and economy have changed markedly since the inception of the idea. It is not at all clear that the liberty which flowered in one historical period can find roots in an age which no longer has the social and economic institutions of that which preceded it. No attempt can be made here to deal with this specific problem. What is being suggested is that the theorist of today must always be prepared to ask historical questions. Only then will he have a basis for comparison and judgment. Only then will he understand where he is now and where he may be going.

The ideological component is no less strong in the study of history than it is in political theory. The view of the past upon which Rousseau and

Marx and Engels build their theories is one of class struggle and the exploitation of man by man. These writers see a somber past, because it is their belief that society ought to move on to a new and better future. It is altogether clear that their accounts cannot be regarded as objective reports. Nor are they meant to be. History assumes importance for political theory only when it is put to imaginative and purposeful use. By the same token, Burke and Tocqueville glorify the past: they see it as an age of harmony, civility, and ordered liberty. They emphasize the deference to authority and the social stability which characterized the old order. Their aim, of course, is to stress the virtues of an earlier age so as to forestall any radical departures on the political and social scene. Burke and Tocqueville, indeed, invent a mythical history and use it as a variety of Utopia. Rather than projecting an idyllic future into which men might be exhorted to move, they recreate a halcyon past to which we ought to return. The ideological overtones in these theories, the implicit judgments passed on the way of life men knew in an earlier period, need not obscure their underlying value. The use—and even the misuse—of history by these writers sharpens their own description and evaluation of the present. Through their reliance on history they make clear the social and economic setting in which political institutions arise and maintain themselves. The past becomes a point of comparison and hence a standard by which new developments may be judged. Without a sense of history the political theorist lacks an awareness of the range and variety of human behavior.[10] With it he begins to discern an order in man's experience and to give perspective to his efforts at analysis.

The history under discussion here is the history of politics and society, of organized power and men as movements. Altogether different from this is another field of intellectual endeavor: the history of political ideas. Politics consists in the deeds men do and the controls societies exert. Political ideas —the thoughts which both theorists and lesser men set down on paper throughout the ages—have only the most speculative of connections with the institutions and behavior which comprise political theory. To say this is to enter an age-old controversy of the academic world. Do the men of ideas have an influence on the conduct of the men of power? It is the judgment of

[10] C. Wright Mills' advice to sociologists should also be taken to heart by students of political theory: "Whatever the problem with which you are concerned, you will find it helpful to try to get a comparative grip on the materials. The search for comparable cases, either in one civilization and historical period or in several, gives you leads. You never think of describing an institution in twentieth-century America without trying to bear in mind similar institutions in other types of structures and periods. That is so even if you do not make explicit comparisons. In time you will come almost automatically to orient your reflection historically." *The Sociological Imagination* (New York: Oxford University Press, 1959), p. 215.

such disparate writers as Plato and Marx that ideas have a negligible impact on political behavior. Nevertheless, there are many students of political theory who sincerely believe that the history of ideas and the history of action stand in intimate relation to each other: it is sometimes argued that ideas influence action; on other occasions it is said that they at least reflect or explain the deeds of the real political world. The consequence of this approach is that historical writers must be studied in relation to the times in which they lived. It is suggested that theories and theorists must be read in the context of the ages they knew and which knew them. Men of ideas, it is argued, can only be seen as products of their times and as participants in an intellectual tradition. This interest in the history of ideas is altogether praiseworthy, and many scholarly men have devoted their lives to it. However, there is some cause to wonder whether this approach does not do an injustice to the historical theorists. For these writers, while no less products of their times than other men, have attained their preeminent stature simply *because* what they have to say has meaning and application far beyond the peculiar historical environment they knew.

The chapters which are to follow will assume that political theory is a body of philosophical and scientific knowledge which, regardless of when and where it was originally written, can increase our understanding of the world in which we live today and will live tomorrow. On this assumption, a whole range of writers from Plato through Mill will be studied without attention to the particular conditions which surrounded them at the time they wrote. This approach is not, it should be said, antihistorical. History is integral to political theory, and the theories of history of men such as Plato and Machiavelli, Rousseau and Burke, Hegel and Marx will be given close attention. But what is being argued is that these theories themselves can and should be studied independent of the role they may have played in the special and arguable field called the history of ideas.

This approach calls for some justification, and perhaps the best way to make a convincing case is to question in several serious respects whether the history of ideas contributes in significant ways to our political understanding.[11] Seven points may be raised; and if they are somewhat less than reverent,

[11] The material in the next several pages appeared originally in an article entitled "*Capital* and Carbuncles: The 'Great Books' Reappraised," in *The American Political Science Review* (September 1954), pp. 775–786. These paragraphs were written with the ardor of youth and a sense of certainty which borders on the dogmatic. They are reproduced here with that spirit intact despite the fact that the passage of years has had some mellowing effect on the author. Indeed, it is now acknowledged that those interested in the historical circumstances surrounding the writing of political theory have a right to at least some assistance in this direction. For this reason, a brief section entitled "The Man and His Times" appears at the head of each chapter which is to follow. The intellectual inspiration for these prefaces derives, in substantial measure, from the author's seminar work with William Ebenstein at Princeton University.

this is because political theory itself stands in need of a forceful defense and perhaps even a sharp break from its traditional method of study.

(1) *"Capital" and Carbuncles.* This approach is primarily biographical. Here we are concerned to discover how a certain author came to write a particular book in a particular way. Thus the fact that Marx had carbuncles is said to have made him vent all the more vitriol on the bourgeoisie in his *Capital.* Or it is concluded that Rousseau's constricted bladder affected his powers of coherent expression at the time he was writing his *Social Contract.* One scholar insists that a familiarity with Machiavelli's personal history will show that *The Prince* is an unfinished document. "Anyone acquainted with the life and character of Machiavelli," he says, "knows that these fragments of his thought, on which a whole theory of conduct has been erected, are nothing but bad-tempered explosions." [12] So to Marx's carbuncles and Rousseau's bladder must now be added Machiavelli's spleen. Once we are aware of the physiological and psychological peculiarities of a theorist, this approach suggests, we will have a fuller grasp of this theory. There is a surface plausibility to this suggestion: no one likes to propose that the personality of an author be divorced from the substance of his writing. Literary biography has long been an underpinning of literary criticism. Yet to make the allowances required by this approach demands that we concentrate on who the man was and not on what he wrote. In the long run, for purposes of political theory, it is probably best that the dissociation be made. The validity of a theory ought to stand or fall on the merits of the written text itself. A literary work can be good, true, or beautiful even if its author is a rogue, a knave, or even an anonymous scribe whose name and character are no longer known to us.

(2) *Lost Laundry Lists.* Many of the historical theorists were extremely prolific authors. Not a few of them lived by their pen, and their collected works fill a lengthy shelf. One of the consequences of this is that students of ideas feel obliged to read and take account of everything a man happened to set to paper. The very fact that a laundry list was written by John Locke tends to make this jotting an important document. It is presumed that the minor efforts of a theorist have, for some reason or other, a claim on our attention. One scholar, for example, has uncovered an article of Hegel's on the English Constitution which appeared in a Prussian magazine in 1831. After a rather painstaking summary of this article, the Hegel scholar makes a rather diffident confession. "On the whole," he says, "Hegel's account of the formal or legal side of the Constitution . . . contains nothing that can be called original or profound." Indeed: "He must join the large group of distinguished and

[12] Gugliemo Ferrero, "Machiavelli and Machiavellianism," *Foreign Affairs,* April 1939, p. 571.

learned foreigners who, while they said much about the English Constitution that was true and interesting, always managed in the end to misjudge it in some fundamental respect." [13] Most students of political theory are content to read Hegel's *Philosophy of History* and *Philosophy of Right*. And with good reason: these two books are systematic works and they contain Hegel's significant political ideas. A student's political understanding is in no way augmented by referring to an obscure article on the English Constitution, even if it was written by Hegel. If he wants to inform himself on the English Constitution, there are a dozen reputable books which will help him. Misjudgments in political analysis are no less misjudgments just because Hegel made them. Nevertheless, the student is entitled to ask which sources are the significant ones. Yet the only answer to this question must be that reason must be judiciously exercised. Marx and Engels' writings are a case in point. To draw together the elements which comprise their political theory one can go to a full-length text such as *Capital*, to polemical books like *The Poverty of Philosophy* and *Anti-Dühring*, to occasional pamphlets like *The Critique of the Gotha Programme*, and even to a speech or two delivered by Marx and to some of Engels' correspondence. The point, of course, is that the student must be discriminating: he must always ask whether minor writings add anything of importance to a writer's theoretical arguments. Those who search after lost laundry lists have ceased to concern themselves with the study of politics.

(3) **The Pursuit of Pedigrees.** For most students of political theory it is enough to note from time to time the similarities between the ideas of two writers. The theories of Burke and Tocqueville, for example, might be compared in order to show that they are interested in the same sorts of questions. However, many historians of ideas are not content with this: they devote their efforts to establishing the actual influence of one theorist on another. Thus one commentator feels entitled to say: "Hobbes has the most direct and obvious influence on the Utilitarians." [14] It is being suggested that Jeremy Bentham and John Stuart Mill read Hobbes' *Leviathan* and that this affected their political theories. Actually there is no evidence that this is so other than a certain similarity in phrasing and emphasis. But this does not prevent scholars from arguing over the alleged influences and intellectual antecedents of theories. Sometimes amateur detective work is brought to bear; one man spent his life compiling a list of all the books which were in

---

[13] Zbyszek Pelczynski, "Hegel on the English Constitution," *Cambridge Journal*, June 1952, p. 519.

[14] John Plamenatz, *Mill's Utilitarianism* (Oxford: Oxford University Press, 1949), p. 12.

Rousseau's library so that he might know the sources of Rousseau's ideas. But any such contentions about influences are difficult to substantiate. St. Thomas Aquinas, for example, freely acknowledges his intellectual debts to Aristotle. Yet the fact that he quotes Aristotle may simply mean that the use of the earlier theorist's words add an air of authority to ideas which St. Thomas would have used even if he had never read Aristotle. Ideas never emerge in a vacuum, to be sure. On the other hand, an intelligent theorist is quite capable of coming to conclusions about political reality without the help of influential predecessors. At all events, the tracing of pedigrees is bound to be speculative, and it contributes very little to our knowledge of politics.

(4) **Nothing New Under the Sun.** "There is not one single new idea in *The Communist Manifesto,*" one commentator says.

The Manifesto is, in fact, an extract from the thoughts of Helvetius, Rousseau, Morelly, Pierre Leroux, Proudhon, Bazard, Enfantin, Buret, Cabet, Dezamy and Considerant on the French side, and from those of Hegel, Heine, Boerne, Gutz-kow, Froebel, Feuerbach, Bruno Bauer, Hess and Weitling on the German side. Marx is as little the originator of socialism and communism as the chairman of General Motors Corporation is the inventor of the automobile.[15]

The student of political theory need not apologize for not having heard of three-quarters of these thinkers who seem to have anticipated Marx's ideas. It is, indeed, impossible to demonstrate that any theorist at all has originated an idea. Of course, the importance of Marx is that he took the thoughts of others and integrated them in a new and persuasive way. Shakespeare did not invent the words of the English language, but he was able to combine them as no one before him had. The difficulty in asserting that there is nothing new is that all roads eventually lead back to Plato and Aristotle. These two theorists, it can be said, sketched out in rough form everything that has subsequently been said about politics. Recently, for example, some students of politics created the term "policy science" to describe a new application in the field of theory. They were quickly reminded by an historian of ideas that their claim to originality was a spurious one. "The idea of 'policy science' is not a new one," he said. "Its first, incomparable formulation is found in Plato's *Republic:* policy, the Platonic Socrates says, can be reasonable and sound only if it is based upon the fullness of scientific insight and knowledge." [16] No one can argue with a proposition such as this: Plato certainly did have something to say about policy, even if it was only a few marginal words

---

[15] Stefan T. Possony, ed., *The Communist Manifesto* (Chicago: Regnery [Gateway edition], 1954), p. xiv.

[16] Paul Kecskemeti, "The Policy Sciences," *World Politics,* July 1952, p. 520.

on the matter. But one consequence of showing that everything has been said before is to discourage contemporary theorists from developing and applying the old ideas. Surely there is more to be said about policy than Plato's brief and generalized remarks. At any rate, the dispute over which writer first expressed which thought contributes very little to an understanding of politics.

(5) *Meaningful Misinterpretations.* The average student of political theory, it would seem, is bent on misunderstanding the ideas in the historical texts. Only a few historians of political thought are equipped to tell us what a particular writer really intended to say. One commentator relates the sad fate of Jean Bodin and his theory of sovereignty at the hands of his readers.

> By the majority perhaps of those in the succeeding centuries who were influenced by Bodin, his statement was read and received as a statement of absolute, unlimited sovereignty freeing the ruler, whether a person or a body of persons, from every restraint except that of his own sovereign will. Nothing was further from the author's real meaning. . . .[17]

Presumably Bodin's real meaning can be known only to those who are familiar with the biographical and historical circumstances which surrounded the writing of his theory. But even if this is the case, the important point is that a writer like Bodin has been remembered by future generations precisely because his theory of sovereignty was misinterpreted. Vexing as it may be to the scholar, students of politics continue to read Bodin because they prefer to believe that his is a statement of unlimited and absolute sovereignty. Were all the subtleties, nuances, and qualifications in that theory to be taken into account, then it might gain in truth, but it would definitely lose in significance. The historical texts which pass the test of time are those which offer striking generalizations about politics. A writer's real meaning is probably more plausible and less colorful than the misinterpretations which his readers are prone to place on him. The upshot of this is that the significance of a political theory lies in the eye of the reader rather than in the actual intention of the author. Machiavelli is again a case in point. From what we know of his personal history, the intention of *The Prince* was to aid in the unification of Italy. However, the average student is concerned with understanding other politics than those of Renaissance Italy, and for these general purposes a reading of Machiavelli can be extremely useful. But the utility of the historical texts will only be demonstrated if the focus is on what the writer says in plain words. The search for hidden intentions and concealed meanings contributes very little to the study of politics.

[17] C. H. Wilson, "Sovereign and Sovereignty," *Chambers Encyclopedia* (New York: 1951), revised edition, Vol. 12, p. 775.

(6) *Representative Reflections.* The history of political thought is concerned with what was on people's minds during various historical periods. It is often assumed, in addition, that a reading of the texts in political theory will give us some insight into what people were thinking at the times these texts were written. No one can deny that when Rousseau was writing *The Social Contract* a lot of other Europeans were also pondering about social contracts. Yet there is a great danger in going on to suppose that *The Social Contract* or any other book was "representative" of the thinking of its age. Many of the most significant texts were the statements of a small minority and actually quite unorthodox by the then prevailing standards.[18] Furthermore, it is almost impossible to say that a given book was the intellectual articulation of a particular party or movement or nation. At the very best, one can suggest that the publication and circulation of a book seemed to run parallel with certain practical political developments. Bentham's works, for example, were being read at the time that many social reformers were at work. But his theory of utilitarianism does not represent what matters were on their minds: what they were thinking about were such mundane things as safety devices in factories and sanitary water systems. Indeed, a book in political theory represents the thoughts of its author and perhaps those of some kindred intellectuals who liked to think in theoretical terms. The vast majority of people in any historical period do not think much at all, and such sentiments as arise in their minds are represented not by learned texts but by the popular press and political oratory. In the final analysis, one of the claims to greatness of the historical writings in that they are unrepresentative of their time; they are not bound by the immediate needs of the period, and they dwell on the enduring questions of politics.

Much the same error is made if it is assumed that a book on theory gives an accurate depiction of contemporaneous institutions and behavior. The Jacksonian America which Tocqueville describes, the Athenian Constitution which Aristotle characterizes, and the British Parliament which Mill depicts are convenient caricatures rather than objective analyses. The descriptions are distorted so as to support theoretical arguments in a more persuasive way. The student who wants to know about the French Revolution as an historical event had best go to sources other than Burke's *Reflections.* For that upheaval was nothing like Burke said it was, for the simple reason that his concern was to persuade his readers that that shattering event should never have occurred. The great books of political theory do not tell us what happened in history. They show how some people chose to view what they imagined had happened, and this is something quite different. The student

[18] See, for example, John Bowle, *Hobbes and His Critics* (London: Cape, 1951).

of politics is obliged to know a good deal about political and social history, but he must not suppose that he can acquire this knowledge from the texts in political theory.

(7) *Influential Intellects.* Historians of ideas are prone to justify their calling not only by suggesting that ideas are representative of a time but also by claiming that ideas have an influence on action. This contention must be taken seriously, and it will be discussed at some length in later chapters. Certainly there is evidence that men of action have been familiar with books of theory. Thomas Jefferson, we know, read John Locke's *Second Treatise* and then sat down to write the Declaration of Independence—undoubtedly an important document. Lenin, we know, read the entire writings of Marx and Engels and then went forth to lead the Russian Revolution—undoubtedly an earthshaking event. But does this mean that the theories of intellectuals have a subtle and indirect influence on the course of these events? Many historians would like to agree with Heine that it was Rousseau and not the politicians who brought forth the French Revolution. "Mark this, ye proud men of action," he said. "Ye are nothing but unconscious instruments of the men of thought who, often in humblest seclusion, have appointed you to your inevitable task. Maximilian Robespierre was merely the hand of Jean-Jacques Rousseau. . . ." [19] Does this mean that there would have been no Declaration of Independence or Russian or French Revolution had Locke or Marx or Rousseau never given Jefferson or Lenin or Robespierre their intellectual inspiration? Most historians will admit that those events would have occurred even if the books in question had never been written. They might suggest that action would have taken a somewhat different direction, but here they can only speculate.

What does stand out, however, is that there have been hundreds of significant events in politics which were inspired by no theory at all. Genghis Khan overran most of Asia without a Rousseau to influence him, and the British embarked on their Imperial adventures more in a fit of absence of mind than in unconscious response to any theory. And if Lenin acknowledged his indebtedness to Marx and Engels, this was probably because he saw that to use their ideas would be effective from an ideological standpoint. The same may be said of Hamilton's and Madison's quotations from Montesquieu in *The Federalist Papers*. Men of action frequently believe that they can endow their deeds with legitimacy in the public eye if they draw on the theories of intellectuals for support.

The danger in attempting to show the influence of theory on practice is

---

[19] Quoted in Karl Popper, *The Open Society and Its Enemies* (London: Routledge, 1945), Vol. 2, p. 102.

that the process actually works the other way around. The politician occasionally uses the words and phrases of a theorist the better to justify his actions. But when he does this, he does not draw on a theory as a theory. On the contrary, he selects those portions which suit his purposes, and then simplifies and circulates them for popular consumption. It is the politician, then, who gives a public reputation to the intellectual. The student of politics does well not to concern himself with the supposed influence of the books he reads. These writings have importance because they are a means to understanding political reality, and they would have this importance even if they were never introduced into the practical arena. In fact, once they are used by men of action, they are so simplified for ideological purposes that they have little value for serious students. There is an important place in political theory for the analysis of ideology, but to engage in this the writer must remove himself from the interplay of interests and comment on the political rhetoric which other men employ. He must, that is, theorize about ideology without becoming an ideologue himself. The elements of political theories which are presumed to have been influential in the world of action are, in fact, simplified slogans which distort rather than clarify reality. If the student turns his attention to the catch phrases which comprise ideology, then he runs the risk of taking their representations at face value. Once he does that, he is talking ideology itself rather than talking about ideology. And in that case he has ceased to be a student of political theory.

The historical texts have their greatest value in that the theories they offer transcend the times and the personalities which produced them. In this sense they are timeless and, in an important respect, anonymous. The reader of Plato and Aristotle no less than the reader of Marx and Mill has every right to ask: What meaning have these ideas for the world of politics I know today? If this is the question he asks—and if he excludes as irrelevant the problems which properly belong to the historians of ideas—he will find himself rewarded with answers which stimulate the mind and inspire the imagination.

POLITICS AND CONSCIENCE

Political theory requires a political conscience. It is no enterprise for those who are unable to care deeply about the world in which they live. To be sure, the play of conscience is prone to distort perceptions and to infuse theory with ideology. This price, however, is one well worth paying. For without the stir of emotion it is impossible to come to grips with the significant questions of an age. The student of political theory must be moved on conscientious grounds if he is ever to think greatly about the world he knows. Too persuasive a concern with the history of ideas or the methods of science can only deflect an individual from developing the commitments to principle which are ultimate keys to understanding. In the final analysis, it is neither historical erudition nor methodological precision which tell us about political reality. Theory exists because there have been men of intellect who saw politics as real problems which cried out for solutions. "The greater political theorists of the past . . . wrote with a practical purpose in mind," Alfred Cobban says. "They wrote to condemn or support existing institutions, to justify a political system or to persuade their fellow citizens to change it; because, in the last resort they were concerned with the aims, the purposes of political society." [20] The central problems of politics are timeless: the aims and purposes of political society are forever in need of discussion. The study of political theory will be sustained in our day only if students bring to it commitments which are both personal and intense. The goal of theory is to enhance the understanding. And great knowledge rises out of those insights which only the engaged mind and the quickened insight are able to create.

[20] Alfred Cobban, "The Decline of Political Theory," *Political Science Quarterly*, September 1953, p. 330.

2.
Plato

THE MAN AND HIS TIMES

Plato was born in Athens in 426 or 428 B.C. His family was an aristocratic one, and it was probably expected that he would devote his career to managing the family properties and holding political office. Yet, as so often happens with young men of superior endowment, he rejected the life of security and prestige which was open to him. The central reason for this decision was that he came under the influence of Socrates. This philosopher and teacher was the center of attention for many of the rich young men of Athens, and Plato soon became his most devoted pupil. When Plato was 28 and Socrates was 70, the teacher was tried by the Athenian courts and sentenced to death. His crime had been to spread subversive ideas among those of impressionable age. This event shocked Plato into a reappraisal of his own life. He embarked upon extensive travels, and when he subsequently returned to Athens, he was determined to carry on the role of his martyred teacher. He founded a school called The Academy and presided over it from 388 to 369. Plato's first writings were, in an important sense, memorials to Socrates. They took the form of reconstructed dialogues which took place among Socrates and his pupils and friends. The teacher would open a discussion by professing to know nothing himself, and he would proceed to pose questions to those who adhered to the conventional Athenian values. Yet these questions were so penetrating and the answers which were given so unsatisfactory that Socrates would be urged to expound some ideas of his own. It is nevertheless clear, at this juncture in the dialogues, that Plato was not confining himself simply to the role of reporter. The positive philosophy which issues from Socrates' mouth is, in the final analysis, Plato's own creation. In The Republic, therefore, Socrates *is the* gadfly who shows the inadequacies of the prevailing dogmas, and Plato is left to spell out a new political theory.

21

The Athens which Plato knew was beginning its decline from greatness. It had lost the Peloponnesian Wars to the Spartans, and this marked the end of an era. But even before that conflict ended in 404, signs of deterioration had already set in. The victory of Sparta was the victory of one social system over another: Spartan oligarchy demonstrated that it was more powerful and more effectively organized than Athenian democracy. The equalitarian and participative society which Pericles had heralded in his Funeral Oration could not muster the discipline and self-sacrifice which were demanded in a time of crisis. In the aftermath of war factionalism further debilitated Athens, and it was in an atmosphere of disillusionment and divisiveness that Plato wrote The Republic. The intellectual problem he set for himself was how to create a society where not simply the ideal of justice but also the facts of social stability and political power might be brought into being. At least in part, he was prepared to draw on the victorious Spartans for his model; the stress on social order and internal discipline are cases in point. But the Spartan oligarchy gave priority to the military virtues, and Plato rejected this emphasis. The society he designed called for rulers who would be philosophers as well as kings and whose task would be to secure justice as well as order. This reconstruction of existing society was avowedly Utopian, and it is not unusual for a prescription such as this to be written in a time of political malaise. The Athens which had once flourished was in no position to reconstitute itself. By the time Plato died in 347 b.c., his theory was purely academic.

2.
Plato

To STUDY POLITICS IS TO STUDY POWER; TO STUDY PHILOSOPHY is to study rationality. The task of political philosophy is to show how power and rationality may be conjoined. The agency for this conjunction is the state. The good state will seek simultaneously to endow power with reason and to enthrone reason on the seat of power.

Plato was the first writer to address himself to political philosophy. As a man of reason, he stood apart from the pressures of contemporary political life. Instead, he sought to draw up a blueprint depicting a state of affairs in which the political imperfections of the existing world would be obviated. Plato was, in a word, a Utopian and his book *The Republic* is a Utopia. As a literary form, a Utopia serves many purposes. Its primary role is to serve as a radical critique of the existing world. Men write of perfect societies because they are exercised over the imperfections they see all around them in the real world. Plato's Utopia, however, constitutes far more than an indictment of the Athens of his day. It is important because it expresses the worries of many who have continued to observe practical politics from Athenian times down to the present day. The ills that Plato sought to identify and cure—ills both of human society and human personality—plague our modern age no less than the ancient.

The Republic is written as a dialogue. Socrates and his friends foregather at the home of a wealthy tradesman for what must be a period of several weeks of unbroken conversation.[1] Three of Socrates' companions have coherent positions to set forward. It is from the lips of Thrasymachus, Glaucon, and Adeimantus that we hear the "practical" point of view. The function they serve in *The Republic* is to hold up as an argumentative foil to Socrates

---

[1] A question which never ceases to intrigue historians of political thought is the extent to which Socrates is voicing the actual sentiments of Plato. For present purposes it will be assumed that one is the spokesman for the other: Socrates' ideas may be considered to be those of Plato.

the prevailing beliefs in Athenian society. The arguments that these men advance are all plausible, and they set the stage for Socrates' rebuttals and reforms. A good place to begin, therefore, is with a summary of what both Thrasymachus and Glaucon have to say about the interrelation of politics and personality. They voice some propositions which recur in one form or another throughout the course of Western political theory.

Thrasymachus speaks of the realities of power. He is the earliest of the Machiavellians—thinkers who address themselves to questions of how rulers can most effectively gain and maintain power. In this approach to politics the standard of successful rulership is given primacy over that of good rulership. The Machiavellian imperative is one running ceaselessly through political theory. Thrasymachus states it in baldest terms. The discussion has opened on a search for a definition of "justice." Socrates' more high-minded friends have been suggesting some rather idealistic meanings for this term, and after a while Thrasymachus can no longer contain himself. "What I say is that 'just' or 'right' means nothing but what is to the interest of the stronger party," he says.[2] And by the stronger party he means, very simply, the man or men who happen to control the instruments of power in society. What his argument comes down to is that whatever "justice" is is defined by those powerful individuals who have the ability to impose their ideas on others. Thrasymachus does not deny that the practical politician's notion of "justice" is frequently what most impractical philosophers would be quick to call injustice. But no matter who bestows the labels, the substance of the conflict is quite apparent. The most profitable course of action for those who call the tune automatically becomes "just" behavior.

By way of an opening rejoinder, Socrates suggests that even an absolute ruler can make mistakes: that he may enact laws which have consequences serving to defeat his own self-interest. Thrasymachus regards this as quibbling. "Do you suppose I should speak of a man as 'stronger' or 'superior' at the very moment when he is making a mistake?" he asks. ". . . The ruler, insofar as he is acting as a ruler, makes no mistakes and consequently enjoins what is best for himself."[3] All rulers make mistakes. The success of a ruler is to be judged by how few of them he makes.

Thrasymachus claims to be concerned only with the way ideas are defined in the real world. If we are going to talk about justice in a political context, then we must face up to the fact that nothing succeeds like success. "I am

---

[2] *The Republic of Plato* (New York: Oxford University Press, 1945), translated by Francis M. Cornford, p. 18.

[3] Pp. 20-21.

speaking of . . . the man who can get the better of other people on a large scale," he says. The despot, for example, "uses force or fraud to plunder the goods of others, public or private, sacred or profane, and to do it in a whole-sale way." [4] If he gets away with it, he can define "justice" in whatever way he pleases and also gain the admiration of the public, which is always ready to applaud success on a grand scale. Indeed there is a stark contrast between the treatment accorded a petty thief who is caught and political tyrant who succeeds. Both may be "unjust" men, but one gets the gallows and the other a triumphal arch:

> If you are caught committing any one of these crimes on a small scale, you are punished and disgraced; they call it sacrilege, kidnapping, burglary, theft and brigandage. But if, besides taking their property, you turn all your countrymen into slaves, you will hear no more of those ugly names; your countrymen themselves will call you the happiest of men and bless your name, and so will everyone who hears of such a complete triumph of injustice. . . .[5]

What is being said here, at least in part, is that moral standards derive their effective meanings from the power relationships in society. The man in the street, no philosopher, is quite prepared to give his approval to the behavior of the successful man of power. What might, in other social contexts, be re-garded by all as sacrilege or even common theft is now seen as legitimate conduct on the part of those who rule. The average man, then, admires in-justice—but only on a large scale—and in so doing turns it into the embodi-ment of "justice." The effective ruler will turn this popular pragmatism to his own advantage. Indeed, he will adopt the public's definition of "justice" as his own.

To hold to any other conception of justice is, Thrasymachus says, "the mark of a good-natured simpleton." [6] But Socrates, undaunted by the label of simpleton, then asks whether success in politics signifies that those who are successful are "positively superior in character and intelligence?" Here Thrasymachus is quick to respond: "Yes, if they are the sort that can carry injustice to perfection and make themselves masters of whole cities and na-tions." [7]

However, we should take notice that Socrates has shifted the ground of the argument ever so slightly. First, he has made Thrasymachus come out and say that political success is prima facie evidence of superior moral and mental

[4] Pp. 25–26.
[5] P. 26.
[6] P. 31.
[7] Pp. 31–32.

qualities on the part of the politician as an individual. But political success, as Thrasymachus would certainly admit, is frequently the result of favorable external circumstances, good fortune in timing, and sheer guesswork. Most successful politicians are fairly intelligent men, but they are not "positively superior" in native intelligence when they are set alongside the men who possess the best brains in their society at the time. The qualities of personality and character which make for political success are not at all the same as those which make for intellectual attainment or moral worthiness. Nor was Thrasymachus trying to suggest that a politician proves that he has either a high I.Q. or an estimable character by virtue of his success on the political battlefield. All that has been proposed is the obvious point that a successful politician shows that he has an aptitude for the political life; and the obvious corollary is that if he is successful, he will be regarded by many of his followers as a man who possesses high intellectual and moral qualities. These comments by Thrasymachus are political in character; they do not pretend to analyze intelligence in general, nor do they claim to expand on abstract questions of moral philosophy. Second, in shifting the ground, Socrates has led Thrasymachus to speak in extreme terms of the politician who is so adept that he can "carry injustice to perfection." It is clear that Thrasymachus would be among the first to grant that nothing in the practical world of politics—not even injustice—is ever carried to perfection. There has never been, nor will there ever be, a ruler who has commanded universal obedience, received unqualified admiration, or set in motion a political system which would operate continuously with no sign of internal dissension. Political success is, of course, a relative matter. Thrasymachus is hardly the sort of man to be blind to the limitations on absolute rule. He is simply making a few rash statements about politics and power, and about morality and public opinion—statements he thought ought to be taken note of by a group of philosophers who have gathered to discuss justice and injustice in a political setting.

But Socrates, as will become more apparent, is less concerned with politics than he is with the human personality. Thrasymachus let slip that he believed the successful ruler would also be a happy man. It is on this admission that Socrates fastens in making his final reply to the ultra-realist position. Discord, he points out, is the bane of any human association—be it "a state or an army or a band of robbers or thieves." Yet a political system in which the ruler is, in the philosopher's eyes, an unjust man will inevitably be one where dissension is the rule rather than the exception. No matter how clever the ruler, and no matter how unremittingly he works at persuading his subjects to accept the values of his regime, the means that he has used will have the "effect of implanting hatred wherever it exists. It must make any set of people, whether freemen or slaves, split into factions, at feud with one another and incapable of any joint action." [8]

What Socrates is saying here is that an absolute ruler can never be completely absolute: feuding factions are always bound to exist, either on or beneath the surface. And he is also saying that there is an essential conflict in such a system between political "justice" and philosophical justice. No matter how successful a ruler may be in terms of manipulating power, he will in the realm of power inevitably engage in conduct that will alienate the philosophers who are the final judges of all politicians. The men of reason, to be sure, do not constitute a political "faction" in the usual sense, yet it is their dissenting voice which stands as an obstacle to unanimous approval for the ways of any ruler. By this avenue, Socrates directs the discussion to what is for him his most compelling argument. The discord which the ruler confronts in his society will also be evidenced in his own personality. "It will produce the same natural results in an individual," he says to Thrasymachus. "He will have a divided mind and be incapable of action, for lack of singleness of purpose; and he will be at enmity with all who are just as well as with himself." [9] The men who define justice disinterestedly—the philosophers—symbolize the conflicts within the ruler's conscience. Trading as he does on injustice, a ruler knows in his own mind that he is violating permanent moral standards. And if he tends to forget this, the philosophers remind him that he is. He has paid a price for his power: this price is, in Socrates' phrase, a divided mind. The man of power cannot be a happy man; his own personality is at war with itself. Thrasymachus has no answer for this. The ruler seeks to aggrandize his own ambitions, yet he wishes that his power be legitimate. He grasps for a moral sanction by evoking the applause of the majority or by insisting that power creates its own morality. But neither of these tactics can work in the long run. Legitimacy must come from other sources, Socrates says, and, what is more, the ruler knows it. Yet the politician will continue to aspire to power, and with each step that he takes his conscience plagues him more. That the unjust ruler is himself an unhappy man is, to Socrates, an unanswerable indictment of the Machiavellian outlook.

It is to Plato's credit that he gives Thrasymachus' argument with such force and plausibility. Plato is a Utopian philosopher, but he also sought to make it plain that he was aware of political realities. What he has done, then, is to build into The Republic various counterarguments to his own theory, which is to follow. Having dealt with the attack on the Machiavellian flank, Plato

[8] P. 35.
[9] Ibid.

then has Socrates turn to a less antagonistic but more difficult set of arguments on another side.

Glaucon feels obliged to enlighten Socrates on the conception of justice held by thinking people in existing society. Glaucon is not, like Thrasymachus, charting out the unpleasant truths about power in human relations. Rather, he is describing the theoretical explanations of human nature and political behavior which are put forward by those who are prone to generalize about politics. In contrast to the primitive Machiavellianism of Thrasymachus, Glaucon adumbrates a "Social Contract" theory—the sort to be elaborated later on by Hobbes, Locke, and Rousseau. Whereas Thrasymachus concentrated on the role of power in defining values, Glaucon is concerned to emphasize the importance of law in any consideration of justice. If we approach the average citizen and suggest to him that he ought to use considerations of justice as his personal standard of political conduct, we find, Glaucon says, that behavior of this sort "is always practiced with reluctance." Indeed, the typical citizen regards justice "not as good in itself, but as a thing one cannot do without." And we are soon forced to conclude that "this reluctance is reasonable." All men live in society. In ideal terms, most men would probably prefer to pursue justice in their conduct as autonomous individuals. But the fact remains that they must live the whole of their lives in the company of others. And it is out of social existence that the institution of law emerges. It is law which tells us what is just behavior. Glaucon traces the development of this idea:

What people say is that to do wrong is, in itself, a desirable thing; on the other hand, it is not at all desirable to suffer wrong, and the harm to the sufferer outweighs the advantage to the doer. Consequently, when men have had a taste of both, those who have not the power to seize the advantage and escape the harm decide that they would be better off if they made a compact neither to do wrong nor to suffer it. Hence they began to make laws and covenants with one another; and whatever the law prescribed they called lawful and right. That is what right or justice is and how it came into existence; it stands halfway between the best thing of all—to do wrong with impunity—and the worst, which is to suffer wrong without the power to retaliate. So justice is accepted as a compromise, and valued, not as a good in itself, but for lack of power to do wrong; no man worthy of the name, who had that power, would ever enter into a such a compact with anyone; he would be mad if he did.[10]

The Machiavellian approach centered on the personality and the characteristics of the ruling few. It gave little attention to the man in the street other than to note the generalized power of public opinion. The Social Contract approach, on the other hand, is concerned with the conceptions of justice

[10] Pp. 43-44.

held by the average citizens who go to make up a society. It is their behavior, not those of the rulers, which must now command our attention.

What Glaucon is saying is that ordinary men are both selfish and rational. They are rational in that they realize that if they are to protect themselves, they must be willing to make important compromises with their fellow citizens. The man who yearns after self-protection must be prepared to grant others this same security. No one will deny that whatever pleasures an individual may gain from hitting someone else over the head can be sadly outweighed by the pains which are incurred when someone else hits him. All men are equal in the sense that they are relatively defenseless, and all are prepared to obey certain common rules which will secure them against the depredations of their neighbors. Rational acknowledgment by all of the powerlessness of each individual leads to the making of a social compact or contract. Men, to put it figuratively, come out of a state of anarchy and enter a state of society. Through the institutions of society and society's government, laws are established. It is these laws which decree what is just and what is unjust behavior. Justice is, therefore, a social instrument. It is never perfect: it is always an uneasy compromise seeking to adjust elementary security which all men, taken collectively, desire with the special needs of individuals. Justice, on these grounds, is an instrumental means and not an end. Justice under law is the means by which the goals of social stability and personal freedom can be adjusted in a rational manner.

The social-contract theory outlined by Glaucon stresses the limitations of human nature. All men, the theory suggests, put their own well-being ahead of that of others. That is, perfect liberty for the individual—no matter what the consequences to society—is a goal worth pursuing so long as you can get away with it. The fact that you can't in fact get away with antisocial behavior does not vitiate the proposition that all men would take unlimited power if by some stroke of chance they had the opportunity. The man of the social-contract theory, then, is a self-centered creature. It is idle to talk of the man who abides by canons of justice, because he does not exist. Indeed, the men we suppose to be just are only that way because they have had no opportunity to be unjust. Men who appear to be looking out for the welfare of the fellow citizens are, in the final analysis, making the best of a compromise situation. Glaucon puts forward the notion of human selfishness succinctly:

If we imagine two men, one just, the other unjust, given full license to do whatever they like, and then follow them to observe where each will be led by his desires, . . . we shall catch the just man taking the same road as the unjust. He will be moved by self-interest, the end which it is natural to every creature to pursue as good, until forcibly turned aside by law and custom to respect the principle of equality.[11]

Human nature is a constant factor in its social context; all men should be viewed as potential tyrants. But the human mind is also a rational instrument: all men acknowledge the necessity of obeying the law. These men are not fit materials for a Utopian society; however, they are capable of living in peace together in a law-abiding society. The means that has been most effective establishing such coexistence is a system of laws which premise and respect the equal worth of all human beings in society.

Socrates listens respectfully to the whole of Glaucon's analysis; and, at the end, when the just and the unjust man are shown to be brothers under the skin, he can only say: "My dear Glaucon, how vigorously you scour these two characters clean for inspection, as if you were burnishing a couple of statues!" [12]

The whole remainder of The Republic is to be an answer to the arguments presented by Glaucon and Thrasymachus. These two men have asserted that both rulers and citizens are imperfect human beings, that society is necessarily a tense compromise in an imperfect world. Socrates does not argue that existing society ought not to be characterized in this way. But what he does want to suggest is that there is another way to approach the institutions of politics and the behavior of men. A different kind of state would not have to fear Machiavellian rulers, nor would it need a Social Contract for self-protection of all its residents. This different state, which Socrates now proceeds to describe, is not the daydream of a moment. On the contrary, it is a detailed blueprint which seeks to provide solutions for the wide variety of problems which are bound to arise whenever men live in society.

THE PLATONIC UTOPIA

Six facets of Plato's Utopian society comprise the core of his political philosophy: class, communism, civility, control, contentment, and consensus.[13] These six features are, of course, interrelated, and no single one can be viewed apart from its connection with the others. The rigid class structure which

---

[11] P. 44.

[12] P. 46.

[13] Plato's Utopia—like Aristotle's Polis—is simultaneously a government, a state, a society, and a community. For this reason, the four terms can be used interchangeably throughout the chapter. While later theorists take pains to distinguish between these institutions—especially between state and society—Plato sees nothing inapposite in having their jurisdictions coincide.

Plato proposes must be juxtaposed against his ideas about the communist organization of property; the stringent controls on human behavior must not be viewed apart from the universal contentment of the population. Only if such a synthesis is constructed will we be able to form an image of Plato's perfect state. Furthermore, each of the elements which Plato chose to include constitutes an oblique criticism of existing societies. We have already seen, in Socrates' brief reply to Thrasymachus, how the discord in the real political world produces social instability and personal unhappiness. A Utopia must solve the problems raised by factionalism, and yet in arriving at a solution it must not create institutions which produce even greater sources of dissatisfaction. Plato's comprehensive solution—the design of a Utopia—must be judged from at least two vantage points. First, we must ask if it embodies a significant indictment of the problems of existing society. Second, we must ask if in its general outline it has the appearance of being a better world than the one in which we now live.

Class. It is impossible to study human society without the conception of class. The only people who seem to deny this proposition are, on the one hand, communist theorists who assert that classes will not exist in communist societies and, on the other, those anticommunists who believe that there are no important class differences in societies which hold to the principles of free enterprise. But most social scientists acknowledge that any complex society will inevitably have gradations—marked by boundaries which vary in their flexibility or rigidity—in its social structure, and that almost all citizens can be pinpointed as belonging to one fairly coherent class or another. The complexities involved in class analysis should never be underrated. We must ask, at the outset, whether we are talking of class in "objective" or "subjective" terms. Does the social scientist label individuals as members of one class or another on the basis of "objective" characteristics which he is capable of perceiving? If so, then how does he handle the "subjective" conviction on the part of people who themselves believe that they belong to a certain stratum in society?

A good case in point is the "middle class." Social scientists can take a group of ten individuals and decide, say, that six belong to the middle class. They do this on the basis of identifiable characteristics exhibited by those persons: level of income, amount of education, area of residence, etc. The bestowing of this label will be done without consulting the individuals in question, except to ask them the objective question about how much they earn, where they live, and so forth. However, there may be two other people in this group of ten who, while they do not possess the objective attributes of middle-class status, nevertheless firmly believe that they do belong to the middle class. Does thinking make it so? We might say that to be middle class you must think of yourself as middle class. But we cannot say that thinking of yourself that way is—in and of itself—sufficient cause for social scientists to put you where you would like to be.

In addition, we must inquire into the relative fluidity of the class structure. Are we talking of an "open" or a "closed" society? How much opportunity is there for an individual—or his children—to move from one class to another, and under what circumstances is such mobility to be observed? These essential questions of class are perennial in political theory. At this early juncture, however, many of them can only be hinted at.

Plato's Utopia is a class society. That is to say, all citizens belong to one of three readily identifiable classes. These are the Guardians, the Auxiliaries, and the Workers. About the last two relatively little will be heard. The Auxiliaries are soldiers and, presumably, minor civil servants. Some of the Workers will be farmers or craftsmen, but the vast majority will be manual or unskilled laborers. It is the Guardian class who command our attention. This group is somewhat hierarchical itself, with ruling Guardians standing at the top and nonruling Guardians beneath them. The latter are invested with important responsibilities, and they act as higher civil servants, while the ruling Guardians are the handful of policy-makers who govern the society. When Plato speaks of the "Rulers," then, he is referring to those selected Guardians who are in the topmost positions. The split between ruling and nonruling Guardians is not a class division as is, say, the gap between Guardians and Auxiliaries. Finally, Plato goes a long way toward indicating that these classes are not hereditary. If a child born to Guardian parents is not of Guardian quality, neither he nor his parents must expect him to inherit their class status. The parents, Plato says, "must, without the smallest pity, assign him to the station proper to his nature and thrust him out among the craftsmen or the farmers." [14] And a child of lowly origins who possesses the requisite characteristics of mind and spirit will be promoted to the Auxiliary or Guardian class. In this sense, it might be more accurate to call the Guardians an "elite" rather than a class. For if opportunity for mobility from class to class exists, then the hereditary aspect is not the governing one. Yet, as will be seen, permanent assignment to classes and education for one's place in a particular class take place at an early age. This means that if a worker's son is to be promoted, he must show his aptitudes at infancy, or not at all. And, concomitantly, a Guardian's son must display his shortcomings early, or not at all. Such a system plainly favors the children of the Guardian class,

[14] P. 107.

and for this reason the term "class" will be employed rather than "elite." [15]
Plato's overriding concern is that the Guardians be wise and good rulers.
"If a man is to be gentle towards his own people whom he knows, he must
have an instinctive love of wisdom and understanding . . ." he says. "So
the nature required to make a really noble Guardian of our commonwealth
will be swift and strong, spirited, and philosophic." [16] Great care must be
taken so that there will emerge in the ruling positions a class of men who
are public-spirited in temperament and skilled in the arts of government. But
the spirit of these men is no less important than their efficiency.

If we want the best among our Guardians, we must take those naturally fitted to
watch over a commonwealth. They must have the right sort of intelligence and
ability; and also they must look upon the commonwealth as their special concern—
the sort of concern that is felt for something so closely bound up with oneself that
its interests and fortunes, for good or ill, are held to be identical with one's own.

So the kind of men we must choose from among the Guardians will be those
who, when we look at the whole course of their lives, are found to be full of zeal to
do whatever they believe is for the good of the commonwealth and never willing
to act against its interest.[17]

The power structure of the Utopia is to be a politics of absolute rule. The
Guardians, as will be seen, are placed in a position where they, and only
they, are capable of understanding what is best for the society. As their policies are based on an awareness of the long-term good of the commonwealth,
there is no provision—nor need there be—for dissent or opposition on the
part of the average citizen. The question of self-government never even
arises in the Utopia: the Guardians are good governors and their wise rule
obviates the need for elections, parties, or popular discussion. Plato does not
make this claim lightly. Indeed, he only puts it forward because he is prepared
to show how and why the Guardians are deserving of their favored position.
They have undergone rigorous training and testing from the time of early
childhood:

We must find out who are the best Guardians of this inward conviction that
they must always do what they believe to be best for the commonwealth. We shall
have to watch them from earliest childhood and set them tasks in which they
would be most likely to forget or be beguiled out of this duty. We shall then
choose only those whose memory holds firm and who are proof against delusion.
Whenever we find one who has come unscathed through every test in childhood,
youth and manhood, we shall set him as a ruler to watch over the commonwealth;

[15] The distinctions between an "elite" and a "ruling class," and between status which
is based on "achievement" as opposed to that based on "ascription," will be discussed more
fully in later chapters.
[16] P. 66.
[17] Pp. 103–104.

he will be honored in life, and after death receive the highest tribute of funeral rites and other memorials. All who do not reach this standard we must reject. And that, I think, my dear Glaucon, may be taken as an outline of the way in which we shall select Guardians to be set in authority as Rulers.[18]

At this point it would be well to answer one question which always arises in discussing Utopias. This classbound, nondemocratic Utopia is the product of Plato's imagination. He is painting a picture for us, the shades and tones of which he has conceived in his own mind. Plato is, in short, an artist, and, like all artists, he is telling us a story. Thus, when he says "we" shall have to watch the candidates for Guardianship or "we" must find out who are the best—when he talks in the second person—he is not deciding that Socrates and Glaucon are to be Super-Guardians who will run the Utopia from behind the scenes. Utopias ought not to be viewed as the author's grand plan for personal power. On the contrary, they are societies which, once set in motion by the Utopian artist, are supposed to run on forever without the intervention of a hidden hand. Nor is it legitimate to claim that Plato is trying to impose his Utopian dictatorship on those of us who prefer democracy. He is no more doing this than Dante was forcing us to live in the Inferno or Swift in Lilliput. We can, in short, take it or leave it. But if we do take it, then we must take it as Plato has laid it out for us.[19] We must accept the rigid class structure, because that feature in the Utopia is necessary if the society as a whole is to realize other and more important ends.

Communism. The communal life the Utopia applies only to the Guardians. Plato's main interest is that they be wise and public-spirited governors. To achieve this end, they must not be tempted to rule in their own interest rather than that of the society as a whole. To be sure, the Guardians constitute a ruling class. But, unlike other ruling classes, they lack motives which would lead them to make policy for their own benefit. In short, they do not possess personal interests either material or psychological.

The chief interests which impel men of power to ignore the public good are economic and social in character. A ruling class which possesses property will tend to make policies which protect their wealth even if those policies inflict harm on the less wealthy majority of the population. And a ruling class which is emotionally concerned about the future of their children will seek to ensure the high status of their offspring even if this means denying opportunity for the children of others to rise. For those reasons, Plato would divest his Guardians of both property and their own children. "None of

---

[18] P. 105.

[19] For further discussion of the Utopia as a literary device in political theory, see Andrew Hacker, "In Defense of Utopia," *Ethics*, January, 1955, pp. 135–138.

them," he says, "must possess any private property beyond the barest necessaries."

They alone of all the citizens are forbidden to touch and handle silver or gold, or to come under the same roof with them, or wear them as ornaments, or drink from vessels made of them. This manner of life will be their salvation, and make them the saviors of the commonwealth. If ever they should come to possess land of their own and houses and money, they will give up their Guardianship. . . .[20]

Other citizens in society may possess property, because they are neither expected to rule nor to have the common good in mind. The farmer may own his own land, and the craftsman his own tools. These possessions might bring their owners to take a shortsighted and self-interested view toward public policy. However, this presents no political problem in the Utopia, because it is the propertied individuals who will have no hand in governing. The prescription of a Spartan life for men of responsibility is a fairly common conception: the church, the military, and the public service have always tended to believe that large salaries and private property dissuade men from an undeviating pursuit of the public interest. Plato enunciates this position in its baldest terms.

The next step is even more drastic. For members of the Guardian class the family is to be abolished. "No one man and one woman are to set up house together privately," Plato says. "Wives are to be held in common by all; so too are the children, and no parent is to know his own child, nor any child his parent." [21] The emotional attachment of parent to child is no less evident in the most rational human being than in the case of the lowest mammal. Mothers and fathers wish their children well, and they seek for them as good a life as they themselves have known or, indeed, a better one. Inheritance laws and private schools are some of the institutions which testify to this desire on the part of parents to safeguard the coming generation. But in Plato's Utopia such a state of affairs would be unbearable. Recruitment to the Guardian class is to be based solely on talent, and not at all on the accident of family pedigree. Therefore, Guardians must be deprived of sons and daughters so that they will not be tempted to use influence to place them in the top jobs. If the society is to survive, then there is no room for mediocrity in high places. In short, no nepotism. There must, of course, be reproduction of the species. But this, Glaucon is told, will be a routine affair:

It is for you, then, as their lawgiver, who have already selected the men, to select for association with them women who are so far as possible of the same natural capacity. Now since none of them will have any private home of his own, but they

[20] *The Republic*, pp. 108–109.
[21] P. 156.

will share the same dwelling and eat at common tables, the two sexes will be together; and meeting without restriction for exercise and all through their upbringing, they will surely be drawn towards unions with one another by a necessity of their nature.[22]

It is doubtful that Plato intended promiscuity. For one thing, the Guardians would be so busy with affairs of state that they would have little time for other sorts of affairs. But more important is the fact that principles of eugenics are to be operative in the Utopia. There must be Guardians for the future, and a scientific effort must be made to see that the best stock in society reproduces itself and transmits its qualities to a new generation who are to be the new ruling class. The enforcement of a eugenics program is a complicated matter, even in a Utopia. The ruling Guardians will have to deceive the nonruling Guardians about what is going on if such a policy is to be effective. Mock marriages and a rigged lottery are to be the techniques employed.

If we are to keep our flock at the highest pitch of excellence, there should be as many unions of the best of both sexes, and as few of the inferior as possible. . . . No one but the Rulers must know how all this is being effected; otherwise our herd of Guardians may become rebellious. . . . We must, then, institute certain festivals at which we shall bring together the brides and the bridegrooms. . . . The number of marriages we shall leave to the Rulers' discretion. . . . I think they will have to invent some ingenious system of drawing lots, so that, at each pairing off, the inferior candidate may blame his luck rather than the Rulers.[23]

The systematic use of deception as a form of political control in Utopia will be examined later on. What is of interest at this point is that, while not all the children of the Guardians—and not even all the children of the ruling Guardians—will pass the eugenics test and hence be elevated to ruling Guardian status, nevertheless Plato still asserts that institutional provision has been made for allowing the children of the lower classes to be admitted to the ruling class. Just when and how this opportunity is to occur, Plato does not say. While logically it is possible to let them in at any time, the whole class basis of the social structure militates against such cooptation. Indeed, Plato has been at more pains to provide against nepotism on the part of the Guardians, a negative safeguard, than he has been to encourage upward social mobility, which is a positive one. The corollary of eugenic control is the control of emotions. Parents must not be allowed to know their own children, for such relationships invariably lead to the building of strong emotional ties. "As soon as the children are born," Plato says, "they will be taken in charge by officers appointed for the purpose." [24]

[22] P. 157.
[23] Pp. 159–160.
[24] P. 160.

These officers will also superintend the nursing of the children. They will bring the mothers to the creche when their breasts are full, while taking every precaution that no mother shall know her own child. . . . They will limit the time during which the mothers will suckle their children, and hand over all the hard work and sitting up at night to nurses and attendants.[25]

With the advent of pasteurization and sterilization, we can presume that the mothers will not even have to be let into the nursery. But, even without these innovations, the idea that each mother is to be a rotating wet nurse gets across the point. The principle of anonymity is to serve the larger end of the efficient state. Emotions must be sublimated so that succession within the Guardian class will be based on the ability of each entrant and not the influence of his parents.

In depriving the ruling class of material comforts and the emotional satisfactions of family life, Plato appears to be falling into the trap which he earlier set for Thrasymachus. The Guardians pay a price for their power: they may not partake of the happiness which is known by ordinary men. "Our aim in founding the commonwealth was not to make any one class specially happy, but to secure the greatest possible happiness for the community as a whole . . ." Plato says. "For the moment we are constructing, as we believe, the state which will be happy as a whole, not trying to secure the well-being of a select few." [26] The point is that it is wrong to ask how the rulers fare in a political system. Anyone who asks this is assuming that the society exists for the happiness of the governing class. Plato's concern is to achieve a state which, taken as an aggregate, will be a happy organism. This aim will be defeated if the comfort of a particular class in the society is given favored treatment. "You must not press us to endow our Guardians with a happiness that will make them anything rather than Guardians . . ." he says. "Men who make only a vain show of being Guardians of the laws and of the commonwealth bring the whole state to utter ruin." [27]

The communist life which is experienced by the ruling class has an important influence on the whole society. The several classes must, in the final analysis, be thought of as component parts of the state. The primary aim for the state is that it be a unified and happy community. If this goal is achieved, then each individual in it may share in the communal well-being. "As the community grows into a well-ordered whole," Plato says, "the several classes may be allowed such measure of happiness as their nature will compass." [28] Does this mean, to return to the earlier question, that the ruling

[25] *Ibid.*
[26] P. 110.
[27] Pp. 110–111.
[28] P. 111.

class will be called upon to sacrifice its own happiness for the greater good of the state they govern? Is Plato's indictment of Thrasymachus' analysis applicable to his own Utopia? The answer has two parts. The Guardians will not be happy, Plato says, if we mean "a happiness like that of a party of peasants feasting at a fair." [29] The austere life of the Guardians will, on the surface at least, be a grim one. But it will be a life filled with satisfactions. There will be pride in having the knowledge that they have brought contentment to others. And, perhaps most important of all, there will be the satisfaction that only contact with philosophical reality can bring.

Within the Guardian class there is to be unqualified equality of the sexes. Men and women are both to have equal opportunity to be ruling Guardians. This principle is not necessarily a startling one, and yet when contrasted with the practice of existing societies, it is quite Utopian. Whether based on fact or prejudice, men have never ceased to argue that women are different. In this they are undoubtedly correct. And from this argument they have usually deduced that difference spells the inferiority of the female of the species—especially when it comes to politics. One of the keystones of Plato's theory of justice is that "different natures should have different occupations." [30] On this basis, the shoemaker does not try to rule and the Guardian does not attempt to make shoes. The three classes in the Utopia are founded on the premise that their respective members possess differing natures. But a principle such as this is a potentially dangerous one, and it must be used with extreme caution. Differences in nature can refer to sex, color, intelligence, or physical strength. A division of labor or of privilege which is based on variations in men's or women's natures cannot be used in an indiscriminate way. "We never meant any and every sort of sameness or difference in nature," Plato says, "but the sort that was relevant to the occupations in question." [31] And it is Plato's view that sex differences are irrelevant when it comes to the qualifications for governing.

If then we find that either the male sex or the female is specially qualified for any particular form of occupation, then that occupation, shall we say, ought to be assigned to one sex or the other. But if the only difference appears to be that the male begets and the female brings forth, we shall conclude that no difference between man and woman has yet been produced that is revelant to our purpose. We shall continue to think it proper for our Guardians and their wives to share in the same pursuits.

To conclude, then, there is no occupation concerned with the management of social affairs which belongs either to woman or to man, as such. Natural gifts are

[29] *Ibid.*
[30] P. 151.
[31] *Ibid.*

to be found here and there in both creatures alike; and every occupation is open to both, so far as their natures are concerned. . . .[32]

Plato's open-mindedness introduces us to an important political contoversy. As Plato himself has shown, we tend to think of individuals in terms of their group memberships. And we just as frequently are prone to label certain groups as superior or inferior. There is often some truth in the suggestion that a particular group is indeed different from others with which it might be contrasted: women taken as an aggregate are physically weaker than men, immigrants are less familiar with the established patterns of culture of their adopted country, manual laborers are not as well educated as managers and professional men. But often we avoid asking if the differences we happen to observe are germane to the function we would like to see performed. Thus Negroes in one area may be deprived of the vote or Catholics in another denied employment just because as individuals they happen to have been born into a group of a certain color or religion. What is being said here is that the natures of these individuals undoubtedly differ from those of the white man and the Protestants who exist around them. But "sameness or difference in nature," Plato reminds us, has to be "relevant to the occupations in question" if we are to use it as a basis for discrimination. Color is not relevant to voting—although education, residence, and property may be. Religion is not relevant to employment—although training, reliability, and congeniality may be.

Perhaps the best way to summarize this problem is to say that we are confronting several questions at once. The questions "Are Men Equal?" and "Are Men Unequal?" are different from "Are Men the Same?" and "Are Men Different?" The decision as to whether any two individuals are the same or different is arrived at empirically: by investigating such attributes as income, education, or physical build. In empirical terms it is almost impossible to show that all members of a group—such as women, Negroes, college graduates—possess common attributes other than the single attribute which caused them to be put in the group to which we originally referred. There are women who are excellent truck drivers and college graduates who can no longer write an English sentence. The problem of whether any two individuals are equal or unequal is answered deductively: by giving the label of "superior" to one whole group and that of "inferior" to another. Any one who falls in the former group by virtue of such attributes as his color or property or religion is automatically deemed "unequal," and in this case superior, to those who fall outside. More will be said of this later. At this point it can only be advised that the equality-inequality and same-different

[32] Pp. 152–153.

questions be kept separate. The whole argument for the political equality of women, then, must be seen as opening the door to a question with far-reaching implications. The communist status of Plato's Guardian class calls for equality of opportunity for all its members. This goal has been reached by no existing society in the world we have known.

Civility. One of the most important goals for the politics of the Western World over the last two thousand years has been the quest for civility.[33] This pursuit is founded on the idea that men ought to live together in a civilized way. This means more than the avoidance of violence or lawlessness. Civility is a positive virtue; it suggests a style of life. That civility usually embraces manners and a cultivation of the social graces is undoubtedly the case. But to stress those features would be to emphasize what are only superficial trappings. Citizens in a civil society do more than behave well; they also behave purposefully. They regard life as an experience which must be rationally planned and carefully disciplined.

Plato's Utopia is an effort to prescribe the rules of the good life in a social setting. He felt it worthwhile to advise in a philosophical treatise that it is appropriate to have one's hair cut regularly. The detailing of such a suggestion is indicative of the range of Plato's concern. Unruly hair is no great tragedy, but the attitude of which such neglect is a symptom can easily cast its influence over into more important realms. In the drive towards creating a civil society, the Guardians are the ones who will set the example:

> They will rediscover rules of behavior which their predecessors have let fall into disuse, including matters supposed to be of little importance: how the young should be silent in the presence of their elders, give up their seats to them, and take dutiful care of their parents; not to mention details of personal appearance, such as the way their hair is cut, and the clothes and shoes they wear.
> It would be silly, I think, to make laws on these matters; such habits cannot be established or kept up by written legislation. It is probable, at any rate, that the bent given by education will determine the quality of later life . . . till they finally mount up to one imposing result, whether for good or ill. For that reason I should not myself be inclined to push legislation to that length.[34]

The state, however, is not a finishing school. Plato is fully aware of the moral and practical limits on overt political intervention in the personal realm. While he readily suggests a broad area of public intervention into the private lives of the Guardians—including the assignment of their marriage partners—he is nevertheless prepared to admit that there comes a point when laws will be unable to affect human conduct. The whole idea of the

[33] For a sophisticated analysis of what is meant by "civility" and a discussion of its place in modern politics, see Edward Shils, *The Torment of Secrecy* (Glencoe: Free Press, 1956), pp. 153–75.
[34] *The Republic*, p. 116.

limited—or constitutional—state is a vital one in political theory. But its statement is not to be found in *The Republic*, and its coherent development was to come long after Plato's time. What Plato is really stressing is the role of custom in shaping behavior. Laws cannot make men civil. Even if legislation on hair-cutting were enacted and enforced, it would not be an appropriate means to achieving the larger end of leading citizens to the good and full life. Plato suggests that education rather than legislation is the institutional setting where civil habits may be inculcated. Social custom and personal habit are the central driving forces in a community. If children are taught the civil life at an early age—and if, when they are adults, society encourages and rewards such conduct—then laws prescribing specific behavior will be superfluous. Plato's Utopia, then, is not simply political or legal in character; it is also a social system and a culture. In the latter role, it strives to make life for all its inhabitants a disciplined and at the same time a full and enjoyable experience. The author of the Utopia displays an encouraging sense of reality when he acknowledges that even in a perfect society there are limits to what laws can accomplish, that a civil society must rise on a foundation of ingrained habit and settled custom.

The institutions which have been discussed—class, property, family—give the main outlines of the Utopia's social structure. These constitute the framework on which depend the philosophical principles which are to guide the state. The good state, Plato says, must embody four virtues: wisdom, courage, temperance, and justice. It is the sum of these, and their delicate interrelation, which impart civility to the society.

Wisdom and courage do not call for any extended analysis at this time. The wise Guardians and the courageous Auxiliaries are, in the act of performing their functions in society, in a position to imbue the rest of their fellow citizens with these characteristics. What constitutes wisdom is, of course, an important question, and Plato will attempt a definition in due course. But so long as the Guardians do their job properly, it is sufficient to say that they are acting with the wisdom that their role calls for and, furthermore, that their possession of wisdom—even though they are only a small minority—imparts this virtue to the whole of society.

The question of temperance raises some interesting problems. Civility, it ought now to be apparent, suggests qualities of character which are usually identified with members of a ruling class and which are only infrequently in evidence among those who belong to the lower orders. Yet a state which embarks on encouraging civility as a social goal must at least bring the lower classes to the point where they will respect—if not adopt—the civil style of life. Hence the need for the virtue of temperance or, to use a word with more political connotation, deference. "Temperance surely means a kind of orderliness, a control of certain pleasures and appetites . . ." Plato says. "Within the man himself, in his soul, there is a better part and a worse; and . . . he is his own master when the part which is better by nature has the worse under its control." [35] This principle should now be writ large. If the state is to be temperate, then the worse part must defer to the better part. Auxiliaries and Workers must give their full and unquestioning obedience to the Guardians. "Our newly founded state . . ." Plato says, "deserves to be called master of itself if temperance and self-mastery exist where the better part rules the worse."

> The great mass of multifarious appetites and pleasures and pains will be found to occur chiefly in . . . the inferior multitude; whereas the simple and moderate desires which, with the aid of reason and right belief, are guided by reflection, you will find only in a few, and those with the best inborn dispositions and the best educated.
> The desires of the inferior multitude will be controlled by the desires and wisdom of the superior few. . . . Furthermore, in our state, if anywhere, the governors and the governed will share the same conviction on the question who ought to rule.
> Temperance is not like courage and wisdom, which make the state wise and brave by residing each in one particular part. Temperance works in a different way; it extends throughout the whole gamut of the state, producing a consonance of all its elements from the weakest to the strongest as measured by any standard you like to take—wisdom, bodily strength, numbers or wealth. So we are entirely justified in identifying with temperance this unanimity or harmonious agreement between the naturally superior and inferior elements on the question which of the two should govern. . . .[36]

Temperance is plainly to be a virtue of the ordinary citizen. It is a habit of obedience, of deference, of respect for his betters. This characteristic is the cement which keeps the society's political foundation in place. The average worker or soldier does not even think to question the fact that he is governed by an exclusive ruling class. He does not demand elections or any of the devices of democratic government, because he readily acknowledges that those who rule him are wiser and better men than he. He obeys because he knows—or senses—that his own best interests will be served if he renders blind obedience. Temperance, then, is evident when the lower—and perhaps themselves uncivil—classes acknowledge without rancor their humble station in society.

The fourth quality of a civil society is justice. The Platonic conception of justice is, for the moral philosopher, the underlying theme of The Republic. However it is important here to analyze justice in its political role. For Plato's

[35] P. 124.
[36] Pp. 125–126.

theory of justice is as much a functional as a philosophical idea. That is, "justice means minding one's own business and not meddling with other men's concerns." [37] Each man in the Utopia has a specific and allotted function to perform. While the society will not suffer any permanent injury if the tailor decides to make shoes or the shoemaker takes up the needle, there will be great damage if either of these semiskilled workers take it in their heads to attempt to govern the state. "When each order—tradesman, Auxiliary, Guardian—keeps its own proper business in the commonwealth and does its own work," Plato says, "that is justice and what makes a just society," [38] Justice is not, then, an independent virtue: it is, rather, the cause and the consequence of the other three. "This quality . . ." Plato says, "makes it possible for the three we have already considered, wisdom, courage, and temperance, to take their place in the commonwealth, and so long as it remains present secures their continuance. . . ." [39] To provide wisdom for the Utopia is the proper business of the Guardians; to impart courage is the function of the Auxiliaries. Justice demands, furthermore, that the shoemaker stick to his last and the farmer to his plough and that neither of them aspire to captain the ship of state. In a word, justice constitutes the functional means by which civility is achieved. Given Plato's prerequisites of a wise ruling class and deferential lower orders, we have the social structure which provides the conditions for achieving a Utopian style of life.

Control. The means by which rulers maintain their control over the ruled takes up much of the study of politics. That Plato's Utopia rests on an intricate mechanism of control has already been shown. It is now time to examine in some detail the techniques by which this end is achieved. Socrates clearly objected to the less than subtle methods put forward by Thrasymachus. Control by imprisonment, exile, or any form of overt punishment has often proved effective. Dissidents can be rendered politically powerless simply by having them locked up; the difficulty here is that even though a man's body may be enchained, his mind is still free. He has not, by virtue of his incarceration, been brought to understand that he was in error when he protested against the powers that be. In short, most political punishment in existing societies is preventive: its aim is to keep the critic from effectively threatening society. Very seldom is it reformatory or rehabilitative in a serious way. Because punishment or the threat of punishment is a form of control which lacks the power to control the mind as well as the body, Plato rejects it. The controls he suggests can dispense with prisons because they

[37] P. 127.
[38] P. 129.
[39] P. 127.

attack the minds of men. If citizens are conditioned to think and behave along lines the state deems proper, then the possibility of deviant behavior will be obviated before it has a chance to occur. The controls which Plato puts forward for his Utopia find their summary in the notion of the political myth. The Rulers implant in the minds of the citizens an image of the world which serves to induce appropriate conduct. Effective communication of the myth requires deception; it calls for conjuring up a distorted picture of reality which, once accepted, will preclude any embarrassing questions being asked about the power structure in society.

This is no simple story of mass manipulation by a cynical ruling class. On the contrary, the structure of controls is double-edged. Not only the Auxiliaries and the Workers, but the Guardians themselves are to be subjected to a thoroughgoing process of conditioning. The minds of the Guardians are to be shaped at an early age. Plato illustrates his point by going back to the formative years when children's stories have their subtle impact. These tales, he says, may be totally unsuited for the ears of future Guardians because their morals can impart approval to dangerous ideas. "The stories in Hesiod and Homer and the poets in general . . ." Plato says, "have at all times composed fictitious tales misrepresenting the nature of gods and heroes." [40] These legends, of course, describe in no small detail the behavior of gods who, to put the matter mildly, are hardly examples of civility for impressionable minds. Murder and theft, rape and incest, war and destruction form major rather than minor episodes in these tales. The fact that it is gods and heroes who indulge in such crimes plainly implies to the child that such acts cannot be wrong. In the Utopia this must be changed:

> Our first business will be to supervise the making of fables and legends, rejecting all which are unsatisfactory; and we shall induce nurses and mothers to tell their children only those which we have approved. . . . Most of the stories now in use must be discarded.
> We shall not tell a child that, if he commits the foulest crimes or goes to any length in punishing his father's misdeeds, he will be doing nothing out of the way, but only what the first and greatest of the gods have done before him.
> If our commonwealth is to be well-ordered, . . . neither young nor old must listen to such tales, in prose or verse. [41]

At this point, once again, we must understand the Utopian method of exposition. When Plato says that "our" first business will be to supervise the making of fables and that "we" shall not tell a child that he is doing nothing untowards, he is not suggesting that he and his friends are behind the controls of the society. He is simply saying that the system, as it develops under

[40] P. 69.
[41] Pp. 69, 70, 72.

its own generative power, will invent means whereby educational censorship can be achieved. Control need not always be the conscious and premeditated manipulation of one man by another. Control is often a social or a cultural pattern which grows up without Machiavellian planning by a power-hungry ruler. Plato is simply saying that censored education for the young Guardians will have to develop in the Utopia if these boys and girls are to have the traits of character necessary for wise rulership. By the time they arrive at adulthood, the Guardians themselves will be the victims as well as perpetrators of a deception. They will have been taught to believe quite sincerely that the gods were righteous and good, and they will pass this deception on to those who come after them. In this way myth as a form of social control will become an established institution in society.

But Plato is plainly worried about the door he has opened. If deception is a necessary device for bringing into being a suitable Guardian class, then such a technique may well become common throughout the society and even indiscriminate in its application. In short, the institutions of control must themselves be controlled. But this is not easy, for the Guardians, once they have reached adulthood, cannot be deprived of the full information on the workings of society which they will most certainly need if they are to govern the state effectively.

If anyone, then, is to practice deception, either on the country's enemies or on its citizens, it must be the Rulers of the commonwealth, acting for its benefit; no one else may meddle with this privilege. For a private person to mislead such Rulers we shall declare to be a worse offense than for a patient to mislead his doctor or an athlete his trainer about his bodily condition, or for a seaman to misinform his captain about the state of the ship or of the crew. So, if anyone else in our commonwealth . . . is caught not telling the truth, the Rulers will punish him for introducing a practice as fatal and subversive in a state as it would be in a ship.[42]

It is a basic principle of organization that communication must be a two-way flow. Plato is concerned not only that the Rulers issue effective commands downward to the citizens; he also wants to make sure that there is an accurate upward flow of information to the Rulers. Political history has shown all too many instances where subordinates have misled, or simply withheld facts from, their superiors. Indeed, whole societies have been weakened because of this communication failure. Plato wishes to ensure that his Guardians will always be aware of the state of the Utopia. Citizens are obliged to speak the truth, not for its intrinsic worth, but because it is necessary if government is to be efficient. However, when it comes to speaking the truth, there is one law for the Rulers and one for the ruled.

[42] P. 78.

If the average citizen must give undistorted reports of social reality, this stricture does not embrace the Rulers themselves. If the problem of control is to be solved, then the ordinary citizen must be deceived about the foundations of the class structure. It has been pointed out that the civil life calls for deference—that the man in the street must accept the authority of the ruling class. Yet such popular acceptance can be sustained only if a political mythology is created which offers a plausible explanation for such obedience and authority. The deference of the lower orders, therefore, must be bolstered by the manipulation of authoritative symbols: a myth which anticipates and gives a satisfactory answer to otherwise embarrassing questions is the only answer.

For this reason, Plato created his famous story about the metallic origins of men. The members of the community must be conditioned to believe that they were not, in fact, born, brought up, and educated in the real world; those experiences, they must be convinced, took place in a dream.

They were the whole time down inside the earth, being molded and fostered while their arms and all their equipment were being fashioned also; and at last, when they were complete, the earth sent them up from her womb into the light of day. So now they must think of the land they dwell in as a mother and nurse, whom they must take thought for and defend against any attack, and of their fellow citizens as brothers born of the same soil. . . . It is true, we shall tell our people in this fable, that all of you in this land are brothers; but the god who fashioned you mixed gold in the composition of those among you who are fit to rule, so that they are of the most precious quality; and he put silver in the Auxiliaries, and iron and brass in the farmers and craftsmen.[43]

This myth serves two vital purposes. On the one hand, it creates attitudes of loyalty to the state. The "motherland" becomes literally the progenitor of all men, and all citizens are bound in brotherhood. On the other hand, the class structure is made palatable: men of iron or brass will accept their lowly station with good grace because they know almost intuitively that gold is the one metal which imparts superior qualities. Finally, the myth will close with the warning moral that "ruin will come upon the state when it passes into the keeping of a man of iron or brass." [44] As the temperate and deferential citizen of the Utopia wishes only for the success and long life of the state, he will not himself want to endanger the collective well-being by aspiring to a political office which he does not deserve.

Whether or not the censorship of children's stories and the myth of metals sound plausible, these devices symbolize an important political principle. It is a Utopian author's privilege, of course, not to try to answer vexing questions

[43] P. 106.
[44] P. 107.

of control. There have been writers of Utopias who have assumed that in their perfect societies all citizens will naturally and spontaneously refrain from stepping on each others' toes and will eagerly pursue the common good of the community.[45] Such Utopias avoid discussion of control because their authors, unlike Plato, find the prescription of deceptive measures a distasteful task. It is to Plato's credit that he confronts this very real political problem head on. Men must be deceived if the good society is to continue in operation. In short, the end justifies this particular means. There is no overpowering evidence that men are harmed by being made to live in a world of myths—so long as the subsequent world of experience does not produce events which give the lie to the myths. Political theorists of all ideological complexions have acknowledged the value of the half-truth and the slight distortion as means to achieving social cohesion and political obedience.

But the practice of deception raises some perplexing questions. Who, first of all, are to be the deceivers and who the deceived? Plato's answer is that deceptions can become institutionalized in the culture and automatically transmitted to ensuing generations. The distorted legends and the myth of metals will, he suggests, be believed both by those who impart them and by those who receive them. On the other hand, if distortions of reality play such a vital role in social control, then we may be forced to conclude that the Guardians know full well that they are tampering with the truth. An intelligent and sophisticated class of rulers cannot be expected to swallow a line which they are using in order to deceive those who are less educated. The Guardians will have access to the old story books; they will know that the gods were not individuals of spotless character. They will superintend the eugenics program, and thus they will know that babies do not sprout from mother earth. It is clear, in practice, that the Guardians will be aware of the fact that they are deceivers. They will have to find ways to keep from becoming cynical about their manipulation of the masses. And they will have to be sure that the truth does not leak out and in so doing upset the equanimity of the otherwise contented citizens.

In addition, the Guardian class will have to be sure that they do not try to deceive each other. Already the Utopia calls for a rigged marriage lottery in which the ruling Guardians hide the truth about the eugenics program from their nonruling colleagues. There is the possibility that even the ruling Guardians, so accustomed to tampering with the truth, may be tempted to

[45] Perhaps the classic instance of a Utopia which exists with neither power nor rulers is William Morris' *News from Nowhere*, written in 1890. For a discussion of this kind of Utopia, see Andrew Hacker, "Original Sin vs. Utopia in British Socialism," *The Review of Politics*, April 1956, pp. 184–206.

be less than candid with one another. Such a situation, as Plato himself admits, would lead to the destruction of the Utopia. But he does not seek to raise or discuss problems such as these.

The whole gamut of questions about control are forever in search of answers; this is why speculation on this aspect of political theory is as necessary today as it was in Plato's time. The Utopia of Plato is perfectly controlled because it is ruled by a class of public-spirited Guardians who do not abuse their powers. Their character is such that even engaging in the crassest of deceptions will not make them cynical or personally ambitious. The institutions of control form Plato's answer to the propositions concerning "human nature" which were set forth by Thrasymachus and Glaucon. The Guardians, through breeding and education, will be able to use the most Machiavellian of controls and yet remain unswerving in their pursuit of the common good. Political power for them is a means and not an end.

Contentment. A Utopia is, by traditional definition, a contented society.[46] Its citizens have achieved a level of happiness unattained by those who of us are doomed to reside in the real world. Nevertheless, it should be made clear that Plato is not by this token a proponent of individualism as a philosophical goal. Indeed, like all communists (and many conservatives), he looks on individualism as a theory which promotes overweening ambition, self-aggrandizement, and excessive materialism and which leads to the disruption of the communal life. The possession of private property, for example, is a hallmark of individualism, and Plato would abolish individual ownership because of its antisocial character.

The contentment of the Utopia, therefore, must be viewed in terms of the happiness of the collectivity. This whole may or may not be more than the sum of its parts: that is a matter of definition. But it is the happiness of the whole which counts. "Our aim in founding the commonwealth was not to make any one class specially happy, but to secure the greatest possible happiness for the community as a whole . . ." Plato says. "We are constructing, as we believe, the state which will be happy as a whole, not trying to secure the well-being of a select few." [47] The ordering idea of the Utopia, then, lies

---

[46] Since the end of World War I there have appeared literally dozens of books—many of them in the guise of science fiction—offering pessimistic predictions of the world our grandchildren will know. Aldous Huxley's *Brave New World* and George Orwell's *1984* are the best-known examples. The mood of these books marks a radical departure from the traditional Utopian efforts. Karl Meyer has called these sketches of a futile future "Futopias." As contributions to political theory, they serve a totally different purpose from the Utopia. If the Futopia descends to the depths of despair, the Utopia rises to the heights of happiness. See Meyer's "O Sacred Old World, That Has Such Robots In't," *The Reporter,* July 6, 1954, pp. 35–37.

[47] *The Republic,* p. 110.

in its unity. The public interest, the common good, the general welfare—any such term—is what should at all times be uppermost in the mind of each individual citizen. The good society is a unified society: its institutions encourage fellow feeling; individual behavior manifests attitudes of altruism and loyalty.

Plato asks Glaucon:

> Does not the worst evil for a state arise from anything that tends to rend it asunder and destroy its unity, while nothing does it more good than whatever tends to bind it together and make it one?
> Are not citizens bound together by sharing in the same pleasures and pains, all feeling glad or grieved on the same occasions of gain or loss; whereas the bond is broken when such feelings are no longer universal, but any event of public or personal concern fills some with joy and others with distress? [48]

His questions are rhetorical, and the answer is clear: "Our citizens," he says, "sharing as they do in a common interest which each will call his own, will have all their feelings of pleasure or pain in common." [49] A prosperous, well-governed, and unified society will be a contented society: each citizen will share in this collective happiness and therefore will himself be happy. If any single person were to seek his personal happiness in a way which would damage the common good, such behavior would be short-sighted and self-defeating for the individual in question. For in disrupting the general welfare an individual, even though in so doing he might obtain temporary pleasures, would in the long run impair the happiness of the whole society—of which he is an integral part.

While he is not an individualist, Plato is concerned—albeit in an indirect way—with the happiness of the individual. When he gives society a higher priority than the individual, this is not because he thinks that institutions have a worth which is inherently higher than that of persons. On the contrary, like all serious political philosophers, Plato is searching for ways and means to give each citizen in society the best that life has to offer. If the path charted out by his Utopia is open to criticism, we must always ask whether it is on the grounds of its practical effectiveness or on the grounds of philosophical principle. The issue may be framed in terms of the debate over individualism vs. collectivism. But it may also be concerned with the question of what is the best way to promote the individual's happiness and development.

One way to proceed further with a question such as this is to inquire into the substantial content of the happiness Plato has in mind. The answer seems

---

[48] P. 163.
[49] P. 165.

to be that it is a contentment which is essentially negative in character. That is, if the citizen is to be happy he must be removed from the sort of experiences which would tend to make him unhappy.

So our laws will secure that these men will live in complete peace with one another; and if they never quarrel among themselves, there is no fear of the rest of the community being divided either against them or against itself. . . . Rid of all these cares, they will live a more enviable life than the Olympic victor, who is counted happy on the strength of far fewer blessings than our Guardians will enjoy. Their victory is the nobler, since by their success the whole commonwealth is preserved.[50]

There will be no wars, no quarrels, no fissures in society. The Utopian citizen will live the serene life. This conclusion is bound to raise some questions about the meaning of happiness. The first might be whether such an existence would soon become boring to the point of frustration. While armed conflict, personal quarrels, and class antagonism are hardly goods in themselves, complete abolition of these antagonisms would also serve to remove sources of enjoyment of life for many people. Plato does not face up to this question. Nor, indeed, do most Utopians, for their aim is to waft us away from the conflicts which plague the real world. But if Plato or any Utopian was pressed on the problem of boredom, he would probably reply that even the perfect society would be marked by lively controversy and debate. However, the disagreements would be about such matters as Bach vs. Berlioz or Cowper vs. cummings. Quarrels about politics and economics would by that time seem irrelevant. Just as in the twentieth century we believe that the once hotly contested arguments between the Guelphs and Ghibellines are now dead issues, so in the Utopia questions of capitalism vs. communism, Democrats vs. Republicans, white supremacy vs. racial equality will have reached the stage of irrelevance. Furthermore, the Utopian writer would say, boredom may be undesirable, but hunger, violent death, and perpetual insecurity are far greater evils. Usually those who find themselves worrying about the possible monotony of the Utopian life are people who are well fed, healthy, and successful in existing society. But most people in this world are not this fortunate. The serenity of a Utopia looks attractive to them, and they do not ask searching questions about the price of admission.

But Plato's most persuasive answer is that his society will be based on the principle of justice. Each citizen will be allowed to develop his potentialities so far as he is able. Not every man who thinks he might like to take a brush to hand is capable of great artistry. The Utopia will take great pains in the crucial matter of job selection as it applies to all phases of life. The

[50] Pp. 166–167.

man who has it in him only to be a competent housepainter will be given that task, and society will encourage him to do it as well as he can. His status and function will be respected by all, and he will not have to apologize for the humbleness of his calling. On the other hand, those who are philosophically inclined or who show an aptitude for administrative responsibilities will be drawn into the Guardian class, and there they will have full opportunity to exercise their talents. The trouble with a classless and uncontrolled conception of individualism, Plato points out, is that it brings failure, frustration, and resentment to far more people than it brings success. The individualist ideology tells all men—from housepainters to philosophers—that the world is their oyster: all are encouraged to ascend the ladder of attainment. But few can succeed, and the many failures feel guilty about their inability to meet a standard of achievement which is applied equally to all.[51] Plato's Utopia does away with the seamy side of individualism. At what cost this is accomplished must be a matter of individual judgment. But one ought to hesitate before disparaging a contented society just because it is contented.

Consensus. It remains only to point out that the citizens of any Utopia must be agreed among themselves on the fundamental principles of social life. In spite of a class structure, there must be concurrence on the goals which are to be pursued and the best means by which to pursue them.

Plato makes explicit two features of the Utopia which will encourage consensus. The first is that there must be no economic extremes. We have already seen that the Guardians are to live without property. Yet there remains the possibility that some of the Workers will, unhampered by the restrictions of communism, be able to enrich themselves quite substantially. What must be prevented, then, is excessive wealth found in the hands of one group and extreme poverty of condition being the lot for another substantial group. "Here, then, are some more evils which must not elude the vigilance of our Guardians and find their way into the commonwealth: riches and poverty," Plato says. "The one produces luxury and idleness, the other low standards of conduct and workmanship; and both have a subversive tendency." [52] While men are often content to accept wide disparities in political power—especially if patterns of deference are strong—they are not nearly as willing to accept marked contrasts in economic well-being. The man whose child does not have enough food can seldom be persuaded that the plenty of the rich is theirs by legitimate title. The solution is not so much to soak

---

[51] For further analysis of the discontents arising from an "open society," see Robert Merton's discussion of "anomie" in his *Social Theory and Social Structure* (Glencoe: Free Press, 1957), revised edition, pp. 131–194.

[52] *The Republic*, p. 112.

the rich as to make sure that the poor man's family has enough to eat. The abolition of poverty is necessary for Utopia as a first step. The initial stage of consensus, then, must be that all are well fed, well housed, and well clothed. Only with this ensured will the citizens be prepared to defer to the rule of those who have been placed over them in the social structure.

The second feature of the Utopia is its size. It must be relatively small. "So we must lay yet another command on our Guardians," Plato says. "They are to take all possible care that the state shall neither be too small nor yet one that seems great but has not unity." [53] And unity is not simply loyalty to the nation, but also the fraternal feeling of all citizens for one another. This cannot be achieved in any meaningful way in a community which numbers over several thousand. In a good society, Plato asks, "are not citizens bound together by sharing . . . any event of public or personal concern?" [54] The answer is that while a village hamlet may be so small that it is dependent on other communities for its welfare or even its existence, the Utopia itself must not grow so large that human relationships become impersonal. All must be able to know—and understand the personal concerns of—everyone else.

Does this mean that his Utopia is inapplicable as a model for states in the twentieth century? Are only Monaco, Andorra, and San Marino able to profit by Plato's strictures? The answer is that a Utopia is a literary representation of philosophical principles: it should not be regarded as a working model. A good analogy is the New England town meeting. While this institution is now all but defunct as an effective organ of government, Americans continue to employ its values as criteria for judging the political performance of a huge nation. Popular participation, rational discussion, and self-government may have only been realities in the setting of the small, isolated, and self-sufficient town, but the ideas themselves are essential to any conception of democracy; therefore, they are adjusted and reapplied to the demands of a new environment. The same procedure holds true for the use to which any Utopia is to be put. No modern society comes near to possessing the consensus demanded by Plato. Yet it is not because of the striking similarity between Utopia and reality, but rather in spite of the vast difference between them, that one embarks on the never-ending attempt to put philosophical ideas into political practice.

[53] P. 114.
[54] P. 163.

POLITICS AND THE PHILOSOPHER

The philosopher's claim to exercise the extraordinary political power which is vested in the Guardian class is certainly not a modest one. While the rulers of the Utopia are the products of selective breeding and rigorous training for high office, their status depends less on these preparations than it does in their possession of a brand of wisdom which is denied to other men. Plato acknowledges to Glaucon that such a proposition requires some defense.

> We must, I think, define . . . whom we mean by these lovers of wisdom who, we have dared to assert, ought to be our rulers. Once we have a clear view of their character, we shall be able to defend our position by pointing to some who are naturally fitted to combine philosophic study with political leadership, while the rest of the world should accept their guidance and let philosophy alone.[55]

This brings *The Republic* to a discussion of epistemology, the question of "What is knowledge?"

Plato's theory of knowledge is one of the most important in the entire history of ideas, and only a brief sketch of its relation to political theory can be given here. Just as we have had to do less than justice to questions of moral philosophy, so we will be compelled to be summary with matters of epistemology. There is, Plato suggests, a vital distinction which ought to be made between "belief," on the one hand, and "knowledge," on the other. The vast majority of men in any society harbor beliefs about both material objects and inanimate ideas. They are not, however, privy to knowledge. The average man will be able to recognize a beautiful woman, a beautiful painting, or a beautiful musical composition when he encounters one. The typical citizen may be able to apprehend a just law, a just administrative decision, or a just judicial opinion. But the man-in-the-street's conceptions of beauty and justice are, to put it simply, no more than adjectival. That is, he can prefix his descriptions of things or relationships with adjectives which give the appearance of imparting a particular quality to whatever it is he is attempting to describe. However, this level of discourse is only the level of belief.

> When people have an eye for the multitude of beautiful things or of just actions or whatever it may be, but can neither behold Beauty or Justice itself nor follow a guide who would lead them to it, we shall say that all they have is beliefs, without any real knowledge of the objects of their beliefs.[56]

What Plato is saying, then, is that there exist philosophic "Forms" which are the "ideas" of Beauty, Justice, Truth, and so forth. A man may discourse on a beautiful poem, and think that he knows what he is talking about. But

[55] P. 181.
[56] P. 188.

only a philosopher knows Beauty—and hence the reality about beautiful poems, beautiful women, and beautiful scenery. (Indeed, the conception of Forms applies not only to ideas like Beauty, but also to material objects. Thus there is the Form of a chair. It contains all which is essential to such functionally different objects as rocking chairs, high chairs, and electric chairs.) The man who does not know the Forms lives not in the world of reality, Plato says, but in a world of dreams.

The essential Forms . . . manifest themselves in a great variety of combinations, with actions, with material things, and with one another, and so each seems to be many. . . . Your lovers of sights and sounds delight in beautiful tones and colors and shapes and in all the works of art into which these enter; but they have not the power of thought to behold and to take delight in the nature of Beauty itself. That power to approach Beauty and behold it as it is in itself, is rare indeed. . . . Now if a man believes in the existence of beautiful things, but not of Beauty itself, and cannot follow a guide who would lead him to a knowledge of it, is he not living in a dream? [57]

Belief, then, is of beautiful things; knowledge is of Beauty. The believer lives in a world of dreams or shadows; the knower lives in the world of Reality. "Knowledge has for its natural object the Real—to know the truth about Reality . . ." Plato says. "The name of philosopher, then, will be reserved for those whose affections are set, in every case, on the Reality." [58]

The difference between the average man and the philosopher, therefore, is that the latter has an objective standard by which to assess all that he sees and does. He does not rely on subjective standards of judgment. The philosopher's evaluations have a superior authority because they are based on a knowledge of the pre-existing and superordinate Forms. Most of us will never come to know the Forms, and we will have to live as best we can manage in a world of pseudo-knowledge. The standards by which we judge things to be beautiful, or actions to be just, will be shifting, superficial, and frequently inconsistent. The average man will claim to be satisfied with perceptions which are no more than belief; or he may be so bold as to claim that even though he is not a philosopher by profession, he is as good as anyone else when it comes to apprehending the Forms. How to deal with these two attitudes—cheerfully making do with the second best or attempting to enter an untenable claim to knowledge—on the part of the average man is a difficult political question. It is another problem involving social control which those who govern average men must face up to at all times— the problem of how to make men admit their ignorance and then to conclude that ignorance is bliss.

[57] P. 183.
[58] P. 185, 189.

The importance of Plato's epistemology for politics should by this time be clear. If we accept the idea that there is a Form of, say, Justice, then the men who dispense justice in a society should be those who know what Justice is. Similarly, if there is a Form of Law, then lawmakers ought to be those men who have a knowledge of Law. Plato's theory of Forms, while it starts as a theory of knowledge, ends up being a political theory. Politics deals with the exercise of power. But all executive, legislative, and judicial power have a substantive content: decisions about administration, lawmaking, and justice involve choices from among real alternatives. Rulers must be sure, first of all, that they have knowledge of existing alternatives; they must, second, know enough to select the right one; and they need, finally, to devise means which stand a good chance of securing the end they have chosen to pursue. The effective exercise of power, therefore, must be founded on full knowledge of human behavior and social institutions. The ruler who has only beliefs to rely on will be ineffective. He will not know what the good society is, and thus he will have no standard on which to base his choices; even if by chance he selects the right goals, he will not know enough to set up means which will lead to the attainment of those goals. Power, to be legitimate, can only be power based on knowledge, not belief.

The theory of Forms appears throughout political theory, although never again in Plato's precise guise. The idea of reason, for example, as employed by Hegel, and that of the laws of history as adumbrated by Marx and Engels, have much in common with Plato's assertion that abstract and absolute Forms exist in—and perhaps even govern—the universe. The search for an external standard of knowledge and morality is one of the chief quests of political theory. No matter how farfetched a theory like Plato's may seem on its face, the forces which move men to think in this way are strong and undying.

Putting together Plato's Utopia and his theory of knowledge is now an easier task. The institutions of Utopia constitute a radical departure from those of existing society, and it remains to ask how men may set foot on the road to perfection. "Our next attempt . . ." Plato says, "must be to point out what defect in the working of existing states prevents them from being so organized, and what is the least change that would effect a transformation into this type of government." [59] The answer lies more in changing men than it does in changing institutions. The difficulty with existing societies is that their men of power are not their men of knowledge, that society's men of knowledge are excluded from her seats of power. In a famous passage Plato lays down the single condition which will bring Utopia into being:

[59] P. 178.

> Unless either philosophers become kings in their countries or those who are now called kings and rulers come to be sufficiently inspired with a genuine desire for wisdom; unless, that is to say, political power and philosophy meet together . . . there can be no rest from troubles, my dear Glaucon, for states, nor yet, as I believe, for all mankind; nor can this commonwealth which we have imagined ever till then see the light of day and grow to its full stature.[60]

The philosopher-king—the man of knowledge and the man of power conjoined in one—is the indispensable requisite for the perfect society. That this conjunction has never been achieved in the political world we know is the chief reason why political philosophy has as important a role to play today as it did in Plato's time. There is no overpowering evidence that, over the course of the centuries, rulers have become progressively more rational. One reason for this, hinted at by Thrasymachus and later to be elaborated on by Machiavelli, may be that the aptitude for the successful exercise of power and the aptitude for the serious acquisition of knowledge are widely different: that the sort of personality who can do one is not the sort of man capable of doing the other.

But, be that as it may, the philosopher-king is symbolic of Plato's political philosophy. The wise ruler, and his counterpart, the rational citizen, turn up again and again throughout the history of political thought. To use such men as theoretical models is not necessarily the sign of a Utopia. Nevertheless, the degree to which these figures are employed is a good index of the Utopian content latent in any political theory. Only Plato is a full-fledged Platonist; but all political thinkers mirror his idealism to some degree. If they did not, they would not deserve the title of thinkers.

After stating that the only hope for achieving political perfection lies in the coronation of the philosopher, Plato rapidly comes to grips with down-to-earth matters in his analysis. In his attempt to show how existing societies corrupt men of philosophical inclinations—and thus put off the dawn of Utopia—he gives a picture of the values and motives which impel men in their everyday behavior in society. Adeimantus opens this phase of the discussion by telling Socrates that the typical philosophers live in ivory towers and hence are of little use to the societies which support them. "As a matter of plain fact, the votaries of philosophy, when they carry on the study too long, instead of taking it up in youth as a part of general culture and then dropping it, almost always become decidedly queer, not to say utterly worthless . . ." Adeimantus says. "Even the most respectable are so far the worse for this pursuit you are praising as to become useless to society." [61]

[60] Pp. 178–179.
[61] P. 194.

The bitter truth of this point gives Plato an opportunity to dilate on the ways society wreaks its toll on the individual—especially the out-of-the-ordinary individual—so as to assimilate him to the standards of the group. Plato concurs with Adeimantus: "The better sort of philosophers are placed in such a cruel position in relation to their country that there is no one thing in nature to be compared to it." [62] However, in the imperfect world we know there is nothing surprising about this. "It would be far more astonishing if they were . . . held in honor by their country," [63] Plato says. But a society which finds that it is not employing to good purpose its men of reason ought not to be so quick to condemn the philosophers themselves. On the contrary, we "must rather blame those who make no use of them." [64] Just as the sick man seeks out the doctor and the doctor is not expected to ply his services in the street, so the philosopher should be approached by those who stand in need of the wise rule he can give them. "All who need to be governed should seek out the man who can govern them," Plato says. "It is not for him to beg them to accept his rule." [65] The philosopher's alienation from politics, then, is a social problem. The fault lies with an obtuse society rather than with the obscure philosopher. If society will not, of its own accord, enthrone a philosopher as king, then there is little that the philosopher himself can do to bring his fellow citizens to take this step. Those who blame their men of reason for failing to be of any use are avoiding the important question. What kind of society, we might ask, is it that fails to create a significant role for its philosophers?

This leads Plato to a consideration of social values. Up until this point he has been taking for granted the Utopian values of reason and knowledge. But existing societies place a high premium on power, property, and prestige. There is, then, a competition between those who uphold these disparate sets of values—we may call them "reason" and "power"—for the loyalty of the best men in any community. It is with some irony that Plato admits that the men who would make the most rational philosophers are also those who are most avidly recruited by those who hold the keys to power. The lures held out to budding philosophers are tempting and seductive.

Everyone, I think, would agree that a nature with all the qualities we require to make the perfect philosopher is a rare growth, seldom seen among men. . . . Consider, then, how many grave dangers threaten to destroy these few. Strangest of all, every one of those qualities which we approved—courage, temperance, and all the rest—tends to ruin its possessor and to wrest his mind away from philosophy. . . .

[62] P. 195.
[63] P. 196.
[64] *Ibid.*
[65] *Ibid.*

And besides this, all the good things of life, as they are called, corrupt and distract the soul: beauty, wealth, strength, powerful connections, and so forth.[66]

Plato is not being an idealist here: he is not saying that if a young person really wants to be a philosopher then he will go ahead and become one no matter what obstacles or temptations are placed in his way. Plato understands that in any society men are products of their environment, and he does not for a moment underrate the attractiveness of wealth and power for a young person of outstanding ability. The attractions in existing society are so great, in fact, that the ranks of erstwhile philosophers are depleted before they have a chance to form. The value of reason may, in academic terms, stand on the highest plateau. But the value of power has tangible rewards to offer, and it has the prestige-laden institutions of society mobilized to implement its recruiting drive. Plato is not at all surprised when a bright young man fails to reject the blandishments of power. The cause of philosophy will undoubtedly suffer, but that is no reason to put the blame on the defector. He is human like the rest of us.

A related aspect of this question is the role which formal education plays in influencing the young in existing society. In Utopia Plato made education one of the chief forms of social control. He was able to do this because the Guardians would take the initiative in creating and transmitting social values. Just the opposite is the case in the real world. By and large, formal education simply serves the function of reflecting and inculcating the prevailing attitudes of the community. Teachers and schools do little more than echo the ideas and beliefs which exist in the outside world. And if there are a few radical educators who question the values of the status quo, there is little chance that their ideas will have much influence. The impact which the institutions of society have on the minds of their students is a more than effective counterweight to their efforts. Yet, for a variety of reasons, society is fearful of its subversive scholars. All manner of evils are blamed on them, and they are forever and again singled out for an attention which goes far beyond their just desserts.

In Plato's time the supposedly disruptive professors were known as "sophists," teachers who instructed the sons of the well-to-do. Plato puts the question squarely to Adeimantus: If our young men are led to take the path of power rather than that of reason, is this behavior on their part to be ascribed to the teaching of the sophists? "Do you hold the popular belief that, here and there, certain young men are demoralized by the private instructions of some individual sophists?" he asks. "Does that sort of influence amount to much?" The answer is that it is society as a whole which sets the

[66] P. 198.

moral tone for young people: the influence of the professors, in comparison, is negligible. "Is not the public itself the greatest of all sophists," Plato asks, "training up young and old, men and women alike, into the most accomplished specimens of the character it desires to produce?" [67] We have here, then, Plato's analysis of the forces which shape personality in existing society. Even if a teacher sought to inculcate the values of reason in his students, he would be fighting a losing battle. If society cherishes the values of power, then contrary teachings will be futile. The young people in our classrooms are not hothouse flowers. They forever come in contact with the world of reality; they know what are the values held by their fellow citizens and they have no doubts about what the ticket to worldly success is.

Whenever the populace crowds together at any public gathering, in the Assembly, the law courts, the theatre, or the camp, and sits there clamoring its approval or disapproval, both alike excessive, of whatever is being done; booing and clapping till the rocks ring and the whole place redoubles the noise of their applause and outcries. In such a scene what do you suppose will be a young man's state of mind? What sort of private instruction will have given him the strength to hold out against the force of such a torrent, or will save him from being swept away down the stream, until he accepts all their notions of right and wrong, does as they do, and comes to be just such a man as they are? [68]

Plato is saying a great deal more here than that professors are ineffectual and innocents are seduced. He is also pointing, in a figurative way, to the impact of public opinion on the mind of the individual. Popular sentiment is only occasionally expressed as vociferously as it is when Plato has the populace crowd together. It is usually an unspoken body of assumptions which are subtly passed on to all members of society. What is more, public judgments of approval and disapproval, of right and wrong, are based on belief and not on knowledge. They constitute a superficial parcel of lowest common denominators—a mixture of myths, prejudices, and slogans. "Is it conceivable," Plato asks, "that the multitude should ever believe in the existence of any Real Essence, as distinct from its many manifestations, or listen to anyone who asserts such a Reality?" [69] The man in the street is unaware of the Forms and suspicious of anyone who claims knowledge of them. "The multitude can never be philosophical," Plato says. "Accordingly it is bound to disapprove of all who pursue wisdom." [70] In the real world the public is not deferential to its betters. On the contrary, it seems to drag the men of reason down to its own low level. Or, as an alternative, it will tolerate them if they

[67] P. 199.
[68] *Ibid.*
[69] P. 201.
[70] *Ibid.*

celebrate and render into pretentious language the prejudices of the common man. But the public has no wish to suffer the subversive ideas of men of reason who take it on themselves to deny the validity of popularly held beliefs.

What bothers Plato nearly as much as the tyranny of the majority is the behavior of some men who pander to the public and actually know better. He is referring to those individuals "who associate with the mob and set their hearts on pleasing it." These men of power are the real destroyers of the potential philosopher. The young man who might otherwise pursue the life of reason will be approached by men of power "who, no doubt, want to make use of him for their own purposes." Because he is a ripe recruit for the citadels of power, "they will fawn upon him with their entreaties and promises of advancement, flattering beforehand the power that will some day be his." [71] Surely these men—and not the professors—are to be blamed if anyone is. Any discussion of "the tyranny of the majority" must, indeed, be accompanied by an examination of the minority within that majority which organizes and directs the activities of the larger group. If we hesitate before ascribing moral responsibility to so vast an entity as "the public," we may nevertheless single out those who make effective the public's great power.

Plato's critique of democracy is an uncompromising one. While purportedly concerned with the seduction of reason, he is actually pointing to the tension between majority power and philosophical knowledge. Like Burke and Tocqueville, he sees only mediocrity in the public mind. Like John Stuart Mill, he sees the majority as a tyrant bent on leveling all superior men and ideas to its own plateau. But he goes even further when he suggests that in the politics of existing society advancement is open only to those who are willing to please the people. The majority are the sovereign, and they bestow their rewards on leaders who will follow them. In addition, Plato points out that under a situation of "mob rule" it is never the mob itself that rules. There must always be a few superior men at the head of—or behind—the crowd who voice its sentiments, respond to its needs, and govern in its name. These demagogues are the rulers who were applauded by Thrasymachus and who will later be analyzed by Machiavelli. They are the men of power who, in the real world, carry the responsibility for seducing or destroying the men of reason. The philosopher-king of the Utopia will also have to keep the multitude in control. The difference between him and the demagogue is that the latter seeks personal power as an end in itself, whereas the philosopher-king takes power only as a means to establishing a good society.

[71] *Ibid.*

Having blueprinted the institutions of Utopia and having shown that philosophers are without honor in existing society, Plato does not become pessimistic. The function of political philosophy is to discuss ideas of the good state. Philosophy is not to be tested by whether these ideas have been or even can be transformed into real political institutions. "When we set out to discover the essential nature of justice and injustice, . . . our purpose was to use them as ideal patterns . . ." Plato says. "We did not set out to show that these ideals could exist in fact." [72] The task of a Utopian architect is to design the best society; it is not to create a workable model of the best possible one. The gulf between "the best" and "the best possible" is a great one. "We have been constructing in discourse the pattern of an ideal state," Plato says. "Is our theory any the worse, if we cannot prove it possible that a state so organized should be actually founded?" [73] The answer is that possibility of attainment is not an issue so long as you make clear that you have been writing a Utopia. The theorist who draws up a plan for revising the terms of office of United States Senators and Representatives might be expected to show that his scheme stood a reasonable chance of adoption, but the Utopian's concern is exclusively with philosophical principles. Plato sought to set up some standards which, without consideration of their being adopted in a programmatic way by any particular society, would nevertheless guide rulers in the exercise of power. As we have seen, it is not necessary or even advisable to approve of Plato's Utopia as an organic entity. The constituent ideas which comprise it—from education to eugenics, from sexual equality to the political myth—represent a whole range of principles which are relevant to political practice in a variety of settings. Because Plato has used the Utopia as an expository device, he is not disillusioned because the real world has been unreceptive to it. He hardly expected it to be welcomed with open arms. Yet he would also be pleased to know that in one form or another his ideas have had a habit of showing up in political thought for 2500 years after his time.

The alienation of the philosopher in the world of power is a perennial problem. The men of reason will never find a happy home in existing society; if they wish to persevere with their chosen way of life and thought, they must develop a sense of inner direction as their chief reliance. The field of philosophy stands alone, abandoned by those who might most be expected to protect her in her hour of need. "Philosophy is left forlorn, like a maiden deserted by her nearest kin . . ." Plato says. "Bereft of her natural

[72] P. 177.
[73] Pp. 177–178.

protectors, [she] is dishonored by unworthy interlopers, who fasten on her the reproach . . . that some who have to do with her are worthless and most of them deserve heavy punishment." [74] Yet a loyal band of brothers will somehow carry on:

> The remnant who are worthy to consort with Philosophy will be small indeed: perhaps some noble and well-nurtured character, saved by exile from those influences which would have impaired his natural impulse to be constant in her service; or it may be a great mind born in a petty state whose affairs are beneath its notice; and, possibly, a gifted few who have turned to philosophy from some calling which they rightly disdain.
> One who has joined this small company and tasted the happiness that is their portion; who has watched the frenzy of the multitude and seen that there is no soundness in the conduct of public life . . .—one who has weighed all this keeps quiet and goes his own way, like the traveller who takes shelter under a wall from a driving storm of dust and hail; and seeing lawlessness spreading on all sides, is content if he can keep his hands clean from iniquity while this life lasts, and when the end comes take his departure, with good hopes, in serenity and peace.[75]

The saving remnant, then, must find its own salvation within those happy few who have come to know reason. And, at the same time, the members of this small fraternity must possess an inner conviction that they—and they alone—are on the right road. A hostile society can be neither persuaded nor conquered; nor ought one to try to escape from its authority or its boundaries.[76] Men of reason must derive their satisfaction not from popular approval but from their own internal conviction. Plato has suggested throughout that this is not an impossibility. Rather than exhorting men to lead the good life, he has taken pains to show how the values of power are always ready to lure away individuals of intelligence and character. Once we are made aware of the drawing power of these temptations, the battle is at least engaged. A society governed by philosophers will not be achieved in the here and now.

---

[74] P. 203.

[75] Pp. 203–204.

[76] Plato at one point does suggest that the public may eventually come to appreciate the "god-like" qualities which the philosophers display in the conduct of their everyday lives. If this comes to pass, he says, the public will "be reconciled to the philosopher and no longer disbelieve our assertion that happiness can only come to a state when its lineaments are traced by an artist working after the divine pattern" (p. 209). However, this eventuality is suggested only halfheartedly by Plato, and it is hard to see how it can counter the arguments concerning the public's obtuseness which Plato has been advancing up to now.
    On the question of whether the dissenter should obey constituted authority in his own society and on the further question of whether it is right to leave your country if it persecutes you, Plato has much to say in his dialogues The Apology and The Crito. These dialogues will not be considered here, but the theoretical questions which are raised in them will be discussed in later chapters.

But each philosopher can make a world for himself if he has the fortitude—an autonomous world in which he is the only citizen.

THE DYNAMICS OF POLITICAL CHANGE: DEMOCRACY AND DEGENERATION

One of the significant omissions in Plato's outline of the Utopia is an explanation of the forces which will serve to keep the ruling class unified. The Guardians are a group of intelligent and highly skilled men and women. The training they have received and the responsibilities they have shouldered in governing the society have plainly taught them to think for themselves. While they are subjected at an earlier stage to a censored form of education, by the time they have assumed positions of power they are able to exercise great discretion in the making of policy. For example, they take charge of the eugenics program, and it is their task to disseminate the political myths among the ordinary citizens. The Guardians, then, cannot be regarded as mindless robots. On the contrary, as individuals they are bound to have personalities of their own. Indeed, if they are the few who have a philosophical aptitude for discovering the Forms, then they surely must have roving and inquiring intelligences.

Out of a ruling class so constituted it is difficult to assume that there will be unanimous agreement on all matters of importance. The Guardians may be at one with each other in the early days of the Utopia, when the pioneering spirit causes them to submerge personal opinions. But as the years roll on, men and women who possess strength of character are bound to develop ideas of their own. While it is likely that very often we would find two Guardians agreeing in general terms on the ends they think society ought to pursue, nevertheless it is also highly probable that we would encounter them disagreeing on the best means which ought to be used to achieve those abstract ends. And it is entirely possible that two Guardians would part company even on questions of ultimate ends: the pursuit of wisdom, for example, as opposed to the pursuit of happiness. Any society, of course, has institutional mechanisms for adjusting differences of opinion. We should suppose that in Utopia no less than other societies there will be meetings to decide on policy, conferences to hear varying viewpoints, and discussions at all appropriate levels within the Guardian class.

Yet there is always the possibility that there will emerge a disgruntled clique of Guardians—a minority which for one reason or another finds itself forever being voted down—and that this group will decide to break the rules of the game. They may attempt to put their policies into operation even though the other Guardians have rejected them; they may sabotage the delicate system of psychological control by letting it be known that the myth of metals is a tremendous hoax; they may even go down to the market place and enlist the support of the ordinary citizens in a move to resort to violent overthrow of the existing regime.

Plato acknowledges that this sort of thing can happen. Revolution is always possible. But it is, he says, always a "palace" revolution. That is, it is a revolt fomented by dissident Guardians, not by the man in the street. "Is it not a simple fact that in any form of government revolution always starts from the outbreak of internal dissension in the ruling class?" Plato asks. "The constitution cannot be upset so long as that class is of one mind." [77] But the single-mindedness of the ruling class is apt to break down, and a disgruntled group of Guardians can inaugurate revolutionary activity. Plato allows for the possibility that a segment of the Guardian class may, in time, tire of the austere life of wisdom and virtue. They may begin to find material possessions and gracious living attractive temptations. Were they ever to reach such a conclusion, they would, of course, be denying the entire rationale upon which the Utopia was set up. Propertied Guardians, Plato says, could not be expected to pursue wisdom and public service unremittingly. At all events, two parties might well form within the hitherto unified society. The revolutionaries stand for "money-making and the possession of house and land, silver and gold." The members of the old guard, "wanting no other wealth than gold and silver in the composition of their souls, try to draw them towards virtue and the ancient ways." [78] Whatever the outcome—stalemate, compromise, or victory for one side or the other—the harm has been done. Unity has been destroyed and Utopia exists no longer.

As a society grows oligarchical—develops a ruling class based on the possession of wealth—two things happen. First of all, the rulers, and especially their offspring, grow soft. "Luxurious indolence of body and mind makes their young men too lazy and effeminate to resist pleasure or to endure pain," [79] Plato says. At the same time, the number of poor grow larger, and they suffer exploitation at the hands of their masters. The constant con-

---

[77] *The Republic*, p. 268.

[78] P. 270. Plato also indicates that the Guardians may become neglectful of the eugenics programs they are obliged to follow. "When your Guardians . . . bring together brides and bridegrooms out of season," he says, "their children will not be so well-endowed or fortunate." While Plato's theory of proper mating seasons is hardly a scientific one, he is making the important point that a disciplined program such as this cannot be allowed to deteriorate lest future rulers lack the high qualities demanded of them (p. 269).

[79] P. 281.

frontation of rich and poor, the extreme contrast between the wealth of the few and the poverty of the many, is bound to erupt in the political arena. Plato depicts the process vividly:

Such being the condition of rulers and subjects, what will happen when they are thrown together, perhaps as fellow-travellers by sea or land to some festival or on a campaign, and can observe one another's demeanor in a moment of danger? The rich will have no chance to feel superior to the poor. On the contrary, the poor man, lean and sunburned, may find himself posted in battle beside one who, thanks to his wealth and indoor life, is panting under his burden of fat and showing every sign of distress. "Such men," he will think, "are rich because we are cowards"; and when he and his friends meet in private, the word will go around; "The men are no good: they are at our mercy." [80]

This is not only a description of the psychology of revolution: it also illustrates the psychology of popular democracy. The man-in-the-street abandons his habit of deference and begins to believe that he is as good as or even better than, those who are placed over him. No longer will political myths about gold, silver, and brass work as a social control. The ordinary citizen has finally seen his rulers for what they really are. While they may not necessarily have grown fat in body, there is a tendency for men long in power to get fat in the head. They become careless about catering to the elemental material and psychological needs of those over whom they rule; they grow out of touch with newly emerging social and political problems. And while being lean and sunburned may be an asset for the poor, what is of course more important is that there are more of them than the rich. (It is of interest to note that Plato makes a time of war one of the catalysts for popular revolution. Political experience has borne this out again and again.) In sum, the poor develop a feeling that Marx was later to describe: class-consciousness. Urged on by their leaders from within their own class, they rebel at the idea of being governed by men who have been shown to be their inferiors. If the ruling class is degenerate, the odds are that they will be unable to defend themselves. "When the poor win, the result is democracy," Plato says. "They will kill some of the opposite party, banish others, and grant the rest an equal share in civil rights and government." [81]

Democracy, according to Plato, is not simply a political system. To be sure, the power of the government is based on majority rule in the sense that governors must be responsive to the wishes and needs of the major portion of the population. But what is more important to Plato's mind is the equalitarianism in matters of taste which permeates such a society. The democratic citizen is—to use the only word possible—an arrogant person: he insists that

[80] *Ibid.*
[81] P. 282.

his conception of the good life is the one which should be tolerated. "When he is told that some pleasures should be sought and valued as arising from desires of a higher order . . ." Plato says, "he will shut the gates of the citadel against the messengers of truth, shaking his head and declaring that one appetite is as good as another and all must have their equal rights." [82] Any suggestion of qualitative superiority is at odds with the ideology of human equality.

The man-in-the-street has just as much warrant to pursue the free life— and to create his own definition of it—as the philosopher, but equal rights for all men entail a good deal more than this when we include in democracy questions of taste. A small minority in society, Plato's "messengers of truth," may wish to engage in pursuits of a higher or more sophisticated order. There would seem to be nothing dangerous in this so long as the minority follows its bent quietly and unobtrusively. However, a democratic society is not usually so tolerant. The resources which the cultured minority must have to pursue its style of life are usually quite demanding. There will therefore arise in the popular mind the presumption that they are enjoying more than their fair share of the pie in order to accommodate their high level of culture. In addition, there is the feeling that the very existence of high culture is a standing sneer at popular culture. It is as if the man-in-the-street were constantly being reminded that the pleasures he enjoys are second-rate. For these reasons the majority of citizens in a democracy tend to feel endangered by the very existence of the minority's tastes. Hence, in the names of democracy, efforts are made to curtail the offensive activities of high culture. In short, when the liberty of the minority conflicts—or appears to conflict—with the liberty of the majority, then the smaller number must give way to the larger. Considerations of quality are required to defer to the ideology of quantity. "In a democratic country," Plato says, "you will be told that liberty is its noblest possession, which makes it the only place for a free spirit to live in." [83] At least, Plato reports, this is the democrat's story. The liberty of a democracy is liberty for those who are contented with accepting the tastes of the majority. This conception of liberty—the democratic conception— deserves less than a sneer.

Who is Plato—or anyone else—to say that the proper role of the average man is to be humbly deferential and to accept the guidance of his self-styled betters? Liberty, all will readily admit, is a precious commodity. Those who claim that it should belong only to the cultured few have the burden of proof on their side. If the liberty of the majority is occasionally a tyrant, if it oc-

[82] P. 286.
[83] P. 288.

casionally tramples on the minority, so it must be remembered that freedom for an exclusive minority has its price as well. This conflict between majority and minority is a never-ending tension of politics—especially of democratic politics. Plato has only raised the question, although in doing so he has made his sentiments on majority rule quite clear.

But triumphant democracy, like all other systems, has within it the seeds of its own destruction. Can, Plato asks, a democracy long survive as a democracy? Its very internal processes as a political system can be self-defeating. Like all political systems, a democracy needs leaders. But the citizens of a democracy make demands of a particular sort on the men who are placed in power. They call for strong leadership, and yet at the same time they call for a government which guarantees liberty for all. This means that the democratic ruler, if he is to be effective, must be as Machiavellian as the autocratic one. He must create the impression that perfect freedom exists in order that he will have the free reign he needs to do his job. What Plato is describing, of course, is the demagogue:

> A democratic state may fall under the influence of unprincipled leaders, ready to minister to its thirst for liberty with too deep draughts of this heady wine; and then, if its rulers are not complacent enough to give it unstinted freedom, they will be arraigned as accursed oligarchs and punished. Law-abiding citizens will be insulted as nonentities who hug their chains; and all praise and honor will be bestowed, both publicly and in private, on rulers who behave like subjects and subjects who behave like rulers. In such a state the spirit of liberty is bound to go to all lengths. . . . The citizens become so sensitive that they resent the slightest application of control as intolerable tyranny.[84]

The political consequence of the heightening sensitivity of the ordinary citizens is that they call for more and more freedom for themselves. The democratic leader, realizing this, tries to channel this energy by creating a scapegoat. It may be a foreign country. It may be a racial or religious minority. Or it may be the rich and well-born who continue to exist in a democratic society. Plato suggests that the latter will be the ones who will suffer. The majority will be urged by their leaders to turn on the well-to-do in the name of liberty. The rich, however, will not remain passive before the onslaught of the poor. "The plundered rich are driven to defend themselves . . ." Plato says, "by any measures they can compass."[85] Thus revolution is matched by counterrevolution. The rich, attacked by the party which claims to speak for the people, are compelled to counterattack ruthlessly if they are to survive: "Even if they have no revolutionary designs, the other party accuses them of plotting against the people and of being reactionary

[84] Pp. 288–289.
[85] P. 291.

oligarchs . . ." Plato says. "When they see the people unwittingly misled by such denunciation into attempts to treat them unjustly, then, whether they wish it or not, they become reactionaries in good earnest." [86] Once the class struggle is engaged in a serious way, the power of numbers is bound to prevail. The poor, with their leader at their head, will overpower the rich.

To consummate this social revolution, it is necessary for the people to follow the dictates of a disciplined party which is led by a single powerful individual. This tolls the death knell of the hitherto existing democracy. "The people always put forward a single champion of their interests, whom they nurse to greatness," Plato says. "Here, plainly enough, is the root from which despotism invariably springs." The democratic idea of perfect liberty for the majority of men leads to its own destruction: "The culmination of liberty in democracy is precisely what prepares the way for the cruellest extreme of servitude under a despot." [87] The man on horseback who plunders the rich in the name of the poor will subsequently turn on his own supporters and will then, in the name of national security and the new society, inflict on them a despotism unequal to any which has gone before. We see in this brief analysis of political change the outlines of the kind of theories which will later be enunciated by such thinkers as Burke, Hegel, and Marx. While Plato's description of degeneration and decay makes no real attempt at a systematic theory, his explanation of the dynamics of political change contains ideas which are extremely useful for an understanding of much that we see around us.

It is clear from the later chapters of The Republic that Plato can be just as much the tough-minded political scientist as he can the Utopian political philosopher. Every political theorist is such a mixture. The student of political theory must therefore be constantly watchful, for it is left to him to distinguish fact from value, description from prescription. Plato's Republic makes a good starting point on which to begin this exercise.

[86] Ibid.
[87] P. 290.

3.
Aristotle

THE MAN AND HIS TIMES

Aristotle was born in 384 B.C. in Stagira, a Greek colony on the coast of
Macedonia. Unlike Plato, he was neither a native Athenian nor of
aristocratic origins. His father was a physician, and this probably placed
his family in the upper-middle class. At the age of 18 Aristotle moved to
Athens, and for the next twenty years he studied at The Academy under
Plato. That Plato was the greatest single influence on him is made evident
by an examination of Aristotle's own writings. But whereas Plato confined
himself almost exclusively to the academic life, his pupil was in continual
contact with the world of practical politics. Beginning in 342, he spent eight
years as a tutor to Alexander, the son of King Philip of Macedon, and later
to be known as Alexander the Great. After this period as counselor to kings,
he returned to Athens where he opened his own school, The Lyceum. Here
he presided for twelve years, at the end of which time he was forced to flee
when his Macedonian connections made him unpopular with the prevailing
Athenian powers. He died in 322 B.C.

Aristotle was a lecturer rather than a writer, and his Politics makes for
less graceful reading than The Republic. Indeed, it is not unreasonable to
assume that the books we now have are little more than expanded lecture
notes. What characterized Aristotle, first of all, is that he was a master of
the several academic disciplines then known to man. His writings and
teachings encompassed theology and metaphysics, ethics and aesthetics,
politics and economics, physics and psychology. In addition, he devised the
formal study of logic. And he also found time for empirical investigation:
during his lifetime he gave close study to the constitutions of more than
150 cities, and this devotion to the facts is at all times evident in his political
theory.

Both Plato and Aristotle conceived of politics in the setting of the city-

69

state. This political jurisdiction, of which Athens and Sparta were foremost examples, is diminutive by contemporary standards. Athens was a little over 1,000 square miles in area and probably had a population of about 300,000. The Greek city-state, moreover, was marked by lines of class and caste which were not questioned or criticized in any serious way. Athens was composed not only of citizens but also of slaves and resident aliens. The latter were free men but were not allowed to participate in politics. And the slaves, of course, had neither freedom nor a political role. For the citizens, however, it was expected that they would be active participants in public affairs. Athenian democracy called for frequent gatherings of the citizen body for legislative purposes. While some public officials were elected, there were also positions of importance which were filled by lot and rotated among the citizens. The emphasis on participation in the city-state cannot be minimized, and it colors the political theories of both Plato and Aristotle. So much was this the prevailing outlook that Athenians did not make a distinction between the public and private spheres of an individual's life. No inherent conflict was seen between the state and the citizen, and even the condemned Socrates agreed that his execution would be in the public interest. The very fact that slaves existed to do the menial labor guaranteed that citizens have the leisure to participate in and reflect on political affairs. Nevertheless, it is questionable whether this condition made the citizen body into what we today would think of as a leisure class. For on the whole the Athenian style of life was a simple one and devoid of comforts. Furthermore, the democracy of Athens, even though restricted to a limited part of the population, was often characterized by excessive behavior and popular tyranny. This caused Aristotle and Plato to have misgivings about self-government, and Aristotle was moved to stress the rule of law as preferable to the rule of men. On the whole, Aristotle was a conservative theorist, and he was not a little uncomfortable in a democratic age. And if he devoted his theory to the politics of the city-state, his analysis appeared just at a time when that political and social institution was declining as an independent entity in the Western World.

3.
Aristotle

If plato can lay claim to being the first political philosopher, then there is little doubt that Aristotle stands as the first political scientist. Aristotle's conception of a science of politics is, when contrasted with later approaches, a straightforward one: it is based on the observation and classification of political institutions and behavior. The *Politics* was written only after he had given close study to the organization and operation of 158 governmental systems. In contrast to Plato, who relied on the deductive method, Aristotle may be called an exemplar of the inductive approach. When he draws a conclusion—and he often does—he makes an effort to demonstrate that this validity can at least be defended on the basis of political experience. Plato's overriding aim was to draw up a blueprint for the ideal system of government. Aristotle's was to suggest the best system possible of attainment—possibility being judged in light of the rules of behavior by which men and societies have abided in the real world. Aristotle does not list all of the 158 constitutions whose operations he studied, nor does he even discuss more than one or two in any detail.

Nevertheless, the fact that he observed a wide variety of political experience is implicit throughout the *Politics*. This is especially the case when he endeavors to classify in a systematic way the institutions and behavior he encountered in the real world. The orderly advance of human knowledge is dependent on classification. Students of politics who aspire to use the scientific method must create categories of analysis for the phenomena they observe in the real world. Aristotle makes explicit his methodological approach at the outset:

Just as, in all other fields, a compound should be analyzed until we reach its simple and uncompounded elements (or, in other words, the smallest atoms of the whole which it constitutes), so we must also consider analytically the elements of which a *polis* is composed. We shall then gain a better insight into the difference from one another of the persons and associations . . . ; and we shall also be

71

in a position to discover whether it is possible to attain a systematic view of the general issues involved.[1]

Analysis of a whole into its component parts is a necessary first step for achieving understanding. We only begin to comprehend a generalized entity called "government" by distinguishing legislative, executive, and judicial functions; "social structure" becomes comprehensible only if we divide it into its constituent institutions; "personality," to have meaning, must be separated into categories such as the id, ego, and superego.

PROBLEMS OF METHODOLOGY

A theoretical category is not a "real" distinction. The real universe does not have convenient labels which are neatly pinned on its component parts— if, indeed, these parts exist at all. A category is a mental construct which the observer draws up for himself so as to better apprehend and explain some aspect of the universe. Because of the subjective element, the process of classification is laden with dangers. One of them is "reification." That is, a student may after a time begin to assume that the category he has invented for analytic purposes actually exist. An example of reification is the "economic man." As a living and breathing human being, he is nowhere to be found in the real world. But by using him as a category—the arbitrary embodiment of some behavioral traits—he helps us to explain a good deal about human behavior. However, if we are tempted to tag the employees of the XYZ Corporation in Cleveland as being "economic men," and if we draw up a scheme to increase productivity on this basis, then we are reifying. We are taking our conceptions out of the realm of analysis and, in effect, are attempting to fit the real world into a straitjacket. This transfer is an abuse of methodology: it assumes falsely that there exists a one-to-one relation between analytic categories and the actual people and institutions which comprise the world. The ideas we employ may be very shrewd, but they carry with them their own limits.

A second danger is that we may create categories for their own sake. We may make analytic distinctions which bear small relation to real differences. We run into this danger when we set up categories for the purpose of establishing a logical or aesthetic symmetry. St. Thomas Aquinas, for example, has a tendency to classify all institutions and behavior in sets of three. But man and society are not governed by magic numbers, and in many cases, while one aspect of reality is better explained by three categories, seven is more

---

[1] *The Politics of Aristotle* (Oxford: Oxford University Press, 1946), translated by Ernest Barker, p. 2.

appropriate for another, and only two for still another. A consequence of the quest for symmetry is to create "residual" classes. Suppose we decide to look at a society from four vantage points: social class, level of education, religion, and race. And suppose that we then divide each of these groupings into its component parts:

Class	Education	Religion	Race
Upper	College	Protestant	White
Middle	High School	Catholic	Negro
Working	Elementary	Jewish	

The first rule is that we ought not to feel obliged to include a "third race" for purposes of symmetry. If there are no Orientals in the particular group of people we are observing, then it is silly to put in such a category just to fill up a box. A second rule calls for consideration of the number of categories involved: there are a total of 54 ($3 \times 3 \times 3 \times 2$) combinations in this classification. If our subject of study is a local branch of a trade union which has 42 members, then it is plain that our analytic scheme is too elaborate. And it ought to be obvious how this kind of procedure can easily get out of hand: if we add four types of national origin, two possible political affiliations, and three classifications for marital status, we are up to 1296 combinations. This is analysis run wild.[2] The possibility of residual categories—that is, categories which do not correspond to reality in a particular case—must be watched. Even though, in terms of logic, an analytic scheme may allow for Jewish Negroes, it is highly doubtful if we should try to "account for" them.

We must, finally, be especially careful about the "levels" of analysis implicit in our categories. In attempting to explain the causes of, say, juvenile delinquency, we may end up with a list having as many as fifteen separate causes for this form of behavior. Such a list is compiled, of course, with the knowledge that there is no such thing as a social cause which exists in isolation from other causes, all of them interrelated. There is, however, the danger of indiscriminate listings. Suppose that among our list of fifteen causes we have on the compilation such headings as "Breakdown of Home Life," "Having Too Much Spending Money," and "Mother at Work." This sort of list is not so much analysis as it is a haphazard intellectual shopping list. We

---

[2] A good example of chaos in classification is found in the "Kinsey Report" on sexual behavior among American males. The sample was secured on the basis of classifications and subclassifications which took account of such social and personal attributes as education, religion, and marital status. However, this listing of categories was carried to such a length that, according to one computation, there were 384,912,000 combinations which were logically possible—over five times as many as there are men in the United States. See W. Allen Wallis, "Statistics of the Kinsey Report," *Journal of the American Statistical Association*, December 1949, pp. 463–484.

might ask, as a first step, whether the categories have been put in what the analysts think is their order of importance as causative factors. Second, we can inquire if an arithmetic "weight" has been assigned to each cause so that we can know how significant each one is in the total listing. And, most important, we must ask searching questions about the levels of causation. That is, in terms of the juvenile delinquency problem we might say that home life has "broken down" because mothers are working; that is, the category, "Mothers at Work," is at a "higher" level than "Breakdown of Home Life" because it is a cause of another cause on our list. There is no easy solution to this kind of problem. It will be raised later on in Aristotle's theory of revolution, when he lists six causes for political upheavals. Indeed, one can ask whether a listing of causes is actually a theory at all. Is the compilation of a plurality of causes an explanation of causation? At this point we can only say that lists of categories are helpful, but they must be approached cautiously and must not be rattled off in an attempt to draw up an exhaustive listing. And at all times the process of classification must be preceded by thorough and systematic observation. This point is one which Aristotle could not stress too often. And this is the departure point for any political science: knowledge of the facts must always precede construction of the theory.

After his methodological preface, Aristotle turns to apply it to the study of politics. His orientation is towards "constitutions." A constitution is first of all the formal system of political institutions and the written body of laws which are operative in a society. But by constitution he also means the informal process of political interaction and the unwritten rules of political behavior which characterize that society. Aristotle is too astute a student of politics to use as his exclusive sources the established institutions and the laws on the statute books. A constitution embodies as well the various ways in which men use laws and institutions to achieve political ends. And this double-edged approach leads to three major considerations to be covered when anyone embarks on political research. That is, Aristotle finds three analytic categories which define the subject matter of political study:

The study of politics . . . (1) has to consider which is the best constitution, and what qualities a constitution must have to come closest to the ideal.

(2) Politics has to consider which sort of constitution suits which sort of civic body.

(3) Politics has also to consider the sort of constitution which depends upon an assumption. In other words, the student of politics must also be able to study a *given* constitution, just as it stands and simply with a view to explaining how it may have arisen and how it may be made to enjoy the longest possible life.[3]

[3] *Politics*, p. 155.

Each of these considerations embodies a methodological approach to the study of politics. The first is ethical: which system of government, we must ask, contains the highest moral quality that is within the realm of attainability? The qualification of attainability indicates that Aristotle is quite prepared to depart from Plato's Utopian method. The second is anthropological: which system, we have to inquire, is so constructed that it makes allowance for the cultural characteristics of the citizens in a given society? The third is historical: how, we want to know, did the system come to take the shape that it now displays, and which are the forces which will lead to its continuance or disintegration? This consideration is ethically neutral; it does not ask if the system under study is good or bad, or if it approaches or runs counter to an attainable ideal.

By this time it should be apparent that Aristotle has no pretensions to being a "pure" political scientist. He is just as concerned to prescribe as he is to describe; his aim is to discuss ethical theory no less than causal theory. In short, like all theorists, he shows a willingness to give attention to both philosophy and science. Unlike most, however, Aristotle is usually quite explicit in differentiating the philosophical from the scientific side of his writing and, in the *Politics* at least, he tries to keep on the scientific track as much of the time as possible. Therefore, it should come as no surprise that Aristotle takes note of political philosophy's integral relationship with political science. Indeed, he goes out of his way to suggest that the scientist has a professional obligation to study philosophy:

We must investigate not only forms which are actually practiced by states that are accounted to be well governed, but also forms of a different order which have been designed by theorists and are held in good repute. The gain of such a discussion will be twofold. In the first place, we shall discover what is right, and what is useful, in our field of inquiry. In the second place, when we proceed to seek for something different from the forms of government we have investigated, we shall not be thought to belong to the class of thinkers who desire at all costs to show their own ingenuity, but rather to have adopted our method in consequence of the defects we have found in existing forms.[4]

Philosophy, then, has important uses for the scientist. He must examine the works of philosophical writers to gain help in setting up his own standards for judgment. In addition, he must verse himself sufficiently in ethical theory so that he will know—and therefore avoid—the pitfalls of Utopianism. The second point is, of course, a veiled slap at Plato. Any effort at prescription, Aristotle is suggesting, must proceed from painstaking descriptive research. Moral theories should have as their aim the amelioration of the ills of societies which actually exist in the real world. The difficulty with Plato's

4 P. 39.

Utopia is that it is not so much a blueprint founded with the idea of re-dressing injustice in the real world as it is a formula which ignores the real world and creates a perfect society from scratch. A Utopia is a solution in the abstract: that is, it is a solution without a problem. There is no evidence, in short, that all existing societies are in need of the drastic reformulation which Plato's Utopia calls for. However, Utopianism is only one of the dangers confronting philosophy in the setting of politics. There are writers who do not seek for perfection in laying down their prescriptions. On the contrary, their fault is that they find the good society far too close to home. They are theorists who, in the course of "addressing themselves . . . to an attainable form, still banish from view the general range of existing constitu-tions, and simply extol the Spartan or some other one constitution." [5] These apologists discover without too much effort that the best possible system has already been attained, that there is no need at all to survey the ex-perience of other societies, and, indeed, that the best possible system happens to be the one that we have right now. Apologism is a recurring problem in political theory: it is the frame of mind which transforms theory into ideol-ogy. It is, for the political scientist, as much of a pitfall as Utopianism. "The sort of constitutional system which ought to be proposed," Aristotle says, "is one which men can be easily induced, will be readily able, to graft onto the system they already have." [6] The type of prescription we should attempt to make, then, is neither the Utopianism of one extreme nor the apologism for the status quo of the other. It is, rather, on a middle ground—a set of reforms which emerge to satisfy already existing needs, proposals which men can agree ought to be grafted onto the system of government they know and are accustomed to.

When we embark on the task of examining actual constitutions, we must be clear in our own minds about the standards of judgment we employ. There are two kinds of questions which we usually find ourselves asking about the behavior of states and legal systems. "The first is whether any of their provisions is good or bad when it is judged by the standard of an *ideal* system," Aristotle says. "The second is whether any provision runs contrary to the principles and character of their constitutions as *actually established*." [7] An example may make this distinction clear. Let us suppose that in a society much of the heavy construction work is done by contracted-out prison labor. How are we to judge the performance of this economic institution? We can, first of all, say that involuntary labor is evil and that no matter how

[5] P. 156.
[6] *Ibid.*
[7] P. 74.

efficiently dams may be built or forests cleared, the institution is itself evil because of the composition of the labor force. In this sense, the criticism we are bringing to bear derives from an ideal standard on our parts that all labor should be free labor. As an alternative method of judgment, we can take for granted that in this particular society prison labor is part of the system for getting construction work accomplished. Then, by implicitly accepting that society's own standard, we can begin to ask such questions as whether the projects are completed on time, if discipline is observed, and if the amount of initiative shown is higher or lower than the authorities think necessary. Here we are judging the system as good or bad not on the basis of an ideal view of free labor, but on the grounds which the society itself sets up: the internal efficiency of an economic institution. This kind of distinction, as Aristotle points out, must be made in all levels of political analysis. To obscure it is to promote confusion of the worst sort.

A NATURAL SCIENCE OF POLITICS

The nature of political life is the chief focus of the *Politics*. Aristotle puts his central emphasis on the institution of the *polis*. This institution is not precisely a state or a society, although it is more nearly the larger unit than the smaller. We might approximate Aristotle's meaning if we think of the *polis* as that entity called "the body politic." The difficulty in defining the *polis* is that neither Aristotle nor Plato found it necessary to distinguish between state and society. In most Western countries we take for granted that within society there are many institutions, of which the state is only one. If there are no other institutions apart from the state in a society, then it is in order to run the two together. This is the question of pluralism, and it will occupy us at no small length throughout the study of political theory. What Aristotle wished to demonstrate is that the "body politic" is a "natural" institution: that is, it is not an artificial device which was consciously created by a group of citizens at a particular time in order to suit particular purposes which they had in mind. On the contrary, Aristotle tries to show that the *polis* is a "natural" association of men and women by pointing out how it grows out of subordinate, but no less natural, associations. If we turn our attention to the nature of man as the basic unit, we soon discover that he as an individual is a creature with certain elemental needs; these needs must be met if he is to live at all. As he cannot survive in day-to-day existence in isolation, let alone reproduce the next generation of the species, he must come into association with others. "The first form of association naturally instituted for the satisfaction of daily recurrent needs is thus the family . . ."

Aristotle says. "The next form of association—which is also the first to be formed from more households than one, and for the satisfaction of something more than daily recurrent needs—is the village." [8] We are clearly ascending an analytical ladder here. If family life satisfies certain human needs, membership in a town or village, consisting of several families, satisfies others. "When we come to the final and perfect association, formed from a number of villages, we have already reached the *polis*—an association which may be said to have reached the height of full self-sufficiency." [9]

It is, above everything else, its self-sufficient character which makes the *polis* a "natural" institution. States may become members of alliances based on multilateral treaties. They may even join worldwide organizations. But these supranational associations are not "natural" because none of the member-states need to belong to such groups—in an imperative sense—in order to achieve full self-sufficiency. They may be helped in economic or military terms by their continuing membership in such bodies. However, that help is more in the realm of convenience than it is a matter of sheer necessity for national survival. The *polis* is as large an entity as Aristotle is prepared to deal with when he speaks of "natural" institutions.

Because it is the completion of associations existing by nature, every *polis* exists by nature, having itself the same quality as the earlier associations from which it grew. It is the end or consummation to which those associations move, and the "nature" of things consists in their end or consummation; for what each thing is when its growth is completed we call the nature of that thing, whether it be a man or a horse or a family.[10]

Several questions are raised here. What does it mean to say that a state or a society "grows out" of lower-level associations? What does it mean, further, to say that the family has as its "end" the fuller development of the state or of society? Aristotle is putting forward here an "organic" conception of politics. This is an important stream in political thought; it was evidenced in Plato and will come later to fruition in the writings of theorists like Rousseau, Burke, and Hegel. A state or a society is viewed as an organism —an entity which is actually alive and in which each component part serves

[8] P. 4.

[9] *Ibid.* Aristotle realizes that his statement that the *polis* is the perfect association will not suit those with an imperialistic frame of mind. "Most men are believers in the cause of empire, on the ground that empire leads to a large accession of material prosperity," he says. The difficulty with imperialism, however, is that it creates the Garrison State to the exclusion of higher pursuits. "Most of the states which make war their aim are safe only while they are fighting," he continues. "They collapse as soon as they have established an empire, and lose the edge of their temper, like an unused sword, in time of peace. The legislator is to blame for having provided no training for the proper use of leisure." (Pp. 318, 320.)

[10] P. 5.

a necessary function. This approach was suggested by Plato when he had the Guardians, Auxiliaries, and Workers each perform roles analogous to the jobs done by parts of the human body. For Aristotle, the citizen, the family, and the village are not individuals or institutions sufficient unto themselves —no more than a finger, a hand, and an arm are able to function separately. The organic theory has consequences of no small importance when we undertake to study the role of the individual and the freedom allowed to private associations in political life.

From his theory of a natural, organic *polis*, Aristotle proceeds deductively to his theory of human nature. It is not by accident that he gives first attention to the body politic and after that is completed focuses his discussion on the individual. "It is evident that the *polis* belongs to the class of things that exist by nature," Aristotle says, "and that man is by nature an animal intended to live in a *polis*." [11] This is, of course, the famous Aristotelian dictum that man is a social animal. This is more than a truism: that men tend to live in the company of others is so obvious as not to bear mentioning. Aristotle is also saying that we must give first analytic priority to man's role as a social animal, and only in a secondary sense may we regard him as an autonomous individual. "The *polis* exists by nature and . . . is prior to the individual," he says. "Not being self-sufficient when they are isolated, all individuals are so many parts equally depending on the whole." [12] The important theoretical question is not whether man is able to exist in isolation, but in what sense he has status as an individual which does not depend on his role in society. Aristotle is not unaware of potential conflicts between an individual and society, but the explicit case for individualism is never made. Man may be a social animal, then, but he is a man as well. Sheep are always found in herds and wolves travel in packs, and yet we do not spend much time commenting on their social nature. The social character of human beings is unique in that it also depends on man's being a conversational and a moral animal.

Nature, according to our theory, makes nothing in vain; and man alone of the animals is furnished with the faculty of language. The mere making of sounds serves to indicate pleasure and pain, and is thus a faculty that belongs to animals in general: their nature enables them to attain the point at which they have perceptions of pleasure and pain, and can signify those perceptions to one another.
But language serves to declare what is advantageous and what is the reverse, and it therefore serves to declare what is just and what is unjust. It is the peculiarity of man, in comparison with the rest of the animal world, that he alone possesses a perception of good and evil.[13]

[11] *Ibid.*
[12] P. 6.
[13] Pp. 5–6.

Whereas an animal grunts out his pleasure or howls to express his pain, a man is more complex in his articulation. He can put into words, rather than grunts, his likes and his dislikes. And, in addition, he can, with his words, state the opinion that a certain course of action is morally good and another is morally bad. Aristotle has sought to establish that man must be viewed as a social, conversational, and moral creature. His needs as a political animal arise from his possession of these characteristics. It is the function of the *polis* and those who govern it to apprehend and satisfy these needs.

Furthermore, the *polis* is "natural" because it looks after the common interest of its members. To employ language which would apply to the human organism, the body politic cannot cut off its nose to spite its face. The politics of the *polis*, then, must be premised on an active awareness on the part of all citizens that if the common interest is to be pursued in a rational way, there must be coherent direction in the society. The patterns of rulership, deference, and consensus which Plato called for are also articulated by Aristotle:

> There must necessarily be a union of the naturally ruling element with the element which is naturally ruled, for the preservation of both. The element which is able, by virtue of its intelligence, to exercise forethought, is naturally a ruling and master element; the element which is able, by virtue of its bodily power, to do what the other element plans, is a ruled element.[14]

The ruling element alluded to by Aristotle is not a ruling class of Guardians in Plato's sense. But by establishing the primacy of brains over brawn as a "natural" relationship, Aristotle is once again depending on his organic theory. It follows that it is "unnatural" for a man with less than average intelligence to aspire to political office. He ought, on the contrary, to leave this job to the "natural" rulers in his midst. While Aristotle does wish to convey this meaning, he does not go to the extremes that Plato did.

The *polis* is so set up as to allow political participation on the part of the average citizen. But this opportunity for participation must be moderated by an awareness of the moral ends of the state. The *polis* which Aristotle is concerned to prescribe for in the *Politics* is an approximation of the good society. This intention of Aristotle's is set out in his opening paragraph. "All associations are instituted for the purpose of attaining some good," he says, "for all men do all their acts with a view to achieving something which is, in their view, a good." Moral purposiveness in individual behavior, he goes on, is writ large in politics:

> We may therefore hold that all associations aim at some good; and we may also hold that the particular association which is the most sovereign of all, and includes

---

[14] P. 3.

all the rest, will pursue this aim most, and will thus be directed to the most sovereign of all goods. This most sovereign and inclusive association is the *polis*, as it is called, or the political association.[15]

On this basis, we must add a new dimension to the previous statements about the rationale of the *polis*. Self-sufficiency—the nourishment and preservation of the organism—is not enough. "The end of the state is not mere life," Aristotle says. "It is, rather, a good quality of life." [16] And the true *polis* cannot assume a passive role in the moral sphere: "Any *polis* which is truly so-called, and is not merely one in name, must devote itself to the end of encouraging goodness." [17] The task of politics is the promotion of the good life. Governments are instituted among men not simply to put out fires, collect garbage, deliver the mail, and direct traffic. Nor do they exist simply to accommodate and adjust differences between competing factions. Laws and government, as we saw, must be judged by two sets of standards, the technical and the moral. Clean streets do not make a true *polis*, nor six-lane highways a good society. Justice and virtue must be discovered and actively encouraged if politics are to be purposeful. Once again we see that Aristotle is not at a far remove from Plato. Yet, despite their areas of agreement, there are crucial differences between the two men.

ARISTOTLE ON PLATO

One of Aristotle's contributions to political theory has to do with a matter of mood. Aristotle puts a high value on moderation, on taking the middle road. One of the disadvantages of taking a middle-of-the-road course is that it lets two other fellows set the rules of the game for you. The moderate, in trying to beat a path between two extreme positions finds that he accepts as limiting cases a set of assumptions which are not his own but the making of others. Even though moderation cannot by itself be a political philosophy, it has social and psychological attributes which offer no small attraction. There are many people who are fearful of extremes just because they are extremes. For them a position which is part-liberal and part-conservative is most satisfying. Furthermore, the moderate finds himself concerned with a discussion of means as much as—or more than—he is with ends. He does not spend time objecting to the ultimate goals which others may propose so much as he does criticizing the methods which they are using to achieve those goals. Taking as given the ends which have been already laid down, the moderate con-

[15] P. 1.
[16] P. 118.
[17] P. 119.

centrates on the most effective ways of making policy. A concern with institutional procedures, for example, is an area in which a moderate is more at home than he is with an argument over what moral purposes the particular institution is designed to attain. It is by understanding the moderate mood that we can best follow Aristotle's analysis of Plato's *Republic*.

It was, Aristotle says, Plato's premise that "the greatest possible unity of the whole *polis* is the supreme good." [18] Aristotle is no enemy to the idea of unity: we have seen how he postulates the common interests of ruler and ruled in an organic society. Yet he feels compelled, after reading Plato, to point out that "a *polis* which goes on and on, and becomes more of a unit, will eventually cease to be a *polis* at all." [19] The trouble with Plato's Utopia is not so much that it is unified; it is that it carries unification to extreme lengths. There is a cost to political effectiveness in social unity, and it increases at an accelerated rate after a point. Aristotle is suggesting that Plato has gone so far past that point that his Utopia is no longer capable of performing the vital political functions. Aristotle turns, first of all, to the institutional framework of Plato's ideal society. In deciding to proceed this way, he is for the moment shelving any criticisms of the assumption which posits the importance of social unity. The discussion is rather made to center on the means which are best suited for attaining both the idea of unity and an effective social organization. "Even if it were the supreme good of a political association that it should have the greatest possible unity," Aristotle says, "this unity does not appear to follow from the formula . . . that the citizens should share children and wives and property with one another." [20]

We are now on ground where the moderate feels more secure. The question is not whether unity is a philosophical good, but rather whether the institutions of communism are appropriate means to that end. Aristotle has some searching questions to ask about the essential stability of a Utopian society. Even Utopian citizens are human:

What is common to the greatest number gets the least amount of care. Men pay most attention to what is their own: they care less for what is common; or, at any rate, they care for it only to the extent to which each is individually concerned. Even where there is no other cause for inattention, men are more prone to neglect their duty when they think that another is attending to it.

The scheme of Plato means that each citizen will have a thousand sons: they will not be the sons of each citizen individually: any and every son will be equally the son of any and every father; and the result will be that every son will be equally neglected by every father.[21]

[18] P. 40.
[19] *Ibid.*
[20] Pp. 40, 43.
[21] P. 44.

Communal property and communal families will, Aristotle says, have the consequence of communal neglect. Plato suggested that his Guardians will be divested of personal interests—or will learn to sublimate them—and will dedicate themselves to the public interest. If the altruism of the Utopian Guardians is supposed to be any sort of guide for the conduct of rulers and citizens in the real world, then Plato is assuming that the average person is capable of undergoing a radical transformation. In short, Aristotle is saying that Plato severely underestimated the qualitative change in human character and personality which would have to take place. "It is a difficult business for men to live together and to be partners in any form of human activity," Aristotle says. "But it is specially difficult to do so when property is involved." [22]

The contrast between Plato and Aristotle should now be clear. Plato chose to tell us how men would act and what their attitudes would be in a perfect society. Aristotle is concerned to start with men as they are in the real world and, using these creatures as his raw materials, to see how far and in which ways they can be improved. Real people have shown that they are self-interested, and one of the most perennial and intensely felt of these interests is private property. The assumption that men can be altruistic partners in a society where all property is under collective ownership rests on far more tenuous grounds than Plato would lead us to believe.

> Legislation such as Plato proposes may appear to wear an attractive face and to argue benevolence. The hearer receives it gladly, thinking that everybody will feel towards everybody else some marvellous sense of fraternity—all the more as the evils now existing under ordinary forms of government (law-suits about contracts, convictions for perjury, and obsequious flatteries of the rich) are denounced as due to the absence of a system of common property.
>
> None of these evils, however, is due to the absence of communism. They all arise from the wickedness of human nature. Indeed, it is a fact of observation that those who own common property, and share in its management, are far more often at variance with one another than those who have property in severalty.[23]

The arguments about unity, about communism, about private property—all of these now begin to take on a new perspective. The fundamental parting of the ways for Plato and Aristotle is over an interpretation of human nature. Is man essentially good—and therefore perfectible? Or is he essentially wicked —and therefore bound by his own perversity to live in an imperfect state? This is the battle later to be fought by Rousseau and Burke, by communism and liberalism, and it remains a vital theoretical issue to this day. Aristotle does not say that man's wickedness is manifested continually. Nor did Plato

[22] P. 49.
[23] Pp. 50–51.

claim that men display their inherent perfectibility under all sets of social conditions. But Plato does say that given the right circumstances, man's capacity for altruism is boundless, while Aristotle, on the contrary, asserts that the destructive features latent within human nature will always be present. Not only will they not disappear with the advent of a Utopian world, but they will serve to prevent that world from ever coming into being.

This disagreement with Plato over fundamentals does not prevent Aristotle from examining particulars. Whether or not one believes that a Utopia is possible, property and the family are real institutions—and political theorists cannot avoid discussing them. It is Aristotle's view that private property ought to be preserved because public ownership simply will not work. He has, in short, concluded that we should keep the prevailing arrangement because Plato's proposed change is less satisfactory than what we have in the status quo. Private property, then, is not an original idea of Aristotle's. His plea for it is more a counterargument to Plato's plea for abolition than it is a positive program of his own. The same mood affects his approach to Plato's abolition of the family. "There is still a further difficulty," he says. "It concerns that part of Plato's scheme which may be called the transposition of ranks." [24] Superior children who were born into the families of Workers were to be taken from their parents and moved up to the Guardian class. Untalented children born to Guardians were to be demoted to Worker status. "How such transposition is actually to be effected is a matter of great perplexity . . ." Aristotle says. "Those who transfer such children, and assign them their new place, will be bound to know who are the children so placed." [25] Human nature, once again, is likely to rear its perverse head. Guardians no less than others are human, and they possess all the instincts of parenthood. They will be as much concerned over the fate of their offspring as anyone else would be. Some of the Guardians will be entrusted with the evaluation program whereby inferior children of the ruling class are demoted to the status of Workers. These selection boards, Aristotle is suggesting, will be besieged by alarmed parents who will want to know what is going to happen to their cruelly misunderstood offspring. In short, the transposition of ranks—especially the downward transposition—is bound to collapse. The self-interest of parents will conquer the public interest; a plan which is intended to be objective and automatic will soon be subverted by the human element. It is important to note that Aristotle is primarily interested in the "how-to" question. He does not go into the question of why the family is worth preserving as an institution. Indeed, were it possible to put Plato's scheme into effect in the real world—that is, were it possible to accommodate

[24] P. 47.
[25] Ibid.

the human element—then Aristotle would have had the ground removed for his basic criticism.

Aristotle's final comments on Plato's blueprint are directed at the ruling class. He is concerned over the fact that a single class is to hold continuous political power. Workers are not to be given a chance to take office, nor will the Guardians ever undergo the experience of having to obey orders given by others. This failure to allow circulation within the social structure can have dangers, for it makes no provision for the aspirations of able and ambitious men, who, for one reason or another, have been denied admission to the ruling class. These outsiders are potential troublemakers:

> There is also an element of danger in the method of government which Plato proposes to institute. He makes one body of persons the permanent rulers of his state. This is a system which must breed discontent and dissension even among the elements which have no particular standing, and all the more, therefore, among the high-spirited and martial elements. The reason which makes it necessary for him to make one body of persons permanent rulers is obvious: "the divine gold which is mixed in the soul" cannot reside at one time in one body of men and at another time in another; it must reside permanently in one body.[26]

Democracy—defined simply as the periodic rotation of rulers by means of popular consent—is designed to anticipate and prevent the discontents of which Aristotle speaks. A study of human nature tells us that there will always be a number of high-spirited individuals who will find reason to object to the way in which the government is being run. Plato's antidemocratic scheme dictates that these dissenters be ignored because they are lacking in wisdom and virtue. But the longer they are ignored, the more apt they are to develop seditious tendencies. The advantage of democracy is that it tries to anticipate such an eventuality. Dissenters are allowed to form their own party, to run for office, and, if elected, to see that policy is made on new lines. Another assumption of democracy is that the heavy burden of political and administrative responsibility will damp down the high spirits and martial airs which the dissenters displayed when they were out of power. Democracy—like the family and private property—has desirable qualities in Aristotle's eyes because it is preferable to the proposed alternative. While Aristotle is neither a democrat nor an antidemocrat, he is prepared to draw on a variety of criteria in assessing the merits of political systems.

There is another criticism to be leveled at Plato's idea of a ruling class. "It is a further objection," Aristotle says, "that he deprives his Guardians even of happiness, maintaining that it is the happiness of the whole state which should be the object of legislation."[27] The price which the Guardians pay for power is their own personal unhappiness. In this sense, Plato said, they are put in

[26] P. 54.
[27] Ibid.

the position of being the servants and not the masters of those over whom they rule. Only by denying themselves the pleasures enjoyed by the average citizen will they be able to apply themselves to the tasks which are their exclusive responsibility. This tragic view of the life led by those in the ruling class may, to some degree, serve to make legitimate their power. But Aristotle looks on this arrangement not as a Greek tragedy but as an ill-conceived political structure. "It is impossible for the whole of a state to be happy unless most of its parts, or all, or at any rate some, are happy . . ." he says. "If the Guardians are not happy, what are the other elements of the state which are?" [28] Can we assume, Aristotle asks, that Guardians, who impose such a stern life on themselves, will not also think it necessary to prescribe austerity for the rest of society? Once rulers have persuaded themselves that selfless dedication to duty is required for the good life, then it is very likely that they will make such an attitude a rule of behavior not only for Guardians, but for all citizens. In such an event, what began as a means will become the end. Plato did not take account of this possibility; but then he did not take account of the foibles of human nature which even Guardians must possess.

Aristotle's conclusion is that Plato's Utopia just will not work. The demands made on its citizens—both Guardians and ordinary individuals—are too high and too inflexible. But not only is the Utopia unattainable to mortal men— not a very surprising criticism of a Utopia—but the specific institutional reforms which are proposed in the blueprint will create more problems than they solve. The changes which Plato proposes will have consequences which their author did not anticipate. And these will be self-defeating: new forms of injustice will arise which will subvert the noble goals which were originally laid out. In short, the citizens of The Republic are asked to pursue unity to a degree which will prove destructive of both themselves and their society.

The life which they are to lead appears to be utterly impossible. The cause of the fallacy into which Plato falls must be held to be the wrong premise on which he bases his argument. It is true that unity is to some extent necessary, alike in a household and a polis; but total unity is not. There is a point at which a polis, by advancing in unity, will cease to be a polis: there is another point, short of that, at which it may still remain a polis, but will none the less come near to losing its essence, and will thus be a worse polis. It is as if you were to turn harmony into mere unison, or to reduce a theme to a single beat.[29]

Whether Aristotle's answer is the final one—to Plato, to all Utopias, and to the recurrent quest for unity and perfection—this judgment can only lie with each student of political theory.

[28] Pp. 54–55.
[29] P. 51.

OLIGARCHY AND DEMOCRACY

Aristotle's critique of Plato has made plain to us many of Aristotle's own assumptions about human nature and the political process. These assumptions—both philosophical and methodological—must now be carried over into our consideration of Aristotle's own theory of government. It was only in the closing chapters of *The Republic* that Plato permitted himself a few casual speculations on the various governmental systems under which men live. Aristotle approaches this area of political science with far greater care than Plato evidenced. Indeed, what we see in Aristotle's approach is an attempt at a science of political behavior. If the crucial step in the scientific method is devising a scheme of classification, then Aristotle's sixfold division of the forms of government must stand as the original essay in political science:

The civic body in every *polis* is the sovereign; and the sovereign must necessarily be either One, or Few, or Many. On this basis we may say that when the One, or the Few, or the Many, rule with a view to the common interest, the constitutions under which they do so must necessarily be right constitutions. On the other hand the constitutions directed to the personal interest of the One, or the Few, or the Masses, must necessarily be perversions.

Among forms of government by a single person Kingship, in the general use of language, denotes the species which looks to the common interest. Among forms of government by a few persons (but more than one) Aristocracy denotes the species . . . because the best are rulers, or because its object is what is best for the state and its members. Finally, when the masses govern the state with a view to the common interest, the name used for this species is the generic name . . . of "Polity."

Three perversions correspond to them. Tyranny is a perversion of Kingship; Oligarchy of Aristocracy; and Democracy of Polity. Tyranny is a government by a single person directed to the interest of that person. Oligarchy is directed to the interest of the well-to-do. Democracy is directed to the interest of the poorer classes. None of the three is directed to the advantage of the whole body of citizens.[30]

The classification may be put in schematic form:

Government in Whose Interest?

Who Governs?	Legitimate Governments In the Interest of the Whole Community	Perverted Governments In the Interest of the Rulers Themselves
One Man	Kingship	Tyranny
A Few Men	Aristocracy	Oligarchy
The Majority	Polity	Democracy

[30] Pp. 114–115.

In employing the first basis for classification—the number of rulers in a given system—we must not make the mistake of construing Aristotle's words too literally. His talk of government by "one man" or a "few men" or "many men" is simply a shorthand device. There is no key to politics in numerical rubrics; it is doubtful, for instance, if there is a prima-facie qualitative difference between a one-man dictatorship and one consisting of a three-man junta. Aristotle makes his intention clear in his comments on oligarchy and democracy; numbers actually symbolize the social classes whose representatives hold the political power in the different systems. "Oligarchy might be defined as the constitution under which the rich, being also few in number, hold the offices of the state," he says. "And similarly democracy might be defined as the constitution under which the poor, being also many in number, are in control." [31] The class basis of a political system, according to Aristotle, is what really matters. It would be a mechanical exercise and just plain wrong to categorize governments simply by counting up the number of rulers. "The factor of number . . ." he says, "is an accidental attribute, due to the simple fact that the wealthy are generally few and the poor are generally numerous." [32] In short, we must not confuse cause and effect. If oligarchy is government by the wealthy and aristocracy government by the virtuous, both are government by "the few" simply because no society has more than a few wealthy or virtuous men among its population.

The second classification in Aristotle's scheme is bound to be rather vague. "Those constitutions which consider the common interest are right constitutions, judged by the standard of absolute justice," he says. "Those constitutions which consider only the personal interest of the rulers are all wrong constitutions, or perversions of the right forms." [33] The introduction of the notion of absolute justice into the scheme would appear to run counter to its supposedly scientific character. This, however, is simply another way of asking whether a particular form of government is "natural." Just as a view of man's nature is implicit in any political theory, so we must inquire whether a governmental form is "natural" in terms of carrying out its obligations to the community. "The good life is the chief end," Aristotle says, "both for the community as a whole and for each of us individually." [34] The chief problem encountered in the pursuit of the good life is that particular individuals—especially rulers—may seek to achieve it for themselves at the expense of the rest of the community. This selfish search for happiness on the part of some

[31] Pp. 115–116.
[32] P. 116.
[33] P. 112.
[34] P. 111.

perverts the "natural" function of government: to provide the good life for all within its boundaries. We must therefore discover whether rulers are selfish or altruistic, interested in their own welfare or of that of the entire community. This means that we must add a philosophical dimension to the scientific one in order to complete the scheme.

Of the six possible combinations, Aristotle's chief interest is in only two: oligarchy and democracy. That these are both "perverted" forms of government systems in which the ruling group governs in its own interest is not surprising considering Aristotle's professed orientation. As a political scientist, his concern is to study political systems as they actually operate. If the systems most in evidence in the real world are perversions of a philosophical ideal, then that is because we have yet to scale the heights of Utopia. The perversity latent in human nature now suggests that men will prefer to live under forms of government which will benefit them directly, that the systems in existing societies reflect the interests of those who have succeeded in attaining power. It is interesting to note that once he embarks on his discussion of oligarchy and democracy, Aristotle no longer feels obliged to point out that they are "perverted" forms. They are, rather, what we have in the real world. To hammer home the fact that they are less than ideal is superfluous.

The distinction between oligarchy and democracy is most easily put in terms of majority and minority rule:

> The proper application of the term "democracy" is to a constitution in which the free-born and poor control the government—being at the same time a majority; and similarly the term "oligarchy" is properly applied to a constitution in which the rich and better-born control the government—being at the same time a minority.[35]

But even though democracy is based on majority rule, it does not exclude the minority of the rich and well-born from political participation or officeholding. Oligarchy, on the other hand, excludes most citizens from these rights by enforcing various written and unwritten qualifications for voting and officeholding. "We may lay it down generally," Aristotle says, "that a system which does not allow every citizen to share is oligarchical, and that one which does so is democratic."[36] In a democracy all citizens, regardless of wealth or class, have the opportunity to participate, but by opening the gates to the majority, a democracy may find that it has drowned out the voice of the rich, the well-born, and the cultured. All men have an equal right to dance, said the Elephants, as they frolicked among the Chickens. Minorities do not lose any of their formal political rights when the democratic floodgates are opened. But the advent of democracy weakens the power of minority groups; indeed, it

[35] P. 164.
[36] P. 171.

may abolish it altogether. When elephants dance among chickens, the result is less a contest among equal parties and more a foreordained victory of quantity over quality.

But the contrast between democracy and oligarchy is not this simple. When we are dealing with an oligarchy, we must not assume that an exclusive group has exclusive power. "Even in oligarchies—and indeed in all constitutions—the majority is sovereign." [37] This is a basic fact of political life which is acknowledged by most political theorists. No matter how oligarchical a government may be in theory, the rulers must—if they are to maintain themselves in power—be responsive to the elemental needs of those they govern.

Another qualification put forward by Aristotle complicates matters even more: "It is not sufficient to distinguish democracy and oligarchy merely by the criterion of poverty and wealth, any more than it is to do so merely by that of number." [38] Doubtless, a scheme of classification would be far neater were we to distinguish democracy and oligarchy solely on grounds of economic class; then we could say that it is the representatives of the poor or the well-to-do who hold political office. There are also minorities in society which are composed of individuals who possess special skills: generals, administrators, technicians. They are neither rich or well-born, yet they often are the men of power in an oligarchical system. And there are also cultured minorities: the men and women who seek governmental power in order to pursue a style of life which stresses high aesthetic or intellectual values. Whenever a minority in a society is shown to have power, we would be wrong to assume that its power rests solely on the basis of wealth. "We have to remember that the democratic and the oligarchical state both contain a number of parts," Aristotle says. "And we must therefore use additional criteria to distinguish them properly." [39] Nor is a democracy a monolithic mass: the many are also broken into groups which possess different political interests. Despite this important qualification, Aristotle does not provide the additional criteria which are needed for a more detailed and comprehensive discussion of democracy and oligarchy. Like Plato, he finds it necessary—in order to get his main point across—to talk of the rich vs. the poor, the few vs. the many. We would do well to follow him on his own terms here, realizing all the time that he knows that the social background of politics is not etched in such stark contrasts.

It is the social structure of the political system which shapes its institutions and the ways they operate. If a society is oligarchical, then law and politics

[37] P. 163.
[38] Ibid.
[39] Ibid.

will reflect the interests of the dominant group in that society. Aristotle makes this argument most clearly when he talks of law and justice. Many thinkers suppose that law and justice are abstract entities which stand independent of the societies for which they provide rules. Insofar as we are concerned only with legal procedures—for instance, with matters of due process—it may be held that law must take an established form in any given system if it is to be law at all. But in the eyes of most men justice has substantive content as well as an abstract form. "In democracies, for example, justice is considered to mean equality . . ." Aristotle says. "In oligarchies, again, inequality in the distribution of office is considered to be just." [40]

What is confusing to outside observers is that rulers in both systems have a tendency to claim that their conception of justice is the only legitimate one.

The advocates of oligarchy and democracy both refuse to consider . . . the persons to whom their principles properly apply, and they both make erroneous judgments. The reason is that they are judging in their own case; and most men, as a rule, are bad judges where their own interests are involved. . . .

But the advocates of oligarchy and democracy are misled by the fact that they are professing a sort of conception of justice, and professing it up to a point, into thinking that they profess one which is absolute and complete. The oligarchs think that superiority on one point—in their case wealth—means superiority on all: the democrats believe that equality in one respect—for instance, that of free birth—means equality all round.[41]

This is the way in which philosophy gets turned into ideology. There is seldom any hypocrisy on the part of the men who rule: they sincerely believe that justice as interpreted in their system is justice in an absolute sense.

Plato and Aristotle both believe that justice exists in an objective sense: it dictates that the good life be provided for all individuals no matter how high or low their status and that estimable qualities of character be encouraged even if only a few in society are capable of attaining them. But democracies and oligarchies are forms of governments where one group rather than another holds the power; as a consequence, each tends to exaggerate or distort that aspect of absolute justice which promotes its own interest. It is no solution to say that the power to define justice should be removed from the hands of self-interested parties. This suggestion is often made in the field of law; for law, no less than justice, ought to be impersonal. "It may perhaps be urged . . ." Aristotle says, "that it is a poor sort of policy to vest sovereignty in any person, subject as persons are to the passions that beset men's souls; and that it is better to vest it in law." [42]

[40] P. 117.
[41] Pp. 117–118.
[42] P. 122.

The difficulty with this very worthy proposal is that law cannot exist independently of the rulers who make, interpret, and enforce it. There is no independent center of power which can enforce an objective law or an absolute justice which is bound to conflict with the vital interests of those who run the political system. Lawyers and judges, no matter how estimable their personal sentiments, cannot divorce law from the interests in society which it serves. The law, in short, is a political instrument, and the consequence of this is clear: "The law itself may incline either towards oligarchy or towards democracy," Aristotle says. "What difference will the sovereignty of law then make in the problems which have just been raised?" [43]

> Laws must be constituted in accordance with constitutions; and if this is the case, it follows that laws which are in accordance with right constitutions must necessarily be just, and laws which are in accordance with wrong or perverted constitutions must be unjust.[44]

This is a statement harboring some important implications, for it suggests that the contours of a society cannot be altered in any significant way by means of legislation. Political theorists are often in sharp disagreement on how far human nature and social custom can be subjected to reform by legal means. The conviction that morality cannot be legislated is plainly in line with Aristotle's view. There is the opposing view that laws have both a coercive power and a moral sanction of their own, that by legislative action within a system the government can transform the main outlines of the system itself. Aristotle has taken his own stand for the present, but there will be others—in particular, Rousseau and Bentham—who will attempt to refute it.

It is now in order to examine Aristotle's theory of democracy. While democracy is a "perversion" of a legitimate governmental form—"polity"—and while Aristotle has many misgivings about the capabilities of the man-in-the-street, nevertheless he does not minimize the advantages of popular participation in politics. "That the people at large should be sovereign rather than the few best," Aristotle says, "would appear to be defensible." [45] And by sovereignty he does not mean the passive theory that rulers should be simply

---

[43] Pp. 122–123. The plural usage should be distinguished from the singular in this area. There is a difference between, say, obeying the "laws" which have been officially promulgated in a society and in respecting the rule of "law" as a political principle. While the latter is meaningless without the former, simple obedience to particular statutes does not by itself signify that the rule of law is operative in a society. For this to be so, there must be widespread understanding of the meaning and importance of the entire legal process for society. This question will be treated more fully in the discussion of sovereignty in the chapter on Hobbes.

[44] P. 127.

[45] P. 123.

responsive to the needs of the people, but rather an active theory which calls on all citizens to actually take a share in the process of self-government.

There is this to be said for the Many: Each of them by himself may not be of a good quality; but when they all come together it is possible that they may surpass —collectively and as a body, although not individually—the quality of the best few.[46]

The idea of a collective political wisdom which is inherent in the body politic is, of course, an accompaniment of the theory of the organic state. It is easy enough to say that the average citizen has neither the wisdom nor the virtue of the select few. But that is the wrong way to set up the question. For the mass of men, when they are taken together, have a collective intelligence which is superior to the judgment of the most philosophical of rulers.

This is one of the arguments for the universal franchise and popular elections. The average voter, if you talk to him alone, will display an ignorance and an irrationality about political matters which is nothing short of pathetic. And there is little doubt that he will proceed to cast his vote on the basis of partial knowledge and a prejudiced outlook. This seeming calamity, however, ought not to cause us too many sleepless nights. For if we take the people as a whole, we will discover that they know best. A million voters, in the process of casting their ballots for one candidate rather than another, will obviously be motivated by nonrational factors, but the final decision—the election to office of one man—will be a rational decision. This, at least, is one of the main reasons why popular elections are thought to be preferable to, and give wiser results than, other methods of selection. Just how this collective wisdom gets distilled out of a million individual follies is a question for both political theory and social psychology. The discussion of issues which is theoretically accompanied by political campaigns is thought of as a process in which citizens have an opportunity to synthesize their partial views. The compromises made necessary when many individuals must come to an agreement on who they want as a leader or what policy they are to pursue is another method for intruding a higher rationality into politics. Or it may be suggested that beneath the level of consciousness each citizen actually wants the public welfare to be advanced. Aristotle does not pursue these questions. Indeed, rather than elevating political wisdom of the public, he asks us to anticipate what might occur if its members are not allowed to participate in government. "There is a serious risk in not letting them have some share in the enjoyment of power," he says. "For a state with a body of disenfranchised citizens who are numerous and poor must necessarily be a state which is full of enemies." [47] Once again

[46] *Ibid.*
[47] Pp. 124–125.

Aristotle gives favorable judgment to a particular institution not so much because of its inherent virtues as because the alternatives are shown to be worse. And, once again also, we see that Aristotle, while aware of the dangers to political stability latent in any disenfranchised body, is not willing to go to the other extreme. The counsel of moderation is to give a vote to the man in the street but not allow him to hold office.

> The alternative left is . . . giving the people the two general functions of electing the magistrates to office and of calling them to account at the end of their tenure of office, but not the right of holding office themselves in their individual capacity. When they all meet together, the people display a good enough gift of perception, and when combined with the better class they are of service to the state.[48]

Even out of this moderate solution there arises a problem—one which later concerned Mill and Tocqueville. If the average citizen is given the vote, and if he is allowed to elect and call to account his rulers, there is no guarantee that he will wish to continue perpetuating members of "the better class" in public office. He may, after a period, decide that he has not been well served by those who are presumed to be his betters. And once he reaches this conclusion, he will insist on putting direct representatives of his own class into power. After the franchise has been universally extended, it is a difficult matter to withdraw this privilege. Indeed, it is no longer looked upon as a privilege: it is now regarded as a right. In short, popular elections can have the ultimate consequence of popular rule.

The average citizen has a fair set of expectations concerning what he thinks he should be getting out of life. We can talk a great deal about the need for superior ability in those who make public policy. But these policies affect the existence of the ordinary man: he is the one who pays the taxes, who dies on the battlefield, who is the gainer or loser at each political juncture. The expert has a role to play in many areas in society, but doubts may be raised as to whether politics should be one of them.

> Each individual may indeed be a worse judge than the experts; but . . . there are a number of arts in which the creative artist is not the only, or even the best, judge. These are the arts whose products can be understood and judged even by those who do not possess any skill in the art. A house, for instance, is something which can be understood by others besides the builder: indeed the user of a house —or in other words the householder—will judge it even better than he does.[49]

The role of experts in politics is far from settled in political theory. That this is so can be illustrated by Aristotle's use of the house analogy. The average homeowner can possess no expert knowledge of strength of materials, land

[48] P. 125.
[49] P. 126.

subsidence, and atmospheric conditions and yet be quite satisfied with the style and accommodations of the house which is built for him. Then, one day, forces unanticipated by him will make their presence known and his castle will come crashing down around his head. The engineer, the geologist, or the meteorologist could have told him it was going to happen, and how catastrophe might have been averted. Or, to add the political dimension, if engineers or geologists had political power, they could tell us just how our houses should be built. There is a whole body of experts—from psychiatrists to plumbers to political scientists—who claim an expertise which ought to be underwritten with political power. It can even be suggested that there remains no sphere where there is not an expert who is the best judge of how the layman ought to conduct his affairs. One of the chief defenses of democracy, however, is to insist on the value of the lay judgment. Even with Aristotle's house analogy, it can well be argued that to take the risk of having your house fall down around your ears is not too high a price to pay for keeping officious experts out of your hair.

Democracy has two faces. Indeed, Aristotle's scientific distinction between the two forms of democratic government is probably more significant for political theory than his philosophical distinction between democracy and polity. Aristotle juxtaposes "populist" and "constitutional" democracy. Majority rule in a constitutional democracy is limited by basic laws which protect the rights of both minority groups and individuals. These limitations do not exist in the case of populist democracy.

> In democracies which obey the law there are no demagogues; it is the better class of citizens who preside over affairs. Demagogues arise in states where the laws are not sovereign. The people then becomes an autocrat—a single composite autocrat made up of many members, with the many playing the sovereign, not as individuals, but collectively.
> A democracy of this order, being in the nature of an autocrat and not being governed by law, begins to attempt an autocracy. It grows despotic; flatterers come to be held in honor. It is popular leaders who, by referring all issues to the decision of the people, are responsible for substituting the sovereignty of decrees for that of the laws.[50]

Aristotle deals here with the subtle question of who actually rules in a populist democracy. As Plato pointed out in his treatment of democracy, we cannot assume that a majority of the people somehow or other spontaneously rule themselves. Populist democracy must have at its helm a popular leader who voices the sentiments and aspirations of the majority. However, it is also plain that such a leader actually does more than bring to the surface the nascent popular will. That leader who rides to power on public sentiment acquires, in

[50] P. 168.

the process of his ascent, a great deal of discretionary power in his own right. The whole study of democratic leadership is still in its infancy.[51] It is, in essentials, just as inchoate in our own day as it was in Aristotle's time.

If populist democracy brings with it tyranny of the majority, the alternative must be some kind of restraint on the popular will. One possibility is that the majority will put restraints on itself. This hope is advanced by Locke, Mill, and Tocqueville; it is one of the assumptions underlying the modern British constitution. Aristotle, however, concentrates on constitutional safeguards. The difficulty with populist democracy is that it is not restrained by laws.

> There would appear to be solid substance in the view that a democracy of this type is not a true constitution. Where the laws are not sovereign there is no constitution. Law should be sovereign on every issue, and the magistrates and the citizen body should only decide about details.[52]

The role of constitutionalism in democracy is a vital theme in political theory.[53] The classic statement for the American experience is, of course, in The Federalist Papers. Aristotle would have the basic constitutional law be supreme—over both the will of the majority and the discretion of the rulers. How the supremacy of the basic law is to be established and respected he does not tell us. A more coherent answer to this question will have to be deferred until theories of Natural Law and liberalism are considered. Both contribute to the underpinning of the constitutional idea.

Another answer to populist democracy is to make certain assumptions about the composition of the social structure. Societies are, by and large, composed of competing groups. Each faction seeks to use political power in the benefit of its own interest. Aristotle talks only of the rich and poor as groups in society, but he has indicated previously that he is not unaware of the role of groups which are not economic in character:

> Factious disputes and struggles readily arise between the masses and the rich; and no matter which side may win the day, it refuses to establish a constitution based on the common interest and the principle of equality, but, preferring to exact as the price of victory a greater share of constitutional rights, it institutes, according to its principles, a democracy or an oligarchy.[54]

In many such situations one or another class actually does win the day and is thus able to use the power of government to promote its own interest. But

---

[51] See Alvin W. Gouldner, ed., Studies in Leadership (New York: Harper, 1950), particularly the essays on "Authoritarian and Democratic Leaders," pp. 389–467. Also of value is the brief analysis of political leadership at the end of James Burns, Roosevelt: The Lion and the Fox (New York: Harcourt, Brace, 1956), pp. 481–487.

[52] Politics, p. 169.

[53] See Carl J. Friedrich, Constitutional Government and Democracy (Boston: Ginn, 1950), revised edition.

[54] Politics, p. 183.

total victory for one group and unconditional surrender by the others are exceptions rather than the rule in most democratic societies. Factions can win political victories, but they are only temporary gains. The group struggle is never-ending, and public policy bends first one way and then another as the winds of power shift. This leads Aristotle to pose a question and to offer an answer:

> "What and what sort of constitution is suited to what and what sort of persons?" In order to answer this question, we must first assume a general axiom which is true of all constitutions—that the part of a state which wishes a constitution to continue must be stronger than the part which does not. Here we have to remember that quality and quantity both go to the making of every state. By "quality" we mean free birth, wealth, culture, and nobility of descent; by "quantity" we mean superiority in numbers. Now quality may belong to one of the parts which compose a state, and quantity to another. . . . Quantity and quality must thus be placed in the balance against one another.[55]

We see, then, that neither the qualitative rich nor the quantitative poor are able to have their own way all the time. A democracy requires the general assent of all the groups which comprise the body politic, and this means minorities as well as the majority. Aristotle assumes that the balance among social groups will be achieved because the groups themselves will be attentive to their particular interests and will mobilize their resources in the struggle for political power. The rich may be few in number, but their wealth is a source of power. The poor may be lacking in money, but their numbers provide power. Other groups may be neither wealthy or numerous, but they may be composed of individuals who react so deeply to particular issues that their intensity of feeling will lend power to their position. And still other groups, drawing on a small core of disciplined adherents, will find that organizational effectiveness is the road to power. These groups will compete against each other to create conditions which are favorable to their particular interests. The assumption underlying this conception of democracy is a politics of balance. A tense and dynamic equilibrium characterizes the relations among groups, and between groups and political authority. In this way the power of

---

[55] Pp. 184–185. It has been pointed out that Aristotle spends far more of his time discussing the "perverted" constitutions than he does their "legitimate" counterparts. However, there are signs that this distinction is not a clear-cut one. For a "polity" is not so much different from democracy as it is a "mixture" of democracy and oligarchy; and "the name is confined to those mixtures which incline to democracy." And an aristocracy is not the opposite of oligarchy, but rather an oligarchical-democratic mixture "which inclines more to oligarchy." (See p. 175.) Thus the desirable constitutional forms are not Utopian forms, but systems which blend the best features of the perverted—that is, extreme—constitutions. We may therefore conclude that the limited democracy of which Aristotle speaks is actually a "polity." While in major outlines it is a democracy, the limitations on majority power are oligarchical features of a moderating character. Aristotle never makes this identity in so many words, but such a conclusion easily follows from his analysis.

the majority is restrained. It is at all times confronted by minorities which can balance the resources at their disposal against the power of numbers.[56] Aristotle gives only the rough outline of political and social pluralism. We will have to wait for Tocqueville to analyze this question, employing a more elaborate approach to the relations between the state and other institutions in society.

The theory of striking an equilibrium between class and class, especially when there is a wide gulf between the interests of the two, is difficult to achieve. Not only are the stakes high in such a struggle, but the conception of justice held by each class can involve the violation of important interests held by the other one. Even if neither class wins permanent victory in this political struggle, the clash of such severely disjoined interests can upset the balance of the society as a whole. For this reason, Aristotle calls for a rearrangement of the social structure, but without any Utopian pretensions: political reform must be possible of achievement if there is to be reform at all.

> We have now to consider what is the best constitution and the best way of life for the majority of states and men. In doing so we shall not employ a standard of excellence above the reach of ordinary men, or a standard of education requiring exceptional endowments and equipment, or the standard of a constitution which attains an ideal height. We shall only be concerned with the sort of life which most men are able to share and the sort of constitution which it is possible for most states to enjoy.
> The issues we have just raised can all be decided in the light of one body of fundamental principles: (a) that a truly happy life is a life of goodness lived in freedom from impediments, and (b) that goodness consists in a mean. It follows that the best way of life is one which consists in a mean, and a mean of the kind attainable by every individual.[57]

The decision to deal with the attainable is but one of several ways to embark on political prescription. Utopian prescriptions, as we saw in the case of Plato, do not seek to provide means by which the ideal state might be achieved. Rather, they lay down principles which may in an indirect way eventually influence policy. Aristotle's aim, unlike Plato's, is to design institutions which can be put into effect in existing society. This sense of the prac-

---

[56] James Madison, in the Fifty-First *Federalist Paper*, employs this sociological limitation as a means of curbing majority power. "The federal republic of the United States," he says, "will be broken into so many parts, interests, and classes of citizens, that the rights of individuals, or of the minority, will be in little danger from interested combinations of the majority." There is no guarantee, of course, that any society will be heterogeneous enough to preclude majority tyranny. Madison could not bring the diverse "parts, interests, and classes" into being: he could only comment on America's good fortune in their existence. Not all societies are so lucky. And some have interests and classes which are so antagonistic that they cannot agree on rules of the game for peacefully settling their differences: too much heterogeneity, Aristotle will point out, is a prime cause of revolution.

[57] *Politics*, p. 180.

tical does not make him any less of a philosopher than Plato, although it is clear that institutions for the real world will have to compromise with the imperfections of human nature. Because politics is the art of the possible, and because the counsel of moderation is an important theoretical principle, Aristotle is led to stress the vital role of the middle class in society. If the class struggle between rich and poor is to be tempered, if the narrow conception of self-interest held by these groups is to be held in rein, then a third constituency must be brought forward to exercise a balance of power.

In all states there may be distinguished three parts, or classes, of the citizen-body —the very rich; the very poor; and the middle-class which forms the mean. Now it is admitted, as a general principle, that moderation and the mean are always the best. We may therefore conclude that in the ownership of all gifts of fortune a middle condition will be the best.

Men who are in this condition are the most ready to listen to reason. Those who belong to either extreme—the over-handsome, the over-strong, the over-noble, the over-wealthy; or at the opposite end the over-poor, the over-weak, the utterly ignoble—find it hard to follow the lead of reason.

It is a further merit of the middle-class that its members suffer least from ambition, which both in the military and the civil sphere is dangerous to states.[58]

Rationality would appear to be the property of those who inhabit a certain social and economic status; men whose stomachs are too full or too empty are apt to see the world in a distorted way and not as it really is. Similarly, those who have much to lose or much to gain will aspire to gain or maintain their power far more avidly than those who are located in the middle class.

This is not to say that all members of the middle class are endowed with a rational outlook, nor is it to deny that many men of moderate means wish to increase their wealth, nor is it to overlook the fact that there are those in the middle class who are prepared to lead the poor to power. Aristotle simply describes a tendency, a pattern of behavior, which seems typical of a certain class. Furthermore, if a society is to develop into a community, if feeling of a common interest is to be infused, then the middle class can play an important moderating role. "A state aims at being, as far as it can be, a society composed of equals and peers; and the middle class, more than any other, has this sort of composition," Aristotle says. "It follows that a state which is based on the middle class is bound to be the best constituted in respect of the elements of which, in our view, a state is naturally composed."[59] The middle class, Aristotle suggests, manifests the spirit of equality and consensus which can serve as a guide for the whole society. Both upper and lower classes lack this spirit: the former because its members are too ambitious as individuals, the latter because it has tendencies to mob behavior. If the civility of the middle-class

[58] Pp. 180–181.
[59] P. 181.

style of life can be brought to permeate all classes, then the most troublesome of society's rough edges may be smoothed over. But Aristotle's main aim is not to idealize any particular class. His interest is to achieve a distribution of power in society which will obviate class struggle, thus ensuring social stability and creating the conditions for pursuing the good life.

It is clear from our argument, first, that the best form of political society is one where power is vested in the middle class, and, secondly, that good government is attainable in those states where there is a large middle class—large enough, if possible, to be stronger than both of the other classes, but at any rate large enough to be stronger than either of them singly; for in that case its addition to either will suffice to turn the scale, and will prevent either of the opposing extremes from becoming dominant.[60]

This, then, is to be the social composition of a democratic society. Ideally, the middle class would be more numerous than either the upper or lower class. Aristotle would approve of a society where the population would be distributed in a ratio between the upper, middle, and lower classes on something of the order of 10–50–40. This means, quite simply, that there is no such thing as a "tyranny of the majority" because there is no majority to be the tyrant in the society. The middle class will ally with one of the other two classes some of the time, and with the other on other occasions. And at all times it will serve to prevent class-consciousness' becoming exaggerated or class differences' becoming exacerbated. "Where the middle class is large," Aristotle says, "there is least likelihood of faction and dissension among the citizens." [61] And how is a numerous middle class to be established and made secure? We are given only a hint for an answer: "It is," Aristotle says, "the greatest of blessings for a state that its members should possess a moderate and adequate property." [62] The role of property ownership in political theory is a central one. Plato talked of its abolition, and Aristotle sought its wide distribution. The argument will be forwarded by John Locke and hurled back by Karl Marx. That a propertied middle class is the chief defense of human freedom and democratic politics is an idea as old as Aristotle. And it is still an idea which demands our serious attention.

SEDITION AND REVOLUTION: CAUSE AND PREVENTION

A theory of political change may be thought of as the lubricant in the engine of political theory. Neither men nor societies will stand still for long,

[60] P. 182.
[61] Ibid.
[62] Ibid.

and in this respect politics is one of the liveliest of the arts. And any discussion of political change must eventually develop a theory of revolution. Academic students of politics have always been grimly fascinated by the spectacle of violent upheaval. Some scholars are fearful of any threat to the social order, and they write their apprehensions into their theories. Others wish to bring about a radical transformation of society, and their theories are used to explain and justify drastic change. And most theorists, no matter what their personal sentiments, are sedentary men of letters for whom the prospect of violence brings on the mixed emotions of repulsion and attraction simultaneously. If Plato made only a few speculative comments on the dynamics of political change, Aristotle is prepared to fill in much of the analysis. Thus he devotes a large section of the *Politics* to this subject. Political change must be viewed from two angles: "We have to consider the general causes which produce changes in constitutions . . ." he says. "In addition we have to suggest the policies likely to ensure the stability of constitutions." [63] Aristotle is not writing a handbook on how to make a revolution; nor, on the other hand, does he feel obliged to dilate on the horrors of revolution once that event has occurred. But he is prepared to give some level-headed advice on how the incipient conditions which spur on revolutionary movements may be detected and how, once they have been detected, they may be extirpated with least pain. In short, while Aristotle is not favorably disposed toward revolutions, he is at the same time no friend to the kind of social and political environment which leads men to rebel.

In line with his analysis of governmental systems, Aristotle frames most of his discussion of revolution in the context of oligarchy and democracy. The conception of justice espoused by each of these systems is filled with revolutionary potential. The distorted and self-interested character of their conception of the good society makes both oligarchs and democrats cling grimly to the power they have or their aspirations for climbing to power.

Democracy arose in the strength of an opinion that those who were equal in any one respect were equal absolutely, and in all respects. . . . Oligarchy similarly arose from an opinion that those who were unequal in some one respect were altogether unequal. . . . Both democracy and oligarchy are based on a sort of justice; but they both fall short of absolute justice. This is the reason why either side turns to sedition if it does not enjoy the share of constitutional rights which accords with the conception of justice it happens to entertain.[64]

The revolutionaries, then, tend to be absolutists. They can know no peace of mind or spirit if they are compelled to live in a society whose institutions

[63] P. 203.
[64] P. 204.

are, by their lights, characterized by injustice. The conceptions of justice and injustice held by such people tend to be ideological rather than philosophical, and the inherent distortions stimulate the tendency to violence. In a revolutionary situation it is not simply ideas, but interests as well, which are at stake. "The cause of sedition is always to be found in inequality." [65] Thus ideas and interests, the ideology of justice and the reality of social inequality, are inextricably tied together. Equality is a two-headed coin: for those on the bottom of the heap it means sharing the power and status of those who are at the top; for those at the top it means turning back a threat to their superior position and resources. Both the desire to rise and the desire to resist are spurs to violence. "There are some who stir up sedition because their minds are filled by a passion for equality, which arises from their thinking that they have the worst of the bargain . . ." Aristotle says. "There are others who do it because their minds are filled with a passion for inequality or superiority, which arises from their conceiving that . . . they are really more than equal to others." [66] In short, "Inferiors become revolutionaries in order to be equals, and equals in order to be superiors." [67] It is important to note that Aristotle sees revolution as originating with either the rich or the poor.

The popular image of revolution, of course, is that of the poor rising up and massacring the well-to-do, but Aristotle would ask us not to forget that democracies have also been subverted by the sedition of those who are outraged over the thought that their presumably superior interests have been treated inequitably by democratic governments. "The ground taken by notables . . . in justification of sedition," Aristotle says, ". . . is the injustice of their having only equal rights although they are actually superior." [68] The aggrieved notables must, of course, enlist the sympathies of at least some of the ordinary public if they are to be successful in overthrowing a democracy. By playing on the indifference to democracy of some, on the resentment of others, and by using their wealth and organizational resources, they may be able to effect a successful reverse of democratic institutions. We have a tendency to think in terms of a cycle of progress: that oligarchy is supplanted by democracy, and then democracy goes on to become a bigger and a better democracy. There is quite enough evidence to suggest that democracy is not part of the march of progress and that a society may well revert to oligarchy at any time. This view is implied by Aristotle, who gives equal attention to both democratic revolution and oligarchic counterrevolution.

[65] P. 205.
[66] P. 207.
[67] Ibid.
[68] P. 211.

Not all revolutions shake the foundations of society. There is a difference between a revolution which transfers power from one section of the community to another and what we might call a "palace" revolution where power changes hands but remains in essentially the same group. "Sometimes sedition is directed against the existing constitution and is intended to change its nature—to turn democracy into oligarchy, or oligarchy into democracy . . ." Aristotle says. "Sometimes, however, . . . the seditious party may decide to maintain the system of government . . . as it stands; but it will desire to get the administration into the hands of its members." [69] While both democracies and oligarchies can be threatened by revolutions of political or social proportions, oligarchies have the additional threat of revolutions inside the "palace" as well.

Oligarchies are prone to two sorts of sedition—the one within the ranks of the oligarchial party itself, and the other between that party and the party of the people. Democracies are only exposed to sedition between the democratic party and the oligarchical; and there are no internal dissensions—at any rate none worth mentioning—which divide democratic parties against themselves.[70]

The analysis of revolutions is one of the most difficult aspects of political theory. A fairly simple classification might talk of three kinds of revolution: the "palace" revolution, the "political" revolution, and the "social" revolution. The first simply transfers power from one group of individuals to another within the same class; the second brings a new class onto the political scene and forces the old ruling class to share its power with it; and a "social" revolution so transforms the structure of society that the old ruling class is destroyed and a new class ascends to power in what is—for all intents and purposes—a new society.

This analytic scheme has the virtue of simplicity, but the dangers in it must not be minimized. They are especially apparent when various theorists are asked to put one of the three labels on actual historical revolutions. For it will emerge that the liberal, the conservative, and the radical tend to see the same events from different perspectives. Was, for example, the French Revolution of 1789 a "palace," a "political," or a "social" revolution? To a conservative like Edmund Burke it looked like the most devastating of social upheavals. On the other hand, a liberal like John Stuart Mill or a radical such as Karl Marx would view it as a violent political transition in which the middle class compelled the aristocracy to share its monopoly of political power. And this is not the only problem of interpretation; while Mill and Marx might agree

[69] P. 204–205.
[70] P. 206.

on the political character of the French Revolution, they would part company when it came to an analysis of its consequences for French politics. Mill would say that it had the result of establishing the realities of representative government and political liberty, that the principles embodied in the Declaration of the Rights of Man were—no matter what dictatorial interludes might intervene in the future—made permanent for all French citizens. Marx would retort that the French Revolution was successful because the propertied middle class, employing the rhetoric of freedom and equality, stirred the members of the working class into revolutionary action and led them to think that by it their lot would be bettered. Freedom, Marx would say, was secured by the French Revolution, but it was freedom only for the property-owning class; in terms of liberty and equality, the working class was no better off than it had been before. The liberal, whose most frequent concern has been with the tension between aristocratic privilege and middle-class liberty, interprets the revolution in one light; the radical, who thinks primarily of the welfare of the working class, sees it in a totally different light.

And not dissimilar to the radical outlook is the view of Machiavelli. Here it is suggested that even supposedly "political" and "social" revolutions do no more than shift power from one set of hands within the "palace" to another. Even though the revolutionary leaders may purport to speak on behalf of the middle class, the working class, or of all the people, once these leaders are successful and come to power they form no less an oligarchical clique than the ruling group which held office prior to the revolution. Despite the revolutionary rhetoric, the Machiavellian insists, the shift of power does not bring with it a wider area of self-government or freedom for society as a whole. For it is an organizational law that political power will always be concentrated in a small group, and even a revolution carried on in the name of democracy is bound to be abortive.[71]

While Aristotle does not go to Marxist or Machiavellian extremes, he is concerned to show that revolutions which claim to upset oligarchical, rule are not always what they seem. We must, as a first step, distinguish between revolutionary threats which emanate from inside and those which come from outside the ruling class:

There are two particular, and most obvious, methods by which changes are brought about in oligarchies. One is the unjust treatment of the masses by the government. Any leader is then an adequate champion, especially when it so happens that the leader comes from the ranks of the governing class itself. . . . Some-

[71] Even though democracy does not result from a revolution, there can be an important change in the composition of the group which holds political power. For a "ruling class" may be supplanted by an "elite." This point will be discussed in the chapters on Machiavelli and Burke.

times an oligarchy is undermined by persons who themselves are wealthy, but who are excluded from office.[72]

Revolutions are not always spontaneous uprisings of the oppressed masses, and even if they are supported by the general public, we must not for that reason assume that the leaders are men of the lower classes. Many revolutions are fomented and led by members of the ruling class; for one reason or another they become dissatisfied with the policies or personalities of the ruling group, and, unable to persuade their fellow oligarchs to change their ways, the dissenters turn in the other direction for support and seek the backing of the man-in-the-street. Thus we have what begins as an internal dispute within one class and ends up as a full-fledged revolution. "Oligarchies are disturbed from inside when their members play the demagogue, for reasons of personal rivalry, . . . by practicing on the masses."[73] It is not uncommon for the dominant group within a ruling class to keep down younger and more ambitious members of the oligarchy. When those in entrenched positions try to exclude those on the fringes from power, such exclusion will be felt to be an abrogation of equal rights—equality, that is, for those who happen to be in the ruling class. "When some of its members try to make an oligarchy still more exclusive," Aristotle says, "those who champion equality of rights are then compelled to enlist the aid of the people."[74] The common people, of course, will be stirred to action by democratic slogans and Utopian promises. If the Old Guard oligarchs are thrown out, the people will be told, then a new era of freedom and justice will prevail throughout the land. The man in the street, lured by these fine words, rallies behind the dissenting New Guard of the ruling class. Because it has popular support, such a revolution is hard to put down, and it is likely that the New Guard will topple the Old. But once the dissenters have attained power, there is no certainty that they will carry out the promises which were made to the masses the day before. Whether there will be concessions, reforms, or a sweeping reconstruction of society depends on a whole variety of factors. The view that the masses bleed, die, and are then cynically defrauded is not a rule applicable to all revolutions. Yet the disillusioning aftermath of many suggests that there is a great deal of truth in the adage "plus ce change, plus c'est la même chose." Aristotle did not elaborate on this aspect of revolutions, for his concern was to describe causes rather than consequences. By way of summary, he could say, "an oligarchy at one with itself is not easily overthrown from within."[75] The

[72] *Politics*, p. 217.
[73] P. 218.
[74] *Ibid.*
[75] P. 219.

trouble, of course, is that ruling classes and elites frequently find it difficult to remain cohesive or unanimous on the ways and means of policy. Plato was aware of this problem, and he tried to devise ways for the Guardian class to keep from falling apart. Even the best organized of modern dictatorships has to worry about internal dissension—not to mention sedition—within the ruling group. In a system where power is concentrated, it is often the men of power themselves who pose the greatest threat to the system.

Aristotle next cites a breeding ground for revolutionary tension which is no stranger to contemporary politics.

> Heterogeneity of stocks may lead to sedition—at any rate until they have had time to assimilate. A state cannot be constituted from any chance body of persons, or in any chance period of time. Most of the states which have admitted persons of another stock, either at the time of their foundation or later, have been troubled by sedition.[76]

Until racial and religious assimilation take place—and generations or even centuries can go by without this taking place—no state can feel internally secure. Many, if not most, of the emerging states in the modern world are composed of racial, national, and religious elements which are strikingly diverse in origin and interest. Ingenious experiments in federalist institutions, as in India, Indonesia, Nigeria, and Burma, have been conducted in an attempt to deal with groups which cling to habits engendered by centuries of independent and autonomous existence. Such groups cannot easily be welded into the institutional framework of a single nation. The result is that while particular stocks are theoretically incorporated into a common state, they often hold apart from its authority. Revolution—in the form of guerrilla warfare or attempted secession or violent overthrow of the constituted government—is a likely consequence. If a state so heterogeneously composed is to survive, it is doubtful whether it can wait for the rebellious citizens to become assimilated in habit and custom to a new political way of life. More often a show of sedition is regarded as the first trial of strength of an emerging government, and it will deploy its resources to meet force with greater force. Aristotle, we should not forget, was not trying to offer a solution; he was simply stating as a matter of fact that ethnic heterogeneity is a breeding ground for revolution. There have been states which have assimilated diverse stocks without sedition or violence. Here, again, it is the peculiar circumstances which determine whether political homogenization will be achieved through peaceful or revolutionary means— or at all.

Democracy itself can be a cause of revolution. It has already been shown

[76] P. 210.

that majority rule in a democracy may be subjected to limitations or it may acknowledge no rein on its powers. Aristotle displayed a preference for a state in which the majority had power but where that power was limited. An inherent problem of democracy is that its democratic tendencies develop of their own accord, and in this growth the restraints on majority rule can become weakened. Whereas at one time the man-in-the-street will defer to the better elements in society, at a later time he may begin to believe the democratic ideology and demand that representatives from his own class be placed in power. The change from limited democracy to unlimited democracy, Aristotle says, can have revolutionary dimensions. Such an upheaval is usually fomented by a demagogue, a man who rouses and assumes leadership of the people. "In democracies," Aristotle says, "changes are chiefly due to the wanton license of demagogues." [77] These leaders urge the electorate to demand the abolition of property qualifications for the franchise and that any citizen regardless of origin be eligible to hold political office. This is the beginning of unlimited democracy. No longer are there institutional barriers between rulers and ruled. What happens, furthermore, is that candidates for office must appeal—or pander—to the sentiments of their constituents. "Where the offices are filled by vote, without any property qualification, and the whole of the people has the vote," Aristotle says, "candidates for office begin to play the demagogue, and matters are brought to a pass in which law itself is included in the scope of popular sovereignty." [78] This is the democratic revolution: if the voice of the people will hear no refusal, then politicians must do as they are bid by their masters. The problem at this point is not whether the average citizen is capable of governing himself; rather, the question is what occurs as a result of unchecked democracy. Aristotle's concern is that fundamental law will be distorted by the whims of popular caprice; he is concerned that rules and institutions which ensure order and morality will be violated in the process of gratifying the whims of the man in the street. If popular sovereignty is unlimited to the extent that it is able to tamper with the basic law whenever the public is so inclined, then it may truly be said that society has undergone a revolutionary change. There may be no violence; indeed, most citizens will probably not realize what has transpired. But the impact of the democratic revolutions will leave its mark on a body politic for generations to come.

If revolutions are to be prevented, they must be anticipated. This means that discussion of what causes sedition is an important first step for any ruler who would avoid disaster. "To know the causes which destroy constitutions

[77] P. 215.
[78] P. 216.

is also to know the causes which ensure their preservation," Aristotle says.[79] Some of the causes of revolution, such as ethnic heterogeneity or the march of democracy, cannot easily be dealt with. At most, symptoms can be alleviated and inevitable transitions rendered less violent. However, there remains a wide area of discretion for rulers who regard it as their task to achieve stability. If they study the conditions which have led to the downfall of other states, they are at least on the way to preserving their own. Aristotle sets down six rules which should always be followed:

(1) The first rule is that the average citizen should be handled with care. This is not to say that the state should be governed solely in his interest; the point is that the ordinary citizen constitutes the seedbed of revolution, and that in order that his revolutionary potential never has an opportunity to flower, rulers should bend over backwards to see that considerate treatment marks their relations with the ruled:

> Some states owe their stability not so much to the solidity of their constitutional systems, as to the good relations in which their officers stand alike with the unenfranchised and the members of the civic body. In such states the unenfranchised are never treated unjustly; on the contrary, their leading members are promoted to share in constitutional rights; and while the ambitious among them are not wronged on points of honor, the rank and file are not maltreated in matters of money and profit. Similarly, in these states, the officers and the other members of the governing class behave towards one another in a democratic spirit of equality.[80]

While rulers may not be disposed to share their power with the ruled, they can go a long way toward anticipating and satisfying popular grievances. Good personal relations and a fraternal spirit can be rules of behavior even though they are not accompanied by a redistribution of political power. The man in the street is to be the recipient of common justice: he is, for example, to receive a fair wage and his taxes should not be oppressive. Ambitious men of humble origins are to be promoted and given honors; in this way potential demagogues are separated from the groups which they might otherwise stir to revolution. In short, Aristotle is suggesting not only that rulers be both fraternal and paternal, but also that the door which gives entry to the ruling group be left slightly ajar for all men of talent. But the talk of justice and equality of opportunity which we encounter in this discussion is not a discussion of philosophical ends; Aristotle's proposals are political means for achieving stability. Indeed, it is hard to know just how far Aristotle is creating a world of deceptive appearances. "A good deal of attention should be paid to the poor . . ." he says. "And if a rich man does them violence, the penal-

---

[79] Pp. 224–225.
[80] P. 225.

ties should be heavier than if he had been guilty of violence against members of his own class." [81] Aristotle is not simply suggesting that the punishment should fit the crime; the punishment is to outweigh the crime in certain cases so that the appearance that justice is being done for the poor man will be firmly implanted in the public mind.

(2) Internal cohesion is frequently accomplished by means of uniting all citizens against a common enemy. The difficulty is that there may be no external threat on the horizon. If this is the case, one must be created:

> The preservation of a constitution may not only be due to the fact that a state is far removed from the menace of any danger: it may also, on occasion, be due to the very opposite. When danger is imminent, men are alarmed, and they therefore keep a firmer grip on their constitution. All those who are concerned for the constitution should therefore foster alarms, which will put men on their guard, and will make them keep an unwearied watch like sentinels on night-duty. They must, in a word, make the remote come near. [82]

This is a suggestion worthy of Machiavelli. There are, in this proposal, a number of problems which at least deserve mention. When a menace is invented and subsequently exaggerated, people tend to look for living embodiments of that threat. While the chief enemies may lie outside the state, there will inevitably be a search for subversives within. This fear of a fifth column—especially when its existence is more imagined than real—can have consequences which are themselves harmful for national unity. Furthermore, there is the danger that if an alarm is fostered, those who thought up this tactic may, out of fear that their bluff will eventually be called, commit their nation to a needless war with the external enemy which was conjured up. [83] In that case the menace has become a real one. Aristotle's strategy is a risky one; nevertheless, it has often proved effective as a means of preventing revolution, and that, after all, is the present concern. In order to deal with the threat of internal revolution, it is frequently necessary to flirt with external dangers which are only slightly less destructive than revolution itself.

(3) The next rule is a simple one and, for that reason, all the more apt to be forgotten. Rulers, Aristotle says, must keep their fingers out of the public till:

> The masses are not so greatly offended at being excluded from office (they may even be glad to be given the leisure for attending to their own business); what

[81] P. 229.

[82] P. 226.

[83] Aristotle was aware of this danger: "We may lay down the rule that confidence should never be placed in devices intended to hoodwink the masses," he said (p. 223). Just how fostering spurious alarms is to be distinguished from hoodwinking the masses is a distinction that Aristotle does not discuss in detail.

really annoys them is to think that those who have the enjoyment of office are embezzling public funds.[84]

Public money is qualitatively different from private money. The public applies a different—and higher—standard of moral conduct to men in public life than it does to men in business. When a businessman bribes a government official, for example, by far the larger share of the opprobrium is heaped on the latter's head. Just why citizens maintain this double standard is a more important question than might appear on the surface. For the answer to it is related to the fact that the state is popularly regarded as the most important of all institutions in society. This means that those who serve it must obey a moral code which is not applied to other men. Robbing the taxpayer, therefore, is not simply a dollars-and-cents matter: it violates a trust over which the public is prepared to become greatly exercised. This is why the charge of corruption in a political campaign has a tendency to drive all the other issues off the platform; the politician who embezzles appears in the worst political light. The whole conception of the politics of "clean government" deserves more study than it has received. By making "corruption" vs. "clean government" the pervasive issue, attention is often deflected from what are, in the final analysis, far more crucial political issues. Nevertheless the average citizen —especially the middle-class citizen—fixes attention on the ruler who has sticky fingers. Aristotle is right in listing this as an important source of dissension, if not necessarily revolution. The charge that governors have defrauded the taxpayers has led to many political downfalls. The ruler who is honest on this count will find that he can frequently have a free hand in pursuing policies which do not lend themselves to public concern. The point, Aristotle is saying, is to be pure in the area where the public demands purity.

(4) If revolution is to be avoided, a political system must have a solid basis of support. It is Aristotle's view that a state will survive only if this base consists of at least a majority of the citizens. "A constitution will tend to be preserved by the observance of . . . the elementary principle which has again and again been suggested . . ." he says, "—the principle of ensuring that the number of those who wish a constitution to continue shall be greater than the number of those who do not." [85] Just how this principle is to be implemented through political institutions is, of course, a question Aristotle has been discussing all along. The ceaseless endeavor of rulers must be to secure the consent of those over whom they rule. Consent can be actively given in the form of a vote, or it can be tacitly bestowed in the sense that if there is no demonstration of protest then such passivity implies consent.

[84] P. 228.
[85] Pp. 231–232.

Further, consent can be granted to a particular system in its institutional entirety, or it can be given to only one particular ruler. If we are to say that a citizen who cast his vote for the candidate who was defeated nevertheless continues to "consent" to his government, then we must enlarge the idea beyond that of obedience to an individual ruler. Aristotle only touches on this problem, and we will have to wait for the Social Contract theorists—Hobbes, Locke, and Rousseau—to explore it more fully.

(5) We have already seen how democracy, by pursuing its populist tendency can cause a revolution in the entire political structure. And an oligarchy, by closing the ruling circle so as to exclude men of ambition and talent, can nurture the seeds of its own violent overthrow. What disturbs Aristotle is that proponents of a particular system consciously or unconsciously strive to push the form of government they prefer to what they believe is its "logical conclusion." Thus there are proponents of democracy who are not content at seeing democracy at work in the political sphere alone: they call for its introduction into economic institutions, voluntary associations, and matters of intellect and taste as well. Similarly, there are those of oligarchical inclination who would extend the exclusive power of the select few into areas where popular consent has hitherto been the rule. Those who insist on going to extremes are inviting revolution: the sudden and drastic extension of power by a majority or a minority is bound to threaten the group which finds it is no longer consulted. To avoid revolution, democrats and oligarchs should both forego striving for a more perfect democracy or oligarchy. On the contrary, both should attempt to adhere to the mean:

Many of the measures which are reckoned democratic really undermine democracies: many which are reckoned oligarchical actually undermine oligarchies. The partisans of either of these forms of government, each thinking their own the only right form, push matters to an extreme. . . . Both oligarchy and democracy may be tolerable forms of government, even though they deviate from the ideal. But if you push either of them further still in the direction to which it tends, you will begin by making it a worse constitution, and you may end by turning it into something which is not a constitution at all.[86]

Aristotle understood that enthusiastic democrats and oligarchs cannot be counted on to restrain themselves simply by appealing to their sense of fair play and moderation. There must be external checks: preferably of both constitutional and sociological character. A constitution may prevent undue extension of power on the part of the majority or minority by laying down as basic law the explicit limits on governmental activity. And a society may be composed of many groups and interests which work in such transitory

[86] P. 232.

combinations so as to prevent any single faction—either majority or minority —from gaining disproportionate political power. Aristotle touched on both of these ideas, and it should be noted that restraining forces such as these are preventives of revolution. If one of the chief causes of revolution is the abuse of power by those in authority, then a political system should seek to provide itself with built-in antidotes for such abuses. Moderating institutions are among the best guarantors of governmental stability and political longevity.

(6) The task of rulers is to secure the consent of the majority of citizens, and this consensus should embrace citizens from all classes. It is therefore the responsibility of governments to educate the governed in how to live politically: citizens must be taught the value of obedience to law, and they must be inculcated with the spirit of the political system which prevails in their society. Unless this is done, there will always be the danger of revolt. One of the lessons of political education which must be learned by those who are to live in a democracy is to accept temporary reverses with a good grace: one of the prices citizens must pay, for example, is to experience having their candidates defeated from time to time. They must be brought to understand that this unhappy turn of events does not presage the end of the world: there will, under the democratic system, be another election in a few years' time and those who were defeated today may be the victorious party later on. Most of the people in this world have never been educated in the politics of democracy: they have not been convinced that willingness to sacrifice short-term gratifications for the long-term good is a desirable attribute. Lacking such education, they may be prone to follow up defeat at the polls by storming the offices of government. The only lasting way to prevent the revolutionary mentality is to teach citizens that head-counting is preferable to head-breaking. The same general strictures on political education apply to those who seek to ensure the survival of an oligarchical or any other kind of system.

The greatest, however, of all the means we have mentioned for ensuring the stability of constitutions—but one which is nowadays generally neglected—is the education of citizens in the spirit of their constitution. There is no profit in the best of laws, even when they are sanctioned by general civic consent, if the citizens themselves have not been attuned, by the force of habit and the influence of teaching, to the right constitutional temper—which will be the temper of democracy where the laws are democratic, and where they are oligarchical will be that of oligarchy.[87]

Political education, especially when it is carried on by the government in power, raises some of the most controversial questions in political theory.

[87] P. 233.

When, for example, does "education" stop and "propaganda" begin? May the state censor or suppress ideas which it feels run counter to the spirit of the constitution? Can we say that a citizen who has been successfully indoctrinated to acknowledge the legitimacy of the political status quo is nevertheless a free man who can make responsible choices of his own? Aristotle does not raise these questions. While he criticized Plato's Utopia for putting too much of a premium on unity and not enough on individual freedom, Aristotle nevertheless does acknowledge that the state cannot follow a complete hands-off policy in the educational realm. How far Aristotle would go in this direction is at least hinted: "Men tend to become revolutionaries from circumstances connected with their private lives," he says. "This suggests that a magistracy should be instituted to supervise those who live in a way out of harmony with the established constitution—who in a democracy do not live democratically; in an oligarchy do not live oligarchically." [88]

Many modern liberals would throw up their hands on hearing such a prescription. A state which meddles in the private lives of its citizens is, we are told, bound to develop the attributes of a totalitarian dictatorship; a state which takes it on itself to decide what kinds of activities are not in "harmony" with its constitution will use its coercive power to force its citizens into a narrow political mold. Such viewing with alarm, while often springing from the most worthy of motives, can be misplaced: all states—totalitarian and democratic, autocratic and constitutional—cannot help but engage in political education. All states constantly scrutinize private behavior and judge whether it is in harmony with public policy. And all states will at one time or another label as "public" actions which some citizens would prefer to think of as "private."

Aristotle's point is that by abstaining from such intervention, real sources of danger to the state can arise; individuals must therefore learn to accept such interference if the entire system of which they are a part is to survive.[89] A democracy which contains too substantial a number of antidemocratic citizens will not last long. The state, acting in the name of the majority, must either educate the dissenters in the blessings of democracy or, that failing, use its power to prevent them from engaging in subversive acts. The whole question is an empirical one: it rests on the degree to which political education is called for and the consequences of its use. To throw up one's hands at any action of the state which might be called "thought-control" is to suppose

[88] P. 227.

[89] See Walter Berns, *Freedom, Virtue, and the First Amendment* (Baton Rogue: Louisiana University Press, 1957) for a contemporary application of Aristotle's argument. The opposite viewpoint will be examined in the chapter on Mill.

that revolutionary thoughts in the minds of individuals will never lead to revolutionary action on their part. While many states have abused their powers in this area, history is also littered with the remains of timorous states which refused to use their power until it was too late. Other writers—Hobbes, Machiavelli, Rousseau, Burke, Tocqueville, Marx and Engels—will go further on this score. Indeed, it is impossible to conceive of a political theory which does not contain, at least by implication, a theory of political education.

Aristotle puts a high value on political stability. He is no less prepared to tell oligarchs how to preserve their oligarchies than he is to tell democrats how to maintain democracies. A democratic revolution which overturned an oligarchy would, for him, be just as bad as an oligarchical counterrevolution which disposed of a democracy. The dangers to be avoided are violence, lawlessness, and disunity. Stability as a political goal must take priority over a preference for democracy, oligarchy, or any other particular system. In arguing against revolution, however, Aristotle is not thereby lending his support to any status quo. He has shown that extreme democracies and oligarchies must reform themselves internally as political systems if they are to avoid revolution; he has also demonstrated that governments which wish to avoid revolution will have to abide by principles of justice, consent, and moderation. Aristotle is reformist in temperament, but nevertheless essentially conservative. And so are most of the theorists in the Western tradition. A John Locke may say that political revolution is, because of the benefits it brings, worth the price that must be paid. A Karl Marx may say that a social revolution is both inevitable and desirable. But the vast majority of Western thinkers side with Aristotle: for reasons which they themselves, in time, will make clear.

THE PHILOSOPHER IN POLITICS

Plato was concerned with the philosopher and the pursuit of philosophical truth. Aristotle is concerned with the citizen and the design of political institutions. The different orientations of the two theorists lead them in different directions. As Plato's successor, Aristotle felt obliged to discard Utopian theorizing and to tackle many of Plato's problems anew. At the end of the Politics, therefore, he turns to the question which engaged his predecessor: the the role of the philosopher in practical politics. Plato had suggested that until existing societies acknowledge that philosophers are the only rightful kings, men of reason should stand apart from politics. Were they to even expose themselves to such affairs, they would find their philosophical purity mortally endangered. Aristotle confronts this question by posing it in Platonic terms:

"Which way of life is the more desirable? The way of politics and action? Or the way of detachment from all external things—the way, let us say, of contemplation, which some regard as the only way that is worthy of a philosopher?"

Here, we may say, are the two ways of life—the political and the philosophic—that are evidently chosen by those who have been most eager to win a reputation for goodness, in our own and in previous ages. It is a matter of no small moment on which of the two sides truth lies: for whether individuals or states are in question, it is always the duty of wisdom to aim at the higher mark.[90]

The trouble with this dichotomy, Aristotle points out, is that because politics deals with power, and philosophy with reason, it is too easy to conclude that politicians should be the only ones to engage in politics. "When it comes to politics," Aristotle says, "most people appear to believe that mastery is the true statesmanship." [91] This overlooks the fact that there is more to politics than power. The state is not simply a dynamo which belongs to the engineers who can manipulate its parts. It is an institution whose purpose it is to promote the good life: "The true end which good law-givers should keep in view . . ." Aristotle says, "is the enjoyment of partnership in a good life and the felicity thereby attainable." [92] Plato had said that the only good state was the Utopia where philosophers were kings; all other states are beyond the pale because power and reason are divorced. Aristotle does not accept this all-or-nothing proposition; he is persuaded that the good state and the good life can be achieved even where philosophers are not kings.

It is the obligation of the philosopher to enter politics. Aristotle does not demand that the man of reason achieve a position of dominance, but the point which should not be forgotten is that the philosopher is a citizen. If the state is to promote felicity, then it is in need of promoters. "Felicity is a state of activity," Aristotle says, "and it is the actions of just and temperate men which are the fulfillment of a great part of goodness." [93] If philosophers claim to know the good, if they claim to pursue goodness in their own lives, then they cannot stand apart from the political arena. Goodness takes on meaning only through good acts; a passive goodness has no meaning in the context of politics.

Goodness by itself is not enough: there must also be a capacity for being active in doing good. If we are right in our view, and felicity should be held to consist in "well-doing," it follows that the life of action is best, alike for every state as a whole and for each individual in his own conduct.[94]

[90] *Politics*, p. 284.
[91] P. 285.
[92] P. 286.
[93] P. 288.
[94] P. 289.

Aristotle is not saying that the philosopher should seek high office. He is not even suggesting that the political involvement of men of reason will guarantee that good laws will be forthcoming. But there is at least the chance that if philosophers take part in politics, then the amount of felicity displayed in public life will be greater than if they do not. And the chances will be heightened if not simply philosophers, but all men of reason participate in politics. The conclusion is that participation by good men is an important step if we are to achieve the good state. "A state," Aristotle says, "is good in virtue of the goodness of the citizens who share in its government." [95]

[95] P. 313.

4.
St. Augustine and
St. Thomas Aquinas

THE MEN AND THEIR TIMES

St. Augustine was born in 354 A.D. in Tagaste, a town in North Africa. While his mother was a Christian, his youth was not only pagan but also a continuous catalogue of libertine experimentation. Later on he embarked on more intellectual quests, sampling the then prevailing doctrines of Manichaeism and Neo-Platonism. At the age of 35 he became a Christian, and shortly thereafter he entered the priesthood. In 395 he was made Bishop of Hippo in North Africa, and he held this position until 430, when he died in that city while it was being besieged by the Vandal invasion.

At the time of Augustine's birth the Roman Empire covered the larger part of the Western World. Yet before his lifetime was over this majestic edifice had crumbled before the invasion of the barbarians from the North. It was the decline and fall of the Roman Empire, then, which constituted the setting for Augustine's political theory. In less than a span of a century Christianity had been transformed from a heretical sect to the official religion of the Roman Empire. Yet less than a hundred years of a Christian Rome had passed before that city fell to the Goths in 410. This defeat was not simply a military disaster but the collapse of a civilization. A whole way of life had been going through a process of decay, and when challenged by invasion from without, it gave way completely.

There must have been some cause for the decline and fall of Rome. The failure of nerve had to be explained in some simple way. The most popular scapegoat, as the inevitable post-mortems were conducted amid the ruins, was Christianity. The otherworldliness and the inherent pacifism of this religion appeared as the force which had weakened the defenses of society. It was to these accusations that St. Augustine rose with his The City

117

of God, which was written between 413 and 426. His approach—on the face of it, an unusual one for a theologian—was to minimize the impact of religious ideas. It was not Christianity which had destroyed Rome, he pointed out, but rather the obsession with material values. His theory displays an impatience with the hypocrisies of social corruption and political power. Despite his repudiation of politics, he does not offer rule by the Church as a possible solution to the world's ills. Rather, his focus is on the discrete individual and that person's ultimate salvation in the face of political chaos. Considering the conditions which surrounded him, it is understandable that St. Augustine felt that this was the most he could say.

St. Thomas Aquinas was born near Naples in 1224 or 1225. He entered the Dominican Order at the age of 19 and subsequently studied in Paris, where he participated in the revival of Aristotelian learning which was then current. His life was spent mainly in teaching and scholarship, and he died in Paris in 1274.

The eight centuries between Augustine and Aquinas saw the gradual reconstitution of political authority and the concurrent rise of the Roman Catholic Church. Feudal kings, whose positions were dependent on the nobles within their jurisdictions, were ascending to power. While this power was hedged with important limitations, the men who held it were aware of the role it would eventually play. At the same time, the Church had assumed a dual role. On the one hand, it was a frankly political organization with the resources to exact widespread obedience. On the other, it was a religious body which gained authority by its reliance on a higher law.

The rise of the feudal kings brought to a head the question of secular versus spiritual authority. St. Thomas saw that the emerging monarchies of Europe would not always be hedged in by the nobility, and he sought to anticipate the threat to the Church which was bound to arise. To meet the impending situation, he created a theory of society which underlined the unity of the social organism and which mapped out the rightful authority of each major institution. His Summa Theologica and On Princely Government are consequently pervaded by the conception of unity.

His theory has an intellectual as well as a political dimension. All human knowledge, he suggested, can be synthesized into a coherent system, and this end may be secured by human reason's coming to know the divine pattern of the universe. Both science and faith have parts to play in such a system of knowledge, just as church and state have legitimate roles in ordering of society. St. Augustine had been attracted to Plato, for his stress was not on reforming prevailing society but on anticipating life in a world to come. St. Thomas, on the contrary, saw in Aristotle's more realistic view a guide for practical politics. Power was not to be rejected; rather, it was to be contained. The Church had to learn the limits of its political resources and to appreciate that adjustment is the key to survival.

St. Thomas' contribution was quickly recognized, and he was canonized half a century after his death on the ground that writings of such stature must have been miraculous in origin.

4.
St. Augustine and
St. Thomas Aquinas

POLITICAL THEOLOGY—THE MEETING-GROUND OF POLITICS AND
religion—has always been an acknowledged branch of political theory. While
primarily prescriptive in orientation, it also makes persuasive claim to being
a descriptive science of man and society. In the Western world political
theology has been predominantly Christian: its central body of theory is
found in the writings of St. Augustine and St. Thomas Aquinas. While it is
of interest to compare similarities and differences in the works of the two
men, it is even more important to examine the ways in which they comple-
ment each other. St. Augustine, for example, discusses general principles of
human nature and political power, while St. Thomas gives specific attention
to such questions as the moral basis of legislation, the limitations on governmental power, and the conditions of social change. If St. Augustine's theory
is sometimes so general as to leave important questions unanswered, we may
look to St. Thomas to pick up much of the unfinished business which his
predecessor left behind him.

GOD, MAN, AND POLITICS

An abiding sense of man's limitations is the hallmark of Christian political
theology. This attitude of mind takes a skeptical view of man's potentiality
for understanding himself and the world in which he lives, and no less of his
ability to order his own social and political affairs. In the realms of both
knowledge and power man will always experience frustration.

To speak of power first, there is—as St. Augustine early points out—no
dearth of this commodity in society. The problem lies in using it purposefully. Man's attempts to master the elemental arts of government, his search
to establish order and justice in his political relations, must always be doomed

120

to failure. The skepticism inherent in political theology should not be equated with a pessimistic or cynical outlook; it signifies, rather, the spirit of realism which must infuse any serious thinking about politics. Both St. Augustine and St. Thomas, for example, stand firmly opposed to any sort of temporal Utopianism: for St. Augustine, to speak of a perfect political system, to imagine that mortal man can understand and resolve all existing problems of power, is to utter a contradiction in terms. Perfection is a quality to be found only in the city of God; the earthly city, even at its height of attainment, will only be a second-best. St. Thomas accepts these assumptions of St. Augustine and goes on to show how actual governments may best strive for limited goals. Even the pursuit of the second-best is a difficult task; certainly it is made to seem far more arduous than Aristotle had supposed. Rulers and citizens must adhere to disciplined rules of conduct if they are to make progress towards achieving even minimal success in government.

Neither St. Augustine nor St. Thomas spends much time talking about freedom or justice, reform or progress. Political life must be understood as one more aspect of the human condition in this Vale of Tears. Man has his rational moments, to be sure, but his irrational behavior is capable of undoing all that has been accomplished in the name of reason. There is good in man, to be sure, but the evil in him can thwart his entry onto the life of virtue. Man, in a word, is a creature of sin: the perversity sewn in him at birth warps his mind and frustrates his action. On the basis of these and related assumptions, political theology develops a political theory noteworthy more for telling us what man cannot accomplish on this earth than for what he can.

One reason why man has such difficulty in using political power for purposive ends is that the human mind itself is an instrument with severe limitations. Rather than detailing the frailties displayed by rulers and citizens —for this will be done in due course—it would be well to show how this stricture affects the theorist who seeks to explain the behavior of rulers and citizens. For if man is a creature of limited reason, the same limitations must apply to a human attempt to construct a theory of politics. A theorist, unless he has made special provision for himself, can be no better than those about whom he theorizes. This is why God plays such an important role in political theology. The invocation of His presence is a tacit admission that it is not within the capacity of the human mind to comprehend all that the senses perceive. For St. Augustine and St. Thomas, an omniscient and omnipotent God always hovers over the political stage. We may see how God is treated as a theorist and then turn to the part He plays as a participant on the actual political scene.

That God is a political theorist follows quite obviously from His omniscience.

He, and only He, possesses a mind capable of understanding the manifold workings of political reality. His knowledge, both moral and scientific, stands as a monument which human theorists may approach only at a respectful distance. In light of this, the political theologian advises his fellow theorists to be humble in their claims and aspirations to political knowledge. The theorist should admit that research conducted by men cannot lead us to a full comprehension of the forces which move men and society. There exists in God's mind not only the rules of morality, but also a comprehensive theory explaining the ultimate questions of political science. Men's minds are too limited in range to discover this theory by themselves; their perceptions cannot achieve the level of understanding attained to by the mind of God. Through the use of reason—a process to be discussed later on—men may gain a vague apprehension of the divine political theory. But they must not be so presumptuous as to think that they have picked God's brains in any thoroughgoing way.

And that God is a political participant follows from his omnipotence. Citizens live in freedom or in slavery, rulers gain power or are deposed, whole societies are rewarded or punished because He so wills. This is intended to be no less than a scientific statement about the workings of politics in the real world. It is clear that the proposition is a deductive one, but the attempt at a deductive science of politics is one of the chief contributions of political theology. God Himself decides just how active or passive a participant He will be: to intervene or to forbear from intervening is His decision. But that He is a power in politics is, according to political theology, a basic axiom of political science. St. Augustine and St. Thomas do not deny that mortal men have wills which are free. Indeed, men are responsible agents who will be rewarded or punished for the choices they make. But if the human will is free, there is also an all-powerful and all-knowing God, and if He does not choose to direct our actions or set the conditions within which we act, He nevertheless has advance knowledge of what we will decide to do. In what sense is human action ever "free"? In what sense is a decision ever "our own"? These are questions which concern not only political theology but all political theory.[1]

The deductive approach of the political theologian obviously stands in conflict with the inductive approach of the political scientist. Both may, although by different routes, come to the same substantive conclusion: they may agree that rulers and citizens are ill-fitted for the rational use of power and that the majority of men are creatures of limited knowledge. Where

---

[1] This question of "free will and determinism," and the related question of the "sociology of knowledge," will be discussed in the chapter on Marx and Engels.

they part company is on the role of God—as both theorist and participant—and on the ability of political scientists to understand reality. This does not mean that the political scientist is an atheist; he would simply render unto God what is God's and to science what is science's. If God does play a role as theorist and participant, the political scientist argues, then it is best to keep it at an entirely separate analytical level from that at which human theorists and politicians operate. In the theoretical realm, the political scientist believes that by imaginative and disciplined use of the inductive method, he and his like-minded colleagues can find answers to the crucial questions posed by the world of politics. He does not try to discover God's political theory—except to heed certain "natural laws" of politics which men have discovered by themselves—and he relies more on research than on reason. If this be arrogance, the political scientist will say, then make the most of it. In the practical realm, he simply does not believe that God intervenes to direct the political affairs of men. If war or tyranny or poverty exist in this world, we cannot settle for saying that this is God's way of punishing a wayward mankind. Such an explanation explains everything and nothing. Political science may not have yet discovered the underlying causes of war, but it will look for the causative factors on this earth rather than in another world. There may be forces we have yet to even begin to understand—ranging from the meteorological to the psychoanalytic—but this is all the more reason to press on with our research.[2]

The political theologian replies to the political scientist not by trying to prove that God participates in the direction of human affairs, but by showing how small a contribution human research has made to our understanding of politics. The response to the scientist's charge is that, quite simply, the "facts" are simply not there for the finding—no matter how much time and effort we spend searching for them. The theologians once more invoke the idea of human limitations: the universe is so complex that only God's mind can comprehend it. He was its architect, and only He can grasp the manifold interrelations which comprise man's political life. The perceptive powers, the elemental senses, of mere mortals are too limited in range and depth for

---

[2] It should also be said, although with some reluctance, that the political scientist often has the suspicion that many of those who talk of God's omniscience and omnipotence are guilty of a form of intellectual laziness. That is, the political theologians seem to be taking a socially respectable but nevertheless easy way of avoiding the difficult tasks of research. It is far simpler to sit back in one's study and assert that man can never attain to God's understanding or that God's will is a causative factor in human affairs. A few imperious sentences, coupled with quotation from scripture, can perform this job in what passes as a learned manner. Having made such pronouncements, the scholar then excuses himself from the hard work—both legwork and brainwork—which is necessary if men are to increase their knowledge of the world in which they live.

us ever to apprehend the fullness of social and political reality. There are too many levels of behavior for our powers of analysis to sort out, too many simultaneous actions for our theories to coordinate, too many concatenations of unpredictable circumstances for us to observe—let alone understand—what is going on around us in society. The geologists may have reached agreement on what causes soil erosion, but political scientists, even after 2,000 years of labor, cannot yet agree on what causes war—war in general or any particular war.

The position of the political theologian is simply one of humility. And humility must not be confused with laziness. There is much that men can know about themselves and their world, but they should, at the same time, admit that there is an even larger realm which is unknowable. The major questions of political science ought not even to be posed as questions; they are too complex for the human mind to handle. Pleas for more time and more resources to develop more systematic methods of analysis simply miss the point: the fault lies not in the infancy of the discipline nor in the primitive analytic tools, but in the inherent limitations of the men who must use them. There is no self-evident proposition which asserts that men must be able to understand the world in which they live. That we must live out the fullness of our lives in at least partial ignorance is as reasonable an assumption as its opposite, which asserts that man's knowledge can know no limits.

The point is not whether the natural and physical sciences have established their beachhead, nor is it whether political science has made progress over the centuries. Both of these propositions are accepted by the political theologian. Rather, the chief question is how much we can ever know about man and society—especially when we begin to sense the depth of our ignorance and contrast what we know with what we would like to know. Then we see that the gulf between achievement and aspiration is breathtaking. So great is the chasm between the known and the unknown that the likelihood is that a man-made bridge will never cross it.

Until political scientists manage to deal with political questions in terms of some significance, men like St. Augustine and St. Thomas will argue that by referring to God's knowledge and God's power we have at hand the only satisfactory way of embarking on the study of political theory.

THE TWO CITIES

St. Augustine's theory is a tale of two cities: the city of God and the earthly city. While in simplest terms these two kingdoms are heaven and earth, it will soon become apparent that they are not dissociated realms. If the city of God is the celestial repose of immortal souls, it is also a sovereign which exerts an influence on the political fortunes of the earthly city. Through the agency of God Himself and through the presence of His missionaries here below, the lives of rulers and citizens of the temporal world are inevitably affected. St. Augustine opens by comparing the two cities.

> The glorious city of God is my theme in this work. . . . I have undertaken its defence against those who prefer their own gods to the Founder of this city—a city surpassingly glorious, whether we view it as it still lives by faith in this fleeting course of time, and sojourns as a stranger in the midst of the ungodly, or as it shall dwell in the fixed stability of its eternal seat. . . . And therefore, as the plan of this work we have undertaken requires, and as occasion offers, we must speak also of the earthly city, which though it be mistress of the nations, is itself ruled by its lust of rule.[3]

The earthly city symbolizes the institutions of power within existing society; it is the world of politics as St. Augustine knew it and as we still know it today. The power of man over man, the instruments used by rulers to control the ruled, the ambition and arrogance of those who quest after mastery: this, in sum, is political life. The city of God, on the other hand, has two arms. First, it is the heavenly kingdom which will exist for all eternity, the supernatural state to which the souls of the righteous will ascend. But St. Augustine goes further: there is, he says, a part of the city of God which exists within and alongside the earthly city. There are a few citizens of the earthly city who are also loyal to God's kingdom. These pilgrims do not in their hearts accept the values of power which society seeks to impose on them. What St. Augustine is saying, of course, is that there is a conflict between the values of power and the values of righteousness. The politics of the earthly city will be corrupt because its rulers are unwilling or unable to accept the values of the heavenly city as guides for conduct. Even if the goals which men of power set down appear worthy in themselves—for example, peace and prosperity—those goals are defeated by the means employed to attain them and the motives which stir men to seek them. St. Augustine pens a sweeping indictment of human perversion and hypocrisy:

> Your desire for peace, and prosperity, and plenty is not prompted by any purpose of using these blessings honestly, that is to say, with moderation, sobriety, temperance, and piety; for your purpose rather is to run riot in an endless variety of sottish pleasures, and thus to generate from your prosperity a moral pestilence which will prove a thousandfold more disastrous than the fiercest enemies.[4]

---

[3] *The City of God* (New York: Modern Library, 1950), translated by Marcus Dods, p. 3.

[4] P. 35.

Time and again political man has shown that he will use political institutions and so define political goals as to facilitate his pursuit of pleasure. St. Augustine's attack is on politics as a whole rather than a specific indictment of the men and women who follow the rules of the political game. For, in contrast to Aristotle, St. Augustine asserts that man was never meant to be a political animal at all.

God created men as equals. In His sight all are equally significant—or insignificant. All men are God's creations and all are possessed of immortal souls. These attributes which men share are fundamental; others which may differentiate them are secondary. In this simple proposition lies the great contribution of Christian doctrine to political philosophy. In laying down this principle, St. Augustine is building an immutable and inviolable status for the individual. If all men are equal, then there is no legitimate reason why any man can be denied the development of his full potentialities as a human being. Those who happen to be in positions of power have no warrant to hold down those of their fellow men who are less fortunately situated. When God created men as equals, He intended that they pursue their equality throughout the course of their lives.

This is prescribed by the order of nature: it is thus that God has created man. For "let them," He says, "have dominion over the fish of the sea, and over the fowl of the air, and over every creeping thing which creepeth on the earth." He did not intend that His rational creature, who was made in His image, should have dominion over anything but the irrational creation—not man over man, but man over the beasts. And hence the righteous men in primitive times were made shepherds of cattle rather than kings of men, God intending thus to teach us what the relative position of the creatures is, and what the desert of sin.[5]

Those who participate in the political life cannot help but act in violation of God's intentions. To gain and maintain power—power over their fellow men —rulers must inevitably establish patterns of superiority and inferiority.

The realms of politics and morality are thus separate and distinct, and St. Augustine calls for a rejection of the values nurtured by the world of politics. One example of what politics compels men to do was detailed by Plato: it is necessary for rulers to distort the truth if they are to obtain effective control. "It is useful for states that brave men believe, though falsely, that they are descended from the gods; for that thus the human spirit, cherishing the belief of its divine descent, will both more boldly venture into great enterprises, and will carry them out more energetically, and will therefore by its very confidence secure more abundant success." [6] That myths are necessary for attaining political success is never denied by St. Augustine. He cites

[5] P. 693.
[6] Pp. 76–77.

their utility simply to demonstrate how elementary morality can be the victim of power politics. And relationships which are founded on power must not only trade in deception; the distorted images of reality become institutionalized and affect the personalities of men in ways which pervert the human character. The conclusion must be that political power does not come naturally to men. St. Augustine agrees with Aristotle in asserting that men are moral creatures. And if men are to be moral, they cannot at the same time be political. Men were intended by God to be shepherds, to preside over the animals of the fields. They were not meant to be rulers, to coerce and deceive their fellow men. Given the instruments of power, men perforce use them badly or immorally. The fault lies not with men, but in the instruments they control—and which in turn control them. Men, in sum, were created as equals. If they act as rulers and subjects, they have transgressed God's intention when He put them on His earth.

The pursuit of the political life, furthermore, will always end in frustration. St. Augustine admits that governments can secure some measure of success in extending and consolidating their power. But the significant consequence of such earthly success as is achieved is that it looks pale indeed when set alongside the countless human and social problems which remain unsolved. Men begin to realize that governments can only alleviate superficial symptoms; the underlying causes of man's ills are not to be cured by political action. St. Augustine points out that the real afflictions are moral, that politics can only palliate man's diseases.

> The earthly city, which shall not be everlasting . . . , has its good in this world, and rejoices in it with such joy as such things can afford. But as this is not a good which can discharge its devotees of all distresses, this city is often divided against itself by litigations, wars, quarrels, and such victories as are either life-destroying or short-lived. For each part of it that arms against another part of it seeks to triumph over the nations though itself in bondage to vice. . . .[7]

What must be stressed is the essential fact of conflict in the political world. Litigations, wars, and quarrels blemish men's relations with each other. And, to make matters worse, the apparent victors in these conflicts are losers also. For the success of victory breeds in them attitudes and traits of character which are destructive of personality. Power begets conflict, and conflict begets immorality.

If successes are doomed to failure, must all politics be written off as a descending spiral with no hope of redemption? St. Augustine, for all his foreboding, was prepared to be more constructive than this. If anything positive is to come out of human government, then men must set limited political

[7] P. 481.

goals for themselves. Power cannot be abolished in the earthly city, but it can be used for the purpose of securing social order. Peace, the absence of conflict, is not only possible as a goal; it is also one sanctioned by God. "God, then, the most wise Creator and most just Ordainer of all natures, who placed the human race upon this earth as its greatest ornament, imparted to men some good things adapted to this life, to wit, temporal peace, such as we can enjoy in this life from health and safety and human fellowship, and all things needful for the preservation and recovery of this peace. . . ." [8]

There is to be no talk of human rights or justice or liberty or rule of law as being the ends of government. States, St. Augustine suggests, err if they try to organize themselves to implement such goals. The consequence is bound to be not a just or a free society, but simply one where there is a greater political jurisdiction in which man will exercise power over man. The responsibility which God has given to earthly rulers is that of establishing order. Men are rational creatures and it will be strain enough on their reason to apprehend God's command and find ways to carry it out. The rationale of order is discovered by proceeding, as did Plato, from the individual to the social whole.

The peace of the body then consists in the duly proportioned arrangement of its parts. The peace of the irrational soul is the harmonious repose of the appetites, and that of the rational soul the harmony of knowledge and action. The peace of the body and soul is the well-ordered and harmonious life and health of the living creature. Peace between man and God is the well-ordered obedience of faith to eternal law. Peace between man and man is well-ordered concord. Domestic peace is the well-ordered concord between those of the family who rule and those who obey. Civil peace is a similar concord among the citizens. The peace of the celestial city is the perfectly ordered and harmonious enjoyment of God, and of one another in God. The peace of all things is the tranquillity of order. Order is the distribution which allots things equal and unequal, each to its own place.[9]

No doubt is left that concord is preferable to conflict, tranquillity to turmoil, and order is to be cherished for its own sake. A stable environment which harbors inequality or injustice is, in the final analysis, superior to a tumultuous one which suffers disruptions attendant on its efforts to resolve the problems of equality and justice. First things come first, St. Augustine is saying, and until order is secured it is unavailing to worry about matters which are plainly of secondary importance.

In many parts of the world the problem of elemental order looms large in the minds of all who inhabit the land. The possibility of imminent violence is a threat which renders all other political preoccupations nugatory. Men

[8] P. 691.
[9] P. 690.

have only to have had a taste of anarchy, to have known the ravages of mob rule, to suddenly awaken to the underlying importance of order in political processes. Men want as much of life as possible to be predictable: they want to know in advance that their homes will not be broken into tonight and that their wives and daughters will not be assaulted tomorrow. One of the tasks of government is to create conditions in society so that the behavior of citizens will be fairly predictable—laws which prescribe and proscribe try to set limits on the range of acts in which our fellow citizens may indulge. The power of government, furthermore, should be used to protect the lives and possessions of peaceloving citizens from the disorderly activity of that part of the community which tends to violence. Sophisticated societies of the Western world are prone to take for granted the effective performance of these official functions. However, in those rare events when social order breaks down, men come to appreciate only too well what they once thought was a self-maintaining mechanism. It takes but a short breath of anarchy to show men the importance of the role their government has been playing all along. And the danger of a lawless episode lies not simply in the possible violence which may be visited on a citizenry. In addition, exposure to apparent chaos may lead men to react in the extreme opposite direction: they find themselves in a position where they will accept the promise of order without asking what price they must pay for it. They are beggars and cannot be choosers, and the man on horseback who undertakes to deliver them will not accept limitations on his terms. If St. Augustine has elected to stress order, it is not without good reason.

In the body of political theory there is a never-ending debate over the role of order in social life. St. Augustine and St. Thomas put a premium on stability; so do Hobbes and Burke. Other theorists, notably Locke and Mill, feel that it is more important to pursue certain goals unremittingly even if the price is political turbulence. The chief of these goals are liberty and equality —although different thinkers define them in different ways—and there are men who are willing to go to the brink of anarchy to obtain them. The men who can say "Give Me Liberty or Give Me Death" feel that social order which is bought at the price of human freedom is meaningless. At this point the debate over order can only be mentioned; the controversy will be carried on in later chapters. What should be emphasized now is that St. Augustine and St. Thomas, as proponents of order, also put a high value on the role of authority in society. High on the list of political virtues stands obedience. The average citizen must not press for what he might think are his rights as an individual: it is for him to obey authority. There is, in St. Augustine's theory, no real sense of compassion for the lot of the underdog. To champion the underprivileged and the powerless, even to admit that they had a cause at all, would simply serve to undermine constituted authority. If the government is to bestow on its citizens the blessings of order, then it must not be subverted by sentiments which would weaken the state through misguided sympathy for luckless individuals.

SLAVERY, SIN, AND SALVATION

Social reform inevitably entails social disruption: attempts to redistribute wealth or to accelerate equality are bound to cause dissension among those in society who have something to lose by such experimentation. The ruler who would secure order must first of all gain the cooperation of those who hold positions of power in society, for these are the people who can help him most, or harm him most if he ignores or threatens their interests. This means that the government should not try to redress the balance of power within the social structure. Those at the bottom of the social pyramid, St. Augustine says, must realize that their misery is a necessary human cost if political order is to be realized. "The miserable . . . do certainly not enjoy peace, but are severed from that tranquillity of order in which there is no disturbance." [10] Nevertheless, so long as the state is able to ensure a stable social order, even the miserable may become participants in the benefits which accrue to all.

Inasmuch as they are deservedly and justly miserable, they are by their very misery connected with order. They are not, indeed, conjoined with the blessed, but they are disjoined from them by the law of order. And though they are disquieted, their circumstances are notwithstanding adjusted to them, and consequently they have some tranquillity of order, and therefore some peace. But they are wretched because, although not wholly miserable, they are not in that place where any mixture of misery is impossible. They would, however, be more wretched if they had not that peace which arises from being in harmony with the natural order of things.[11]

The poor and the downtrodden must realize that a hierarchical society is the natural order of things, that by being the stolid base of the pyramid they will share in the only way possible the tranquillity and peace which is their succor.

The conjunction of order, inequality, and obedience is a major theme in political theory. It is spelled out more fully in St. Augustine's theory of slavery. It has already been noted that God intended men to be shepherds, not masters over one another. Yet St. Augustine could not avoid the unpleasant fact that slavery has always existed in one form or another: the total mastery

[10] P. 690.
[11] Ibid.

of one man by another is a part of current no less than past history. This institution exists in the earthly city because of the sinfulness of man. "The prime cause, then, of slavery is sin, which brings man under the dominion of his fellow—that which does not happen save by the judgment of God, with whom is no unrighteousness, and who knows how to award fit punishments to every variety of offence." [12] If slaves languish in bondage, it is because they are sinful creatures: they, no less than others, are responsible moral beings and God has punished them for their transgressions by delivering them over to the rule of others.

Does St. Augustine really mean this? On first glance it looks as if he is using divine punishment as a means to obtain social control just as Plato used the myth of metals. Are all slaves so sinful as to deserve this punishment? Are there no exceptions among them? St. Augustine is fully aware of the logical danger in such generalizations. "There are," he admits, "many wicked masters who have religious men as their slaves." [13] The only way to establish a semblance of equality here is to point out that sinful masters are sufferers also—although their affliction is of a different quality. If the slave carries chains on his body, his master is oppressed in spirit. And even the virtuous slave may be heartened by this knowledge: his consignment to bondage may have been a terrible accident, but he is really better off than the man who lays the whip across his shoulders. "And beyond question it is a happier thing to be the slave of a man than of a lust; for even this very lust of ruling, to mention no others, lays waste men's hearts with the most ruthless dominion." [14] Men who have power are destroyed by the instruments they wield. Men who are subjected to power are freer than their masters. The downtrodden should understand that their bodily suffering, their obedience to authority, is part of a greater scheme of things.

When men are subjected to one another in a peaceful order, the lowly position does as much good to the servant as the proud position does harm to the master. But by nature, as God first created us, no one is the slave either of man or of sin. This servitude is, however, penal, and is appointed by that law which enjoins the preservation of the natural order and forbids its disturbance; for if nothing has been done in violation of that law, there would have been nothing to restrain by penal servitude. And therefore the apostle admonishes slaves to be subject to their masters, and to serve them heartily and with good-will, so that, if they cannot be freed by their masters, they may themselves make their slavery in some sort free, by serving not in crafty fear, but in faithful love, until all unrighteousness pass away, and all principality and every human power be brought to nothing.[15]

[12] P. 694.
[13] *Ibid.*
[14] *Ibid.*
[15] *Ibid.*

While St. Augustine's argument applies specifically to chattel slavery it has, of course, been used to rationalize every sort of autocratic rule. The oppression of one group in society by another—rich over poor, white over black, commissars over proletarians—has been justified by insisting that hierarchy is necessary for order and that in a better world neither power nor obedience will be necessary. Here we can see the invisible point at which political theology can be transformed into ideology. A theory of the limitations of man and society can be put to use by a group intent on exacting cheerful obedience from those who might otherwise have cause to protest. But the point at issue is order. The point St. Augustine does not discuss is which group or class benefits from a particular order. For his concern is that society as a whole be stable: to secure this end even slaves must be brought to realize that to challenge their lot will upset the balance of an ordered society.

Nothing which has been said about the harshness of servitude or the imperatives of obedience should be construed as a contradiction of St. Augustine's theory of human equality. Despite sin and slavery, all men are inherently equal in the sight of God. Despite the primacy of order and authority, the individual's soul remains inviolate. And, despite the follies and frustrations of political life, man is a rational creature. If the equality, the individuality, and the rationality of men seem more a matter of theory than practice, this is because St. Augustine is a political scientist who cannot ignore the power and perversity which exist in human relations. Equality is an assumption; to make it at all is a major step in political theory. And, St. Augustine says, men are equal in that they all possess qualities of mind and spirit which differentiate them from the animals: "If we were irrational animals, we should desire nothing beyond the proper arrangement of the parts of the body and the satisfaction of the appetites—nothing, therefore, but bodily comfort and abundance of pleasures. . . ." [16] However, man is a rational creature; more should be expected of him, and more is generally forthcoming.

> As man has a rational soul, he subordinates all this which he has in common with the beasts to the peace of his rational soul, that his intellect may have free play and regulate his actions, and that he may thus enjoy the well-ordered harmony of knowledge and action which constitutes, as we have said, the peace of the rational soul.[17]

This statement concerning human reason displays an optimism which is rather startling in St. Augustine. The proposition that man is able to harmonize knowledge and action is similar to the description of Plato's

---

[16] P. 692.
[17] Ibid.

Guardians. Has St. Augustine, for all his sense of human limitations, fallen into Utopianism? The answer is that "rationality" or "reason" only has meaning in political theology if it is shown to be consonant with God's wisdom. Man may increase his knowledge of himself and the universe, but these increments can only be made with God's help. "Owing to the liability of the human mind to fall into mistakes," St. Augustine says, "this very pursuit of knowledge may be a snare to him unless he has a divine Master, whom he may obey without misgiving. . . ." [18]

Just as Plato's conception of rationality relied on knowledge of the Forms, so St. Augustine's calls for an understanding of God's will. And it has been the failure of rulers and citizens to heed His commands which has lowered man's political life to its sorry state. Men of power have the potential to act with reason, but they have not utilized it. Seduced by the blandishments of earthly power and comforts, they fail to seek divine guidance. "The citizens of the earthly city," St. Augustine says, ". . . being deprived of His unchangeable and freely communicated light, and so reduced to a kind of poverty-stricken power, eagerly grasp at their own private privileges, and seek divine honors from their deluded subjects. . . ." [19] Once more we see the tension between power and rationality which was described by Plato. Men are rational creatures, St. Augustine says, but they do not use their reason in the sphere of politics. And because of the small likelihood of creating rational government in the earthly city, St. Augustine turns his eyes to the city of God. In that eternal kingdom there would be no conflict between power and rationality, because the power of man over man would have no need to exist.

Yet the city of God must not be thought of as a Utopia. Utopian writers, such as Plato and Rousseau and even Marx, designed their societies for the men who walk this earth. The Utopian believes that it is possible for society to progress and for men to perfect themselves; he affirms that men can mobilize their intelligence and good will to transform existing institutions so that the conflicts of today will be rendered obsolete in a happier tomorrow. St. Augustine, on the contrary, holds out no such hope for earthly progress or reform. The premises on which human politics are founded make it impossible for the power which man exercises over man ever to be endowed with legitimacy. The earthly city is doomed to be a spiritual vacuum so long as it exists.

Two cities have been formed by two loves: the earthly by the love of self, even to the contempt of God; the heavenly by the love of God, even to the contempt

[18] *Ibid.*
[19] P. 345.

of self. The former, in a word, glories in itself, the latter in the Lord. For the one seeks glory from men; but the greatest glory of the other is God, the witness of conscience. . . . In the one, the princes and the nations it subdues are ruled by the love of ruling; in the other, the princes and the subjects serve one another in love, the latter obeying, while the former take thought for all. . . .[20]

What binds the city of God together as a body politic is not power, but love. Its "princes" do not use coercion or the threat of coercion to exact obedience from their subjects. Obedience is cheerfully given because laws are administered in the spirit of the common good rather than the rulers' own interests. The ideal of fraternity, of the brotherhood of man, has always played a major role in political philosophy. That it rules the city of God might well be expected. But it is also clear that in human political relationships, love is not enough. The relations between man and man are made tolerable and even civilized by fraternal spirit. But actual societies cannot count on the power of altruism, nor can political order be secured through brotherhood alone. St. Augustine has abstracted out love—the worthiest of human motives—and has made it the exclusive relationship between citizens in the city of God. Plainly, he realizes the impracticality of what he has done: the city of God is not made for mortal men. Only angels can dispense with the institutions which humans require for ordering their social existence. This otherworldliness, however, is not to be construed as a theory of despair. St. Augustine is sure in his own mind of the existence of the city of God: righteous men will surely ascend to heaven and there experience the joys of perfect government.

A secular Utopian like Plato would agree that current generations of men will never see the ideal society that the future holds in store: centuries of human progress might be required before Utopia is established on earth, and even then no promises can be given. St. Augustine, in offering men the prospect of heavenly repose, holds out a different kind of hope: the earthly city will not reform itself, but when we have served our term there, we may pass on to the city of God. In both cases, however, we will all be dead before the advent of the perfect society is upon us.

THE CONSPIRACY OF THE GODLY

There are two arms to the city of God: in addition to the angelic host, the heavenly kingdom has its representatives on earth. These pilgrims believe in the values of the city of God: they deny the legitimacy of earthly power, and they seek to convert their fellow citizens to this heretical view. St. Augustine, in describing the pilgrims, outlines a theory of conspiracy: the small minority

[20] P. 477.

who have, by one means or another, come to perceive the ultimate truth about politics and morality are—to put the matter bluntly—political subversives. They harbor doubts about the virtues of the heads of states, the values of material prosperity, and the goals and motives of political life. They owe their allegiance to another state—a state, furthermore, which is confident that it will preside over the funeral of the earthly city. The conspiracy which St. Augustine describes is an international one; it disregards national boundaries and customary political allegiances. "This heavenly city," he says, ". . . while it sojourns on earth, calls citizens out of all nations, and gathers together a society of pilgrims of all languages, not scrupling about diversities in the manners, laws, and institutions whereby earthly peace is secured and maintained. . . ."[21] To the members of this international conspiracy, loyalty to the city of God takes priority over national loyalties. The righteous of the world are to unite in a revolutionary vanguard. But is there to be a revolution?

The virtuous citizen, it will be recalled, was advised by St. Augustine to obey constituted authority even though that authority does not reflect God's will. It would appear, then, that the conspirators are being asked to obey two masters. They must be good citizens of the earthly city, because only by so doing will order, the attainable goal of existing societies, be secured; and they must be missionaries of the heavenly city to prepare themselves for the better life which is to come.

> The earthly city, which does not live by faith, seeks an earthly peace, and the end it proposes, in the well-ordered concord of civic obedience and rule, is the combination of men's wills to attain the things which are helpful to this life. The heavenly city, or rather the part of it which sojourns on earth and lives by faith, makes use of this peace only because it must, until this mortal condition which necessitates it shall pass away. Consequently, so long as it lives like a captive and a stranger in the earthly city, . . . it makes no scruple to obey the laws of the earthly city, whereby the things necessary for the maintenance of this mortal life are administered.[22]

The conspirators, then, do not resist the authority of the earthly city in any overt way. They obey the laws and act as model citizens. But at the same time they quietly exploit the favorable conditions around them in order to sustain and strengthen what is their primary allegiance, the city of God. Their task is not to make a revolution but to prepare the way for one. They do not constitute a clear and present danger, but one that is vague and remote. The conspirators remain above ground in their role as citizens and under ground in their role as members of an international movement. While their actions

[21] P. 696.
[22] Pp. 695–696.

signify that they are loyal to the earthly city, in their hearts they are loyal only to the city of God.

WHY MEN NEED GOVERNMENT

St. Thomas carries on with St. Augustine's assumption concerning political goals: "The welfare and prosperity of a community," he says, "lies in the preservation of its unity; or, more simply, in peace." [23] The step from order to unity is an important one; it adds to St. Augustine's abstract principle an institutional underpinning. And St. Thomas takes these ideas and makes them the beginning—not an end-point—of a systematic theory of politics. For St. Augustine order was the sole achievement which might reasonably be expected of earthly governments. Citizens should ask no more than that domestic tranquillity be bestowed upon them. To demand more would be to tragically overestimate man's ability to use power without abusing it. St. Thomas, on the other hand, proceeded from the idea of order to a notion of unified government, and then to a theory of law. Human political systems might be no more than second-best when contrasted with the sublime government of the city of God: however, this is no reason to draw so starkly limited a picture of man's potentialities for improvement.

It is St. Thomas' view that human governments are capable of learning political lessons from the city of God. Rather than stressing the contrast between the two cities, we should acknowledge that both kingdoms are integral parts of God's universe and both are bound by His law. Even if the governments of men number among the least significant segments of the Divine creation, the fact remains that earthly political arrangements constitute a vital component of the Divine scheme. St. Thomas makes this point clear by analogy: the role played by a temporal ruler is comparable to that of God's sovereignty over the universe as a whole. "We must now consider what God does in the universe, and thus we shall see what a king should do . . ." he says. "Just as the creation of the world serves as a convenient model for the establishment of a city or a kingdom, so does its government allow us to deduce the principles of civil government." [24]

St. Thomas' method is an avowedly deductive one: to say that God's government of the universe is the blueprint for earthly government is to state a principle which can be neither proved nor disproved by the experimental tests available to men. Such a proposition is either a self-evident truth to the

---

[23] *On Princely Government*, in *Aquinas, Selected Political Writings* (Oxford: Blackwell, 1954), edited by A. P. D 'Entreves and translated by J. G. Dawson, p. 11.

[24] *Ibid.*, pp. 69, 73.

eye which beholds it or it is a string of words without meaning. The point about the deductive method, however, is that its usefulness to the student of politics need not rest wholly on the plausibility of its major assumptions. For the actual deductions—the statements about the political world which are claimed to flow logically from the initial premises—are capable of offering many insights. St. Thomas' postulate is that the universe is a seamless web: the basic rules of government apply throughout the whole of God's creation, and they should serve as a constant guide to human rulers as they design political institutions and command their fellow men. In other words, human rulers are expected to be cognizant of the dictates of both the Natural Law and the Divine Law. St. Augustine doubted whether men of power would use their reason to apprehend God's commandments. St. Thomas, more optimistic, finds reason to believe that they will perceive the higher values. For him, then, the task is to show how God's law and human law may be conjoined.

In all of St. Thomas' political writing, the emphasis is on the need for unity in the direction and control of government. "Man is naturally a social and political animal, destined more than all other animals to live in community," he says.

> The fellowship of society being thus natural and necessary to man, it follows with equal necessity that there must be some principle of government within the society. For if a great number of people were to live, each intent only upon his own interests, such a community would surely disintegrate unless there were one of its number to have a care for the common good. . . .
> Wherever there is an ordered unity arising out of a diversity of elements there is found some such controlling influence.[25]

Man, a social animal, lives in society, but societies are inhabited by individuals who possess conflicting interests. If that society is to survive as an entity, then political power must be created and exercised so as to ensure that those interests will be subsumed under the pursuit of the common good. So runs St. Thomas' logic. Social unity must be secured by political unity: and political unity calls for concentrated power.

> The most important task for the ruler of any community is the establishment of peaceful unity. Nor has he the right to question whether or not he will so promote the peace of the community. . . . For no one ought to deliberate about the ends for which he must act, but only about the means to those ends. . . . That which is itself a unity can more easily produce unity than that which is a plurality. . . . So government by one person is more likely to be successful than government by many. Furthermore, it is clear that many persons will never succeed in producing unity in the community if they differ among themselves. So a plurality of

[25] *Ibid.*, pp. 3, 5.

individuals will already require some bond of unity before they can even begin to rule in any way whatsoever. Again, that is best which most nearly approaches a natural process, since nature always works in the best way. But in nature, government is always by one. Among members of the body there is one which moves all the rest, namely, the heart: in the soul, there is one faculty which is pre-eminent, namely reason.[26]

Once more the argument by analogy comes into play: the rule of a single man is comparable to the heart's command over the body. St. Thomas' reliance on analogy is not to be thought of as merely a flight of poetic fancy. On the contrary, it is a way of underlining the deductive truth that all things in God's creation are related in their structure and function. Government is not an isolated institution; it is part of the natural order of things. And to be natural, its leadership must be unitary. St. Thomas, like Machiavelli and Hobbes who are to follow him, and unlike Plato and Aristotle who preceded him, gears his discussion to a single individual who holds the reins of power in society. To talk of one man rather than a class or an elite, to stress personality rather than social structure—emphases such as these are not universal in their applicability. When bureaucratic organization is ascendent, a single man, no matter how strong his personality, is unlikely to be the focus of political discussion. Nevertheless, in many parts of the world today the single ruler who stands at the summit must be given the spotlight of political analysis. If St. Thomas leans too far in this direction, other theorists will redress the balance.

To answer the question why men need to be governed, we must explore St. Thomas' theory of human nature. There are three aspects of man's behavior which deserve examination on this score.

(1) St. Thomas pursues Aristotle's theme that man is an integral part of nature; he therefore has certain needs in common not only with his fellow men but also with the animals and substances which surround him on this earth.

For there is in man, first of all, an inclination to good in accordance with the nature which he has in common with all substances, inasmuch, namely as every substance seeks the preservation of its own being, according to its nature. . . .

Secondly, there is in man an inclination to things that pertain to him more specially, according to that nature which he has in common with other animals. . . .

Thirdly, there is in man an inclination to good according to the nature of his reason, which nature is proper to him. Thus man has a natural inclination to know the truth about God, and to live in society. . . .[27]

[26] *Ibid.*, pp. 11, 13.
[27] *Summa Theologica*, in *Basic Writings of Saint Thomas Aquinas* (New York: Random House, 1945), two volumes, edited by Anton C. Pegis, Vol. II, p. 775.

Few people would deny that these qualities are "natural" to all men, although some might raise questions about the inclination to know God's truth. Like a tree which is blown by the storm and then seeks to right itself, men seek to preserve their own lives and well-being. Like all animals, men seek to perpetuate their own species. But, unlike plants and animals, men have a moral sense: they not only act, but they aspire to act rightly and to have others believe that they are acting rightly. The important point for political analysis is that man-the-substance, man-the-animal, and man-the-moral-agent must find a way to live together with a minimum of discord. In his first role, every man is a potential murderer: he is capable of killing others in order to save his own life. In his second role, he is a potential libertine: to perpetuate the species, he may fall prey to impulses which will inflict damage on the lives of others. The rationale for government, then, is that the two basic roles which men play must be controlled so that they do not do violence to the third. The moral life will only be complete if its values are not dragged under by men's "natural"—and essentially antisocial—impulses.

(2) The next facet of human nature is similar to that contained in St. Augustine's theory. It reflects the qualified optimism of Christian doctrine. "Man . . . acts by intelligence," St. Thomas says. "Every man is endowed with reason, and it is by the light of reason that his actions are directed to their end." [28] Does this mean that St. Thomas is prepared to say, any more than St. Augustine, that men are both intelligent and rational in their political behavior? The answer is that St. Thomas' is a theory of human nature in isolation —of each individual's potentialities taken alone in abstraction—but not of man's political nature. Men may be intelligent and rational, but they are also social. Intelligence and rationality describe the individual in a hypothetical Robinson Crusoe situation: if there is only one citizen in a "society," then there obviously can be no conflicts. Put men in a society, however, and you create conditions which require political direction. "The diversity of human interests and pursuits makes it equally clear that there are many courses open to men when seeking the end they desire," St. Thomas says. "Man needs guidance for attaining his ends." [29]

Here St. Thomas is echoing St. Augustine's individualist doctrine. He is saying that men are, without a doubt, possessed of reason and that they are capable of acting intelligently. But as a political scientist, St. Thomas is forced to add that the behavior of individuals undergoes a transformation when they develop interests at variance to those of their neighbors. Men who display reason and intelligence when they are by themselves do not carry these virtues

[28] *On Princely Government*, p. 3.
[29] *Ibid.*

into social situations. The reason for this is that societies are aggregates of individuals with heterogeneous interests; such diversity breeds conflict, and men are not prone to resolve their conflicts of interest by rational argument. The isolated individual, then, is a person of reason, but the same individual, when he becomes a member of society, cannot be counted on to act rationally. When confronted with questions of social and political policy, his mind reacts in ways which are markedly different from those he uses in dealing with his strictly personal problems. In social situations the interests of one man take on an irrational dimension when they are pitted against those of another. If such divergent interests are to be resolved peacefully, then men— no matter how rational they are as individuals—must accept political authority.

(3) It has been remarked more than once that if all men are "equal," no political theory has ever sought to deny the very obvious "differences" which exist among them. The equality of man posited by the Church Fathers means that all are of equal value in the eyes of God: men can never be "unequal" in that overriding sense. However, there are inequalities—that is, differences —not only of material wealth and physical strength, but also in men's ability to know truth and act with virtue. And while all men have souls, not all develop their full potentialities to an equal degree. "As regards the soul, there would have been inequality as to justice and knowledge . . ." St. Thomas says. "Hence some would have made a greater advance in justice and knowledge than others." [30] This was, of course, Plato's position—although Plato did not temper his view by making all men equal before God. It follows from this that those men who lack the qualities of justice and knowledge—and they are undoubtedly the majority of mankind—must accept the leadership of those few in their midst who can point out appropriate courses of action. Only through government can the values of the good life be transmitted to the average man.

Men, then, must be ruled. As creatures of natural instincts, their otherwise uninhibited behavior must be channelled and controlled. Nor are the majority of men sufficiently endowed with knowledge and justice to discover the good life for themselves; they must be guided by those who are equipped with these virtues. And while as individuals men are possessed of reason, the conflicts of human interests which arise in the social state blind them to rational choice. On these premises St. Thomas builds his argument for political authority. And it follows from this that the ruled have an obligation to render obedience to those empowered to rule over them.

[30] *Summa Theologica*, Vol. I, pp. 920–921.

TYRANNY AND REVOLUTION

If the need for government is granted, then means must be found for the effective exercise of power. For St. Thomas the solution is to vest authority in one man who is strong of mind and virtuous of spirit. If power is fragmented, many ends will be pursued and none will be secured. "A social life cannot exist among a number of people unless under the governance of one to look after the common good," he says. "For many, as such, seek many things, whereas one attends only to one." [31] That St. Thomas puts his reliance on a single individual is, of course, an implicit commentary on those who stand in need of his rule. "The multitude of human beings . . ." he says, "are not perfect in virtue." [32] Only a select few in society possess the requisites for wise and virtuous leadership: in short, the attributes of the philosopher and the king, the aptitudes for rationality and power, must be discovered within the population.

It is not surprising that only one out of many will meet this requirement. "It requires outstanding virtue for a man to control not only himself, but others also . . ." St. Thomas says. "In every art or science, those who can control others aright are more praiseworthy than those who merely carry out the directions of others with competence." [33] The accents here are clearly Platonic. St. Thomas is calling for a man who shows adeptness in handling others; for political purposes this is a praiseworthy virtue. And he also requires a man of inner discipline and moral stature. There may be a few such men in society; certainly there will not be many. And in order that the goal of unity be achieved, it is best that one man both exercise and embody governmental authority.

There is good reason for St. Thomas' great concern over the caliber of the man who is to shoulder this responsibility. Men must be ruled, but they must also be ruled justly. Power must be exercised, but it must not be abused. "Since government by one person, being the best, is to be preferred . . ." St. Thomas says, "it is necessary that whoever of the possible candidates is proclaimed king shall be of such character that it is unlikely that he will become a tyrant." [34] No less than Aristotle, St. Thomas is concerned over the possibility that strong government may degenerate into tyrannical government. And, like Plato, he puts his faith in the careful selection of those who

---

[31] *Ibid.*, Vol. I, p. 922.
[32] *Ibid.*, Vol. II, p. 792.
[33] *On Princely Government*, p. 49.
[34] *Ibid.*, p. 29.

will be vested with power. For the internalized moral sense of the ruler is what stands between the citizens and oppressive rule.

There is, however, an additional protection; and it is one that Plato and Aristotle did not speak of. God is a participant in the political process, and He can reward or punish the men who exercise power over their fellows. No ruler can ever forget that Divine judgment is being passed upon him, nor can he be unmindful of the eternal prize which will be his if his tenure of office meets God's standards. "Now it is right," St. Thomas says, "that a king should look to God for some reward."

This conclusion can also be demonstrated by reason. For there is a firm conviction in the minds of all who think rationally that blessedness is the reward of virtue. Virtue in anything else can, in fact, be described as that which perfects its possesser and renders action beneficent. . . . But because an intellectual nature desires that which is universally good, it can be made truly happy only by the possession of such a good that its attainment leaves nothing further to be desired. For this reason, blessedness is called the perfect good, as though containing in itself all that is desirable. But no earthly good can do this. . . . There is no permanence in earthly things and nothing earthly can, in consequence fully satisfy desire.

Rather, we consider them happy who rule wisely, who prefer the suppression of evil to the oppression of people, and who carry out their duties, not from a desire of empty glory but for love of eternal blessedness. . . . God alone, therefore, can satisfy the desire which is in man and make him blessed. God alone is fitting reward for a king.

"So great is the reward of heavenly blessedness promised to kings for the just exercise of power, that they should strive with all care to avoid tyranny," St. Thomas sums up. "Nothing in fact, should be more dear to them than to be raised to glory in the heavenly kingdom with that same regal dignity which surrounds them on earth." [35] God, in short, is on the side of the citizen, and the ruler had better forbear from becoming a tyrant if he wants to get into heaven.

That men of power are judged not only by those over whom they rule but also by God, is a sentiment which pervades all societies. And there is good evidence that rulers adhere to this belief no less than others. One has only to look at the pains they take to ensure that they are at one with God's will. Officeholders promise God that they will govern faithfully; legislative sessions open with prayers asking for Divine guidance; and in many countries the clergy are consulted to discover whether acts of state are consonant with canons of faith and morals. Nor should this be brushed aside as empty ritual or pandering to popular prejudices. St. Thomas is stating a manifest psychological fact: men of power are men of uneasy conscience. The judgments

[35] *Ibid.*, pp. 43, 45, 47.

they must make are weighty ones, and their power is for evil as well as for good. Rulers are called upon to interpret the law in circumstances where emotion and interest can easily thwart the processes of justice; they set the conditions under which men will know freedom or have it withdrawn; they decide that some men will die while others will live. Such responsibilities are a crushing burden on those who shoulder them. Can anyone doubt that the president who decides that an atomic or hydrogen bomb must be dropped on an enemy city or the judge who sentences to death a prisoner convicted on circumstantial evidence will wonder how his decision will affect his disposition in an afterlife? St. Thomas is undoubtedly correct in assuming that all rulers, in some sense or another, want to go to heaven; he is right in saying that the desire for an approbation higher than mortal man can bestow tempers the tendency to abuse power.[36] For men of power, despite all the monuments built for them or all the boulevards bearing their names, will eventually agree with St. Thomas that "there is no permanence in earthly things." So long as men are creatures of conscience, the internalized restraint can be looked to as a hedge against tyrannical rule.

But St. Thomas is no Plato: he is not a Utopian and he is not talking of philosopher-kings. While the ideal ruler in the real world will be a man of upright character, virtuous conscience, and God-fearing proclivities, there is no absolute guarantee that these attributes will always be evident in men of power. That a tyrant may emerge and that oppressive government may be the lot of the governed is altogether possible. Power can corrupt the character of a ruler, and his fear of God's punishment may be neutralized by the heady experience of lording authority over his fellow men. The checks suggested by St. Thomas may not be sufficient: wisdom, virtue, and justice may give way to tyranny. Is it then permissible for citizens to remove from office such a tyrant? Is revolution to be allowed in St. Thomas' scheme of things?

If the tyranny be not excessive it is certainly wiser to tolerate it in limited measure, at least for a time, rather than to run the risk of even greater perils by opposing it. For those who take action against a tyrant may fail in their object, and only succeed in rousing the tyrant to greater savagery. Even when action against a tyrant meets with success, this very fact breeds strife and grave discord among the populace, either in the moment of rebellion or after his overthrow when opinion in the community is factiously divided as to the new form of government. Again, a community sometimes succeeds in deposing a tyrant with the help of some other ruler, who in turn seizes absolute power. But fear of sharing

---

[36] The idea that rulers are men of conscience—indeed, that they bear not only their own consciences but also the spiritual burdens of those over whom they rule—is stated masterfully in "The Legend of the Grand Inquisitor" in Dostoevsky's *Brothers Karamazov*. For a discussion of this and related themes, see Andrew Hacker "Dostoevsky's Disciples: Man and Sheep in Political Theory," *The Journal of Politics*, November 1955, pp. 590–613.

the fate of his predecessor drives him to even greater severity against his new subjects. Thus it is often the case with tyranny that a new tyrant is worse than the old.[37]

The instance of nonexcessive tyranny might be called Case I. Here St. Thomas advises against revolution for three reasons: (1) You may fail; and if you do, the tyrant will wreak his vengeance on you with even greater severity than before. (2) You may succeed; but those who banded together to make the revolution will differ on the constitution of the new regime, and the community will be divided and unrestful. (3) You may succeed only by enlisting the aid of an outside power; and once the revolution has triumphed, he may step in as a new and more severe tyrant. Hence St. Thomas's advice in Case I is: Don't do it.

Case II would be where the tyranny becomes so excessive as to be intolerable. In this instance:

> It has been argued that it would be an act of virtue for the more powerful citizens to kill the tyrant, even exposing themselves to the peril of death for the liberation of the community. . . . But this does not agree with Apostolic teaching. For Peter teaches us to obey not only good and temperate rulers, but also to bear reverence to those who are ill-disposed. . . . It would indeed be dangerous, both for the community and for its rulers, if individuals were, upon private initiative, to attempt the death of those who govern, albeit tyrannically. . . . The consequence of such presumption is more likely to be the loss of a good king to the community than any benefit from the suppression of tyranny. It seems then, that the remedy against the evils of tyranny lies rather in the hands of public authority than in the private judgment of individuals.[38]

In Case II, St. Thomas offers three arguments against the violent overthrow of an intolerable government: (1) St. Peter has instructed us to obey all rulers, be they tyrants or just men. (2) If one condones revolution as a general practice, then any malcontent's interpretation of what constitutes tyranny is as valid as anyone else's. This means that the door is left open for the overthrow of good as well as bad rulers. It is better to put up with tyrants than to face the possibility, by countenancing the principle of revolution, of having virtuous governors deposed by those who do not recognize virtue. (3) At all events, the responsibility for deposition lies with public authority itself. There frequently exist procedures such as impeachment, expressions of no confidence by those near the ruler, and limitations on tenure of office, which can rid a society of an unwanted ruler. Again, St. Thomas' advice in Case II is: Don't do it.

Case III involves the situation where revolution seems all but impossible.

[37] *On Princely Government*, p. 29.
[38] *Ibid.*, p. 31.

That is, neither the duly constituted procedures for removal can be used nor is outside help available. Here St. Thomas says:

> Finally, when there is no hope of human aid against tyranny, recourse must be made to God the King of all, and the helper of all who call upon Him in the time of tribulation. For it is in His power to turn the cruel heart of a tyrant to gentleness. . . . As for those tyrants whom He considers unworthy of conversion, He can take them from among us or reduce them to impotency. . . . But for men to merit such benefit of God they must abstain from sinning, because it is as a punishment for sin that, by divine permission, the impious are allowed to rule. . . . So guilt must first be expiated before the affliction of tyranny can cease.[39]

In Case III there are also three possibilities. (1) If those who are subject to tyranny invoke Divine intervention, God may soften the heart of the tyrant. (2) Or God may strike the tyrant dead, or deprive him of his political strength. (3) And there is the possibility that the very existence of a tyrant is a sign that God wishes to punish a wayward community. Therefore, the remedy suggested in Case III is: Pray to God, and mend your own ways.

There is no "right to revolution" in St. Thomas. As was the case with St. Augustine, there is no encouragement of revolution nor is approval ever given to acts of political disobedience. In fact, if tyranny is shown to exist, St. Thomas suggests that the fault may lie with those who are suffering tyranny and not in the tyrant who is God's agent. St. Thomas' chief objection to revolution is that it is an act of disorder. It is a form of change so fraught with violence and uncertainty that the community suffers greater harm from the attendant disruptions than it would were the existing regime allowed to remain in power. There can, furthermore, be no justice without order; and there can be no order without obedience to constituted authority. Revolutions—whether violent in character or not—destroy the stability upon which orderly human relationships must be founded. St. Thomas is no friend of tyranny, and he realizes that tyrannical government may oppress the human spirit. But a concerted attempt to remove a tyrant will surely bring, both in in its act and in its wake, instability and strife. Between the evils of tyranny and revolution, St. Thomas unhesitatingly chooses the former.

Few writers are as candid as St. Thomas in their discussions of this question. Aristotle took a detached view and confined himself to an analysis of the causes and prevention of revolution. John Locke speaks approvingly of turning rulers out of office, but his comments are so measured that it is hard to imagine that such an act will disrupt society in any major way. Karl Marx assumes that the proletarian revolution is both inevitable and desirable, but the transitory dictatorship which follows it will be succeeded by a Utopian

[39] *Ibid.*, pp. 33, 35.

communist society. And Edmund Burke, who is closest to St. Thomas, concludes that all revolutions are evil, but he also suggests that what stirs them up is never legitimate protest but usually hypocritical propaganda. St. Thomas is willing to admit—and here he and Burke part company—that tyranny can indeed be intolerable. One of the reasons he counsels against revolution, in fact, is that its aftermath may result in more severe tyranny than was experienced before. These are not the prescriptions of a purblind conservative: they are the words of a prudent student of politics who is prepared to analyze the ways and means of achieving the good society. In such a society order is the first requisite. The aftermath of revolution is chaos. The French Revolution led not to a powerless paradise, but first to the Reign of Terror and then to the despotism of Bonaparte. The Russian Revolution led not to classless contentment, but to the Bolshevik hegemony and the despotism of Stalin. No one will deny that the evils in the regimes of both Bourbons and Romanoffs were removed by the act of revolution. But the question St. Thomas would ask is, quite simply, at what price? In both of these cases the *ancien régime* was at least an ordered society: it was a predictable system of personal relationships, and in it each man knew his privileges and obligations. Once these relationships were shattered, the conditions in which men might pursue the good life ceased to exist. In a state of chaos, where custom has been abrogated and authority destroyed, it is impossible for an individual to develop his potentialities. Order, in short, is the precondition for civilized existence.

THE RULE OF LAW

A theory which calls for one-man rule, which expects unquestioning obedience to authority, which refuses to sanction opposition to tyranny—such a theory has all the makings of absolute and autocratic government. But this is not all that St. Thomas had to say. His abiding claim to the attention of students of political theory lies in his role as a legal theorist. Government, he says, must at all times operate under the rule of law.

Law, for St. Thomas, is a far broader conception than that used by legislators, lawyers, or judges. His intention is to create a legal framework which will encompass the governance of all aspects of the universe. This system of law, then, does not specify behavior for all circumstances, nor is it a catalogue of procedural rules. Rather, it is an overarching scheme with several interrelated parts, each of which has a particular purpose. There are, in St. Thomas' theory, four kinds of law: (1) The Eternal Law; (2) The Natural Law; (3) Human Law; (4) Divine Law. St. Thomas weaves so intricate a theory of the interconnection of man and nature, of the natural and supernatural, that only a jurisprudence of some complexity can serve his over-all purpose.

Eternal Law is more the concern of the theologian than the political philosopher. "The very notion of the government of things in God, the ruler of the universe, has the nature of a law." [40] The student of politics does not regard it as his province to study the Law of Gravity or Kepler's Law or Newton's Second Law of Thermodynamics. He simply takes the existence of these and other aspects of the Eternal Law for granted. Needless to say, the workings of the Eternal Law can have grave consequences for public policy. If this Law states that the atmosphere can contain only a certain amount of Strontium 90 and still be safe for human health, then the testing and use of thermonuclear weapons may be a "violation" of the Eternal Law; and this will have consequences for all who live on this planet. The conservation of mineral resources, timber lands, and water tables are also areas where those who make public policy must be governed by the rules of the Eternal Law.

Natural Law, St. Thomas said, "is nothing else than the rational creature's participation of the Eternal Law." [41] What has been done is to draw a distinction between the rational and the irrational inhabitants of the universe. Rivers, insects, animals, and machines are distinguished from man, who is the only rational creature. St. Thomas found it necessary to specify a form of law which applies to men as rational beings, as well as to the irrational qualities which they share with plants and animals. That is to say, Eternal Law by itself covers only one aspect of human behavior; the Natural Law is needed as a supplement.

Now among all others, the rational creature is subject to divine providence in a more excellent way, insofar as it itself partakes of a share of providence, by being provident for itself and for others. Therefore it has a share of the eternal reason, whereby it has a natural inclination to its proper act and end; and this participation of the Eternal Law in the rational creature is called the Natural Law.[42]

Here we have the key assumption of St. Thomas and of all Natural Law theorists who are to follow him. It is the idea that all men are "naturally" inclined to act in ways which are, in the final analysis, appropriate not only for themselves but also for those around them. Man is a part of nature, and he will incline to follow the Natural Law. To be sure, this inclination is often thwarted by human perversity or so discouraged by social institutions that it is not given an opportunity to show itself. Yet the existence of this propensity in men and the assumption that there are means and ends which are

[40] *Summa Theologica,* Vol. II, p. 748.
[41] *Ibid.,* Vol. II, p. 750.
[42] *Ibid.*

objectively right are what set Natural Law theories off from political theories which do not see fit to rely on a higher law.

Human Law is the field of "public law" which is concerned with political institutions, public policy, and the administration of justice. This legal system embraces the creation and enforcement of laws made by men to govern men. Human Law, according to St. Thomas, has three chief characteristics: (1) "It belongs to the notion of Human Law to be ordained to the common good of the state." (2) "It belongs to the notion of Human Law to be framed by the one who governs the community of the state." (3) "It belongs to the notion of Human Law to direct human actions." [43] This should make plain the fact that St. Thomas is more concerned with Human Law in prescriptive terms than he is to describe what law is actually like in the governments of the real world. To state that Human Law should have as its goal the common good is to state a norm rather than relate a fact. That it should be framed by a man who has this common good as his only aim is, again, more a philosophical than a scientific proposition.

This is made apparent when we see that St. Thomas' real concern is with the relationship between Human Law and Natural Law.

The human reason needs to proceed to the more particular determination of certain matters. These particular determinations, devised by human reason, are called Human Laws. . . . "Justice has its source in nature; thence certain things came into custom by reason of their utility; afterwards these things which emanated from nature, and were approved by custom, were sanctioned by fear and reverence for the law." [44]

There need not be an opposition between Human Law and Natural Law because the one originates in the minds of men and the other in the mind of God. If certain Human Laws show themselves to have a utility over the course of time, then we may assume that they have been consonant with the Natural Law all along. The notions of custom and social utility are important intermediaries in the over-all legal system.

To complete the legal foundation, St. Thomas says, "besides the Natural and the Human Law, it was necessary for the directing of human conduct to have a Divine Law." [45] The distinction between Divine and Natural Law was thought necessary for a number of reasons. While Natural Law deals with man in his capacity as a rational creature in an ordered universe, Divine Law applies to him as one of God's subjects who must render obedience to Divine

[43] *Ibid.*, Vol. II, p. 788.
[44] *Ibid.*, Vol. II, p. 751.
[45] *Ibid.*, Vol. II, p. 752.

authority. That is, the Natural Law takes note of man's natural inclinations to behave rationally, and it provides the guidance which these human propensities should need if they are to have the freedom to develop. Divine Law, on the other hand, is a table of commandments: "Man is ordained to an end of eternal happiness," [46] St. Thomas says. This means that a Divine Law is needed to direct man's soul. Man, however, must take the responsibility of making moral choices, and he is a fallible creature. Thus the Divine Law—unlike the Natural Law—is a body of commandments. It is, furthermore, directed at the inner motives and motivations of men. Human Law can only deal with external behavior; a Divine Law is needed to judge what goes on in our minds and hearts. And it is, finally, a code to govern man, who is a creature of sin. "Human Law cannot punish or forbid all evil deeds . . ." St. Thomas says. "In order, therefore, that no evil might remain unforbidden and unpunished, it was necessary for the Divine Law to supervene, whereby all sins are forbidden." [47] Divine Law, then, is in its form like Human Law: it is a legal code, all of its statutes having been drafted by God. The Ten Commandments are, of course, the best-known instance of the Divine Law. Directives of this character are laid down by God so that humans will have guide lines to follow if they wish to be moral persons. And rewards and punishments are meted out to those whose inward motives and outward behavior come within the pale of His law. Divine Law is God's way of motivating both citizens and rulers in areas where Human Law cannot reach.

Of chief interest to the political philosopher is the relationship between Human Law and the Natural Law. It is already clear that in St. Thomas' theory those who exercise political power—the men who create and enforce Human Law—have no temporal limits on their authority. What, therefore, makes the power of these rulers legitimate? The answer is that not only is a ruler charged with making the laws, but he must make them well. And the quality of his performance can be judged against an objective standard.

What, first of all, is the definition and function of law? "Law is nothing else than an ordinance of reason for the common good, promulgated by him who has care of the community . . ." St. Thomas says. "The proper effect of law is to lead its subjects to their proper virtue." [48] Law is rational in character because God has created a rational universe, and the laws which affect men are derived from the Eternal Law which He drew up to give order to His creation. The progression is, at heart, a logical and a simple one: "Since, then, the Eternal Law is the plan of government in the Chief

---

[46] *Ibid.*
[47] *Ibid.*, Vol. II, p. 753.
[48] *Ibid.*, Vol. II, pp. 747, 759.

Governor, all the plans of government in the inferior governors must be derived from the Eternal Law . . ." St. Thomas says. "The Natural Law is nothing else than the rational creature's participation of the Eternal Law." [49] And, as the final step in the progression, the laws enacted by men should carry over the rationality which God inculcated in the Eternal Law and which the Natural Law carried on. "It belongs to the notion of Human Law," St. Thomas says, "to be derived from the Law of Nature." [50]

Here we have the core of Natural Law theory. It is, of course, prescriptive in its orientation. St. Thomas calls on rulers to enact only laws which are derived from the Natural Law. Only if this prescription is followed, will Human Law be legitimate and human lawmakers have unquestioned title to their positions of power. If Human Law is to reflect the Natural Law, then it must take account of the elemental needs and inclinations of men. If it is to be "natural," a law cannot violate human nature in any important respect. St. Thomas earlier outlined the three essential components of man's nature. He shares with all substances the will to hold on to life; therefore, "Whatever is the means to preserving human life, and of warding off its obstacles, belongs to the Natural Law." He shares with all animals the will to reproduce his kind; therefore, "Those things are said to belong to the Natural Law which nature has taught to all animals, such as sexual intercourse, the education of offspring and so forth." And as a rational creature he has a will to know truth and live in society; therefore, "Whatever pertains to this inclination belongs to the Natural Law: e.g., to shun ignorance, to avoid offending those among whom one has to live, and other such things regarding the above inclination." [51] As a substance and as an animal, there is no question that man will be governed by the dictates of the Natural Law: men will in all political and social conditions seek to preserve and perpetuate themselves. But as a rational creature who should quest after truth and live amicably in society he needs more than the Natural Law. Only if Human Law is sympathetic to these inclinations and only if it encourages the rational development of the individual will the commands of the Natural Law have been obeyed. If Human Law tolerates ignorance or conflict, then men's lives will be frustrated. They will live as substances and animals, but their earthly existence will not experience fulfillment.

The good lawmaker, then, must apply his reason to the discovery of the Natural Law and the manner in which it applies to the society he governs. He may not, therefore, act as a free agent: he has no warrant to enact Human

[49] *Ibid.*, Vol. II, pp. 766, 750.
[50] *Ibid.*, Vol. II, p. 788.
[51] *Ibid.*, Vol. II, p. 775.

Law which is arbitrary or oppressive. At all times his first question must be whether the laws he enacts reflect the dictates of the Natural Law.

REASON AND CUSTOM

How is a ruler to know what is "natural"? The first answer is that man has reason. Some men—and it is to be hoped that those who exercise power are within this group—have so disciplined themselves that they can use their reason to apprehend the essential rules of natural justice. Knowledge of what is "natural," in short, is available to mankind. It is not dependent on Divine revelation: an angel does not have to appear with a message from God in hand. On the other hand, as St. Augustine pointed out, men must invoke the powers of prayer and the attitude of humility if they are to use their ability to reason to the utmost. It is not enough that the human mind be clear-headed, disciplined, and imaginative: communication with God, the creator of the Natural Law, must be established if a knowledge of His Law is to be acquired. Prayer and piety are essential. All men are capable of coming to such knowledge, but in the world we know it is probable that only a few will achieve that goal. A society should be judged by how far its rulers can be numbered within this rational minority.

The theory of Natural Law, while prescriptive in its consequences, is clearly an instance of a deductive science of behavior. Just as physicists speak of the "natural laws" of motion, so St. Thomas would say that the Natural Law which will guide men to the moral life is a scientific theory. The problem which arises is one that is perennial in politics. The physicists, through the experimental method, can verify or at least make plausible, their "natural laws." But can a political scientist use such methods to gain agreement on interpretations of the Natural Law? He cannot, because the deductive method relies not on experimentation but on reason. Reasonable men tend to differ on their definitions of right behavior, and no laboratory apparatus exists by which their quarrels might be settled. Because men are subjective in their judgments and because the Natural Law is an objective phenomenon, St. Thomas feels it necessary to show how reasonable men may be guided to an understanding of it. It is bootless for individuals to argue over who has "really" utilized his reason in an effort to know the Natural Law. It would be better to conduct such an analysis in a social setting, which is where, after all, it belongs.

A rational lawmaker, St. Thomas says, will give careful study to the character of his citizens and the social conditions which are operative at his historical time. He should understand that the Natural Law never calls on rulers to come in conflict with the basic needs of men. This means that Human Law which is to reflect the Natural Law must always be in harmony with the human personality and the social setting. "Laws imposed on men should also be in keeping with their condition . . ." St. Thomas says. "Laws should be possible both according to nature and according to the customs of the country." [52] A law which violates custom is also, in all likelihood, violative of the Natural Law. The reason for this should be clear. Men become accustomed to the traditional patterns of behavior in their society: if they are commanded to alter their way of life in a radical manner, there is a good likelihood that both they and the community as a whole will suffer moral and political disintegration. The sharp break will lead to psychological tensions and social conflict.

St. Thomas empoys a specific example to illustrate this theory. The Natural Law does not specify that a society must adopt any particular economic system. It does not decree that the institution of private property is either "natural" or "unnatural." Its existence or absence should be the province of Human Law, and all that is asked is that economic arrangements be in accord with the conditions and customs of the country in question.

The common possession of things is to be attributed to Natural Law, not in the sense that Natural Law decrees that all things are to be held in common and that there is to be no private possession: but in the sense that there is no distinction of property on grounds of Natural Law, but only by human agreement; and this pertains to positive law, as we have already shown. Thus private property is not opposed to Natural Law, but is an addition to it, devised by the human reason.[53]

St. Thomas was unwilling to make any sweeping generalizations about individual as opposed to collective ownership of property. What we have to ask is whether, in a given place and at a given time, men need to own private property in order to develop their fullest potentialities. In circumstances where it can be rationally demonstrated that they do, then it can be said that private property is a legitimate "addition" and hence should be regarded as an institution derived from the Natural Law. In other cultures such an institution would be disruptive of customary patterns of behavior. There are parts of the world where communities are so constituted that all facets of life are integrated with common ownership of property; this is particularly the case in many primitive societies where the getting of food is the principal occupation. Citizens in such societies do not feel the need for private property that is experienced by members of more advanced communities. Or as even advanced societies reach certain stages of bureaucratization many citizens

[52] *Ibid.*, Vol. II, p. 792.
[53] *Ibid.*, in *Selected Political Writings*, pp. 169, 171.

reshape their goals so as not to include property ownership as a requisite. These topics will be discussed more fully in later chapters. What is important to note now is that it is not at all legitimate to assert in a dogmatic way that a particular institution is prescribed by the Natural Law and to claim that only if it is universally applied will men know their full realization. Custom and conditions must always be the intermediary between Human Law and the Natural Law. An institution which fits "naturally" in one society may be both artificial and stultifying in another.

St. Thomas assumes that the experience of men is cumulative: as societies develop through time, they retain practices which have proved useful, they eventually discard that which ceases to serve a function, and they are in a constant process of modification and adjustment.

> In practical matters, for those who first endeavored to discover something useful for the human community, not being able by themselves to take everything into consideration, set up certain institutions which were deficient in many ways: and these were changed by subsequent lawmakers who made institutions that might prove less frequently deficient in relation to the common welfare.
> On the part of man whose acts are regulated by law, the law can be rightfully changed because of changed conditions among men, to whom different things are expedient according to the difference of their conditions.[54]

Social change is legitimate, so long as it does not involve an abrupt breach of custom. For St. Thomas, innovation is a slow and cautious procedure. Men develop habits and prejudices which they come to cherish. Law must follow custom. And the lawmaker must wait for circumstances to demonstrate clearly the need for innovation. The burden of proof lies on the would-be innovator: he must give satisfactory evidence that it will benefit the general welfare. "Human Law is rightly changed insofar as such change is conducive to the common welfare." [55] But the community is not a set of building blocks: it is not as if a mason were to remove one stone and put another of similar dimensions in its place. Rather, we are dealing with an organic body, and the process of innovation—even if each change seems salutary on its merits—can be harmful if it is exercised too mechanically.

> The mere change of law is of itself prejudicial to the common welfare, because custom avails much for the observance of laws, seeing that what is done contrary to general custom, even in slight matters, is looked upon as a rather serious offense. Consequently, when a law is changed, the binding power of law is diminished, insofar as custom is abolished. Therefore human law should never be changed, unless, in some way or other, the common welfare be compensated according to the extent of the harm done in this respect.[56]

[54] *Ibid.*, in *Basic Writings*, Vol. II, pp. 800–801.
[55] *Ibid.*, Vol. II, p. 802.
[56] *Ibid.*

What this adds up to is that custom is very often, in fact, an expression of the Natural Law. Men are rational, and over time they develop their patterns of behavior in ways which satisfy their basic needs. For this reason rulers must be wary of breaking the cake of custom, for in so doing they may be abrogating the Natural Law. But custom, as we know, is frequently irrational, and it takes no effort to discover social practices which continue to be followed even though they no longer serve any useful purpose. The answer here—and it is one that will be elaborated on by Edmund Burke—is that behavior which seems irrational on the surface may actually serve a latent function in the lives of those who engage in it. An old example is that of sailors who offer up sacrifices to the sea gods for a safe voyage. Knowing that they have done their duty to the gods, the chances are that they will be more self-confident while at sea and thus better able to weather whatever storms may come. The custom of sacrificing, then, is "irrational" in one sense; but it is "rational" in another because it performs an important function in the well-being of men's lives. A second example may indicate how the breach of even seemingly unjust custom may work an over-all harm. A community may have a practice whereby older people, once they feel they are no longer useful, will go off and hurl themselves into the nearest volcano. They will perform this act quietly, automatically, and without any remorse or protest. This custom serves a need: it solves the "old age" problem for the society. If a ruler, in the name of justice, makes this custom of voluntary suicide illegal, and if he creates social sanctions which aid the enforcement of the new law, he will find himself with a whole host of problems. He will have to feed and house the nonproductive oldsters and tend them with new and special medical facilities. Resentments will grow up among the younger generation, which feels it oppressive to carry their grandparents' burdens. It might, in the final analysis, be said that the reform was not a mark of progress but of retrogression. The new law, in abolishing one seemingly "unnatural" practice may have created many more problems which serve to thwart human development.

Does this mean that any custom which can be shown to serve a social function ought to be considered a "natural" practice? After all, every custom can be construed as functional in the broad sense that it makes for "social cohesion." Ought we therefore to say that the high infant mortality rates, the unbalanced diets, and the painful ceremonial rites which some societies have developed over centuries are "natural" simply because they are accepted without protest? In other words, can a custom ever be criticized on moral grounds? Can, in fact, the Natural Law and established custom be in conflict? [57] The answer must be that for a custom to be considered "natural" it must be practiced willingly and ungrudgingly by all members of a community. Once an old man decides that he would prefer to live on to a ripe age rather than immerse himself in molten lava, his very act of questioning the traditional practice is evidence that the custom is—for him at least—no longer an established one. Similarly, if the institution of slavery is to be regarded as a customary arrangement, then slaves as well as masters must cheerfully accept its existence. There is always the danger that the "way of life" which one section of a community claims is the traditional pattern for the whole society will actually be denied by another group in the society. In this case it is difficult to discover the "established" customs and to cite practices which are "natural."

Much of one's view here depends on whether the theorist sees the class struggle or the harmony of interests—to use the two extreme cases—as operative in the society. St. Thomas sees harmony rather than conflict and is therefore able to rely on the fact of custom as supportive of the Natural Law. He also regards men's needs as fairly constant and consequently believes that the traditional institutions which satisfy these needs ought to be respected and maintained by Human Law. The use of the Natural Law in this way, and the reliance on custom as an intermediary, shows that St. Thomas' theory is essentially a conservative one. Liberals show less reverence for custom, and one reason for this is that they take a different view of man's ability to adjust to new experiences.[58] One way for rulers to deal with this problem in practical terms is to make sure that innovations are always made to appear as extensions of existing practices rather than breaks with them. But this matter is in Machiavelli's province, and will be considered in the next chapter.

The quest to discover laws and institutions "natural" to men had best

---

[57] David Spitz has suggested that the Natural Law and established customs often do not live easily together. "These are not always compatible standards," he says. "In a particular situation they may even stand in direct opposition to each other. For the first . . . is an appeal to principle, to an allegedly objective criterion independent of group or national practice. The second is an appeal to subjective experience, to what communities have done and believed." "Conservatism and the Medieval Mind," *Dissent*, Summer 1959, p. 282.

[58] John Stuart Mill, for example, has this to say: "It would be a great mistake in any legislator not to shape his measures so as to take advantage of such pre-existing habits and feelings when available. On the other hand, it is an exaggeration to elevate these mere aids and facilities into necessary conditions. People are more easily induced to do, and do more easily what they are already used to; but people also learn to do things new to them. Familiarity is a great help; but much dwelling on an idea will make it familiar, even when strange at first. There are abundant instances in which a whole people have been eager for untried things." *Representative Government*, p. 181.

begin with an examination of human customs. In those traditional and ingrained patterns of behavior rulers will find the earthly expressions of the Natural Law. Manifestations of the Natural Law will differ throughout time and country, but its basic fabric is always the same. What it provides for at all times and places is the free development of men in their role as rational creatures. Those who frame Human Law must be students of the unchanging nature of man; here they may be guided by the words of St. Thomas. But they must also study the changing needs of men and society; here St. Thomas leaves them to their own reason.

Obedience to the precepts of the Natural Law, then, is the answer to the question of how power becomes legitimate. St. Thomas' explanation is but one of several. Not only does it differ from those of Plato and Aristotle in important respects, but it will differ even more from the democratic theories of Locke, Rousseau, and Mill. Indeed, whether democracy and Natural Law can be reconciled is one of the great controversies of political theory.[59] Democracy holds that the people are capable of deciding on what is their own best interest. Natural Law calls for an extraordinary exercise of reason—presumably by extraordinary men—to discover what is the best government for the community. Rousseau and Burke, Mill and Tocqueville, will carry this discussion on. In addition, Natural Law, with its deep respect for custom, has a clear connection with conservative theory. It ought to be obvious at this point that the theories of St. Thomas and St. Augustine carry within them the seeds of ideology: that distorted descriptions and interested prescriptions can rise from their writings just as easily as from the theories of less saintly writers.

[59] For a discussion of Natural Law vs. democracy in the context of contemporary American politics, see Walter Lippmann, *The Public Philosophy* (Boston: Little, Brown, 1955).

5.
Niccolo Machiavelli

THE MAN AND HIS TIMES

Niccolo Machiavelli was born in Florence in 1469 and in an Italy which was a patchwork quilt of independent and antagonistic states. His career was a political one, and many of his life's efforts were devoted to securing public office. From 1498 to 1512 he was Secretary of Chancery for Florence. There, under a republican regime, he handled affairs for the Departments of War and Interior and also served as a diplomatic correspondent. Toward the end of this time the Medici family was again rising to power in Italy. The Florentine Republic lost out in a struggle with the Pope, and the consequence was that the Medici were restored as rulers of Florence. Machiavelli was on the wrong side, and he lost his job and was imprisoned on the charge of conspiracy. After his release he retired to the countryside and there wrote The Prince in 1513 and The Discourses in 1521. The Prince was dedicated to "Lorenzo the Magnificent" and it appears as an ingratiating request for sympathy, forgiveness, and a job. For Machiavelli longed to return to the political life, and he was as anxious to serve the Medici as he had been to work for the Florentine Republic. But no post was offered to him, and it was only late in life, a few years before his death in 1527, that he was given the sedentary task of writing a history of Florence. For a man who so confidently lay down the rules for political success, his own political career ended in failure.

Renaissance Italy was poised between the feudalism of the Middle Ages and the system of nation-states which characterizes the modern world. Technological advances and new forms of economic organization had gone far toward weakening the feudal structure: increased trade, expanded markets, and the growth of cities all contributed to a redistribution of political power. Territorial jurisdictions were becoming more farflung and this presented a challenge to the localism of the feudal order. In

157

northern Europe the institution of a national monarchy was developing, and its power was beginning to be regarded as absolute. However, the Italy which Machiavelli knew was not sharing in this transformation. The country was a collection of small states, not the least of which were under the control of the Papacy. If the Pope could not command the loyalty of all the Italian princes, he had sufficient military strength to act as an important balance of power. The Italian states were in a condition of continual conflict, both among themselves and within their own borders. One consequence was that Italy was constantly being invaded by Germany, France and Spain; and these intruders were as often as not invited in by one or another of the warring factions. There existed no single power strong enough to unite Italy, and the status of the Papacy, in Machiavelli's eyes, was an obstacle preventing the secular states from joining together as a single nation. In sharp contrast to its sycophantic dedication, the closing chapter of The Prince is a stirring plea that all Italy be united, that political power be used to create one nation. But this end, like his careerist ambitions, was not to be secured in Machiavelli's own lifetime—or for many centuries to come.

If the Italy of the Renaissance did not experience political success, its cultural and intellectual life was of magnificent proportions. The break with the medieval outlook was a sharp one. No longer was it to be the lot of men to find happiness and salvation in a world to come. On the contrary, man could shape his destiny in his life, and by his own efforts he might come to know a creative and satisfying existence. At the same time, the pervasive authority of the Church was brought into question, and secular rulers found less and less occasion to apologize for their exercise of power. The intellectual rebirth brought a new appreciation of Greek and Roman culture and a diminished role for Christian ideas. But the most signal development was the discovery of the individual. Its political manifestation is to be seen in The Prince, an egoistic and arrogant book. If men, and men of power in particular, are to persuade themselves that they have status as individuals, then it follows that they will act to maintain their personal interests. The corruption and the cruelty which Machiavelli saw in Italian politics were rampant expressions of an emerging human ego. This ego had been confined for almost a thousand years, and its sudden release would understandably lead to excesses. Machiavelli understood that men were now on their own and would have to shape their own political future. He had sufficient faith that the pursuit of self-interest would be enlightened and that power would be guided by human reason.

5.
Niccolo Machiavelli

MACHIAVELLI IS THE FIRST WRITER TO EMBARK ON THE EXPRESS
task of describing the world of politics as it actually operates. Plato and
Aristotle, St. Augustine and St. Thomas—all of these theorists offered perceptive insights into the functioning of political behavior and institutions.
But at the front of their minds they had fairly clear-cut notions of what
constituted good behavior and good institutions. The result of this duality
of purpose is that in their writings the real and the ideal are often confused.
Or, to put it more precisely, the theorist's description of the real world becomes distorted insofar as his main concern is to set us on the path to the
ideal. The pursuit of a political science, in these cases, runs the risk of being
a secondary interest. Plato tended more to political philosophy than Aristotle,
St. Thomas more than St. Augustine. But none of them embraced the realist
spirit with the ardor or consistency that Machiavelli displays.

Realism is a necessary first step in any attempt to make a science out of
politics. We have already seen its beginnings in Socrates' friend, Thrasymachus, and the conception of theory based on the empirical method was
developed further by Aristotle. Realism rests on the assumption that the
student of politics must focus his attention on what men do rather than
consume his time listening to what men say. If we observe men's behavior, we
will discover that while they talk quite highmindedly about political goals,
their political acts bear little relation to those worthy utterances. Aristotle
said that man is not only a social animal, but also a conversational animal.
The realist approach assumes that a large part of political conversation is no
more than self-interested rationalization. It is no small waste of time to listen
to talk of purported philosophical principles if we are soon to discover that
these lofty propositions are not effective guides to action. And it is even
more futile to study propositions which profess to be descriptive if we learn
that they give a distorted picture of the way men behave. Rather than

159

listening, then, the student should get out in the field and watch the political process at work. A second postulate of the realist approach is that the driving force behind political behavior is the desire on the part of men to gain and maintain power. Political power is construed as the ability to make others act as you would like them to act. To the realist point of view, power is the substance of political science: the power of man over man. Just as the economist presumes that the businessman is motivated by the drive to enrich himself, so the realist looks on the politician as being impelled by the drive to exercise power over his fellow men. If these models—both the economic and the political—are oversimplified descriptions of social behavior, it will remain to be seen how far more complicated explanations bring us closer to the truth.

A further postulate of the realist approach is that it is possible to divorce the spheres of morals and politics. In saying this, the realist is saying a number of things. It sometimes is contended—and other theorists besides Machiavelli are prepared to make this claim—that the only way to theorize about the world of politics is for the theorist to step outside that world; he must suspend his own moral judgments as far as is humanly possible. A theorist, to be sure, is no different from any other human being: he has his own ideas about good and evil, right and wrong. However, if he is to understand and describe the world as it really is, he must not allow these preferences of his to intrude into his studies. If he does, he will find that he is judging rather than explaining, prescribing where he should be describing.

The realist insists that not only is a neutral stance necessary; it is also, he says, quite possible. Men can develop the study of politics into a scientific discipline if they are aware of the force of their own prejudices, if they have the strength to discuss in a detached way behavior which they find distasteful, and if they at all times give highest priority to the discovery of truth— wherever and whenever it may be found. The political theorist is called upon to emulate the physicist, who has no moral feelings about the electrons or the paths they trace, or the biologist, who neither loves nor hates the amoeba. The withholding of value judgments about the subject of study has contributed to making physics and biology scientific disciplines. In a like way, the student of politics can, if he tries, forbear from investing man and governments with the qualities of good and evil. We will only understand the political world which surrounds us if we are as objective about it as the entomologist is about the lives he beholds in an ant hill. There is no denying that men understand ant life better than they do their own; the lesson, the realist says, should be clear.

A POLICY SCIENCE

The divorce of morals and politics has another aspect. In the course of his writings Machiavelli offers counsel to whatever rulers will take the time to read his books. The suggestions which he makes are based on the assumption that political advice need not contain a moral content. Machiavelli's set speech to his reader goes something like this: (a) *if* you wish to gain or maintain power for whatever reason or purpose you have in mind, (b) and *if* these are the conditions under which historical circumstances or limited resources compel you to operate, (c) *then* this is the best way to achieve the ends that you want. The political theorist, in this case, is taking on the role of the professional specialist. Analogous examples come readily to mind. The doctor: (a) *if* you wish to regain your health, (b) and *if* you can take three months off from your job, (c) *then* take these pills and go to the Bahamas. Or the scientist: (a) *if* you wish to blow up the world, (b) and *if* you are prepared to spend only so much money, (c) *then* build this sort of bomb. The point, of course, is that the first proposition in the formula is bound to involve a decision about values. But Machiavelli is prepared to take as "given" the fact that a politician wishes to gain or maintain power, just as a doctor does not ask the patient whether the pursuit of health is a good thing. Why a man wants power, what he intends to do with it once he has it—these are questions which the specialist must avoid. The doctor does not ask his prospective patient what he intends to do with his life after he has been cured, nor does he pass judgment on the career the patient will follow when he gets better. And he certainly does not make leading the good life afterward a condition for giving treatment. Machiavelli takes the same stance: moral judgments are for the political participant; professional judgments are for the political scientist. It is the latter's job to tell the practitioner how to achieve the goal he has elected to pursue.

The formula, however, can be a deceptive one. It has three parts, and the middle proposition is an important connecting link. For the conditions imposed by historical circumstances and available resources will operate on the other two parts. They will, first of all, put limits on the goals which are attainable at any point in time. The specialist, in pointing this out to the politician, can therefore affect the actual ends which are pursued. Permanent officials in the British Civil Service, for example, have a way of telling Cabinet Ministers, "Oh sir, you can't do *that*." They are not questioning the moral content of the goal; they are simply saying that resources are not available for carrying it out. Or the specialist can point out the price—in financial or other terms—which would have to be paid were the goal in question to be achieved. In this way the goal may be modified, and in this way also the specialist has an influence on ends as well as means. Furthermore, circumstances and resources usually give a wide range of discretion to the professional. There is no single way to secure political stability or draft a peace treaty or deliver the mail. Having a series of choices before him, the specialist is free to advise one set of policies rather than another. While alternative plans may secure the objective, they will do it in different ways. And what happens as a result of using one set of means rather than another will, in the final analysis, affect the shape that the end will take. Machiavelli takes full advantage of the freedom of choice which is open to the specialist. Whether the specialist, in taking advantage of this freedom, can still insist on the division between morals and politics is a question which is bound to recur.

If politics is to be a science, it must have its own axioms. Aristotle postulated that man is a social animal, but this is rather obvious and is really on a level with the law of gravity. St. Thomas said that man is a moral animal. This is not so obvious—indeed, it is rather controversial—and ought therefore to be put on a par with Boyle's Law. Machiavelli's first axiom goes further than those of his predecessors; it deals with matters at the level of social and political organization, and it also claims to be based on the facts of political life. "In all republics, however organized," Machiavelli says, "there are never more than forty or fifty citizens who attain a position that entitles them to command." [1] In all political systems, regardless of time or place, the few will rule and the many will be ruled. This applies no less to democracies than it does to autocracies or dictatorships, no less to free societies than to oppressed ones. This dictum is not ethical in character; on the contrary, it states a fact of political life which has been operative since politics began. Any conception of morality, any conception of democracy or freedom, must build with this fact as its foundation.

That Machiavelli's law is inductively based has already been suggested. It is built on the fact that politics is organizational: political ends can be achieved and means can be mobilized only if men organize themselves for this purpose. And the initial principle of organization is the division of labor. Just as an army must divide the work between generals and privates, so in political life some must rule and others be ruled. Within the framework of this law there can be a variety of governmental systems. Like Aristotle,

[1] *Discourses on the First Ten Books of Titus Livius*, in *The Prince and the Discourses* (New York: Modern Library, 1940), p. 163.

Machiavelli will speak of democracies as well as oligarchies. He will certainly grant that the public can make its influence felt on the policies and personnel of government. And he will talk, furthermore, of free societies as well as oppressive ones. Men can know liberty as well as authority if they design their institutions rationally. But all that Machiavelli says must be viewed in the context of the basic organizational law. There are things a majority can do in the political sphere, but there are also things it cannot do. Machiavelli does not regard these questions as moral in character: he does not, for example, worry over whether the public should be allowed in on the decision-making process for ethical reasons. The principles to be laid down, then, are scientific ones: they are based, as far as possible, on empirical investigation. But both science and investigation are built on and derived from the assumption that power gravitates to the hands of a minority.

It follows from this premise that Machiavelli will direct the bulk of his attention to the ruling minority. Both the *Prince* and *Discourses* are written for this limited audience, and the former is specially designed as a handbook for those who wish to exercise power effectively. This, of course, is not new. Plato devoted most of *The Republic* to a consideration of the Guardian class, and St. Thomas directed his attention to the rulers who would interpret and implement the Natural Law. What sets Machiavelli off is that he does not rely on the conception of a ruling class as Plato did, nor does he follow St. Thomas in demanding virtue in those who rule. Machiavelli will follow St. Thomas in discussing the single person—the prince—who holds the reins of power. But this man will be analyzed in the context of a broader idea. This is the notion of an elite, and it would be well to contrast it with that of a ruling class.

A ruling class is a hereditary institution. It is recruited for the most part on the basis of birth: its members gain entry through the simple process of being the offspring of the right parents. They are raised and educated apart from the rest of society, and much of their education is premised on the fact that they will eventually have the responsibility of rulership. Once born and educated into this style of life, they move effortlessly into positions of power and prestige in society. The chief mainstay of a ruling class is, nevertheless, wealth. But it is inherited wealth, and very usually wealth based on the ownership of land. This old wealth brings with it a social status which is not acquired by other means. Members of a ruling class, then, assume their status because of *who* they are. They have power because they bear traditional family names and because they are connected through property ownership with an ancient part of the country. Not all members of a ruling class are clever or virtuous or even capable of exerting leadership in society.

However, within this class there are usually some who can take on the responsibilities and handle them well. And, it should be recalled, class education trains the oncoming generations for the power they will inherit. At all events, no one expects that recruitment by accident—for that is what dependence on birth results in—will produce no idiots or immoralists. That is not the point. As Burke and Tocqueville will show, the merits of class rule are displayed more in consequences for society as a whole than they are in the innate superiority of the few who have exclusive power.

The idea of an elite is newer to political theory and less easy to describe in coherent terms. If membership in a ruling class is signified by who a person is, membership in an elite is gained by what an individual is. That is, an elite is functional: its members have power or status because of the functions they are capable of performing, the jobs they are able to do. The key to an elite, then, lies in its members' skills. These may be learned, like those of the doctor or engineer. Or they may be inherent in the personality of the individual, like a good bedside manner or a salesman's knack of persuasion. The point about an elite based on skills, of course, is that the demand for different skills varies through time and place. If at one period there is a need for certain skills, then those who have them will be drawn into the elite. At a different occasion or at another place, the very same individuals might find themselves outside the elite group because their skills were irrelevant to the needs of the time. Just as the inheritance of name, wealth, and status is important for the maintenance of class rule, so opportunity for social mobility is a requisite of elite rule. If position is to be based on skill, then those with the appropriate training and competence must be allowed to move into the elite as their talents are needed. While a ruling class can justify itself on grounds other than skill, an elite must demand talent of its members or perish. This is why there can be no such thing as a hereditary elite: if the father has his status because he is an efficient administrator, then the son must display equal efficiency if he is to attain to his father's level.[2]

There are several possible confusions in the elite idea. For this reason it is necessary to make several distinctions. First of all, there are what might be called the "objective" elites. These are the individuals in any given group who, either by objective test or the esteem of those around them, are deemed to be the "best" in that group. Thus, among journalists and jazz musicians, professors and prostitutes, architects and astrologers, there is always a small

[2] The classic statement of elite theory, which will be drawn on throughout this chapter, is Vilfredo Pareto's The Mind and Society (New York: Harcourt, Brace, 1935), 4 volumes, edited by Arthur Livingston and translated by Andrew Bongiorno.

minority who are considered superior. We may therefore speak of the "elite" of journalists or the "elite" of prostitutes. But once we have said this, for political purposes at least, there is little more to say. The elite architects and professors and jazz musicians do not band together in any combined elite: at the very most, it can be said that they are found together between the covers of *Who's Who in America* or *The New York Times Index*. Machiavelli is interested in only one of the many elites to be found in a society: the minority which is "best" at the exercise of political power. Of all those who attempt to rule their fellow men, only a few succeed. These are the people Machiavelli is addressing himself to and talking about. And within this "political" elite we find a governing and a nongoverning segment. The former consists of those who currently hold the reins of power. The latter are potential challengers: men waiting in the wings to depose the incumbents when the time is ripe. The "political" elite, then, is a special case of the "objective" elite. And if the skills of power are harder to describe than the skills of dentistry, Machiavelli's importance lies in his attempt to show how men succeed at the political game.

No clear-cut distinctions can be made, of course, between a ruling class and an elite. Every dominant group combines ascription and achievement. No ruling class is closed to the talented entirely, and no political elite demands that all its members demonstrate extraordinary skills. Furthermore, a ruling class and an elite can live side by side in a single society, sometimes sharing power amicably and sometimes in mortal combat with each other. In some countries the ruling class will absorb the elite into its membership; in others it will expire rather than admit the intruders. Ruling groups, by and large, show both class and elite tendencies. If Machiavelli emphasizes talent, Burke will stress inheritance at a later stage.[3]

Machiavelli's concern is with the individuals who comprise—or who seek entry to—the political elite. Indeed, his attention is directed at most times to the individual who has attained the top rung of the political ladder and who wants to stay there. However, just as a businessman deserves to be called successful on the basis of whether or not his enterprise makes a profit, so a ruler succeeds only so long as his government is in power. This means

---

[3] An excellent study of class and elite in contemporary America is E. Digby Baltzell, *Philadelphia Gentlemen* (Glencoe: Free Press, 1958). Baltzell uses inclusion in the *Social Register* as evidence of "upper-class" status and inclusion in *Who's Who in America* as evidence of "elite" status. In 1940, the year studied by Baltzell, there were—in the twelve cities with *Social Registers*—38,450 family units listed in those volumes. In the same twelve cities there were a total of 12,570 individuals who were listed in *Who's Who*. Of those listed in *Who's Who*, 23 per cent were also listed in the *Social Register* and 77 per cent were not (See table on p. 29). This book has an excellent discussion of the "overlap" between class and elite in both local and national terms.

that Machiavelli is as much interested in the stability of the state as he is in the careers of the elite. Political survival—of men and governments—becomes Machiavelli's ultimate test. The aim of the state is not to promote freedom or virtue or the good life for its citizens. Its goal is to stay in operation. If its survival value is increased by its being a free state, then it should be free. But it might just as easily be oppressive by the same token. Machiavelli believes in human liberty and the rule of law. But he adheres to these values because they are conducive to political stability and survival. If he talks the language of political philosophy on occasion, it is only because he has first laid the groundwork of a political science.

A MODEL OF MAN

"For it may be said of men in general," Machiavelli says, "that they are ungrateful, voluble, dissemblers, anxious to avoid danger, and covetous of gain. . . ." [4] It is on the basis of statements like this that Machiavelli's realism has been called pessimism, his science cynicism. The chief reason why his generalizations are so forbidding is that Machiavelli is not so much a general theorist as he is a political model-builder. When he talks of "man," for example, he is referring to an abstraction which might be called "political man." That is, all the variables in the human personality except those which are directly relevant to the political process are held constant.

Plato's and St. Thomas' theories of human nature tried to embrace the whole personality of an individual: social and political, animal and ethical elements were all integrated into an overreaching scheme. And because man's moral and political natures were so intertwined, both Plato and St. Thomas could easily imagine occasions where successful political behavior might come in conflict with standards of morality. If morals and politics are integrated in the personality, they said, then they must be in external behavior as well. And out of their quests for such a synthesis rose their theories of politics.

Machiavelli, on the other hand, recognizes two standards. Take the matter of ingratitude. In terms of personal morality an individual should always be grateful for kindnesses rendered him. But we are on slippery footing if we try to transfer this moral imperative to the political realm. For, as a matter of simple and everyday fact, man—when he acts in his capacity as "political man"—just does not exhibit gratitude to his rulers. An unemployed man may vote for Franklin Roosevelt in 1936 because he thinks that with a Democratic administration he will stand a better chance of finding a job.

4 *The Prince*, in *op. cit.*, p. 61.

And within a short time he finds employment and things begin to look better. In 1952 the same man votes for Dwight Eisenhower because he thinks the Republicans will lower taxes. Do we expect this citizen to be grateful to the party of Roosevelt for sixteen years? Or do we take it for granted that his question to the parties will be: "What Have You Done For Me Lately?" An even better example is what occurred in Great Britain in 1945. The war in Europe being over, Parliament dissolved and there was the first general election in ten years. There is no doubt that every Briton looked on Winston Churchill as the man who saved the country in its darkest hour. And the Conservative Party sought to capitalize on this sentiment by putting up posters with Churchill's picture throughout the country with the caption, "Let Him Finish The Job." The voters responded by electing a huge Labour majority in the House of Commons for the first time in history. Do we "blame" the Republican voter of 1952 or the Labour voter of 1945 for failing to show gratitude? The answer, which is all that Machiavelli is saying, is that we do not. Neither rulers nor citizens count on or expect gratitude in politics. Moral standards which apply to individual behavior are not applicable to the political role.

Politics, so viewed, is a system of rewards and penalties, and performance is judged on the current record and future expectations. The rules of this game are often rigorous ones, but both rulers and citizens are expected to give as well as they get. Notice Machiavelli's advice to a ruler who has recently conquered another state: "In taking a state the conqueror must arrange to commit all his cruelties at once," he says, "so as not to have to recur to them every day, and so as to be able, by not making fresh changes, to reassure people and win them over by benefitting them." [5] It is taken for granted that a new ruler will have to deal severely with those who might endanger his regime: Machiavelli does not blanch at the thought of cruelties; indeed, he accepts them as necessary. And execution, expropriation, and imprisonment will perforce be the lot of those whose loyalty is in question. That, in short, is the way the political game is played. On the other hand, the conqueror cannot rule his new territory effectively if his new subjects are surly, unrestful, and uncooperative. They have a resource to match his power: their willingness or refusal to accept his rule. Therefore, the ruler had better get his cruelties over with as soon as possible so as to assure the citizens that benefits and not blood will flow from his authority. This is in itself a limitation on the ruler: like it or not, he must put down the sword and begin to depend on other means. Politics, then, is a hardheaded business: it is a serious game in which the scores are carefully recorded by both sides. Talk of

[5] *Ibid.*, p. 35.

things like gratitude only obscures the fact that morality is relevant only so long as it pays.

If Machiavelli concentrates his attention on the ruling minority, this does not mean that he ignores the majority who are ruled. The mass of men and women in any society, however, are characterized more by their inertia than anything else. This does not mean that they can be counted on to be passive in all circumstances. But what it does mean is that they react rather than act, and that their behavior can usually be predicted by a sophisticated ruler. Indeed, this predictability of human behavior forms one of the scientific claims of Machiavelli's theory. It is not that the man-in-the-street is either stupid or ignorant. He knows what is happening politically, and he knows what he wants from his government. However, this knowledge and these wants are usually drawn in terms which are essentially simple. For one thing, they are often negative: men ask not so much for freedom as the absence of oppression. A citizen "who becomes prince by the favor of the populace," Machiavelli says, "must maintain its friendship, which he will find easy, the people asking nothing more than not to be oppressed." [6] And most men are concerned more about their personal integrity and their material possessions than they are about the political system under which they live. "Whenever one does not attack the property or honor of the generality of men," Machiavelli says, "they will live contented, and one will only have to combat the ambition of a few, who can be easily held in check in many ways." [7] The public, furthermore, desires to be free, but the vast majority defines freedom simply in terms of security. "The prince . . . will find that a small part . . . wish to be free for the purpose of commanding," Machiavelli says. "While all the others, who constitute an immense majority, desire liberty so as to be able to live in greater security." [8] The lesson is clear: what the mass of men want is to retain their property and their self-respect, to be guaranteed a reasonable degree of security, and not to be oppressed. A talented ruler should be able to provide these conditions. His real worry will stem from the threats to his power presented by those who would seize his throne. The public, however, is a lethargic giant. This ungainly, domesticated creature can easily be placated. A ruler need not stay up nights fretting about the power which lies dormant in its muscles—so long, that is, as he sleeps with one eye open.

Machiavelli is suggesting, as all theorists must in one way or another, that stable government has to be founded on consent. The consent may be

[6] Ibid., p. 37.
[7] Ibid., pp. 66–67.
[8] Discourses, p. 163.

active or passive, the product of habitual deference or skillful manipulation. Machiavelli's theory of consent assumes a rather primitive level of political awareness. The questions men ask, the demands that they make—these involve their property, their security, their integrity rather than matters of political policy or systems of government. In a word, if they do not feel oppressed, they will readily give their consent. Most men never in their lives stop to wonder whether or not they ought to obey a particular ruler or a certain law. They are creatures who are prone to passive acquiescence. The ruler who provides the social, economic, and psychological satisfactions which his subjects demand will find that in the political realm he will have a remarkably free hand.

To call the mass of men "nonpolitical" is simply to point out that they have neither the time, the energy, nor the inclination to think much about politics. Furthermore, anyone who wishes to master the complexities of the political process must devote much study and thought to the hard facts which comprise political reality. Politics, as needs no emphasis here, is the happy hunting ground of myths and half-truths. To create for one's self a relatively undistorted image of the political world takes no small amount of disciplined effort. Few are willing to exert themselves that hard. And the man-in-the-street is content to live in a world of appearances. "The great majority of mankind are satisfied with appearances, as though they were realities," Machiavelli says, "and are often even more influenced by the things that seem than by those that are." [9]

This is, of course, the language of Plato. But Machiavelli intends to put this idea to work:

Let a prince therefore aim at conquering and maintaining the state, and the means will always be judged honourable and praised by everyone, for the vulgar is always taken by appearances and the issue of the event; and the world consists only of the vulgar, and the few who are not vulgar are isolated when the many have a rallying point in the prince.[10]

Machiavelli's theory of control, then, can be summarized in three propositions. First, the mass of men have certain elemental needs, and their obedience cannot be counted on until these needs have been satisfied. A ruler cannot even begin to think about using political power until he has ensured the continued presence of these basic social and psychological conditions. Second, once the mass of men have been so benefited, they will happily leave political power in the hands of a minority. Having secured this tacit consent, a ruler will find that he has a wide area of discretion in which he

[9] *Ibid.*, p. 182.
[10] *The Prince*, p. 66.

may act as he pleases. He will also find that he has the power to create for the public an image of politics which strengthens his own position. Third, when a ruler has both political power and the ability to communicate his own version of reality, he will find it easier to consolidate his status. Indeed, he may be able to redefine popularly held conceptions of honor, security, and freedom from oppression so that the public believes it continues to have these possessions in hand even though their substantive content has been altered.

From Plato through Machiavelli all theorists have insisted that power must be exercised rationally. Some have said this because they wished power to serve moral ends; others simply because they wanted it to be used as effectively as possible. To be effective, power must be accompanied by an understanding of reality, an ability to predict the consequences of acts, and a coherent view of what is within the realm of possibility. Machiavelli does not waste time speculating on whether men are rational or irrational, nor does he worry over inherent capabilities in this direction. His implication, however, suggests that rulers can behave rationally whereas the mass of men cannot. This is not because rulers have knowledge of the Forms or the Natural Law: Machiavelli would deny that such abstractions exist. Rather, rulers have superior knowledge and understanding by virtue of their location in the social structure. Having access to more information, being the ones who initiate communications rather than those who receive them, having shouldered organizational responsibilities—for these reasons rulers can take a more rational view of the world. The mass of men, on the other hand, live in a crowd: they are forever prey to emotions and half-crystallized sentiments. Their social location is one which lives off distorted images and momentary whims. Because society is so structured, there is always the danger that the public, acting on impulse, may misconstrue reality and do itself irreparable harm.

> The people often, deceived by an illusive good, desire their own ruin, and, unless they are made sensible of the evil of the one and the benefit of the other course by someone in whom they have confidence, they will expose the republic to infinite peril and damage. And if it happens that the people have no confidence in anyone, as sometimes will be the case when they have been deceived before by events or men, then it will inevitably lead to the ruin of the state.[11]

The mass of men—because they live in a mass—are incapable of deciding on policies which will secure their own best interests. They may know what they want, but they do not know how to achieve it. They must therefore be brought to the point where they will bestow their confidence on a ruler

[11] *Discourses*, p. 247.

who can make rational policy for them. Just what a ruler must do to gain the people's confidence is Machiavelli's next concern.

A HANDBOOK OF POWER

Much can be learned about a theory by asking where the theorist sits. John Locke and John Stuart Mill, for example, put themselves down with the man-in-the-street and look on politics from the standpoint of how the average citizen is affected. Plato and St. Thomas, on the other hand, are concerned to stand apart and look on the political system as a whole. Machiavelli takes neither of these views: he regards the political process from the standpoint of the favored few who rule. And because he is concerned with the ways and means of rulership, with the organization of political power, he tends to take a different viewpoint about traditional questions of political philosophy. Aristotle, it will be recalled, analyzed oligarchical and democratic systems from the standpoint of such values as virtue and justice. Machiavelli, too, speaks of oligarchy and democracy—however, his usage is to refer to societies where the "nobility" have power, on the one hand, and where "the people" have it, on the other. (The "nobility" here are not to be thought of as a wise or virtuous minority: rather, they are the dominant minority in society in terms of holding effective power.) From the vantage point of a ruler, the difference between oligarchy and democracy lies in the security of tenure which one system affords as opposed to the other. That is, a ruler must ask whether he will be more secure if he relies for his support on the nobility or on the people. Oligarchy is a preferable system in Machiavelli's eyes if having the nobility as a constituency proves safer for the career of the ruler; democracy is better if the people provide a surer base.

In an oligarchic system the ruler must gain the loyalty of the small group of men who can, by virtue of the power they have, lend their support to his regime. Such a ruler will be the head of state, but he will find himself dependent on the powerful men who surround him. The ruler in a democracy must secure the consent of the majority of citizens: as individuals they are weak, but if they are mobilized as a constituency they form a powerful basis of support. He must, if he elects to rely on the people, be attentive to their needs. And these needs, of course, are different from those of oligarchical groups. The question resolves itself to which of the two constituencies is less threatening in the demands it makes on the ruler. Machiavelli analyzes the ways in which both systems confer power on a ruler and the problems arising in each.

When the nobility see that they are unable to resist the people they unite in exalting one of their number and creating him prince, so as to be able to carry out their own designs under the shadow of his authority. The populace, on the other hand, when unable to resist the nobility, endeavour to exalt and create a prince in order to be protected by his authority. He who becomes prince by help of the nobility has greater difficulty in maintaining his power than he who is raised by the populace, for he is surrounded by those who think themselves his equals, and is thus unable to direct or command as he pleases. But one who is raised to leadership by popular favour finds himself alone, and has no one, or very few, who are not ready to obey him. Besides which, it is impossible to satisfy the nobility by fair dealing and without inflicting injury on others, whereas it is very easy to satisfy the mass of the people in this way. For the aim of the people is more honest than that of the nobility, the latter desiring to oppress, and the former merely to avoid oppression. It must also be added that the prince can never insure himself against a hostile populace on account of their number, but he can against the hostility of the great, as they are but few.[12]

The question is not a philosophical one: the two systems are to be judged not on the basis of which is the good society or which best encourages the moral life for its citizens. The point at issue is which system of government facilitates the ruler's freedom of action. Machiavelli appears to think that on this score democracy is best: a ruler surrounded by men equal to him in stature and talent will always run the risk of a palace revolution, whereas the people can be controlled from a distance and their needs are less sophisticated. But in either event the ruler can only maintain his power if he has the consent of a constituency. Because democracy seems preferable in terms of effective control, Machiavelli turns to the techniques a ruler must use to acquire the acquiescence of the people as a whole. It should be clear by now that in Machiavelli's theory there is no incompatibility between autocratic rule by one man and a democratic system of government. All systems, democracy no less than others, are instances of minority rule. Questions of consent, constituency, and control must always be seen in this perspective. Four major rules of rulership are worth citing.

(1) A ruler must be a strong man, and he must be prepared to exhibit his strength when the necesssity arises. His responsibility is to govern the state, to ensure its stability and survival. For this reason, he must be willing to employ means of an ungentlemanly character. "A prince," Machiavelli says, "must not mind incurring the charge of cruelty for the purpose of keeping his subjects united and faithful." [13] Seldom can power be exercised without either the charge or fact of cruelty. Only in a Platonic Utopia will the consensus be so harmonious that harsh measures will not be needed to keep dissidents in order. Indeed, as St. Augustine pointed out, the earthly city

[12] *The Prince*, p. 36.
[13] *Ibid.*, p. 60.

is kept united by power: love of man for man is a luxury that only the city of God can afford. Machiavelli agrees with this precept. And he puts the question in a straightforward manner: "From this arises the question whether it is better to be loved more than feared, or feared more than loved." Should a ruler seek to be first in the hearts of his countrymen?

The reply is, that one ought to be both feared and loved, but as it is difficult for the two to go together, it is much safer to be feared than loved, if one of the two has to be wanting. For it may be said of men in general that they are ungrateful, voluble, dissemblers, anxious to avoid danger, and covetous of gain; as long as you benefit them, they are entirely yours; they offer you their blood, their goods, their life, and their children, as I have before said, when the necessity is remote; but when it approaches, they revolt. And the prince who has relied solely on their words, without making other preparations, is ruined; for the friendship which is gained by purchase and not through grandeur and nobility of spirit is bought but not secured, and at a pinch is not to be expended in your service. And men have less scruple in offending one who makes himself loved than one who makes himself feared; for love is held by a chain of obligation which, men being selfish, is broken whenever it serves their purpose; but fear is maintained by a dread of punishment which never fails.[14]

That political behavior is marked by ingratitude has already been made clear. Indeed, the mass of men will take advantage of any sign of weakness on the part of a ruler. They are all summer soldiers and sunshine patriots. So long as the going is good they will profess undying loyalty and eternal affection, but when the chips are down they will forget the vows made in a palmier day. Because of this, a ruler must treat his citizens like children: they are easily spoiled by love, and what is worse their love is a fickle one. Love, then, is no safe basis for political authority. A ruler who spares the rod will spoil his constituency. The childlike citizens, however, understand punishment. They may fear the whiphand, but they need not hate it. Fear can engender respect: it is more likely to do this than motivate hatred. And citizens can be shown that firmness will establish the conditions necessary for the bestowal of future benefits. The ruler who yearns after love will find that his tenure is dependent on the transitory emotions of his subjects. Love, after all, can turn into hate with a speed which defies comprehension. Machiavelli's cardinal precept is that the ruler must always have the upper hand; he must retain the initiative at all times. The danger with love is that it must spring from the heart of the lover: the loved one, for all his virtues is at the mercy of another's emotions. "Men love at their own free will, but fear at the will of the prince . . ." Machiavelli says. "A wise prince must rely on what is in his power and not on what is in the power of others." [15] The firm ruler

[14] *Ibid.*, p. 61.
[15] *Ibid.*, p. 63.

keeps the offensive at all times; in this way he, and not his subjects, decides which suit is to be trump.

(2) Neither cruelty nor fear should be used for their own sake. Every act, harsh or otherwise, should have a political purpose, and one of the chief areas where firmness is needed is in dealing with the internal opposition. Any political policy—indeed, any system of government—is bound to benefit one section of the community and harm another. A ruler must always keep a watchful eye on those who get the short end of the stick; this is especially the case if the aggrieved parties are accustomed to a better deal. For those who feel injured can become a major troublespot. "Whosoever undertakes to govern a people . . . without making sure of those who are opposed to this new order of things," Machiavelli says, "establishes a government of very brief duration."[16] No ruler is entitled to assume that the dissidents constitute a "loyal opposition." The happy experience of several Western democracies must not be used as a basis of generalization. In Britain and America and a handful of other countries the party which loses an election takes stock stoically and prepares for the next contest a few years hence. Most nations in the world do not have parties, do not have elections, and if they have either there is no guarantee that the victorious faction will not decide to call off all future elections and outlaw all competing parties.

Machiavelli notes that a constitutional consensus cannot be taken for granted. And he also says that political changes attendant on the inauguration of a new regime will probably give rise to an opposition movement which more likely than not will be subversive and conspiratorial. This can occur even if the reforms work in the direction of granting a larger measure of freedom to the public. For the new freedom will be thought of by many men as the new oppression. What is meat for one citizen is poison for another, and its effect can be lethal for the ruler who does not keep an eye open for the wiles of the disaffected.

> The state that becomes free makes enemies for itself, and not friends. All those become its enemies who were benefitted by the tyrannical abuses and fattened upon the treasure of the prince, and who, being now deprived of these advantages, cannot remain content, and are therefore driven to attempt to reestablish the tyranny, so as to recover their former authority and advantages.[17]

The problem of counterrevolution accompanies that of revolution throughout political theory. Machiavelli does not chide the ruler who wishes to introduce revolutionary reforms: in fact, the prince who selects the majority of the public as his constituency will probably have to engage in redistri-

---

[16] *Discourses*, p. 162.
[17] *Ibid.*, p. 161.

butive measures for their benefit. All that Machiavelli does is advise that the danger of counterrevolution may arise if such a goal is pursued, and firm action is needed to deal effectively with the problem of subversion. "Princes . . . will never be safe so long as those live whom they have deprived of their possessions . . ." he says. "Old injuries can never be cancelled by new benefits." [18]

The prescription is simple enough: kill off the leaders of the oppositions, especially those who look as if they will harbor grudges, and render the disgruntled powerless. Such stern steps are necessary to ensure the safety of the regime. Scruples in this matter will only endanger the state; in any event, they will not be reciprocated, for the opposition will take advantage of the sign of weakness and will plot to overthrow the new order. Just how many dissidents must be executed, exiled, or imprisoned, just how long the reign of terror has to last—this is not detailed. It was noted earlier that Machiavelli advised that all cruelties be committed at once so the blood may be washed away and a new era of good feeling inaugurated. But this may be easier said than done: those who profited by the old regime may be numerous and well organized. If stability is to be gained, then a period of cruelty may be the necessary price. No state, Machiavelli says, can tolerate in its midst those who plot its overthrow. A ruler must be firm if he is to have a regime to rule.

(3) A steady thread throughout the Machiavellian fabric is the dissociation of morals and politics. This is not only a methodological precept for the political theorist, but also a rule of behavior for the political practitioner. A ruler, Machiavelli says, must not be governed by conventional ethical standards, for these will be so many millstones round his neck. But he must be skillful at using the language and symbols of conventional morality, for he will find them a powerful technique. In short, a ruler must suspend his own ideas about good and evil; and, while he realizes that they have an influence on the conduct of others, he must not succumb to them himself. "It is necessary for a prince who wishes to maintain himself to learn how not to be good," Machiavelli says, "and to use this knowledge and not use it, according to the necessity of the case." [19] This does not mean that a ruler should do evil rather than good at every possible juncture. That would be a counsel of caprice, and to carry it out would be an act of personal indulgence.

Machiavelli has nothing against the rules of conventional morality as such: he simply asks that the ruler not be bound by these rules. The pursuit of conventional morality can often be effectively used as a means to a more im-

[18] *Ibid.*, p. 407.
[19] *The Prince*, p. 56.

portant end. The ruler is in trouble, however, if he regards moral strictures as ends in themselves. A time-honored moral principle is that men ought to keep their promises. Of this precept, Machiavelli takes a less than conventional view. "The experience of our times shows those princes to have done great things who have had little regard for good faith, and have been able by astuteness to confuse men's brains . . ." he says. "A prudent ruler ought not to keep faith when by so doing it would be against his interest."[20] Working on the premise that the average man expects that promises will be kept by those in authority, a ruler who breaks his word at propitious moments will be able to profit by the confusion which ensues.

This is but another instance of gaining the initiative rather than allowing it to rest with the public. But Machiavelli is saying more than this: rules of morality must be jettisoned from time to time if the prince is to govern greatly. Deception is necessary, but not simply to gratify a ruler's penchant for perversity. On the contrary, the strength of the state lies in his hands, and if he abjures morality it is to serve a higher goal. In a famous passage, Machiavelli indicates why it is important to seem to be one thing and to actually be another:

It is well to seem merciful, faithful, humane, sincere, religious, and also to be so; but you must have the mind so disposed that when it is needful to be otherwise you may be able to change to the opposite qualities. And it must be understood that a prince, and especially a new prince, cannot observe all those things which are considered good in men, being often obliged, in order to maintain the state, to act against faith, against charity, against humanity, and against religion. And, therefore, he must have a mind disposed to adapt itself according to the wind, and as the variations dictate, and, as I said before, not deviate from what is good, if possible, but be able to do evil if constrained.[21]

The key phrase here—and it is the key phrase for the whole prescriptive side of Machiavelli's theory—is, "in order to maintain the state. . . ." To achieve this end, the ruler is justified in using any and all means. This standard, traditionally called *raison d'etat*, clearly flies in the face of theories which call upon governments to promote the virtuous life.

Plato, for example, would rather talk about a nonexistent Utopia where justice reigns than talk about existing societies which foreswear moral goals. St. Augustine writes off the earthly city because it does not pursue ethical values. And St. Thomas puts on rulers the obligation of implementing the Natural Law. For all of these theorists a state which does not encourage morality is a state not worth preserving. The virtues of faith, charity, humanity, and religion are, they would say, the very reason for having a state at

[20] *Ibid.*, pp. 63, 64.
[21] *Ibid.*, p. 65.

all. Machiavelli, of course, denies all this; and his reply, if he chose to make one, would take two directions. If he wanted to defend himself, he would remind the philosophers that he said a prince should "not deviate from what is good, if possible." Immorality is not being prescribed: rulers should always do good rather than evil if the former is within the realm of possibility. If cruelty is compounded beyond a certain point, the ruler will be working against his own interests. Good ethics make for effective government most of the time, after all. What bothers the critics are the times when exceptions to this rule are called for. But it is unlike Machiavelli to take the defensive on any question. On the positive side he would reply that it is not possible for the good life—or any sort of life—to be encouraged by the state if that state is not capable of surviving. The first, and continuing, task is to create the conditions of stability: if this is not accomplished, then no political goals are possible.

Machiavelli's theory is designed as a groundwork in power for all political philosophies. Every state, no matter what ends it elects to pursue, must begin with the notion of *raison d'etat*. And it would be a mistake to construe Machiavelli's idea as running counter to other theories of politics. Plato's Guardians were supposed to promote justice, but they used deception to consolidate their power: the censored children's stories, the myth of metals, the loaded marriage lotteries were all Machiavellian devices. Aristotle's state existed to promote virtue, but he advised rulers to exaggerate and encourage public insecurity by raising the specter of external dangers to the community. St. Augustine and St. Thomas made order their first requisite, and they condoned slavery and tyranny if those institutions were necessary for stability. Machiavelli's reply, and he may be pardoned for being somewhat smug, is that all theories of politics are Machiavellian if they have any claim to being political. And he would go on to say that talk of the immorality of certain techniques is, in the final analysis, downright hypocritical. Power used to maintain the state is neither moral nor immoral: states should be judged not by the power they use to stay in business but by what they define as their business once the enterprise has been solidly established.

(4) One of the most effective techniques available to a ruler is to make use of the sentiments which already exist in the minds of the citizens. And the most deeply rooted of these are religious sentiments. A ruler should not be a religious man himself, but he can take advantage of these beliefs in others. First of all, he must act as if his only desire is to uphold the foundations of religion in society.

Princes and republics who wish to maintain themselves free from corruption must above all things preserve the purity of all religious observances, and treat them with proper reverence; for there is no greater indication of the ruin of a country than to see religion condemned. . . . It is therefore the duty of princes and heads of republics to uphold the foundations of the religion of their countries, for then it is easy to keep their people religious, and consequently well conducted and united. And therefore everything that tends to favor religion (even though it were believed to be false) should be received and availed of to strengthen it, and this should be done the more, the wiser the rulers are, and the better they understand the natural course of things.[22]

The teachings of religion, especially those of Christianity, are a great help in making men submissive citizens. Did not St. Augustine and St. Thomas counsel men to put up with oppression in this world because they would know freedom in the world to come? "Our religion," Machiavelli says, "places the supreme happiness in humility, lowliness, and a contempt for worldly objects . . . if our religion claims of us fortitude of soul, it is more to enable us to suffer than to achieve great deeds." [23] This, of course, is the ideal religious outlook for the average man: ideal, that is, from the ruler's standpoint. It is preferable that citizens not be stirred to do great deeds, especially great political deeds like upsetting constituted authority. A religion which instills the ideas of humility and lowliness is the stout ally of any ruler. But he must employ this means of control with sophistication. When subjects are exploited by their rulers to the extent that they become aware that they are being exploited, then, as Marx and Engels will point out, they tend to become cynical about religious teachings. Rather than suffering in silence, they grow caustic about pie in the sky. Religion is a convenient foundation on which to build public obedience. But Machiavelli realizes full well that man does not live by piety alone: material benefits must always accompany spiritual benefices.

The techniques which Machiavelli suggests are detailed with the assumption that the elemental needs of men must be understood. Man is not infinitely manipulatable. He is, on the contrary, a creature with likes and dislikes, habits and prejudices, of his own. If he is to be subjected to political control, then the controlling agency must meet him at least partially on his own ground. This implicit tug of war between ruler and ruled, the shifting to and fro of offensive and defensive, gives an idea of the dynamic character of Machiavelli's theory. Men are, for example, tradition-bound creatures: they prefer the old to the new, the predictable to the unpredictable. If a ruler wishes to embark on a program of change, he can surmount traditional roadblocks: to be successful he must show an awareness of the conservative sensibilities of those he governs.

[22] *Discourses*, pp. 149–150.
[23] *Ibid.*, p. 285.

He who desires or attempts to reform the government of a state, and wishes to have it accepted and capable of maintaining itself to the satisfaction of everybody, must at least retain the semblance of the old forms; so that it may seem to the people that there has been no change in the institutions, even though in fact they are entirely different from the old ones. For the great majority of mankind are satisfied with appearances, as though they were realities, and are often even more influenced by the things that seem than by those that are. . . .[24]

So long as the outward forms are left inviolate, so long as traditional symbols are not destroyed, a ruler will find that he is able to alter the substantive content of institutions. Citizens do not care so much about the wine as they do about the label on the bottle. It is possible to have courts without justice, elections without contests, and religion without theology—but the forms and symbols of courts, elections, and religion must be sustained and exalted. Men can be deceived not because they are stupid, but because they care deeply about few things and are indifferent about most. The skillful ruler begins by working in the zone of indifference. He experiments in an effort to find out whether his subjects are genuinely concerned about an institution or whether they are only attached to the symbolic veneer. If he discovers that it is the appearance men cling to, he can embark on revolutionizing the traditional structure while retaining the traditional form. Machiavelli's theory allows for radicalism—so long as it looks like conservatism.

LIBERTY, LAW, AND MAJORITY-RULE

Machiavelli, like Aristotle, focuses his attention on two forms of government: oligarchy and democracy. In both systems the underlying principle is the same: the few govern and the many are governed. What distinguishes the two is whether the effective constituency is a privileged minority or the majority of the people. Machiavelli does not assume that the minority is wise or virtuous, nor does he suppose that power in their hands will be exercised either rationally or effectively. Indeed, rulers have been advised to secure their power by using the majority as their constituency rather than depending on an ambitious and suspicious minority. Similarly, Machiavelli seems willing to give the average man his due whenever possible: no sympathy is shown towards the patronizing tone used in discussing the so-called masses. "The general prejudice against the people," Machiavelli says, "results from the fact that everybody can freely and fearlessly speak ill of them in mass, even while they are at the height of their power." [25] It is all too easy to inveigh against the mob and shudder at the hegemony of the great unwashed.

[24] *Ibid.*, p. 182.
[25] *Ibid.*, p. 266.

This has been fashionable in political theory from the time of Plato to the present day: talk about tyranny of the majority is a staple in the conversational diet of the Western world. Machiavelli is neither for nor against the majority. As a political scientist, he understands that many of the philosophies of majority tyranny are built not on political fact but on ideological ogres. What begins as a logical construct ends as an emotion-laden song of doom. The realities are different: the licentious majority seldom acts in the ways the philosophers say it will; and if it displays weaknesses, they are little different from those exhibited by privileged minorities.

If Machiavelli is not a democrat with the faith of a Rousseau, neither is he a liberal with the commitment of a Locke. The hallmark of the liberal is that he values the freedom of the individual above all other standards. While Machiavelli favors human freedom, he does not give it the priority that liberalism demands. He realizes as a matter of fact that many men do cherish liberty, and for this reason he sees fit to discuss it. For if men expect a certain condition of life, then a state must find ways of satisfying that expectation. It has already been pointed out that freedom can have different meanings for different sections of society. To a few it connotes the freedom to command, perhaps even the freedom to oppress the many. To the majority of men it signifies freedom from oppression, the freedom to know personal security.

But, no matter how the idea is construed, it is perennial in politics. "All the legislators that have given wise constitutions to republics have deemed it an essential precaution to establish a guard and a protection to liberty," Machiavelli says.[26] And the problem of liberty must be approached in much the same way as was the problem of power. With the previous question it was asked what would be the most effective constituency for a ruler to use as a basis of support. Now not rulers but lovers of freedom must make the same inquiry. "As every republic was composed of nobles and people, the question arose as to whose hands it was best to confide the protection of liberty," Machiavelli says.[27]

This discussion is best handled in terms of practical politics rather than abstract philosophy. The crucial point is what will be the consequences if one group rather than another is made the custodian of liberty: in particular, how will the privileged minority react if this responsibility is handed over to the majority? Neither majority nor minority stewardship is an unmixed blessing in this area, but the minority can cause more trouble if it is not allowed jurisdiction.

[26] *Ibid.*, p. 121.
[27] *Ibid.*

There are strong reasons in favor of each, but, to judge by the results, we must incline in favor of the nobles. . . . The preference given to the nobility, as guardians of public liberty, has two advantages: the first, to yield something to the ambition of those who, being more engaged in the management of public affairs, find, so to say, in the weapon which the office places in their hands, a means of power that satisfies them; the other, to deprive the restless spirit of the masses of an authority calculated from its very nature to produce trouble and dissensions, and apt to drive the nobles to some act of desperation, which in time may cause the greatest misfortunes.[28]

The majority, on the whole, are more tolerant; they are more willing to see this power in the hands of the minority than the latter are prepared to be ruled by the majority. The danger to be avoided, in Machiavelli's eyes, is not majority tyranny but minority counterrevolution brought on by the fear of majority tyranny. If, therefore, the minority is allowed its way, its fears will vanish and, in addition, responsibilities of office will temper their ambitions. This analysis follows from the fact that the kind of freedoms after which privileged minorities seek can easily be frustrated by a public which cannot comprehend the more sophisticated expectations held by the smaller group. The minority, that is, has more to lose than the majority: they feel more intensely about their freedom as a condition for the good life as they define it. This intensity of feeling, then, would lead them to react more violently were they to be deprived of their liberty. Machiavelli is not saying that the privileged few are the best defenders of freedom; he is simply pointing out that society will be disrupted if they are not allowed their head.

Indeed, Machiavelli paints no flattering portrait of those whom birth or talent have raised to privileged positions. He is as aware of their frailties as he is of the virtues in the average man. "Individual men, and especially princes, may be charged with the same defects of which writers accuse the people," he says. "For whoever is not controlled by laws will commit the same errors as an unbridled multitude." [29] Machiavelli has no preconceived preference for either majority or minority rule. On the contrary, like Aristotle, he is impressed with the need for rule of law. Whichever men govern, they must be controlled by legal means which are beyond the manipulation of any particular individuals or groups. The intimation of constitutionalism here expands somewhat on the Aristotelian analysis. If a ruling majority can be corrupted, so can a ruling minority. All men are frail, and all forms of government need legal restraints on their rulers if both liberty and stability are to be secured.

[28] *Ibid.*, pp. 121–122.
[29] *Ibid.*, p. 261.

The tone which Machiavelli uses in *The Discourses* is quite different from that employed in *The Prince.*

The character of the people is not to be blamed any more than that of princes, for both alike are liable to err when they are without any control. . . . Contrary to the general opinion, then, which maintains that the people, when they govern, are inconsistent, unstable, and ungrateful I conclude and affirm that these defects are not more natural to the people than they are to princes. To charge the people and princes equally with them may be the truth, but to except princes from them would be a great mistake. For a people that governs and is well regulated by laws will be stable, prudent, and grateful, as much so, and even more, according to my opinion, than a prince, although he be esteemed wise; and, on the other hand, a prince, freed from the restraints of the law, will be more ungrateful, inconstant, and imprudent than a people similarly situated. The difference in their conduct is not due to any difference in their nature (for that is the same, and if there be any great difference for good, it is on the side of the people); but to the greater or less respect they have for the laws under which they respectively live.[30]

Democracy on the whole is preferable to oligarchy, and the overriding condition of stable government is that the rule of law be sovereign. This was, of course, Aristotle's prescription. To talk of government of laws and not of men is not as unrealistic as may appear at first glance. To be sure, men make laws, men administer laws, and men interpret laws: the human factor is obviously present at all times. Yet laws come to have a power of their own which is independent of the men who make, administer, and interpret them. This is especially true if the legislative, executive, and judicial functions are not lodged in the same agency: rules are the product of many hands and many minds, if the legislative process has various way stations to pass in the governmental structure. The consequence, only implied by Machiavelli, is that obedience to law is more than simply obedience to the men who contribute to its passage. Because law is the resultant of settled procedures, because it requires the approval of several institutions, because it is developed over time—for these reasons a piece of paper called a law takes on an authority of its own. If citizens feel obliged to obey these pieces of paper, Machiavelli says, government will have a stable foundation. And the case seems to be that the majority which consists of average citizens can more easily be brought to respect the authority of law than can a privileged minority. The latter, perhaps, consider themselves too worldly to be deceived by the legal mystique, or they may have designs on using the law to their own advantage by endowing their special interests with official authority. Whatever the reason, Machiavelli feels that rule of law fares better in a democratic political environment.

And he goes even further in modifying the strictures laid down in *The*

[30] *Ibid.,* pp. 262–263.

Prince. If the average man does not have the ability to hold the reins of power himself, average men taken as an aggregate demonstrate rational qualities in selecting their rulers and in judging political policy. Indeed, they do better at this than members of a privileged minority. "The people," Machiavelli says, "show more wisdom in their selection than princes." [31] There is no claim being made that the public is well informed or even particularly intelligent about political matters, but citizens do form general impressions about the quality of their leaders, and on the whole their impressions make good sense. All of the people cannot be fooled all of the time, and the average voter can usually sense if a candidate is a fool or a knave. "In the election of their magistrates, they make far better choices than princes," Machiavelli says, "and no people will ever be persuaded to elect a man of infamous character and corrupt habits to any post of dignity." [32] And this rational behavior extends to policies as well as personnel:

> As to the people's capacity of judging of things, it is exceedingly rare that, when they hear two orators of equal talents advocate different measures, they do not decide in favor of the best of the two; which proves their ability to discern the truth of what they hear. And if occasionally they are misled in matters involving questions of courage or seeming utility, so is a prince also many times misled by his own passions, which are much greater than those of the people.[33]

Can these propositions be squared with Machiavelli's previous assertions that the people are deceived by appearances, stupefied by religion, and susceptible to manipulative control? The answer, first of all, is that these strictures apply to all men equally: to members of privileged minorities as well as to the man in the street. But the average citizen has an advantage here over his supposedly superior cousin, for his wants are simple and they can be satisfied without elaborate programs. This means that the average man need only express his wants in a vague way, and he is readily capable of knowing if they are being attended to. Because of this, rationality comes rather easily: the simpler the demands, the simpler they are to fulfill. Privileged minorities, on the other hand, suffer many disabilities. For one thing, their wants are diffuse and complex, and it is far harder to devise policies to secure their attainment. The more sophisticated the conception, the more apt is its achievement to be frustrated. Furthermore, minorities tend to be creatures of vested interests and hence are blinded to reason: their perceptions are distorted by ambition, greed, and a whole host of irrational forces. Machiavelli, then, is prepared to make the general public the repository of a collective

[31] *Ibid.,* p. 509.
[32] *Ibid.,* p. 264.
[33] *Ibid.,* pp. 263–264.

rationality. But this is less a paean of praise to popular virtues than it is a lecture on the limitations of the privileged few.

For Machiavelli does not deify democracy. For all their inherent rationality, the people tend to let their emotions get the upper hand. They will, for example, develop an exaggerated idea of national power and overcommit their states' resources. "There is no easier way to ruin a republic, where the people have power, than to involve them in daring enterprises," Machiavelli says. "For where the people have influence they will always be ready to engage in them, and no contrary opinion will prevent them." [34] It has been remarked that democracies are the most warlike governments, and there is a grain of truth in this idea. If the man-in-the-street is told that he is good enough to select his own rulers and make public policy, he may soon conclude that he and his country have the right to dictate to other nations the virtues of the democratic way of life. Democracy, in a word, tends to ego-inflation, and this tendency can have dire consequences for a state. For the average citizen seldom stops to ask if his country has the resources which would be necessary to make the world over in its image. A related drawback of majority rule is that the arrogance of the average man can weaken political leadership. Having been informed that the institution of one-man-one-vote rests on the assumption that any one man is as good as any other man, the citizen soon begins to act on this flattering theory. The frequent result is that a premium is put on mediocrity in high places; this is especially the case when a nation is resting on its laurels. "Men of rare and extraordinary merit are neglected by republics in times of peace and tranquillity . . ." Machiavelli says. "There are always in such times many other citizens, who want to be, not only their equals, but their superiors." [35]

The tendency for what starts as equality to end as leveling is one of the chief criticisms of democracy. Plato remarked on it, and Tocqueville and Mill will put it at the center of their theories. Whether this problem rises usually in tranquil times, as Machiavelli says, or whether it is a permanent feature of majority rule will have to be discussed at a later time. Finally, Machiavelli returns to speculate on the basic conditions which are required if democracy is not to be self-defeating. The vast majority of mankind has lived in servitude since the dawn of history. It would be a great mistake to attribute to any general public qualities which are only developed after centuries of experimentation and growth. The abilities to understand the processes of government and to appreciate the values of freedom are not nurtured overnight. A people recently liberated from the heavy yoke of op-

[34] *Ibid.*, p. 248.
[35] *Ibid.*, p. 462.

pressive rule cannot be assumed to have the qualities necessary for self-government. Citizens, Machiavelli says, must learn to govern themselves in a way which is bound to be slow and painful.

A people may well be compared to some wild animal, which (although by nature ferocious and savage) has been as it were subdued by having been always kept imprisoned and in servitude, and being let out into the open fields, not knowing how to provide food and shelter for itself, becomes an easy prey to the first one who attempts to chain it up again. The same thing happens to a people that has not been accustomed to self-government; for, ignorant of all public affairs, of all means of defense or offense, neither knowing the princes nor being known by them, it soon relapses under a yoke, oftentimes much heavier than the one which it had but just shaken off.[36]

If there is much to be said for democracy, these sentiments must not be applied indiscriminately. Only in countries which have reached a certain stage of political maturity will the majority be an effective constituency for stable government. A people which has recently deposed a tyrannical regime will not know how to use its new-found freedom. In the ensuing chaos, as St. Thomas took pains to point out, a new tyrant will rise to take advantage of the situation. Few revolutions which are fought under the banner of democracy actually lead to the democratic goal. If majority rule is to be effective and stable rule as well, then time and experience are necessary conditions.

The virtues of democratic government will come into their own only if the state has strong leadership. The majority may form the principal constituency, but they must be led. The analysis of power and the discussion of democracy are in agreement here. In the final resort, we must return to the man whose task it is to hold the state together and guide its fortunes. "A sagacious legislator of a republic, therefore, whose object is to promote the public good, and not his private interests," Machiavelli says, ". . . should concentrate all authority in himself." [37] The man who leads the people has more to do than find out where they want to go: he must show them how to get there. And if what they want calls for firm and determined action, then he must be willing to take such steps. If citizens are left to govern themselves, the nation will be a ship without a rudder, and it will not take much of a storm to bring it to grief. But political survival, Machiavelli says, requires more than a strong leader at the helm. Stability comes only with material prosperity and the spirit of progress. And these, in turn, are the products of a free society. "Only those cities and countries that are free can achieve greatness," he says.[38] Does this mean that

[36] *Ibid.*, pp. 160–161.
[37] *Ibid.*, p. 138.
[38] *Ibid.*, p. 287.

a state which oppresses its citizens can never rise to greatness? This would appear to be Machiavelli's final judgment. And how far this is a conclusion derived from the rigorous use of the scientific method, and how far Machiavelli has allowed his notion of the ideal to cloud his vision of the real—that decision must rest with each reader.

LIONS AND FOXES

By this time it should be obvious that Machiavelli's writings are more than handbooks for princes. While political skill and political success are themes which are returned to again and again, it is easy to see that Machiavelli is at work on a theory of politics which is far from narrow in its dimensions. He now proceeds on an even grander scale, for he seeks to underpin his political theory with a conception of history and a psychological system which will give meaning to the previous discussions.

Plato's theory of history was a downward-sloping one: Utopia would degenerate in oligarchy, and that into democracy, and that into tyranny. Machiavelli's, as will be seen, is more a cyclical theory: change moves neither up nor down, but to and fro between different governmental systems. If Machiavelli does not predict steady degeneration, at the same time he is not willing to proclaim the march of progress. Nor is there a moving spirit behind the course of events: God is not invoked as a political participant, and no Platonic Form called History proceeds relentlessly with its own design. Yet a theory of historical change there must be. For Machiavelli has run the risk of allowing a ruler to believe that if he is clever enough and follows all the strictures in the handbooks, he will be able to handle any and all situations; he may, indeed, get the impression that he can meet all challenges with an appropriate response and consequently hold power indefinitely. Actually, Machiavelli is keenly aware of human limitations. There comes a time when even the most skillful of rulers finds himself out of a job, for the game of politics is played in an arena where the rules are constantly changing. Social and psychological variables are forever permuting and combining in new and unforeseen ways. The upshot is that the realm of certainty—the sphere of behavior which can be foreseen and mastered by even a very clever ruler—is often uncomfortably small. This expanse of the political unknown is governed, says Machiavelli, waxing metaphorical, by Dame Fortune. Rulers may use their power and authority to propose: but she often takes it on herself to dispose. Men are not able to predict or control circumstances as they conspire to combine in their fortuitous fashion. Dame Fortune's work may be understood, at least in a general way, but it cannot be made subservient to human authority.

This, of course, brings Machiavelli to the puzzle of free will vs. determinism raised by the theologians. His full statement deserves attention.

It is not unknown to me how many have been and are of the opinion that worldly events are so governed by Fortune and by God, that men cannot by their prudence change them, and that on the contrary there is no remedy whatever, and for this they may judge it to be useless to toil much about them, but let things be ruled by chance. This opinion has been more held in our day, from the great changes that have been seen, and are daily seen, beyond every human conjecture. When I think about them, at times I am partly inclined to share this opinion.

Nevertheless, that our free will may not be altogether extinguished, I think that it may be true that Fortune is the ruler of half our actions, but that she allows the other half or thereabouts to be governed by us.

I would compare her to an impetuous river that, when turbulent, inundates the plains, casts down trees and buildings, removes earth from this side and places it on the other; everyone flees before it, and everything yields to its fury without being able to oppose it; and yet though it is of such a kind, still when it is quiet, men can make provisions against it by dykes and banks, so that when it rises it will either go into a canal or its rush will not be so wild and dangerous. So it is with Fortune, which shows her power where no measures have been taken to resist her, and directs her fury where she knows that no dykes or barriers have been made to hold her.[39]

This is a middle-of-the-road position. Machiavelli grants a larger role to the free will of men than does St. Augustine or St. Thomas. Nevertheless, men are no more than dyke-builders, and there will come a time when Fortune's impetuous flood will refuse to be held by man-made barriers. Men ought to work to arrest the tide of events, for the task need not always be hopeless. Machiavelli makes no plea for fatalism, for he knows that an area of human freedom can be developed: if he did not believe this, he would not have written his books in an effort to influence men of power. The admonition, then, is to understand as best we can the work of Fortune: to use our power to order events where we can and to be philosophical about the circumstances we cannot control.

The political applications of this view of history follow readily. Men are creatures of the times in which they live. They can control the destinies of states and their fellow citizens if they attune their policies to the conditions of society and the human personality with which their moment in history confronts them. "Men in their conduct, and especially in their most prominent actions, should well consider and conform to the times in which they live," Machiavelli says. "And those who, from an evil choice or from natural inclination, do not conform to the times in which they live, will in most instances live unhappily, and their undertakings will come to a bad end."[40] The

---

[39] *The Prince*, p. 91.
[40] *Discourses*, p. 439.

prescription, of course, is that rulers must bend their efforts to be both sociologists and social psychologists—to understand the social and psychological needs of a population is imperative, if power is to be used effectively. Yet Machiavelli is not sanguine about the ability of rulers to master the realities of their time. His warning that knowledge is power will fall on the deaf ears of men who cannot or will not hear. At no time has Machiavelli suggested that rulers are men of superior knowledge or intelligence to the general run of mankind.[41] They have an aptitude for power and possess organizational skills, but these are specialized talents in the final analysis, and they do not imply a general understanding of social processes. Machiavelli, like Plato, is forced to conclude that in existing societies power and rationality are divorced: men of reason and men of power stand apart from each other, and neither benefits by the aid the other might give him.

Nevertheless, Machiavelli turns to his discussion of political psychology with the brave hope that it may enlighten men of power. There are, in his psychology, two dominant personality types. These may be called the Lions and the Foxes. Different sets of social and political conditions call for the talents of different types of personalities: in one period one type will be demanded; at another a different type will be called for. The ideal ruler will be aware of this fact, and he will be adept at changing his personality to suit the occasion.

> You must know, then, that there are two methods of fighting, the one by law, the other by force: the first method is that of men, the second of beasts; but as the first method is often insufficient, one must have recourse to the second. It is therefore necessary for a prince to know well how to use both the beast and the man. . . .
> A prince being thus obliged to know well how to act as a beast must imitate the Fox and the Lion, for the Lion cannot protect himself from traps, and the Fox cannot defend himself from wolves. One must therefore be a Fox to recognize traps, and a Lion to frighten wolves.[42]

To talk of men and beasts, of Lions and Foxes—this is the language of poetry rather than of scientific psychology. Yet it is interesting to note how useful these poetic notions can be and how political theory has relied on them. A Lion, we may assume, lives by force; this may be brute force or, alternatively, the force of his personality. He attracts a following by the sheer impact of his

---

[41] Vilfredo Pareto, who carries the Machiavellian tradition into the twentieth century, makes this point explicit: "Ruling classes, like any other social groups, perform both logical and non-logical actions, and the chief element in what happens is in fact the order or system, not the conscious will of individuals . . ." (*The Mind and Society*, para. 2254). That Pareto chooses to talk in terms of classes and groups rather than individuals is something which will be commented on later in this chapter.

[42] *The Prince*, p. 64.

person; and in times when men need a striking figure behind whom they can rally, a Lion will ascend to power. A Fox, on the other hand, lives by his wits. He can devise the programs and policies which, because they are designed and administered efficiently, provide for the detailed needs of a society. There are times when men do not feel that they need an impressive personality to lead them; they are more concerned with efficient administration and honest government. A Fox can be an anonymous ruler: he may be no more than a name or a title to his subjects. In addition, a Fox is usually adept at bureaucratic in-fighting: he knows how to succeed in the power struggle of officialdom by organizing factions and monopolizing resources. Machiavelli understands that the qualities which make for Lions and Foxes are at opposite ends of the personality pole. But he understands no less well that political conditions are so variable that one week the public will call for a Lion and the next will want a Fox. If a ruler wants to stay in power for more than one week, he must have a dual personality. "Those of our princes who have held their possessions for many years, must not accuse Fortune for having lost them, but rather their own remissness." [43]

How many rulers can carry off such an act? Machiavelli's whole tone conveys the impression that few men have the ability to shift psychological gears when the occasion demands—or even to know that the time for such a shift has arrived. Such rulers may be remiss, but their failings are so judged because Machiavelli is holding up a high standard. "One sees a certain prince today fortunate and tomorrow ruined, without seeing that he has changed in character . . ." Machiavelli says. "The prince who bases himself entirely on Fortune is ruined when Fortune changes." [44] Men, then, do not change their character: Lions and Foxes, no less than leopards, seem incapable of changing their spots. Machiavelli has done his duty: he has told rulers what they must do if they are to ride with Dame Fortune. That this advice is not heeded is probably not a surprise to Machiavelli. "I conclude, then, that Fortune varying and men remaining fixed in their ways, they are successful so long as these ways conform to circumstances, but when they are opposed then they are unsuccessful." [45]

Machiavelli's polarized psychology has enough truth in it, oversimplified though it may be, to warrant serious attention from students of politics. The notions of the Lion and the Fox denote tendencies in individuals: no one person is wholly a Lion or wholly a Fox, and most are neither. It is certainly clear that varying circumstances both call for and throw up different person-

[43] *Ibid.*, p. 90.
[44] *Ibid.*, p. 92.
[45] *Ibid.*, p. 94.

ality types. This is best illustrated in the case of revolutions. To organize a revolution—to mobilize a movement, to stir men to action, to perpetrate the violent overthrow of the existing regime—this clearly calls for a Lion in the position of leadership. But once the revolution has succeeded and the new order must face the task of feeding the population, administering economic policy, and providing everyday services—then a Fox is needed. Machiavelli's theory is best tested at the point when the violence has subsided and the new state must be put on the tracks: is the Lion of the barricades able to assume the Foxlike responsibilities which must be shouldered in the new era? A few Lions can make the shift—although it may be questioned if they were really Lions even in the revolutionary era—but many will not or cannot.[46] Indeed, it is probably easier for a Fox, by using the resources of mass media and public relations, to create a Lionlike image of himself in the public's mind than it is for a Lion to learn the Foxlike skills of administration. Yet in times of serious change, public relations is not enough: if the public wanted a Lion, they will not settle for a glossed-over Fox. This was clearly the fate of Herbert Hoover: a skilled administrator, who could not demonstrate the personal leadership which the American electorate of 1932 both wanted and needed. Not only, Machiavelli would say, was Hoover wrong for his time, but it was also likely that Fortune would pick his successor and thrust greatness upon him. "It certainly is the course of Fortune, when she wishes to effect some great result, to select for her instrument a man of such spirit and ability that he will recognize the opportunity which is afforded him." [47] If the times present a challenge, Machiavelli is saying, they will also cast to the top a man capable of meeting that challenge. Dame Fortune gives no guarantee that she will always bring forward an emissary to end a depression or win a war. But Machiavelli bids us be optimistic: "Not knowing the aims of Fortune, which she pursues by dark and devious ways, men should always be hopeful, and never yield to despair." [48]

If we put together Machiavelli's historical and psychological theories, we emerge with a systematic explanation of political change. But it is in order to at least remark on what is being done when these two conceptions are synthesized. For Machiavelli's theory of history and his theory of personality are

---

[46] Harold Lasswell, another modern Machiavellian, talks of "agitators" and "administrators" as political personality types. In his scheme, such men as John Cobden and V. I. Lenin are set down as examples of individuals who could fill both roles. See *Psychopathology and Politics*, in *The Political Writings of Harold Lasswell* (Glencoe: Free Press, 1951), p. 54. James Burns says that Franklin Roosevelt also had such a dual personality. *FDR: The Lion and the Fox* (New York: Harcourt, Brace, 1956), *passim*. While Lenin and Roosevelt were plainly Lions, they were rather subdued compared with populist leaders like Huey Long or William Jennings Bryan.

[47] *Discourses*, p. 382.

[48] *Ibid.*, p. 383.

both determinist theories. In the former it is the "conditions of the times"— brought into being by Dame Fortune—which govern the political arrangements that a society will have. Societies are constantly changing, although the tempo will vary according to time and place. New social conditions arise and bring with them now political problems, which in turn call for new forms of leadership. These imperatives of history are unrelenting: the dynamic of change which Machiavelli postulates has some of the features of Hegel's dialectic in it. Machiavelli does not commit himself on what causes change; he does not, like Marx, ascribe it to economic and technological developments. Questions of causation must be left in the hands of Fortune—the female counterpart of St. Augustine's and St. Thomas' God. The theory of personality is also determinist. Virtually all rulers are either Lions or Foxes, and they are consequently prisoners of their own psychological make-up. Individual character structure is on the whole extremely inflexible. Machiavelli's psychological analysis is not a far remove from Freud's; however, Machiavelli does not speculate on the forces which make one man a Lion and another a Fox. He does not discuss heredity or social conditioning, parental influences, or infantile sexuality. Here, too, unknown factors can be ascribed to Fortune. A theory which seeks to synthesize two determinisms does not come up with a double determinism; on the contrary, irresistible force meets immovable object, and each must necessarily give way somewhat if both are to live in the same theory. For the individual ruler the consequence is that his freedom of action is curtailed both from without and from within. Social and historical conditions will determine if his type of skills are needed at this moment of time, and his own personality structure will govern whether he can do the job which is called for. The key to success is obvious: be born with the right character at the right period in history. If an individual is a Lion, he must pray that Fortune will decree that society will need forceful and highly personal leadership. Only at such a juncture will Lionlike talents be appreciated. If a Lion is born into an age made for Foxes, he had better take up gardening and hope that a change of wind will come in his lifetime. Machiavelli has already shown rulers how they may exercise power in the area of freedom open to them; it is only fair to also indicate what are the boundaries which limit human action.

Political change proceeds through the conjunction of historical and psychological forces. All societies will experience a circulation of rulers. In one epoch Lions will govern and Foxes will stand in the wings; in the next, Foxes will supplant Lions. The political elite consists of all those—both Lions and Foxes—who have an aptitude for exercising power. At one time the Lions' techniques will be needed, and they will be the governing elite; at the next the Foxes' skills will be wanted, and the Lions will be thrust off the stage into the nongoverning elite.[49] The circulation can be fast or slow, peaceful or violent. It may be achieved by elections or by revolution or by some intermediate method. It should also be made clear that the circulation of rulers is inevitable and never-ending; it is a law of history supported by a law of psychology. It is not legitimate to assume, for example, that there may emerge Foxes who are clever enough to anticipate and cope with all problems which may arise in the body politic. There are limits on what can be achieved by even the most adroit of administrators. For the man-in-the-street is a creature of variable emotion, and even the citizens of advanced societies arrive at a point when they want a personality rather than a policy. The great catalyst for the circulation is public opinion—usually a vague and often an unarticulated opinion, but one which knows what it wants from government and knows whether it is getting it.

Machiavelli does not do more than hint at his theory of circulation. He does not indicate what social conditions call for what kind of ruling personality, nor does he say, for example, that democracies demand Lions and oligarchies prefer Foxes.[50] And the relation of public opinion to this whole idea must be inferred by the reader. Other writers—notably Hegel and Marx—will enunciate theories of history, but none of them go into the psychological aspect in the way that Machiavelli does. If his tale of Lions and Foxes seems too simple an explanation of personality and rulership, it nevertheless remains to be said that few theorists have been able to improve on his rudimentary first steps.

THE MEANING OF ELITE RULE

In company with St. Thomas and Hobbes, his predecessor and successor on these pages, Machiavelli puts a single ruler at the center of the political process. The urge to centralize the ultimate source of authority, either for ethical or practical reasons, is an understandable one. At the same time it is clear that no one man can govern effectively unless he has an organization at his disposal. Plato's Guardian class was such a political machine, and it was so well organized that its creator saw no need to put a leader at its head. It is,

[49] The idea of circulation of elites is developed in all its fullness by Pareto, *op. cit.*, para. 2179.

[50] Max Weber's analysis of the kinds of social structure which accompany varying types of authority is the classic in this field. His comparison of "charismatic" and "bureaucratic" authority helps to complete the approach which Machiavelli employs. See *From Max Weber* (New York: Oxford University Press, 1946), edited and translated by H. H. Gerth and C. Wright Mills, pp. 196–252.

then, a simple fact of political life that one man cannot possibly reach—and therefore cannot control—every citizen in a society. He must have a hierarchy of disciplined and loyal followers—members of a governmental or party structure—who will see that his policies are actually carried out at the grass-roots level. If organization solves important problems, it creates them too. Near the top of the structure must be lieutenants who are given both discretion and responsibility. These men are potential rivals for the ruler's job if they are persons of talent; if they are yes-men or time-servers, then they impair the efficiency of the organization.

Machiavelli is mistrustful of political organizations, and he seems to prefer a ruler who stands by himself. This man will reach the public by identifying his personality with the government in the mind of every citizen. "A wise prince," he says, "will seek means by which his subjects will always and in every possible condition of things have need of his government, and then they will always be faithful to him." [51] A Lion may be able at the height of his popularity to so project an image of himself to the public at large. But can a Fox establish this identification and secure continued obedience on its basis? Machiavelli does not discuss these matters, and they form a major gap not only in his theory but in most of those we consider. No longer is the study of organization confined to ward bosses, and no longer does the study of bureaucracy bring to mind only civil servants wrapped in red tape. In the modern world, where advanced technology and social interdependence are the rule, questions of organizational structure become as important as the traditional substance of political theory. For the organizational life and the bureaucratic personality are realities which shape our behavior as much as if not more than the forces we usually study.

Now is the time to return to certain questions about the elite which were raised early in this chapter. Machiavelli's theory does not rely on a ruling class, and now it would appear that he does not talk of a ruling elite either. Nowhere is there a discussion of a coherent group of men who hold or aspire to hold political power in society. Only once does he come close to talking about an organized group. "In every republic there are two parties," he says, "that of the nobles and that of the people." [52] But the structure and functioning of the nobles' party is never examined, and it would be wrong anyway to equate it with a political elite. On the contrary, the point about elite rule in Machiavelli's theory is that it describes a process rather than an institution. That is, it tells us that political power tends to gravitate to men of talent, that effective government calls for special skills. The use of the elite notion, then,

[51] *The Prince*, p. 39.
[52] *Discourses*, p. 119.

does not suggest that the men who possess these superior talents join together in an organized group. Men with such aptitudes may be widely scattered, of varying persuasions, and even in conflict with each other.[53] Machiavelli does not try to show that there is an organized elite. What he does suggest is that there are in any society a group of elite individuals: various men who gain positions of power not because of their birth and breeding but because of their possession of talent. The elite idea, therefore, describes a process of selection and recruitment. And it is a democratic process in the special sense that social and family origins are rendered irrelevant: men are elevated for what they can do rather than because of who their parents are. The development of a democratic elite process presupposes, of course, equality of opportunity for all persons of talent to ascend to positions of power. This theme, too, is not elaborated upon by Machiavelli, but both Burke and Tocqueville will pursue it at a later stage.

There is a second feature to the elite theory which has even more important implications for political theory, especially democratic theory. In Machiavelli's writing the center of the political stage is dominated by a perpetual circulation of elite rulers. From this emphasis there arises the strong presumption that the exchange of power from elite to elite is the only thing which counts in the political process. What role, then, is to be ascribed to the great mass of men who never attain to membership in the elite? Machiavelli, at first glance, seems not neglectful of the man-in-the-street. He warns rulers never to forget the power which inheres in the public, and he discusses such matters as democratic government, popular elections, and the various ways in which the ruled influence those who rule them. Nevertheless, in the final analysis any weight assigned to these factors does not outweigh Machiavelli's initial premise: it is an elite which rules; the people never rule themselves. No matter how many outward forms of democracy are created, no matter how much lip service is paid to the public's power, self-government remains an impossibility. One way to put Machiavelli's comments on both democracy and popular consent in their proper perspective is to use an analogy, one that is not as farfetched as might first appear. The relation between the ruler and citizens in a state may be compared with that between a warden and convicts in a prison. The warden, to begin with, does not have complete freedom of action: on the contrary, he has undertaken to do a job, and he must carry out the functions

[53] Some writers have held that men who hold seats of power in dominant institutions in society are bound to develop a "community of interest" even if they never come together to decide on common policies in an organized way. Two major books which present this idea in a persuasive way are C. Wright Mills, *The Power Elite* (New York: Oxford University Press, 1956) and Floyd Hunter, *Top Leadership U.S.A.* (Chapel Hill: University of North Carolina Press, 1959).

which are required of his office. He must make sure that the convicts are fed and clothed, that they receive adequate exercise and recreation, and that they are allowed the informal and minor infractions of official regulations which make life bearable in a prison. So long as the warden provides for these material and psychological needs, the convicts will be reasonably content and will accept his authority. A skilled and sympathetic warden, furthermore, will use the resources at his disposal to the utmost of his ability and he need not be in constant fear of a rebellion by the prisoners. However if he neglects their needs—if he, for example, cracks down too hard and no longer winks at the small freedoms which are in circumvention of regulations—the convict population may express its discontent through action. There may be hunger strikes, bedlam in the cell blocks, or a group of prisoners may even seize the warden and hold him as hostage in their demand for better conditions.[54] And even if there is no willful neglect on the warden's part, such factors as a heat spell or overcrowded conditions which are beyond his control may make the convicts unhappy and lead them to give violent vent to their dissatisfaction. Even if the state troopers are at hand to put down a riot from the outside, it may be too late so far as the safety of the warden is concerned. In one sense, to draw this analogy to a close, a prison is a "democracy": the effective authority of the warden is based not on the revolvers of the prison guards but on the "consent" of the convicts. But if we succumb to the temptation to call a prison "democratic" in any sense at all, we are making the mistake of taking one element in the democratic process and giving that factor a far greater importance than it warrants.

The prison analogy, in short, ought to show that democracy should not be sold too cheaply. If too low a standard is set for democratic performance, then democracy may be discovered not only in prisons but in totalitarian countries, slave camps, and even zoos. And it should be clear by now that the level of "democracy"—government by the governed or by the "consent" of the governed—which Machiavelli talks about is a rather primitive one. Rulers ascend to power and are deposed, but it is not because a self-governing public has first given and then withdrawn its consent on any grounds which could be called rational. What occurs, rather, is that there comes about an alteration in the condition of society, a change developing independently of political policies and beyond the control of either citizens or rulers. This change arouses in men new needs and new expectations which they feel acutely but do not fully understand. They sense that it is time for a shift in those who rule them,

---

[54] See Gresham M. Sykes, *The Society of Captives: A Study of a Maximum Security Prison* (Princeton: Princeton University Press, 1958), for an excellent analysis of the "politics" of prison life.

and they will follow an emerging leader who seems to them to symbolize the new order of things.[55] But this is more an unconscious historical process than it is a conscious choice from among alternatives on the part of individual citizens. Consent, if it is to be part of the democratic process, must be a far more sophisticated process than Machiavelli makes out. Locke, Rousseau, and Mill will show how institutionalized participation and rational discussion are needed if citizens are to approach self-government. Machiavelli did not claim to be writing a democratic theory; if he does suggest that governments are based on the "consent" of the governed, this thought is advanced at such a primitive level that its democratic content is nonexistent.

The meaning of elite rule is a negation of democracy. It does not matter what ideological label is attached to a governmental system: "democracy" and oligarchy are sisters under the skin. It does not matter which personality types hold political power: the differences between Lions and Foxes are hidden by the fact that both stand apart from the mass of men. The man-in-the-street will never and can never be an effective political participant. He is doomed to be a follower throughout history: to have policy made for him but not by him. He stands in the valley and watches Lions and Foxes throw thunderbolts at each other in their competition to capture the seat of government. He is a passive spectator, or at best an instrument activated by others for their own ends. In "democratic" or revolutionary epochs the citizen may find himself approached by Lions, who will use the rhetoric of equality and self-government in their drive to enlist popular support as a means of unseating the ruling Foxes. But if the public sides with the Lions and carries them to victory, it will soon discover—if it is interested in making such a discovery—that the new state is no more democratic than the previous regime. The personnel at the summit have changed, but the structure of power remains oligarchical as always; the "democrats" might conquer, but not democracy, which perishes at the moment of its adherents' triumph.[56] Democracy is a slogan—a word men can utter but a process they can never practice. The

---

[55] See Gaetano Mosca: "When we say that the voters 'choose' their representatives, we are using a language that is very inexact. The truth is that the representative *has himself* elected by the voters. . . ." *The Ruling Class* (New York: McGraw-Hill, 1939), edited by Arthur Livingston, and translated by Hannah D. Kahn, p. 154.

[56] This proposition is a paraphrase of Robert Michels, who develops Machiavelli's ideas into a theory he calls the Iron Law of Oligarchy. "The majority of human beings, in a condition of eternal tutelage, are predestined by tragic necessity to submit to the dominion of a small minority," Michels says. "Leadership is a necessary phenomenon in every form of social life. Consequently it is not the task of science to inquire whether this phenomenon is good or evil, or predominantly one or the other. But there is great scientific value in the demonstration that every system of leadership is incompatible with the most essential postulates of democracy." *Political Parties* (Glencoe: Free Press, 1949), pp. 390, 400.

man in the street may eventually derive both material and spiritual benefits as the elites circulate above his head. The competition between Lions and Foxes is bound to produce an ameliorative residue for the community as a whole. And these benefits should never be underrated: freedom of speech, intellectual liberty, religious toleration, economic prosperity, and technological progress. But these symbols of the good life should not be equated with democracy, to do that is to succumb to rhetoric which blinds men to the realities of power.

6.
Thomas Hobbes

THE MAN AND HIS TIMES

Thomas Hobbes was born in Malmesbury in 1588, the son of an Anglican clergyman. The family was not well-to-do, and a prosperous relative intervened to send him to Oxford at the age of fifteen. Hobbes was an extraordinarily bright youth, and even while a student he perceived the limited value of the Aristotelian exercises which preoccupied his teachers. On leaving the university, he became a tutor to the children of the powerful Cavendish family, and he remained under their patronage for most of his life. This position enabled him to travel extensively on the Continent and to meet the leading scientific and literary figures of his time. Hobbes clearly traveled in powerful circles for most of his adult life, and he was sympathetic to the manner of life he encountered there. Nevertheless, his own political position was never clearly defined. On the one hand, he was unwilling to support the preferred position which the Church of England had under the Stuart monarchy, and, on the other, he was hostile to the democratic and parliamentary aspirations of the Puritans. He was consequently in trouble with both camps at one time or another, and he felt compelled to exile himself from England on two notable occasions. His books, The Citizen and Leviathan which were published in 1642 and 1651, were favorable to the idea of monarchical government, but the latter was too secular in tone to suit the Stuarts. And, no less ironically, while his writings were critical of parliamentary government, he discovered that life under Cromwell's Protectorate was not as oppressive as he might earlier have imagined. Finally, to finish a career where theory and practice never quite came into focus, Hobbes made peace with the Restoration after Charles II ascended the throne; and he died very comfortably in bed in 1679 at the age of ninety-one.

His reaction against the scholasticism of Oxford led him to the new scientific work which was emerging on the Continent. Galileo's laws of

199

motion, in particular, held a strong attraction for him, and Hobbes' political theory gives evidence of this new way of thinking. The universe is composed of atomic particles which are constantly colliding against one another, and the men who inhabit the earth may be looked upon as atoms in continuous motion. But autonomy and movement, followed by inevitable collision, result in an all-pervasive human selfishness and a feeling of fear. Men give highest priority to their personal interests, and in so doing they can never be sure that they will survive the depredations they visit on one another.

This rudimentary science of politics was apparently borne out by the actual experience of the England Hobbes knew. Since the turn of the seventeenth century the country had been without an effective government, and the authority of the Stuart monarchy was being challenged from several sides. There was widespread dissatisfaction over the privileged status of the Anglican Church, and new sects were building constituencies for themselves and demanding recognition. A commercial transformation was bringing forward new men of power who were denied the social and political preferment they thought their due. Religious and economic forces thus meshed with political demands that the King share his power with a legislative body representing at least the ascending elements in society. The civil wars which marked this period made it an era of insecurity for all Englishmen. Citizens had good reason to live in fear and at times in fear of violent death. In such a climate Hobbes' call for a strong sovereign authority was a significant one. The demand that citizens constitute and then obey a political power was an answer to the condition of near-anarchy then prevailing. While the requirements he imposed were harsh ones, Hobbes established the idea of the sovereignty of the state for once and all in political theory.

6.
Thomas Hobbes

With Hobbes there comes a new departure in political theory: the politics of individualism. This is not to say that earlier theorists did not care about the welfare of the individual citizen, nor is it to say that they failed to voice a respect for the average man. Previous theories, however, focused their main attention in other directions. Plato, St. Thomas, and Machiavelli, for example, were chiefly concerned with the strength and stability of the state. These three writers also devoted the greater part of their time to discussions of the ruling minority. Plato and Machiavelli offered detailed analyses of the social and psychological attributes of those who rule, but they had very little to say about the character of the vast majority of men and women who make up society. St. Augustine postulated the equality of all men, and St. Thomas spoke of the reason with which all men are endowed; but the first was a religious more than a political assumption, and the second a potentiality more than an actuality. Finally, all the earlier theorists joined with Aristotle in asserting that man is a social animal and that he can only find the good life in a political and social setting. In terms of emphasis, they would all be prepared to say that what is good for the community is good for the individual rather than to suggest that what is good for individuals—taken singly and then added together—comprises the common good.

If Hobbes marks a departure, it is a gradual one. Many of the ideas of his predecessors linger on in his theory: the ideas of reason, of equality, of the strong state, and even St. Thomas' conception of the Natural Law are all to be found in Hobbes' writing. What differentiates him is that he begins his political theory with a political psychology that embraces all men. When Hobbes subsumes the first eleven chapters of *Leviathan* under the heading "Of Man," he is emphasizing the fact that he is describing the general characteristics of *all* human beings. Rulers and ruled, wise and ignorant, rich and poor, all have common physiological and psychological qualities which disparities of class, status, or power do not alter. There is no specific analysis of

201

an elite or a ruling class in Hobbes' theory. The focus is on man, on the one hand, and on the state, on the other. The central theme of the theory is the relationship between the discrete individual and political authority.

THE PSYCHOLOGY OF INDIVIDUALISM

The eleven chapters entitled "Of Man" appear at first glance to be little more than a catalogue of character traits. Attitudes, emotions, and patterns of behavior are elaborately defined, described, and put into relation with each other. A sample of the human qualities which Hobbes lists gives an idea of the range and scope of his study:

Anger, blushing, covetousness, despair, envy, felicity, giddiness, hunger, impudence, joy, kindness, laughter, motion, natural lust, opinion, power, rage, speech, true religion, understanding, valor, wit.

The point for our present purposes is not whether this aggregate of attributes adds up to a scientific psychology, for Hobbes' theory of personality is designed to serve as a preface to his political theory. What is important is that he has chosen to begin in such a straightforward way with a consideration of the individual viewed apart from society. This emphasis on the individual, in short, stands for a political outlook which is bound to be reflected throughout the whole of Hobbes' theory.

Two important themes emerge from this approach. The first is the fact of human equality. It is not a theological deduction, but the observation of everyday experience, which tells us that men are equal.

Nature hath made men so equal in the faculties of the body and mind; as that though there be found one man sometimes manifestly stronger in body, or of quicker mind than another; yet when all is reckoned together, the difference between man, and man, is not so considerable, as that one man can thereupon claim to himself any benefit, to which another may not pretend.[1]

It is not just the fact that all men have souls which makes them equal. Nor is it that all men are equally significant in the eyes of God which puts them on a plane. On the contrary, it is an empirical fact that the faculties of body and mind of men are really much the same. Such differences of physique or intelligence as are occasionally displayed are, in the final analysis, unimportant. Unimportant for what? Hobbes' answer to this question is both normative and descriptive. Because men's differences are not considerable, no individual can claim preferred treatment on account of his superior brawn or brain. The benefits which men need for the good life are needed by all men: if one man

[1] *Leviathan* (Oxford: Blackwell, 1946), edited by Michael Oakeshott, p. 80.

claims preferential consideration, his demand is no more legitimate than that of any other man.

Out of this assessment clearly grows a prescriptive theory: privilege must give way to equality of treatment. On the descriptive side, Hobbes points out that the claims to superiority uttered by some men have little basis in political practice. "As to the strength of body, the weakest has strength enough to kill the strongest, either by secret machination, or by confederacy with others . . ." he says. "And as to the faculties of the mind, . . . I find yet a greater equality amongst men, than that of strength." [2] The notion that a man weighing 100 pounds can kill a man weighing 185 is not arguable. But the equality of mind of a man with an I.Q. of 100 as against a man with an 185—that is something different. Plato and St. Thomas stood firm in insisting that intelligence is not equally distributed throughout the population, and most political theorists have in one way or another accepted this assessment. Hobbes' denial is based on the facts he observes. Most men believe that they are as intelligent as those around them, and this belief is itself a social fact which will have political consequences. "For such is the nature of men, that howsoever they may acknowledge many others to be more witty, or more eloquent, or more learned," Hobbes says, "yet they will hardly believe there be many so wise as themselves; for they see their own wit at hand, and other men's at a distance." [3] The subjective belief in intellectual equality stands higher in Hobbes' theory than any objective test which might show a range of scores. For men act on their beliefs whether they be well- or ill-founded. And human action is what constitutes politics in the everyday world. Furthermore, Hobbes' man can now be seen as a proud, even arrogant, creature. He is impressed with his own excellence and, as will later be seen, has a coherent idea of his own self-interest.

A second theme arising from Hobbes' psychology is that man is an active creature. The earlier theorists, including Machiavelli, made the individual out to be, on the whole, a passive spectator of the political process. He might, in democratic or revolutionary eras, be roused to activity, but he is then manipulated by leaders who play on his sentiments and his uncomprehended needs. Hobbes, on the other hand, gives great emphasis to human activity. Man is constantly in motion, and these movements are purposive. He speaks of what he calls "voluntary" motion and its dependence on a reflecting mind: "There be in animals . . . voluntary motion, as to go, to speak, to move any of our limbs, in such manner is first fancied in our minds . . ." he says. "And because going, speaking, and the like voluntary motions, depend always upon

[2] *Ibid.*
[3] *Ibid.*

a precedent thought of whither, which way, and what, it is evident, that the imagination is the first internal beginning of all voluntary motion."[4] Once more it is in order to point out that this elementary exposition of psychology is not as important as its underlying purpose.

The ideas that man is active, that he moves voluntarily, that he has a mind of his own—these are what are significant. This conjunction of thought and action is summarized in Hobbes by the idea of *"will."* "In deliberation, the last appetite or aversion immediately adhering to the action, or to the omission thereof, is what we call the will . . ." he says. "For a voluntary act is that which proceedeth from the will, and no other."[5] Political theory cannot do without the conception of "will"; we find ourselves compelled to talk of "free will," "the general will," "the will to power," and "last will and testament" even if we are vague in our minds about the meaning of this everyday term. What "will" stands for is a mental decision to act, with the high probability that action will follow from the thought. To talk of "will" is not to talk of what men might do or think they would like to do: it is to refer to the fact that human action is actually going to be forthcoming. The "will" which each man possesses, then, is the motor which joins mind and body. Where there is a will, there is a way; and because there is a will, men must be expected to be active creatures.

The strands of equality and human pride, activity and will, come together to make man a political participant. Not just the Lions and Foxes of the political elite, but all men, seek after power. The power men desire is not necessarily over their fellow men; it is the power to make themselves secure, and that, of course, often comes to the same thing. Human activity is, then, a will to power:

> I put for a general inclination of all mankind, a perpetual and restless desire of power after power, that ceaseth only in death. And the cause of this, is not always that a man hopes for a more intensive delight than he has already attained to, or that he cannot be content with a moderate power, but because he cannot assure the power and means to live well which he hath present, without the acquisition of more.[6]

It is clear that if each man is active, each man seeks power, and each man considers himself the equal of everyone else, then not a few social problems are bound to arise. All men seek security, to live and to live well, and can only achieve this goal by commanding the power to control the environment in which they reside. If all have this desire, then not all can attain it. Nor will

[4] *Ibid.*, p. 31.
[5] *Ibid.*, p. 38.
[6] *Ibid.*, p. 64.

moderation be an effective stance, for the man who stands still will find his neighbors attaining their own security by impinging on his. Hobbes etches the human portrait this way because he is fully aware of the vexing questions which are raised when men must live in proximity to each other. And the picture of society which emerges is an aggregate of autonomous and willful individuals. There is no idea of the organic community as found in Plato and St. Thomas, where each knows his proper station and men defer to their betters. For Hobbes, society is an association, not an organism; the whole is the sum of the parts and no greater. Individuals are not lorded over by some greater-than-human authority which decrees that mortal social arrangements are part of an eternal scheme. Hobbes' individualism is empirically based and secular in orientation; as a theorist, he reports what he sees and his prescriptions are within the realm of possibility.

Men desire power, but this desire is doomed to frustration as all men pursue it simultaneously. The result is inevitably that all men are creatures of fear: they are afraid of those around them, for they know that their motivations are the same as their own. Out of this view of man and men's relations with each other, Hobbes constructs his political theory. Men want power and yet they lack power: in this all are equal. To depict this state of affairs as vividly as possible, Hobbes creates two analytical constructs: the "state of nature" and the "social contract."

THE STATE OF NATURE AND NATURAL LAW

The-state-of-nature–social-contract model is, at heart, a straightforward device. It is posited that man once lived, without society or government, in a natural state. This state of nature eventually proved to be either impossible or undesirable to maintain. Therefore, at a specific time the inhabitants of the natural state came together and consciously agreed to set up social and political institutions. This agreement is called a social contract, or sometimes a social compact or a covenant. It marks the beginning of society and political authority.

This analysis of the origins of states and societies must not be thought of as either history or anthropology: none of the social-contract writers claim that this is the way things really occurred. If pressed, they would probably go along with Aristotle's view that social and political life was a slow development growing out of the family and the kinship group. The historical or anthropological accuracy of the state of nature and social contact is not up for discussion. The ideas are used in much the same way that St. Augustine and St. Thomas use divine intervention: to provide answers to questions which are important and yet beyond the range of empirical research. They are also used in the way that Plato employed the Utopian technique: to depict in a graphic form behavior and principles which are fundamental to a theory. Thus, when Hobbes talks of a one-time state of nature, he is actually trying to evoke in our minds an image of men living without government; in this way his positive aim, the demonstration of why men need government, is achieved. Occasionally Hobbes tries to persuade us that the state of nature was real and that it still exists in some places. "The savage people in many places of America . . ." he says, "have no government at all, and live at this day in that brutish manner." [7] However, he does not elaborate on this; which is just as well, because the American Indians clearly had both social and political institutions. If Hobbes tends to reify his constructs, it is only because he wants to give a firm empirical foundation to his theory. The question, however, is not whether the state-of-nature–social-contract model was ever real, but whether it tells us new things about social and political reality.

To understand why we now live under government, we must imagine what life would be like without such established authority. Here Hobbes is ready to give a straightforward answer. "The natural state of men, before they entered into society, was a mere war, and that not simply, but a war of all men against all men," he says.[8] Because there is no common power in society which men are forced to respect, life is one long depredation in which lawless creatures are doomed to a bleak existence. In a famous passage Hobbes describes the warlike state:

> In such condition, there is no place for industry; because the fruit thereof is uncertain: and consequently no culture of the earth; no navigation, nor use of the commodities that may be imported by sea; no commodious building, no instruments of moving, and removing, such things as require much force; no knowledge of the face of the earth; no account of time; no art; no letters; no society; and which is worst of all, continual fear and danger of violent death; and the life of man, solitary, poor, nasty, brutish, and short.[9]

This depiction rests its case not so much on material poverty or cultural barrenness, as on the continual fear of violence and death which men experience in the state of nature. Men are prisoners of fear because society has no common power with which to punish those who disturb the peace of their neighbors. If the means of punishment are at hand, then order can be secured and men can live at ease with each other. The point is not to try to abolish fear,

[7] *Ibid.*, p. 83.

[8] *The Citizen* (New York: Appleton-Century-Crofts, 1949), edited by Sterling P. Lamprecht, p. 29.

[9] *Leviathan*, p. 82.

for that is impossible, but to have men stand in awe of a common power rather than one another. "The dispositions of men are naturally such, that except they be restrained through fear of some coercive power, every man will distrust each other," Hobbes says.[10]

We can now observe Hobbes' psychology in practice. Men are so possessed by the will to power and the yearning for security that they will ravage the persons and property of those about them in an effort to aggrandize themselves. Only a superior coercive power will thwart these antisocial impulses; only an agency which can effectively punish or threaten punishment will create conditions in which men may live in mutual trust. This is, Hobbes suggests, no deductive proposition about human nature. On the contrary, it is the record of human experience. If we look at the way men behave in the states we know, it ought not to be hard to imagine how they would act were there no state at all.

We see even in well-governed states, where there are laws and punishments appointed for offenders, yet particular men travel not without their sword by their sides, for their defenses, neither sleep they without shutting not only their doors against their fellow subjects, but also their trunks and coffers for fear of domestics. Can men give a clearer testimony of the distrust they have of each other, and all, of all? [11]

If things as we know them are not quite as bad as Hobbes makes out, it should not be forgotten that in many parts of the world today men do keep a gun by their side for just the reason that Hobbes states, and even in those societies we call civilized there is little sign that the locksmith's is a dying trade. We may begin to take our fears for granted: to assume that locking one's car and avoiding certain dark streets is a matter of course. But the fears remain, whether we are conscious of them or not, and they wreak their toll on our personalities by creating tensions and anxieties which we attempt to discharge in permissible ways. In putting stress on the fears of men in the state of nature, Hobbes exposes the Achilles' heel of the political personality. The war of all against all must end if men are not to drive themselves mad.

It will not do to say that in this jungle the fittest will survive and progress will march onward over the bodies of those incapable of standing the competition. For men are not animals, and there are limits to the strains they can put up with. Even the apparent victors in the state of nature can never consolidate their conquests: new adversaries always appear on the horizon, for every man is an enemy. Constant wakefulness can only lead to physical exhaustion, and even the strongest have a rear guard exposed to the knives of

[10] *The Citizen*, p. 11.
[11] *Ibid.*

their neighbors. In short, the state of nature is a state with perfect liberty: all men are absolutely free to do as they please—with themselves and to each other.

> The right of nature . . . is the liberty each man hath, to use his own power, as he will himself, for the preservation of his own nature; that is to say, of his own life; and consequently, of doing anything which in his own judgment and reason he shall conceive to be the aptest means thereto.[12]

Clearly, freedom in a state of nature can have no real meaning. "In the state of nature, to have all, and do all, is lawful for all." [13] On this basis, one is free only to stand guard over one's self twenty-four hours a day, 365 days a year. Talk of competition or survival of the fittest has a hollow ring in such circumstances: for in the state of nature the stakes are no less than death. For competition to be meaningful, there must be a mediating power, a rule-maker who stands apart from the competitors. And this the state of nature does not have.

When all is lawful for all, the notion of law itself is rendered vacuous. And this more than anything else disturbed Hobbes. For, like St. Thomas, he bases his theory on the rule of law and the conjunction of law and political power. To make vivid the importance of legal institutions, Hobbes uses the Machiavellian approach. A state of nature, he says, is a state without morality: it is possible to theorize about human relationships without intruding ethical considerations. The state of nature is a hypothetical construct, and we must now hypothesize a moral vacuum. "To this war of every man against every man, this also is consequent: that nothing can be unjust," Hobbes says. "The notions of right and wrong, justice and injustice, have there no place. Where there is no common power, there is no law; where no law, no injustice." [14]

Does this mean that we have returned to Thrasymachus after so long: that the definition of justice lies with the stronger party? Hobbes' answer, at least in part, is that a political theory has to be about politics. It is idle to talk of right and wrong, justice and injustice, as abstract categories, for if these standards exist without the means of their enforcement, then we are left with the Utopianism of a Plato or the other-worldliness of the theologians. If justice is to be operative in a real society, then there must be legal institutions to see that justice is actually done. And these institutions must be real courts and real judges whose decisions are enforced by the power of the state. Hobbes is insisting that justice will be no more than philosophical rhetoric until power is created to give it a basis in human law. And law, the mediating ele-

---

[12] *Leviathan*, p. 84.
[13] *The Citizen*, p. 28.
[14] *Leviathan*, p. 83.

ment between power and justice, derives its authority from the policeman's nightstick. "Before there was any government," Hobbes says, "just and unjust had no being." [15] There need be no quarrel with this proposition so long as we are not asked to accept its converse as well: so long, that is, as it is not being said that the existence of *any* government whatever automatically makes for a just society. At this stage Hobbes does not commit himself on what consequences will occur when a common power is established. He is only saying that there is no point in talking about law or justice in a state of nature. Unenforceable standards cease to be standards at all.

That law is the creation of human governments has been established. But Hobbes is not content to stop here. There is also in his theory a conception of the Natural Law which is, in fact, far more detailed in its specifications than that enunciated by St. Thomas. The Natural Law, furthermore, exists in the state of nature even though its influence on men's conduct is palpably meager. What made Hobbes decide to introduce the Natural Law into an environment where it could clearly have little effect? The answer is that men are no less men just because they must cower in fear in the state of nature. The equality of mankind, which causes such disruptions when men must fend for themselves, also contains the prescription that every individual has a full claim to lead the life of a reasoning being. The Natural Law lays down the conditions for this life and forbids such conduct as will be destructive of human existence. "A Law of Nature," Hobbes says, "is a precept or general rule, found out by reason, by which a man is forbidden to do that which is destructive of his life." [16]

The Natural Law, because it may be apprehended by reason, is within the grasp of all men. Hobbes parts company with St. Thomas by asserting that every individual, and not just a ruling minority, is capable of perceiving the Natural Law. The argument that the reason of the average man is too beclouded for him to grasp the subtleties of the Law of Nature is rejected by Hobbes. He is well aware that ambition and self-interest can obscure man's reasoning powers. Hobbes faces this criticism squarely and then attempts to answer it.

Perhaps some man . . . will say that the deduction of these Laws is so hard, that it is not to be expected they will be vulgarly known, and therefore neither will they prove obliging: for laws, if they be not known, oblige not, nay, indeed are not laws.

To this I answer, it is true that hope, fear, anger, ambition, covetousness, vainglory, and other perturbations of mind, do hinder a man so, as he cannot attain to the knowledge of these Laws, whilst those passions prevail in him: but there is no

[15] *The Citizen*, p. 129.
[16] *Leviathan*, p. 84.

man who is not sometimes in a quiet mind. At that time therefore there is nothing easier for him to know, though he be never so rude and unlearned, than this only rule, that when he doubts, whether what he is now doing to another, may be done by the Law of Nature, or not, he conceives himself to be in that other's stead.[17]

Men may be willful and self-interested, but they have moments of solicitude when they are able to put themselves in the other fellow's shoes. This ability to empathize demonstrates that even the least sophisticated of persons can know the precepts of the Natural Law.

St. Thomas gave to the Natural Law a coercive power of no small proportions: rulers were expected to abide by its precepts in their promulgation of human law, and if they did not, they would be denied entry to the Heavenly Kingdom. Hobbes is unwilling to invoke divine intervention as the only safeguard. On the contrary, obedience of the Natural Law is a matter of each individual to settle with his own internalized standards of conduct. "We must therefore conclude," Hobbes says, "that the Law of Nature does always and everywhere oblige in the internal court or that of conscience." [18] It is an integral part of Hobbes' theory that men, whether in the state of natural or civil society, have a moral sense. They are naturally good—or at least not as sinful as St. Augustine or Machiavelli made them out to be—and if their failings in the state of nature become exaggerated, it is due to the impossible conditions of anarchy and war. If men seek pleasure, avoid pain, and use antisocial means to achieve these ends, this is a statement about human psychology. It does not counteract the proposition that man is a moral creature as well.

They are merely sensible creatures, that they have this disposition, that immediately as much as in them lies, they desire and do whatsoever is best pleasing to them, and that either through fear they fly from, or through hardness repel those dangers who approach them, yet they are not for this reason to be accounted wicked.[19]

In a state of nature men spend so much time at war with their neighbors that it is easy to conclude that they are naturally wicked. Yet, curiously enough, it is not in the state of nature, but in civil society, that man's natural goodness is given a genuine chance to make itself manifest. Natural man—the man of reason and conscience—comes into his own only under a system of political authority. Here Hobbes is at one with Aristotle and St. Thomas.

"The Laws of Nature are immutable and eternal," Hobbes says.[20] And he then proceeds in Leviathan to list them in all their fullness. As there are al-

---

[17] *The Citizen*, p. 55.
[18] *Ibid.*, p. 56.
[19] *Ibid.*, p. 12.
[20] *Leviathan*, p. 104.

most twenty of these laws, it will suffice to set down only a representative sample:

That every man ought to endeavor peace, as far as he has hope of attaining it.
That a man be willing, when others are so too, as for peace and defense of himself he shall think it necessary, to lay down this right to all things; and be contented with so much liberty against other men, as he would allow other men against himself.
That men perform their covenants made.
That every man strive to accommodate himself to the rest.
That no man by deed, word, countenance, or gesture declare hatred or contempt of another.
That every man acknowledge another for his equal by nature.
That such things as cannot be divided, be enjoyed in common, if it can be.
That all men that mediate peace be allowed safe conduct.[21]

These precepts, then, range from a law as general as the Golden Rule to a directive specifying that a man carrying a white flag not be shot at. They are clearly rules for civilized men, and they are plainly intended to create a harmonious society where individuals may live at peace with one another. We may raise once more the troublesome question of why Hobbes discusses the Natural Law in the context of the state of nature. It should now be obvious that the Natural Law is designed for men in society, not men in anarchy. And this is just the point. Through the use of their reasoning powers, men slowly begin to see that they must abolish the state of nature. They intuitively know that they ought to abide by the Natural Law—their consciences tell them that—and they must find the means of quitting a condition which gives free rein to their lower nature. "The Natural Laws, though well understood, do not instantly secure any man in their practice," Hobbes says, "and consequently, that as long as there is no caution had from the invasion of others, there remains to every man that same primitive right of self-defense." [22] There is an impulse in man, then, to rise above his primitive self. There are all the ingredients in the Natural Law—the keeping of the peace, the mutual giving up of freedom to a common power, the performing of covenants, the acknowledging of equality—for the institution of a government which will abolish the war of all against all. This government will, of course, make laws. The Natural Law, even though inoperative in the state of nature, is prior to government. It cannot be said, therefore, that the Natural Law is born with the creation of government; rather, the political conditions are created whereby it may be given meaning. The Natural Law is eternal and immutable: it exists in the consciences of men, and so long as men walk this earth it will be among them.

[21] *Ibid.*, pp. 85, 93, 100, 101, 102.
[22] *The Citizen*, p. 63.

The two-dimensional model, that of the state of nature and the social contract, signifies why men choose to live under government. The choice arises from the conflict between psychology and social psychology: individual men are so constituted that they will destroy each other and themselves if put in proximity. Yet they are capable of solving this dilemma, and it is to this solution that Hobbes now turns.

CONSENT AND SOVEREIGNTY

Machiavelli's conception of consent was—admittedly rather crudely—compared to the grants of power convicts give to their wardens. In his eyes, citizens gave or withdrew their consent in an unthinking way and on the basis of their primal urges. Hobbes, as has been seen, thinks far more highly of the capabilities of the average man. And he extends this generous view to the theory of consent which underlies his theory of government. This consent of the governed is active, conscious, and reflective. It is, in addition, institutionalized: government is founded on a contract which all citizens take out with one another, a formal petition or resolution in which they expressly agree to submit to the authority of a common power. The idea of institutionalized consent marks a departure from the rather inchoate notions of earlier thinkers. Man is a creature of will, and therefore his government should be based on an express sign of approval. The vote, of course, is the chief institution of consent, and it expresses the will of those who participate. The ballot, in fact, can only have meaning if we postulate that men want to make, and are capable of making, choices about the disposition of power in society. Hobbes has been making just this assumption: man, as a creature of will, is aptly prepared for taking on the role of a consenting citizen.

The consent of the governed can only be the foundation of government if citizens are rational. Plato and St. Thomas, for example, did not rely on consent; rather, they found the legitimacy of government in the virtue and wisdom of the few who ruled. Power became rational because the ruling minority was composed of men of reason. To depart from this standard, as Hobbes does, a theorist must proceed to claim that reason is found in the entirety of the population. Aristotle said this of democracy, but he did not commit himself on the question of popular consent. Because Hobbes assumes the equality of all men, and because he says that all can know the precepts of the Natural Law, he has no difficulty in concluding that a government founded on consent will be both rational and legitimate. There is no place for a privileged elite in Hobbes' theory. But there is a place for concentrated power, and this will have a lot to do with the character of consent. For Hobbes does not talk of regular elections or town meetings or any of the mechanisms of participation which we associate with popular government. Locke and Rousseau will broaden the operation of institutions of consent at a later stage. The major first step which Hobbes takes is to found government on an express contract, a document which indicates the purposes men wish their government to pursue and their agreement to do what is necessary to help their government achieve these ends. The contract, then, is a vote, but it is not a continuing ballot. Once popular consent has put the train on the tracks, it will move of its own power. Whether citizens can ever flag down this engine is open to serious question.

The reason why men contract together has already been made clear. In agreeing to obey a government, they agree to accept formal restraints on their activities. But political power will have to be exercised purposively: it will be used to protect human life and thereby create the conditions for civilized existence.

The final cause, end, or design of man, who naturally love liberty, and dominion over others, in the introduction of that restraint upon themselves, in which we see them live in commonwealths, is the foresight of their own preservation, and of a more contented life thereby; that is to say, of getting themselves out from that miserable condition of war, which is necessarily consequent . . . to the natural passions of men, when there is no visible power to keep them in awe.[23]

Hobbes makes no Utopian promises here: men love liberty, but they love to dominate their fellow men as well. If citizens consent to live in a commonwealth, they will attain to a more contented life; however, their basic character structure will not be changed. The fundamental guarantee given by the social contract is that human life will be preserved: citizens will once and for all be absolved from the fear of violent death which plagued their lives and stultified their personalities in the state of nature. But fear cannot be abolished simply by creating political institutions. The yearning for power continues to exist in men, and if this tendency is not to express itself in anarchic ways, then fear must continue to be employed as a control. Men must now stand in awe of their political sovereign. If they are to be made secure from the unpredictable forays which occurred in the state of nature, then they must submit to the awesome but predictable power of political authority.

Power must be met with power. This is the price of civilization. Every citizen is a potential menace to society, and, taken together, a population is a seedbed of anarchy. Only a powerful government, founded on the consent of men's higher natures, will keep in check the antisocial behavior which is

[23] *Leviathan*, p. 109.

latent in the lower natures of these selfsame individuals. For men to be delivered from a state of chaos they must lay down their arms and deliver themselves over to a sovereign. This, then, is the social contract:

> The only way to erect such a common power, as may be able to defend them from the invasion of foreigners, and the injuries of one another, . . . is to confer all their power and strength upon one man, or upon one assembly of men, that may reduce all their wills, by plurality of voices, unto one will: which is as much as to say, to appoint one man, or assembly of men, to bear their person; and everyone to own, and acknowledge himself to be author of whatsoever he that so beareth their person, shall act, or cause to be acted, in those things which concern the common peace and safety; and therein to submit their wills, everyone to his will, and their judgments to his judgment.
>
> This is more than consent, or concord; it is a real unity of them all, in one and the same person, made by covenant of every man with every man, in such manner, as if every man should say to every man: "I authorize and give up my right of governing myself, to this man, or to this assembly of men, on this condition, that thou give up thy right to him, and authorize all his actions in a like manner." This done, the multitude so united in one person, is called a Commonwealth.[24]

This contract, like most such documents, has a lot of fine print in it and deserves a careful reading. Each citizen divests himself of the unchecked power which characterized his behavior previously and hands it over to those who are charged with governing. Each citizen strips himself of the right of governing himself which he exercised in the state of nature and makes government the repository of all rights. And because citizens submit this way of their own free will and out of rational choice, the government they establish is endowed with legitimacy. The authority of the state derives from the contract which all make with all; the sovereign is not party to the contract, but rather the result of it. He is hired to do a job: to secure the common peace and the public safety. And his employers agree that if he is to accomplish his task, then they must be willing to obey the man they have retained. Finally, although Hobbes allows that the sovereign may be an assembly of men as well as one man, it is clear that he prefers the single ruler as the seat of sovereignty. If real unity—the goal of all theorists up to this time—is to be achieved, then the concentration of power in a single man is the best form of government.

The notion of sovereignty has been a standby in political theory for many years. First brought to the fore by Hobbes, students of the subject have regarded it as a major element in the understanding of states and citizens. But in recent years it has tended to lapse into the background. The reason for this is that later generations of theorists have viewed sovereignty as a fiction, and on the whole not a very useful fiction. Sovereignty describes a condition of supremacy: a sovereign acknowledges no higher authority, its word is the

[24] *Ibid.*, p. 112.

final word. Clearly both past and recent history have been marked by events which are bound to be discussed in the context of sovereignty. Presumably the growth of the American nation has been accompanied by the developing relation between several "sovereign" states and the "sovereignty" of the national government. The discussions of federalism at the Constitutional Convention were infused with the idea of sovereignty, and how conflicting conceptions of political supremacy might be resolved was the great nexus of debate both then and later. In the arena of international relations, the idea of "national sovereignty" is omnipresent as there develop treaty organizations which appear to gain jurisdiction over the internal affairs of member nations. Thus, while political theorists have been abandoning their talk of sovereignty, governors from Baton Rogue to Sacramento and foreign ministers from Quebec to Jakarta have continued to discourse on it with no sign of abating. One obvious reason for this is that sovereignty lies more in the realm of ideology than it does of theory. It is a rallying cry more than an explanation: a persuasive justification for the status quo or rhetoric to arouse sentiment for a new allocation of power. Thus, both states which are slipping and those which have recently attained to power speak of the sovereignty which inheres in their being. Usually, of course, the orators who speak this way are speaking about something else; they are talking about power.

The chief theoretical difficulty with sovereignty is that it conveys two ideas at once. And the confusion of these ideas in a single term is what has made the conception so hard to apply. For there is *legal* sovereignty, on the one hand, and *political* sovereignty, on the other. To discover the political sovereign in a society—and the "discovery" of the seat of sovereignty was long thought to be a task of political science—one must ask what person or what institution has supreme power. Machiavelli's theory is really an essay in political sovereignty, even though he does not use the term. The prince is advised to arrange things so that there exists no power with the resources to supersede his own. Plato, too, sought to impart political sovereignty to the Guardian class; its power was to be supreme and no other groups in society could question or override it. Yet we know that power is never absolute: rulers must always make concessions in order to keep their office. Certainly there has never been a ruler who had the power to do everything he would have liked to have done. This argument, while true, tends to miss the point. A ruler may be hedged in by all manner of limiting factors: public opinion, his party organization, and even the repressive forces within his own personality. But the question to be asked is whether there exists apart from him a coherent center of power which can veto his commands. Public opinion is too nebulous to be called a discrete obstacle to political sovereignty. The

American system of government, of course, provides a wealth of examples in this sphere. The first to come to mind is the power of the Supreme Court to declare laws of Congress invalid: because this power is deposited in a coherent institution and is always available for use, it is impossible to say that Congress has political sovereignty—although there are many other reasons for saying this as well. Indeed, because of federalism, the separation of powers, periodic elections, and the existence of the Constitution itself, it is impossible to find America's political sovereign. The search for a supreme power is bound to take a circular path leading nowhere. And to call "the people" the political sovereign is to say everything and nothing. To ascribe that power to the Constitution is to evade the problem in a similar way.

Legal sovereignty, on the other hand, is somewhat easier to talk about. Every society must have a source of law which is final and definitive. Institutions must be developed which will arbitrate conflicts between state legislatures and the national Congress, the Congress and the administration, private associations and governmental bodies, traditional precepts of the common law and legislative innovations. Courts, of course, are the chief agency for this arbitration, but even they may be compelled by legislators and administrators to interpret the law in particular ways. The discovery of the legal sovereign, the man or institution whose word is law, may end up being a very difficult task. Nevertheless, the law itself, at any given time and on any given matter of importance, is usually settled and its word is known. The law will change through time, but at a certain moment there is always an institution to tell us what it is or where to find it. The existence of a documentary Constitution, while always open to interpretation, facilitates the knowledge of what is legal. So does a body of legal precedent. In some countries the legal sovereign is a single ruler who draws up his edicts and hands them down from the breakfast table. In others it is a legislature which does not recognize the authority of courts to invalidate its statutes. And in still others it is a complex network of procedures among and between separated institutions of government. But at all times the legal sovereign must be governmental: no political party, no private association, no individual may make law.

The juxtaposition of political and legal sovereignty clearly presents more problems than can be solved. If it is shown that a certain bill was drafted in the offices of a private association and that that group used its resources to compel legislators to vote it into law, then where does sovereignty lie in this case? The political power rests with the private group, and yet that group's power can only be cloaked with legality if its will is put into statutory form and given a stamp of approval by the legal sovereign. It is plain that legal sovereigns are frequently figureheads: governmental agencies which impart legitimacy to centers of private power. Furthermore, there will always be powers behind the throne: men of lesser office or no office at all who put words in the mouths of those charged with making the law. Even on the international scene there are governments-in-exile which claim to be legal sovereigns—and are often so recognized by other nations—while political supremacy effectively rests with the new regimes. Any discussion of sovereignty must be a mixture of both legal and political considerations, and yet any attempt to speak the two languages at once is bound to be confusing.

When Hobbes talks of sovereignty, he means legal sovereignty first and foremost. The intention of the social contract is to create an undisputed fount of law. While the legal sovereign should be underwritten by political power, Hobbes wishes to show that rule of law is the only basis on which men can live together in a civilized way. Aristotle, St. Thomas, and Machiavelli all said that the rule of law ought to govern relations between man and man, but they did not elaborate on the way in which a stable legal order might be secured. In taking up this challenge, Hobbes creates a ruler who derives his authority to make law from the consent of those who will have to obey. The state of nature existed without law: "Where there is no common power, there is no law," Hobbes said. The social contract, therefore, is an analytic attempt to conjoin power and law; Hobbes does not divide his discussion of sovereignty into political and legal components, because in his mind they are to meet in a single person. As a theoretical model there can be no objection to this; its difficulties in practice are, of course, legion. The next step, therefore, is to see what use Hobbes makes of his model.

Power is given to the sovereign by the people. Unlike Machiavelli's ruler, it cannot be said that he saw his opportunity and seized the reins of government at a propitious moment. Hobbes' citizens submit because they agree among themselves that there is a specific job which needs to be done. "The office of the sovereign . . ." he says, "consists in the end for which he was trusted with the sovereign power, namely the procuration of the safety of the people." [25] And this means that the citizens may hold the sovereign to the terms of his office. Admittedly, he is charged only with securing peace and safety: he is not obliged to provide the good life, but only the basic conditions under which the good life may be developed. However, he is given power so that he may establish his legal authority. If he neglects the public safety and uses his power to promote his own interests, then his laws are no longer vested with the consent of the governed. Obedience is to law and not to power; this is what distinguishes Hobbes from Machiavelli.

And may citizens overthrow a tyrant? The reply is that they need not

[25] *Ibid.*, p. 219.

obey him if he fails to protect them from violence and death. "The obligation of subjects to the sovereign," Hobbes says, "is understood to last as long, and no longer, than the power lasts by which he is able to protect them." [26] While this is no sanction for revolution in any sweeping sense, it allows citizens greater freedom to disobey than St. Thomas did. The social contract was drawn up by individuals to accomplish a specific end, and they are entitled to cancel that document if the man they hired proves unequal to the job. If the sovereign cannot or will not use his power to ensure peace, then subjects may dismiss him and form a new contract with a new ruler. Hobbes does not say more than this on the matter of obligation of citizens to obey, and it is clear that he assumes that the cancellation clause in the contract will not have to be invoked very often. And it is apparent that tyranny as such is no ground for nullifying the agreement. The sovereign may have to be oppressive, he may have to deprive citizens of various freedoms, in order to secure the public safety. The contractors know this in advance when they agree to form a commonwealth, and they may not create new reasons for reneging on the contract once they have tasted sovereign authority. Consent, in the final analysis, is initial and not continuing: it establishes civil government and may be used again later on for one and only one eventuality.

AUTHORITARIAN RULE

In turning to a consideration of what life is like in Hobbes' commonwealth, the overwhelming fact is the concentrated power of the sovereign. The area of freedom which individual citizens have seems to be woefully small, and the sweeping powers of the ruler are to be rendered unquestioned obedience. But if there is power, it is rightful power: the commands of the sovereign are not capricious edicts but are laws invested with full and majestic authority. Only in this way can Hobbes assert that the citizen is obliged to obey.

As men, for the attaining of peace, and conservation of themselves thereby, have made an artificial man, which we call a commonwealth; so also have they made artificial chains, called "civil laws," which they themselves, by mutual covenants, have fastened at one end, to the lips of that man, or assembly, to whom they have given the sovereign power; and at the other end to their own ears. These bonds, in their own nature but weak, may nevertheless be made to hold, by the danger, though not the difficulty of breaking them.[27]

Laws, it would seem, are fictions: artificial chains by which citizens agree to imagine that they are bound. They are weak because they exist only in men's minds; but they hold tight because men are rational enough to realize

[26] *Ibid.*, p. 144.
[27] *Ibid.*, p. 138.

that if they break the laws, then they endanger their own safety. The objective power of the sovereign, while pervasive, needs to rest on the subjective ascription of legality which citizens invest in that power. Law, therefore, must have this subjective element: it must be recognized by those who will be called upon to obey it. Otherwise, it is naked force, and Hobbes realizes full well that force alone cannot secure effective government. This raises the idea of legal sovereignty above the level of a truism. "The legislator in all commonwealths is the only sovereign . . ." Hobbes says. "For the legislator is he that makes the law." [28] That statement by itself tells us very little, for law cannot possibly be made by a nongovernmental body. The legislative agent must, by definition, be the legal sovereign. However, Hobbes is adding to this proposition when he says that law, if it is to be worth calling law, must be based on the obedience of citizens who acknowledge that the law ought to be obeyed. In this way, Hobbes seeks to show that the sovereign's power must at all times be regarded as legitimate. If he is authoritarian, if he demands absolute obedience, the fists of mail are covered with the velvet gloves of consent and legality.

Hobbes now proceeds to outline the powers of the sovereign. His jurisdiction, first of all, is universal: all citizens are his subjects, and all must render obedience. What about those who did not sign the social contract? The reply is that they are bound by the agreement of the others. So long as a majority of the community voted to set up a sovereign, the minority is obliged to obey. "Because the major part hath by consenting voices declared a sovereign, he that dissented must now consent with the rest." [29] Were a dissenting minority to remove themselves from the reach of the sovereign, then they would sooner or later set up their own lawmaking agencies. This would mean that the society had two legal sovereigns, a logical impossibility; and when they inevitably came in conflict, the society would be at war with itself, a political calamity. The institution of majority rule is based on the equalitarian principle: minorities cannot ask that this principle be breached, because in so doing they would endanger the entire society. This question will be raised again when the matter of freedom of association is discussed.

Furthermore, the citizen has no rights against the state. The sovereign is

[28] *Ibid.*, p. 173.

[29] *Ibid.*, p. 115. However: "Most men think that the consents of all are contained in the votes of the greater part; which in truth is false. For it is not from nature that the consent of the major part should be received for the consent of all . . ." (*The Citizen,* p. 85). If Hobbes is of two minds on the question of how far and under what circumstances a majority vote binds the dissenting minority, it is because every student of politics is ambiguous on this point. It would appear that if the commonwealth is to have effective government, then all in society must acknowledge its legality whether they signed the contract or not.

instituted by the citizens and he is, as an artificial man, symbolic of the individual wills of all his subjects. "Because every subject is by this institution author of all the actions, and judgments of the sovereign instituted . . ." Hobbes says, "he that complaineth of injury from his sovereign, complaineth of that whereof he himself is author: and therefore not to accuse any man but himself." [30] If a citizen is oppressed by an arm of the government, he should not protest, but rather acknowledge that he is oppressing himself. The citizen has no rights against the state, because it is illogical to speak of rights directed against an extension of your own person. If you hit your left thumb with a hammer held in your right hand, you do not ask redress from the hammer. Rights do exist in Hobbes' society, but they are the possession of the sovereign. Hobbes lists twelve of these rights: ten are powers which might be expected to inhere in any state. Two, however, are worth pointing out:

To be judge of what opinions and doctrines are averse, and what conducing to peace.
The whole power of prescribing the rules, whereby every man may know what goods he may enjoy and what actions he may do without being molested by any of his fellow-subjects.[31]

If it is assumed that the state has these rights, and if it is also postulated that citizens have no inherent rights of their own, then it is in order to ask why the language of rights is used at all. When it is said that the state has the "right" to judge which opinions are subversive, all that is being said is that the state *will* make such a judgment. In fact, Hobbes' use of the term "rights" here is synonymous with the term "power"—or, actually, "lawful power."

This is an example of what happens when a theory invests the state with a personality, even a fictional personality. For then the state takes on the attributes of an individual, and it can match its "human" claims against those of other individuals. In fact, the state has the power to act, and very often it will go ahead and use that power. But to call those powers of the sovereign "rights" is to open the door very wide to a state of affairs where individuals count less than impersonal institutions. An example of this problem is the modern business corporation. In constitutional law it is considered a fictional "person" and hence entitled to protections under the Fourteenth Amendment. Does this mean that a corporation, as a person, has political "rights" which it should be allowed to exercise? It has been proposed that corporations have the right to free speech and therefore they can spend their money on political propaganda just like anyone else. But a corporation can have a bank-

[30] *Leviathan*, pp. 115–116.
[31] *Ibid.*, pp. 116–117.

roll of hundreds of millions of dollars to spend; it can have hundreds of thousands of employees to speak as its voice: is it really a person just like anyone else? It has been said that a corporation is no more than an extension of its stockholders' and employees' personalities, that the political rights it asks for are really the extended rights of citizens whose interests are spoken for by the corporation. But stockholders buy their shares one day and sell them the next, with little thought of the corporation's political position, and the vast majority of the company's employees may disagree with the political outlook of the corporation, especially if it is formulated by top management. These considerations are raised simply to show the difficulties which arise when fictional "persons" are created and then endowed with "rights." Both states and corporations—and trade unions and churches and political parties —have obvious powers to secure ends that they pursue, and very frequently (always, in the case of states) these powers are lawful. But it would be more satisfactory from the standpoint of political theory if rights are reserved for— or withheld from—living and breathing individuals. This notion of the rights of man will be taken up in the next chapter, when Locke's theory is discussed.

If the subject has no rights under the social contract, he nevertheless has an area of freedom in which he may do as he pleases. Had he rights in this area, then his freedom would be absolute and no action of government could ever abrogate his specified liberties. But because Hobbes' citizen has handed over his rights to the sovereign, he may only have back such freedoms as the sovereign sees fit to give him and for only so long as the sovereign wills.

The liberty of a subject, lieth only in those things, which in regulating their actions, the sovereign hath pretermitted [i.e., omitted to mention]: such as is the liberty to buy, and sell, and otherwise contract with one another; to choose their own abode, their own diet, their own trade of life, and institute their children as they themselves think fit; and the like.

Because all the motions and actions of subjects are never circumscribed by laws, nor can be, by reason of their variety, it is necessary that there be infinite cases, which are neither commanded, nor prohibited, but every man may either do, or not do them, as he lists himself. In these, each man is said to enjoy his liberty. . . .[32]

Freedom, for Hobbes, is the sphere of action which the all-powerful state allows to its citizens. And freedom, for that reason, is the creation of the state: it does not exist independently of it. Just as justice must grow out of law, so liberty must grow out of political power.

Two factors emerge from the analysis. The first is that Hobbes' state is authoritarian, but it is not totalitarian. That is, the sovereign does not try to

[32] *Ibid.*, p. 139; *The Citizen*, p. 151.

regulate all facets of human and social life: economic, residential, family, and other decisions are left to the individual. Plato's state, it will be recalled, stooped so low into human affairs as to regulate the length of hair that the Guardians might wear. Hobbes' freedom, while extended at the sufferance of the ruler, is clearly an extensive one compared with that of other theories. Second, the reason why an area of freedom is opened to citizens is that it is politically impractical for the state to keep all phases of human behavior under its direct control. Men are too active and their interests are too varied for even the most efficient sovereign to enforce a comprehensive plan of social behavior. Hobbes eschews totalitarianism, then, for practical reasons rather than as a matter of principle. His view is much like Aristotle's critique of Plato: unity is desirable, but an attempt at too much unity will weaken rather than strengthen the state.

It follows from all that has been said so far that sovereignty is indivisible. As a legal proposition, this is self-evident and dictated by logic. As a political proposition, it must be shown how the state secures supreme power. Already the reasoning powers of men have been appealed to: they are asked to agree to obey the law because it is in their own ultimate interest. Furthermore, rights accrue, under the social contract, to the state, and it parcels out such freedoms as it feels are necessary.

Hobbes now turns to a principle which is intended to strengthen governmental power by weakening competing powers in society which might threaten political sovereignty. "The sovereign in every commonwealth," he says, "is the absolute representative of all the subjects, and therefore no other can be representative of any part of them, but so far forth as he shall give leave." [33] Here Hobbes is enunciating one of the cardinal principles of absolute rule. In a society there can be only one representative institution, and that is the state. All citizens have agreed to regard the sovereign as an extension of their personalities and as the repository of their rights. This means that loyalty is to be rendered exclusively to the state: there is no room left over for other associations in society which might compete with the state for the allegiance of citizens. It has already been seen that the sovereign must demand complete obedience to his laws: there is no allowance for individuals who take a lighthearted view of political authority. Similarly, associations which, by their very existence, divide the loyalties of citizens are dangers to the commonwealth. Such groups are "factions," and they are inherently divisive.

If it be the duty of princes to restrain the factious, much more does it concern them to dissolve and dissipate the factions themselves. Now I call a faction a

[33] *Leviathan*, pp. 146–147.

multitude of subjects gathered together either by mutual contracts among themselves or by the power of some one, without his or their authority who bear the supreme rule. A faction, therefore, is as it were a city in a city. . . .[34]

If there are to be lesser associations than the state within the society, then they may only exist by the leave of the sovereign. Only he may decide whether a private group works with or at cross purposes to the ends of the commonwealth. This view clearly runs counter to the pluralism which Aristotle suggested earlier: a great hedge against both tyranny and revolution, he said, is a plurality of groups in society. The competition among associations, Aristotle claimed, would prevent the accumulation of oppressive power in the hands of any single person or group. This view, to be explored in great detail by Tocqueville later on, is now regarded as one of the foundations of a free society. Yet Hobbes rejects it. First of all, the very idea of a city within a city, of ancillary bodies making "private laws" which bind their members, contradicts his conception of an indivisible legal sovereign. And on political grounds, he finds himself unable to assume that private associations will tend to their own business and not make incursions on the power of the state. The loyalty which resides in the body politic, Hobbes seems to be saying, is a constant sum: any loyalty drawn off by private groups is loyalty lost to the sovereign. And this means that factions are bound to sap the strength of the state by weaning away citizens from their obligation of political obedience. Hobbes cites various of these factions—churches and political parties—and then explains how the former are dangerous to the state's existence:

Factions for government of religion, as of Papists, Protestants, etc. or of state, as patricians and plebeians of old time in Rome, and of aristocraticals and democraticals of old time in Greece, are unjust, as being contrary to the peace and safety of the people, and a taking of the sword out of the hand of the sovereign.

For if one command somewhat to be done under penalty of natural death, another forbid it under pain of eternal death, and both by their own right, it will follow that citizens, although innocent, are not only by right punishable, but that the city itself is altogether dissolved; for no man can serve two masters, nor is he less, but rather more, a master whom we believe we are to obey for fear of damnation, than he whom we obey for fear of temporal death.[35]

What emerges is that Hobbes does not trust the motives of private associations: like Machiavelli, he sees in them a dangerous potential for revolutionary activity. And he clearly understands that these groups are political in character: while they may claim to be religious or economic or fraternal in purpose, they are bound to deal eventually in the commodity of power. Churches, to Hobbes' mind, are political institutions: they have laws, ruling hierarchies,

[34] *The Citizen*, p. 149.
[35] *Leviathan*, p. 155; *The Citizen*, pp. 75–76.

and sanctions over their members. Indeed, the sanction of threatened damnation can prove to be more effective than the political punishments the state may mete out. Any exercise of such religious power takes the sword out of the hand of the sovereign; for this reason, the state must strike first and dissolve those institutions which threaten its supremacy.

The sovereign, then, is the comprehensive institution in society. For Hobbes, as for Plato and Aristotle, state and society are conjoined in a single body. But Hobbes differs from Plato and Aristotle in important respects. First of all, his society is not an organic conception: it is an association of individuals, based on a contract which is voluntary and man-made. Thus Aristotle might tolerate competition among various parts of the *polis* because he knew that despite their antagonisms they were still integrally related to the social organism. Second, Hobbes makes his sovereign social as well as political out of choice; he realizes that it does not have to be this way, but he concludes that the merger will serve his larger end. It did not even enter Plato's mind that his Utopia failed to distinguish state and society; Hobbes has considered the possibility of a division, and he has rejected it. For a society composed of many cities and many sovereigns would undo all the work that has been accomplished by the social contract. There would be no guarantee that political supremacy would remain with the sovereign: competition among social groups could easily revert into a state of war. This is also why Hobbes gives the sovereign the power "to be judge of what opinions and doctrines are averse and what conducing to peace."

If factions are a threat to the public safety, so are factious ideas in the minds of citizens. Subversive thoughts can lead to subversive actions. "The actions of men proceed from their opinions," Hobbes says, "and in the well-governing of opinions, consists the well-governing of men's actions." [36] This means that the state must suppress those individuals who urge their fellow citizens to question the fundamental legitimacy of the sovereign power. This is an abuse of freedom which can be especially dangerous when aimed at unsettling the mind of the average citizen; and the sovereign must be on guard against such a threat.

> Another infirmity of a commonwealth is . . . the liberty of disputing against absolute power by pretenders to political prudence, which though bred for the most part in the lees of the people, yet animated by false doctrines, are perpetually meddling with the fundamental laws, to the molestation of the commonwealth.[37]

Hobbes is as well aware as Machiavelli that absolute government will give rise to dissension, protest, and even sedition. Yet he does not prescribe the harsh

[36] *Leviathan*, p. 116.
[37] *Ibid.*, p. 218.

measures which are called for in *The Prince*. He cannot do this, because, unlike Machiavelli's, his commonwealth is founded on the express consent of the governed. Even though the sovereign is given a free hand so long as he ensures internal peace, even though disgruntled minorities are bound by the majority vote, Hobbes is at all times as concerned with the legitimacy of the law as he is with the supremacy of political power. His task of reconciling power and consent is a far harder one than Machiavelli's: to combine authoritarian rule with as much freedom as possible, to concentrate power while respecting the individuality of each citizen—so difficult are these endeavors that Hobbes' attempt at a solution becomes one of the most intricate and involved of all political theories.

EDUCATION FOR OBEDIENCE

Any theory which seeks to reconcile values which are in inherent conflict with each other is bound in the final analysis to give greater priority to one of the stated goals. Hobbes' is no exception to this rule. If his psychology is individualist, his politics are absolutist; and when a choice has to be made between the individual and the absolute state, the latter is always accorded preference. It is for the citizen to obey: if he has the power to reason, he must not use it to think about controversial political issues. Freedom of speech, freedom of association, freedom to protest: none of these are rights, and all are permissible only if the state decides that their use will be politically innocuous. Indeed, even that prized possession of the individual, the conscience which led him to apprehend the Natural Law in the state of nature, is no longer to be relied upon in civil society. "With him that lives in a commonwealth," Hobbes says, ". . . the law is the public conscience." [38] Men may not appeal to their own understanding of the Natural Law as justification for questioning the acts of rulers. It is one of "the mischiefs that have befallen mankind," Hobbes says, ". . . that the knowledge whether the commands of kings be just or unjust belongs to private men." [39] These private men were sufficiently endowed with reasoning powers that they could come together and draw up a contract creating civil society; they were aware enough of the precepts of the Natural Law that they could draft a document embodying the rules by which men might live together. But just as they gave up their rights in that contract, so they gave up their privilege of judging right from wrong in the political sphere. The law, the creation of the sovereign, defines justice and injustice. It is not for the citizen to reason why.

[38] *Ibid.*, p. 211.
[39] *The Citizen*, pp. 8–9.

If the sovereign is a tyrant, then that is the luck of the draw. Like St. Thomas, Hobbes hopes that the ruler will be a pious man and fearful of divine retribution. "The sovereign . . ." he says, "is obliged by the Law of Nature, and to render an account thereof to God, the author of that Law, and to none but Him." [40] But Hobbes has not once said that rulers need be men of wisdom and virtue. He does not follow Plato in laying down rules for the recruitment and training of a Guardian class; he does not go along with St. Thomas and say that those who rule are the virtuous minority in society; he does not even pursue Machiavelli's tack that rulers have superior political skills. The anonymous individual who is the sovereign is, in the final analysis, more an office than a person.

All that Hobbes can do is utter the hope that rulers will be guided by the Natural Law. Once a commonwealth is established, the Natural Law comes out of the consciences of individuals and into the public domain; it is now for the ruler, who is the sole source of legal authority, to embrace the Natural Law in the laws which he promulgates. This, at least in theory, will provide a hedge against tyranny. Hobbes demonstrates logically that the Natural Law can only be expressed through the sovereign.

> The Law of Nature, and the civil law, contain each other, and are of equal extent. For the Laws of Nature . . . are not properly laws, but qualities that predispose men to peace and obedience. When a commonwealth is once settled, then they are actually laws, and not before; as being then the commands of the commonwealth; and therefore also civil laws; for it is the sovereign power that obliges all men to obey them. . . . The Law of Nature therefore is a part of the civil law in all commonwealths of the world. Reciprocally also, the civil law is a part of the dictates of Nature.[41]

This is a logical proposition: it tells why the Natural Law must be underwritten by civil law and why, through implication, it is no longer allowable for private citizens to define and act on the Natural Law independently. But the logic does not say that all rulers will model their laws after the Natural Law. That is a prescription which is beyond the power of logic to decree. Hobbes can therefore only turn to exhortation: power carries its obligations and rulers have an obligation to govern justly. "It is their duty in all things, as much as possibly they can, to yield obedience unto right reason, which is the Natural, Moral, and Divine Law." [42] But the only duty for which they are institutionally accountable to the citizens is the duty to protect them all from violent death. If they fail in this, they may be unseated by a dissolution of the contract. But all other duties—including the duty to be a rational and

[40] *Leviathan*, p. 219.
[41] *Ibid.*, p. 174.
[42] *The Citizen*, p. 142.

just ruler—are only to God. Hobbes' own logic forces him to this position: he would like the sovereign to obey the Natural Law, but he cannot allow citizens the right to depose rulers who flout it.

Hobbes acknowledges that there is no guarantee that a sovereign will do his duty to God, and there is much evidence from political history that he will not. "The monarch may diverse ways transgress against the . . . Laws of Nature," he says, "as by cruelty, iniquity, contumely, and other like vices." [43] Even so, there can be no room for conscientious objection or civil disobedience. If submission seems intolerable, it must nevertheless be rendered for that is the foundation stone of the social contract.

> Must we resist princes, when we cannot obey them? Truly, no; for this is contrary to our civil covenant. What must we do then? Go to Christ by martyrdom; which if it seems to any man to be a hard saying, most certain it is that he believes not with his whole heart, that Jesus is the Christ, the Son of the living God (for he would then desire to be dissolved, and to be with Christ), but he would by a feigned Christian faith elude that obedience which he hath contracted to yield unto the city.[44]

Not only does Hobbes follow St. Thomas here in counseling full obedience, but he also follows Machiavelli by bringing in religious arguments for political submission. The sovereign can play on the religious sensibilities of his subjects and seek to convince them that there is no middle ground between Christian obedience and the way of the martyr. Hobbes does not for a moment claim that life in the commonwealth will be an easy one. We are talking about the real world, not about Utopia. "The state of man can never be without some incommodity or other,"[45] and better to have the incommodity of a tyrant who brings peace and safety than the incommodity of the state of nature which brings the freedom to suffer violent death.

Finally, Hobbes can enter the claim that the sovereign, no matter how tyrannical, is legitimate in the sense that Aristotle described. He does not seek power for his own pleasure, nor does he ignore the interests of those over whom he has absolute rule. "The city was not instituted for its own, but for the subjects' sake . . ." Hobbes says. "The safety of the people is the supreme law." [46] The sovereign is a stern father who, if he oppresses his children, oppresses them for their own good. Hobbes remains steadfast and consistent in affirming that, despite the possibility of tyrannical and irrational rule, sovereignty must remain inviolate. Citizens had their opportunity to consent

[43] *Ibid.*, p. 94.
[44] *Ibid.*, p. 208.
[45] *Leviathan*, p. 120.
[46] *The Citizen*, p. 142.

when they drew up the contractual agreement. After that moment consent is no longer part of the political process.

Nevertheless, Hobbes realizes that the difficult life of the authoritarian state may engender unrest. It has already been noted that seditious factions and dangerous ideas are to be outlawed. Yet the state cannot remain on the defensive. Putting out brushfires is not enough: it must make an affirmative effort in the direction of political education so that obedience will become habitual. And if dangerous ideas are to be extirpated in a lasting way, then citizens must be given persuasive reasons rather than threatened with punishment. "It is therefore the duty of those who have chief authority to root perverse doctrines out of the minds of men, not by commanding, but by teaching; not by the terror of penalties, but by the perspicuity of reasons." [47] This is a long step forward from Plato and Machiavelli: rulers are not advised to purvey half-truths, but rather to teach their subjects obedience in a rational way. If the people are to be convinced as well as persuaded, if they are to understand as well as accept, then they must be educated to a knowledge of the political system of which they are a part.

The people are to be taught first, that they ought not to be in love with any form of government they see in their neighbor nations, more than with their own, nor, whatsoever present prosperity, they behold in nations that are otherwise governed than they, to desire change.

They are to be taught that they ought not to be led with admiration of the virtue of any of their fellow-subjects, how high soever he stand, or how conspicuously soever he shine in the commonwealth; nor of any assembly, except the sovereign assembly, so as to defer to them any obedience, or honor, appropriate to the sovereign. [48]

Hobbes does not go into any detail about the ways and means of political education, other than to say that it should be pervasive: "I therefore conceive it to be the duty of supreme officers to cause the true elements of civil doctrine to be written, and to command them to be taught in all the colleges of their several dominions." [49] This is a touchy subject, of course, and it is recurrent in political theory. Is Hobbes talking about education or is he talking about indoctrination? If citizens are to be led to love their form of government and defer only to the sovereign, then is the educational process to encourage them to think for themselves or to embrace only the truths which are handed down to them? All political education involves some absolutes—even if it is the absolute principle that freedom to dissent should be tolerated

[47] *Ibid.*, p. 146.
[48] *Leviathan*, pp. 221, 222.
[49] *The Citizen*, p. 147.

—and students must be conditioned so that they will accept the ideas and institutions on which their system of government is premissed.

Hobbes prefers to use reasons rather than myths in this process because he has an underlying respect for the individual citizen. What he would say is that "once upon a time" each citizen did a very enlightened thing: he participated in a contract which took him out of the state of nature and put him in civil society. That was a rational action, and it has freed him from fear of violent death since that time. The difficulty is that as the years go on, men forget that political life provides for their bodily safety. They are proud creatures, and they begin to think of the strong sovereign as an oppressor who tyrannizes for no good reason.

For all men are by nature provided of notable multiplying glasses, that is, their passions and self-love, through which, every little payment appears a great grievance; but are destitute of those prospective glasses, namely moral and civil science, to see afar off the miseries that hang over them, and cannot without such payments be avoided.[50]

Political education is an effort to minimize the passion and self-love of a prideful people and inculcate in them the rudiments of moral and political science. They must learn why the state exists, and what would occur if it disappeared. They must be taught why obedience is a virtue, and what are the consequences of sedition. In short, political education tries to impart the long-term view to men who are prone to be shortsighted in their judgments. Clearly the textbooks for such a political science course would not be censored legends or ideological tracts: they would, on the contrary, be the rough-sledding Leviathan and The Citizen. In Hobbes' view, these tomes justify authority and obedience in a rational way; the rulers who embody authority and demand obedience have a duty to teach this political theory to those whom they rule.

A SYSTEMATIC THEORY

Hobbes' theory generates a power of its own: it is propelled by its own force in a way that is quite dissimilar to the other writings which have been considered up to this point. For Hobbes' model is, in reality, a self-contained and internally consistent political system. Other theorists have, in the course of their writing, discussed a wide variety of middle-range ideas; and some of them, notably Plato and St. Thomas, have come close to designing a systematic scheme. But it is Hobbes who has created a theory which embraces a psychology, a sociology, and a political science, and which integrates these into a coherent theoretical framework. His theory of personality meshes with his

[50] *Leviathan*, p. 120.

social and political theories; and at all times he can be seen working back and forth in an effort to show how one feature of the system is related to the others. Few theorists embark on such a grandiose project: of the writers to be considered here only Marx and Engels rival Hobbes' pretensions.

It is fascinating to note how Hobbes virtually drags the reader *into* his model: one must accept each element of the system—individualism, the state of nature, the social contract, sovereignty, the Natural Law—because each hinges logically on all the rest. Before the reader knows it, he is rolling along in an elaborate snowball, and he must travel in the direction in which Hobbes has pushed it.

Difficulties arise when an attempt is made to abstract middle-range ideas out of Hobbes' theory. The notions of individualism and sovereignty, for example, are important parts of Hobbes' system, and they are also general terms in the vocabulary of political theory. Yet Hobbes' use of these ideas is so intertwined with other aspects of his theory that what might start as a healthy amputation ends as a rather gory mutilation. That is to say, Hobbes' conception of individualism is exactly tailored to the specifications of the rest of his system. If we want to talk about individualism in a general way—outside the context of a state of nature or an authoritarian state—then Hobbes' explanation can display severe limitations. Indeed, a pitfall of a systematic theory can be that if the reader sees fit to reject one of its basic premises, then he is tempted to dismiss the system as a whole. Do men fear violent death above all things? If one agrees, then Hobbes' theory follows with an unrelenting logic. If one disagrees with that initial assumption, then there often is the disposition to say that the whole edifice is built on sand. These strictures about systems are offered as an admonitory epilogue to Hobbes; they may also serve as a prologue to Marx and Engels.

Yet, lest one conclude that a system can be brought toppling to the ground simply by kicking away one block close to the bottom, it should be pointed out that Hobbes covers himself at most critical junctures. The theory is, first of all, a model. Particular facets of personality and particular institutions are abstracted from political reality, and they are then magnified and manipulated so that their workings under various circumstances can be observed. The role of fear will serve again as an example. The picture which Hobbes paints of the state of nature—and it is a sort of reverse Utopia where nothing works out —is intended to show that the life of constant fear is the one thing which men seek to escape at any price. To those who protest that they cherish liberty and would rather suffer death than lose it, Hobbes would reply that they have never really been faced with the horrors of a state of nature and so they are in no position to make such a commitment. It is, however, altogether in order to say that Hobbes is being far too single-minded: it can be suggested that while fear looms large in our lives, we are moved by other considerations as well. Hobbes would not dispute this so long as primacy is granted to the feature of the human personality which he emphasizes in his model. While he considers many dimensions, he has, like all serious theorists, committed himself to a single one as the most important causal factor. If not fear, he implicitly challenges his reader, then what is it which causes political men to act as they do?

And yet, for all this, Hobbes draws a complex personality: man is a proud and willful individual; he is active and self-interested. Although his passions may obscure his vision, he has the power to reason, and he is capable of appreciating the advantages of the long-term view. And all men, furthermore, are equal: this is a fact based on careful observation, and it is integral to Hobbes' system. The value of any one man's life stands on a parity with the life of any other man. And to show that these are not simply noble words, Hobbes builds his theory of the absolute state in order to preserve all human life. Absolute rule, indeed, becomes necessary because there are no privileged classes or elites in Hobbes' model. If the fears of all men are to be allayed with equal effectiveness, then political power and legal authority must be concentrated in an agency capable of providing for the public safety in a comprehensive way.

Finally, Hobbes has made a significant contribution by a crucial omission. Plato, Aristotle, and the theologians gave the state a moral as well as a political purpose. Hobbes' state has the responsibility of securing and organizing political power so that it can guarantee the public safety. And there its job ends. Hobbes does not make it the function of the state to promote virtue or to transform citizens into good men. In saying this, he departs in a radical way from his predecessors—Machiavelli, of course, excepted. This tells us that Hobbes respects the individual sufficiently to allow him to find the good life wheresoever he may. Men are to create their own conception of freedom and—within the limitations required by the power of the state—pursue it on their own. If the state indulges in political education, it is solely for the purpose of teaching men to obey political authority as a general principle.

The state's educational concern, to use a distinction once common in constitutional law, is procedural rather than substantive. The substance of freedom is a private pursuit. If men have no political rights in Hobbes' commonwealth, they have the private right to develop their personalities along lines of their own choosing. "The right of nature," Hobbes says, ". . . is the liberty each man hath, to use his own power, as he will himself, for the preservation of his own nature."[51] This private right existed in the state of nature and it is

[51] *Ibid.*, p. 84.

carried over into civil society. Once men are in society, the state will, of course, forbid many actions and require others, but it will not set down an official code of personal morality. This means that Hobbes' authoritarian state forbears from being totalitarian: it draws the line between the political and the personal, the power which is necessary for the public safety and the freedom which is necessary for the individual's development. Freedom, then, is the freedom to do as you please:

By liberty, is understood, according to the proper signification of the word, the absence of external impediments: which impediments, may oft take away part of a man's power to do what he would; but cannot hinder him from using the power left to him, according as his judgment, and reason shall dictate to him.[52]

In employing this conception of freedom, Hobbes has released the individual from another conception of the same idea. For Plato and those who take his general view, freedom is the liberty to do the right thing: to pursue Virtue, to abide by the Natural Law, to obey the General Will, to be in step with the forward march of History. Hobbes' individualistic conception of freedom turns men loose; it frees them from external impediments, especially the rapacities of the state of nature. Once so liberated, they must create the good life for themselves. Immediately the question arises as to whether men are capable of this. Can they discover the good life without the intervention of a political agency which will teach them the knowledge of virtue and reality? Hobbes is sufficiently impressed with his proud and willful men that he believes they will use their freedom to achieve worthwhile ends. Other theorists are less sanguine than Hobbes about men's ability to use freedom without political guidance: the chief function of the state, in their eyes, becomes the moral one of defining freedom and leading men to the right conduct which is the true exercise of that freedom. Locke, Bentham, and Mill are in essential agreement with Hobbes. Burke, Hegel, and Marx follow the earlier definition. Rousseau and Tocqueville attempt to reconcile the two. And the dialectic of freedom will go on so long as political philosophers continue to talk.

[52] *Ibid.*

7.
John Locke

THE MAN AND HIS TIMES

John Locke was born in 1632 in the West Country of England, an area notable for its Royalist sympathies. His father supported the Parliamentary cause, yet, despite the harrassment he suffered, he was able to send his son first to the Westminster School and then to Oxford. After graduation, Locke continued at the University as a philosophy tutor until 1684, when Charles II had him removed for political reasons. During this time he developed scientific and medical interests and was one of the founding members of the Royal Society. As was the case with Hobbes, he was fortunate enough to obtain the friendship and support of a powerful member of the nobility. In Locke's instance it was the Whig Earl of Shaftesbury, who subsequently became Lord Chancellor of England. He assisted his patron in drawing up a constitution for the Carolina colony in America, and on this occasion Locke was able to conjoin theory and practice by explicitly writing the principle of religious toleration into that document. But the Earl of Shaftesbury was essentially opposed to the monarchy, and when his patron was dismissed, Locke was forced to flee to the Continent. He spent six years in Holland and had a chance to see a free society in actual operation. Following the fall of the Stuarts and the invitation to William of Orange to become king, Locke returned to England, where he was welcomed. He was given a number of high political offices, and he ended his career as Commissioner of Trade and Plantations. He died in 1704.

The Protectorate had lasted little longer than Cromwell himself, and in 1660 there seemed no other alternative but to restore the Stuarts to the throne. If Hobbes had seen virtues in Charles II, it was nevertheless clear that that monarch was committed to arbitrary rule. He was unwilling to share his power with Parliament, and he

233

sought to impose his religious views on the nation. This went on for thirty-five years, after which Charles II was succeeded by his brother who was even more highhanded. In addition, James II was a Roman Catholic, and all indications were that he was intent on undoing the Protestant Reformation. The economic and religious forces which had brought on the Puritan Revolution forty years earlier had continued to grow throughout this period. If Cromwell had provided a temporary answer to their quest for representation, it was still plain that they had been unable to consolidate their gains through deep-seated institutional reforms. By 1688, however, important political lessons had been learned. In that year Parliament took the unprecedented step of deciding to ask William of Orange to become King of England. This decision, now known as the Bloodless Revolution, was a milestone in constitutional history. James II saw that the country wished to be rid of him, and he unobtrusively and unprotestingly slipped away to France, never to return.

The Revolution of 1688 was based on what at the time could be construed as popular consent. Powerful sections of the country wanted Parliament to be sovereign and now, unlike the case with the Puritan Revolution, they were prepared to write this principle into the basic law. William of Orange was not allowed to ascend the throne until Parliament had declared him the rightful monarch, and with this step the conception of "divine right" was replaced with that of constitutional monarchy. A Bill of Rights was drawn up in the following year, and this limited the power of the throne in financial and military matters. Dissenting religious sects were allowed far more freedom than they had hitherto enjoyed. In this period, then, was seen the birth of two principles which have underpinned Anglo-Saxon politics for three centuries: government by consent and government by constitution. The Parliaments which followed 1688 were by no means representative of all the people: the franchise extended to but a fraction of the adult population, and the nobility had substantial power. Yet the idea was established that men who are ruled may pass judgment on those who rule over them. And at the same time there was set down the principle that the powers of government are limited, that there are areas of human life into which neither King nor Parliament may legitimately intrude.

Locke's Second Treatise of Civil Government is usually looked on as a rationalization for the new Whig order. That he identified himself with that party and its political aspirations is a matter of record. His book was published in 1690, two years after the Revolution, and it is understandable that he prefaced it by heralding the era to come. Yet it is also the case that Locke had been at work on his theory before the precipitating event, and it is obvious that it is no pamphlet of the moment but a set of considered ideas. While its publication coincided with a turning point of history, it is a volume which began before and has lived long after the times which produced it.

7.
John Locke

LIBERALISM AS A POLITICAL THEORY FINDS ITS CONCRETE EXPRES-
sion in the writings of John Locke. This theory, as will be seen, has more than
one meaning: in fact, some of the most diverse ideas and individuals have
claimed the liberal label for themselves. Nevertheless, there is a common core
which stands at the center of all conceptions of liberalism. For this theory
stands for freedom: the free individual, as well as that individual's freedom
from external restrictions and his freedom to do what he believes is right. In
this sense Hobbes clearly is a liberal, and so are Aristotle and Machiavelli.
Yet if a theory is to be called "liberal" in a meaningful sense, it must put the
free individual at the center of the theory—and keep him there. Hobbes'
man had frequently to give way to the claims of an authoritarian state, and
Aristotle and Machiavelli were concerned with human freedom only part of
the time. It is Locke who not only regards the ideas of individualism and equality as important, but who also frames his theory of government so as to give
primacy to the free lives of the citizens who are served by that government.

The essential freedom in Locke is a permissive one: it is freedom from the
state. States and governments are coercive institutions, and, no matter how
much they may make claim to being representative, their actions are bound to
thwart the behavior of individual citizens. Laws are directives to do this, to
forbear from doing that. And if government is effective, violation of the laws
will result in punishment—an even greater restriction on freedom.

If men are to be free, ways must be found to limit the powers of government, to constitute governments so that citizens will be able to ensure that
limits will be observed, and to recognize the freedoms of men which are prior
to governmental powers. Locke discusses all of these subjects in the course of
his theory. Some of them have been noted earlier: Aristotle and Machiavelli
spoke of governments limited by the "rule of law." St. Thomas and Hobbes
said that the Natural Law might direct rulers away from paths of tyranny.

236

But it is Locke who states that citizens are able to do something positive to secure governments which will not oppress them. And he underpins this view by asserting a theory of the rights of man: rights which all men have, both in a state of nature and in civil society, against their government. Locke takes over the individualist conception of man which Hobbes put down in great detail, and he then proceeds to give it a firm place in the political process by postulating that man's individualism must always be bulwarked by political recognition of his inherent rights. The rights of men, then, take priority over the powers of the state. To exercise these rights, men must be freed from economic, religious, and other restrictions which states are so prone to enact. And if it is an elemental rule of politics that power must be opposed by power, then Locke attempts to show how men's rights may be underwritten so that the state will have to give way to their claims.

VARIETIES OF LIBERALISM

Liberalism has become so common a term in the vocabulary of politics that it is a brave man who will try to give it a precise definition. It is a view of the individual, of the state, and of the relations between them. But, apart from the rudiments which have been outlined, there is little agreement on the content of this idea. Therefore, it would be well to outline the major conceptions of liberalism, for in the final analysis each student of politics is going to have to choose his own definition for himself.

(1) *"Reformist" Liberalism.* This is the popular—and partisan—conception of liberalism which is always juxtaposed against "conservatism." The reformist liberal is prepared to move fast, whereas the conservative wants to proceed slowly and cautiously. The liberal is willing to experiment with legislation and political processes, while the conservative wants to give established institutions every chance to prove that they can do the job. The reformist thinks of the present as a prelude to the future; the conservative regards the present as a product of the past.

It is obvious that this kind of liberalism expresses a mood rather than a coherent policy, a sense of tempo rather than a specific political direction. Yet at the current time it is also clear that liberalism does stand for a fairly specific ideological view. The modern liberal is very much aware of social and economic problems—as he perceives and defines them—and he looks to the government as the major instrument for the solution of these problems. He is convinced that private individuals either cannot or will not confront these matters, and therefore the state must intervene if they are to be attended to. Health, housing, education—all these and perhaps more must be the subjects of collective action.[1] This means, of course, that the state will necessarily grow in size: taxes must be raised to finance new governmental functions, more civil servants must be hired to administer the new services, regulations must be drafted and enforced so that the government will be able to achieve the new goals that it has set out for itself.

How can reformist liberalism be called "liberal" if it requires an increase in state power rather than a limitation on it? The answer to this question is the old proverb, "One man's meat is another man's poison." There is a conflict between reformist liberalism and the free market conception of liberalism which will be considered shortly. The reformist says that the government can actually be a liberating agency. It can redistribute wealth, it can provide public services, and it can protect the weak from the depredations of the strong. In this way the power of the state is used to provide the conditions for achieving the good life for the vast majority of the citizens. Big government, in short, ensures the little man a freedom he did not know before: freedom from starvation, from sickness, from ignorance, from fear.

But the state is using its power to establish these guarantees; it is not relying on voluntary or individual action. This means that in the process of bestowing public benefits on the majority, a minority in society is bound to feel the whiplash of state power. Those whose wealth exceeds the average will be subject to heavier taxation, those who own businesses will be subject to regulation, those who prefer to do without governmental aid may nevertheless be compelled to accept it, or at least to abide by the rules which accompany the aid program. The state, the argument runs, may coerce a few, but it frees the many. And if it did not undertake these responsibilities, then the majority would be coerced by centers of power other than the state. But can big government not also oppress some of the little people who make up the presumably benefited majority? That possibility exists, the reformist admits, but it is less likely than the oppression the little man would suffer were not the state prepared to protect him. This dialogue between liberal and conservative is a familiar one. And it revolves about an important conception of human freedom in our day.

(2) *"Free-Market" Liberalism.* It is no surprise that this brand of liberalism is often regarded as a part of contemporary "conservative" doctrine. For the liberalism of the free market has a history stretching back to at least the time of Adam Smith. Originally it was a radical theory: it called for the liberation of businessmen from the restrictive regulations which governments imposed on economic activity. These restrictions, based on mercantile and even feudal

[1] The best recent statement of reformist liberalism is John Kenneth Galbraith, *The Affluent Society* (Boston: Houghton Mifflin, 1958).

ideas, prevented rising commercial and industrial interests from developing in new directions. Accompanying this protest there grew up a body of thought which postulated that both individuals and society as a whole would manifest their finest potentialities only if the state kept its hands off private economic activities. While businessmen, allowed to expand without official interference, would be the direct beneficiaries, the entire nation would also profit from the burgeoning investment and production.

Free-market liberalism, clearly, became the ideology of a section of the community which had much to gain by a weakened state. Indeed, it is part of this theory that the state is a coercive instrument which is bound to inflict injury whenever it undertakes to use its power. However, the free-market conception did ascribe to public authority certain important functions: it must provide courts so that contracts will be respected and conflicts resolved; it must provide a police force so that property will be safeguarded; it must maintain armed forces so that foreign investments will be protected. Yet free-market liberalism must not be viewed as a wholly economic theory, even though that was its largest single component. If men were to be free to own and operate their businesses as they saw fit, they also needed political freedoms so as to ensure a government sympathetic to these ends. Hence, in the effort to secure a free market, it was also argued that freedom of speech and freedom of association were necessary guarantees. That is, a free economy needs a free government to sustain it. The courts which were created to sanctify contracts would also be available to safeguard political freedoms. The free-market theory, then, was the expression of a new and rising section of society: one that called for an expanded suffrage and a free press as means to achieving economic freedom. It is important to note the conjunction of a political and an economic outlook, and to observe that it was the product of the business class. That class formed a coherent constituency which was prepared to fight for freedom in the face of governmental opposition. In those societies which do not have a business class concerned with establishing a free-market environment, it may be wondered what alternative constituency there is available to oppose the state in the name of liberty.

Despite the venerable history of free-market liberalism it must not be thought that it is an outdated theory. On the contrary, it has powerful spokesmen in our own day, even though the feudal and mercantile restrictions are no longer on the statute books. The interesting thing is that the limited-state notion is now turned against those who would raise that edifice called the welfare state. Once again a large governmental structure is termed coercive and destructive of fundamental liberties. Therefore, the reformist liberals and the free-market liberals are at odds with one another: the former call the latter "conservatives," and the latter reply that they are the "true" representatives of the liberal idea. The argument over terms is not important. What is important is the fact that free-market liberalism is still the ideology of businessmen even though they are no longer parvenus claiming admission to seats of power. Thus the free-market idea is no longer radical; rather, it is a defense of the status quo more than anything else. And even though the enemy—an interfering government—remains the same, the character of business institutions has altered immensely since Adam Smith's time. If competition is a hallmark among free-market liberals, nowadays it is often competition among a handful of giant firms. If weak government is a tenet of the ideology, then government can be strong enough to bestow tariffs, contracts, and monopolistic privileges to the favored. What has occurred is that the free-market rhetoric has stayed constant while economic conditions have changed. Nevertheless, while modern businessmen do not think of themselves as "liberals," the free-market ideas they espouse are part of the liberal heritage.

Free-market liberalism, then, is an example of a body of thought where theory and ideology cannot possibly be separated. It is also an example of the development of ideas alongside events: indeed, it demonstrates the fact that political rhetoric has a disturbing habit of standing still while the ground underneath it is shifting.[2]

(3) *"Utopian" Liberalism.* Liberalism is more than a political platform or an economic ideology. It is also a theory of human nature, and this theory has a way of infusing all liberal thinking about politics and economics. The liberal view of man is that he is, quite simply, a perfectible creature. He is endowed with reason and resourcefulness, and with the will to improve himself. Utopian liberalism is beyond a doubt the most optimistic of political theories. It explicitly rejects the doctrine of original sin laid down by the theologians. Man is not evil, but inherently good. If his political performance has not been up to par, this is because his benign nature has been corrupted by unjust institutions. Man is not ignorant, but capable of acquiring an understanding of the universe and all its workings. If human sciences at the present time leave much unexplained, this is because men's minds have been fettered by superstition and ideology. And men are perfectible: they may attain to their finest potentialities by virtue of their reason and their goodness. The society of the Utopian

---

[2] There have been a number of restatements of free-market liberalism in recent years, but the definitive work is still Friedrich A. Hayek, *The Road to Serfdom* (Chicago: University of Chicago Press, 1945). For a discussion of the ways government has worked against a free market by encouraging monopoly, see Walter Adams and Horace M. Gray, *Monopoly in America: The Government as Promoter* (New York: Macmillan, 1955). And for a witty analysis of usages of the rhetoric of free-market liberalism in an age of economic concentration, see Thurman W. Arnold, *The Folklore of Capitalism* (New Haven: Yale University Press, 1937).

liberal consists of enlightened individuals who have the freedom to pursue their own self-interest and yet who refrain from coercing each other in the course of this pursuit. This liberalism differs from Plato's Utopianism in that it applies to all men and not simply to the ruling class; for the Utopian liberal all men are good, all men are rational, all men are perfectible. This is a theory of human nature, and not an analysis of a specific class. Furthermore, while Plato's Utopia was a camera-eye portrait of a perfect society at some distant date, the liberal notion of society is a dynamic one. History is ·progress: the onward and upward march of enlightened individuals. History is the never-ending story of reason's conquest of ignorance, good's victory over evil. Finally, whereas Plato developed a communism in which the citizen would subordinate his interests to the larger purposes of society, Utopian liberalism is individualist in orientation. The free man stands at the center of this theory: states and societies are associations he establishes for his convenience but not for ends higher than his own.

The Utopian view of human nature, as was said, is evident in all the varieties of liberalism. The reformist liberal has faith that men are enlightened enough to use the institutions of government to benefit themselves and yet to forebear from using those institutions as coercive instruments. The free-market liberal assumes that if men are liberated from restrictions on their activity, they will pursue their self-interest in an enlightened way and thereby enrich society as a whole. The Utopian assumptions find their original expression in the theories of both Hobbes and Locke. They are carried forward by Bentham, Tocqueville, and Mill as liberal thought takes on new dimensions. They are also developed by Rousseau and Marx in directions which are frequently unsettling to those who worry whether the liberal view is susceptible to abuse.

The original criticism of the Utopian view of human nature was found in the writings of the political theologians. And Machiavelli tried to indicate that it simply did not square with the facts of life. However, the great reply lies with Edmund Burke, for his theory of conservatism raises serious questions about the liberal attitude towards man's capabilities.[3] It is one thing to show that men are not equal, not rational, not good. But is also important to show

---

[3] Few liberals, of course, admit to their Utopian bias. Therefore it falls to conservative writers to make this admission for them. Four liberal assumptions, according to Russell Kirk, are: "(1) The perfectibility of man and the illimitable progress of society. . . . They deny that humanity has a natural proclivity toward violence and sin. (2) Contempt for tradition. Reason, impulse, and materialistic determinism are severally preferred as guides to social welfare, trustier than the wisdom of our ancestors. . . . (3) Political levelling. Order and privilege are condemned; total democracy, as direct as practicable, is the professed radical idea. . . . (4) Economic levelling. The ancient rights of property, especially property in land, are suspect. . . ." See *The Conservative Mind* (Chicago: Regnery, 1953), p. 9.

what happens politically when a society operates on the assumption that men are perfectible. For out of the Utopian view grows an exaltation of the average man which is bound to have consequences for certain values which have been traditional in society. It is one thing, in short, to talk of men as the Utopian liberals do: it is quite another to act as if that talk were a sound basis for political action. Both Burke and Tocqueville will expand these ideas. They will be answered by Rousseau and Mill. It would be wrong to accuse the Utopian liberals of political naivete: they know that human progress moves in fits and starts, that war and tyranny are no less present in our own time than in the past, that men continue to be selfish and irrational despite all efforts to educate them in opposite directions. The point is not that we have uncovered man's Utopian nature already—that is patently not the case—but that this is a possible and desirable goal to strive for. The liberal mood is optimistic: improvement, progress, perfectibility—these are within the reach of all men and societies, and they are best achieved by political means.

(4) *"Democratic" Liberalism.* If reformist and free-market liberalism have a tendency to take on the character of ideology, and if Utopian liberalism tends to emphasize philosophy to the exclusion of scientific considerations, then democratic liberalism at least makes an attempt to be a political theory in the textbook sense. The heart of democratic liberalism is the balancing of two values: democracy and individual freedom. Or, to put it another way, a society should be governed by the twin principles of majority rule, on the one hand, and minority rights, on the other. There were evidences of democratic liberal thought long before Locke: in Aristotle, in Machiavelli, in Hobbes. Aristotle and Machiavelli both granted that the general public tended to show greater common sense about political matters than did exclusive minorities. While neither called for unrestricted majority rule, they were sensible to the constructive role which average citizens might play. At the same time, Aristotle and Machiavelli were concerned about the freedom of those individuals whose tastes might run counter to prevailing sentiments in society. For this reason, protections had to be raised which would ensure freedoms to individuals despite the predilections of those who held political power. Both writers spoke of the "rule of law" as standing above the word of any particular ruler. While they did not elaborate on the institutional or constitutional forms which would secure "rule of law," it was clear that freedoms had to be guaranteed by procedures which could not be overridden by the rulers of the day. Most liberal theories conclude by placing a higher premium on individual liberty than they do on democratic government. While Locke does not juxtapose these two values in an explicit way, both Tocqueville and Mill make the tension between them central to their theories. Locke does espouse both

majority rule and individual rights, and it is important to note that he and Tocqueville and Mill all feel obliged to sanction democracy, even though their chief concern is to establish free societies.

The reason for the dilemma which democratic liberals impose upon themselves is not hard to find. They want a free society in which all men will know liberty. But the average man's conception of freedom is frequently at odds with that of certain individuals who wish to live in ways which are not socially approved. Therefore, the majority, in securing its own freedom, may make decisions which trample on the liberty of various minorities. This is, of course, the problem of the tyranny of the majority which Plato raised and which never ceases to be discussed. There are some liberals who for this reason reject any talk of majority rule: they consider individual freedom to be so important that democracy presents too great a danger to it to be tolerated. However, most liberals are also democrats, and this is because they are unwilling to make qualitative distinctions about the superiority of one man's freedom as opposed to another's. If the majority, composed of average men, defines its freedom in a rather rough-and-ready way, who is to ask them to give up their liberty so that an allegedly superior minority may pursue its more sophisticated tastes? Liberalism stands for the freedom of all men, not simply the freedom of a cultured or a wealthy minority. Unfortunately, most men only feel secure in their freedom if alternative definitions of freedom are extinguished: it is difficult for one section of society to be contented if it knows that attitudes and activities antithetical to its own tastes are present in another part of the community. Majority rule, freedom for the great mass of average men, is a legitimate component of liberalism because freedom must be bestowed even on average men. Yet the freedoms of minorities and lone individuals cannot for this reason be thrust by the wayside. There are various ways of attempting to reconcile majority and minority freedoms. If Locke suggests some procedures in a tentative way, others will proceed further towards a solution of this perennial problem.

That there are common features in these various conceptions of liberalism should be plain by now. The two which stand out are, first, the free life is the prime pursuit of politics and, second, the state's task is to eschew coercion and to encourage the conditions for that free life. The contrast between reformist and free-market liberalism has shown how time and circumstances can change men's view of the substantive content of freedom. The principles of Utopian and democratic liberalism demonstrate that there exist certain fairly fixed psychological and political assumptions to which all liberals adhere. Few liberal theorists adopt any single one of these approaches unreservedly. It would be hard in this day, for example, to find anyone to hold to the Utopian outlook in an unqualified way. Nevertheless, all liberals are, in one way or another, a mixture of reformists, democrats, Utopians, and proponents of the free market. If the proportions of the ingredients vary, the basic recipe is always the same.

LOCKE VS. HOBBES

Like Hobbes, and for much the same reason, Locke opens his theory by postulating that men once lived in a state of nature. The existence which they led in that natural state, taken together with the motives which impelled them to leave it, provide the philosophical underpinning for the civil governments which replace the previous condition. Locke paints his picture in tones far more temperate than those used by Hobbes:

> To understand political power aright, and derive it from its original, we must consider what state all men are naturally in, and that is a state of perfect freedom to order their actions and dispose of their possessions and persons as they think fit, within the bounds of the law of nature, without asking leave, or depending upon the will of any other man.
> A state also of equality, wherein all the power and jurisdiction is reciprocal, no one having more than another. . . .[4]

There is no talk of this being an unbearable condition: men are not observed to live in fear of violent death, nor is life described as being solitary, poor, nasty, brutish, and short. The perfect freedom of Locke's state of nature seems, in fact, to work out reasonably well. Men do not appear to abuse their liberty, and they do not go about threatening the lives of their neighbors. "Though this be a state of liberty, yet it is not a state of license . . ." Locke says. "The state of nature has a law of nature to govern it, which obliges every one; and reason, which is that law, teaches all mankind who will but consult it, that being all equal and independent, no one ought to harm another in his life, health, liberty, or possessions."[5] Hobbes' state of nature also had a Law of Nature, but men were so concerned with elemental survival that they could not afford the luxury of abiding by its tenets. Locke gives no guarantees that men will consult the Natural Law, but on the whole he seems more sanguine about their ability to live in peace with one another.

However, this is still a state of nature: there are no political institutions and no common authority. This means that each man consults, interprets, and acts

---

[4] *Second Treatise of Civil Government*, para. 4. Locke numbered each paragraph in this essay, and therefore the references may be found in any edition. The edition used here is in *The English Philosophers from Bacon to Mill* (New York: Modern Library, 1939), edited by E. A. Burtt, pp. 403–503.

[5] Para. 6.

on the Natural Law according to his own lights. Furthermore, he judges the behavior of his fellow citizens on this self-defined basis. "The execution of the law of nature is in that state put into every man's hand," Locke says, "whereby everyone has a right to punish the transgressors of that law. . . ." [6]

Is there really a meaningful difference between Hobbes' and Locke's conceptions of the state of nature? One has its inhabitants ravaging their neighbors in the search for security; the other has them meting out mutual punishment in the name of reason which each man defines for himself. If every man is seen to impinge on the freedom of every other man, then the social consequences would seem to be the same no matter what motives inspire these invasions. Where each man sets himself up as judge, jury, and policeman—no matter how reasonable he may think he is acting in these roles—the end result ought to be no less anarchic than Hobbes' war of all against all. Yet Locke insists that he does not want to have it this way, and a theorist is entitled to design a hypothetical state of nature whichsoever way he wishes. For Locke has more than one reason for not wanting to equate the state of nature with a state of war. "The state of nature and the state of war, which however some men have confounded, are as far distant as a state of peace, good-will, mutual assistance and preservation, and a state of enmity, malice, violence and mutual destruction, are from one another," he says.[7]

The real dispute is not whether men in the state of nature have reasoning powers—for both Hobbes and Locke grant that they do—but whether they have the will to live according to the dictates of their reason. Locke believes that the state of nature need not necessarily be warlike because he has faith in men's willingness to forbear from resorting to force. Despite the lack of a common judge, the result need not be anarchic.

> Men living together according to reason, without a common superior on earth with authority to judge between them is properly the state of nature. By force, or a declared design of force, upon the person of another, where there is no common superior on earth to appeal to for relief, is the state of war, and 'tis the want of such an appeal gives a man the right of war. . . . Want of a common judge with authority puts all men in a state of nature; force without right, upon a man's person, makes a state of war.[8]

What Locke is saying is that life need not be unbearable in the state of nature, and consequently we ought not to assume that men are relentlessly driven to establish a government to protect their lives. On the contrary, a state of na-

[6] Para. 7.

[7] Para. 19. We can safely assume that the "some men" referred to here are Hobbes and various of his disciples. It is really immaterial that Locke does not mention Hobbes by name, for our concern is with the opposition of ideas and not of the individuals who wrote them.

[8] *Ibid.*

ture can be a quite reasonable place; therefore, if men do decide to form a common authority, the decision is not pressed upon them by fear of violence and death.

Why, then, do men quit the state of nature? If freedom and equality can be made operative by the use of reason, then there would appear to be no need to set up a government at all. While a state of war might occasionally break out, this seems to be the exception rather than the rule. Yet as a political theorist Locke has some reservations about man's ability to act as an objective judge. Men are passionate and egoistic creatures, and the processes of justice may be undone as personal considerations enter. "It is unreasonable for men to be judges in their own cases, . . . self-love will make men partial to themselves and their friends," Locke says. "And on the other side, . . . ill-nature, passion, and revenge will carry them too far in punishing others; and hence nothing but confusion and disorder will follow." [9] These human frailties can clearly lead to abuses of power.

Nevertheless, the confusion and the disorder which society may experience are still a far remove from Hobbes' state of war. Men can put up with inconveniences such as these, and they can work steadily at developing reasonable resolutions of disputes. What is most important, however, is that they will want to think twice before they give up the liberty and equality which they know in the state of nature. The cure for confusion and disorder may in the end be far less palatable than putting up with these inconveniences. Locke wants any decision to form a government to be a cautious and measured one. It may be far more inconvenient to find oneself living under an absolute monarch than suffering the discomforts of the state of nature.

I easily grant that civil government is the proper remedy for the inconveniences of the state of nature, which must certainly be great where men may be the judges in their own case, since 'tis easy to be imagined that he who was so unjust as to do his brother an injury, will scarce be so just as to condemn himself for it. But I shall desire those who make this objection, to remember that absolute monarchs are but men, and if government is to be the remedy of those evils which necessarily follow from men's being judges in their own cases, and the state of nature is therefore not to be endured, I desire to know what kind of government that is, and how much better it is than the state of nature. . . .[10]

The restrictions of governmental authority, Locke would agree with Hobbes, are preferable to the terrors of a state of war. But the state of nature is not necessarily a state of war. This means that if government is to make an advance on the state of nature, it must be a government which will maintain the freedom and equality that men originally knew. Certainly the inconveniences

[9] Para. 13.
[10] *Ibid.*

which men experienced when there was no common judge are less oppressive than the absolute rule of Hobbes' sovereign. Locke suggests that liberty may be more important than life, that some prices are too high to pay for order and safety. The solution Hobbes offers raises questions about the lot of the individual, and its answers are less than satisfactory.

> For if it be asked, what security, what fence is there, in such a state, against the violence and oppression of this absolute ruler, the very question can scarce be borne. . . . As for the ruler, he ought to be absolute, and is above all such circumstances; because he has the power to do more hurt and wrong, 'tis right when he does it. To ask how you may be guarded from harm and injury on that side where the strongest hand is to do it, is presently the voice of faction and rebellion.[11]

It can now be seen why Locke has tried to make his state of nature as pleasant as possible. He wants men to be in a strong enough bargaining position so they can lay down conditions about the kind of government they will live under if they decide to quit the state of nature. The chief condition is that the individual's freedom will continue to be respected and secured. Hobbes' men could not quibble about terms: they would only be ensured protection from violent death. Because Locke's state of nature is not so fearsome, its inhabitants can bide their time: they can pick and choose among governments so as to make sure that they are actually profitting from their move into civil society.

The social contract which Locke describes is not much different from Hobbes'. First of all, citizens can no longer be judges and policemen as the spirit moves them. "Every man entered into civil society," Locke says, "has quitted his power to punish offenses against the Law of Nature in prosecution of his own private judgment." [12] The contract itself is then spelled out:

> Wherever, therefore, any number of men so unite into one society, as to quit everyone his executive power of the Law of Nature, and to resign it to the public, there, and there only, is a political, or civil society. And this is done wherever any number of men, in the state of nature, enter into society to make one people, one body politic, under one supreme government, or else when anyone joins himself to, and incorporates with, any government already made. For hereby he authorizes the society, or, which is all one, the legislative thereof, to make laws for him, as the public good of the society shall require, to the execution whereof his own assistance (as to his own decrees) is due. And this puts men out of a state of nature into that of a commonwealth, by setting up a judge on earth with authority to determine all the controversies and redress the injuries that may happen to any member of the commonwealth.[13]

[11] Para. 93.
[12] Para. 88.
[13] Para. 89.

The hallmark of this commonwealth is not the sword, but the scales: not a sovereign whose sole obligation is to protect life, but a supreme government which is to settle conflicts and redress injuries. While Hobbes' sovereign might do away with internal differences in the society for the sake of establishing order, Locke's government tolerates controversy and only seeks to act as a judge among conflicting parties. Here we see emerging one of the tenets of liberalism: the state has certain duties to perform, but it must not use its power beyond the boundaries set down by the contract. Citizens set up their government, but only for specified purposes. That government, therefore, cannot claim that it needs a free hand in order to secure public safety. On the contrary, Locke is persuaded that no government at all is preferable to the oppressive order which an absolute ruler might promise.

A further distinction between the two contract theories is worth noting. Locke allows, far more readily than Hobbes, that citizens may dissolve the social contract. This will be discussed later on. One reason why Hobbes objected to such a dissolution was that that act would plunge men back into the state of war—that is, if the contract were broken, not only government but society as well would disappear. Hobbes' choice, as usual, is between order and anarchy with no middle ground. Locke, on the other hand, makes the contractual process more elaborate. The original contract—the one which brings men out of the state of nature for the first time—is similar to Hobbes' in that it establishes a society and a government concurrently. Indeed, at that point there is no important difference between social and political institutions. However, Locke's contract actually has two parts in it: one sets up society and the second sets up a government. This is made clear when the discussion turns to the possibility of dissolving the government. When such an eventuality arises, this affects only the political part of the contract. "He that will with any clearness speak of the dissolution of government ought, in the first place, to distinguish between the dissolution of the society and the dissolution of the government," Locke says.[14] This distinction is one that Hobbes was unwilling to make. Locke, however, sees nothing inapposite in breaking the political part of the contract and having the social part remain intact. That is, men may dissolve their government but they may remain in society: they need not return to the state of nature. Indeed, if the only way to get rid of a government were to destroy the society as well, then changes of rulers would be all but impossible, and we would be back at Hobbes' absolute sovereign once more.

The importance of the two-stage contract goes to the heart of liberal political theory. From Plato through Hobbes, theorists were not concerned to distin-

[14] Para. 211.

guish between state and society as different institutions. The jurisdictions of these two entities were identical, and this meant that the state was jusified in extending its power into whatever parts of society it felt was necessary. The liberal theory of the state, however, cuts down the allowable sphere of political activity. The state is but one of several institutions in society: alongside it stand religious, economic, educational, and other institutions which have existences and purposes of their own. Because the state is a political and not a social agency, it must confine its activities to areas which are properly political. It has no warrant—under Locke's contract—to interfere with matters outside the political province.

All this is implied, further, by Locke's statement that even if a government is dissolved, the society remains in existence. Churches, schools, businesses, private associations—all these are not dependent on the state for their continued being. Liberal theory, in addition, assumes that each individual plays two roles: he is a resident of a society and a citizen of a state. The loyalties which he incurs as a citizen do not flow over into all aspects of his social life. On the contrary, as the owner of a business, the member of a church, or the father of a family he has obligations which are additional to—and occasionally in conflict with—those of political citizenship. This means that the individual can find his freedom not through obedience to the state but by a voluntary choice of the activities he may wish to pursue in society. Liberal political theory, therefore, is less political—less about the state—and more social and individual. A free society, one free from governmental interference, is the refuge for free men.

After all the efforts of writers, culminating with Hobbes, to establish the strength of the state, it is Locke who sets about to weaken that instituion and limit its powers. This is done not out of Utopian design, but rather to give each individual an area of freedom in society which is impervious to political control. But it is clear that a social contract with two stages is not a sufficient guarantee that the state will observe limitations. Power must be met with power, as Aristotle emphasized when he stressed the role of the middle class, and this means that institutions in society must develop strength so they can ward off possible inroads on the part of a tyrannical state. Locke does not develop a conception of countervailing social institutions in any explicit manner: the notion of basing a free society on a pluralist foundation will be elaborated by Tocqueville and Mill.

What Locke does do, however, is lay down the first foundation for pluralism. He has already indicated that the state exists to promote the free life of individuals; he has suggested that there are limits on the state's legitimate powers. And now he adds to these a factor designed to elevate the importance of the individual and give him the power and status to achieve his freedom. This factor is private property.

PROPERTY AND PERSONALITY

"The great and chief end," Locke says, "of men's uniting into commonwealths, and putting themselves under government, is the preservation of their property.[15] Just what Locke means by property is one of the vexing questions of political theory. At first glance it would appear that a lofty philosophy of freedom may well be degenerating into an ideological defense of business interests. But this is not Locke's meaning at all. When he speaks of property, he intends that its possession and benefits will be accorded to all citizens—not in equal portions perhaps, but broadly enough so that property will have a meaningful role in the lives of all men. It would be well, before examining Locke's analysis, to give some attention to the traditional and contemporary conceptions of this institution; for the term itself is used so variously that any student of politics must try to settle his own thinking on the matter before approaching someone else's theory.

(1) Property, of course, is one's home, one's car, one's wristwatch, and one's toothbrush. In this sense everyone can claim to be a property-owner: if nothing else, of the clothes on his back. However, this conception of property is not of much relevance for political theory. Ownership of a household full of goods, while providing material comfort, does not give an indication of the source of those things, or the means by which they are sustained or replaced. In short, it takes more than a paid-up mortgage and a savings account at the local bank to be a "man of property." In a technical sense, individual possessions are called "personalty," and they ought to be distinguished from property.

(2) Property, in its most important sense, is the ownership of a source of wealth. Until recently this was interpreted as an individual's ownership of an enterprise: a factory, a store, a farm, or real estate. Such a person would own and operate his holdings at a profit; after he had added value to the goods he manufactured or the services he provided, there would be a surplus which he could count on keeping for himself. The ownership of instruments of production or distribution—this was Marx's definition, and it has been used by non-Marxists as well—combines possession and labor. That is, the owner gives of his time, effort, and imagination to his enterprise. It is the product of his own savings, and it remains profitable because of the initiative he displays in managing its affairs. Whether it be a small shop or a landed estate, a large factory or a fleet of trucks, the personality of the owner is interwoven with the

[15] Para. 124.

management of the productive instruments. And this property must be not only wealth-producing, but also material and tangible. Whether it consists of buildings or machines or inventories of goods, the property-owner ought to be able to list an actual "net worth" in his "assets" column.

(3) But property need not be ownership of material objects. It can also be of symbols which stand for such ownership. The most obvious of these symbols is money: if you have $10 million in the bank, not only do you earn interest on it, but you could buy a factory with it tomorrow and start collecting its profits. However, most people do not collect money; rather, they invest their cash in profitable enterprises and get a return on these investments. What is owned, of course, is pieces of paper: stocks and bonds. There are important differences between owning tangible productive instruments and owning symbolic shares in those instruments. Both the symbols and the material realities can be wealth-producing. Indeed, many people get higher incomes from their shareholdings than others do from their personal ownership of enterprises.

First of all, however, the shareowner does not manage the enterprise of which he is part owner. He may never have seen it, and he may not even know what are made in its factories. While he and his fellow investors are legal owners of the business, they have only the most formal of rights when it comes to having a say on how the company is run. Individuals with very large holdings can gain seats for themselves or their representatives on the board of directors, but most shareholders are not of that status. The average owner of stocks and bonds settles for his quarterly checks from an anonymous corporation treasurer. In theory, he has hired executives to manage the business for him; in practice, they set aside enough money each year as dividends so there will not be a fuss at the stockholders' annual meeting. The shareowner may like to think that eight drill-presses and fifteen feet of the assembly line are "his"; but he cannot dictate how they will be used, and he certainly cannot remove them from the factory. If anything, his shares symbolize money he has loaned to the corporation, to do with as it pleases until the shareowner sees fit to call back his loan.

In addition, because shares in a corporation are diffused among thousands or even hundreds of thousands of holders, a personal sense of identification with the enterprise is extremely difficult to establish. Many shareholders buy stocks on the advice of a broker, for they do not have the knowledge to judge the qualifications of the management or the prospects of the industry. And any loyalties to a company are usually left by the wayside if it is deemed profitable to take one's cash out of one firm and put it into another.

Finally, a person may own shares in many companies—as one does by investing in a "mutual fund"—and in this sense it is impossible to regard one's property as anything more than interest-bearing loans. Are shares legitimately to be construed as property? They must be, simply because they are sources of wealth. While this kind of property does not inspire the personal attachment to the wealth-producing process that ownership of an enterprise does, it is nevertheless the definition of property for a growing segment of the population. The ownership of shares can give to the holder a stake in the welfare of the economy, and his income from his holdings can give him the sense of security aspired after by all who would become men of property. However, there is a danger in being too facile in thinking of shares as property. The man with $10,000 invested in stock may receive dividends of $800 each year; that is hardly the meaning of property. At least an investment of $150,000 is needed before we can ascribe to shareholding the status of property in any significant sense.

(4) It follows from this that a corporation itself is a piece of private property. Owned by thousands of anonymous stockholders and managed by salaried executives, it nevertheless has a status of its own as a private institution in society. This is best observed when government officials try to regulate the company or union negotiators seek to impose working conditions: at these junctures the executives insist that the company is private property and hence protected against intrusive bureaucrats, that managerial prerogatives are a matter of right and not to be surrendered to labor bosses. The managers will say, furthermore, that they are no more than trustees, doing a job as best they can for the shareholders. At all events, the men who manage corporations base their freedom of action on the fact that these institutions are themselves property and hence to be accorded all the rights to which such holdings are entitled by law and custom. But, with shareholding so diffused and with the buying and selling of stocks at such a rapid tempo, the reality seems to be that a corporation is property without effective owners. The salaried managers make the decisions, and the shareholders collect their dividends. Perhaps it would be best to adjust our thinking and admit that it is possible to have "ownerless" property. What is interesting is that corporate businesses run by salaried managers nevertheless invoke the rhetoric of entrepreneurial property as legitimizing devices. Our society's chief justifications for private property were designed to explain the enterprises where ownership and management were in the same hands. In an age of ownerless institutions of property, a new theory is clearly needed. And it might be added that not only corporations, but also churches, universities, foundations, and trade unions are attaining to the status of aggregations of unowned wealth.

(5) Finally, an individual has property in his own person. This is not the ownership of a tangible enterprise, nor is it shares in a safe-deposit box. A few

examples will make this clear. A soldier who is disabled in wartime is entitled to a pension because had he not been incapacitated he would have had the potentiality for creating wealth with his own person. A worker has earned seniority through long service with one company, and his employer cannot deprive him of the preferred treatment which is accorded to a man whose person has been on the premises longer than others. A doctor and a lawyer have property in the medical and legal trainings which are incorporated in their persons, and they cannot be unlicensed or disbarred without due process at the hands of their professional colleagues. And an actor may have property in his handsome features and thus take out insurance totaling millions of dollars against the eventuality of their disfigurement. These illustrations make their point, but they do not go so far as to demonstrate that all men are guaranteed a return on their willingness to work. Men may have property in their persons, but if there is no demand for their labor, they have no right to a job. Indeed, the examples which were given are actually illustrative of investments of time or money which inhere in the persons of various individuals. Not all men have such investments in their persons, and to the extent that they are lacking these individuals do not possess a property value. At times when labor is scarce, then every "able body" is a property and can command a price; when there is a surplus of labor, only the fortunate can take advantage of the property in their persons. In the final analysis, then, this conception of property hinges on the interplay of supply and demand, on individual bargaining advantage, and on the social approval accorded to certain talents and skills. No individual can assume that there will *always* be a demand for the property in his person—except, perhaps, a girl with a pretty face and an attractive figure. Locke, however, did not talk of things like this.

    In turning to Locke's discussion of property, it is important to ask at each juncture what kind of property is being considered. If Locke is occasionally vague or ambiguous on this score, this is because we all tend to think of property in terms closest to our own interests. At all events, Locke seeks to construct a defense of private property as an institution. That it needs defending ought to be apparent. Plato believed that property obscured men's reasoning powers, and he therefore denied it to the Guardians. Aristotle approved of property, but he said that any class which became too wealthy would constitute a threat to political stability. St. Thomas refused to assert that property is sanctioned by the Natural Law and claimed that it is an "addition" enacted by human legislators. And Hobbes allowed his citizens to own property, but he gave the sovereign the power to regulate the ways in which it was employed. All these theorists, in short, have expressed reservation about property. And not only theorists, but actual property-owners have never been absolutely sure in their own minds that their holdings are legitimate ones. An uneasy conscience tends to accompany wealth, especially if there is in society any significant group which does not share in that wealth. For this reason, theories justifying property are always in the making. They serve the purpose, first of all, of salving the consciences of the rich, and they also are employed to persuade the propertyless that even though they do not share in this institution they still ought to grant its legitimacy. It is easy to see how theories of property are apt to turn into ideology: "What is good for property is good for the entire society," is more an attempt at rationalization and persuasion than it is an essay in description and analysis.

There are, as will be seen, perfectly valid theoretical explanations of private property. One has already been advanced: that political freedoms cannot be detached from economic freedom, that an independent business class can form a hedge against a tyrannical state. However, it is incumbent on any student of this emotion-laden subject to try to disentangle theory from ideology.

Locke asks two related questions. The first is, quite simply, why have private property at all? The second is, how can those who have attained to the status of property-owners justify their privileged position? Unlike Aristotle, Locke does not call for a broadening of the property-owning class. Indeed, he does not suggest what its dimensions already are. Nor does he say, as Rousseau will, that property-ownership has become concentrated in too few hands and hence can no longer enter a claim to legitimacy. What Locke does do is to lay down a series of justifications for the institution itself. These defenses have varying sources, but they all point in a single direction: that property-ownership is necessary if men are to have the wherewithal to lead the good life.

(1) First of all, God has put men on this earth and He has given them reason so that they may make use of the earth's resources. God, as St. Thomas pointed out, did not commit himself on whether public or private ownership of these resources is best suited for the virtuous life. This would depend on the time and circumstances, and on the stage of social development and the degree of scarcity of resources.

Locke opens his discussion by granting that God originally gave property to all men in common:

> God, who hath given the world to men in common, hath also given them reason to make use of it to the best advantage of life and convenience. The earth and all that is therein is given to men for the support and comfort of their being. And though all the fruits it naturally produces, and beasts it feeds, belong to mankind in common, as they are produced by the spontaneous hand of nature; and nobody has originally a private dominion exclusive of the rest of mankind in any of them as they are thus in their natural state; yet being given for the use of men, there

must of necessity be a means to appropriate them some way or other before they can be of any use or at all beneficial to any particular man.[16]

The appropriate means for making use of the resources which God has given to men is, Locke says, for individuals to develop them so they can actually sustain life. For Locke is no less a proponent of individualism than Hobbes: if there is a job which requires doing, then it is best that individuals undertake the task. There is no assumption that society or the state are better fitted or more legitimately entitled to handle the ask of producing goods and providing services. God, then, has given men the raw materials: he has, for instance, put a mineral like bauxite in the earth. But only men can dig it out, transform it into aluminum, manufacture airplanes, and distribute these products to one another. If this is to be done, then mines, mills, factories, and sales agencies must be created. And the best way to accomplish this is to allow individuals to come into possession of the land and materials so they will have the means—and the incentive—to turn earth into usable commodities. To say that private ownership is the most appropriate means for turning God-given resources into human benefits follows from the individualist bias: better for men, acting voluntarily, to carry out this task than for it to be left to collective ownership and operation. Nevertheless, this argument is a deductive one: it is not shown empirically that private hands are more efficient or morally superior to public control. Aristotle claimed that individuals would give greater attention and care to property they themselves owned, and that resources held in common would be neglected and their potentialities would remain undeveloped. This raises the vital question of incentives; it is implicit in Locke's analysis, but it is not brought to the surface.

(2) The next defense is at an altogether different level. This may be called a labor theory of value, although more appropriately it is a labor theory of property rights.

> Every man has a property in his own person; this nobody has any right to but himself. The labor of his body and the work of his hands we may say are properly his. Whatsoever, then, he removes out of the state that nature hath provided and left it in, he hath mixed his labor with, and joined to it something that is his own, and thereby makes it his property.[17]

This justification would appear to be confined solely to agricultural property. "As much land as a man tills, plants, improves, cultivates, and can use the product of, so much is his property," Locke says.[18]

However, landed property is only an illustration of a more general principle.

[16] Para. 26.
[17] Para. 27.
[18] Para. 32.

Men earn their right to property by mixing their labor with inert materials and thereby giving those materials a higher value and a greater usefulness. This occurs not only at the agricultural stage, but also in mining, manufacturing, and distribution. "God gave the world to men in common; but . . . it cannot be supposed He meant it should always remain common and uncultivated," Locke says. "He gave it to the use of the industrious and rational . . . , not to the fancy or covetousness of the quarrelsome and contentious." [19] This means that the industriousness of an individual, the initiative and imagination he displays in cultivating resources, can give him title to ownership. The labor need not be physical: it can also be the intellectual labor of planning and managing. However, Locke does demand that the owner put in a good day's work on his enterprise. There is no allowance for the rentier, the absentee-owner, the speculator, or the anonymous shareholder in this theory. Furthermore, the property owner's reward is to be no more than he and his family can actually use: they may live well, but they should not make so much that there is cash left over.

What Locke is stressing is that ownership is justified by its productive character: if men are to make money, their profits can only be explained by their having added something to the commodities available to society. If a man builds a house, for example, he is entitled to call it his own and to charge rent on those who occupy it. But after thirty years of collecting rents he will not only have paid for the house and compensated himself, but he will have enough left over to build a new house. If he is to be industrious and rational, as Locke demands, he should tear down the old house and put up a new and better one: this would be a progressive use of his property right. Were he simply to collect rents for another thirty years, he would not be justifying his earnings by a show of industry. He might profit, but society would suffer because he was abusing his property right by resting on his laurels.

Locke's theory puts heavy obligations on the property-owner. He stresses the labor of the individual to the exclusion of other factors. This approach was to be used not only by Marx, but also by the classical economists. A product, for example, is the sum of the pains, sweat, and toil of the workmen who have contributed to its final form.

> For 'tis not barely the ploughman's pains, the reaper's and thresher's toil, and the baker's sweat, is to be counted into the bread we eat; the labor of those who broke the oxen, who dug and wrought the iron and stones, who felled and framed the timber employed about the plough, mill, oven, or any other utensils, which are a vast number, requisite to this corn, from its sowing, to its being made bread, must all be charged on the account of labor, and received as an effect of that.

[19] Para. 34.

Nature and the earth furnished only the almost worthless materials as in themselves.[20]

This conception, while it fits well with Locke's previous statements, has a number of important gaps. Locke clearly wishes to see that the ploughman, the reaper, and the baker are repaid for their labor: their wages should be included in the loaf of bread. But, unfortunately, there is the interplay of supply and demand. Consumers may not want the bread they have produced, and if it grows moldy on the shelves, this means that human labor will go unrewarded. Or buyers may be willing to pay only a certain price for it, and the farmers and middlemen may end up receiving less than adequate payment for their labor. Presumably rational production and pricing would avoid these problems, and perhaps Locke is assuming that an "invisible hand" will ensure to all who labor a fair return. But economists have had reason to question this free-market assumption in recent years, and the artificial price supports demanded by farmers—plus production controls—show that productive labor cannot count on automatic compensation.

In addition, Locke's theory has no place for the role of investment funds in the productive process. The ploughs, the mills, the ovens he speaks of are expensive items, and the money to buy and replace them must come from somewhere. If owners are only allowed to keep as much in the way of profits as they can use, then they will have no surplus cash for capital goods. It is because of the need for large sums of money for capital equipment that the corporation came into being: it had to borrow funds so as to construct machines by which it would produce wealth on an efficient and substantial scale. The lenders—stock- or bondholders—clearly demanded payment for their loans, and these sums have to be included in the price of a commodity even though they represent no one's labor. They do represent a commodity—money —which the manufacturers need no less than they need labor; and they also represent the risk that investors take, for if the enterprise fails, then the lenders' money is lost. The "unearned" profits which go to investors do not fit into Locke's scheme. And since the modern corporation is largely based on such an investment pattern, it is difficult to find a place for it in this part of Locke's defense of property. However, there are other facets to his justification, and in these corporate property may find bases for legitimatization.

(3) Property is political as well as economic, and therefore Locke gives it a place in his theory of the contract. In this theory, the idea of consent looms large—far larger, certainly, than it did in Hobbes' model. The way in which Locke bases government on the consent of the governed will be examined later on. At this point it is important to see how property is based on consent.

[20] Para. 43.

As men lived together and as they enlarged the use of their resources, they began to acknowledge that a division of labor and consequently of property was necessary among individuals. "As families increased, and industry enlarged their stocks . . ." Locke says, "by consent, they came in time to set out the bounds of their distinct territories, and agree on limits between them and their neighbors, and, by laws within themselves, settled the properties of those of the same society." [21] Actually this agreement took place in the state of nature: the laws of property of which Locke speaks were not official, but rather informal agreements among reasonable men. This emphasizes the fact that the right to property is prior to government: it is a Natural Right which men possess at birth. Government can and should recognize this right, and it may embody it in statutory form. But even if a government is dissolved or abolished, that right remains with each individual. This agreement, furthermore, does not require that property holdings be equal:

> The consent of men have agreed to a disproportionate and unequal possession of the earth—I mean out of the bounds of society and compact; for in governments the laws regulate it; they having, by consent, found out and agreed in a way how a man may rightfully and without injury possess more than he himself can make use of by receiving gold and silver, which may continue long in a man's possession, without decaying for the overplus, and agreeing those metals should have a value.[22]

In saying this, Locke is making some important additions to his theory of property; and these additions impart a good deal more sophistication to his previous explanations of that institution. In the state of nature men already agreed that the property holdings of one man might be larger than that of his neighbors. When the contract is concluded, and state and society are formed, then government gives legal recognition not only to property, but also to the pattern of property distribution which existed prior to the contract. And citizens give their consent, in addition, to the creation of a money economy: one of the functions of a government is to establish a currency and to underwrite its stability. The consequence of this is that the dictum that men may own only so much as they can make use of goes by the wayside. If their property produces a profit, then owners may put these earnings into gold or silver, the value of which is backed by the authority of the state. And it is further clear that this surplus money will not be hoarded or spent entirely on consumer goods; it will be used for the investment purposes which have been discussed already. While Locke does not say so in so many words, he is suggesting that substantial investment in an economy cannot be carried out unless there is a government which can stand behind a national currency. Not

[21] Para. 38.
[22] Para. 50.

only gold and silver, but also paper money and stock certificates and bonds must be able to circulate freely and with predictable values. Property without money is bound to be limited in scope, and its products cannot be distributed or exchanged with any degree of efficiency. For this reason, the property men have even in an amicable state of nature will never reach its full productive potentialities. One motive for setting up government, then, is to provide the legal basis for economic expansion. Money must have a foundation in law, and investment hinges on a money economy. In Locke, therefore, we see the emergence of the politics of a capitalistic society. The state must be strong enough to provide legal underpinnings for private investment, and yet not so strong as to interfere with the free decisions of men who wish to risk their money to make a profit for themselves.

One of the more interesting themes in political theory is the tracing of the gradual development of the idea of consent in political relations. All systems are perforce based on the consent of the governed, because no army or secret police has ever been created which can long keep a whole population in unwilling subjection. If there is "consent" in Machiavelli's theory, it is at the primitive level of satisfying the elementary social and psychological needs of the rather simple-minded average man. If this idea appears in Hobbes, it is expressed once in the formation of society and is not called upon after the sovereign has ascended to power. And the "consent" in Hobbes is not so much a measured act as an impulsive desire to escape the threat of violent death at any price. Locke develops the idea, and he makes it more rational and creates institutions which give it more substantial meaning. Nevertheless, it will fall on Rousseau and Mill to endow consent with sufficient attributes so it becomes a coherent element in democratic government.

What Locke is saying is that property is legitimate because men who must live in its midst have consented to its existence. And they have agreed, furthermore, that they harbor no objections to its unequal distribution. The men who engaged in this act of consent are the hypothetical men of a hypothetical state of nature: the hypothetical great-grandfathers of all of us. This raises the question, which Locke will later undertake to answer, of why and how far the decisions of men long since dead are still binding on us the living. And it also leads us to wonder whether consent is not being confused with habit. If men do not object to either the existence or the unequal distribution of private property, is this because they have rationally considered the alternatives or because they accept these features of the society into which they were born as a matter of habit and custom? Rousseau will insist that consent must be an active process, one renewed each day in men's lives; while Burke will claim that genuine consent is found in the established customs which men unconsciously develop over generations and centuries. Furthermore, Locke defends property through consent only part of the way: he has also said that property is sanctioned by God and earned by men. This raises a problem considered in the discussion of St. Thomas: if an institution derives from God's will, then that is sufficient justification for it. Indeed, human objections to such an institution are insufficient warrant to override the precepts of the Natural Law. Locke, then, is covering both his flanks: property is sanctified by both Divine approval and popular consent. And to this he adds that men earn their right to property by mixing their labor with it—what might be called a utilitarian justification.

In introducing these three defenses, is Locke making too much of a good thing? It is one thing to try to reconcile or synthesize three discrete themes in political philosophy; it is another to simply add one on top of another to please all factions. A lawyer very often takes just this approach. He will say to the judge and jury, "I intend to prove, first, that my client was not at the corner of Third and Main at the time that the murder took place; second, that the gun which he held in his hand was not loaded; and third, that he shot the victim in self-defense." The lawyer says this because he wishes to show that his client is innocent of the violation of not one, but actually three separate laws. In a similar way, Locke is appealing to the "laws" of God, of democracy, and of utility. The fact that these laws have different foundations and often are in sharp conflict with each other may damage his philosophical consistency but it strengthens his political case.

(4) To this triad of reasons Locke adds a fourth. Property is justified because it is going to emerge in society whether we like it or not. Men are creatures who seek material comfort and security, and they will be found to bend their efforts in the direction of enriching themselves. Not all men may have the will or ability to acquire and develop property, but there will be enough such individuals to establish and maintain this institution in any society. "Find out something that hath the use and value of money amongst his neighbors," Locke says, "you shall see the same man will begin presently to enlarge his possessions." [23] Man, then, is an entrepreneurial animal—or at least some men are. If a man finds that he can increase his wealth, then he will proceed to do so. And it follows from this that men will not waste their time and efforts in activities which do not give an economic return. Locke asks us to imagine a farmer in Darkest America: will this man toil behind the plough simply for the pure enjoyment of it?

For I ask, what would a man value ten thousand or a hundred thousand acres of excellent land, ready cultivated, and well stocked too with cattle, in the middle

[23] Para. 49.

of the inland parts of America, where he had no hopes of commerce with other parts of the world, to draw money to him by the sale of the produce? [24]

The answer, of course, is that a man will only cultivate his property in the expectation of financial reward. Where men require a material incentive for their efforts, and where the acquisition of wealth leads to the desire for more wealth—in such a society property is bound to arise. For property ownership is the best way yet discovered for a man to make money: no annual salary bestowed by any organization has yet to approach the wealth which can be acquired through property. (Even the Queen of England, who gets a handsome salary from Parliament, has substantial property holdings of her own.) Locke is not putting the role of "economic man" at the center of his theory. Locke's individual, actually, craves freedom more than he does money. But the two go together, and this conjunction will be discussed shortly.

Nor is Locke setting down a conception of human nature in the elaborate way that Machiavelli or Hobbes did: the middle-of-the-road comments on man in the state of nature show that Locke does not want to emphasize either men's good side or their predatory character. He is simply saying that there is an acquisitive element in human nature which will lead men to acquire and make use of property. This will not be true of all men in all times or places. There are some societies where productive property is generally held in common; the inhabitants of these less developed cultures seem to be content with sharing the fruits of a collective enterprise. Whether they will retain these attitudes in the face of outside pressures and expanding economic opportunities is, of course, another question. And even in advanced societies there are individuals —teachers, ministers, civil servants, scientists—who seem content to find their rewards in the satisfactions of their work and the service they render to others. Nevertheless, in the modern world most individuals are attracted by the prospect of property ownership. If they do not want to own and manage their own enterprise, they at least would like to possess some of the symbols of property— money, stocks, bonds—in far larger measure than they now enjoy.

Why is property so important in political theory? From Plato to the present day it looms large in the writings of those who would explain the behavior of men and societies. One reason, as has been noted, is that the discussion of property is not so much theoretical as it is ideological. The defense of property is uttered on behalf of those who have it; the attack is leveled by those without it and who believe they suffer from the power which it gives to the fortunate few in whose hands it lies. Perhaps the best way to avoid the emotions and interests which surround this subject is to try to explain how it is that property figures so importantly in our thinking about politics. The best place to do this

[24] Para. 48.

is in the context of Locke and liberal theory, for there the relation between private property and the free development of the individual personality is made most clear.

The organic community which Plato, Aristotle, and St. Thomas presupposed gave every citizen an acknowledged status. Each person knew his station in life: he knew what was expected of him in the way of duties, and he knew, furthermore, what he might expect from his rulers. In addition, citizens tended to remain in the class into which they were born, and they did not harbor aspirations to rise to a higher level in society. If in actuality such communities were not as contented and class-bound as Plato depicted in his Utopia, at least the rate of social change was slow enough so that most men could live out their lives with settled expectations and a fairly secure status. The organic community is not possible in the modern world—although Rousseau and Burke will try to show how features of it can be incorporated in modern institutions. Societies have grown in size; the tempo of life has become accelerated; and—above all—technological development has rendered obsolete the class lines and patterns of deference which characterized the organic conception. If there are division of labor and interrelation in the industrialized world, they follow rules of their own making and not the philosophical models of the theorists. This transformation of society calls for a theory of individualism. With the disintegration of the organic community, each individual must stand on his own. He cannot hide behind class membership or seek protection in his social status.

Machiavelli's theory of an elite based on what men can do rather than who they are fits in this pattern. So does Hobbes' notion of atomistic citizens who associate together on the basis of a voluntary contract. And to these ideas Locke's emphasis on property makes a logical addition. It was the entrepreneurs who, in their pursuit of wealth, advanced technology so that it destroyed the organic relationships of men. In organic communities men did not need property because they gained their security through their settled class membership and their socially ascribed status. Once these disappeared, they had to seek new institutions on which to base their security. The answer was to replace class and status with the individual ownership of property. Ironically enough, then, it was the inroads made on the old order by the pioneers of property which eventually caused all men to feel the need of personal ownership. One way this change has been described is to talk of the change from "status" to "contract"; another has been to speak of the transition from "Gemeinschaft" to "Gesellshaft" associations.[25] What is being suggested is that the relations which bind

---

[25] The ideas of Gemeinschaft and Gesellschaft ("communal collectives" and "societal collectives") originate with Ferdinand Toennies. See his "Estates and Classes," in Reinhard Bendix and S. M. Lipset, Class, Status, and Power: A Reader in Social Stratification

men together undergo a qualitative transformation. Whereas once they were based on ingrained custom and tradition, now they are based on temporary agreements for the purpose of getting a specific job done. Property is an institution which not only utilizes contract and the *Gesellschaft* association, but it is also one which is able to provide a measure of security for individuals who have no traditional patterns of expectations on which they can rely.

The modern individual, then, is an insecure and helpless creature. His lonely and undefended position is a fact of life which he cannot avoid and may never forget. For this reason, the pursuit of property looms large in his life. What can property do for a man? Perhaps the best way to begin explaining the functions of property is to use one or two metaphors. The property a man owns is, first of all, a pedestal. If all men are equal, as Hobbes and Locke both insist, then all men are equally insignificant. Every individual is a small fish in a big pond, and consequently subject to the buffeting of his neighbors. Yet, despite this threatening situation, both liberal theory and the practical world expect all men to stand on their own two feet. Any individual who wishes to rise in the world cannot assume that his family name or his place of birth or even his native talents will give him the stature he desires. But property can. If all men are standing in their stocking feet, the man of property stands higher. The wealth or the wealth-producing instruments he owns give him a pedestal—a pedestal of power—on which he can stand. Elevated above the ordinary run of powerless men, he need not fear them: as individuals they cannot reach him to pull him down, and even a collective effort on their part can be matched by the resources which his property has to offer. Property, in a word, adds an additional dimension to a man's stature: it renders him larger and stronger than his fellows, and hence it protects him from their depredations on his person. And because it gives him this security, it allows him to turn his attention to developing the finer aspects of his personality. Unconcerned, as most men are, with the worrisome thought of where the next meal is coming from, he can devote his time and energy to the finer things of life. Property, to introduce a second metaphor, is also a hedge. It demarcates a certain area—large or small, depending on the size of the property holding—in which its owner may do as he pleases. Whether the hedge includes inside it a landed estate or a factory or store, the man who claims title can act as he wills in the area he may properly call his own. To be sure, modern governments may prescribe conservation measures or safety regulations or minimum wages and maximum hours of work for employees. And trade unions may win the power to decide working conditions and production

---

(Glencoe: Free Press, 1954), pp. 49–63. The movement of legal relationships from "status" to "contract" is stated by Henry Maine, *Ancient Law* (Oxford: Oxford University Press, 1931). These ideas will receive further discussion in the chapters on Tocqueville and Marx.

schedules. Nevertheless, the property-owner continues to have a wide area of freedom in making his own decisions about operating his enterprise. If governments or trade unions wish to interfere, the burden lies on them to show that property rights ought to be infringed. Locke is correct in saying that property is ordained by popular consent: if an outside agency wishes to invade a man's property, it must persuade the public first that such an incursion is justified. Within the confines of this hedge, then, a property-owner may come to know freedom: freedom from external interference and freedom to do as he pleases and thinks right. Without such a hedge to protect him, he finds that such freedom as he can obtain is directly at the sufferance of his none-too-tolerant neighbors. Both as a pedestal and as a hedge, property is an artificial institution which gives its owners a power they would not otherwise have. Men who desire security must seek to become more than equal to their fellow citizens. If they are not to be lost in a lonely and anxiety-ridden crowd, they must obtain the means to climb out of it. Property is that means.

In addition, the property a man owns gives him the raw materials with which to apply and develop his personality. The individual who owns a business which is altogether his can express his own character in the things he manufactures, in the organization of men and materials, in the atmosphere he creates in his enterprise. The Ford Motor Company was an extension of the personality of Henry Ford; the candy store on the corner can reflect the individuality of the small businessman who owns and manages it. This function of property, of course, applies to the enterprise where the owner and manager are the same man. The person who owns shares in a company deals in the symbols of property and not the reality of production and distribution. Most men seek an outlet for their creativity; yet the modern world with its bureaucratic routine robs work of its individual character. While hobbies and social activities give some release, there is good reason for believing that much in our personalities remains pent up and frustrated. The man of property has materials—not to mention other men—which he can manipulate in ways which have substantial meaning. He works for himself, not for others; and his labors are in directions of his own choosing. Whether this be myth or not, the attraction of property appeals to those who are compelled to be individuals and yet who find that the decisions which guide their lives are made by others than themselves.[26]

[26] Many small owner-managers have less freedom than we would like to believe. Vital decisions affecting their businesses are made by their suppliers, customers, and the institutions which extend them credit on severe conditions. See C. Wright Mills, *White Collar* (New York: Oxford University Press, 1951), and Arthur J. Vidich and Joseph Bensman, *Small Town in Mass Society* (Princeton: Princeton University Press, 1958). For a discussion of the way in which owning a business becomes an ideal for industrial employees, see Eli Chinoy, *The Auto Workers and the American Dream* (Garden City: Doubleday, 1955).

Furthermore, property ownership gives the individual a tangible sense of identification. Just as the Stanleys were always associated with the County of Derby—because they owned most of it—in eighteenth- and nineteenth-century England, so a Rockefeller may identify himself with a great industrial complex. And even the Smith who owns Smith's Hardware Store will find that he is given an established role by those in society who recognize the function that he and his enterprise perform. The search for identity is particularly strong in an individualist society, because men may no longer rely on their family name or inherited station. Each man must create his own identity, in his own eyes and in the eyes of those around him. Some try to achieve this end by associating themselves with impersonal institutions—General Electric, Yale University, the United States Navy—with the hope that some of the institutional identification will rub off on them. However, this can never succeed entirely, except perhaps for the few who rise to top positions in such organizations. The best means to establish an identity—and this is far more a psychological than an economic process—is to create an image of one's self in one's property. If most men cannot be Stanleys, heirs to the Earldom of Derby, at least some men can be a Conrad Hilton of Hilton Hotels, a Henry Kaiser of Kaiser Aluminum and Chemicals, or a Jack Warner of Warner Brothers Pictures.

Finally, property gives to its owners a link with posterity. With property go laws of inheritance which allow a man to pass on to his children that which he earned and owned in his lifetime. No matter what the explanation for it may be, most men want their names and works to live after them. How many fathers have sired sons for no reason other than that the family business will know yet another generation of life? If property is an extension of a man's personality, it gives him further security by bestowing the knowledge that even the hands of time need not call a halt to the labors he has started.

If a sense of security, if the opportunity to develop their personalities, if meaningful freedom—if all these are given to men of property, then what of those who do not possess it? It may well be suggested that the owners of property know security and freedom because they stand on the shoulders of the propertyless to breathe a better air. Locke does not discuss this other side of the coin; he assumes that all would be men of property and that none need be the losers. Other theorists—Rousseau, Tocqueville, and of course Marx and Engels—will concern themselves with those who do not share the blessings of property. Whether they call for a more equitable distribution, its abolition, or simply a frank awareness of its social and psychological consequences, all theorists of property are dealing with an institution which has political ramifications in all societies in all ages.

THE RIGHTS OF MAN

With Locke and with liberal theory the idea of human rights comes to the center of the political stage. It has just been seen how property rights are of central importance in Locke's writing, and how this right exists in a state of nature as well as in civil society. Indeed, one of the reasons why Locke opens his theory with the state-of-nature model is because he wants to show that men possess their rights even before governments come into existence. And, in contrast to Hobbes, Locke does not write into the social contract that citizens must give up their rights to their sovereign. In Hobbes' theory all that individuals retained was the right of self-defense, which meant the right to get rid of their ruler if he did not protect them from violent death. Locke's citizen keeps not only the right to life, but the rights of liberty and property as well. These possessions, which men have both in and out of government, are what give strength to the liberal conception of individualism. Most theories profess to esteem the individual: they wish to see that he is treated with justice and guaranteed a wholesome life. But only a few go further than this and claim that the individual has a *right* to just treatment and the good life. Locke, in making this departure, is endowing all men with an attribute which previous theorists saw fit to withhold. It would be well, therefore, to examine the conception of rights with some care.

In beginning, a warning which was made in the course of the discussion of Hobbes' theory ought to be repeated. If confusion is to be avoided, rights must be ascribed only to individuals. To say that governments or states or societies have "rights" will raise more analytical problems than it can ever hope to solve. Locke talks of the "right" of a government, but it is clear that he is referring to the power of such an agency to perform its proper functions. Indeed, he says just that. "Political power," he says, "I take to be a right of making laws with the penalties of death, and consequently all less penalties, for the regulating and preserving of property, and of employing the force of the community in the execution of such laws, and in the defense of the commonwealth from foreign injury, and all this only for the public good." [27] Here Locke is simply saying that a government *will* make laws, mete out penalties, preserve property, and defend its citizens from foreign attack. He is also saying that a government *ought* to do these things. But he does not suggest in the course of his theory that governments have "rights" in a similar or related sense to the way that individuals do. Indeed, it is the rights of citizens which bind the state and limit its activities. Were the state to claim a reciprocal and opposing "right" against

[27] *Second Treatise*, para. 3.

its citizens, then the political process would come to a standstill—or, more likely, the state would always win in such a matching game.[28]

And if rights are the possessions of individuals, they are held by all individuals without exception. Just as the state of nature and the social contract postulate human equality, so does Locke assume that equality governs the sphere of rights. After laying down that "all men by nature are equal . . ." he says, "that equal right that every man hath to his natural freedom . . . was the equality I there spoke of." [29] There is a difference, then, between a right and a privilege. The latter may be extended to a few selected individuals—wiser men, abler men, more virtuous men—by the state or by some theory that has ways of recognizing superiority. But a right does not discriminate among its possessors: no tests are given to discover if an individual "deserves" to have it or whether he has "earned" it. "The sum of all we drive at," Locke says, "is that every man enjoys the same rights that are granted to others." [30]

However, it would be a mistake not to approach this stricture in a common-sense way. To assert that one man enjoys the same rights as are accorded to all others is simply to say that equal conditions must apply. If voting is a right and not a privilege, then all must have the vote. Considerations of wealth or intelligence or virtue cannot be referred to when the franchise is bestowed. If only men may vote, then its claim to being a right is severely weakened; but at least all women, regardless of race or creed or marital status, must be denied the ballot. If a literacy test is required in order to be registered, then it must be an examination that all citizens are capable of passing if they undertake to study for it. Clearly a rule of reason applies here. A state may say that in order to vote all citizens must pay a poll tax of $300, and all are capable of saving up money so they can pay that assessment. Yet such a law plainly discriminates against the less wealthy, and a vote in that context is not a right but a privilege for the rich.

Locke's meaning should be apparent. If whole groups of citizens are denied certain freedoms on the basis of sex or color or religion or wealth, then it is

[28] In his *Letter on Toleration* Locke poses just this question. The state or its ruler may close down churches, censor newspapers, and put bans on foreign travel by citizens. "What if the magistrate believes that he has a right to make such laws, and that they are for the public good," Locke asks, "and his subjects believe the contrary?" The problem develops: "Who shall be judge between them?" And Locke's answer: "God alone." In *Second Treatise of Civil Government and A Letter Concerning Toleration* (Oxford: Blackwell, 1948), edited by J. W. Gough, p. 154. If the resolution of right against right is in God's hands, then it means that either citizens must submit to tyranny or they will overthrow the government. In either event the conception of rights is no longer operative: the discussion is of power.

[29] *Second Treatise*, para. 54.

[30] *Letter on Toleration*, p. 159.

improper for those who have those freedoms to speak of them as rights. Indeed, the whole question of property rights—and their attendant freedoms and securities—becomes complicated when there exist poor men who have small chance to join the ranks of the propertied. All men, we may say, have the right to open a business and compete with large corporations and even to put them out of business. To many people, however, this seems empty rhetoric.

A right, in simplest terms, is a freedom. And it is also a claim: an individual's claim that those around him—including the state—will respect his wish to exercise that freedom. The corollary, of course, is that each citizen has the obligation to defer to the rights of his neighbors. Rights clearly cannot exist except in a framework of mutual rights and obligations. Yet Locke does not speak much of the latter, for a stress on obligations can, as with Hobbes, lead to the individual's subservience to the state and the limiting of his own freedom. Liberal theory emphasizes the rights of men, and conservative theory, as will be seen with Burke, underlines men's obligations. Nor is it a satisfactory answer to say that rights and obligations ought to be "balanced." The only way to approach this problem in a meaningful way is to talk about it at a less abstract level.

Specific questions must be asked about particular rights. Does it appear, we must inquire, that one group in society seems to end up with the rights most of the time while another group is left standing with all the obligations? Or when we juxtapose conflicting claims, do we give equal weight to both, whereas to do this is to defeat purpose with abstract logic? For example, we can say that a neighbor of mine has a right to make political speeches in a sound truck and I have the obligation to tolerate his unwelcome noise. And against this we can say that I have a right to privacy and he has an obligation to respect my desire for quiet. Anyone who tends to "equate" these rights and obligations is treading on dangerous grounds: the right to free speech, it might be suggested, has a higher standing than a right to auditory comfort—my obligation to put up with his sound truck is therefore greater than his obligation to leave my neighborhood at peace. At all events, this is contentious ground, and that is as it should be. One man's right can be not only a nuisance but downright oppressive to another. Locke does not explore the question of conflicting claims to rights because he is concerned to establish their very existence. But Mill and Tocqueville will continue this aspect of the discussion. And it follows, finally, that a man's claim to a right may not be acknowledged or respected by the state or by his neighbors. Rights may exist in theory, but not in practice; on paper, but not in the eyes of the local policeman.

Two sorts of questions arise about the political status of rights: one is philosophical and the other is practical. What must be examined is, first, the *source* of rights, and, second, the *enforcement* of rights. After that the relation between these two aspects should be discussed. The best way to begin is to set the whole matter down in the form of a diagram:

THE SOURCES OF RIGHTS

	Natural Rights: rights men think they ought naturally to have.	*Legal Rights:* rights a state recognizes as belonging to its citizens by law.
ENFORCEMENT OF RIGHTS	(1)	(3)
Enforced Rights: rights a state or society actively secures for all citizens.	Rights men think they ought to have are secured to them by state power or society's tolerance.	A state or society uses its power to secure to citizens rights which the state has recognized by law.
	(2)	(4)
Unenforced Rights: Rights a state or society neglects to secure or denies to some or all citizens.	Rights men think they ought to have are not secured to them by state power or society's tolerance.	A state or society fails to use its power to secure to citizens rights which the state has recognized by law.

The problem of deciding where rights originate is a controversial one in political theory. The Natural Rights doctrine which Locke employs postulates that all men are born with certain inherent rights: God gives these to His children just as He gives them arms and legs, eyes and ears. Men are placed on this earth to lead a life, and they must have certain freedoms if they are to live that life to its fullest potentiality. God not only brings men into the world, but he also endows them with the innate authority to attain the best that life has to offer. This, Locke says, is expressed in the Law of Nature.

> Man being born, as has been proved, with a title to perfect freedom, and an uncontrolled enjoyment of all the rights and privileges of the Law of Nature equally with any other man or number of men in the world, hath by nature a power . . . to preserve his property—that is, his life, liberty, and estate—against the injuries and attempts of other men. . . .[31]

Natural Rights, then, are derived from the Natural Law. They give men title to their lives, their liberties, and their estates: in short, their property is a Natural Right. In saying that these rights exist in the state of nature, Locke is saying that men would have them under any circumstances—whether they lived under

---

[31] *Second Treatise*, para. 87.

a government or did not. In the state of nature, a right is a claim against one's neighbors: it calls on them to forbear from interfering with a freedom which an individual wishes to exercise. It also, once men are in society, is a claim against the state: it calls on it to refrain from intruding its power in an area where the individual claims personal freedom of action. This raises the question of whether citizens, in entering a social contract, can sign away their Natural Rights to the state. Hobbes, of course, said that this was just what they did. Locke, on first glance, seems to say that the citizen does hand over at least one of his rights. "He has given a right to the commonwealth to employ his force for the execution of the judgments of the commonwealth whenever he shall be called to it." [32]

However, this is not so much the abdication of a right as it is giving the state permission to draft the citizen in the event that his help is needed to fight a war or put down insurrection or simly to help in the enforcement of laws. A state must have power, and it must often use its citizens to lend strength to its power. Locke would say, then, that an individual cannot give up his Natural Rights—to life, to liberty, to property—to the state. If he signs such a contract under duress or through miscalculation, the agreement is invalid. For what God has given to men is a gift which is to last the length of their lives; they may not divest themselves of it voluntarily, nor may states deprive them of it. In fact, the man who seeks to give up his Natural Rights, even though he thinks he is acting voluntarily, is stripping himself of the attributes he needs if he is to be a man at all. And the state which attempts to deprive men of their Natural Rights is creating a condition whereby its citizens will not be men but rather something less than human. A man's Natural Rights, therefore, inhere in his personality: they are immutable from the day of his birth and non-transferable throughout his lifetime.

The obvious question to arise is whether Natural Rights are objective or subjective. How do we know that God has endowed men with them? St. Thomas, who seemed to know what God had in mind, never made mention of them. Must we take Locke's word for it? Clearly it cannot be proved in any inductive manner that these qualities exist in men. If they are objective—if they actually exist—then their existence must be self-evident to all reasonable men. However, Edmund Burke was a very reasonable man, and it did not appear self-evident to him that Natural Rights either existed or ought to be secured to all men. Furthermore, there is the danger that men will take advantage of the Natural Rights idea and go about claiming that God has given them title to all manner of freedoms. Liberty can become license, property can become exploitation. And this is just what worried Burke: men may either consciously

[32] Para. 88.

or unconsciously give a socially abusive interpretation to the freedoms allowed them by their Natural Rights.

About all that can be said on this score was said in the analysis of Natural Law—a theory as open to abuse as Natural Rights. What men "naturally" need to find the good life must be discovered by reason. Capricious interpretations are self-serving ideology; they are not dispassionate attempts at scientific theory. The fundamental needs of men are grounded in their personality and in the way that personality reacts to the social environment of their age. In this sense, knowledge and intelligence are required if the expression of Natural Rights suitable to a particular time and place are to be determined. But Natural Law theory is better able to achieve this than Natural Rights theory. St. Thomas gave to wise and virtuous rulers the task of interpreting the precepts of the Natural Law and applying them in human law. These men, trained in the customs of their society and removed from the pulls of self-interest, were well equipped to exercise reason in this area. Natural Law is a social conception, and it is to be used to govern society as a whole. The concept of Natural Rights, on the other hand, is part of the doctrine of individualism. It is not for rulers—wise or virtuous or neither—to tell citizens what their Natural Rights are and what are legitimate expressions of them. On the contrary, no such higher authority can claim such a power. This means that it is left to each man to ascertain what freedoms his Natural Rights allow to him. But has the average man the reason to use these rights in a temperate and socially benevolent way? If not just superior men, but all men may devise their own interpretations then society is apt to suffer. This concern is grounded further in the fact that Natural Rights theory does not employ custom as a mediator in the interpretative process. By placing a premium on the cultural status quo, Natural Law allayed any fears that it might be used to upset the established structure of society. In this sense, as was indicated, it was essentially a conservative theory. Natural Rights, however, puts a premium on the development of the individual personality, even if that development calls for a modification of customary patterns. This means that the doctrine is liberal and even revolutionary. If individuals claim that society as it has been hitherto constituted stultifies their growth, then they may invoke Natural Rights to justify their attempts to reform society. This is how the free-market liberals used the Natural Right of property to call for abolition of feudal and mercantile restrictions on commercial and industrial development. The conclusion must be, therefore, that Natural Rights theory is more susceptible to subjective—and self-interested—interpretations than Natural Law theory. Individualism, as both Hobbes and Locke have made clear, gives full respect to the reason of all men regardless of their social standing. To endow these men with Natural Rights is to open the door to conflict, self-interest, and ideology. It is also to open the door to progress.

Natural Rights are theoretical freedoms which men think they ought to have. Whether they are right or wrong in assessing their true needs, the fact remains that they hold these beliefs and would like to act on them. But rights are not made effective simply because some theory prescribes them. They must be underwritten with power if they are to have meaning for an individual who lives in society. The state of nature, Locke says, recognizes men's Natural Rights, but it has no constituted authority which can ensure to men the enjoyment of them. This is, then, the *second* alternative on the diagram which was sketched earlier. There is no state power to secure Natural Rights to an individual and society's tolerance is a weak reed to lean on in so important a matter.

If man in the state of nature be so free, as has been said, if he be absolute lord of his own person and possessions, equal to the greatest, and subject to nobody, why will he part with his freedom . . . ? To which, it is obvious to answer, that though in the state of nature he hath such a right, yet the enjoyment of it is very uncertain. . . . This makes him willing to quit this condition, which, however free, is full of fears and continual dangers; and it is not without reason that he seeks out and is willing to join in society with others, who are already united, or have a mind to unite, for the mutual preservation of their lives, liberties, and estates, which I call by the general name, property.[33]

The answer is to move from the *second* to the *first* alternative, to set up a society with political power which will provide the conditions for the enjoyment of Natural Rights by all. But it is not possible to move to the *first* alternative without embracing the *third* as well. It is, of course, conceivable that men might go from an anarchic state of war into a tolerant society and yet forbear from setting up a state. In such a social—but not political—situation men could count on social recognition of each other's Natural Rights. But this possibility, while logical, is not very real. Locke had men move into society and government at the same time, and this means that it is incumbent on the government—not society—to secure Natural Rights to its citizens. This is done by means of legislation: the state enacts a Constitution or a Bill of Rights or simply ordinary statutes which give to citizens their Natural Rights in the guise of enacted law.

With this shift to the *third* alternative, we are now in the realm of legal rights. Rights, in this case, are the freedoms which the state says citizens are entitled to have. This general view is called the "positive" theory of law, and it was expressed in Hobbes' conception of sovereignty. Not simply laws, but also rights are what the duly-constituted legal authority says they are. It is not

[33] Para. 123.

God, but men who bestow our rights. These men may be a single ruler, a judicial tribunal, a legislature, a constitutional convention—or a combination of these and other men and institutions as well. Legal rights need not be given and taken away in a capricious manner: as the discussions of "rule of law" have shown, men's claims to just treatment under law may be safeguarded by political checks, due process, and appeals to higher authority.[34] There can be no quarrel about at least the language of legal rights: by referring to a Constitution or a statute book or judicial decisions, a citizen may know just what his rights are. Of course, there are bound to be constant disputes over the meanings of words: a right to free speech may be recognized in law, but a policeman may decide that picketing a store is not covered by that right. Nevertheless, so long as there are courts and mechanisms for amending the law, citizens are able to engage in the continual process of discovering their legal rights and creating new ones for themselves. Because the legislative process is so constituted, legal rights are far less ambiguous than Natural Rights. Why not abandon the idea of Natural Rights altogether and settle for saying that our rights are what the state tells us they are?

The answer is that men have their own ideas about what their rights are, and they are not content to let the state tell them the scope and limits of their freedom. Rights have a moral content, and the Natural Rights idea is a doctrine men can appeal to when they disagree with their government's interpretation of allowable freedom. Even if there are established procedures for amending laws or Bills of Rights, these are often too slow and cumbersome to satisfy citizens who feel they have been wronged. And it is often difficult to replace the judges or legislators who have the power to tell us what our legal rights are. What Locke seeks to do with Natural Rights is similar to St. Thomas' approach to the Natural Law: Locke wants to see governments use their power to give legal recognition to Natural Rights. If they do this, then they are using their power legitimately. Indeed, they are using their power for the purposes intended in the social contract. In short, individuals enter government and society the better to enjoy their Natural Rights.

Though men when they enter into society give up the equality, liberty and executive power they had in the state of nature into the hands of society, to be so far disposed of by the legislative as the good of the society shall require; yet it being only with an intention in everyone the better to preserve himself, his liberty and property (for no rational creature can be supposed to change his condition with an intention to be worse), the power of the society, or the legislative constituted by them, can never be supposed to extend farther than the common good, but is

[34] Despite his advocacy of limited government, Locke does not make specific proposals for constitutional safeguards. However, he does suggest that the legislative and executive functions can be separated, and this institutional step can be an important one in the direction of limiting governmental power. See paras. 143 and 144.

obliged to secure everyone's property by providing against those . . . defects . . . that made the state of nature so unsafe and uneasy.[35]

This, then, is Locke's prescription: that the state should use its enforcement powers to secure legal rights, which are Natural Rights made official. Once men have quit the state of nature they must look to the state to legislate both effectively and morally.

But there is a danger that the state may fail to put men's Natural Rights on the statute books. In this case we are still with the *third* alternative in the diagram, but that alternative is now disjoined from the first. A state or a ruler which fails to recognize Natural Rights by law has usurped its contractual authority and abused the power given to it. "As usurpation is the exercise of power which another hath a right to, so tyranny is the exercise of power beyond right," Locke says, "and this is making use of the power anyone has in his hands, not for the good of those who are under it, but for his own private, separate advantage." [36] Locke, no less than Hobbes or St. Thomas, is well aware that the state may flout the precepts which God has directed be followed in the exercise of political authority. However, in Locke's theory the citizen has far greater latitude for making a legitimate protest against tyrannical rule, and his rights in this area will be explored later on.

In addition, a state may enact rights into law—and they may be legal expressions of genuine Natural Rights—and then may fail to enforce them with any degree of regularity. The right to vote, the right to worship, the right to own property—all these may be embodied in the Constitution and carved in granite and yet be ignored by those charged with the business of enforcement and regulation. In this event we have descended to the *fourth* possibility in the diagram. And Locke warned against such a descent. "The supreme power" cannot take from any man any part of his property without his consent," Locke says. "For the preservation of property being the end of government, and that for which men enter into society, it necessarily supposes and requires that the people should have property." [37] In order that government not sidestep the basic rights they have accorded to citizens, Locke introduces the notion of consent. If the right to property is a Natural Right, then it can only be abridged if the property-owning individual consents to such an abridgment. If a state does not put its own power and its legal authority behind a Natural Right, then a citizen can invoke his own power and authority to safeguard that freedom. Clearly the whole idea of Natural Rights gives greater theoretical power to the individual than any other single idea in political theory. Indeed, his freedom

[35] Para. 131.
[36] Para. 199.
[37] Para. 138.

is so extensive that it may be wondered what is to prevent perpetual disobedience to political authority. If every citizen's reason may be pitted against the determinations of enacted law, if express consent is required before the state may exercise its power in economic and related spheres—if this is the case—then it is hard to see how government can acquire the authority even to safeguard the rights of individuals, which is after all its primary obligation. Locke will try to answer these questions at a later stage, when he examines the political source of state power. For if he talks of consent, he also talks of majority rule.

An individual's rights, in Locke's theory, are claims against the state. The fear expressed in the previous paragraph was that the state might confiscate the property of a citizen. This raises a number of considerations. First of all, if the citizen's rights are counterclaims against official power, then there should be means short of revolution for his freedoms to be secured. What this means is that there should be an authority higher than the state which will compel the state to grant the individual his free exercise of his rights. What is this higher authority? St. Thomas and Hobbes advised men to pray to God if they wished to be liberated from tyranny. Machiavelli and Aristotle spoke of an abstraction called the "rule of law" which would overrule oppressive acts by a governor.

But if "rule of law" is to be operative, then there must be established institutions to give it effect. Some of these have been mentioned: judicial review, separation of powers, due process. For this reason it is often worthwhile to distinguish between the *state* and the *government*—something which heretofore has not been done. The government is composed of the legislative and executive branches, and it makes the day-to-day policies which regulate the lives of citizens. The personnel of government, furthermore, are of transitory tenure, and they are expected to conduct their affairs with an eye towards prevailing sentiment in the society. The state, on the other hand, has a more permanent foundation. It embodies the courts and other agencies which are concerned with interpreting the law; its personnel have either life tenure or at least terms long enough to separate them from the play of public opinion. In addition, the state represents the Constitution, the common law, and the political traditions of the society. While Locke did not distinguish between government and state, it is clear that such a distinction is implicit in his theory. For if the government —the legislature or the administration—infringes on a citizen's rights, then he may in a free society appeal to the state to have these injuries redressed. In liberal theory, then, not only must state and society be separated, but if the rights of men are to be secured, a further institutional separation must be made. This is why it is important that the judicial process must stand apart from the legislative struggle. For if the courts are the guardians of rights, then they must have an authority different from the assemblies which make laws. The alternative to this government-state divorcement is to hope that the government will restrain itself, that it will voluntarily refrain from impairing the rights of individuals. Whether this legislative self-restraint will be evidenced in an atmosphere of majority rule is a matter which concerns all those who wish to safeguard human rights.

And if rights are levied against one's government, it may be asked whether they are entirely political in conception. Cannot other individuals, or even "society" as a whole, acting independently of the government, deprive an individual of his freedom? Liberal theory, at least as expressed in Locke, tends to see only the government as the potential threat to a citizen's rights. Other institutions—and this would include the relations between friends and neighbors—are voluntary in character, and if a man finds himself coerced by an employer or a priest, he can always quit his job or leave that church. Obligations to one's government are not only based on a promise of obedience, but the state has a power greater than other institutions to enforce its will on citizens. Nevertheless, it is quite clear that social pressures can operate to limit a person's freedoms. The power of public opinion, the discipline at one's place of work, the subtle influences of a neighborhood—all of these and more may deprive an individual of his liberty. Locke acknowledges that not only the state, but private citizens may so coerce each other. As an example, he cites the disabilities which society can inflict on persons of an unpopular or unorthodox religion. "No private person," he says, "has any right in any manner to prejudice another person in his civil enjoyments because he is of another church or religion." [38]

Does this mean that the state will step in and compel an employer to consider all job applicants by objective standards and without regard for religion? If a fair employment practices commission is set up and if the coercive power of the state is at hand to make that commission's decisions effective, then we may say that in this case an individual has rights against other individuals in society and that the state is prepared to secure to him these rights. However, Locke does not develop this point at all. One reason for this may be that it opens up wide areas of conflict. In the example just stated the government is curtailing the property rights of one man in order to secure the civil rights of another. Whenever a state seeks to make rights social as well as political, it is bound to favor some groups in society and deprive others. Yet Locke's silence leaves important questions unconfronted. Tocqueville and Mill will return to the problem of an oppressive society's impact on individual freedom. They

[38] *Letter on Toleration*, p. 132.

both see that even if men live under a free government they can still have to put up with a tyrannical society.

A theory of rights, then, has philosophical and practical components. But clouding any analysis of this subject is the suspicion that a good part of the talk about rights—both by political theorists and ordinary men—is ideological in motive and consequence. If men want rights, if they demand freedom of action, their concern is not so much with "rights" or "freedom" as abstract goods as it is with those things which the rights or freedom will secure to them. Men desire property, religious liberty, political power, and similar goals. They want property, for example, for reasons which are largely psychological in origin; the same sort of argument can be made about religion or power. In this case all allusions to rights are political rhetoric: part of the strategy of achieving ends which are thought good. Both Machiavelli and Marx, if asked to discuss the matter of rights, would probably say that it is a smokescreen for something else. The citizen who utters the phrase "I have a right to . . ." is really saying no more than "I want. . . ."

In the four alternatives set down in the opening diagram, the meanings might be somewhat as follows: (1) I want to keep my property, and I want the state to continue protecting my possession of it. (2) I want to keep my property, and I want the government to stop taxing away my profits. (3) I want to continue exercising the vote, which the law recognizes as mine, and I want the state to continue protecting my exercise of it. (4) I want to be allowed to vote, which the law permits me to do, and I want the government to stop barring me from the polls on the basis of an unfair literacy test. An individual, then, may want to maintain the status quo or he may want to secure a new state of affairs which he believes will be more desirable than the current situation. But in either event both Natural Rights and legal rights are being looked at from the subjective standpoint of the person who is claiming a freedom.

This approach has political utility because it leads us to an understanding of the actual liberties which men feel they need and an insight into the groups which are competing for power. Talk of rights tends to be universal: *all* men have a right to property or a right to vote, even though these freedoms may not loom large in their own estimation of what is important. Wants, on the other hand, tell us about what is on men's minds, and they give an indication of how political power and the governmental process is actually being used by some people to secure freedoms they think desirable. Nevertheless, this subjective approach does not tell the entire story. Legal rights, especially if they are enforced, are objective: whether all or only a few men want them, they are on the statute books and they are secured by the local policeman. It would be a gross caricature to call the Bill of Rights an Enumeration of Wants. In a sense it is, but it also has an existence and an authority of its own which gives it a role in society larger than the self-interested demands of individual citizens. The ideological component of any theory of rights can never be overlooked. But states and governments, laws and constitutions, are more than institutions at the service of an ideology.

THE CONSENT OF THE MAJORITY

Liberalism's strength lies in its theory of the individual; its weaknesses are displayed when it comes time to construct a theory of the state. If men are characterized by their freedom, their equality, and their independence, then the problem arises of how to put such men in the role of citizens—a role which necessarily calls for obedience and submission. Locke's answer is to place heavy reliance on the doctrine of consent. "Men being . . . by nature all free, equal, and independent," he says, "no one can be put out of this estate, and subjected to the political power of another, without his own consent." [39] Both Hobbes and Locke use the social contract to drive home the fact that governments must be founded on a basis of consent. Men who are by nature free and equal may only legitimately become citizens if each one has agreed to accept this status. In the realm of theory there is nothing wrong with postulating that hypothetical citizens unanimously give their approval to a hypothetical contract. But what direction must we take when we move into the world of political reality? In facing up to this question Locke is compelled to be as explicit as possible about the meaning of consent.

First of all, Locke is unwilling to say that the consent of a previous generation is binding on today's citizens. "Whatever engagements or promises anyone made for himself," he says, "he is under obligation of them, but he cannot by any compact whatsoever bind his children or posterity." [40] Each man has his own life to live, and his own freedom to define and pursue; consequently, every individual—presumably when he reaches the age of twenty-one—must affix his signature to the contract which was drawn up at the origin of the society. In this way mere geographical residence becomes political citizenship.

And thus the consent of freemen, born under government, which only makes them members of it, being given separately in their turns, as each comes to be of age, and not in a multitude together. People take no notice of it, and thinking it not done at all, or not necessary, conclude they are naturally subjects as they are men.[41]

[39] *Second Treatise*, para. 95.
[40] Para. 116.
[41] Para. 117.

Actually, such formal and individual consent seldom takes place. It does in the case of adult immigrants who must take a specific pledge of allegiance when they become citizens of their adopted country. But Locke is correct in saying that most individuals take no notice of this change in their status. What he wants to do, quite simply, is to emphasize the fact that consent is individual: another person, living or dead, cannot commit a citizen to the basic contract.

This brings Locke to a second feature of consent. If most people do not realize that they are consenting at a certain point in their lives, then is it proper to call this unconscious acquiesence a sign of "consent"? A theory which requires that consent be individual should, one might suppose, demand that such approval be based on conscious premeditation. Yet Locke is too keen a student of human behavior to ask that men be so rational and so engaged in the political process that they ponder deeply before making all commitments. Men have many concerns, and their political involvement cannot claim all of their time. Silence does indeed often signify consent, and any theory of this subject must make provision for unspoken agreement to the policies and personnel of government on the part of citizens. Hence Locke distinguishes between "express" and "tacit" consent. The former is manifested by voting, public debate, and obedience which results from conscious deliberation and choice. Most consent, however, is beneath the level of conscious awareness. The problem, as Locke sees it, is: "How far anyone shall be looked upon to have consented, and thereby submitted to any government, where he has made no expression of it at all." And the answer:

> Every man that hath any possession or enjoyment of any part of the dominion of any government doth thereby give his tacit consent, and is as far forth obliged to obedience to the laws of that government during such enjoyment.[42]

But is mere residence in a locality—the mere fact that one has not packed up and emigrated—sufficient evidence that an individual has granted his consent to the prevailing regime? Locke's idea of tacit consent is more a rule of thumb than it is an analysis of the significance of silence in the political process. Tacit consent may, in fact, be sullenness: beneath the closed lips may be unspoken discontents and misunderstood grievances.

On the other side, Locke's notion lends an air of authority to the unthinking and habitual acquiescence on the part of those who are easily pleased. If a large majority are tacitly contented and a small minority are expressly discontented, then are sheer numbers to carry the day when the intensity and articulation are so disproportionate? This question is not answered by Locke, but Tocqueville will give full discussion to the ways an elephantine majority can unconsciously

[42] Para. 119.

make its power felt in society. And Burke will conjoin the doctrine of tacit consent with habit and custom to give it a central position in conservative theory. The doctrine is easy to criticize but difficult to dispense with. So long as men are silent, uninterested, or simply busy at other things than politics, any theory will have to account for consent at a variety of levels.

If a ruler needed the unanimous consent of his subjects before he could take office, if each citizen were obliged to obey only those laws he saw fit to consent to—in such circumstances no government could ever establish its authority. Well aware of this, Locke now moves from individual consent to majority rule. Unanimity and personal exemptions are made to apply only to the signing of the original contract. After that moment a new principle comes into force: consent is henceforward defined as the consent of the majority. Rulers are legitimate, and laws are binding on the whole community, if a simple majority gives them its consent. "The majority have a right to act and conclude the rest . . ." Locke says. "It being one body must move one way, it is necessary the body should move that way whither the greater force carries it, which is the consent of the majority." [43] Locke's espousal of majority rule follows logically from his assumptions about human equality. Each man is to count for one, and no one is to count for more than one. This evaluation applies not only to the intrinsic worth of individuals, but also to their participation in the exercise of political power.

The alternative to majority rule must be minority rule of some sort; but at no time does Locke speak of the existence of a wise or virtuous or talented minority which has a prior claim to a position of political superiority. Let us suppose that there is a community of 100 citizens and each person is "worth" ten "units." If a ballot gives the result of 64:36, then the score is 640 units to 360, and the larger one carries the day. But imagine that somehow or other the side favored by the minority of 36 is deemed the winner. This would mean that the 36 are considered to be a "qualitative" majority, or actually the equivalent of 51; and that the 64 are a "qualitative" minority, or actually the equivalent of 49. The consequence, therefore, is that each person in the 36 is now "worth" 14 "units" and each person in the 64 is "worth" 7. Can a quantitative minority justify a claim to being a qualitative majority: to being worth twice as much, man for man, as its neighbors? Locke did not see how such a claim could be established. The only time this might be allowed would be if the original contract stipulates that on some occasions an extraordinary majority—more than 50 per cent plus one—is needed for victory. "Whosoever . . . unite into a community must be understood to give up all the power nec-

[43] Paras. 95, 96.

essary to the ends for which they unite into society, to the majority," Locke says, "unless they expressly agreed in any number greater than the majority." [44]

Express agreements about extraordinary majorities were, of course, written into the American Constitution. The Senate, by its very existence, gives a greater "unit worth" to the citizen of Alaska than it does to the citizen of California. The process of amending the Constitution gives a minority the chance to stand in the way of majority sentiment. And so long as Congressional districts vary in size—a matter left to state legislatures—rural voters will be overrepresented to the detriment of urban and suburban voters.

Locke does not expand on the uses to which this device might be put. Minorities which profit from it usually claim that it protects them from oppression at the hands of the majority. On the face of it, the requirement of an extraordinary majority does not lead to minority rule; it only puts obstacles in the way of unlimited majority rule. Yet insofar as it allows a minority to maintain a status quo which they prefer, then the status quo is ruling—and that may be just what the minority would preserve were they to have a positive rather than a negative power. The point about all this is that extraordinary majorities are written into the original contract, and they are not dependent on consent at a later time in the society's history. Nor is there any guarantee that these clauses will protect all minorities, and not just those fortunate enough to be able to take advantage of them.

Human equality calls for majority rule. But human liberty, or at least the freedoms of some individuals, may be impaired by a government with majority support. From Plato through Mill, theorists have expressed their anxiety about majority tyranny. Some of these fears, as Machiavelli pointed out, may be misplaced, and talk of minority "rights" is often rhetoric intended to protect vested interests. Apart from his comment on extraordinary majorities, Locke does not worry about abuses of majority rule. Indeed, he regards that institution as a salutary protection of the rights of the individuals who comprise the majority. Citizens must be able to hold their government at bay, for it has the power to turn them into slaves. The best way to restrain the government is to require that its laws be based on the consent of those who will have to obey those laws. And this consent, expressed in majority rule, is evidenced not simply in the original contract but periodically throughout the life of the state. Locke, then, is a democratic liberal: he advocates putting political power in the hands of the majority. His faith in human reason extends down into the broad base of the social pyramid, and he has made plain that when he speaks of equality he is willing to put it into action.

[44] Para. 99.

At the same time, Locke's liberalism calls for a free society. Even if the government is moved by the power of the majority, it must nevertheless limit the use of its ability to coerce. The state is supreme, Locke says, but the good state observes certain limitations:

First, it is not nor can possibly be absolutely arbitrary over the lives and fortunes of the people.

Secondly, the legislative, or supreme authority, cannot assume to itself a power to rule by extemporary arbitrary decrees, but is bound to dispense justice, and decide the rights of the subject by promulgated standing laws, and known authorized judges.

Thirdly, the supreme power cannot take from any man any part of his property without his own consent.

Fourthly, the legislative cannot transfer the power of making laws to any other hands; for it being but a delegated power from the people, they who have it cannot pass it over to others.[45]

What is to prevent a legislature, speaking for the will of a majority, to do any one or all four of these things? On this score Locke is silent. The rights of men, which he has raised to so high an eminence in his theory, can be torn down by a government which sees little or no value in these freedoms. Yet what is Locke to do? If he sets up certain minorities with the task of protecting rights and the power to secure their continual existence, then the individuals belonging to those minorities are given a superior status in society.

It is not fair to ask for an airtight solution to this dilemma. When freedom and equality are juxtaposed in such sharp terms, not all can be gainers and none losers. Mill and Tocqueville will face this problem of majority rule and minority rights at a later time and with new approaches. At this juncture it may be observed that exhortation is a necessary part of political philosophy. Just as St. Thomas exhorted rulers to obey the precepts of the Natural Law, so Locke calls on governments to voluntarily restrain its incursions on men's Natural Rights. Whether the appeal is to the conscience or to the sense of self-interest of men of power, an appeal is what it is. If there were perfect institutional safeguards against abuses of power, we may rest secure they would have been discovered long ago. Because there are no cut-and-dried solutions, writers of political theory must approach the human variable as best they can. Men of power have, on occasion, been known to listen to reason; the man in the street has, on occasion, checkreined his impulses and displayed a mature tolerance. If political philosophers tend to write sermons between the lines of their theories, they do this because they cherish the hope that men will know the truth when they hear it and will act on that knowledge when the case is made persuasively.

[45] Paras. 135, 136, 138, 141.

A RIGHT OF REVOLUTION?

Have men a right to overthrow a government which deprives them of their freedom? St. Thomas denied this because he believed the act and consequences of revolution to be destructive of political order. Hobbes was unwilling to say that governments were obliged to grant freedom, and hence the excuse for revolution could not arise. Locke's essential ambiguity on this subject has caused no end of controversy among students of political theory. He does say that the people have the power—although not the right—to remove a government whose policies they find curtailing their essential liberties.

The legislative being only of fiduciary power to act for certain ends, there remains still in the people a supreme power to remove or alter the legislative when they find the legislative act contrary to the trust reposed in them; for all power given with trust for the attaining an end, being limited by that end, whenever that end is manifestly neglected or opposed, the trust must necessarily be forfeited, and the power devolve into the hands of those that gave it who may place it anew where they think best for their safety and security. And thus the community perpetually retains a supreme power of saving themselves from the attempts and designs of anybody, even of their legislators whenever they shall be so foolish or so wicked as to lay and carry on designs against the liberties and properties of the subject. . . .[46]

Whether or not this statement has revolutionary implications depends on the reading which is given to it. If the removal of the legislative is violent, if the alteration of the form of government undermines the traditional constitutional structure, then Locke is clearly saying that citizens may take it on themselves to make a revolution. But if all that is being said is that every four or five years the voters have a chance to remove their lawmakers, as is the case in constitutional democracies, then the worst that happens is that Democrats replace Republicans, or Conservatives take office and Labour moves to the opposition benches.

It would have been well had Locke made explicit the distinction between "state" and "government." To remove a "government"—that is, the elected personnel and the officials they appointed—is a normal constitutional procedure. To remove a "state"—elected officials, judges, civil servants, and even private citizens identified with the political structure—usually involves violence and a dictatorial aftermath. In either event Locke acknowledges that citizens can dismiss their rulers. "When the government is dissolved," he says, "the people are at liberty to provide for themselves by erecting a new legislative, differing from the other, by the change of persons, or form, or both, as

[46] Para. 149.

they shall find it must for their safety and good." [47] The ground has already been prepared for this act by introducing two clauses into the original contract: one applies to society, and the other to the government. Even if the citizens dissolve the contract with the government, they still remain in society and have a vantage point from which to install new lawmakers. Locke, then, has anticipated the dissolution of government, and this might be construed as tacit approval on his part for such a move should it become necessary. Indeed, his measured tone and matter-of-fact approach gives the reader to believe that if revolution is being discussed it is not a very violent affair and not really disruptive of society.

But matters are not this simple. For Locke understands that tyranny is common among states and that constitutional procedures are not always available for getting rid of oppressive rulers. To remove those in authority is, in many instances, a revolutionary matter. Unlike St. Thomas and Hobbes, Locke has talked of men's Natural Rights and their political freedom. He has said that the only proper basis of government is the consent of a majority of the governed, and the state is obliged to secure to men their basic liberties. If he feels so deeply about these matters, then what prevents him from condoning violent revolution as a means of unseating tyranny when all other methods fail? The simple answer is that Locke backs down at the last moment. He admits that if the state uses illegal force—that is, does not protect Natural Rights—then the people may well resist political authority. "If . . . the majority of the people . . ." he says, "are persuaded in their consciences that their laws, and with them, their estates, liberties, and lives are in danger, and perhaps their religion too, how they will be hindered from resisting illegal force used against them I cannot tell." [48] But this is no more than a factual statement: if a large enough group is oppressed by a tyrannical state, they will eventually rise up and overthrow it. This will be especially the case if they are politically conscious about what they feel are their economic and religious—and, one might add, their national—freedoms. Yet the interesting thing is that Locke does not applaud such behavior. On the contrary, he apologizes for having no suggestions about how revolutions of this sort might be prevented.

In the final analysis, Locke is tempermentally very much like St. Thomas. The thought of violence shocks him; the prospect of actual resistance to political authority conjures up in his mind no less an image than Hobbes' state of war. "This will unhinge and overturn all polities," he says, "and instead of government and order, leave nothing but anarchy and confusion." [49]

---

[47] Para. 220.
[48] Para. 209.
[49] Para. 203.

So long as change is orderly, so long as a government is replaced with another much like it and the fabric of society is left undisturbed—in this event citizens may change their rulers. But if they get bolder ideas, they will find no sanction for them in Locke's theory.

Liberalism's ambiguities are its virtues. Locke's theory cannot possibly attain to the logical consistency of Hobbes' model, because it tries to pursue too many discrete goals at the same time. Government must be limited, but it must be strong enough to secure rights to its citizens. The majority should determine the course of governmental policy, but the interests of minorities should not suffer. Men may acquire unequal amounts of property in the economic sphere, but this ought not to affect equality in the political realm. Freedom from tyranny is an end all societies should aim for, but the anarchy and confusion attendant on resistance to authority are to be avoided. Perhaps the great omission in Locke's theory—the one which leaves unresolved so many of his problems—is a consideration of social structure. What kind of society is to give rise to the men and governments that liberalism requires? Apart from his theory of property, Locke says little about social classes or social institutions; his political analysis wears the air of universal application, and yet it may be suited only for societies at a certain level of historical development. This is not so much a criticism of an important theorist—for Locke has opened many new doors which can never again be closed—as it is a preface to the directions liberal theory will take with succeeding writers.

8.
Jean Jacques Rousseau

THE MAN AND HIS TIMES

Rousseau was born in 1712 in Geneva, a city still infused with the stern morality of John Calvin, who had presided there over a century before. His family was French and had taken refuge in Switzerland during the persecutions of the Huguenots. Nevertheless, the Calvinist influence appeared to have had little impact on the Rousseaus. The father was a person of eccentric tendencies: he started as a watchmaker but soon gave up this sedentary trade to become a dancing master. He took none of his jobs very seriously, wandering off on random travels as the spirit moved him. Rousseau's mother died in childbirth, and the father took over the rearing of the son. Part of the boy's education consisted in being read the most lurid of adventure stories all through the night. If this led to a disregard for such conventional matters as keeping regular hours, it also inspired limitless imagination. Rousseau refused to apprentice himself to a trade in Geneva, and at the age of sixteen he ran away from home and city. Unlike Hobbes and Locke, he had neither steady employment nor noble patronage. His life was an unending series of wanderings throughout Europe, and there were times when he knew real poverty and deprivation. Indeed, there was one period when he was reduced to petty thievery in order to keep alive, and others when he lived off a procession of women who were prepared to play the role of a mother he never knew. Rousseau did marry, but as a family man he was notoriously unfaithful, and his irresponsibility was evidenced by his farming out his children because he was unwilling to provide for them. Yet, for all these displays of antisocial behavior, Rousseau's personality was sufficiently engaging that doors were again and again opened to him and forgiveness bestowed.

He entered the ranks of political theorists in 1749 when, at the age of 37, he submitted an entry in an essay contest sponsored by the Dijon Academy. The question to be answered was, "Has the Revival of the

287

Sciences and the Arts Helped to Purify or to Corrupt Morals?"
Rousseau said that corruption had been the result, and he expounded the
thesis that the alleged advances of civilization had served to suppress all
that was good and creative in man. His essay won first prize and gave him
wide attention. He followed it with the Discourse on the Origin of Inequality
and The Social Contract, which appeared in 1755 and 1762. These works
gained him admission to the salons of Paris, where he mingled with the
intellectuals and publicists of the time. But he was not of the class which
sponsored these gatherings and his exposure to it in no way made him an
aristocrat. Rousseau was always a poor man, and while he might have
been invited to a great home for an afternoon or an evening, no French
counterpart of the Devonshires or Shaftesburys took him under their
wing. Rousseau's books were always objects of controversy, and if at some
times they were acclaimed by the intelligentsia, at others they were banned
or burned by official decree. He died in poverty and poor health in 1788.

The French Enlightenment to which Rousseau contributed was an intellectual awakening similar to that of the Italian Renaissance. While the
best-known writers and their immediate audience may have had privileged
backgrounds, there was a tendency to take a skeptical view of the basic
assumptions on which society was founded. A significant symbol of the age
was the question posed by the Dijon Academy for its essay contest, and no
less revealing is the fact that Rousseau's answer received the prize. Most of
the thinkers, however, confined their criticism to the intellectual realm;
if they did attack actual institutions, their target was the church. It was
Rousseau who went farther and, in the eyes of some, too far. His theory
brought into question the economic and political structure of society:
private property and absolute government were both described as
impediments to the good life. For man's essential goodness to be revealed
required a revolutionary transformation of prevailing institutions.

Whether Rousseau should be called a socialist or a democrat in the
modern understanding of those terms is a matter of debate. His talk of
liberty and equality was frequently qualified by less than complimentary
references to the common man. The French Revolution, which was to
come a decade after his death, extolled the principles Rousseau had
outlined, yet its impetus came neither from the aristocracy which had
underwritten the thinking of the Enlightenment nor from the common
people whose potentialities were to be released by a reordering of society.
On the contrary it was the rising middle class which sought social status
and political power and which was prepared to use Rousseau's rhetoric
as a theoretical rationale for their aspirations.

8.
Jean Jacques Rousseau

POLITICAL THEORY HAS NEVER BEEN PARTICULARLY HOSPITABLE
to democracy. The majority of theorists tend to regard the public as a potential
mob and democratic government as incipient tyranny. Even those writers who
show signs of sympathy towards the doctrine of majority rule—Aristotle, Locke,
Tocqueville, Mill—are in the final analysis prone to give higher priority to
political freedom and individual rights as values. In all of their theories it is
the majority that is asked to give way so that the pursuit of freedom may be
unhampered. Even Locke, who professes adherence to unqualified majority
rule, spends so much more time developing his theory of the rights of man
that there can be no doubt as to where his chief concern lies. Of this tributary
of political theory, then, the mainstream is decidedly liberal; it is only
secondarily democratic.

Rousseau is an unabashed democrat, and because of this he plays a dissenter's role in Western political theory. This is no insignificant commentary
on the Western political tradition itself. While political theorists have been
emphasizing limited government and individual rights, the emerging aspiration in the real political world has been for majority rule and an unfettered
state. Cloistered thinkers from Plato to Locke have, in reality, been speaking
for a small minority: the rights and freedoms they justify have meaning for
men of wisdom or wealth or high social status. This minority, the theorists suggested, is worth protecting: its members possess qualities which promote the
stability or the virtue of society. But minority rule, minority rights, and minority virtue have never received much sympathy in the minds of most citizens.
The average man has a higher opinion of himself than the theorists are prepared to entertain—and in recent years this average man has begun to act
effectively on the basis of this opinion. The only writer who wholeheartedly
gives the man-in-the-street a political philosophy is Rousseau. And this is because Rousseau has an image of the common man which most closely accords
with the image the average man holds of himself.

289

Rousseau's theory, to put matters simply, may be expressed as a "U." The top of the left-hand side of the "U" is the *State of Nature*, an idyllic paradise in which natural men led lives of simple pleasure. At the bottom of the "U" is our present condition, *Civil Society*, which is characterized by inequality, human corruption, and illegitimate power. At the top of the right-hand side of the "U" is *Community*. This is a political society which men may achieve if they realize the causes of their current discontents and if they come to understand the true arrangements of political democracy and human freedom. At all three of these points, however, Rousseau adheres to a consistent view of human nature. The natural man, the corrupted man, the democratic man— all are essentially the same creature. They look different, to be sure, but this is because different environments have imposed their ways of behaving on them. At the close of the *Discourse on the Origins of Inequality*, Rousseau tries to frame the problem with which he is dealing. "That men are actually wicked, a sad and continual experience of them proves beyond doubt," he says. "But, all the same, I think I have shown that man is naturally good." [1] How can one acknowledge that men are wicked in their behavior and yet at the same time say that they are good in nature? Indeed, what does it mean to say that men are naturally good?

THE MEANING OF EQUALITY

Aristotle believed in the "wickedness of human nature," St. Augustine and St. Thomas affirmed the doctrine of original sin, and Machiavelli stated that men in general are "ungrateful, voluble, dissemblers, anxious to avoid danger, and covetous of gain." How, against such an arsenal of opinion, can Rousseau attest to man's underlying goodness? Original sin, as was seen, summed up the basic fact of human perversity. Even in the best-ordered of political or social arrangements there will always be at least a few individuals who will throw sand in the gears. Out of malice or stupidity, out of vanity or misunderstanding, there will perpetually exist people who will not act in accord with the conventional conception of right behavior. Social harmony will always remain an unattained ideal because of the human failings of some dissenting citizens. It was in this vein that Aristotle criticized Plato's Utopia. It was for this reason that St. Thomas defined the goal of politics as the achievement of order in an imperfect world.

Rousseau has observed the same men and the same perversities as have the

[1] *A Discourse on the Origin of Inequality*, in *The Social Contract and Discourses* (London: J. M. Dent, 1913), translated by G. D. H. Cole, p. 222.

theorists who preceded him. The wicked behavior of mankind has hardly escaped his eye. Yet this, he says, is a superficial view of man in society:

> If we look at human society with a calm and disinterested eye, it seems, at first, to show us only the violence of the powerful and the oppression of the weak. . . . The mind is shocked at the cruelty of the one, or is induced to lament the blindness of the other; and as nothing is less permanent in life than those external relations, which are more frequently produced by accident than wisdom, and which are called weakness or power, riches or poverty, all human institutions seem at first glance to be founded merely on banks of shifting sand. It is only by taking a closer look, and removing the dust and sand that surround the edifice, that we perceive the immovable basis on which it is raised, and learn to respect its foundations.[2]

Those who take wicked actions as evidence of a wicked nature are misled by the sands which cover the foundation. The trouble with most theories, Rousseau says, is that they fail "to distinguish properly between what is original and what is artificial in the actual nature of man." [3] For too long we have been taking appearances for actuality. On the basis of superficial evidence there is constructed a superficial conception of human nature and, as a corollary, an arbitrary framework of the Natural Law. "Modern writers begin by inquiring what rules it would be expedient for men to agree on for their common interest," Rousseau says, "and then give the name of Natural Law to a collection of these rules, without any other proof than the good that would result from their being universally practiced." [4]

The difficulties with Natural Law theories are many, but the chief one is that they take man as he is found in society and then proceed to generalize about him in a purportedly "scientific" way. But social man is already a corrupted man: he is a product of an environment which compels him to act as a competitive and self-interested creature. Anyone who wishes to talk meaningfully of human nature and Natural Law must abstract man from his social setting. The basic material for theory must be natural man, a creature unconditioned and uninhibited by the constricting rules of social life. "As long as we are ignorant of the natural man," Rousseau says, "it is in vain for us to attempt to determine either the law originally prescribed to him, or that which is best adapted to his constitution." [5] The individual as he is in a state of nature leads Rousseau to avow man's inherent goodness. The evil which men do is the product of environmental forces; society twists the minds and behavior of individuals so that in their search for security they commit antisocial acts.

[2] *Ibid.*, p. 158.
[3] *Ibid.*, p. 155.
[4] *Ibid.*, p. 157.
[5] *Ibid.*

As with Hobbes and Locke, Rousseau's notions of natural man and the state of nature are logical or analytical abstractions: they make no claim to having an anthropological or historical basis. As far as Rousseau is concerned, men have always lived in society—indeed, in a whole variety of societies. What students of politics must do is ask themselves which facets of individual behavior are the inevitable products of social existence, and which are elements of man's nature that exist independently of his social conditioning and experience. To even begin to ask such a question the student must utilize the deductive rather than the inductive approach. "Let us begin then by laying facts aside, as they do not affect the question," Rousseau says. "The investigation we may enter into, in treating this subject, must not be considered as historical truths, but only as mere conditional and hypothetical reasonings, rather calculated to explain the nature of things, than to ascertain their actual origin. . . ." [6]

To ignore the facts, to abstract out a hypothetical natural man—this is a mental *tour de force* which is bound to raise many an eyebrow. Yet such a logical exercise is not as extravagant as might be thought. The economist, as was observed earlier, is compelled to talk of an "economic man" whose desires are plainly a caricature of those found in real life. Similarly, sociologists will, for example, assign the role of "mother" to a woman, and they will talk of her as if she did not play many other roles as well. In fact, such analytical constructs are absolutely necessary if we are to make any progress in the social sciences at all. Men and women have many roles and are the products of many social and psychological forces. Yet we cannot talk of all of these roles or forces in the same breath. We are compelled to analyze behavior into its component parts and to hope that if we do this sensibly we will still remember that the whole is more than the sum of the analytic parts. At all events, Rousseau is trying to draw a picture of presocial man. If we begin to understand this abstracted person, then we will see what traits of character he has before society begins to mold him.

The general direction of social conditioning, as Rousseau will make clear, is inequality. Natural men stood in a position of equality towards each other. Rousseau makes the distinction between natural or physical inequality on the one hand, and moral or political inequality on the other:

I conceive that there are two kinds of inequality among the human species; one, which I call natural or physical, because it is established by nature, and consists in a difference of age, health, bodily strength, and qualities of the mind or of the soul: and another, which may be called moral or political inequality, because it depends on a kind of convention, and is established, or at least authorized, by the consent

[6] *Ibid.*, p. 161.

of men. This latter consists of the different privileges which some men enjoy to the prejudice of others; such as that of being more rich, more honored, more powerful, or even in a position to exact obedience.[7]

Natural or physical inequalities are clearly human *differences*. No political theorist, no matter how carried away with his equalitarianism he might be, has ever argued that men are the *same*. All theorists take note of the variations in strength, intelligence, and temperament which are found in all aggregates of men. The question of human equality has been raised, in one form or another, in connection with all the theories which have been discussed so far. It might therefore be in order to make some comments which draw together what has already been said. First of all, there is the equal-unequal and similar-different juxtaposition:

	Basis of Judgment	
	Empirical	*A priori*
Qualities Which Men Share	Similar	Equal
Qualities Men Do Not Share	Different	Unequal

The differences in these approaches have been discussed in the chapters on Plato and the theologians. One difficulty is that most theorists do not bother to distinguish, say, inequality from empirical differentiation. For this reason the student must take note of when one meaning is being conveyed and when another is intended. Furthermore, there is the question of whether a priori equality can be "proved" by citing evidence of overriding similarities among men, as Hobbes believed, or whether it can be "disproved" by adducing significant differences, as Plato sought to do. Men, of course, can be simultaneously different and equal if a theorist wishes so to regard them. But they cannot be similar and unequal, for inequality must be based on some dissimilarity of possessed qualities—even if those qualities are not visible to the naked eye. The important point, however, is to understand what uses a theory makes of these ideas and observations. Neither the empirical nor the a priori approach is, of itself, more compatible with freedom or justice or even democracy. Therefore, we should now turn to the equal-unequal dichotomy and take note of some of its political consequences. For the idea itself always connotes the viewpoint of superiority and inferiority, and how this view is expressed depends on who is looking at whom:

Unequals, depending on usage and situation, can be either favored or deprived individuals in a society. Aristotle, for example, spoke of members of an oligarchy as unequals, while in modern political contexts inequality is

[7] *Ibid.*, p. 160.

	SUPERIORITY "The Downward View"	INFERIORITY "The Upward View"
	(1)	(2)
The Democratic View	Equals: The First-Class Citizens Who Are a Majority of the Society	Unequals: The Second-Class Citizens Who Are a Minority in the Society
	(3)	(4)
The Oligarchic or Aristocratic View	Unequals: The Superior Individuals Who Are a Minority in the Society	Equals: The Men in the Street Who Are a Majority of the Society

generally reserved for those persons lacking the advantages that most men have. While in the democratic view it is possible that the equals will be a minority—as in some counties in Southern states where Negroes are in a majority—what this usually means is that we are referring to a subcommunity which is actually oligarchic even though the whole society is democratic. The vantage point of the person who is talking about equality is of great importance, for it establishes the tone in which his sentiments are expressed; and that tone can have practical ramifications. If the equalitarian is a member of either (1) or (3), then he addresses himself *downward* to his fellow citizens in (2) and (4) and says, in effect, "You're as good as I am." If the proponent of equality is himself in (2) or (4), he addresses his sentiments *upward* to those in (1) and (3) and says, in so many words, "I'm as good as you are." [8] The downward expression evidences the compassion of a privileged citizen who believes that either a majority or a minority of his fellow men have suffered injustice which ought to be redressed. The upward expression of equalitarian sentiments embodies the impatience and the envy, the anger and the arrogance of men who are bent on rising even if it means toppling the dominant group which currently has superior status.

Rousseau's tone is one of compassion. Burke, on the other hand, discusses the arrogance of those who claim equality for themselves where they do not deserve it, and he fears that their successful rise will lead to the leveling of institutions which embody important social values by virtue of their unequal qualities. If these men who look upward from (2) and (4) are guilty of envy and arrogance, so may those who look down from (1) and (3) be culpable of a dog-in-the-manger outlook. The problem of equality, as with all other

[8] Clinton Rossiter has a good discussion of these two views of equality, especially as they relate to conservative and liberal theory. See his *Conservatism in America* (New York: Knopf, 1955), pp. 63–98.

questions of political theory, can only be made meaningful if it is set in the context of personal interests, social structure, and historical development.

A theory which propounds the superiority of some men and the inferiority of others will usually stress these differences among men. And a theory which tends in an equalitarian direction wil underplay the great gaps, for example, between the intelligence of some individuals as opposed to that of others. In political theory we are interested in what Rousseau calls "moral" or "political" equality or inequality. The idea of moral equality was raised by St. Augustine and St. Thomas when they asserted that all men had immortal souls, that all men were equally significant—or insignificant—in the sight of God. This assertion could only be made, of course, if the theorist was prepared to assume the existence of the soul and of a God. Yet equality does not have to rest on theology. Rousseau invokes neither the soul nor God to support his view that natural men are equals. On the one hand, he assumes that the equality of all humans is self-evident; on the other, he shows that such inequalities—that is, differences—which we observe are the result of social and political forces which debase some men and elevate others. It will be recalled that Aristotle and St. Augustine suggested that individuals who happened to be born as slaves were, somehow or other, naturally inferior. Rousseau, on the other hand, postulates equality because he sees that all alleged evidences of inequality are the consequence of artificial gradations in society. A slave is deemed inferior because a society tolerates the ownership of one man by another. A member of a particular race is deemed inferior because a society prevents members of that race from elevating themselves.[9]

Rousseau was impatient with all talk of moral inequality. He was persuaded that men are equally worthwhile, equally deserving of a mature respect, and equally capable of governing themselves. Whoever questions this would be warned that until social restraints are removed, we will not have given men a chance to demonstrate their essential equality. Nor is this discussion confined to the realm of deductive reasoning. The practice of giving one man one vote and no more than one vote is based, in large measure, on Rousseau's thinking. The professor of astrophysics and the day laborer are empirically different in terms of their intelligence, knowledge, and breadth of experience. Then why not give the astrophysicist ten votes and the laborer one? There are many ways

[9] Indeed, those who decide who may enter the doors of opportunity often put up barriers against supposedly inferior groups in society on the grounds that they are unfit for superior status. In this process the inferiority of the disadvantaged group is defined by the fact that its members rank low on the social scale. This logical exercise is rather like the boy who shot both his parents and then pleaded for mercy on the grounds that he was an orphan.

to approach such a question, but not the least is that despite their differences they are still equal.

THE ORIGIN OF INEQUALITY

Rousseau's description of life in the state of nature is an amoral idyll. Natural men and women, unrestrained by society's laws or conventions, pursue their lives in privacy and peace. Morality does not exist, because human relations are infrequent and free of coercion. The savage has no need to threaten his fellow men for there is nothing to steal or to gain. Rousseau says all this as graphically as possible, because he wishes, as a start, to offer a corrective to Hobbes' notion of a warlike state of nature where existence was solitary, poor, nasty, brutish, and short.

> Above all, let us not conclude, with Hobbes, that because man has no idea of goodness, he must be naturally wicked; that he is vicious because he does not know virtue; that he always refuses to do his fellow creatures services which he does not think they have a right to demand; or that by virtue of the right he truly claims everything he needs, he foolishly imagines himself the sole proprietor of the whole universe.
> Savages are not bad merely because they do not know what it is to be good: for it is neither the development of the understanding nor the restraint of law that hinders them from doing ill; but the peacefulness of their passions, and their ignorance of vice.[10]

The natural man which Rousseau sets up is a creature of peaceful ignorance. He does not know what it is to be good, but then he does not know what it is to be bad. For morality is a product of society. If Hobbes' natural man is seen to violate rules of morality, then Rousseau would want to know why a creature in a state of nature is made to steal or cheat or seek power over others. Rousseau would reply that what Hobbes is describing is not a natural state at all, but, rather, a rudimentary civil society. In a natural state men live in peace with each other. And because they do we can then assume that man's underlying nature is also peaceful. Human traits of jealousy, covetousness, greed, and the will to power are all acquired characteristics—and acquired only in society. Remove man from society and his natural goodness will display itself.

It was not a conscious or premeditated act which brought men out of the state of nature and into civil society: things simply began to happen, and it was more by accident than by design. Nor should the motives which impelled the first social act be construed as evil ones. What happened was that a fortui-

---

[10] *Discourse*, pp. 181–182.

tous occurrence had unanticipated consequences. It was all, according to Rousseau, very simple:

The first man who, having enclosed a piece of ground, bethought himself of saying "This is mine," and found people simple enough to believe him was the first real founder of civil society.[11]

Why did that pioneering savage put up a fence around the land he was tilling? We do not know. Perhaps it was to keep animals out or to prevent the drifting of snow. But why, more importantly, did that savage begin to speak the language of private property? Until he did, the words "mine" and "thine" were unknown to human vocabularies. The motive forces behind the new fences and the new words cannot be ascribed to fear or selfishness. For there was no objective need for this innovator to put up a wall or stake a personal claim. There was plenty of land to go around, and none of his neighbors had been endangering his security or comforts.

The origins of property, like many momentous developments, were matters of chance. But once the deed had been done it could not be undone, for the men who claimed title to property soon assumed the role of employer. Not being able to work their land all by themselves, they had to hire others to work for them.

So long as men remained content with their rustic huts, . . . and confined themselves to such arts as did not require the joint labor of several hands, they lived free, healthy, and honest, and happy lives, so long as their nature allowed, and as they continued to enjoy the pleasures of mutual and independent intercourse. But from the moment one man began to stand in need of the help of another; from the moment it appeared advantageous to any one man to have provisions for two, equality disappeared, property was introduced, work became indispensable, and vast forests became smiling fields, which man had to water with the sweat of his brow, and where slavery and misery were soon seen to germinate and grow up with the crops.[12]

Whereas once two natural men once stood on a plane of equality, we now have superior and subordinate in civil society. The great institution for inequality is, then, private property.

What troubles Rousseau most of all is not so much the social as the psychological consequence of life when property and inequality hold sway. Men were thrown in constant contact with each other, they became interdependent, and they began to obey the rules of conduct which emerged as necessary for social life. Yet because the central organizing principle in society was property, self-interest—the defense of one's own—became the guide for behavior. Men were "taught by experience that the love of well-being is the sole motive of

[11] *Ibid.*, p. 192.
[12] *Ibid.*, p. 199.

human actions." While they might occasionally form "some kind of loose association" to protect common interests, on the whole "every one sought his own private advantage, either by open force, if he thought himself strong enough, or by address and cunning, if he felt himself the weaker." [13]

What had happened was that with property there developed not only materialism, self-interest, and inequality, but also the human ego. Men developed a conception of the self which would, in time, work to their own disadvantage. For a social system based on private property sets an egoistic standard for success, and it implants this standard in all individuals. Men come to feel that they must own property, be superior to other men—in a word, be successful. This is, of course, the seamier side of individualism, but it is the side that Rousseau chooses to emphasize. Not only did men come to judge themselves as successes or failures by social standards; they also became compulsive about the way they were viewed by those who lived about them.

Each one began to consider the rest, and to wish to be considered in turn: and thus a value came to be attached to public esteem. Whoever sang or danced best, whoever was the handsomest, the strongest, the most dextrous, or the most eloquent, came to be of most consideration: and this was the first step towards inequality, and at the same time towards vice. From these first distinctions arose on the one side vanity and contempt and on the other shame and envy: and the fermentation caused by these new leavens ended by producing combinations fatal to innocence and happiness.[14]

For every man who is successful there must be a man—or more than one—who is a failure. For one who gains public esteem there must be one who fails to achieve it. Yet all are indiscriminately taught to pursue success, and all are educated to crave popular approval. The fruits of individualism may be enjoyable for the few who are victors, but they cannot be shared by all. Yet victory is not that sweet: even those who meet the standards of society become victims of vanity and contempt—both underlying signs of the insecurity which besets even those who appear to have emerged at the top.

In short, all men fall prey to the frailties of their own ego. Relying, as they must in an individualist environment, on the strength of their own personalities, they build defenses to hide the basic weakness of the self. Life becomes an elaborate pretense: if an individual cannot display all the prizes that society demands, then he must go through never-ending rationalizations to persuade others that success has been attained.

It now became the interest of men to appear what they really were not. To be and to seem became two totally different things; and from this distinction sprang insolent pomp and cheating trickery, with all the numerous vices that go in their

---

[13] *Ibid.*, p. 194.
[14] *Ibid.*, p. 197.

train. On the other hand, free and independent as men were before, they were now, in consequence of a multiplicity of new wants, brought into subjection, as it were, to all nature, and particularly to one another; and each became in some degree a slave even in becoming the master of other men: if rich, they stood in need of the services of others; if poor, of their assistance; and even a middle condition did not enable them to do without one another. Man must now, therefore, have been perpetually employed in getting others to interest themselves in his lot, and in making them, apparently at least, if not really, find their advantage in promoting his own.[15]

Relations between man and man in an individualist-oriented society cannot be based on love, spontaneity, or generosity. Rather, all men assume the roles of either exploiters or the exploited. Life becomes a dangerous game in which men cheat each other in an outright manner, or devise ways to persuade others that it will be to their advantage to support one's own designs. The common coin is not altruism, but rather self-interest.

One reason for the rise of egoism is that as society becomes more complex, men's wants increase more rapidly than the means of satisfying them. Men's expectations rise, and they begin to feel that the successful life depends on possessing more and more material comforts. But today's luxury becomes tomorrow's necessity; and as the tempo increases, man's reach is forever bound to exceed his grasp. Life seems more comfortable, more conveniences are available, but expectations always run behind attainment. "These conveniences lost with use almost all their power to please, and even degenerated into real needs," Rousseau says, "till the want of them became far more disagreeable than the possession of them had been pleasant." [16] The prize of individualism is material prosperity, but the price of this prosperity is continual frustration. The senses are comforted, but the mind and soul are twisted in the process. Men seek to conquer each other rather than experience the joys of the fraternal life. In this cold war no one wins: victors can never be sure that the vanquished will remain in their place and mastery means nothing if servants are not servile.

The threats and anxieties which arise in civil society are not only psychological; they are also political. The ethic of individualism and the institution of property sets men in competition with each other, and this competition soon becomes cutthroat. If all are to play a game, then the game must have rules. What is needed, in short, is a rule-making institution: a state. Just as the man who put up the first fence created society, so, Rousseau says, a new pioneer comes along to suggest that society cannot exist without political authority. This trailblazer speaks the language of Hobbes, and it is worth listening to his blandishments in their fullness.

[15] *Ibid.*, p. 202.
[16] *Ibid.*, p. 196.

After having represented to his neighbors the horror of a situation which armed every man against the rest, and made their possessions as burdensome to them as their wants, and in which no safety could be expected either in riches or in poverty, he readily devised plausible arguments to make them close with his design.

"Let us join," said he, "to guard the weak from oppression, to restrain the ambitious, and to secure to every man the possession of what belongs to him: let us institute rules of justice and peace, to which all without exception may be obliged to conform; rules that may in some measure make amends for the caprices of fortune, by subjecting equally the powerful and the weak to the observance of reciprocal obligations. Let us, in a word, instead of turning our forces against ourselves, collect them in a supreme power which may govern us by wise laws, protect and defend all the members of the association, repulse their common enemies, and maintain eternal harmony among us."

Far fewer words to this purpose would have been enough to impose on men so barbarous and easily seduced; especially as they had too many disputes among themselves to do without arbitrators, and too much ambition and avarice to go long without masters. All ran headlong to their chains, in hopes of securing their liberty; for they had just wit enough to perceive the advantages of political institutions, without experience enough to enable them to foresee the dangers. The most capable of foreseeing the dangers were the very persons who expected to benefit by them; and even the most prudent judged it not inexpedient to sacrifice one part of their freedom to ensure the rest; as a wounded man has his arm cut off to save the rest of his body.[17]

The differences between Rousseau and Hobbes are not just academic quibbles about which labels ought to be attached to what fictional constructs. In Rousseau's eyes, what Hobbes calls a "state of nature" is really a "civil society." And what Hobbes calls "civil society," Rousseau will proceed—in The Social Contract—to call the "state." Hobbes has society emerge from the state of nature as the result of a contract, and this society has embodied in it all the political and legal characteristics of a sovereign state. Rousseau has society develop from the state of nature by what might be called an inevitable accident, and the state will later come into existence as the result of a specific contract. Once again a schematic representation may be of some help:

	Hobbes	Locke	Rousseau
The First Transition: From a State of Nature to Civil Society	A Single Contract which puts men into Society, and . . .	A Two-Part Contract, one part of which puts men into Society, and . . .	An informal and nonlegal agreement, which puts men into Society.
The Second Transition: From Civil Society to the State	. . . simultaneously puts them into the State, without distinguishing between State and Society.	. . . the second part of which (actually a second contract) puts them into Civil Government.	A Two-Part Contract which formally reconstitutes Society and also puts men into the State.

[17] Ibid., p. 205.

And, once more, the questions of importance center on the uses to which the various analytic stages and transitions are put. Hobbes had a forbidding picture of the state of nature prior to society and the state to show that if men did not have a common authority to hold them in awe they would fall victim to their own baser instincts. Rousseau has created a benign state of nature prior to society and state to demonstrate that even without social or political restraints—and probably because of their absence—men can live in harmony and peace with each other. And Hobbes, by basing society and state on a contract which assumes men's overriding need for authority, makes that agreement all but irrevocable. Rousseau, along with Locke, sees the state as an addition to society, not an integral part of it; and he puts self-government ahead of strong government. This means that if men wish to alter the form of their political system they can dissolve the governmental part of the contract and draw up a new one without destroying society. Indeed, continual dissolution and recreation is precisely what Rousseau will propose in *The Social Contract*.

The transition from state of nature to society in the *Discourse on the Origin of Inequality* is political as well as social. And in building a state on top of society, men jumped out of the frying pan of cutthroat competition into the fire of political tyranny. This transition, then, is not a contract. It is informal and accidental, nonlegal and, in fact, founded on a gigantic swindle. In no sense are rational or informed processes of consent at work, and in no sense are the resultant society and state to be considered legitimate institutions. Men felt or were persuaded that they needed a common power to secure what would pass as justice and to establish what would look like peace. So obvious and so pressing were these needs made to appear that individuals were willing to accept strong authority without asking what price had to be paid. That price might be the very freedoms which men sought to have secured to them; but few took such a far sighted view, and most of those who did wagered that they had more to gain than to lose by pledging their obedience. Had men been rational, Rousseau says, "it would have been inconsistent with common sense to begin by bestowing on a chief the only things they wanted his help to preserve." [18] But they were not rational: they had become so blinded by their lust for material comfort and by their desire to rise above the heads of their fellow men that they were unable to ask profound political questions. "The first expedient which proud and unsubdued men hit upon for their common security," Rousseau says, "was to run headlong into slavery." [19]

When security depends upon property and social status, then the yearning for its preservation can have the effect of defeating the ethic of individualism.

[18] *Ibid.*, p. 208.
[19] *Ibid.*

The very basis of individualism is irrational, and we ought not to be surprised if men who profess it are capable of destroying it. This, Rousseau would say, is the stage at which modern societies have arrived. We live in a social framework which is based on property and inequality, and we live under a state which is founded on coercion and legal authority. Rousseau would not argue with Hobbes on this score: we do indeed have Leviathan, and he is a creature of our own making. The motives which led us to submit to him may have been irrational and contrary to our underlying nature: it is a combination of chance and design which have led to the ascendancy of illegitimate power. Yet the misfortunes which have befallen the modern world have not eradicated man's essential goodness.

The natural man is dormant, but he never becomes extinct. "Original man having vanished by degrees," Rousseau says, "society offers to us only an assembly of artificial men and factitious passions." [20] We are wearing masks to which we have become so accustomed that we think them parts of ourselves. Indeed, we are so impressed with what we consider to be material and intellectual progress, that we forget that the benign savage who lies deep in all of us has been brutally assaulted by the artifacts of his own making. Our so-called progress brings suffering which we do not fully understand: we aspire to be superior, and we deplore the consequences of inequality when they are inflicted on us. In raising inequality out of equality we have not only built a towering mountain but also alongside it a bottomless pit. "All the inequality which now prevails," Rousseau says, "owes its strength and growth to the development of our faculties and the advance of the human mind." [21] Those who sit astride the mountain created by man's intelligence and skill are ever fearful that they will tumble into the gaping abyss at its foot. And those in the lower depths scramble over each other to attain the success and avoid the stigma of failure by which society judges all men. If this is progress, then Rousseau has small use for it.

Furthermore, the politics of inequality only consolidate this anxious condition. Law lends a specious authority to property, and the state enforces artificial distinctions among men. We may not be able to return to our natural state, and civil society may be a necessity. But if this is so, then the great obligation of the state is to civilize once more—to make legitimate—relations between citizens. Rather than authorizing inequalities based on property, it must promote equality based on the inherent identity of all men. This is the foremost task of politics. If we are to bring out what is best and what is natural in every human being, then the democratic state is the only way to

[20] *Ibid.*, p. 220.
[21] *Ibid.*, p. 221.

reconcile social existence with political authority. From the *Discourse on the Origin of Inequality* it is therefore a logical step to *The Social Contract*.

COMMUNITY AND LEGITIMACY

Rousseau's political theory—like Plato's earlier—is a theory of society. If men are to live the good life, they must learn to live in a community. The notion of community is infuriatingly vague; philosophers and social scientists have spent much effort in an attempt to make clear just what this entity is.[22] A definition of social structure can be framed in terms of class or institutions: we can talk of rich people and poor people, old families and new families, individuals of high status and low status; or we can describe churches and corporations, universities and trade unions, political parties and civic associations, and similar institutions. Society, then, is composed of people and groups, and its major outlines can be perceived by a skillful classification of individuals and institutions and their mutual relations—not so a community. Groups of people can live together in a specified geographical area; they can set up institutions for the attainment of certain goals; they can agree on ways and means for resolving conflicts among interests—but, for all this, it may truthfully be said that while many aggregates of individuals are societies, they have yet to achieve the status of community.

The chief requirement for community is *consensus*: an unarticulated agreement among individuals on how life ought to be lived, an unspoken concord on what constitutes right behavior. The quest for community, which is the quest for consensus, lay at the heart of Plato's theory—so much so that Aristotle felt compelled to point to the dangers of extreme unity and any monolithic conception of the good. Indeed, Plato was so concerned over the need for consensus that he was prepared to have his Guardians indulge in thought-control in a premeditated way to ensure that all citizens would think the right thoughts and act in approved ways. But consensus need not be the product of Machiavellian engineering on the part of rulers. It can develop slowly and unconsciously over generations, even centuries. This, as we will see, is what Edmund Burke had in mind when he talked of "prescription."

Rousseau does not advocate a planned or manipulated Utopia like Plato's, yet at the same time he does not wish to allow time and tradition to develop its own consensus in an unplanned way. While he has much in common with both Plato and Burke, Rousseau goes his own way in the search for

[22] A summary of the classical and contemporary literature is to be found in Sebastian de Grazia's *The Political Community* (Chicago: University of Chicago Press, 1948). De Grazia's own analysis of community is itself an original and provocative contribution to political theory.

community. He begins with the assumption that most significant aggregates of individuals do in fact possess a common interest; some groups show this more so than others, but all have tendencies which serve to unify rather than divide. The main argument behind this assumption is, of course, the equality of all men. Their essential identity leads us to acknowledge that, in many instances, what is good for all is good for one.

All men are creatures with needs which are, at base, the needs of all other human beings: the need for security, for love, for self-respect, for freedom, and for the good life. If any of these are denied to any citizens, then all suffer. For this reason their attainment must be a common project. Out of this grows the further assumption of consensus: all men, whether they know it or not, whether they act in ways which show it or not, agree on the basic rules of conduct for social living. A consensus is both unanimous and inarticulate: every member of a community, simply by virtue of living within its boundaries, is attuned to the general body of principles which guide behavior for that community. No one is excepted. Everyone "knows" what these principles are, even though they may be at such an ultra-high wave length that it is impossible for the average citizen to "hear" them all the time or to articulate them most of the time. This unconscious agreement on principles makes a community.

Yet we must not forget that many a society has not had the time or favorable circumstances which allow for the ironing out of deep-seated conflicts; many a society is riven with class or racial or national differences which render impossible an agreement on principles which may apply with justice to all citizens. Rousseau, as will be seen, lays down the conditions which a society must meet if it is eventually to transform itself into a community. Furthermore, there is the perennial danger that an established community will cease to perpetuate its consensus, and hence lapse into the status of society—if it is possible for even that to be retained.

These, then, are the tasks which Rousseau sets for himself: how does a society become a community, and how does it stay that way? In the course of this analysis there emerges a theory of democracy and a theory of political freedom. Both of these ideas must be viewed—and can only be viewed—within the context of a communal setting. Democracy and freedom without community are, according to Rousseau, dangerous delusions. The autonomous individual of Hobbes and Locke can be neither a free nor a democratic man; individualism, by liberating man from the sanctions of communal values, gives him a spurious freedom and a purposeless self-government which are so empty of principle as to be meaningless.

This needs to be said because the theories of Hobbes and Locke are, on first appearance, far more plausible than that of Rousseau. The freedom to do what you like without external restraint, the right to choose and consent to your rulers—these are common-sense conceptions and ones held by most Western theorists. Rousseau, on the other hand, gives new meanings to the old words. At first sight these meanings are curious, even outrageous. Yet, after we begin to understand what he is getting at, it becomes clear that both freedom and democracy have additional dimensions which the common-sense theories have overlooked. While Rousseau's way of stating his case is often bizarre, he has something important to say. To learn the truth we must often go out of our way to understand an alien language.

Political obligation has, for many years, been a classical question of political philosophy. Why, the average citizen is entitled to ask, should I obey these particular rulers or those particular laws? The only acceptable answer in political philosophy is that the power which underwrites the authority of the state or the rulers or the laws is legitimate power. Only to power which is rightful is the citizen obliged to bend his knee. Great controversies, of course, spring from differing conceptions of legitimacy. Every theorist we have thus far considered has had a criterion for judging whether or not a government is legitimate. Plato required that power be exercised rationally; St. Thomas demanded that rulers attune their policies to the dictates of the Natural Law; Hobbes asked that security for the citizens and legal stability be provided; Locke posited that the inherent rights of men be protected. Rousseau addresses himself to this question on the opening page of *The Social Contract:*

Man is born free; and everywhere he is in chains. One thinks himself the master of others, and still remains a greater slave than they. How did this change come about? I do not know. What can make it legitimate? That question I think I can answer.[23]

Man's transition from freedom to slavery was discussed—as a historical fiction—in the *Discourse on the Origin of Inequality.* When Rousseau says that he does not know how this change came about, he is simply saying that he has no pretensions to being either a historian or an anthropologist. What he does know, as a political scientist, is that modern man's potentiality for full development is frustrated by his repressive social institutions. What he does believe, as a political philosopher, is that he can tell us how to create a political system which will organize power in a legitimate way.

To begin, Rousseau rejects the standards for legitimacy set down by his predecessors. Quite clearly he opposes the notion that might makes right. This was, in essence, the view of Thrasymachus in *The Republic* and Machiavelli in *The Prince.* If we take the position that rightful power is successful

---

[23] *The Social Contract,* in *The Social Contract and Discourses, op. cit.,* p. 3.

power, then legitimacy becomes contingent on the interest of those who have gained access to the seat of government. "If force creates right, the effect changes with the cause," Rousseau says. "Every force that is greater than the first succeeds to its right [and] as soon as it is possible to disobey with impunity, disobedience is legitimate." [24] The might-makes-right viewpoint can be a useful one when it comes to describing the process by which men seek to gain and maintain power; this is especially true when it is construed not in a simplistic or vulgar sense, but as an explanation of the way in which the power structure influences the prevailing values in society.

However, it must be understood that such analysis, while often worthwhile, is not political philosophy. The philosophical approach to legitimacy deals not with how things came to be as they are—for that is the province of political science—but rather with how they ought to be in the present and in the future. The political scientist tends to regard talk of legitimacy as ideology: as used either by the "outs" who wish to gain power or by the "ins" who seek to maintain their power. The political philosopher acknowledges that theories of legitimation are often used in ideological ways; nevertheless, he still has the task of sorting out which claims to power are rightful and which are not. This may involve ploughing through what Rousseau was driven to call at one time "a mass of inexplicable nonsense." [25] But unless we are to lower Plato or St. Thomas to the level of an editorial writer or a campaign orator, we must grant that the discussion of legitimacy is appropriate to serious students of politics.

Second, Rousseau discards the idea that peace, security, or stability is the touchstone for legitimacy. In doing this, he is parting company with Hobbes and, to some degree, with St. Thomas. Those who put a premium on peace and order will soon find themselves condoning a benevolent despot—if such an unusual ruler could ever be found. The whole notion of tranquillity as a legitimizing factor seems, to Rousseau, to confuse ends and means:

> It will be said that the despot assures his subjects civil tranquillity. Granted: but what do they gain . . . if the very tranquillity they enjoy is one of their miseries? Tranquillity is found also in dungeons; but is that enough to make them desirable places to live in? [26]

One way to put this is that life, liberty, and the pursuit of happiness are not three co-equal goals. Life, while of course a necessary prerequisite, is only a means to the attainment of liberty and happiness. A government which ensures tranquillity will see to it that citizens are not in constant danger of losing their lives. No one will gainsay the performance of this vital function; what can be

[24] *Ibid.*, p. 6.
[25] *Ibid.*
[26] *Ibid.*, p. 7.

questioned is whether providing such peace is sufficient to endow a government with legitimacy. For, as Rousseau said, tranquillity alone is less a blessing than a misery; to it must be added the *kind* of life which citizens will lead once they have been brought to the point where they have no longer to fear violent death.

Furthermore, Rousseau finds inadequacies in the historical or traditionalist argument for legitimacy. Here he is opposing Locke and, as we will see in the next chapter, Edmund Burke. Both Locke and Burke said that government is founded on a contract, and hence is based on consent. Locke saw this agreement as being reached many generations ago, and as binding future generations so long as they do not expressly say that they are dissatisfied with political arrangements as they stand. Burke's "contract" never involves articulated consent at all, but rather rests on an unconscious acquiescence among those dead, those living, and those yet to be born. Rousseau regards consent as a living and an ever-active process. In entering a political contract, an individual "alienates" himself: he agrees to give up his freedom to do certain things in return for certain protections—which will ensure an even greater total freedom—from the state. This alienation is a uniquely personal act; it requires an individual to decide to fragment his liberty, and even his personality, as part of a calculated political risk. Because consenting to authority is such an important decision, Rousseau cannot see how the consent of long-dead ancestors can—even by means of tacit consent—bind those who are now living.

> Even if each man could alienate himself, he could not alienate his children: they are born men and free; their liberty belongs to them, and no one but they has the right to dispose of it. Before they come to years of discretion, the father can, in their name, lay down conditions for their preservation and well-being, but he cannot give them irrevocably and without conditions: such a gift is contrary to the ends of nature, and exceeds the rights of paternity. It would therefore be necessary, in order to legitimize an arbitrary government, that in every generation the people should be in a position to accept or reject it; but, were this so, the government would be no longer arbitrary.[27]

If a father cannot commit his children to obey the government, then it follows even more strongly that a contract concluded in, say, 1789 cannot bind citizens in the 1960's—almost two centuries later. For Rousseau, each person must consent to authority expressly and frequently. His conception of a contract clearly goes further than that of either Hobbes or Locke in this respect. And it is on this highly individual and highly participative notion of consent that Rousseau builds his own conception of legitimacy. In a word, a government, if it is to be legitimate, must be a democratic government.

[27] *Ibid.*, pp. 7–8.

Rousseau's contract draws a contrast between precontractual and post-contractual man: on the one hand, the natural man who existed in an idyllic state of nature, and, on the other, a political man who is bound to obey conventional laws. But the distinction is not this simple, for in leaving the natural state, there is no guarantee that the political life will be an improvement on what went before. Indeed, the *Discourse on the Origin of Inequality* observed that the transition from the state of nature to life in society was a distinct misfortune. The social contract which instituted political authority was, to put it bluntly, a hoax perpetrated by the owners of property in order to consolidate their hold on the mass of the population. The upshot was that such a government did not encourage, but rather frustrated, the good life. The purpose of *The Social Contract*, therefore, is to suggest to men a method for delivering themselves from the difficulties they were in at the end of the *Discourse*. Men have left the state of nature for good, and there is no way to return. They have, furthermore, become accustomed to social life and material well-being. The task, therefore, is to create a political system which will make power legitimate: if power can be made a servant rather than a master, then it will be possible to rediscover much of the freedom which men knew in the state of nature. In short, Rousseau, acting as both a political philosopher and a political scientist, is seeking ways to organize political life so that men can rise out of the slough of social and psychological despond and use power as a means to achieve freedom.

The new state—a state which is to be free, democratic, and legitimate—is admittedly an artificial device, created by men for men. And states should not be thought of as "natural" developments. In postulating this Rousseau is clearly at odds with Aristotle, Hegel, and Burke. If states were simply the end product of a series of historical evolutions—or even accidents—then it would be difficult to call any one state legitimate and deny that title to another. We have already seen that men in a state of nature have no warrant to exercise power over each other, and it has also been indicated that might cannot make right: "Since no man has a natural authority over his fellows, and force creates no right, we must conclude that conventions form the basis of all legitimate authority among men." [28] Conventions are purposeful acts; they signify the ways men organize their relations so that given ends may be secured. A state is the prime example of such a man-made convention.

On this basis Rousseau suggests a method for setting up a legitimate state. He begins by stating the problem which has to be solved; he proceeds to show the steps which must be taken; and he then lays down the final and formal act which all citizens must perform to obtain membership in the state:

[28] *Ibid.*, p. 7.

The problem is to find a form of association which will defend and protect with the whole common force the person and goods of each associate, and in which each, while uniting himself with all, may still obey himself alone, and remain as free as before.

Each regains his original rights and resumes his natural liberty, while losing the conventional liberty in favor of which he renounced it. These clauses, properly understood, may be reduced to one—the total alienation of each associate, together with all his rights, to the whole community; for, in the first place, as each gives himself absolutely, the conditions are the same for all; and, this being so, no one has any interest in making them burdensome to others.

Finally, each man, in giving himself to all, gives himself to nobody; and as there is no associate over which he does not require the same right as he yields others over himself, he gains an equivalent for everything he loses and an increase of force for the preservation of what he has.[29]

These paragraphs—like all contracts—call for a close reading. The striking characteristic of this political contract is that apparently everyone gains and no one is a loser. Men agree to subordinate themselves to authority, and yet all remain as free as they were before they undertook this obligation; conventional liberty is given up, but in its place natural liberty is resurrected. What makes this possible is not any inherent magic in the contract but rather Rousseau's premise that all men are dealing, and will deal, with each other on the basis of absolute equality. All men will equally agree to accept political authority, and each will be as liable to coercion as any other. All men will equally turn over their rights to the state, and each will know that none of his fellow citizens will have the power to harm him. And all men will equally become both governors and governed, and each will acknowledge that the power to compel the obedience of others is matched by one's own obligation to obey. Human equality is the first requisite for democracy, and Rousseau puts this condition at the heart of his theory. Freedom—the freedom of democratic men—can only exist when all men face each other on a parity not only of esteem but also of power.

At this point it would be well to show that Rousseau considers his contract to be a moral one; it establishes a legitimate state. Legitimization, however, touches not only political institutions, but the individual citizen as well. "The passage from the state of nature to the civil state produces a very remarkable change in man . . ." Rousseau says, "giving his actions the morality that formerly lacked." [30] It follows that man can only become a moral creature once he participates in the contractual process. The individual, then, needs the state, for the state contains the institutional conditions within which the good life can be led. Whereas in the state of nature man had natural liberty—the

[29] *Ibid.*, p. 12.
[30] *Ibid.*, p. 15.

freedom to do as he pleased without restraints from others—in the political state he now possesses moral liberty. It is this new freedom, Rousseau says, "which alone makes him truly master of himself." [31] Moral liberty is not negative: the freedom *from* hinderance by our fellow men. It is, on the contrary, positive: the freedom *to* know what is right and proceed to do it. "The mere impulse of appetite is slavery," Rousseau says, "while obedience to a law which we prescribe to ourselves is liberty." [32]

This conception marks a departure from Hobbes' and Locke's definition of freedom. It involves three explicit conditions, all of them are necessary: (1) obedience, (2) obedience to law, (3) obedience to law which we have participated in enacting. In the combination of these requisites freedom becomes not simply a void in which men might do as they please; it becomes a disciplined path of action which is moral, political, and democratic. Any animal or any savage will experience sensual gratification if he is allowed to run loose rather than be chained up. Only political man—that is, moral and civilized man—is capable of knowing that freedom should be used to perform right actions. To do right men must obey the law—not any law, but only those which are legitimate; only those which they have helped to enact. The mediation of the state, through the legislative process, shows each citizen what is right. Citizens participate in framing laws; but whereas as autonomous individuals they behave like amoral animals, as citizens taking part in a joint endeavor they legitimize authority and liberate themselves. How this complex procedure is set in operation is the theme of *The Social Contract.*

But before turning to this, it should be noted that the new state is based on "an equality that is moral and legitimate." [33] The state of nature eventually deteriorated because it allowed human differences to get out of hand; men who were stronger or more cunning were able, if they so chose, to make a better life for themselves. Equality in the good society can best be imagined if it is contrasted with the specious legal equality of existing systems. Where, as was discussed in the *Discourse,* legal equality is accompanied by differences in wealth then the fact of economic inequality renders legal equality a sham and a delusion. If equality is to be both moral and legitimate, then the status and property of citizens must be brought to a parity. What must be avoided is the spurious equality of an inequalitarian society. "Under bad governments," Rousseau says, "this equality is only apparent and illusory; it serves only to keep the pauper in his poverty and the rich man in the position he has usurped." Under good governments, "men, who may be unequal [i.e., different] in strength or intelligence, become every one equal by convention and legal

[31] *Ibid.,* p. 16.
[32] *Ibid.*
[33] *Ibid.,* p. 19.

right; . . . from which it follows that the social state is advantageous to men only when all have something and none too much." [34]

The social contract, then, is a man-made convention: its purpose is to rescue men from the injustice which characterizes contemporary politics. Having descended from the coercionless state of nature to an inequalitarian civil society, Rousseau now shows men how they can purposefully ascend to a better political world. It is impossible to return to the left-hand side of the "U"; but in climbing the right-hand side, men may approximate some of the conditions of the state of nature and at the same time live at peace under political authority. To make this ascent, as we have seen, it is first of all necessary to equalize men's property and power as much as possible. After that has been done, a substitute must be found for the natural legitimacy which characterized the state of nature. The legitimacy of the state of nature was based on its having emerged untainted by human self-interest. A legitimate government is far more difficult to achieve, for it is a convention of men and men must strive to raise this institution about the strife of particular interests. The social contract cannot abolish the differences among men: strong and weak, intelligent and stupid individuals will continue to exist. But it can do something else: "The fundamental compact substitutes, for such physical inequality [i.e., differences] as nature may have set up between men, an equality that is moral and legitimate." [35] The new state replaces the natural legitimacy of the state of nature with the moral legitimacy of the social contract.

Men must now live under authority, something they were able to do without in their natural state. However, they need not cavil at this, because the new authority which binds them has a moral sanction. The basis of this legitimacy is that the government which they must obey is self-government. Rousseau puts more reliance on the democratic method than any other theorist. Unless a government is democratic, he says, a citizen has no obligation to obey. And only through democracy, he says, can men recapture the freedom which their fathers once knew in the state of nature. If men are to break the chains forged by society's repressions, if they are to develop their full potentialities as individuals, then they must learn to live democratically. The legitimacy of a democratic state is not, to Rousseau, a philosophical turn of phrase: it is the precondition of the good life.

SOVEREIGNTY AND THE GENERAL WILL

For introducing the twin ideas of "sovereignty" and the "General Will" into his writings, Rousseau has received no great thanks from students of political

[34] *Ibid.*, p. 19, 19n.
[35] *Ibid.*, p. 19.

theory. As was seen in the case of Hobbes, "sovereignty" is a word of several meanings, perhaps no meaning at all. The "General Will" is a notion unique to Rousseau, and it is, at one and the same time, so crucial to his theory and so vague in its connotation that the student more often than not wishes that Rousseau had found some other way of expressing his central idea. Yet this ought not to surprise us: one of the lessons of political theory is, after all, that the most important questions for which we seek answers are the most difficult to set down in a coherent way.

The social contract is a process whereby each individual—as was noted previously—gives up his political independence on the condition that all his fellow citizens do the same:

> Each man, in giving himself to all, gives himself to nobody; and as there is no associate over which he does not acquire the same right as he yields others over himself, he gains an equivalent for everything he loses and an increase of force for the preservation of what he has.[36]

It is the social contract which brings the political sovereign into being. The political power which existed prior to the contract was based on the illegitimate suzerainty of the rich over the poor. The new state is equalitarian in that all have agreed to obey all. Furthermore, each man divests himself of a part of his personality—the political part—so that this feature of his identity is merged with the similar quality of all other citizens. "At once, in place of the individual personality of each contracting party, this act of association creates a moral and collective body . . ." Rousseau says. "This public person, so formed by the union of all other persons . . . is called by its members *state* when passive, *sovereign* when active. . . ."[37]

The sovereign and the state, then, are a single institution. But whereas the state is an institution, the sovereign is a process as well: the state takes on the additional role of sovereign when its citizens actually are in the process of making political decisions. Sovereignty is state power when it is being exercised—and exercised democratically. Rousseau's theory emerges as an organic one: the sovereign is a "person", a being in its own right which is a synthesis of the political lives of all citizens. This relationship works two ways: if the sovereign is composed of all the citizens, each citizen also has in himself the quality of the sovereign. To be sure, he can only act as sovereign when he acts in unanimous concert with all other citizens. Nevertheless, the state, when it acts as sovereign, is ultimately as dependent on him as he is on it. Rousseau tries to state this interwoven relationship:

[36] *Ibid.*, p. 12.
[37] *Ibid.*, p. 13.

This formula shows us that the act of association comprises a mutual undertaking between the public and the individuals, and that each individual, in making a contract, as we may say, with himself, is bound in a double capacity; as a member of the sovereign he is bound to the individuals; and as a member of the state to the sovereign.[38]

As part of the sovereign he has the right, in association with his fellow citizens, to participate in the process of self-government. As part of the state, he has the obligation to obey the dictates of the state when it acts as sovereign. A state, in sum, is sovereign when it embraces all citizens on the basis of a contract which makes provision for self-government as well as for obedience.

Hobbes and Rousseau disagree on the process whereby legitimate authority is created, but both insist that the sovereign is the only source of law. While Hobbes' sovereign—a single man—was above the law, Rousseau's sovereign— an organism consisting of all men—is itself the law. Citizens must obey the sovereign; however, it must never be forgotten that those who render obedience to the law are the same people who enacted it. If the citizens, assembled as sovereign, find a law distasteful, they will not disobey it: rather, they will repeal it and put a better one in its place. The point worth remembering is that the sovereign is a legal body as well as a political one: when it has gone through the appropriate processes, its decisions are the law of the land for all citizens. The legal quality of sovereignty is important because it fits in with Rousseau's conception of freedom as obedience to legitimate authority. Thus, it is only through the laws that citizens can become free. It is here that one of the most notorious phrases in all of political theory arises. Men ought to be free, Rousseau says, and if they are so misguided as to question the right path to freedom then they must be forced to be free.

The sovereign, being formed wholly of the individuals who compose it, neither has nor can have any interest contrary to theirs; and consequently the sovereign power need give no guarantee to its subjects, because it is impossible for the body to wish to hurt all its members.

This, however, is not the case with the relation of the subjects to the sovereign. . . . In fact, each individual, as a man, may have a particular will contrary or dissimilar to the General Will which he has as a citizen.

In order then that the social compact may not be an empty formula, it tacitly includes the undertaking, which alone can give force to the rest, that whoever refuses to obey the General Will shall be compelled to do so by the whole body. This means nothing less than he will be forced to be free; for this is the condition which, by giving each citizen to his country, secures him against all personal dependence. In this lies the key to the working of the political machine; this alone legitimizes civil undertakings, which, without it, would be absurd, tyrannical, and liable to the most frightful abuses.[39]

[38] *Ibid.*

[39] *Ibid.*, pp. 14–15.

What does it mean to be "forced" to be free? This statement could not possibly be found in the theories of Hobbes or Locke, for individualism defined freedom as absence of external restraint. The citizen of Hobbes or Locke was a man who was freed from the coercion of his fellow men or the state; enjoying this liberty, he was free to do whatever it came into his head to do so long as he did not impinge on the freedom of others. Rousseau regards the individualist conception as purposeless: why go through all the trouble of creating order out of chaos, why go through all the bother of setting up a state, if the end product is no more than to allow men to gratify their whims and pursue their fancies? Surely, Rousseau argues, the monumental task of politics is not to raise a majestic political edifice so that men may be "free" to pursue aimlessly whatever they happen to find pleasurable at the moment. On the contrary, the acts of a sovereign are more than bureaucratic regulations; the laws which the sovereign enacts are considered judgments which emanate from a legitimate authority. They should be obeyed, first of all, because they reflect the will of all the citizens: as acts of a democratic body, laws are the self-will of each citizen writ large. And they should be obeyed, secondly, because true freedom can only be attained if we live our lives in a purposeful and disciplined way. Once the sovereign has enacted a law, it would be not only foolish but also contrary to his own realization of freedom for a man to disobey it.

Freedom, for Rousseau, must be exercised under law and with the approval of the community. The man who sets off on his own volition to define freedom will, in all likelihood, content himself with behavior which is inferior in quality and unchallenging to his potentialities. Furthermore, such a man may take undue advantage of a self-defined freedom and use it as a means to coerce others; in doing this, he would revive the war of all against all which existed before the social contract established political sovereignty.

In being forced to be free, then, men gain the equivalent of the freedom they knew as natural men in the state of nature. By pursuing freedom under law, the right road to freedom is followed, and men are able to live together in peace and fellowship. "Each regains his original rights and resumes his natural liberty, while losing the conventional liberty in favor of which he renounced it," Rousseau says. "These clauses, properly understood, may be reduced to one: the total alienation of each associate, together with all his rights, to the whole community." [40] The conventional liberty which is given up is the freedom to do as you please: the natural liberty which is resurrected by the social contract is the freedom to do what is right.

The sovereign, then, is a lawmaking body with the ability to compel obedience. The whole idea that if men are to know freedom they may have to

[40] *Ibid.*, p. 12.

be coerced into obeying the law—while it appears in political theory as early as Plato—has a strange ring to it. If sense is to be made out of this notion, it must be discussed in the context of the General Will. But before coming to that, however, several questions should be asked about the scope and limits of state action.

Whether Rousseau—or any political theorist—harbors in his writings the germ of totalitarianism rests, in the final analysis, on what is said about the allowable limits of the state's activity in society. From Aristotle through Machiavelli and up to Locke, the liberal and constitutional strands in political theory have postulated that there is a portion of men's lives into which no state should intrude its power. Rousseau would appear, on first reading, to sanction a state which might claim authority over the total personality of every citizen. The words are surely there: ". . . the total alienation of each associate, together with all his rights, to the whole community." Does this mean that Rousseau's man, unlike Locke's man, must forfeit all his rights to the sovereign? The answer to this question is a matter of great dispute among students of political theory. Some see a totalitarian state where the citizen, deprived of his rights as an individual, is told what his freedom is and is then forced to behave as the state thinks best. But there is another point of view which suggests that what Rousseau is saying is not as simple as this. We have already seen that Rousseau views men in not one, but several roles. That is, at one time all men are makers of the law, and later on, in a different role, they must obey the law. Similarly, men are "political" only part of the time. The organic sovereign is a public person, and citizens, when they participate as part of the sovereign, are acting in their political capacity.

> But besides the public person, we have to consider the private persons composing it, whose life and liberty are naturally independent of it. We are bound then to distinguish clearly between the respective rights of the citizens and the sovereign, and between the duties the former have to fulfill as subjects, and the natural rights they should enjoy as men.[41]

Men are not political all of the time. They are also private citizens with natural rights of their own. In short, the alienation of rights is not a total deprivation. "Each man alienates," Rousseau says, "only such part of his powers, goods, and liberty as it is important for the community to control." This certainly indicates that there are limits to the claims of the state over the lives of the citizens. But, immediately after saying that, Rousseau goes on to warn: "it must also be granted that the sovereign is the sole judge of what is important." [42]

[41] *Ibid.*, p. 24.
[42] *Ibid.*

Before throwing up our hands and concluding that Rousseau's sovereign will abolish personal liberty and make alienation total, we ought to recall how a proposition of this kind should be read. First of all, it is clear that Rousseau, unlike Locke, gives the state the potential power to label all behavior "political behavior" and therefore makes all conduct susceptible to official regulation. The private rights which Rousseau's citizens possess are not inalienable: they are a residue and their exercise, the state has decided, will not harm the public good. And rights that the state today permits to remain in private hands it may tomorrow transfer to the public domain. After admitting this, however, we must go on to ask what is undesirable about the state's deciding what should be public and what should be private? If the alternative is that all citizens should be judge of what rights they need for the good life as they themselves define it, then it is likely that we would end up once again in a fearful state of nature much like that of Hobbes. If the alternative is that there are some essential rights—such as property, speech, religion—which must remain outside the pale of state interference, then a series of constitutional protections are needed to stand between the individual and governmental power. Not even Locke was prepared to set up institutions of state or society that could prevent the government from violating the basic rights of citizens.

The notion of an independent and powerful judiciary which can limit government interference is not in any of the standard writings of political theory. What the theorists argue is either that the individual has rights which ought not to be tampered with or that the good state will exercise self-restraint even though it has the authority to extend its power wherever it pleases. Locke would not put obstacles in the way of majority power, and yet at the same time he was a staunch exponent of the rights of individuals. What the question comes down to is whether Rousseau's state, with its potentiality for uncurbed interference in the lives of its citizens, will in fact exercise self-restraint in the use of its power. Its vestment of sovereignty is, in its forms, no different from Hobbes': it is the sole judge of whether an individual's claims to private rights are to be allowed. Yet if a theorist remains silent about particular applications of state power, then a student is hard put to know how that theoretical state might act in a particular situation. There is much anxiety about the potentiality for tyranny in Rousseau's theory of democracy: more so, in fact, than there is in Hobbes' theory of one-man absolute rule. The reason for this concern stems from the over-all mood which Rousseau strikes when he discusses the exercise of political power: this mood, to the minds of many students, is too reasonable in its assumption that power will not be abused. Both Hobbes and Locke acknowledged that the state might be arbitrary or despotic. Yet this thought seems never to enter Rousseau's mind, and it is his failure to speak to this point which is worrisome. A state can have a totalitarian "look" even though the theorist who created it professes sentiments of democracy, equality, and freedom. Perhaps what stirs fears in Rousseau's writing is his theory of the General Will.

Will, as was pointed out in the chapter on Hobbes, is the possession of an active individual. It is the tendency to action, the thought or feeling which results in actual behavior. By stressing the quality of will in each person, Hobbes sought to demonstrate that all individuals have an autonomy of mind which is conjoined with purposeful acts. But can a state or a society or a community have a "will"? Most liberal and individualist theorists would deny this: will, in its meaningful sense, belongs only to discrete individuals and cannot be attributed to collections of individuals. Rousseau, however, is unwilling to accept this point of view. To his mind there is, in a community, a force called the General Will, and it is no less real than the wills possessed by individuals. If the sovereign is the state in its active mood, the General Will is the motor power behind the acts of the sovereign.

The ideal state, as it is described in *The Social Contract*, must exist within the framework of a cohesive community: it is viable only when citizens are agreed on the fundamental principles of what constitutes appropriate behavior. This agreement which binds men into a community is, as was pointed out earlier, its consensus. Consensus is all but impossible to describe or define: it is, in the final analysis, an atmosphere which pervades a group of people who live together. An exhaustive listing of common attitudes and patterns of behavior will, of course, help to describe this atmosphere, but a consensus is understood better by what people do not do rather than by what they do, by what they leave unsaid rather than by what they say. For this reason, a consensus cannot be equated with public opinion: public opinion is too superficial, too ephemeral, to encompass the sentiments which tie together a community and motivate it to sustained action. The consensus embraces national and religious feelings, traditional habits and customs, institutional loyalties and interests, not to mention the psychological forces which find common expression at a certain time and place. The degree to which these sentiments are shared by all citizens marks the degree to which they have attained the communal life.

Because Rousseau postulates the desirability of such basic agreement, some of his political ideas take on a more benign aspect. Being "forced" to be free, for example, is not so terrifying a thought if it is known that the people who do the coercing and the people who are coerced both share fundamental beliefs about right conduct: in this case such compulsion is on matters of details and not on matters of substance. A state which acknowledges no restraints over the power it has over citizens is less fearsome when both governors and the governed agree on common principles: in this case the rationale for authority will be accepted by those who must heed its dictates. It is in the context of consensus, of a communal setting, that Rousseau's notion of the General Will should be viewed.

> The first and most important deduction from the principles we have so far laid down is that the General Will alone can direct the state according to the object for which it was instituted, i.e. the common good: for if the clashing of particular interests made the establishment of societies necessary, the agreement of these very interests made it possible. The common element in these different interests is what forms the social tie; and, were there no point of agreement between them all, no society could exist. It is solely on the basis of this common interest that every society should be governed.[43]

This is as close as Rousseau comes to defining what he means by the General Will, and—all things considered—he conveys his meaning quite clearly. A society is an aggregate of individuals, and even in the best of societies there will be diverse interests. A community possesses a common interest—a General Will—which rises above and reaches below the particular interests of individual citizens. What Rousseau is suggesting is that the state, a political agency, has the responsibility of transforming society into a community. It must give coherent expression to the common interest in the sentiments which all citizens share, and it must be sufficiently strong to mediate among opposing interests. Even in a cohesive community there can be the propertied and nonpropertied, farmers and city dwellers, native-born citizens and recently arrived immigrants. Social change brings an expansion of population and a division of labor, and this inevitably leads to diversity of interests. If in a state of nature all men were equal and possessed only the elemental interest of self-preservation, an advanced society pays for progress with the coin of conflict.

Most states, of course, recognize the existence of diverse interests, but many try to gloss over underlying conflicts—and not a few will use political power to promote some interests at the expense of others. The good state, according to Rousseau, will be aware of interests; however, it will attempt to subsume them under—and direct them toward—the common good. This can only be achieved in practice if the interplay of interests is comfortably within the framework of a consensus. "The common element in these different interests is what forms the social tie," Rousseau says. Thus there can in a community be manufacturing, agricultural, commercial, financial, and similar propertied interests. There can also be a section of the community which owns no property and works for others to earn a living. But so long as all citizens share the sentiment that the institution of private property is worthy of preservation,

[43] *Ibid.*, p. 20.

then conflicts among individuals and groups can be mediated in a peaceful and constructive way. There can be dissent as long as it is inside the boundaries of the consensus.

If a minority of significant size—thirty or forty per cent of the citizens— rejects the idea that private property is legitimate, then a consensus no longer exists; and the life of the community itself is in no small danger. When Rousseau says "it is solely on the basis of this common interest that every society should be governed," he is postulating a consensus which is sufficiently broad to encompass and transcend particular interests. Indeed, he is saying that the consensus must be flexible and tolerant enough so that freedom may thrive within its borders. In terms of property, for example, farmers and manufacturers and retailers, owners and employers and employees, all should put the general welfare of property above the well-being of their own particular relation to that institution. In existing societies this larger view tends to be rendered more lip service than actual support: under the aegis of the individualist ethic less attention is paid to the ties that bind than to the conflicts of interest which divide. These tendencies, Rousseau believes, can be corrected if a sense of community is imparted to citizens; if the General Will comes to the fore as a political force.

"The General Will is always right and tends to the public advantage," Rousseau says.[44] To say this is simply to say that a community cannot work against its own consensus. The communist who advocates and actively works for state expropriation in a community where all others approve of individual ownership—such a man is necessarily wrong. So is the atheist who shouts that God does not exist and that churches should be taxed out of existence. Both of these deviates are working at cross purposes to the norms of the community, and hence to the General Will. While it is too simple to say that the communist and atheist are wrong because they have been "outvoted," Rousseau at a later stage comes close to asserting just that. And what should be done about the communist amidst the capitalists, the atheist amidst the God-fearing? At this juncture Rousseau's dictum must be applied: the dissenters should be forced to be free. Through persuasion preferably, and if necessary through sanctions applied by the state and the community, they must be shown that they are wrong and that the General Will is right. True freedom can only grow out of an acceptance of right knowledge.[45]

[44] *Ibid.*, p. 22.

[45] An approach similar to this is taken by some psychoanalytic writers when they discuss political deviation. See the late Robert Lindner's studies of two of his patients, one a communist and the other a fascist. Their communism and fascism were, according to Lindner, expressions of personality disorders. After extensive psychotherapy, both were cured and became normal American citizens with normal political outlooks. *The Fifty-Minute Hour* (New York: Rinehart, 1955), chaps. 2 and 4.

That this theory embraces a moral relativism is partially true. To be sure, Rousseau adheres to certain fixed values which transcend all societies: the values of democracy, equality, community, and human freedom. But it is no less clear that various societies have their own ways of defining and developing the applications of these values. Each community evolves its own consensus over time, and in this sense a community's morality is an environmental product. An individualist consensus might spell freedom in one community; a communist consensus could be the definition of liberty in another: and while in the former a communist would have to be forced to be free, in the latter an individualist would be compelled to change his ideas if he was to know freedom. Before raising the obvious objections to such relativism, it should be made clear that Rousseau is writing as a social scientist. This, he is saying, is how a community must operate if it is to be a community at all: this, he is saying, is how values are created and enforced if they are to be meaningful in men's lives. There is little to be gained in attempting to create institutional schemes which are capable of universal application. The forms which democracy or freedom will take depend on such factors as the stage of technological development, the amount of social mobility, the intensity of national sentiment, and so forth. If a society is to be democratic or free, then it must be allowed to develop its own institutions and ideas; and this development is bound to be within a cultural setting which provides its own opportunities and limitations. A General Will, unlike the Natural Law, varies in its precepts from community to community.

The General Will is an attempt to conjoin the idea of consensus with the fact of political power. One consequence of this endeavor is to render irrelevant some of the traditional questions of political theory.

> It can no longer be asked whose business it is to make laws, since they are acts of the General Will; nor whether the prince is above the law, since he is a member of the state; nor whether the law can be unjust since no one is unjust to himself; nor how we can be both free and subject to the laws, since they are but registers of our wills.[46]

Despite Rousseau's refusal to utilize the Natural Law, his similarity to St. Thomas is striking. In the good state, law and custom are bound together. The acts of the General Will are not simply statutory but also expressions of the customs of a community. For this reason, we cannot ask "who" is responsible for a community's customs, nor whether rulers are bound less or more than ordinary men by them or if they are just or unjust. A law may or may not be in accord with justice. But a custom cannot be judged in the same way, for any standard by which it might be evaluated is the product of the community

---

[46] *The Social Contract*, p. 30.

itself, and the community is little more than a composite of those selfsame customs. In other words, if customs are to be called unjust—as one is tempted to label the practices of infanticide, slavery, or human sacrifice—then the charge must be leveled by someone who stands outside that community and who feels justified in judging other men's customs by an external standard. Because Rousseau speaks only of the self-contained community, he takes that community's customs as "given": they constitute the framework within which freedom and justice are defined. But the similarity with St. Thomas must not be overdrawn. Natural Law depends on a wise and virtuous ruler who will apprehend its precepts, and as a theory of politics it tends in conservative directions; the General Will is expressed by all citizens in their collective capacity, and it makes for a radical departure in political theory.

In theory, the General Will is absolute and omnipotent. "The social compact gives the body politic absolute power over all its members," Rousseau says. "And it is this power which, under the direction of the General Will bears . . . the name of sovereignty." [47] Yet this is only an academic statement of sovereign power; the logic of Rousseau's theory cannot allow for a center of either power or authority which might check or restrain the General Will. For at the same time Rousseau is ready to acknowledge that in all communities there are customs—he calls them "conventions"—which have grown up over time. And these established ways of doing things necessarily set limits on the legislative power of the General Will. "The sovereign power . . ." Rousseau says, "does not and cannot exceed the limits of general conventions, and . . . every man may dispose at will of such goods and liberty as those conventions leave him." [48]

For Hobbes, liberty was the area where an absolute ruler decided that laws were unnecessary; for Locke, it was found in men's Natural Rights which existed prior to the creation of the state. Rousseau finds freedom within the community itself: the state is a creature of the community, and it is bound not to conflict with the customary patterns of behavior which bind the community together. Just as the General Will draws on custom to strengthen its political power, so is it no less restrained by custom. If it is the task of the state to give expression to the consensus of the community, at the same time the community circumscribes the authority of the state. The General Will, in sum, is as much a servant of the community as it is its master. This is made quite clear when Rousseau lays down the social and cultural conditions within which the state must operate. "What people," he asks, "is a fit subject for legislation?" Not any random collection of citizens may govern themselves by the

[47] *Ibid.*, p. 24.
[48] *Ibid.*, p. 26.

General Will. On the contrary, they must live in a community which adheres to clear-cut specifications.

One which, already bound by some unity of origin, interest or convention, has never yet felt the real yoke of law; one that has neither customs nor superstitions deeply ingrained, one which stands in no fear of being overwhelmed by sudden invasion; one which, without entering into its neighbors' quarrels, can resist each of them singlehanded, or get the help of one to repel another; one in which every member can be known by every other, and there is no need to lay on any man burdens too heavy for a man to bear; one which can do without other peoples, and without which all others can do; one which is neither rich nor poor, but self-sufficient; and, lastly, one which unites the consistency of an ancient people with the docility of a new one.[49]

This, of course, is a Utopian expectation. Rousseau is setting up an ideal: like Plato, he does not actually believe that existing societies will be able to fill most or even all of the specifications which he sets up. Rousseau's purpose is to create a body of principles toward which men and societies may work. Even a nation with a population of 100 million or more, a nation with a sharply graded social structure, a nation with a history of oppressive rule—all of these can at least endeavor to approach the ideals of democracy, freedom and the General Will which Rousseau holds up as goals.

LEGISLATION AND THE LEGISLATOR

In the democratic state all men should participate in the legislative process. Yet before this statement can be completed a whole host of problems are raised: men are creatures with particular interests, and these may cloud their vision of the General Will; public policy is a complex matter, and the average citizen may not know how to achieve the ends he desires; in short, men are good, but they are not always rational.

The General Will is always right and tends to the public advantage; but it does not follow that the deliberations of the people are always equally correct. Our will is always for our own good, but we do not always see what that is; the people is never corrupted, but it is often deceived, and on such occasions only does it seem to will what is bad.[50]

This general view was taken by Plato and Aristotle, who in many respects share Rousseau's view of human nature and the organic society. Aristotle, for example, was quite willing to let citizens convene in a legislative body in order to decide on public policy. While, like Plato, he had grave doubts about the average man's rationality, he nevertheless saw more good than harm in demo-

[49] *Ibid.*, p. 41.
[50] *Ibid.*, pp. 22–23.

cratic government. Plato's pessimism about popular rationality led him, of course, to rule by a class of philosopher-kings. Rousseau, like all who espouse democracy, cannot come down definitely on one side or another. Self-government calls for participation by the man-in-the-street; good government calls for the rational exercise of power. These two ideal values cannot be reconciled in any altogether satisfactory way. But Rousseau does state the dilemma of the democrat, and he does come to a conclusion of his own.

How can a blind multitude, which often does not know what it wills, because it rarely knows what is good for it, carry out for itself so great and difficult an enterprise as a system of legislation? Of itself the people wills always the good, but of itself it by no means always sees it. The General Will is always in the right, but the judgment which guides it is not always enlightened. It must be got to see objects as they are, and sometimes as they ought to appear to it; it must be shown the good road it is in search of, secured from the seductive influences of individual wills, taught to see times and spaces as a series, and made to weigh the attractions of present and sensible advantages against the danger of distant and hidden evils.

The individuals see the good they reject; the public wills the good it does not see. All stand equally in need of guidance. The former must be compelled to bring their wills into conformity with their reason; the latter must be taught to know what it wills. If that is done, public enlightenment leads to the union of understanding and will in the social body: the parts are made to work exactly together, and the whole is raised to its highest power.

This makes a legislator necessary.[51]

The great problem raised by Plato is resurrected once more, but this time it is posed not by a philosopher-king but by a professed democrat. A democratic citizenry, much as we may respect its members as individuals, turns into a blind multitude when it is confronted with the complex business of making laws. But their blindness applies to means, not to ends. Legislation deals with the solving of problems, and in this process there are two steps involved: the first is to understand that the problems actually exist and to desire that they be solved; the second is to devise the specific means which will bring about the solution of those problems. The public, Rousseau says, wills the ends. But it does not know how to create the means for attaining those ends. Rousseau, then, has not departed from his basic, and democratic, premise. Men acknowledge the fundamental rightness of the General Will; they defer to its supremacy over their own particular wills.

It might be said that the average man has a kind of sixth sense—a political and moral sense—which sows in him the desire to act in right directions. The trouble is that the judgment, the perception, the understanding of the public is clouded by irrational influences. The General Will exists, to use modern phrasing, at the level of the collective unconscious. Legislation, on the other

[51] *Ibid.*, p. 31.

hand, must be a product of reasoning at the conscious level. This means that the public must be shown how to transform their intuition of the good into coherent policies which will achieve the ends which they sense to be right. What is needed is not a philosopher-king—for the General Will is not ignorant of political philosophy—but a legislator who will guide the public.

Guidance is not dictation: "The wise legislator," Rousseau says, "does not begin by laying down laws good in themselves." [52] His job is to help the people to help themselves. He does this by raising their unconscious sense of the good to the rational level of consciousness. Once this has been done, he suggests to them means whereby they may secure the ends which they themselves have been willing all along. The relation between legislator and public is remarkably like that between psychoanalyst and patient in classical Freudian theory.

And, just as in psychoanalysis the analyst uses myths—the Oedipus Complex, the Death Wish, the Pleasure Principle—to persuade and to gain authority over his patient, so must the legislator employ fictional symbols to bring the public to believe that they should accept his ideas. Here Rousseau does not cavil at the Machiavellian argument for delusion.

> Wise men, if they try to speak their language to the common herd instead of its own, cannot possibly make themselves understood. There are a thousand kinds of ideas which it is impossible to translate into popular language. Conceptions that are too general and objects that are too remote are equally out of its range: each individual, having no taste for any other plan of government than that which suits his particular interest, finds it difficult to realize the advantages he might hope to draw from the continual privations good laws impose. . . .
>
> The legislator therefore, being unable to appeal to either force or reason, must have recourse to an authority of a different order, capable of constraining without violence and persuading without convincing.
>
> This is what has, in all ages, compelled the fathers of nations to have recourse to divine intervention and credit the gods with their own wisdom, in order that the peoples, submitting to the laws of the state as to those of nature, and recognizing the same power in the formation of the city as in that of man, might obey freely, and bear with docility the yoke of the public happiness. [53]

First Rousseau referred to the public as a "blind multitude," and now he adds insult to injury by calling them a "common herd" as well. Only a wise legislator can understand the complexities of the legislative and administrative processes: the public is unable to ever share this wisdom. In order that the people may get the kind of laws they really want—but which they sense only in the vaguest way—the legislator must have a free hand to write and enforce legislation along rational lines. However, Rousseau is neither Plato nor Hobbes: he is, on the contrary, talking of a democracy. The legislator is not a king or a

[52] *Ibid.*, p. 35.
[53] *Ibid.*, p. 34.

prince or a dictator: under the sovereignty of the General Will no single man or group of men, no matter how rational, have authority to rule the rest. "He . . . who draws up the laws has, or should have, no right of legislation," Rousseau says. "The people cannot, even if it wishes, deprive itself of this incommunicable right." [54]

This means that the legislator cannot establish his authority by force or by fear. At the same time, he cannot assume that the public is intelligent enough to be swayed by rational arguments in favor of particular legislative or administrative policies. Therefore, he must persuade without convincing: he must use emotion-laden symbols so that behind their facade he may be free to plan his program of legislation. By invoking the approval of a deity or by appealing to patriotic sentiments, he endeavors to gain a blanket consent for his specific actions.[55] Once more the psychoanalytic analogy is useful. The analyst has no power to compel his patient: the patient can walk out of the room if he likes, and stop returning for treatment—or he can decide to go to another analyst. It is therefore necessary for the analyst to establish authority over the patient not by force or even by reason—for the patient cannot understand psychological subtleties—but by persuasion. Once the analyst has secured the confidence of the patient, then he may begin to assume that the patient will follow his prescribed course of treatment. But these arts of persuasion are a blend of fact and fiction, of reason and emotion, of science and myth. Rousseau's legislator must be adept not only in the science of legislation but also in the art of engineering popular consent.

The epithets "common herd" and "blind multitude" ill fit a democratic theory, yet Rousseau does not, despite his use of them, sneer at the average man. All men are naturally good, but their goodness does not endow them with legislative talents. Human equality insists on the equal worth of all men, but it does not imply that all are possessed of rationality to the same degree. It is a sign of Rousseau's optimism that, while holding fast to his belief in human goodness, he also acknowledges the limitations of a political public. And it is to his credit as a democrat that he seeks to achieve rational legislation and at the same time leave ultimate power in the hands of the people. The legislator is not a Platonic philosopher-king, a Machiavellian ruler, or a Hobbesian sovereign. He is an expert and he is responsible to the General Will. However, if the politics of democracy are not to thwart effective government, this expert

---

[54] *Ibid.*, p. 33.

[55] Rousseau cites Machiavelli: " 'In truth,' Machiavelli said, 'there has never been, in any country, an extraordinary legislator who has not had recourse to God; for otherwise his laws would not have been accepted: there are, in fact, many useful truths of which a wise man may have knowledge without their having in themselves such clear reasons for their being so as to be able to convince others.' " *Ibid.*, p. 34n.

must be allowed a free hand so that legislative and administrative means will be found for attaining political and philosophical ends.

THE REQUISITES OF SELF-GOVERNMENT

"If we take the term in the strict sense, there never has been a real democracy, and there never will be . . ." Rousseau says. "It is unimaginable that the people should remain continually assembled to devote their time to public affairs." [56] In a strict—in fact, in a Utopian—sense, a true democracy must be a perpetual town meeting. Each citizen must participate directly and continually in the process of self-government. Because such political involvement is, to use Rousseau's word, unimaginable, real societies which profess democratic goals are prepared to settle for a "republican" form of government. Rather than all citizens taking a direct part in the governmental process, elected representatives are allowed to speak and act in the name of their constituents.

If a society is large, specialized, and busy, it is obvious that it must settle— if it can—for representation. The importance of a Utopian ideal such as direct democracy is that it sets a standard: it is very easy to adopt the institutions of representative government and to thereby assume that a political system is only one remove from the democratic goal. The difficulty, as Rousseau will point out shortly, is that representative institutions have a tendency to get less and less representative: unless a society constantly asks itself to what extent its government is approximating the Utopian democratic standard, it will have no way of judging whether its parliaments and congresses, or cabinets and presidents, are reflecting or perverting the popular will. Therefore, even though Rousseau can say that there never has been and never will be a real democracy, he still, in drawing the outlines of his ideal state, chooses to employ the assumption that men are capable of governing themselves in a direct way. If the Ancient Greeks could assemble in the market place to practice pure democracy, then that in itself is sufficient proof that such a system is not beyond the limits of human nature.

The sovereign, having no force other than the legislative power, acts only by means of the laws; and the laws being solely the authentic acts of the General Will, the sovereign cannot act save when the people is assembled. The people in assembly, I shall be told, is a mere chimera. It is so today, but two thousand years ago it was not so. Has man's nature changed? [57]

The very idea of a government as "the people in assembly" may or may not be chimerical. The point is that just as Rousseau has drawn up certain Utopian

[56] *Ibid.*, p. 55.
[57] *Ibid.*, p. 74.

requisites for his society, so he bases his conception of democracy on an institutional arrangement no less ideal. The state's power can only be legitimately exercised through laws; laws must be the expression of the General Will; the General Will is operative only when all citizens gather together in a meeting. Rather than argue over whether government by the people in assembly is realistic or even possible, it would be better to take this idea as a philosophical standard; once this is done, then we can proceed to ask whether legitimacy is in evidence to the degree to which a society's laws are the product of democratic government.

The whole effort of Rousseau is to bring the particular wills of individuals and the General Will of the community into harmony. This means that the former must make themselves subservient to the latter; however, this submission does not result from the naked exercise of authority, for all individuals realize in their hearts that it is the General Will which is right. The means by which citizens are brought to take this broader view is through personal participation: more than any other political theorist, Rousseau stresses the importance of the average citizen's involvement with affairs of state.

The better the constitution of a state is, the more do public affairs encroach on private in the minds of the citizens. Private affairs are even of much less importance, because the aggregate of the common happiness furnishes a greater proportion of that of each individual, so that there is less for him to seek in particular cares. In a well-ordered city every man flies to the assemblies: under a bad government no one cares to stir a step to get to them, because no one is interested in what happens there, because it is foreseen that the General Will will not prevail, and lastly because domestic cares are all-absorbing. Good laws lead to the making of better ones; bad laws bring about worse. As soon as any man says of the affairs of the state: "What does it matter to me?", the state may be given up for lost.[58]

Rousseau is saying a good deal more here than that in a good state the citizens participate in the process of self-government. He is also erasing the boundary between public and private life which was so important a theme in Locke's political thought. In a good society, Rousseau says, a citizen has not much need of a private life, for by virtue of living in a good society he will be able to partake of the common happiness. Such a citizen so identifies his wellbeing with the public well-being that he can live his total existence as a public man. Indeed, a private life becomes more a liability than an asset in such an environment: the individual who tries to stand alone, who seeks to create his own values, who demands to be left to himself—such a person will find himself not free but enchained. By rejecting the values of the community and its demand for participation, he will be lonely, alienated, and anomic. While a Locke and a Mill may talk of the rights of man and the importance of a private

[58] *Ibid.*, pp. 77–78.

life, these individualists forget that the ordinary citizen prefers the security which comes of working in unison with his fellows. Rousseau is saying that true freedom can only come through self-government; and self-government requires participation—so much and so constant participation that the citizen has little time for a life of his own. Each man, then, hies himself off to the assembly with enthusiasm; for in gathering with others he finds that in his personality his public and private selves are merged, and in this process he reaches the height of political development. Security and freedom become indistinguishable.

It is obvious that political participation is the exception rather than the rule in many societies. The height of involvement for most citizens in a democracy is the act of voting. Few are active in the policy-making process, and even fewer work actively with the political parties. In short, most citizens do have the attitude toward politics which Rousseau expressed in the question, "What does it matter to me?" The reasons for such indifference cannot be examined at this point.[59] What is relevant is the psychological consequence of political indifference for the modern citizen. The man who does not participate is not a whole man: Rousseau has pointed out that only by participating in the making of the law which will govern your life—only then can you rise above the status where you are the servant and another man is your master. The man who eschews politics soon finds that he is no longer master of his fate: because he refuses to take part in the process of self-government, he discovers that the manner in which he must live his life is dictated to him by others. Such a man cannot be free, for he is forever subject to the authority of others: such a man cannot be a whole personality, for he has lost control of the conditions which control his existence. The only answer is political participation. Indeed, only in the subjugation of one's private life can one rise to a greater and more meaningful freedom.

The case for universal and intensive participation in politics, then, is a two-sided one. Approached negatively it says that if citizens do not make self-government a reality, if they do not take advantage of the opportunity to make the policies which will direct their own lives, then they will be prey to rulers who will exercise power arbitrarily. On the positive side, Rousseau is saying that political involvement is necessary for the full development of the individual personality. The healthy man is a democratic man, for such a person has none of the feeling of powerlessness, the sense of frustration, which is the lot of those who are subject to the rule of another. The price of participation may

---

[59] For a suggestive discussion of political participation and nonparticipation in the United States, including an analysis of who are the active participants and why, see Robert Lane, *The Political Life* (Glencoe: Free Press, 1959).

be high: time must be spent studying laws, attending meetings, debating issues. Its reward is not simply the absence of arbitrary rule: it is also the creation of a liberated personality.

If Rousseau would have every citizen spend his lunch hour at the legislative assembly, it follows that this responsibility cannot be delegated to a representative. Of course, Rousseau's ideal society was to be so small that each citizen would know his compatriots, and all of them could fit in one meeting hall. In a large state democratic government, at its very best, must still be representative government. The town meeting where all participate directly is replaced by indirect participation: citizens elect legislators, and the legislators are supposed to enact into law the will of the citizens. Rousseau is aware of the necessity for representation. What disturbs him is that we tend to take it for granted and seldom stop to think about the ways in which representation distorts the democratic process. To emphasize this fact, Rousseau asserts that neither sovereignty nor the General Will can in the final analysis be represented:

> Sovereignty, for the same reason as makes it inalienable, cannot be represented: it lies essentially in the General Will, and will does not admit of representation: it is either the same, or other; there is no intermediate possibility. The deputies of the people, therefore, are not and cannot be its representatives: they are merely its stewards, and can carry through no definitive acts.[60]

That an individual's will does not admit of representation is one of the great neglected truths of political theory. The General Will, it will be recalled, lies deep in the mind and heart of every individual in a community. It emerges, in the form of sovereignty, at such times as all individuals are gathered together. If this kind of talk has a mystical ring, it is only because the methods of social psychology are still too imperfect to describe or explain clearly what we mean by the "atmosphere" which pervades a cohesive political community. But the fact remains that wills cannot be represented. The only person who can truly speak for Smith is Smith himself. For Smith is 10,000 roles, interests, attitudes and emotions: no other person can transmit Smith's will unless he has lived Smith's life. Yet an American congressman is called upon to speak for almost 400,000 citizens, and a British Member of Parliament almost 100,000. Rousseau would say, then, that if you are a farmer and your representative is an urban lawyer, he cannot know or represent your will.

This is the reason why there are sporadic calls for "functional representation." Under such a system legislative apportionment would not be based on geographical districts but on occupational groupings: farmers, schoolteachers, doctors, industrial workers, would all have representatives who would speak

[60] *Social Contract*, p. 78.

for their special interests. Presumably the plan could be so arranged that additional social dimensions could be added and that specific representation for Negroes, Methodists, suburbanites, and stamp collectors could be provided. Without going into the merits of this proposal, it is easy enough to see that its theory is based on the idea that arbitrary geographical districting does not represent the wills of citizens. If a man is the owner of a drugstore, then much of his will as an individual lies in his role of druggist. If this will is to participate in policy-making, then institutional provisions must be made for its inclusion. As matters now stand, a single congressman is called on to represent druggists, dentists, and interior decorators. And he simply cannot manage to do this.

Even if nostrums like functional representation or proportional representation were adopted, the basic problem would still remain. Each individual has a unique will: this will is his personality, the composite of all his qualities. No other man can be you. While representation is a necessity in any large society, Rousseau is trying to remind us just what it is which is suppopsed to be represented. If he sets his standard too high for actual political practice, he is doing this so that existing societies can have a goal toward which to aspire and against which to judge their representative institutions.

THE COMMUNITY AS REPOSITORY OF TRUTH AND FREEDOM

Rousseau's argument for popular participation and against legislative representatives gives rise to his views on political parties and pressure groups. These associations come between the citizen and the state, he says, and by acting as refracting mechanisms they distort the General Will. Such groups Rousseau calls "factions" or "partial societies," and they tend to draw the citizen's loyalty away from a wholehearted pursuit of the common good.

If, when the people, being furnished with adequate information, held its deliberations, the citizens had no communication one with another, the grand total of the small differences would always give the General Will, and the decision would always be good. But when factions arise, and partial associations are formed at the expense of the great association, the will of each of these associations becomes general in relation to its members, while it remains particular in relation to the state; it may then be said that there are no longer as many votes as there are men, but only as many as there are associations. . . . It is therefore essential, if the General Will is to be able to express itself, that there should be no partial society within the state, and that each citizen should think only his own thoughts. . . .[61]

[61] Ibid., p. 23.

If a citizen could be isolated from his neighbors when he takes part in the political process, he would make his decisions without having his mind distorted by the importuning of special interests. Men are inclined to be public-spirited if left by themselves: they are even willing to subsume their own preferences to the common good. Difficulties arise when interest groups begin, on the one hand, to tell an individual what his interests are, and, on the other, to speak for him in the legislative process. A dentist who stands by himself, Rousseau would say, is just as good a citizen as anyone else and he may be counted on to think about the public welfare in a generalized way. But if the same man joins with other dentists in an association, then a change will take place in his political outlook. His membership in the association will ultimately cause him to think of himself as a dentist first and as a citizen second. Indeed, his group affiliation will tend to inflate in his own mind his special status as a dentist and the interests which he has apart from his fellow citizens. Finally, the dental association will begin to speak politically for its members: it will press for laws which favor dentists but not the general welfare; it will take on the job of political participation and incline the individual dentists to abdicate their responsibilities as citizens. The association will assert that "what is good for dentistry is good for society," and in leading its own members and even society to believe this it will distort their perception of the common good. This, then, is what occurs when "partial societies" come between the citizen and the state.

Furthermore, isolated citizens all count as equals, for each participates only on the basis of his citizenship—which he shares equally with all others—and not on the basis of a special role. When private associations intrude, they turn the legislative process over to the interplay of interest groups; and because these groups are not equal in membership or resources, some associations benefit, to the detriment of others. No longer are individuals counted, but management is pitted against labor, farmers against food processors, race against race, and religion against religion. In politics, Rousseau is saying, we should endeavor to maintain our general role as a citizen of the commonwealth. We all tend to fall into special roles, and partial associations exaggerate our special interests, to the damage of ourselves and the common good. The dentist, Rousseau would say, is actually harmed by his dental association: it warps his personality and perverts his politics. Actually the dentist should understand that "what is good for society is good for dentistry," and he should play down his special role and work for the public good.

It is of course true that no dentist is summed up by his dental role. He may be, for example, a Baptist, a Mason, a baseball fan, and a veteran as well. Not only will he belong to a dental association, but he will also have memberships in his church, his lodge, his veteran's post, and the Milwaukee Braves Boosters Club. Like all of us, this dentist is a man of many roles and several associations. All of his groups may want to influence and speak for him, but no single one of them can claim his total loyalty. Rousseau understands that men have special interests—be they religious, economic, fraternal, or the Milwaukee Braves—and that associations are bound to arise to promote these interests. "If there are partial societies," he says, "it is best to have as many as possible." [62] The more associations or pressure groups there are, the less powerful any single one will be and the less chance there will be that strong special interests will obscure the general welfare.

But this suggestion that power be diffused is only a second-best remedy. Rousseau is not happy with partial societies for they distort the democratic process. The substitution of groups for individuals robs participation of its highly personal character: it leads citizens to abdicate their political responsibilities, and it diverts them from expressing the General Will. Rousseau, in short, rejects the politics of pluralism: he repudiates the argument that out of the discussion and conflict, the bargaining and compromise, of organized interests will emerge the general welfare. He cannot see how the clash of self-interested factions will do anything other than produce a lopsided and inequitable legislative result. The pluralist process is what Rousseau calls the "will of all." It differs from the General Will because its motivation is the special interests of diverse pressure groups and its end product emerges from the tugging and hauling of the political arena. The General Will, on the other hand, springs from individual citizens untainted by group affiliations and from the desire in each citizen that only the common good be served. Yet the General Will can be—at least arithmetically—derived from the "will of all."

There is a great deal of difference between the will of all and the General Will; the latter considers only the common interest, while the former takes private interest into account, and is no more than a sum of particular wills; but take away from these same wills the pluses and minuses that cancel one another, and the General Will remains as the sum of the differences. [63]

The question of pluses and minuses cancelling each other out is a difficult one. What Rousseau seems to object to in the "will of all," the pluralist clash of interests, is the process itself. Even when the General Will is operative, there will be differences of opinion among individual citizens. But these differences can be cancelled in a straightforward and equalitarian way, whereas with the group struggle the result is more apt to be the survival of the strongest. Rousseau's cancellation theory may be illustrated by taking a hypothetical

[62] *Ibid.*
[63] *Ibid.*

community consisting of only ten individuals. In their political capacity they are considering a revision in the minimum-wage law, which now stands at $1.25 per hour. Each of the ten first of all asks himself what the new minimum wage should be: ideally he poses this question in terms of what is good for the community as a whole, not with a view of what is good for his own interest. The ten judgments—or votes—come out as follows:

Citizen	Revision Downward	Revision Upward
A		1.35
B		1.30
C	"MINUSES"	1.45
D		1.35
E		1.40
F	1.15	
G		1.30
H	1.10	
I	1.15	"PLUSES"
J	1.20	

When the ten opinions are combined, the result is a decision to raise the wage from $1.25 an hour to $1.27½. This is of course a simplified illustration, and it inevitably contains a number of assumptions which are worth mentioning. First, the decision to raise the wage by 2½¢ takes into account the sentiment of the minority as well as the majority. This need not be the case. There might, as one step, be a vote on whether to revise the wage upward or downward: in this case, those wishing to raise the wage would win six to four. Then, as the next step, the majority party might caucus to discover how high the upward revision should be: the arithmetic mean of the six comes out to a raise of about 11¢. Finally, the six would then agree to vote in a $1.36 wage over the protests of the four who wanted a downward revision. However, Rousseau would say that to do this would be to pit faction against faction, not individual against individual. Therefore the "minuses" must be taken into account in every stage of the cancellation process: this means that even though the wage is raised, it is not raised so high as to violate minority opinion. Second, it is assumed that the feelings of all ten citizens on this matter are of equal intensity. There are not one or two to whom this is a heart-and-soul matter, while to others it is just another vote. Again, Rousseau would say that all the voters are acting in their capacity as citizens of the commonwealth: they are not playing the part of individuals with special interests. For this reason there is no variation in intensity of feeling, for all citizens feel equally strongly about the promotion of the public good. Third, the range of votes goes from $1.10 to $1.45, a span of only 35¢. And 70 per cent of the citizens' opinions fall within a span of 20¢. No one wants to reduce the wage to the starvation level, and no one wants to raise it so high that it will have inflationary consequences for the economy as a whole. Here Rousseau would say that the cancellation idea can only be operative if there is a fundamental consensus among the members of the community. Revising the wage upward to $1.27½, then, is the General Will. It is not the "will of all," because individuals are voting as public-spirited citizens, not as parties with special interests. To be sure, most issues cannot be reduced to arithmetic terms with the ease that this one has been. But Rousseau is adumbrating a principal here, and simplicity is usually the best way to convey the major idea behind a general theory.

Within each citizen, Rousseau says, there is the deep-seated desire to promote the public welfare. Personal interests and factional groupings can serve to cloud a person's mind and distort his perception of the common good. If the general interest is to be pursued unremittingly, there must be an agency which will bring individual citizens to know and act on the long-term interests of the community as a whole. This agency is, of course, the General Will; and it can be made to emerge, as was seen, by the process of voting. In determining what the General Will actually is, Rousseau says, "the vote of the majority always binds all the rest." [64] This idea, however, must not be construed too literally: the conditions which were attached to the vote on the minimum wage show that voting must follow a careful pattern.

In that case, however, the "defeated" minority did not harbor any major disagreement toward the victorious majority. But what of the individual dissenter who finds, when the ballots are tallied, that he is the only one out of

[64] *Ibid.*, p. 88.

step? Rousseau is concerned with this problem and he addresses himself to it at some length.

> But it is asked how a man can be both free and forced to conform to wills that are not his own. How are the opponents at once free and subject to laws they have not agreed to?
>
> I retort that the question is wrongly put.
>
> The citizen gives his consent to all the laws, including those which are passed in spite of his opposition, and even those which punish him when he dares to break any of them. The constant will of all the members of the state is the General Will; by virtue of it they are citizens and free.
>
> When in the popular assembly a law is proposed, what the people is asked is not exactly whether it approves or rejects the proposal, but whether it is in conformity with the General Will, which is their will. Each man, in giving his vote, states his opinion on that point; and the General Will is found by counting votes.
>
> When therefore the opinion that is contrary to my own prevails, this proves neither more nor less than that I was mistaken, and that what I thought to be the General Will was not so. If my particular opinion had carried the day I should have achieved the opposite of what was my will; and it is in that case that I should not have been free.[65]

That the dissenter is "mistaken" in his conception of the General Will follows from all that Rousseau has been saying up to this time. Truth lies with the community, which is to say it lies with the majority. A dissenter may be "right" by some other standard, but in terms of the life of this particular community he is wrong. He must admit that he is mistaken and be prepared to be educated by his neighbors. Rousseau is not advocating persecution: on the contrary, he is calling for the enlightenment of those who live in the shadows. The dissenter's independence of mind is not an expression of true freedom: it is, rather, a neurosis—a distorted picture of social reality and an impulse to act in socially destructive ways. It is the obligation of the community to cure him; it is his obligation to submit to treatment.

This approach to truth and freedom assumes, as did Hobbes, that each individual has a will of his own. But Rousseau departs from Hobbes in postulating a distinction between a citizen's "real" will and his "deceived" will. The "real" will is operative when an individual is in tune with the General Will, with the consensus of his community. The "deceived" will manifests itself when he pursues special interests to the detriment of the community's wellbeing. The idea of a "real" will has ominous accents for many students of political theory. Cannot a dictator or a demagogue say that the "real" will of this subjects is the glory of the state—and thus lead them on with the aid of an aggressive or totalitarian ideology? Modern rulers have a tendency to claim the role of interpreter of a nation's "real" will, and irrationalism, oppression, and war have followed in the wake of such claims. Rousseau's answer would be that

[65] *Ibid.*

no ruler can tell a citizenry what the General Will is: the legislator, it will be recalled, was specifically not given this task. The General Will arises from the community as a whole, and each citizen develops his own "real" will by himself. Indeed, Rousseau's theory contains the basic assumption of self-government: that the average citizen is capable of ruling himself in an effective way. Within the public mind, Rousseau is saying, there is the knowledge of the long-term good for the community. The man-in-the-street knows what he wants in general terms, and his aspirations are always in accord with the public welfare. If men are permitted to take part in the democratic process, if they are not deceived by interests or factions, then neither a philosopher-king nor a ruler who claims to know the Natural Law is needed.

Aristotle and Machiavelli both saw the wisdom of this position: ruling minorities, they said, have a greater tendency to use political power to aggrandize their own interests than does the majority. Until the sort of rulers postulated by Plato and St. Thomas come on the scene, it is best to put our trust in self-government by the average man. Rousseau approaches the matter in a positive way: majority rule, he says, is not simply to be accepted because minority rule never seems to turn out well. On the contrary, the community has within itself the knowledge of the good life and the ability to act on it. The average man wants peace and prosperity, freedom and justice, community and truth. And he can sense when he is being confronted with schemes and schemers who would violate these basic goals. He may be deceived for a time; he may be hoodwinked by persuasive orators and Utopian programs: but in the long run he sees through men and movements which are harmful to the community. Rousseau's democracy is an article of faith: faith in the citizens who will submerge their special interests and who will govern themselves in accord with the General Will. Existing societies do not give men the opportunity to exercise their "real" will: the structure of society and the political process foment self-deception in individuals and degrade the democratic system. If democracy has given itself a bad name at some times and places, the fault lies with a society which works counter to the democratic idea. The fault never, Rousseau says, should be ascribed to individuals: they have the potentiality for effective self-government if only a community is so constituted as to give them a chance.

Nevertheless, there is bound to be some misgiving about Rousseau's treatment of the dissenter. Is he the only one who is out of step? History has thrown up enough examples of men who thought and spoke before their time, who were proved at a later date to have been right when society was wrong. Furthermore, the dissenter who starts as a party of one may convince others of the truth as he sees it, and eventually yesterday's heresy may become tomorrow's majority view. To treat the dissenter as mistaken, to educate him to the social orthodoxy, is to assume that truth is static and that freedom has been permanently achieved. Rousseau's picture is, indeed, a static one: the concensus of a community, as he draws it, is an unchanging body of sentiments. It will fall to Hegel to show how a consensus evolves over time, how ideas clash with ideas to bring forward new truths. And John Stuart Mill will stress the importance of the dissenter and show why society must—for its own good— tolerate his heretical ideas. Rousseau's discussion of truth and freedom must be viewed in the context of a stable and homogeneous community. If the General Will, as expressed in a majority vote, is always right, this is because values—while undoubtedly subject to influence by outstanding individuals— are ultimately given their force by social acceptance.

THE DEMOCRATIC MAN

Is Rousseau calling for an extraordinary kind of citizen? It would be more accurate to say that he is calling for an extraordinary set of political and social conditions. All citizens have a higher and a lower nature, and the former can be brought out if the environment is so constructed that the citizen is rewarded when he makes a short-term sacrifice for a long-term good. Most citizens dislike paying taxes, and if allowed to vote on them, they would lower such levies to the vanishing point. But at the same time all citizens wish to be provided with good roads, schools, hospitals, and recreational facilities. In short, they want both lower taxes *and* public services. If given the chance, the average citizen in average circumstances will vote down a new tax. Yet it would not be unrealistic to argue that the "real" will of this citizen is his desire for schools and hospitals, and that he does not "really" want lower taxes because he cannot get the schools and hospitals without them. If you sat down and discussed the need for hospitals with an average citizen he would eventually admit that they are needed and he would like to see them built. But it is doubtful, given the conditions of contemporary society, that he will act consistently on this belief. The problem is twofold: to bring the citizen to understand the dictates of his "real" will, and then to get him to conduct himself in accordance with it. Both are difficult to achieve, but the second is by far the harder.

By postulating that the General Will lies within each citizen, Rousseau is simply saying that we all have a higher nature which can be brought to the surface. He is not suggesting that the General Will is a myth invented by an ambitious ruler who wishes to stir his nation to feats of conquest. For Rousseau the General Will is based in the hearts of all citizens: it arises there and is developed slowly by education, custom, and tradition. To be sure, rulers can play on the irrational sentiments which all men possess. But if these sentiments do not express the consensus of the community—the enlightened pursuit of the common good—then the ruler is manipulating the particular wills of citizens; he is not expressing the General Will.

Rousseau's writings are marked by a tendency to ambiguity and internal inconsistency which has infuriated generations of political scientists. The fault lies, of course, not so much with Rousseau as with the difficulty of his subject. Democracy and freedom are not disposed of in clear and consistent phrases. It would be well, in closing, to admit these defects and, indeed, to set down an example of one of the most glaring of them. Rousseau is writing for those of us who live amidst the imperfections of existing society. The world we know is plagued by discord and apathy, self-interest and irrationality. It is hard to believe that out of such conditions a free and democratic community might emerge. Yet, Rousseau reminds us, the goal he sets for the future once existed in the past.

> In Greece, all that the people had to do, it did for itself; it was constantly assembled in the public square. The Greeks lived in a mild climate; they had no natural greed; slaves did their work for them; their great concern was with liberty. . . .
> What then? Is liberty maintained only by the help of slavery? It may be so. Extremes meet. Everything that is not in the course of nature has its disadvantages, civil society most of all.[66]

The good citizen—enlightened, participating, public-spirited—has need of leisure and economic security which are generally available to only a fortunate minority. Does this mean that citizens of the caliber Rousseau demands will only emerge if society provides slaves to hew the wood and draw the water? Perhaps the freedom for some must be paid for by the slavery of others. This is a disturbing thought to hear from an avowed democrat and a proponent of human freedom. Yet Rousseau is to be commended for exhibiting one of the more annoying skeletons in freedom's closet: its bones will continue to rattle through the theories of Burke, Mill, and Tocqueville.

And but a few pages later Rousseau's other face appears. The ideal of self-government is found when simple men come together to rule themselves: neither philosophers nor slaves, but humble tillers of the soil are the stuff of which democracy is made.

> As long as several men in assembly regard themselves as a single body, they have only a single will which is concerned with their common preservation and general well-being. In this case, all the springs of the state are vigorous and simple and its rules clear and luminous; there are no embroilments or conflicts of interests;

[66] *Ibid.*, p. 79.

the common good is everywhere clearly apparent, and only good sense is needed to perceive it. Peace, unity, and equality are the enemies of political subtleties. Men who are upright and simple are difficult to deceive because of their simplicity; lures and ingenious pretexts fail to impose upon them, and they are not even subtle enough to be dupes. When, among the happiest people in the world, bands of peasants are seen regulating affairs of state under an oak, and always acting wisely, can we help scorning the ingenious methods of other nations, which make themselves illustrious and wretched with so much art and mystery? [67]

Which is the "real" Rousseau? That decision belongs to each student of politics.

[67] *Ibid.*, p. 85.

9.
Edmund Burke

THE MAN AND HIS TIMES

Burke was born in Dublin in 1729 of a middle-class Protestant family. After attending Trinity College, he migrated to London with the intention of practicing law. However, this interest soon faded, and he embarked on a career of writing and politics. He entered the House of Commons at the age of thirty-seven and remained there for most of the rest of his life. Burke was not an aristocrat and consequently had no safe seat in his own right. This meant that he had to rely on the good will of those who had it in their power to put a man in Parliament. Such a career was no easy matter for an individual with ideas of his own, and he was able to keep the favor of the handful of merchants who comprised the Bristol electorate for only six years. Fortunately, he obtained the less critical patronage of the Duke of Newcastle, who kept him in the House of Commons until 1794. Burke was always aware of his middle-class status, yet this did not diminish his admiration for the role which the aristocracy played in British politics and society. While positions of power and prestige were bestowed on people less talented than himself, he acknowledged that his birth did not entitle him to preferment. He died, not far from bankruptcy, in 1797.

Burke's interests ranged over the political issues of his day, and the bulk of his writings are reprinted speeches and tracts for the times. He was not a systematic theorist in the sense that Hobbes or Locke or Rousseau was, and his daily involvement with the business of the House of Commons did not give him the leisure for deep reflection. Yet if he did not examine his own assumptions in an explicit way, the clarity of his style allows the reader to ascertain just what these principles are. Burke's commentaries on three national revolutions give a good idea of the tenor of his thought.

The Revolution of 1688 had given power to Parliament, and the following century had given Parliament to the Whig Party. Burke himself was a Whig; but this was a "modern" Whiggism, and by the time he reached the House of Commons he noted a severe deterioration in the state of his party. If one of

341

the principles of the Bloodless Revolution was that Parliament was henceforward to share power with the monarch, no account seems to have been taken of a king like George III, who was a strong-willed man and who insisted on making the legislature an instrument attuned to his own purposes. What angered Burke was that his party acquiesced to this state of affairs and acted as a rubber stamp on George III's behalf, accepting in return the small change of royal favors. Burke was by no means a democrat. Indeed, he had told the voters of Bristol that he would not act simply as their instructed emissary but would serve what he himself conceived to be the national interest. However, he saw that the great bulk of the Whig Party was thinking not of the welfare of the nation so much as of the king's pleasure. A balanced constitution, Burke insisted, requires an independent legislature, and it must consist of men of talent and principle who have committed themselves to governing a nation. If legislators are subservient to the special interests of either kings or commoners they are betraying the Revolution which brought them into being.

If this kind of criticism brought Burke no favor with his Whig colleagues, his views on the American Revolution were even less popular. He defended the colonists' war for independence on the ground that they were fit to govern themselves. The British had shown their incapacity to rule a territory across 3,000 miles of ocean, and the Americans who sought to run their own affairs seemed in Burke's eyes to be men of substance with legitimate political grievances. If the colonists were prone to invoke ideology, there was enough common sense in their demands to warrant overlooking the rhetorical excesses. If there were strong economic and social undercurrents to the revolution, Burke was nevertheless persuaded that it was a demand for political reform not far different from that which arose in England in 1688.

Far different was his reaction to the events across the Channel. George III and the Whig Party may have doubted the loyalty of their Irish critic, but the publication of his Reflections on the Revolution in France in 1790 made him the hero of the court and club. For to Burke's mind the French Revolution was social rather than political: not only were old rulers supplanted by new men of power, but the entire structure of society and the foundations of traditional authority were being destroyed. Here was untutored democracy running wild, with no thought given to the abilities of those who would exercise power. That these new men were members of the prosperous middle class did not impress Burke. For in France he saw the havoc which is wreaked on a nation when ideology is enthroned and tradition cast by the wayside.

The defense of aristocratic rule and an ordered society was the theme of all Burke's writings. He criticized the Whig Parliament because it was not aristocratic enough; he welcomed America into the family of free nations because he thought he saw in the new country the makings of responsible government.

9.
Edmund Burke

FROM THE TITLE ALONE EDMUND BURKE'S *Reflections on the Revolution in France* would appear to be an essay about a particular historical event which can be located in space and time. Its abiding claim on the attention of students of political theory, however, rests on far broader grounds. Burke's book is a statement of the philosophy of conservatism, a critique of liberal and democratic theories, and an analysis of human nature and the structure of society. While the allusions to what occurred in France in 1789 are of some historical interest, political theorists have concerned themselves with what emerges from "between the lines": a body of principles about political behavior which bear on our own century as well as Burke's.

That it was an actual revolution which excited Burke to take his pen in hand is of some importance. Aristotle was troubled by Plato's Utopia, and he tried to show how too perfect a unity would be harmful to both citizens and society. Locke was upset by Hobbes' theory of absolute rule, and he attempted to demonstrate that human freedom was no less important than internal security. Burke, however, is not writing in reply to Rousseau's theory, or in answer to any particular theorist. Rather, he is replying to a revolution. The tyranny, the demagogy, the mob behavior he describes—all of these actually happened: they are not the hypothetical chapters from an academic text. While Burke would undoubtedly claim that the democratic revolution he deplores is an expresssion of Rousseau's ideas, the fact remains that the subject for analysis is not theoretical political words but rather actual political deeds.

Yet this down-to-earth approach is, interestingly enough, complicated by a further factor. All of the political theorists up to this time who have criticized tyrannical rulers have assumed that the targets for their criticism were practical-minded men who sought power in order to aggrandize their own interests. The tyrants depicted by Aristotle, St. Thomas, Machiavelli, and Locke did not claim that their hunger for power was a pursuit of the public interest. With Burke there is a new departure: his anxiety over the democratic and revolutionary leaders he sees in action is compounded by the fact that these self-styled

343

tribunes of the people are themselves men of ideas. Were they tyrants desiring power for its own sake, they might be dealt with in one of the various ways provided by traditional political theories. But the new men of power described by Burke regard themselves in all sincerity as the heralds of a new philosophical era. The democracy and the liberty and the equality which are their revolutionary goals seem at times to come straight from the textbook of Rousseau.

Burke's objection, then, is to the practical pursuit of Utopia. There is nothing wrong with a Plato or a Rousseau—or a Marx or an Engels—penning a Utopian dream for the consumption of their fellow intellectuals. But when these ideas fall off the ivory tower and into the hands of the politicians, then the troubles begin. For revolutionary leaders do not use the textbook ideals as theoretical principles so much as they fashion them into rigid blueprints to be imposed on an actual society. The consequence of this practical Utopianism, as Burke will make plain, can be devastating. The traditional structure of society will be dismantled for no other reason than that a theory calls for the radical transformation of men and institutions: patterns of behavior which have developed over centuries will be thrown over as political power is used to give effect to Utopian principles.

Burke's criticism, therefore, is of the facts of revolution and democracy; but it is also of the ideas in men's minds which give shape and direction to these facts. Thus we are confronted with the spectacle of a theorist attacking practical men because they are guided by theoretical considerations. Burke's preference, apparently, is for politicians who are not encumbered by ideas: they should be prudent men of action, not dreamers of abstract thoughts. Yet is this what Burke—or any theorist—really wants? Perhaps Burke's troubles stem from the fact that the politicians he sees are implementing some one else's ideas and not his own. For Burke has a program no less than other writers, and there is a hortatory quality to his words. The opposition, therefore, may not be between theory and practice so much as it is between good theories and bad theories. But this point will be developed at a later stage.

VARIETIES OF CONSERVATISM

Conservatism, like liberalism and democracy, is not only a political theory, but also an ideology and an outgrowth of institutional arrangements. And, it goes without saying, more than a single meaning has developed for the term. Some of these meanings were considered at the time when the various conceptions of liberalism were discussed: then the liberal-conservative opposition was set up in terms of disparate views of human nature and governmental power. But it was also shown that conservative policies shift ground as the years go by: the conservatives of 150 years ago adhered to mercantile economic policies; today they espouse the free-market economy; and there is no predicting what conservative policies will be 150 years from now.

In dealing with conservatism, then, a distinction must be made between principles and policies. The former—be they ideological, organizational, or philosophical—involve a fairly fixed set of values throughout the course of history. In terms of policy, however, we must not expect conservatives to have a permanent commitment to the views they support at any given time or place. The conservative theorist, while he professes an attachment to his principles, is less bound to his policies of the day than a liberal is to his. It is not a matter for surprise that, year by year, conservatives cease defending certain ideas and institutions, and begin to accept—even to champion—arrangements they once bitterly opposed. Liberals and democrats, monarchists and constitutionalists, socialists and communists—all these will come and go as historical circumstances change. But there will always be a conservative "party," either emerging or established, among both thinking and practical men. The reasons for this will appear as the varieties of conservatism are examined.

(1) *"Status-Quo" Conservatism.* Despite all protestations to the contrary, this form of conservatism is bound to be more ideology than theory. It is the generalized rationalizations for keeping things as they are which are uttered by or on behalf of those who are faring well within the status quo. The existing scheme of things may be feudal or capitalist, democratic or liberal, socialist or communist, but in every social or political system there emerges a group in society which has much to lose and little to gain by social change or political reform. These individuals, no matter whether they are kings or commissars, will develop a rhetoric which attempts to demonstrate that the prevailing system— the system by which they profit—is the embodiment of universal truth and justice.

This conservatism, then, can be found in all societies. For example, there are conservative communists who give their own interpretation to and then invoke the writings of Karl Marx to counter the claims of radical communists who assert that in a communist society incomes should be on an equal plane. Even societies which seem radical or revolutionary soon develop vested interests, and out of these spring the conservative mentality.[1] For men of power and privilege feel obliged to justify their status with high-sounding words: few individuals are capable of saying, either to themselves or to others, "I am rich, I like being rich, and my having wealth needs no defense." On the contrary, they wax philosophical. "My wealth is not for my personal enjoyment," they say. "It is socially productive; it is legitimate payment for the heavy responsibilities I

---

[1] For an interesting 'radical" communist critique of the "conservative" forces at work within the Soviet Union today, see Vladimir Dudintsev's novel *Not By Bread Alone* (New York: Dutton, 1957), translated by Edith Bone.

bear; in fact, not simply myself but everyone profits because things are as they are."

Those who are intent on keeping their wealth, their status, or their power usually understand that they maintain their privileged positions only at the sufferance of the poor, the humble, and the powerless. To secure the consent of their fellow citizens who have not done so well within the status quo, they devise conservative theories which are disseminated throughout society in an effort to render legitimate the fortunate circumstances of a privileged minority. Whether it is the phrases of St. Thomas or Karl Marx which are invoked, the motive and the intended consequence behind the invocation are the same. It will not be hard to see how Burke's theory can easily become the ideology of those who are successful and who do not particularly want to share the fruits of their success with their less worthy neighbors.

(2) "*Organizational*" *Conservatism.* States, governments, and political parties are by definition forms of organized activity. If an organization is to gain or maintain power, if it is to work to achieve ends of its own choosing, then it will soon discover that ways and means begin to loom as important in its life as do ends. An organization, to do an effective and substantial job, must employ the principle of division of labor, yet specialists have a tendency to become wrapped up in their specialty and to pursue it at the expense of larger organizational goals. An organization is composed of individuals who develop outlooks and interests of their own; in their concern for their own status and security they will tend to interpret and act on the organization's programmed aims in terms of their personal aspirations. An organization has at its disposal only limited resources, be they money or men or materials; this means that goals must be compromised and ends must be adjusted to the means available for their fulfillment. And it follows from this that an organization must nurture its clientele or constituency, for its power and authority depend on the consent of employees or customers or voters, and these clients or constituents make demands which force the organization to temper its policies. Finally, an organization develops a life and an instinct for survival of its own. Internal problems and politics emerge to occupy the time and energy of members. A political party or a legislature, for example, may have to worry more about keeping members in line than about what it will do if and when it has power. At the same time, an organization evolves positions, routines, and an attitude of mind which have a power and existence in their own right regardless of what the organization was originally set up to accomplish.[2]

[2] See the essays in Robert K. Merton, *et al.*, eds., *Reader in Bureaucracy* (Glencoe: Free Press, 1952), especially those in Section 3 entitled "Bureaucracy and Power Relations," pp. 114–178. Also amusing and relevant is C. Northcote Parkinson, *Parkinson's Law and Other Studies in Administration* (Boston: Houghton Mifflin, 1957).

What this adds up to, of course, is that the more highly organized political and social activity becomes, the more the forces of conservatism emerge. Political goals may be radical or liberal or democratic, but when men organize themselves to implement these goals, the process of organization brakes the pursuit of the original aims. There develop inertia, interests, and ideologies which are quick to give plausible reasons why things once thought desirable now cannot be done. All politics, to be sure, is not organizational; and all organizations are not conservative—at the outset. However, the tendency is there, and it is a marked one. Yesterday's idea is today's movement, and today's movement is tomorrow's bureaucracy. This does not mean that politics are getting more conservative as every day passes; rather, as Machiavelli pointed out, ideas and men are always rising to challenge prevailing bureaucracies. What calls for emphasis, however, is the fact that much of what we call conservatism is organizational in character and origin. We are dealing not so much with a theory or even an ideology, as with unplanned patterns of behavior which individuals pursue when they work in an organizational environment. Because organizations do not usually avow their conservative tendencies in any explicit way, their political impact can easily be neglected. It would be well, therefore, to regard states and governments, parties and interest groups, in organizational terms; in this way it is possible to understand the resistance to change which is endemic in societies.

(3) *"Philosophical" Conservatism.* Once ideological and organizational factors are set to one side, it is possible to discuss conservatism as scientific description and disinterested prescription. Whether such a divorcement can ever be made is problematical: students of conservatism show great alacrity in identifying their principles with concrete and selected practices. Is it possible, for example, to celebrate the principle of property without seeming to defend a particular group of property owners? Is it possible to discuss the merits of social stratification without appearing to plead for those currently at the top of the pyramid? All that can be said is that if such an intellectual feat can be performed, Burke's attempt shows a skill and a persuasive power that merits admiration. The principles of philosophical conservatism—unlike those of status-quo conservatism—are abstract as well as concrete. History and tradition, religion and authority, and property and social order should be respected; society should display variation and yet organic unity; man is prey to his passions and his reason is a limited quality; ideas should come as the product of experience and not be arrogant essays in Utopia. These and related principles will be elaborated upon by Burke. It is clear that some of them—such as respect for property and religion—call for institutions and attitudes which are not present in all societies. To the extent that they are not, such a society is failing to

adhere to the principles of philosophical conservatism. All defenses of a status quo, in short, do not have a philosophical content.

What is the relation between the theorists who adumbrate conservative principles and the ordinary people who claim to adhere to them? This question has a special importance in the context of philosophical conservatism, for there is a great intellectual gulf between the philosophers of conservatism and the man-in-the-street who employs conservative rhetoric. In terms of sheer power of intellect there are few thinkers to rival Edmund Burke. What is troublesome is that the average man who gives voice to conservative sentiments has a tendency to intolerance, chauvinism, and rigidity which is greater than that of the average liberal. The conservative in the street tends to sense conspiracies about him, to have an affinity for strong and masterful leadership, and to harbor less than flattering opinions about minority groups and unorthodox ideas.[3] The average conservative, in fact, tends to be a perpetual source of embarrassment to conservative philosophers: the theorists are in constant search for a group of citizens—men of power or ordinary people—who express genuine conservative principles in their thinking and behavior. That such a group is increasingly difficult to find in modern society suggests two facts: that philosophical conservatism has much of the Utopian in it and that practical conservatism is generally the ideology of the successful or the threatened. This problem, of course, is not unique to conservatism. Democratic theorists tend to stress the liberal or constitutional features of democracy, while practicing democrats emphasize unlimited majority rule and the equality of quality. And while liberal writers talk largely of freedom in terms which would secure its blessings to all men, practical liberals are inclined to favor a class structure which strengthens the freedoms of an allegedly superior minority in society.

One further point may be made by way of introduction. In this chapter and the two which have preceded it, three dominant ideas have been discussed: liberalism, democracy, and conservatism. That these have many points of contact with each other should be more than obvious: the theories share many values and they draw on each other at critical junctures. If Locke's liberalism is democratic, Rousseau's democracy is liberal. Furthermore, the liberalism of Tocqueville and Mill have strong conservative features. Nevertheless, it is fair to say that conservatism and democracy have the least in common: as theories of politics, they begin with such disparate assumptions about man and

---

[3] The classic work in this area is T. W. Adorno, *The Authoritarian Personality* (New York: Harper, 1950). Also see Herbert McClosky, "Conservatism and Personality," *The American Political Science Review*, March 1958, pp. 27–45. It should also be noted that the supposedly "liberal" constituency in society suffers from many of the same disabilities. See Seymour M. Lipset, "Democracy and Working-Class Authoritarianism," in his *Political Man* (New York: Doubleday, 1960), pp. 97–130.

society that their areas of agreement are extremely small. This does not mean that there cannot be a conservative "party" in a democracy; on the contrary, most viable democracies have an effective conservative element within their borders. What it does mean is that the actual political systems we see around us ought not to be confused with theoretical models. Most real conservatives do not trouble their minds much with philosophical problems about things like human nature, and most real democratic governments do not require that all their citizens believe in the philosophical principles of democracy. If there are violent arguments between a Burke and a Rousseau, it is at the level of political theory. And because both men are good political theorists, their ideas have much to do with the political reality we all know. Therefore, while the controversy between conservatism and democracy may be more sharply etched in the realm of ideas than it is in the real world, such a caricature is salutary in that it points to the tensions and conflicts which we feel all the time and might otherwise not understand.

THE LESSONS OF POLITICAL EXPERIENCE

Burke is not impressed with the traditional vocabulary of political theory. Words like "freedom," "justice," and "equality," phrases like "Natural Rights" and the "General Will"—all of these must be discussed in specific contexts if they are to merit serious consideration. The word "liberty," for example, has a noble ring, but no number of rhetorical flourishes can make it a positive blessing in all circumstances.

I cannot stand forward, and give praise or blame to anything which relates to human actions, and human concerns, on a simple view of the object, as it stands stripped of every relation, in all nakedness and solitude of metaphysical abstraction. Circumstances (which with some gentlemen pass for nothing) give in reality to every political principle its distinguishing color and discriminating effect. The circumstances are what render every civil and political scheme beneficial or noxious to mankind. . . .

Is it because liberty in the abstract may be classed among the blessings of mankind, that I am seriously to felicitate a madman, who has escaped from the protecting restraint and wholesome darkness of his cell, on his restoration to the enjoyment of light and liberty? Am I to congratulate a highwayman and murderer, who has broke prison, upon the recovery of his natural rights? [4]

Freedom is not an abstraction: freedoms are the acts of men, and we must at all times ask whether the individuals with whom we are dealing are capable of intelligent action. There are some men who can use the gift of freedom with prudence; there are others who will inevitably abuse it. And the latter include

[4] Edmund Burke, *Reflections on the Revolution in France* (London: Dent, 1910), p. 6.

not only madmen and murderers, but also apparently normal and law-abiding citizens whose passions may overpower their reason. In discussing human liberty the student of politics should always inquire: about which people are we talking, with what time and what place are we dealing? In one society the freedoms of speech and assembly will be the healthy means to self-government; in another they will spell opportunity for demagogues who are intent on overthrowing an established regime.

Liberal theorists who speak of human liberty and the rights of man focus their attention on the free individual. Each person is born with inherent rights, and it is the function of government to secure those freedoms to all citizens. The individual, in liberal theory, is prior to both government and society; he is, furthermore, a rational creature who requires freedom so that he may develop the full potentialities of his personality. Guided by the doctrine of Natural Rights, government is seen as a liberating rather than a coercive agency in society. Burke, on the other hand, is not prepared to argue about man's inherent rights: he does not quarrel with Natural Rights as a theory; what he does object to is the subjective and undiscriminating way in which men lay claim to them. For men are creatures of passion as well as reason, and they have need to a political authority which will control their impulses no less than they need a bill of rights to remove restraints on their activities. Freedom is a positive good, but every whim, fancy, or momentary urge is not thereby to be condoned. An indulgent government, which accepts every man's valuation of his own freedom, will unleash passions that can only result in social havoc. What must be realized, Burke says, is that a government's first task is not to secure liberties to citizens incapable of handling them. Its primary job, rather, is to exercise power so that human passions will be subdued. Control and even coercion are in order if men's arrogance is not to lead them to anarchy: only when power has accomplished this purpose can we commence talking of rights and freedom.

Government is not made in virtue of natural rights, which may and do exist in total independence of it; and exist in much greater clearness, and in a much greater degree of abstract perfection: but their abstract perfection is their practical defect. By having a right to everything they want everything. Government is a contrivance of human wisdom to provide for human wants. Men have a right that these wants should be provided for by this wisdom. Among these wants is to be reckoned the want, out of civil society, of a sufficient restraint upon their passions. Society requires not only that the passions of individuals should be subjected, but that even in the mass and body, as well as in the individuals, the inclinations of men should frequently be thwarted, their will controlled, and their passions brought into subjection. This can only be done by a power out of themselves; and not, in the exercise of its function, subject to that will and to those passions which it is its office to bridle and subdue.[5]

[5] P. 57.

The distinction between "rights" and "wants" is an important one, and one not sufficiently appreciated by liberal theory. A right is a demand for freedom which a citizen consciously feels in need of and which he claims so that he may better pursue an end of his own choosing. The claim to a right, in short, is consciously felt and rationally motivated. A want, on the other hand, is an objective condition which an individual must experience if he is to enjoy the good life. The point about wants is that the citizen himself is frequently unaware of what troubles him and of what is needed to remedy his dissatisfaction. A human want, for example, is the need for the passions of individuals to be checked by an external power. Few citizens realize that they and their neighbors ought to be so bridled, but the fact that they are unconscious of this want does not make it any the less real. At the conscious level citizens want freedom; at the same time they need to be subdued so they may enjoy freedom in an ordered society. For this reason Burke can say that government exists to satisfy human wants, and at the same time he refuses to say that government rests on a basis of popular consent. Were consent to be the foundation stone of political authority, then government would be hard put to deny citizens their rights; for few individuals would allow themselves to be subdued today for the promise of a better tomorrow. This is why Burke calls for a government which, in relation to the governed, is a "power out of themselves": as an agency over and above its citizens, it will be able to ignore their momentary whims and provide them with the conditions they need if they are to enjoy freedom and order.

Indeed, all talk of self-government is misconceived from the start. Democracy assumes a natural man who is selfless and rational. As a theoretical model, this may have some value, but real societies are characterized by diversity of interests, competition for power, and human passions. These are the inevitable accompaniments of social development, and no Utopian sweep of the pen can abolish them. The larger a society grows, Burke says, the further natural man recedes in the background and the greater will human differences appear.

Indeed in the gross and complicated mass of human passions and concerns, the primitive rights of men undergo such a variety of refractions and reflections, that it becomes absurd to talk of them as if they continued in the simplicity of their original direction. The nature of man is intricate; the objects of society are of the greatest possible complexity: and therefore no simple disposition or direction of power can be suitable either to man's nature, or to the quality of his affairs.[6]

When sturdy peasants govern themselves underneath the branches of an oak, we are dealing with a sufficiently small and homogeneous community so that self-interest and public interest may effortlessly coincide in an enlightened

[6] P. 59.

General Will. However, as society grows more complex, the complexities in man's nature are brought out. The division of labor leads to heterogeneity of interests, and as men become attached to their interests, they develop a selfish as well as an altruistic side to their character. A political theory which shuts its eyes to the intricacies of human nature, which glosses over the potential for evil in men, has little applicability in complex societies. Modern man faces modern problems, and they can only be solved by a realistic approach to political power. Politics is an experimental science, Burke says, and we can devise effective institutions of government if we take the practical view and are careful to eschew dogmatic approaches.

The science of constructing a commonwealth, or renovating it, or reforming it, is, like every other experimental science, not to be taught a priori. Nor is it a short experience that can instruct us in that practical science; because the real effects of moral causes are not always immediate; but that which in the first instance is prejudicial may be excellent in its remoter operation; and its excellence may arise even from the ill effects it produces in the beginning. The reverse also happens: and very plausible schemes, with very pleasing commencements, have often shameful and lamentable conclusions. In states there are some obscure and almost latent causes, things which appear at first view of little moment, on which a very great part of its prosperity or adversity may most essentially depend. The science of government being therefore so practical in itself, and intended for such practical purposes, a matter which requires experience, and even more experience than any person can gain in his whole life, however sagacious and observing he may be, it is with infinite caution that any man ought to venture upon pulling down an edifice, which has answered in any tolerable degree for ages the common purposes of society, or on building it up again, without having models and patterns of approved utility before his eyes.[7]

Burke's conception of a science of government is not the orthodox one. For it is a science without scientists: the experimentation, the systematic exploration through trial and error, which is required for successful results—these are not the productions of identifiable individuals. The experience on which Burke's science of government must draw is not found in technician's notebooks or in theorist's treatises. On the contrary, he is talking of the accumulated social experience of centuries of political practice. No single individual, no matter how extensive the studies of his lifetime, ought to presume that his small wisdom is a match for the experience of ages. Social and political development have taken place, as it were, in a gigantic laboratory. Through history men have tried to govern themselves in a multitude of ways: some of these ways have been found wanting, and they eventually perish; others meet the challenges which confront them, and they survive to do battle again. If a social or political system endures for an extended period, then the presumption must be that it has passed a sort of laboratory test: it contains the means of adjusting itself to

[7] P. 58.

new situations as they arise. But these mechanisms of adjustment are the product of slow and often silent historical growth, and for this reason they may not always be apparent to the naked eye of the political analyst. For this reason, too, he who tampers with society does so at great risk: in his attempts at reform he may be undermining the subtle instruments of social survival. "The things which facilitate or obstruct the various ends which are to be pursued by the mechanism of civil institutions . . ." Burke says, "require a deep knowledge of human nature and human necessities." [8] If policy-makers are to be rational, they must be students of human and social needs: they must examine the experience of governments with an eye toward understanding men's capabilities and limitations. Not metaphysical dogma, but a science of human nature and social institutions must be the wellspring of political action.

That Burke's theory is conservative by this time needs no arguing. The burden of proof is placed on the shoulders of he who proposes change: the would-be reformer must demonstrate in a persuasive way that the change he champions will be one for the better. The conservative is in the enviable position of not having to offer a defense: the status quo speaks for itself, for it is the proven product of history. The innovator may point to the injustices of the present, but he must also argue for an unknown and unpredictable future. The conservative will always ask: How do we know that your plans for the future will be better than going along as we have been? The answer must be that we cannot know; no assurances can be given.

"A disposition to preserve and an ability to improve, taken together, would be my standard of a statesman," Burke says. "Everything else is vulgar in the conception, perilous in the execution." [9] This is no obdurate defense of the status quo: preservation and improvement are twin principles. Indeed, change must be accepted in timely and judicious quantities if conservative values are to have meaning. "A state without the means of some change is without the means of its conservation," Burke says. "Without such means it might even risk the loss of that part of the constitution which it wished most religiously to preserve." [10] Statesmen who refuse to replace a nail in the horse's shoe will soon discover that the rider, the dispatch, and the battle are all lost. But, despite these nods in the direction of reform, Burke's theory must not be given a misplaced emphasis. The burden of proof still rests on the reformer, and he must build on the existing structure rather than renovate its foundations. "A good patriot and a true politician," Burke says, "always considers how he shall make the most of the existing materials of his country." [11]

[8] P. 58.
[9] P. 153.
[10] Pp. 19–20.
[11] P. 153.

The attack, then, is leveled at those theorists and politicians who would force a break with the past in order to lead men to a Utopian future. These men would demolish the standing edifice in order to raise a new temple in the name of progress. To them nothing old is sacred: if freedom, justice, and equality—as defined by themselves—are to prevail, then outmoded institutions must be consigned to the scrapheap of history. "I cannot conceive how any man can have brought himself to that pitch of presumption," Burke says, "to consider his country as nothing but carte blanche upon which he may scribble whatever he pleases." [12] While the arrogance of such reformers is galling, even more disturbing is the shallow modernity of their arrogance. They are prepared, if given the power, to impose on men and society a scheme which was conceived in a short moment of history. Disregarding the lessons of centuries and the proved worth of ancient institutions, they see all political problems as contemporary and their solutions as the work of an hour.

This kind of thinking is not discouraged by the social-contract theories, especially those of Locke and Rousseau. For in those writings citizens are given the power and the right to reform the structure of political authority and even to abolish their governments for a momentary grievance. Burke attacks the assumptions behind this way of thinking.

Your literary men, and your politicians, and so do the whole clan of the enlightened among us, . . . have no respect for the wisdom of others; but they pay it off by a very full measure of confidence in their own. With them it is a sufficient motive to destroy an old scheme of things, because it is an old one. As to the new, they are in no sort of fear with regard to the duration of a building run up in haste; because duration is no object to those who think little or nothing has been done before their time, and who place all their hopes in discovery. They conceive, very systematically, that all things which give perpetuity are mischievous, and therefore they are at inexpiable war with all establishments. They think that government may vary like modes of dress, and with as little ill effect: that there needs no principle of attachment, except a sense of present conveniency, to any constitution of the state.

They always speak as if they were of opinion that there is a singular species of compact between them and their magistrates, which binds the magistrate, but which has nothing reciprocal in it, but that the majesty of the people has a right to dissolve it without any reason, but its will. Their attachment to their country itself is only so far as it agrees with some of their fleeting projects; it begins and ends with that scheme of polity which falls in with their momentary opinion.[13]

Innovators do more than throw the baby out with the bathwater: they leave us with no more than an empty promise that they will refill the tub with champagne for all.

The reply to this is that change must be approached in organic terms. That

[12] *Ibid.*
[13] Pp. 84–85.

is, if the political and social organism is to undergo an operation and survive that ordeal, then the grafting or amputation must be carried out with full consideration for the well-being of the whole patient. A praiseworthy example, Burke suggests, is Great Britain: constitutional innovations are accepted only in terms which do not violate the standing institutions of government and society. "We . . . wish to derive all we possess as an inheritance from our forefathers," he says. "Upon that body and stock of inheritance we have taken care not to inoculate any scion alien to the nature of the original plant." [14] And if Britian was a good conservative model in Burke's own time, it remains so to this day. It is one of the few major powers which, since the advent of industrialization, has experienced no violent revolution within its borders. Constitutional government, a respect for tradition, and civility of behavior have characterized British politics from Burke's time to our own. If Great Britain, despite its interludes of liberal and socialist reform, remains a conservative nation, much of the reason for this is found in Burke's theory. His analysis of social structure and social control give an understanding of how countries like Britain can achieve stability over long periods of time. Whether the British experience and the Burkean prescription are suitable commodities for export to less favored lands is, of course, another matter.

That Burke has much in common with St. Thomas, Hobbes, and Rousseau is quite clear. But it is also obvious that he is synthesizing many of their ideas as he creates a new theory of politics. Like St. Thomas and Rousseau, for example, he stresses the power of customs and conventions. "If civil society be the offspring of convention, . . . that convention must limit and modify all the descriptions of constitution which are formed under it," he says. "Every sort of legislative, judicial, or executory power are its creatures." [15]

Patterns of social behavior which are unplanned and often accidental must modify and limit governmental power. This, of course, is anathema to the rational reformer, for the basic assumptions of reform are that political institutions are the creations of rational men and that those men may arrange them howsoever is necessary to achieve their political ends. And an accompanying assumption is that beneath the distorted mask and vestments there exists a natural man who will only know rational freedom when institutions are remade to accord with his natural inclinations. Burke, of course, rejects the idea of a natural man: it is idle to suggest that men can be stripped down to that primitive condition ever again, and it is pernicious to suggest that he can be reconditioned to live happily in whatever new society a reformer may happen to devise. We must take men as we find them, and they are the products of

[14] P. 29.
[15] P. 57.

and captives to social custom. Governments must be built on the base of such citizens, and this means that laws and institutions must adjust themselves to the conventions of society and the people who have practiced them for generations. The only way for government to rise above convention is to press its policies forward by violent means, and this is a possibility that Burke does not care to consider. Society is the master, therefore, and government is its servant; in this Burke shares common ground with Rousseau. But Burke's society is a product of the experience of history, while Rousseau's is capable of radical impulses and violent shifts of opinion. For the one, society acts as a brake on the power of government: for the other, it can supply fuel for greater political potency.

And, like St. Thomas, Burke believes that social and political systems are part and parcel of the natural order of the universe. "Our political system is placed in a just correspondence and symmetry with the order of the world," he says.[16] The important deduction from this premise is that every feature of government serves a purpose: whether we realize it or not, all of our institutions have been put there for a reason. We are frequently tempted to call obsolete or superfluous some political agency, but, unbeknownst to us, that agency may be one of the cements which holds the entire system together. The handing out of postmasterships for patronage purposes may, for example, appear to hamper the efficiency of the post office. But, on the other hand, it may be one of the cheapest ways to reward those who give their time and effort to keeping our party system going. The same thing may be said of such apparently non-rational practices as religious observance, regional loyalties, and class allegiances. To tamper with them is to violate the reflection of a natural order which is found in our political and social institutions.

To destroy any power, growing wild from the rank productive force of the human mind, is almost tantamount, in the moral world, to the destruction of the apparently active properties of bodies in the material. It would be like the attempt to destroy (if it were in our competence to destroy) the expansive force of fixed air in nitre, or the power of steam, or of electricity, or of magnetism. These energies always existed in nature, and they were always discernible. They seemed, some of them unserviceable, some noxious, some no better than a sport to children; until contemplative ability, combining with practic skill, tamed their wild nature, subdued them to use, and rendered them at once the most powerful and the most tractable agents, in subservience to the great views and designs of men.[17]

The power of religious feeling can be mobilized to forestall oppressive rule by an autocratic state; the power of national sentiment can be employed to turn back the appeal of an alien ideology. Similarly, family and regional loyalties,

[16] P. 31.
[17] P. 154.

dispositions to preserve ethnic and local customs—all these can be of value in securing political order. The point is that powers like these serve rational purposes for a society even though their cruder manifestations may seem to be wholly irrational. He who would root these powers out of the minds of men will be hard pressed to find substitutes as effective. To say that the state is "natural" is to say that its development has been guided by a higher reason. The symmetry and order which characterize political systems are not, however, the conscious plans of mortal men. Human reason is too frail an instrument to accomplish so monumental a task.

THE FRAILTY OF HUMAN REASON

The wisdom and virtue which guide the course of government and politics are to be found not in individuals but in the social organism. Burke chooses to stress the collectivity rather than the individuals who comprise it for two reasons. The first, which has already been discussed, is that the social whole is more than the sum of its individual parts. A society has a life of its own which is the product of its history, its culture, its geography, its national tradition. The men and women who reside inside its borders at any given time are but passing players on a stage of history. To focus on them alone would be to ignore the deep and powerful forces which govern the lines along which that society has moved in the past and will move in the future.

The second reason for Burke's social emphasis is that he takes a skeptical view of the intellectual potentialities of the individual. Hobbes thought little of man's ability to master his social environment, but he at least credited him with the wisdom to draw up a contract which would provide order and law. Machiavelli viewed most men as passive creatures who could be controlled with bread and circuses, but he also noted that a few men could use their intelligence to achieve power and prestige. Burke's indictment of man as a political actor is more comprehensive than either Hobbes' or Machiavelli's. As an individual and as a member of a political public, man is subject to passions which militate against the rational fulfillment of political goals. "History consists for the greater part," Burke says, "of the miseries brought upon the world by pride, ambition, avarice, revenge, lust, sedition, hypocrisy, ungoverned zeal, and all the trains of disorderly appetites which shake the public." [18] The great battles of politics, Burke says, may look as if they are fought in the name of religion, morals, laws, prerogatives, privileges, liberties, and the rights of man. But this is a shallow view. Derivative slogans actually conceal the residual appetites. It is the pride, the ambition, the avarice, which reside in the hearts

[18] P. 137.

and minds of men individually and collectively which make for the tensions characterizing politics. These vices, as Burke calls them, are constant and unalterable: they are, one might say, the political expression of original sin.

Human diversity, in short, leads to social perversity. As Rousseau pointed out, heterogeneity of interests among men lead to political factions and entrenched disagreements: he thought that a homogeneous community would bring the abolition of both diversity and perversity. Burke rejects this solution, not because it is communitarian, but because it is Utopian: it seeks to abolish that which cannot be abolished. Tyranny is not the product of tyrants, but of the passions which lie in every citizen. "You would not cure the evil by resolving that there should be no more monarchs, nor ministers of state, nor of the gospel," Burke says. It is the passionate public which needs to be saved from itself: "Wise men will apply their remedies to the causes of evil which are permanent, not to the occasional organs by which they act." [19]

Burke is not, like many thinkers, concerned about the ideas of freedom or justice, equality or law. To take these ideas seriously is to take at face value the rationalizing slogans of self-interested men. The real focus of political theory must be on the unconscious and ununderstood forces which move all men at all times. From this it follows that the primary task of politics is that of control: ways and means must be found to harness and channel the appetites of an irrational public.

If Burke is to be called an irrationalist, it is well to be clear on our meaning of that term. His purpose is not to applaud the irrationality of men: rather, it is to recognize its existence. This recognition does not imply approval. However, it will lead to prescriptions on how best to utilize forces of irrationality in order to achieve rational ends. In short, Burke is trying to be rational about the irrational. He is attempting, first, to understand and, second, to control the appetites and passions which can lead men to self-defeat. But even here there are limitations. There is only so much we can know even about ourselves: our self-knowledge is a tiny particle compared with our monumental ignorance. For all his talk of an experimental science, Burke himself makes no claim to possessing a superior intelligence. If we read back over his own words, we will see that he describes more often than he explains, he asserts more than he analyzes. Indeed, as we will see later on, he uses the metaphors of the poet rather than the language of the scientist. The reason of men—including himself—much though they may prize it, is often a delusion. "Wisdom is not the most severe corrector of folly," he says. "They are the rival follies, which mutually wage so unrelenting a war." [20] To put wisdom and folly, reason and un-

[19] P. 138.
[20] P. 155.

reason, on a parity is simply to say that our understanding is so meager that the wise man and the fool are brothers under the skin.

Let us say that a perfect understanding of the social and political process—possessed only by God—rates a score of 100. The wisest students of society and politics have, for all their efforts, achieved a score of no more than 10. The man-in-the-street may be said to have attained a 2, although that is a generous estimate. Wisdom and folly, then, stand in a ratio of 5:1. If that is the only ratio which is borne in mind, then our wise men are clearly far superior in understanding to their fellow citizens. Burke, however, asks us to take note of the fact that our presumed men of wisdom fall 90 points short of perfection, and they are not much better than the average man who is 98 points short of the mark. Both are ignorant, and to argue over 8 points is rather idle in a case like this.

Nor does Burke's indictment end here. It may well be that our reason, simply because it embodies an attempt to rise above the myths and prejudices which infuse the political thinking of most men, will be altogether too rational. It may devise plans in circumstances where behavior cannot be planned; it may set goals which men cannot even begin to attain. Yet if such reason is pursued unremittingly, it may lead not only to failure but also to consequences which were not predicted at the outset. What Burke is saying is that not only is there irrationality in most attempts to use our reason: there is also a wisdom in what appears to be our folly. Seemingly foolish behavior which persists year in and year out will develop patterns of behavior that build confidence and make for security and order. "A prudent man . . ." Burke says, "would think the superstition which builds to be more tolerable than that which demolishes." [21] Prudence, then, stands for a recognition of the limits of our reason. It also entails a respect for the unplanned and unconscious wisdom in the customary behavior which exists in any society. It is a wisdom created without the intervention of wise men, and therefore one which can be participated in by the average man as well as—and, indeed, with more ease than—the philosopher.

The science of government, Burke said earlier, requires more experience than any person can gain in his whole life. This means, as was noted, that we have a science without scientists, for even the most astute student of politics will reach his grave long before he can secure a grasp of the operations of politics. If this is true for the theorist, it is even more the case for the practitioner. Would-be architects and custodians of any government must be conscious of their transitory status. No one man, no group of men can create a state: no year, no generation can give at its birth the heritage which a govern-

[21] P. 156.

ment requires for longevity and stability. "Political arrangement, as it is a work for social ends, is to be only wrought by social means," Burke says. "There mind must conspire with mind. Time is required to produce that union of minds which alone can produce all the good we aim at." [22] The minds which conspire to produce a body politic are numberless and timeless. We ought not to point to any particular group—such as the Founding Fathers of 1787 or the Bolsheviks of 1918—and give them credit for strength and stability of nations existing in our own day. Such men may have set the engine on its tracks, but they could do no more than give it a starting push. Rather, it is the faceless millions who make up a nation who, through their consent to authority and their belief in a common heritage, create a society and a government. In this sense Burke is an equalitarian: all men are equally creatures of a limited reason, but all men also partake of—and contribute to—the wisdom of an ageless society.

With this in mind, we may now examine Burke's conception of a social contact. Like that of Hobbes, Locke, and Rousseau, it is an equalitarian document: all citizens participate in its making. But, unlike its predecessors, it is not the conscious creation of rational citizens. If society is created for a purpose, this end is not necessarily to be achieved by asking men to think through and act on their own conception of that goal. Indeed, too much rationality, as has been seen, can lead to its own downfall. And, because Burke's contract is a growth of many years and the product of many minds, there must be no talk of its being based on active consent and thereby revokable when the consent of citizens is withdrawn.

Society is indeed a contract. Subordinate contracts for objects of mere occasional interest may be dissolved at pleasure—but the state ought not to be considered as nothing better than a partnership agreement in a trade of pepper and coffee, calico or tobacco, or some other such low concern, to be taken up for a little temporary interest, and to be dissolved by the fancy of the parties. It is to be looked upon with other reverence; because it is not a partnership in things subservient only to the gross animal existence of a temporary and perishable nature.

It is a partnership in all science; a partnership in all art; a partnership in every virtue, and in all perfection. As the ends of such a partnership cannot be obtained in many generations, it becomes a partnership not only between those who are living, but between those who are living, those who are dead and those who are to be born.

Each contract of each particular state is but a clause in the great primaeval contract of eternal society, linking the lower with the higher natures, connecting the visible and invisible world, according to a fixed compact sanctioned by the inviolable oath which holds all physical and all moral natures, each in their appointed place.[23]

[22] P. 165.
[23] Pp. 93–94.

Society has within it science and art, virtue and wisdom, but these properties were not created by scientists or artists, by wise or virtuous men. Any individual of talent builds on the foundation laid for him by generations of predecessors: any man of reason adds his few grains to the great stock which has accumulated before him. And society, furthermore, is an entailed inheritance which will pass on to those as yet unconceived. Citizenship does not begin at birth, nor does it end at death. In these terms, all talk of consent, of representation, of democracy and self-government fades into irrelevancy. The contract is historic rather than contemporary, tacit rather than express. And overarching government and society is the natural order of the universe. The Natural Law prescribes the forms of political and social institutions. If we are to speak of consent at all, it is consent as it is expressed through history and custom.

We must take men as we find them in society, Burke says. "No artificial institution whatsoever can make the men of whom any system of authority is composed other than God, and nature, and education, and their habits of life have made them." [24] Pride, ambition, avarice, and a host of frailties mark the human breed. Reason is a weak reed in an ocean of ignorance. What makes life possible is that the passions of men can be controlled: society develops unconsciously customs and patterns of behavior which make for order and predictability. Like Rousseau, Burke puts his faith in the wisdom of the collectivity. Unlike Rousseau, however, his citizens are not men of reason or even beneficence. They can live together only because they are capable of accepting the authority of society. It is not an authority of their personal making, but it nevertheless merits obedience. And Burke, for all his talk of the great primaeval contract of eternal society, is not willing to leave the matter of social control to chance. Men of passion and unreason must be brought to submit to government by institutions which take account of the frailties of human nature. Not any form of society will suffice to this end. On the contrary, Burke has clearly in mind the kind of social structure which needs prescribing.

CLASS SOCIETY AND MASS SOCIETY

Neither Hobbes nor Locke had a systematic theory of social structure. Hobbes granted that rulers and ruled had a different status in society, but he did not do more than hint at this. Locke stressed the role of property in the life of men, but he did not proceed from this to a discussion of propertied and propertyless elements in society. Rousseau was well aware of discrepancies of class, status, and power in the contemporary world; however, he believed that

[24] P. 38.

these were the hallmarks of an unreconstructed society. The community that Rousseau held out as a goal would have no classes, no degrees of status, no inequalities of power. If he did acknowledge the stratified character of existing societies, it was as an aberrant phase in human history. Burke sees much the same world that Rousseau did in his *Discourse on the Origin of Inequality*; but, rather than call for its abolition, he subjects it to careful scrutiny. What is an aberration for Rousseau is a prescription for Burke: social institutions are the outcome of an orderly development over time. To inveigh against classes or property, against authority or power—this is to dismiss lightly forms of social control which have demonstrated their utility since the day when man and man first decided to live together. It is with this attitude that Burke turns to the question of political power in society.

That there ought to be a ruling class is a self-evident proposition for Burke. This class, as will be seen, is both social and political in its composition and functions. If there is to be a legislative assembly, for example, then its membership must be drawn exclusively from a particular section of society. Too many legislatures bow to the arguments for a universal suffrage and, as a next step, to the plea for equal opportunity for all citizens to hold political office. Assemblies composed of common men, Burke suggests, will exercise power in a common way. Or, more frightening, they will be swept along by their momentary impulses: congresses and parliaments, like any mob, can easily be swayed by demagogues and led by tyrants. Tyranny of the majority frequently receives its best expression in hasty legislation enacted by an equalitarian assembly. For this reason, Burke, like Aristotle, finds it necessary and desirable to limit access to legislative power to those who can be trusted to exercise it with humility. "Nothing can secure a steady and moderate conduct in such assemblies," he says, "but that the body of them should be respectably composed, in point of condition in life, of permanent property, of education, and of such habits as enlarge and liberalize the understanding." [25]

Here is the first institutional departure from democracy. There are in society, Burke says, those who because of their property and education and general outlook are well-fitted to handle political power. Whether Burke believes, like Plato, that there can come into existence a superior breed of men, or whether, like Machiavelli, he is pointing to those whom birth or talent have raised to privileged positions—this question will be considered shortly. What is important is that not all men are qualified to partake of political power or hold the reins of government. The equalitarian theorist talks of the basic identity of all men, and he is eventually lead to affirm that one man is as fit to govern as is another: the worth, the value, the honor and the capabilities

[25] P. 39.

of all men are equated. But where the proponent of human equality sees identity, Burke sees significant differences. A few are fit to rule; the many are fit only to be ruled.

> In asserting that anything is honorable, we imply some distinction in its favor. The occupation of a hair-dresser, or of a working tallow-chandler, cannot be a matter of honor to any person—to say nothing of a number of other more servile employments. Such descriptions of men ought not to suffer oppression from the state; but the state suffers oppression, if such as they either individually or collectively, are permitted to rule. In this you think you are combating prejudice, but you are at war with nature.[26]

There is no sermonizing here about the dignity of all mankind. All that the butcher and baker and candlestickmaker should expect from politics is that they not be oppressed. Burke, like Plato and Aristotle, believes that self-government by the majority, or the exercise of power by direct representatives of the majority, will have dire consequences. A populist legislature may have persuaded itself that it seeks only to obtain liberty, justice, and equality for the downtrodden masses. But in pursuing this goal it will find itself oppressing the cultured and propertied minority who are the strength of the state. The ends which popular government invariably seeks will never, ironically, be achieved by the politics of democracy. Those ends, such of them as can be secured by men in this world, will be best brought about by the class which is suited to handle power. The hair-dresser and the tallow-chandler must learn to stand down; they must learn to defer to their betters in these matters.

Plato's ruling class was, for all intents and purposes, an inbred and hereditary caste: if their internal gold was invisible to the naked eye, it was used to segregate man from man much as the color of skin does in many modern societies. On the other hand, Machiavelli's ruling class was not bound by birth and breeding. As was pointed out, it might more properly be called an elite open to those who had an aptitude for the game of power and the will to play it. Burke's ruling class, as will be seen, is based largely on the possession of inherited property. Yet he is prepared, as grudgingly as was Plato, to admit to positions of power men of talent who would benefit both themselves and the established ruling class by their ascent.

If any single outlook divides the liberal from the conservative, it is his approach to the question of equality of opportunity. Both liberal and conservative—unlike the democrat—accept the existence of class gradations in society. The liberal believes in an open society: careers should be open to the talents. The man of ability, the liberal asserts, should have every chance to gain education, property, status, and power. Mobility should be facilitated at

[26] P. 47.

all times: the talented must be encouraged to rise, the inept compelled to fall. Accidents of race and creed, birth and parentage should not hold down an individual of merit. The conservative is not inhumane, nor does he lack compassion. Nevertheless, he is wary of the liberal's enthusiasm for an open society and unimpeded social mobility. Burke is not dogmatically opposed to equality of opportunity, but he wants the path to be a difficult one:

> I do not hesitate to say that the road to eminence and power from obscure condition ought not to be made too easy, nor a thing too much of course. If rare merit be the rarest of all rare things, it ought to pass through some sort of probation. The temple of honor ought to be seated on an eminence. If it be opened through virtue, let it be remembered too, that virtue is never tried but by some difficulty and some struggle.[27]

To the liberal, and certainly to the democrat, these words have a hardheaded ring. Because of their great good fortune in having been born into a privileged class, power and eminence automatically devolve on a small group in society. Members of this favored class must pass no test of merit or virtue: luck in the lottery of birth puts them on a nonstop elevator to the summit of the social edifice. Yet for those individuals of humble parentage who aspire to rise in society Burke demands that their struggle be arduous and their ascent made difficult. There is clearly a double standard at work here: those born into the purple may stay at the top without justifying their worthiness; those born beneath the salt must pass a vigorous test if they are to rise to eminence.

If the road of opportunity is to be a rocky one, then Burke is prepared to defend this course. Real merit only emerges if a real test is administered: if mobility is facilitated, then men of superficial talents will ascend to positions they cannot handle. And, just as important, the best will not be brought out in those of high potentialities. "Difficulty is a severe instructor, set over us by the supreme ordinance of a parental Guardian and Legislator, who knows us better than we know ourselves . . ." Burke says. "He that wrestles with us strengthens our nerves, and sharpens our skill." [28] These words, or words like them, are frequently heard to fall from the lips of a self-made man. A man who has climbed to great heights against arduous odds will often acknowledge that his character profited in no small measure from the difficulties he encountered. To be sure, the struggles he surmounted will have defeated others: for everyone who makes the ascent there will be a hundred who fall by the wayside and a thousand who never embark the climb at all. But a test designed to produce excellence must necessarily reject the many who are mediocre.

And what of the double standard? That Burke does not deign to test those

[27] P. 48.
[28] P. 163.

who are so fortunate as to be born to power and eminence would seem to be palpable injustice. For even the most conservative interpretation of the laws of heredity will grant that mediocrity and worse will at some time or another appear in the best of families: a name or a title does not necessarily impart virtue to its bearer. The short answer is that Burke is too occupied with larger issues of justice and freedom to concern himself with the injustices which might occasionally be inflicted on those born to lowly status. He is, first of all, not a little fearful of the new man, the recent arrival on the scene of power. "Considerate people, before they declare themselves, will observe the use which is made of power," Burke says, "and particularly of so trying a thing as new power in new persons." [29] The man who makes the climb in his own lifetime will have been obsessed with his personal career for the larger part of his adult life; he will have inevitably judged all opportunities in terms of his personal interests. His eyes have been necessarily fixed on himself, for if he is to succeed in a difficult world, then he must judge conditions and events as they affect his own progress. Such a man, once successful, will tend to take a limited view of the purposes to which his power might be put. Even when secure—and it is doubtful if he will ever feel secure—he will never feel safe about assuming wider responsibilities. Furthermore, in his climb he will have expended much psychic energy, and he will have got in the habit of unremitting activity. It is doubtful if such a man can late in his life learn to use the leisure and contemplation which are needful for those who would do great things. This is why the conservative is chary of the newly rich and the newly arrived. Through no fault of their own, they are unable to use their power in responsible ways. There are, of course, exceptions. But for each statesman who has risen from the ranks there are too many others who abuse their new status in society.

This means, then, that the new entrants to the ruling class must be few in number in any generation. They must by no means be allowed to gain disproportionate power: indeed, their share must be a small, almost indiscernible, one, for the prescriptive members of the ruling class, the men and women who have been born and bred into it, are the carriers of a nation's traditions. They are the prime defenders of the institutions of law and government, of religion and custom, which have given the society its strength. The wisdom and virtue of this class does not lie in its wise and virtuous members so much as it resides in the ruling class as a timeless institution. This class educates its members to its political, social, and national responsibilities: it gives them property, but it also gives them the leisure and the environment in which to take the long and considered view. These are not philosopher-kings, nor are they men of excep-

[29] P. 7.

tional talents as individuals. Rather, they are men who, because of advantageous surroundings and lifelong conditioning, are capable of using power with prudence. The freedom and justice of a society are in the custody of such a class. If equality of opportunity is facilitated, then a historic ruling class can become transformed into an elite which, for all its talents, has never become accustomed to serving the greater ends of freedom and justice. This, then, is the conservative case against unhampered opportunity: it is also the reply of a ruling class to those who call for government by a circulating elite.

Society, in Burke's view, is a great chain of being. Beneath the apex of the social pyramid is not a confused multitude of autonomous individuals. On the contrary, men are of varying talents, and society calls on them to play a variety of roles. There is, overarching this diversity, a social order which gives a rational arrangement to its many interests and classes. Burke's analysis is a reply to the theories of individualism, and he draws for authority on the writings of Plato and Aristotle.

The legislators who framed the ancient republics knew that their business was too arduous to be accomplished with no better apparatus than the metaphysics of an undergraduate, and the mathematics and arithmetic of an exciseman. They had to do with men, and they were obliged to study human nature. They had to do with citizens, and they were obliged to study the effects of those habits which are communicated by the circumstances of civil life. They were sensible that the operation of this second nature on the first produced a combination; and thence arose many diversities amongst men, according to their birth, their education, their professions, the period of their lives, their residence in towns or in the country, their several ways of acquiring and fixing property, and according to the quality of the property itself, all which rendered them as it were so many different species of animals.

From hence they thought themselves obliged to dispose their citizens into such classes, and to place them in such situations in the state, as their peculiar habits might qualify them to fill, and to allot to them such appropriated privileges as might secure to them what their specific occasions required, and which might furnish to each description such force as might protect it in the conflict caused by the diversity of interests, that must exist, and must contend, in all complex society. . . .[30]

Society is far more than an aggregation of units: it is a complex arrangement of variable personalities interlocked in a variety of orders and classes. We must admit, first of all, to the innate disparities of human nature: the differing aptitudes, temperaments, and inclinations of men create a diversity of one kind. And the interests and characteristics men acquire in the course of their life in society—their differing ways of making a living, regional loyalties, family arrangements—make for a diversity of a second kind. When these natural and social differences are permuted and combined, a whole array of classes appears

[30] Pp. 180–181.

in society. Furthermore, while there may be a major "horizontal" diversion between the propertied few and the nonpropertied many, Burke also points to the "vertical" differentiation between kinds of property: agricultural and commercial, manufacturing and financial, rural and urban, debtor and creditor. This, he implies, obviates any clear-cut class struggle between rich and poor; for men of property form not a solid phalanx, but are themselves a heterogeneous group. Indeed, it is its heterogeneity which characterizes the whole of society. And this diversity should not be given a grudging acceptance, but rather ought to be warmly welcomed.

However, this diversity must not be accompanied by mobility between classes: the stations in which men are placed should be relatively fixed over time. Each man, according to his qualities and the role he plays in society, should accept his appropriate situation with its privileges and its obligations. Undue fluidity within the body politic will strain established expectations, and it can, as was point out earlier, intrude unqualified individuals into the ruling class. Burke wishes to avoid the advent of a "mass society," which he sees latent in the doctrine of individualism. The ordered heterogeneity he prescribes, with its impediments to social mobility, imparts to each citizen the feeling that he belongs to an organic community and that he performs a necessary function in society. Every person is able to identify himself with a viable element in the social order: a class, a guild, a locality. There is a danger that, in the worthy names of freedom and equality, misguided men will upset this stratified pattern. "The metaphysical and alchemical legislators . . ." Burke says, "have attempted to confound all sorts of citizens, as well as they could, into one homogeneous mass." [31] The idea of a mass society stands in total opposition to that of a class society. A mass society is composed of a lonely crowd: men without identities or loyalties, who search vainly for a source of authority. Such men are easily victimized by demagogues, for they have been freed from prescriptive rules and yet they are unable to put this freedom to use. Furthermore, the variety of interests and classes which once acted as buffers between the state and citizens is now destroyed: the individual may be reached directly and effectively by political authority, as there are no intermediate associations in society to act in his defense.[32]

It should be clear how Burke can see the danger of mass society tendencies in theories like those of Hobbes, Locke, and Rousseau. And Tocqueville and Marx will give further attention to this vexing problem. While Marx sees the rise of a mass man as the inevitable consequence of industrialization,

[31] P. 181.

[32] See R. A. Nisbet, *The Quest for Community* (New York: Oxford, 1953) for an elaboration of this idea.

Tocqueville hopes that a plurality of social interests will temper the onrush of homogenizing forces. Yet if pluralism is a solution, it should be noted that the conservative and liberal conceptions of this theory are quite different. Burke's plurality of orders and classes is an integral part of an organic social scheme; in this he shares Aristotle's and Plato's assumptions. Liberal pluralism, on the other hand, calls for free associations, social mobility, and a permissive state: there is no talk of organic unity, nor is it required that groups fit into some kind of "natural" scheme. There is a real conflict here about the definition of society and the meaning of freedom. Whether the choice must be between the extremes of a class society and a mass society, whether a free society and individual liberty are opposing ideas—these problems will arise more than once as the discussion proceeds.

INSTITUTIONS OF SOCIAL CONTROL

If men are to be arrayed in a variety of classes, and if each citizen is to accept his assigned station in life, matters as grave as these cannot be left to chance. There must emerge forms of social control which will preserve the class distinctions necessary in a stratified society. The institutional controls prescribed by Burke are three: property, religion, and prejudice.

Property. If a ruling class is to have effective control over the reins of government, it must acquire the means of securing the respect of those over whom they rule: its legitimacy, in other words, needs to be established in the public mind. Burke saw that a self-perpetuating class—one which has held power in society for generations and perhaps even for centuries—is able to evoke consent through the established agencies of habit and custom. The way in which such continuity of rule is ensured is by safeguarding the institution of inherited property. This institution gives its owners a sense of security, and it allows them to develop the habits necessary for the responsible use of power. Property, then, should be looked on as more than material goods. If there is wealth involved, it is only as a means to a higher end.

The power of perpetuating our property in our families is one of the most valuable and interesting circumstances belonging to it, and that which tends the most to the perpetuation of society itself. It makes our weakness subservient to our virtue; it grafts benevolence even upon avarice. The possessors of family wealth, and of the distinction which attends hereditary possession, are the natural securities for this transmission.[33]

When a conservative like Burke speaks of property, he has in mind a fairly specific kind of property-holding. To begin with, it is family wealth: a fortune,

[33] *Reflections on the Revolution in France,* p. 49.

bound by primogeniture and entail, which is passed on inviolate from eldest son to eldest son. Such wealth, to play its part, must be fairly substantial: family fortunes and their income must be large enough to give significant social power to those who own and preside over them. Furthermore, it is preferable that the property be based on land. If this is so, then the family, by virtue of its control over a discrete territorial area, can establish personal relationships of authority with its tenants: mutual obligations of master and servant, even lord and vassal, can take firm root. If a society's territory is divided into hereditary and propertied domains, then each citizen will learn to accept authority which is visible and close at hand. Also, this means that families of property will have responsibility for legislative seats and ecclesiastical livings: politics and religion will fall into harmony with the patterns of property.

Only landed property can set up such straightforward lines of authority and control between employer and employee, priest and parishioner, legislator and constituent. These relationships, based as they are on landed tenure, are founded on historical patterns of status rather than on voluntary contracts. The limitations on property based on manufacturing or commercial ownership lie in its ephemeral character: the owner of a factory or a store cannot establish forms of control over his employees in the same way that the owner of land can. The "company town," owned by a single family, has been the closest modern approximation to traditional landed property, and that is all but a thing of the past in an age of labor mobility, industrial diversification, and corporate ownership. In addition, the ownership of a manufacturing enterprise can be a temporary and impersonal matter: companies are bought and sold with great ease; the public at large is admitted to partial or total ownership; few families are able for long to maintain managerial control over the firms their grandfathers once owned outright.

Nevertheless, there have been some interesting attempts to apply Burke's prescriptions to the corporation ownership and management of manufacturing property. The social control which property brings was admitted not only by Burke, but by contemporary executives who wish business to face up to its social responsibilities. A factory is not a feudal fief, but there are signs that "corporate communities" of today can come in many respects to resemble the landed status systems which Burke had in mind. Whether this will come to pass in any comprehensive way is something only the future can tell.[34] What is important to note is that society is passing through the age of economic individualism and entrepreneurial property: ownership and management are

---

[34] These ideas are stated and expanded by the late Russell Davenport in "The Greatest Opportunity on Earth," *Fortune*, October 1949, pp. 65 ff. Also see William H. Whyte, Jr., *The Organization Man* (New York: Simon and Schuster, 1956) and Andrew Hacker, *Politics and the Corporation* (New York: Fund for the Republic, 1958).

now divorced; large, impersonal corporations now hold the great weight of propertied power. Neither the family patriarch nor the autonomous entre-preneur are the major figures on the modern scene. With the advent of large national corporations, as yet imperfectly understood institutions, modern so-cieties may be seeing the revival of conditions for a society not unlike those which Burke called for in an earlier time.

If property is the institution which creates the social power of a responsible ruling class, then there can be no loose talk of equalizing wealth. The man-in-the-street must be brought to understand that he benefits, albeit indirectly, from the existence of great fortunes in the hands of others. He is governed well because his governors have been schooled in the traditions of their class: a class which is prepared and fitted to assume responsibility for the welfare of society as a whole. Burke is therefore prepared to say that there should be a distinct gulf between the few who own property and the many who do not. And a concerted effort must be made to cloak with legitimacy the property of the few so that the many without it do not object to their underprivileged status.

The characteristic essence of property, formed out of the combined principles of its acquisition and conservation, is to be unequal. The great masses therefore which excite envy, and tempt rapacity, must be put out of the possibility of danger. Then they form a natural rampart about the lesser properties in all their gradations. The same quantity of property, which is by the natural course of things divided among many, has not the same operation. Its defensive power is weakened as it is diffused.

The body of the people must not find the principles of natural subordination by art rooted out of their minds. They must respect that property of which they cannot partake. They must labor to obtain what by labor can be obtained; and when they find, as they commonly do, the success disproportioned to the endeavor, they must be taught their consolation in the final proportions of eternal justice.

Of this consolation whoever deprives them, deadens their industry, and strikes at the root of all acquisition as of all conservation.[35]

The average citizen must be safeguarded from the impulses of his own rapacity: he must be taught to respect the property in which he cannot and should not share. And even if his own life of toil brings him but a small return, he must be persuaded that in another world lies eternal bliss.

These imperatives follow logically from Burke's previous discussion of social structure. A stratified society is founded on deference: the many must defer to the wealth, the eminence, and the power of the few. Deference is not consent in its express form: rather, it is the tacit product of custom and habit. Out of this custom and habit is derived the legitimacy of the ruling class: it embodies authority because men over time have become used to ascribing authority to it. The great political problem of a class society is how to maintain patterns of deference, and Burke's answer is that if a ruling class has substantial prop-

---

[35] *Reflections on the Revolution in France*, pp. 48, 240–241.

erty, it has the opportunity to shoulder and carry out great responsibilities. It can use its wealth, its power, and its leisure to rule wisely and virtuously. It can understand the expectations of those who are ranged beneath them, and it can exert every effort to satisfy their expressed and unexpressed needs. It can, in short, do the job it is supposed to do.

Yet, for all the good intentions a ruling class may have, it is always beset with difficulties: its members can degenerate in character and ability and fail to let in judicious numbers of new recruits; it can gratify its own desire and neglect those of the rest of society; it can divide into warring factions and upset the equilibrium of the social structure; or it can be faced with totally new problems—war, industrialization, nationalism—which, try as it will, it cannot solve. Some of these difficulties may be surmountable; others obviously are not. Romantic though Burke may at times appear, he shows a clear understanding of the institutions by which social control can be secured if it is going to be secured at all. Property, while by no means a perfect or the only instrument, does contain great potentialities for the perpetuation of a class society.

Religion. The irritations which surround human reason produce a gaping vacuum in men's lives. For the average man is unable to live by his intellect alone, and yet he strives for a certain knowledge of himself and the universe. When the reason of individuals proves inadequate to the task of providing the explanations men desire, religion steps in with answers for questions which were hitherto uncomprehended. The more one doubts the potentiality of man's reason, the more reliance one places on religion. It should be obvious that Burke, like the theologians, makes large provision for religion in his theory. It is important for both theory and practice: the conservative theorist uses religious doctrines to underpin his explanations of politics and society, and less sophisticated versions of these doctrines play a vital role in the lives of ordinary citizens and in the political process. In their attempts to give legitimacy to their deeds, both established regimes and movements which seek to attain power are prone to claim that they are fulfilling God's will in the world of politics.

Indeed, it is not infrequent that competing factions will both claim divine sanction: it is not uncommon, for example, to observe the old order invoking the doctrine of Natural Law to impart authority to its power, while potential usurpers call on Natural Rights to lend legitimacy to their claims. Which title is the real one? The answer, as always, is that authority lies in the eye of the beholder. If the two camps are appealing for support to the same constituency, then each individual must establish for himself the criterion on the basis of which he will ascribe legitimacy. At all events, it is plain that the invocation of religious authority has been considered one of the most effective devices for securing popular consent. From Plato to Machiavelli, and through to Rousseau and Burke, theorists have advised rulers to use religious explanations to pacify discontent and legitimize power.

This is possible, Burke says, because men are so constituted that they are always receptive to religious doctrines. One evidence of this is that despite the palpably self-interested use to which such doctrines have been put time and again by political movements, men continue to forget abuses and are ever ready to be persuaded by a new set of religious incantations. Religion, then, is not an alien or artificial intrusion. On the contrary, Burke says, men are by nature animals prepared for religious instruction:

> We know, and it is our pride to know that man is by his constitution a religious animal; that atheism is not only against our reason, but our instincts; and that it cannot long prevail. . . . We know, and what is better we feel inwardly, that religion is the basis of civil society, and the source of all good and of all comfort.[36]

Indeed, men need religion: were they to depend solely on the explanations they could derive from the power of their own minds, their lives would forever be filled with gnawing doubts and frustrating uncertainties. Furthermore, as will be seen, religion provides a solace for earthly grievances which, if left unexplained, might lead to grave social disorders.

Considering Burke's skeptical view of human reason and his emphasis on the need for authority, it is not surprising that he stresses the importance of religion. It is, he says, one of the two foundations on which the Western world stands:

> Nothing is more certain, than that our manners, our civilization, and all the good things which are connected with manners and civilization, have, in this European world of ours, depended for ages upon two principles; and were indeed the result of both combined; I mean the spirit of a gentleman, and the spirit of religion.[37]

The spirit of a gentleman—the civility inherent in a hereditary ruling class—has already been discussed. The spirit of religion not only helps to perpetuate the class which preserves the virtues of civility; it also serves as a means of control for society as a whole.

There can be no question that Burke's theory of society will deny the good things of life to many individuals. That these instances of personal injustice are necessary for the attainment of a higher social justice is, unfortunately, not always the most persuasive of arguments. The poor as well as the rich, the ambitious as well as the established, the frustrated as well as the satisfied must be taken into account. For those who have not done well within the system are

[36] Pp. 87–88.
[37] P. 76.

potential troublemakers. If these would-be rebels are to remain contented with their humble stations in life, they must be led to believe that worldly ambition is a misconceived goal and that material comforts, social prestige, and political power are but momentary gratifications in man's immortal journey through time.

It is especially in a class society that men must be taught to accept seeming injustice stoically, for the opportunity to rise in the social structure cannot be held out as a goal. Yet such a society may have all the conditions of poverty and frustration which make for violent social protest. And, ironically, it is the intricate patterns of privilege and responsibility which is found in a class society that can least stand questioning of this kind. The answer, to Burke, is the infusion of the religious spirit. If religion is the underpinning of public knowledge and belief, then its authority can be used to give legitimacy to apparently inequitable social arrangements. As an institution of social control, Burke says, one should never minimize the importance of religion:

It is the public ornament. It is the public consolation. It nourishes the public hope. The poorest man finds his own importance and dignity in it, while the wealth and pride of individuals of every moment makes the man of humble rank and fortune sensible of his inferiority, and degrades and vilifies his condition. It is for the man in humble life, and to raise his nature, and to put him in mind of a state in which the privileges of opulence will cease, when he will be equal by nature, and may be more than equal by virtue, that this portion of the general wealth of his country is employed and sanctified.[38]

Here, in sharp focus, is an example of Burke's rational approach to irrational behavior. He sees as clearly as anyone that the class society he has been prescribing cannot conceal from those in the lower orders the inferiority of their condition. The average man is well aware that his status is a vile and degraded one, and no rosy-hued "educational" campaigns can make him oblivious to the hunger or powerlessness he experiences as part of his everyday life. And his inferior condition is made all the more apparent to him because he can see with his own eyes the privileged way of life enjoyed by those born to more fortunate circumstances. Burke shuts his eyes to none of this: a consolation is needed, and religion can fill that role. This public ornament is designed, however, for "the man in humble life." Whether or not the intellectual Burke believes in God or an afterlife, he is prepared to utilize religious doctrines as a means of political and social control over those in society who might upset the established order in their attempt to secure redress for their very real grievances.

Does Burke expect the ruling class—a class whose existence is far from being a humble one—to hold their religious beliefs as unquestioningly as the man in

[38] P. 95.

the street? There is no easy answer for this question, for Burke nowhere ascribes to his ruling class the cold calculation that Machiavelli required of his governing elite. There will be some among a ruling class who understand that popular religion is being used for purposes of political expediency: these men will understand what is happening, and they will acknowledge, perhaps regretfully, the need for such a program of control. However, it seems probable that most members of the ruling class will be devout worshippers, and, although they may not need a consolation to the same degree that their inferiors do, they will believe in God because, like all mortals high and low, they harbor doubts and uncertainties which cry out for answers.

Prejudice. In addition to developing habits and customs, a society creates over time a mythology about itself, its inhabitants, and the world. These myths may be religious in character—but they are also likely to be racial, or even economic or political in content. Every society has its myths, and every society to some extent lives by them. A myth is not pure fantasy: it always has some basis in historical or contemporary fact. But it is enough of a distortion of reality to cause concern to those rational individuals who would have their fellow men live by reason alone. Burke, as we have seen, finds himself at odds with theorists and practitioners who celebrate human reason. All the more serious, therefore, is the criticism he levels at those who would reconstruct society so as to exorcise the myths and illusions which have grown up over time. Here again Burke is trying to be rational about the irrational. Myths may not be rational in their content, but the functions they serve are themselves both rational and important.

It is with this idea in mind that Burke indicts men who would attempt to put their theory of human reason into social and political practice. Such rational reformers will inevitably produce consequences more harmful than the doubtful good they are intending.

> All the pleasing illusions, which made power gentle and obedience liberal, which harmonized the different shades of life, and which, by a bland assimilation, incorporated into politics the sentiments which beautify and soften private society, are to be dissolved by this new conquering empire of light and reason. All the decent drapery of life is to be rudely torn off. All the superadded ideas, furnished from the wardrobe of a moral imagination, which the heart owns, and the understanding ratifies, as necessary to cover the defects of our naked, shivering nature, and to raise it to dignity in our own estimation, are to be exploded as a ridiculous, absurd, and antiquated fashion.[39]

It is plainly irresponsible to wipe out men's illusions in the name of abstract reason if it is obvious that most men are not capable of living up to the rational standard which the reformers set for them. And even if they were capable of

[39] P. 74.

this, they would still search for security and a sense of identity which only their myths can give them. Men must submit to power, yet their illusions of political authority can compensate their egos so that the impact of power is softened. Men must accept their class status, yet illusions of the social responsibilities of their betters can rationalize for them their lowly station in life. And, through a variety of kindred myths, the harsh outlines of the political process can be assimilated to the habits and customs of social life. Burke mistrusts reason not because he is an obscurantist, but because he senses that what passes for reason in some quarters is itself a distortion of reality—and an unhealthy one at that. The men of reason single out one small element in the human character and exaggerate its role out of all proportion. At the same time, they neglect the basic needs of men: needs which, though themselves capable of rational analysis, can only be satisfied through irrational instructions.

Burke's own summary of his position is worth reading in its entirety:

> I am bold enough to confess, that we are generally men of untaught feelings; that instead of casting away all our old prejudices, we cherish them to a very considerable degree, and, to take more shame to ourselves, we cherish them because they are prejudices; and the longer they have lasted, and the more generally they have prevailed, the more we cherish them. We are afraid to put men to live and trade each on his own private stock of reason; because we suspect that this stock in each man is small, and that the individuals would do better to avail themselves of the general bank and capital of nations and of ages.
>
> Many of our men of speculation, instead of exploding general prejudices, employ their sagacity to discover the latent wisdom which prevails in them. If they find what they seek, and they seldom fail, they think it more wise to continue the prejudice, with the reason involved, than to cut away the coat of prejudice, and to leave nothing but the naked reason; because prejudice, with its reason, has a motive to give action to that reason, and an affection which will give it permanence.
>
> Prejudice is of ready application in the emergency; it previously engages the mind in a steady course of wisdom and virtue, and does not leave the man hesitating in the moment of decision, skeptical, puzzled, and unresolved. Prejudices render a man's virtue his habit; and not a series of unconnected acts. Through just prejudice, his duty becomes a part of his nature.[40]

It would be well to be clear on the fact that Burke uses the term "prejudice" in a far more general sense than is now commonly employed. An anti-Semitic mentality or a white-supremacy outlook constitutes a very narrow application of this idea. These uses of prejudice, furthermore, can tend to divide a community more than they unite it: while a society may achieve a temporary solidarity by persecuting Jews or discriminating against Negroes, these scapegoating exercises are divisive in character, and the psychological tensions they create are greater than the unity they achieve. Prejudice, in Burke's terms, is the whole accumulation of untaught sentiments which resides in every mem-

[40] P. 84.

ber of a society. No educational curriculum, no matter how skillfully devised; no program of propaganda or indoctrination, no matter how cleverly managed —none of these can be sufficient substitutes for the way in which birth, growth, and experience in a society instills in men attitudes and motivations which shape their minds and direct their behavior. Men only dimly understand and seldom analyze their love of country, pride in nationality, reverence for tradition, and respect for religion. Formal education may supply supportive materials, but men can take their share of the bank and capital a society has acquired over time only by living and learning.

Prejudice, then, is a social product: the growth of many years and the unrecounted experience of mankind. Life in society passes on to each inhabitant a pattern of prejudices which he neither willed to learn nor can will to discard. Prejudice, furthermore, is a spur to action: it is a force within each person which impels him to translate his feelings into behavior. When Burke says that prejudice has a motive to give action to reason, he means that deeply felt sentiments will, in a real sense, move a man's body in ways that rational thought cannot. The man of contemplation may or may not force his reason to the conclusion that a war is a just one, that the enemy should be defeated. The man of prejudice, spurred on by love of country and hatred of tyranny will rush out to slaughter his nation's foes. All of us are, to some degree, men of both contemplation and prejudice. But it is the latter role, Burke says, which produces action when action is most needed. To know the good is not sufficient when to do the good is what national survival requires.

As an institution of social control, prejudice subsumes both property and religion. If employed with skill, it can be either a stimulus to action or a force for inertia. But, above this, it leads men to defer and to obey. Prejudice, if it is to be put to significant use, must be in the social or national interest: it cannot turn servant against master or citizens against their rulers. It is, clearly, a dangerous tool: one as likely to abuse as to salutary use. This, once more, is why Burke is not willing to allow the play of prejudice to chance: within the ruling class there must be some who understand the force of prejudice as it operates in men and who know how to channel it in directions which are constructive. They must know the myths and illusions which have power; they must not employ symbols for one end if they are geared to serve another.

And, as was the case with religion, we must not ascribe Machiavellian qualities to Burke's ruling class: it will suffice to say that it cannot be totally oblivious to the sources of its power.[41] And if prejudice consists of untaught feel-

---

[41] Conditioning need not be manipulative. The transmission of prejudice can be achieved without premeditation or cynicism on the part of the conditioners. "In the older systems both the kind of man the teachers wished to produce and their motives for pro-

ings, its political aspect is that of unreflecting consent. There is no Bill of Rights in Burke's society: freedoms of expression are neither constitutionally protected nor socially encouraged. Too much public talk, too much discussion of political affairs, can only be harmful. "It has been the misfortune . . . of this age," Burke says, "that everything is to be discussed, as if the constitution of our country were to be always a subject rather of altercation than enjoyment." [42] Discussion can unsettle prejudices and rob them of their motive power. If men are to obey established authority, then new ideas must be given a rather frosty welcome. Burke does not pursue this theme, and it is clear that he is not prepared to push it too far. Much of what he says is in reaction to the radical liberals and democrats who see a positive virtue in having everything discussed.

For all his talk of social control, Burke never mentions specific controllers. There are none of Plato's Guardians, and not even a Hobbesian Sovereign. The ruling class has the responsibility of perpetuating its own power and preserving freedom and social order. Yet Burke offers no Machiavellian advice to members of that class; nor, on the other hand, does he imply that there exists an invisible hand which will infuse the ruling class and its property with legitimacy or will promote religion and prejudice. Visible hands must work at this job; but too much conscious or premeditated intervention may do violence to the natural and orderly development of society. The problem is to devise a balance whereby natural forces and political power will share responsibility for social and political control. Burke is too realistic to adopt Plato's Utopian scheme and too distrustful of man's reason to be fully Machiavellian. He does not ascribe to the members of the ruling class individual talents or aptitudes which are superior to those possessed by the rest of society: what he does say is that their secure status enables them to act virtuously and responsibly and to take the long-term view of the political good.

Burke recognizes the need for political power: he neither conceals it nor seeks somehow to do away with it. His chief concern is with philosophical ends rather than political means: while power is important, its exercise is not central to his theory in the way that it is to Machiavelli, Hobbes, and Marx. Burke's main interest, rather, is in the establishment and perpetuation of a free society.

---

ducing him were prescribed by . . . a norm to which the teachers themselves were subject and from which they claimed no liberty to depart. They did not cut men to some pattern they had chosen. They handed on what they had received: they initiated the young neophyte into the mystery of humanity which overarched him and them alike. It was but old birds teaching young birds to fly." C. S. Lewis, The Abolition of Man (London: Bles, 1947), p. 43.

[42] Reflections on the Revolution in France, p. 88.

FREEDOM AND CIVILITY

Burke's conception of freedom departs from the liberal and democratic views: the former outlook defines freedom in terms of the rights of the individual; the latter emphasizes the participation of all men in the process of self-government. For Burke, however, freedom is neither individual nor political so much as it is social and historic. It is a condition which develops over the passage of time and is always to be discovered in the fabric of society: freedom is "an entailed inheritance derived to us from our forefathers, and to be transmitted to our posterity." [43] What this means is that most societies probably already have in their possession all the freedoms they require for the good life. In reply to those who champion the rights of man and the continual struggle for freedom, Burke answers that there is more to be lost than to be gained.

> I was indeed aware, that a jealous, ever-waking vigilance, to guard the treasure of our liberty, not only from invasion, but from decay and corruption, was our best wisdom, and our first duty. However, I considered that treasure rather as a possession to be secured, than as a price to be contended for. I did not discern how the present time came to be so very favorable to all *exertions* in the cause of freedom. [44]

If there is a problem concerning freedom, it centers or how to conserve what we already have; it does not involve the discovery or creation of new freedoms for new people. Only those freedoms which have been tested by time and have thereby demonstrated their lasting utility can be recognized as meaningful. And these, of course, are the freedoms which a society already possesses: they are not the hypothetical liberties which some men claim are needed for a happier future. Such claims should be regarded with skepticism: the language of freedom rolls easily off irresponsible tongues. It is best to presume that a society which has slowly adjusted its institutions to new conditions through history is one which has been developing in harmony with the natural order of the universe. Burke's conception of freedom should be viewed in the context of history and social development:

> By a constitutional policy working after the pattern of nature, we receive, we hold, we transmit our government and our privileges, in the same manner in which we enjoy and transmit our property and our lives. The institutions of policy, the goods of fortune, the gifts of providence, are handed down to us, and from us, in the same course and order. Our political system is placed in a just correspondence and symmetry with the order of the world, and with the mode of existence decreed to a permanent body composed of transitory parts; wherein, by the disposition of a stupendous wisdom, molding together the great mysterious incorporation of the human race, the whole, at one time, is never old, or middle-aged, or

[43] P. 31.
[44] P. 51.

young, but, in a condition of unchangeable constancy, moves on through the varied tenor of perpetual decay, fall, renovation, and progression.[45]

Burke's description of society, it would appear, is virtually immune to criticism. How can one propose to reform a body which is in a just correspondence and symmetry with the order of the world? How can one speak of injustice in a system produced by a stupendous wisdom molding together the great mysterious incorporation of the human race? What use are human programs for improvement when society of its own power will move from decay and fall to renovation and progression? The freedoms of society grow as society itself grows: they are natural developments, not the artifacts of men. The great task for lovers of freedom is to preserve that which they have: their great enemy lies in the spirit of innovation in our midst which would destroy our inheritance and thrust on men purported liberties which they do not need and do not know how to use.

The tragedy of the modern age is that the freedoms which only a few are capable of handling have been indiscriminately bestowed on all men. The language of liberty has been made a vulgar one: the prudence and virtue which must accompany liberty if it is to be made lasting and meaningful have been jettisonned in order that freedom may be made palatable to a wider constituency.

In some people I see great liberty indeed; in many, if not in the most, an oppressive, degrading servitude. But what is liberty without wisdom, and without virtue? It is the greatest of all possible evils; for it is folly, vice, and madness, without tuition or restraint. Those who know what virtuous liberty is, cannot bear to see it disgraced by incapable heads, on account of their having high-sounding words in their mouths.[46]

The task is not to give new—or even the traditional—freedoms to new men. They will not accept the concomitant responsibilities which must accompany them, nor do they possess the qualities of character which puts the exercise of freedom at the service of the common good. Those who talk of freedom for all will bring oppression, degradation, and servitude on the social order: talk of Natural Rights and self-government is, in the final analysis, irresponsible. Instead of speaking of freedom for men, we should concentrate on its precondition, free government.

It is wrong to think that a society of liberated citizens will automatically produce, as an arithmetic sum, a free government. This is to regard freedom wholly in terms of the removal of restraints, and such an idea can only be self-defeating. "To form a free government; that is, to temper together these op-

[45] Pp. 31–32.
[46] P. 241.

posite elements of liberty and restraint in one consistent work," Burke says, "requires much thought, deep reflection, a sagacious, powerful, and combining mind." [47] Real freedom has as much to do with restraint as it does with liberation: it calls for the vesting of power and authority in a ruling class which can impose restraints and ration freedoms in harmony with the needs of society. A free government and a democratic government, therefore, are not synonymous. In a democracy leaders must be expressly responsive to the demands of the governed: to keep their power they must satisfy short-term claims even at the price of long-term disaster. A democracy cannot, if it is to be truly democratic, produce a prudent and virtuous freedom. "When the leaders choose to make themselves bidders at an auction of popularity . . ." Burke says, "they will become flatterers instead of legislators; the instruments, not the guides, of the people." [48] If society is to be free, then the man-in-the-street needs strong leadership. This leadership should, of course, respond to the elemental needs of ordinary citizens, but it must be secure enough to be able to ignore the capricious demands—demands often voiced in the language of rights and liberty—of the people. This is why a ruling class, buttressed by powerful social controls, is required for a free society.

The freedoms of which Burke writes are clearly not the freedoms of speech, press, or assembly; nor are they freedom from arbitrary exercise of power by the government. Burke's major concern is the survival of a society whose chief attribute is its civility. In its passage through history, society has developed the features of civilization and culture which more and more distinguish men from the lower animals. The creators and carriers of civility have always been a minority: they are the ones who create the institutions and the style of life which, in time, is transmitted downward to all members of society. The members of this minority are the benefactors of every individual. Whether they be artists or men of letters, scientists or creators of wealth, statesmen or philosophers—this is the group which gives a society its freedom. It provides our material comforts, uplifts our understanding, and advances our tastes.

If all men are to be free, then this minority must be protected and encouraged. Its best shield is a secure ruling class; and the carriers of civilization, the creators of freedom, are in dire need of such a shield. For the average man does not understand or appreciate the benefits of a free society which will ultimately accrue to him: the freedoms of which his grandchildren will one day partake are now incomprehensible to his narrow and unimaginative mind. The tendency of a democracy is to discourage—and even oppress—this important minority. "In a democracy, the majority of the citizens is capable of exercising the most cruel oppressions upon the minority . . ." Burke says, "and

[47] P. 242.
[48] Ibid.

that oppression of the minority will extend to far greater numbers, and will be carried on with much greater fury, than can almost ever be apprehended from the dominion of a single sceptre." [49]

The solution can only be to withhold political and social power from the majority today, in order that the whole society gain tomorrow. This means that freedom should be the province only of those who belong to the ruling class or who merit protection by that class. This minority is capable of using its freedom in a creative way; and, for this reason, it is all the more susceptible to popular oppression unless it is shielded by political power. Burke, therefore, can only discuss freedom in the context of a class society: to speak of reconciling democracy to civility is to ignore the experience of history and the nature of man.

Burke's political theory uses as its model a society which is old and established. A nation which has but recently come into existence, or one in the process of accelerated social change, is poorly suited to follow the precepts Burke lays down. Except for a few sheltered corners of the globe, hardly any societies have experienced—or will in the future experience—the luxury of gradual and cautious development. Burke's prescriptions are not meant for a recently emancipated colony in Africa or an Asian nation undergoing the tremors of sudden industrialization. The importance of his theory, then, lies in its values: the principles of tradition and authority, class and civility, are enduring and of wide application. Even in an age characterized by democracy and industrialization Burke's ideas are recurrent. While old ruling classes may be replaced by new elites, it is interesting to note how these elites strive to achieve the qualities of the class they have supplanted. Even the commissars of a Soviet state eventually begin to talk of history, stability, and tradition, and they seek to perpetuate the social order through their property and children.

This translation of Burke's ideas in the modern world must not be strained, and it is futile to ask if Burke would "approve" of the new uses of his old principles. Nevertheless, there is a conservatism in the world we now know: it subsists in a new social and political environment, and its values are bound to wear a new face. The best place to examine the compromises and tensions of modern conservatism is in the writings of Alexis de Tocqueville, for he confronts Burke's principles with the fact of a democratic society in a new nation.

POETRY AND POLITICS

Burke talked at one time of an experimental science of politics, but it soon became apparent that his conceptions of science and experimentation were closer to the thinking of St. Thomas than they were to that of Machiavelli.

[49] Pp. 121–122.

Burke's science is deductive, and its experiments take place in the great laboratory of human history. Indeed, it is not science but rather poetry which best describes his method; not the measuring stick, but rather the metaphor is the means of communication on which he relies.

"Your literary men and your politicians," he says, "are in no sort of fear with regard to the duration of a building run up in haste." A country's constitution, in this instance a bad constitution, is seen as a poorly constructed house. "We have taken care," he says, "not to inoculate any scion alien to the nature of the original plant." Another constitution, this time a good one, is described as a flower or a tree. Burke does not mean that a constitution is actually a building or a plant. Nor is he simply suggesting that it might be fruitful to compare a constitution with these objects. Metaphors are used when the thing or the relationship which a writer wishes to describe is so abstract or complex that ordinary descriptive language will not achieve the desired communication.[50] Metaphors are often able to conjure up in our minds the image of a concrete object or a dynamic process which is familiar to us. All of us can create for ourselves a mental picture of a jerry-built tenement. We would have difficulty, however, in imagining so complex a thing as a constitution: we have neither the specialized knowledge nor the perceptive powers to understand what one is or how it works. Burke might use all the prosaic words in the world in an attempt to describe a constitution, and yet in the end we might still have no coherent idea of what he was trying to get across to us. The alternative he chooses is to take things we are already capable of imagining— such as buildings and plants—and show us through the use of metaphors how a vague thing like a constitution has much in common with the everyday things we have experienced.

The problem which needs to be solved is one of communication from mind to mind: how the abstract ideas in Burke's head are to be transmitted to the heads of his readers. There are dangers in the poetic approach. The image of "a building run up in haste" may not depict for us what it does for Burke. Many urban tenements, for example, look quite solidly put together from an external view, yet Burke's concern may not be so much with outward appearances as with hidden flaws. If the writer's and the reader's experience of building construction differ, then the metaphor may fail to serve its intended purpose. In fact, it may backfire. The person who wishes to convey his idea by

---

[50] "Metaphors must thus be viewed as expressing the vague and confused but primal perception of identity, which subsequent processes of discrimination transform into a conscious and expressed analogy between different things, and which further reflection transforms into the clear assertion of an identity or common element (or relation) which the two different things possess." Morris R. Cohen and Ernest Nagel, *An Introduction to Logic and Scientific Method* (New York: Harcourt, Brace, 1934), p. 369.

quoting the proverb, "A rolling stone gathers no moss," may be assuming too much: do or do not his listeners believe that a stone ought to be covered with moss? Despite these difficulties, theorists are compelled to rely on metaphors. Poetry cannot claim to be precise communication, but it can be effective communication when the subject matter is too abstract or complex to be described by ordinary prose.

There will always be poetry. The question is whether or not there is a place for it in political theory. If Burke sees it as a solution to the problem of communication, other theorists have other answers. Jeremy Bentham, whose writings will be considered in the next chapter, suggests that a quantitative approach will be both precise and effective. Whether mathematics constitutes an advance on metaphor is a question all students of politics ought to ponder.

10.
Jeremy Bentham

THE MAN AND HIS TIMES

Bentham was born in 1748, the son of a well-to-do London lawyer. He began life with two initial advantages: a fine mind and the prospect of a private income. Evidence of his mental qualities emerged when he was reading Latin at the age of four. His formal education at the Westminster School and Oxford University had little influence on him, as he was by that time developing ideas of his own. He prepared for the bar, but possession of financial means allowed him to pursue his personal interests. Bentham did not undertake a political career, but if he chose not to serve in Parliament, he nevertheless sought to influence those who did. His London home was an intellectual center, and his writings found an audience among people who mattered. For Bentham's voice was that of a new radicalism, and he was in tune with the political developments of his time. He died in 1832, shortly before the passage of the Reform Act which gave the franchise to the class to whom he had been addressing his ideas.

The industrialization of Europe, particularly in England, was giving rise to a middle class which was underrepresented in national politics. The commercial middle class which had preceded it had not the social or economic base from which to issue an effective challenge to the established order. Despite the Revolution of 1688 and subsequent constitutional reform, political power tended to gravitate back to the landed aristocrats who controlled not only the House of Lords but the House of Commons as well. However, the emerging entrepreneurs of industrial capitalism would not settle for being represented by someone else. The economy they sought to create required a new political outlook, and the traditional conception of a "balanced" constitution did not impress them. This industrial middle class, whatever its motives, was prepared to give voice to the rhetoric of democracy and to seek the support of the man-in-the-street. Burke might have deplored the rise of the ideology and interests of this new force in society, but he was attacking the machine age and the odds were against him. Bentham's political writings are not polemical, and on first reading it may appear that he is championing no cause at all. He was, nevertheless, the spokesman for a new approach to politics.

There are two emphases in Bentham's A Fragment on Government and The Principles of Morals and Legislation, which appeared in 1776 and 1789. The first is his preoccupation with the role of law in society. Earlier political writings had taken for granted a traditional social structure based on landed property, ascribed status, and hereditary monarchy. Industrialization, however, changes the character of property ownership and increases the tempo of social mobility. Such a transformation can only give rise to a demand for a government sympathetic to new conditions. The industrial entrepreneurs, in particular, wanted a free hand in producing goods and making money. At the same time, the power of government had to be used to ensure that contracts would be honored, and this required a uniform and predictable system of law. Bentham stressed the need for political institutions which would enact rational legislation adapted to the changing needs of the time. Politics, therefore, was not to be guided by an uncritical reverence for tradition but by the conscious will of reasonable men. The second emphasis in Bentham's writing is a positive view of public administration. If Burke railed against Whig blunders, Bentham sought the ways and means of governing a nation efficiently. He was an ardent proponent of penal reform, and the civil servants who were to concern themselves with municipal sanitation and factory regulation proudly styled themselves as "Benthamites." It is interesting to note that his theory was used both by entrepreneurs who sought freedom from regulation and by bureaucrats who were concerned with an efficient public service. Bentham's idea that law and administration can be instruments for bettering the human condition created a link between political theory and concrete political institutions. Bentham wrote as a technician in an age of technology. Yet it is not difficult to see that a human compassion and an enthusiasm for social progress are the forces behind his prescriptions for reform.

10.
Jeremy Bentham

With Jeremy Bentham's theory of utilitarianism emerges
an outline of the modern state. Like Machiavelli, Bentham is concerned with
the specific tasks which a government is called upon to perform. But, unlike
Machiavelli, his interest is in a government which will do its utmost to secure
the happiness of all its citizens, and not simply that of a privileged class or elite.
And Bentham, like Machiavelli, talks the language of a science of politics. But
whereas the "policy science" of Machiavelli had as its end the security of tenure
of rulers, Bentham's seeks to provide ways and means for maximizing the contentment of the whole society. In Bentham's theory, then, there is an interplay
between a science of government and the practice of politics. Good legislators
should be informed by the political and psychological precepts of utilitarian
theory. There is no place for philosopher-kings in Bentham's writings, but
there is a call for both intelligence and sophistication on the part of those who
will exercise political power.

THE QUANTITATIVE METHOD

The language of science is number, and its grammer is measurement. Scientists only communicate with each other if they use forms of expression which
are capable of conveying identical meanings to everyone. There is no need to
point out the vagueness and ambiguity of words, especially political words. If
precision is to be achieved in communication, then precise symbols have to be
employed. Whereas words like "democracy" and "freedom" mean all things
to all people, the symbols "4" and "376" are able to convey the same thing to
all persons. This explains why political scientists use the language of number as
frequently as they do; while the quantitative method can be overused or even
abused, it is nevertheless an important step in the direction of precise communication.

In the discussion of political theology in an earlier chapter it was indicated that there exists no small difference of opinion between the proponents of what might be called common sense, on the one hand, and those who adhere to inductive science on the other. In the eyes of many students a quantitative science of politics has yet to win its spurs: in the course of its researches it has yet to come up with findings which are either new or startling. The elaborate apparatus of number and measurement, it is claimed, has done little more than confirm the obvious. The scientists are quick to retort that students who have relied on common sense have been settling for too little. Many speculative insights have a brilliant ring when first enunciated, but all too many, when subjected to testing, have been shown to be dead wrong. If our concern is with truth, the scientists say, then hypotheses about behavior must be phrased in precise terms and be capable of systematic review.

This is not, however, the place to get embroiled in an abstract controversy over methodology: it would be better to select a single example and examine it in fairly specific terms.

Common-sense Method	*Quantitative Method*
"Most Voters Support the Same Political Party that Their Fathers Did."	"67.4 per cent of the Voters Support the Same Political Party that Their Fathers Did."

The common-sense approach postulates, quite simply, that an intelligent observer draws on his experience—both personal and vicarious—and then makes a judgment about behavior as he sees it. The quantitative method would appear, at first glance, to be a great advance on this. For what does the phrase "most voters" mean? It can signify anything from 50.1 per cent to 99.9 per cent. In most spheres of knowledge, vagueness like this would hardly be tolerated. If we are to increase our political understanding, then words and phrases like "most," "many," "by and large," and "tends to" must be discarded. The substitution to be hoped for is a quantitative one: 67.4 per cent has the virtue not only of truth but also of precision. This is not to say that the common-sense proposition is false: in this case it happens to be true.[1] The indictment of the "most voters . . ." proposition is simply that it is not good enough: the gap between 50.1 per cent and 99.9 per cent has to be filled in. Only the hard and systematic confrontation of the facts will lead us to the precise figure that tells us what we want to know.

[1] The layman's common sense is based on an experience—and an intelligence—which is often not broad enough to handle questions which are more complicated than they seem at first glance. Common sense might conclude, for example, that "Southern soldiers were better able to stand the climate in the hot South Seas islands than northern soldiers." But a study of the facts showed that just the opposite was the case. For this and other examples, see Paul Lazarsfeld, "*The American Soldier*—An Expository Review," *Public Opinion Quarterly*, Fall 1949, p. 380.

How was the 67.4 per cent arrived at? This is a long story, and only its outlines can be given here. In order to conduct a study of voting behavior, a group of researchers selected the upstate town of Elmira, New York, as their point of focus. This city has a population of approximately 52,000. The 67.4 per cent, then, refers only to the voters of Elmira, New York. The study was done in connection with the 1948 presidential election: the 67.4 per cent, therefore, tells us about party affiliations as they stood in that year. Out of the total population of the town, interviews were conducted with a sample of 1,000 voters: the 67.4 per cent, it appears, is computed on the basis of 2 per cent of Elmira's residents. And of the 1,000 in the sample, only 792 were able to identify the partisan preferences of their fathers and were at the same time willing to express their own to an interviewer. The 67.4 per cent, in the final analysis, is a report on 366 Elmira Republicans and 426 Elmira Democrats who were interviewed in 1948. And out of this sample, 304 Republicans and 230 Democrats said that they were following in their fathers' political footsteps.[2]

The objections which come to mind are many and immediate. Elmira, New York, is not the whole of the voting world, and it is probably not even representative of that universe. The year 1948 is but one moment of recent history. A 2 per cent sample, no matter how skillfully it may have been drawn, is still only a sample. What people tell strange interviewers and what they really have in mind may be totally different. The list of protests could be extended for many pages. The main point, however, is that the figure of 67.4 per cent obtains its precision from the fact that the research which produced it was limited to a time and space-bound sample. Nevertheless, it is impossible to interview over sixty million American voters. In all cases where there are no public records giving official information on all members of a community, it is necessary to employ a sample. When voters register, they are not asked for their fathers' political affiliations: if we want this data, it is necessary to put the question directly to a selected group of citizens. The researchers who conducted the Elmira study are not unaware of the difficulties inherent in the methods they employed. However, they would say that it is far better to have a figure like 67.4 per cent derived from an interviewed sample than to have nothing at all.

---

[2] Bernard R. Berelson, *et al.*, *Voting: A Study of Opinion Formation in a Presidential Campaign* (Chicago: University of Chicago Press, 1954). The figures cited here are from pp. 6, 89, and 381. The illustrative figure of 67.4 per cent is not stated explicitly in the book, but it can be derived from Chart 37 on p. 89 if the responses for both parties are combined. *Voting*, it should be said, is an important and sophisticated book; and it is a major contribution to recent political science. If it is playing the part of a straw man here, it nevertheless deserves respectful attention from all students of politics.

The quantitative approach never ends with a single study: indeed, a piece of research is a beginning rather than a climax. The figure of 67.4 per cent is neither permanent nor sacrosanct. The search is for true knowledge: to discover how many people, in this case, vote as their fathers did. And knowledge here refers not to one town or one year, but to a generalized proposition about "hereditary" voting. The quest for scientific truth, then, is a never-ending one. And in actual practice "truth" is defined in terms of what one's competent colleagues will agree to as being true. The Elmira researchers, for example, published their findings: they indicated how they designed and carried out their study, and they then presented the data which they obtained. Before the ink is dry, the entire fraternity of political scientists have jumped on such a study like a pack of ravenous wolves. Why, for example, was the town of Elmira especially chosen? Why the year 1948? How was the sample selected? How competent were the interviewers? These and a score of other questions are fired: and the original researchers try their best to show that their findings are valid—that it is legitimate to generalize from one time and one place, that the sample is a good one, that the interviewers were well trained and competently supervised. Through this public dialogue—in book reviews, articles, professional meetings, seminars—both researchers and critics educate each other. And from this mutual education emerges scientific truth. Science, then, is social. Only through discussion and public criticism can scholars come closer to agreement on what is actually true.[3] The theorist who relies on his intuition, on his common sense, has no means of showing his colleagues how he came to his conclusions or why they have a claim to being accepted as valid. Some of his fellow scholars may share the general direction of his thinking, but he has no method they can test and no findings which are susceptible of verification. Scientific truth, then, is decided by a "majority vote." The electorate, to be sure, consists of a limited and highly trained group of individuals who are competent to judge the work in their field. Through the process of constant experimentation and self-criticism, a body of agreed-upon truth is determined,

[3] "Among other things, science must have, at its core, a publicly agreed body of knowledge. It is thus a social and cultural phenomenon, depending on the existence of institutional means for the free expression of opinion and criticism. An alchemist, a magician, or a witch-doctor may use the most dispassionate observational technique but is bound to keep his researches secret: a scholar or a scientist must publish his results, however inaccurate they may be. . . . Thus, 'writing-up' one's work is not just a chore to be done after the experiments are completed, but is a vital part of the research. Sometimes the only way to decide what one has really discovered is to write a paper, give a lecture, or otherwise persuade a critical audience of its significance." John Zinman, "What is Science About?" *The New Statesman*, August 8, 1959, p. 168. Also: "Objectivity is closely bound up with the social aspect of scientific method, with the fact that science and scientific objectivity do not and cannot result from the attempts of an individual scientist to be 'objective,' but from the cooperation of many scientists." Karl Popper, *The Open Society and Its Enemies* (London: George Routledge, 1945), Vol. 2, p. 205.

modified, and enlarged. Can the presumably competent majority be wrong? It can, but it will not be wrong for long. Scientists, no less than other men, develop vested interests in established approaches to work and in their perceptions of reality. A majority of men deemed competent may not be able to understand a radical breakthrough which occurs in their own time: a new theory may be called unsound, or even crackpot, and its creator will be a voice in the wilderness. However, if the new facts are really facts, then the majority will eventually have to acknowledge the validity of the new theory. The problem of how to treat new departures is a recurrent one in science: tolerance and skepticism must find a balance if the wheat is to be winnowed from the chaff without undue delay.

No attempt is being made here to compare the quantitative method in political science with those employed in the natural and physical sciences. Such comparisons are dangerous, and they can impose methodological steps without regard for the varying quality of the subject matter in the different sciences. For instance, it is one of the canons of the traditional sciences that reported experimental facts be capable of reproduction, that other scientists be able to go through the same paces and come out with identical findings. This is why such a premium is put on precise measurement and on painstaking description of methods.[4] But in political science there is no experimentation in the controlled sense, and it is impossible to reproduce a study in any exact manner. The good people of Elmira, for example, cannot be locked in a laboratory so that forces extraneous to the study at hand will be held constant. This means that peculiar circumstances ranging from the level of humidity to the level of employment may have had an influence on the study's findings. And were a group of researchers in Michigan to attempt to test the Elmira facts by doing a similar survey in Saginaw, it is clear that even if they used the same techniques they would hardly be "reproducing" the original "experiment."

This limitation on a science of politics is not a fatal one. For the concern is

---

[4] "Experimental facts must be reproducible, or their discoverers will be called liars. Theories must be made logical, or their begetters will be called fools. A theological or ethical statement may be accepted or rejected according to taste or temperament; a recipe for making gold must work. But, if empirical knowledge depends on evidence, this is not always available in the perfect form of pointer readings, photographs, and mathematical calculations. Sometimes there are no eye-witnesses, as in cosmology and geology; sometimes we have only statistical inferences, as in economics; sometimes all the witnesses are tainted, as in politics and sociology. Thus, the methods of the sciences must be adapted to the object of study." John Zinman, *op. cit.* For a sophisticated and well-written discussion of the over-all use of logic and the scientific method in the study of society, see Ralph Ross and Ernest van den Haag, *The Fabric of Society* (New York: Harcourt, Brace, 1957), especially pp. 193–308. In introducing this chapter on Bentham, only those aspects of the scientific method directly relevant to utilitarianism have been discussed.

not with Elmira or Saginaw, but with the validity of a proposition about political behavior. The figure of 67.4 per cent is not validated by sending a new team of scholars into Elmira for a recheck: it is modified by new research which attempts to correct some of the difficulties in the previous work. Inspired by the Elmira study, therefore, a group at the University of Michigan conducted a nation-wide survey in 1952.

Elmira Study	Nation-wide Study
"67.4 per cent of the Voters Support the Same Political Party that Their Fathers Did."	"78.7 per cent of the Voters Support the Same Political Party that Their Parents Did."

The University of Michigan study, which interviewed voters in every state in the union, had a sample of over 2,000. Of these, 1,044 could identify their parents' affiliation and were also willing to express their own. In this case, 282 Republican voters had Republican parents and 540 Democrats had mothers and fathers who were Democrats.[5] That the Michigan survey phrased its question in terms of both parents, whereas the Elmira one asked only about fathers simply shows that researchers on a given project will decide themselves what they think is important. Actually, both surveys show that the number of "split" households are few in number, so it is probably safe to assume that in Elmira the fathers represented the mothers' affiliations as well. But this is just an instance of the vexing situation where, because of variations in the wording of questions, precise comparisons are made difficult.

Which is it to be: 67.4 per cent or 78.7 per cent? The answer, of course, is that the question should not be put in this way. Both figures are available for students of politics; both are tentative approaches to true knowledge in this area. The nation-wide study does not "refute" the Elmira survey, nor does it even replace it. Together they form part of the ever-growing body of quantitative data about political behavior. This information should be subjected to constant criticism and modification, for truth in political science never stands still and is always provisional. What the scientists are sure in their minds, however, is that either 67.4 per cent or 78.7 per cent is preferable to a vague statement like "most people. . . ."

The emphasis here has been not so much on the logic of the scientific method as on the discovery of true knowledge in the study of politics. One further comment may be made on this matter. Verifying a proposition, it has

[5] Angus Campbell, *et al.*, *The Voter Decides* (Evanston: Row, Peterson, 1954). The figures cited here are from pp. 99 and 230. The illustrative figure of 78.7 per cent is not stated explicitly in the book, but it can be derived from Chart 7.5 on p. 99 if the responses for both parties are combined. This book, needless to say, ranks with *Voting* in the literature of political science. The data from *Voting* were available to the authors of *The Voter Decides* even though the two books were published in the same year.

been said, is a matter of convincing one's colleagues that a particular generalization is true. There is a difference between demonstrating that a theory is true and showing that a theory works. And this distinction is crucial to politics, for in that area effectiveness often tends to be confused with truth.

An example may be taken from the no man's land between the natural and social sciences: psychoanalysis. There is a great body of psychoanalytic theory: systematic explanations of human behavior devised by thinkers such as Freud, Jung, Adler, Rank, Horney, and Sullivan. These theories offer plausible reasons why individuals behave as they do, and not a few political scientists have drawn on them in an attempt to better understand political behavior. But psychoanalytic theories are not intended as academic exercises. On the contrary, they were originated and continue to be used for clinical purposes. That is, a psychoanalyst's chief job is to cure mental disorders; it is not to create theoretical explanations for their own sake. A Freudian analyst will, in the course of treating a patient, suggest that his malfunctionings stem from Oedipal longings which unconsciously have been repressed. Before undergoing analysis, the patient did not know that he had an Oedipus Complex, and he certainly did not know that he was repressing important impulses. As a result of treatment, therefore, he learns just why he has been behaving as he has: he gains a theoretical understanding of his behavior, whereas before he had only a confused idea that something was wrong. Psychoanalysis, then, is a form of education. And upon acquiring this knowledge the patient begins to recover: his insights into his own functioning permit him to channel his drives in constructive directions. Through his own efforts and with the help of the analyst, he is now cured.

Does the fact that patients are cured through Freudian treatment serve to demonstrate the validity of the Freudian theory of the Oedipus Complex? The answer is that it does not. Cures show that Freudian explanations are effective: they do not show that the theory is true. This may be made clear by transposing to a similar situation. A native approaches his tribal witch doctor and complains of pains in his back. The doctor, after appropriate incantations, declares that his patient is possessed of an evil spirit. If he will sit on a riverbank by the full moon's light and recite the prescribed prayers, then the pains will disappear. The patient follows the witch doctor's instructions to the letter, and the pains do go away.[6] That primitive medicine and primitive

---

[6] For a discussion of psychoanalysis in primitive societies see Erik H. Erikson, *Childhood and Society* (New York: Norton, 1950). Richard Jenkins notes that a given patient might be presented with Freudian, Adlerian, or Rankian explanations as part of treatment, and any one of them would be successful. "I am convinced," he says, "that any one of these interpretations—and others as well—might be used therapeutically." "Research in Psychotherapy," *American Journal of Orthopsychiatry*, January 1948, p. 115.

psychoanalysis were often effective is an established fact. But does this mean that the theory about demons or evil spirits is true? The point, of course, is that it is the over-all situation which leads to cure: the psychosomatic basis of illness, the authority which the analyst has in the eyes of the patient, and the inherent plausibility of the theoretical explanation which is offered. The theory of the Oedipus Complex is plausible and its use in psychoanalysis is effective. But the fact that it works in effecting cures does not verify its truthfulness. Indeed, it is doubtful if a theory of human behavior such as Freud's can ever be verified to the satisfaction of most social scientists. They may applaud or decry the Freudian ethic, but then they are passing judgment on an ideological fact and not on a scientific theory.

In practical politics the focus is on the effective use of power rather than on the pursuit of academic truth. Yet with Bentham no less than Plato it is realized that men who would govern well must govern wisely. They must know the facts, and even if they do not understand why citizens behave as they do, they must be sophisticated enough to predict the consequences of policy and sensitive enough to assess the needs of the individuals and groups which comprise a society. Nevertheless, political wisdom may be a product of intuition more than theoretical understanding. An effective ruler who brings happiness to his citizens probably is not following a Theory of Felicity in his making of policy. There is the danger that students of politics will find validations for theories in instances where their supposed applications have been successful. In politics, as in psychoanalysis, power has its own logic. The man of power, as Thrasymachus suggested, can make his own truth by imposing conditions which appear to verify his assertions about reality. This is rather like the professor who put a flea on his desk and commanded it to jump. It jumped. He then pulled all the legs off the flea and once again told it to jump. It stood still. "And this," said the professor, "proves my theory that a flea's sense of hearing resides in its legs." All that is being suggested here is that particularly where power is involved—psychoanalysts over patients, rulers over citizens, professors over fleas—a student must be careful about questions of verification and truth.

There are, in effect, two realms: one is science, and the other is engineering. The first is the realm of the man who would understand; the second of the man who commands. These kingdoms do not always or necessarily overlap. The civil engineer may have to read the textbooks of theoretical physics, but the political practitioner does not have to read Machiavelli or Bentham. Both Machiavelli and Bentham have written theoretical explanations of political behavior and handbooks in political engineering. It may well be that a science of politics can exist only on the pages of a book—that when its precepts are put in practice, the impact of power vitiates all trace of scientific method or truth. This problem will recur as Bentham's theory is examined on the succeeding pages.

POLITICAL UNDERSTANDING AND POLITICAL REFORM

Like most theorists who have faith in the scientific approach and the inductive method, Bentham is a thoroughgoing optimist. "The age we live in is a busy age; in which knowledge is rapidly advancing towards perfection," he says. "In the natural world, in particular, everything teems with discovery and with improvement." [7] Through the disciplines of the natural and physical sciences men have come to understand themselves and the universe to a far greater degree than existed in any previous age. Bentham therefore proposes to create a science of politics: in particular a science of legislation. But what is to be the purpose of such a science? For it is important to know whether it is to be a "pure" science, whose only aim is to help us understand the behavior of lawmakers, or whether it is to be "applied" science, precepts on the ways and means of framing effective laws.

"Correspondent to discovery and improvement in the natural world," Bentham says, "is reformation in the moral." [8] Yet discovery and improvement are two separate processes: the first is a matter for political science, the second a matter for political engineering. Through his causal linkage of the two, Bentham makes it quite clear that he will be as much interested in reforming society as he will in understanding it. Furthermore, laws which are based on scientific principles will, in the final analysis, be more effective than those which are not. To secure this practical end, Bentham undertook to create a science of human behavior. For too long a time, he says, theorists have concerned themselves with the logic of political ideas. But men are more creatures of behavior than they are creatures of reason: a political logic, therefore, should concentrate on man's propensity to act. "There is, or rather there ought to be, a logic of the will, as well as of the understanding," Bentham says. "The operations of the former faculty are neither less unsusceptible nor less worthy than those of the latter of being delineated by rules." [9]

The traditional role of logic has been to set standards for clear and consistent thinking. It is Bentham's aim to move from the logic of ideas to the

[7] *A Fragment on Government,* in *A Fragment on Government and The Principles of Morals and Legislation* (Oxford: Blackwell, 1948), edited by Wilfrid Harrison, p. 3.
[8] *Ibid.*
[9] *The Principles of Morals and Legislation* in *op. cit.,* p. 123.

logic of behavior. The latter he calls the "logic of the will," and its most important part is the science of legislation.

The science of law . . . is, to the art of legislation, what the science of anatomy is to the art of medicine: with this difference, that the subject of it is what the artist has to work with, instead of being what he has to operate upon.[10]

To the distinctions previously made—science vs. engineering, pure science vs. applied science, discovery vs. improvement—is now added that of science vs. art. While the terms change, the essential meaning remains the same. And it is important to introduce the distinction between the clinical and the political arts. The physician, in the operating room at least, has complete control over the body of his patient: in this environment he can have a free hand to work such improvements as he sees fit. The legislator, on the other hand, can never put the body politic under anaesthetic and thus be at liberty to introduce whatever reforms he likes. Political engineering, then, must put up with limitations brought about by a refractory subject matter. Once again, the strictures laid down by Machiavelli are relevant. Bentham's science is to be a pure science; however, its goal is not understanding as an end in itself, but rather the creation of principles which can be applied in the form of laws. These principles, in sum, will be both true and effective.

What has beclouded the study of political and legal science up to this time is the habit of moralizing. Theorists seem unable to do one thing at one time. All theory, to be sure, has elements of science and elements of philosophy in it. However, description and prescription should be dealt with in separate places, and the propositions of each sort should be clearly labeled as such. The terms Bentham uses are "exposition," on the one hand, and "censorship," on the other.

There are two characters, one or other of which every man who finds anything to say on the subject of Law, may be said to take upon him;—that of the Expositor, and that of the Censor. To the province of the Expositor it belongs to explain to us what, as he supposes, the Law is: to that of the Censor, to observe to us what he thinks it ought to be. The former, therefore, is principally occupied in stating, or in enquiring after facts: the latter, in discussing reasons. . . . To the Expositor it belongs to show what the Legislator and his underworkman the Judge have done already: to the Censor it belongs to suggest what the Legislator ought to do in the future. To the Censor, in short, it belongs to teach that science, which when by change of hands converted into an art, the Legislator practices.[11]

Bentham is at least expressing the explicit intention of keeping the roles of expositor and censor separate and distinct. He is the first political theorist to

[10] *Ibid.*
[11] *Fragment*, pp. 7–8.

show so great a concern for this divorcement, and his care in the matter is inspired by his interest in scientific accuracy. The theory which thoughtlessly blends description and prescription does great harm to the descriptive part. If a writer is much exercised over how the world ought to be, then he will tend to paint his picture of what is in emotional colors. The radical theorist's radicalism will depict a world marked by inequality and injustice; the conservative theorist's conservatism will show a world of proved institutions and established customs. The descriptions given by philosophers and ideologues are tainted: indeed, such theorists are so occupied with moralizing that there is a suspicion that they have not done their empirical homework.

Bentham spares little irony in his reference to the ignorance of most political philosophers: "No wonder then, in a treatise partly of the expository class, and partly of the censorial, that if the latter department is filled with imbecility, symptoms of kindred weakness should characterize the former." [12] Bentham fully intends to be a moralist: he has already said that his aim is to reform the methods and substance of legislation. However, such prescriptions as he offers will be firmly grounded on a sophisticated description of human behavior. In fact, it is his aim to devise a science of ethics: a guide to right action can be developed through the use of the scientific method.

Most moral philosophies have not had such a foundation. "The various systems that have been formed concerning the standards of right and wrong . . ." he says, "consist all of them in so many contrivances for avoiding the obligation of appealing to any external standard, and for prevailing upon the reader to accept of the author's sentiment or opinion as a reason for itself." [13] There must be an objective measure if conduct is to be labeled good or bad: it is not sufficient for a theorist to draw on his intuition and then proclaim that he has discovered a "self-evident" proposition. Natural Law theories, for example, are at heart subjective. "A great multitude of people are continually talking of the Law of Nature," Bentham says, "and then they go on giving you their sentiments about what is right and what is wrong." [14] If the Natural Law is subjective rather than objective, then the burden lies on Bentham to devise a system which has the attributes of objectivity. And this he quite confidently turns to do.

A science of behavior must start, as Aristotle pointed out, with a scheme of classification. Until categories of analysis are established, the phenomenal world is an inchoate mass of things and relationships. This process Bentham calls "arrangement":

[12] *Ibid.*, p. 14.
[13] *Principles*, p. 140.
[14] *Ibid.*, p. 141n.

It is matter of arrangement to distribute the several real or supposed institutions into different masses, for the purpose of a general survey; to determine the order in which these masses shall be brought to view; and to find for each of them a name.[15]

The classification of data is an elementary first step in the scientific method. "To understand a thing," Bentham says, "is to be acquainted with its qualities or properties." [16] And the dangers inherent in this process were fully discussed in connection with Aristotle's theory: symmetrical and superfluous categories, reification, undifferentiated levels of analysis, and so forth. To avoid these logical and methodological pitfalls, the theorist cannot impose an artificial scheme of classification on objects which have a natural order.

Despite his harsh words about Natural Law theories, Bentham admits to the existence of something called "human nature." But if we are to rely on that which is natural to man, it is hoped that the discovery will be based more on empirical observation that on a priori reasoning.

That arrangement of the materials of any science may, I take it, be termed a natural one, which takes such properties to characterize them by, as men in general are, by the common constitution of man's nature, disposed to attend to: such, in other words, as naturally, that is readily, engage, and firmly fix the attention of any one to whom they are pointed out.[17]

Bentham is clearly seeking to strip his argument of any metaphysical overtones: the word "naturally" means no more than "readily." And the idea is that a scheme of classification should be such as to gain the ready agreement of any reasonable man. The science of behavior to be outlined is, at heart, a simple and straightforward one. It has no theological or historical apparatus underpinning it, and it does not depend on elaborate metaphors like the social contract or the state of nature. Indeed, the obvious character of the theory is all the more testimony of its essential truth. Not simply wise or virtuous men, but all individuals can see that Bentham's is the natural explanation of human behavior.

Institutions, action, and attitudes are broken down into their component parts so that they may be better understood. Bentham's *Principles of Morals and Legislation* is, in large measure, an essay in classification. His breakdown of classes and attributes is far greater than those of either Aristotle or Hobbes. Some examples of the kinds of things he classifies and the number of subgroups he creates are all that can be given:

[15] *Fragment*, p. 23.
[16] *Principles*, p. 312n.
[17] *Fragment*, p. 24.

"Circumstances Influencing Sensibility"	32
"Sanctions of Pain and Pleasure"	4
"Simple Pleasures"	14
"Simple Pains"	12
"Good Motives"	4
"Bad Motives"	5
"Cases in which Punishment is Groundless"	3
"Cases in which Punishment is Inefficacious"	6
"Offenses Against Property"	13
"Offenses Touching the Condition of a Guardian"	17
"Offenses Touching the Condition of a Husband"	21

This is but a small sample of the kinds of categories which Bentham sets up as a means of analyzing human psychology and political policy. The subgroups of each classification are first listed and then described in great detail. The subgroups of two of his categories may be illustrated to give the flavor of his method:

Circumstances Influencing Sensibility	*Offenses Touching the Condition of a Husband*
1. Health	5. Polygamy
2. Strength	12. Dissipation in Prejudice of Matrimonial Wardship
3. Hardiness	
8. Steadiness of Mind	16. Wrongful Withholding of Connubial Services
10. Moral Sensibility	
20. Pecuniary Circumstances	20. Wife-stealing
28. Education	

Bentham's book at times has more the look of a catalogue for automobile parts than it does that of a treatise in political theory. He calls his approach "the exhaustive method," and he is not unaware that this phrase can have more than one meaning.

Doubtless such a method is eminently instructive; but the fatigue of following it out is so great, not only to the author, but probably also to the reader, that if carried to its utmost length at the first attempt, it might perhaps do more disservice in the way of disgust, than service in the way of information.[18]

There are serious questions about this method of approach. How do we know that there are thirteen "offenses against property" and only thirteen? Why not five or ten or fifteen? There is an air of confidence pervading Bentham's classifications which is difficult to dispel and hard to controvert. Number is the language of science, and to hear that there are precisely thirty-two "circumstances influencing sensibility" is to listen to the voice of authority. But is there really a difference between "strength" and "hardiness" which corresponds to reality? Bentham's model errs, if it errs at all, on the side of comprehending all possibilities so that the omission of none will be risked.

[18] *Principles*, p. 312n.

Like a cautious lawmaker, he wishes to anticipate all eventualities which may arise. Whether this so encumbers the model that its main determinants are obscured is a chance that Bentham has to take.

In addition, there is implicit in the arrangement the assumption of multiple causation. If we ask what is it that affects men's "sensibility" and makes it what it is, Bentham is prepared to give us thirty-two possible or actual causes. To apply this scheme in studying human behavior it would be necessary to deploy the thirty-two causes according to their relative importance in varying situations. If, on a scale of 100, equal weight were given to each cause, then all would carry a gravity of 3.13. But it is obvious that on some occasions "moral biases" figure more vitally than "quantity and quality of knowledge." Perhaps in those circumstances the one should be given a weight of 7.34 and the other reduced to 2.09. The problem of weighting is integral to the multiple causation approach.[19] Some theorists have avoided this dilemma by adumbrating single-cause models. Thus Marx would pluck "pecuniary circumstances" out of Bentham's list of thirty-two causes and would give it star billing. Freud, on the other hand, would assign primary causation to "sex." There is no simple answer to this matter. If single-cause theories smack of purblind dogmatism, multiple causation looks as if it is evading the significant questions.

Bentham is not unaware of these difficulties: "To search out the vast variety of exciting or moderating causes, by which the degree or bias of a man's sensibility may be influenced, to define the boundaries of each, to extricate them from the entanglements in which they are involved, to lay the effect of each article distinctly before the reader's eye, is, if not absolutely the most difficult task, at least one of the most difficult tasks, within the compass of moral physiology." [20] Men have yet to reach agreement on this question

---

[19] While modern political scientists show a marked tendency to indulge in model-building, they are extremely hesitant when it comes to the matter of assigning "weights" to the variables they set out. This omission tends to rob such constructs of any value they might have for other scholars who might wish to test them or put them to their own uses. One courageous exception was the late E. L. Thorndike. In his two books, Your City (New York: Harcourt, Brace, 1939) and 144 Smaller Cities (New York: Harcourt, Brace, 1940), he devised a "G-Score" to determine the "goodness of life" in various cities. Each city received a score so that it could be ranked against others. Thorndike used such statistical indices as the infant death-rate, public expenditures for teachers' salaries, frequency of home-ownership, and circulation of certain magazines. Most important, he assigned a numerical weight to each index so that more important elements had a greater statistical influence. The infant death-rate, for example, was minus 12 whereas the per capita number of automobiles was plus 4. Only if such assignments are made can one's fellow scientists begin to discuss the validity of the model. Thorndike did not claim that his weights were the embodiment of ultimate truth, but he at least opened the doors for meaningful consideration of the subject.

[20] Principles, p. 166n.

which lies at the heart of political and psychological theory. But the scientific method does not pretend to give eternal and definitive answers: it establishes a process by which knowledge may be increased.

Bentham is pointing to a path rather than anticipating its ultimate destination. Despite his self-assured air, the outline he offers is a tentative one. "It is not to be expected that this process should be strictly pursued . . ." he says. "It may, however, be always kept in view: and as near as the process actually pursued approaches to it, so near will such process approach to the character of an exact one." [21] The emphasis is on the approach rather than the end of the journey: the student who is disappointed because he never achieves absolute precision in his descriptive efforts is doomed to perpetual frustration. If the scientific method is used with cautious perseverance, then our understanding is bound to be enhanced. And this is all that Bentham is asking for.

UTILITARIAN LEGISLATION

Bentham's great contribution to political theory is the doctrine of utilitarianism. This theory is an attempt to link the scientific method to the making of political policy. There are three separate facets to the utilitarian approach. First, it is a psychological theory, an explanation of the functioning of the human personality. Second, it is a theory of government, an explanation of the functioning of political and legal institutions. Third, it is an applied science, an explanation of how lawmakers may so direct human activity that the general welfare will be maximized. These three parts are, of course, in intimate relation to each other. Bentham's politics are based on his psychology; his applied science is based on his theoretical principles. Utilitarianism is an effort to conjoin a descriptive psychology with a prescriptive political theory. The good state will maximize the public well-being, and good lawmakers will frame legislation that calculates the sources of felicity within individuals and for society as a whole. Bentham defines utilitarianism in terms of happiness:

By the principle of utility is meant that principle which approves or disapproves of every action whatsoever, according to the tendency which it appears to have to augment or diminish the happiness of the party whose interest is in question: or, what is the same thing in other words, to promote or to oppose that happiness. I say of every action whatsoever; and therefore not only of every action of a private individual, but of every measure of government.[22]

Happiness—the maximizing of pleasure and the minimizing of pain—is the standard by which behavior should be judged. An individual should perform

[21] *Ibid.*, p. 153.
[22] *Ibid.*, p. 126.

an action if it looks as if it will make him a happier person. A government may properly compel its citizens to perform certain actions if the consequence will be a greater measure of pleasure to a particular person or the total society. Finally, an outside observer may pass judgment on the acts of individuals and governments on the basis of whether they serve to maximize happiness or pleasure.

This formula, Bentham suggests, is a scientific means for selecting among alternative courses of action. All men, it may safely be said, desire happiness; everyone, given the choice, would select pleasure and reject pain. "With respect to actions in general, there is no property in them that is calculated so readily to engage, and so firmly to fix the attention of an observer, as the tendency . . . which may be styled the common end of all of them," Bentham says. "The end I mean is happiness: and this tendency in any act is what we style its utility." [23]

That men place the highest value on happiness should be evident to anyone who has observed individual or collective behavior. This basic assumption of utilitarianism is not difficult to accept for the obvious reason that words like "happiness" and "pleasure" are general enough to cover most eventualities. The martyr is actually happiest when he is unhappy; the masochist experiences pleasure when he is in the throes of pain. These instances are not paradoxical: they simply demonstrate that the key terms are susceptible of varying meanings. Bentham is vague in his use of terms at this point so that he will have room in which to develop his theory in its fullness at a later stage.

By utility is meant that property in any object, whereby it tends to produce benefit, advantage, pleasure, good, or happiness (all this in the present case comes to the same thing) or (what comes again to the same thing) to prevent the happening of mischief, pain, evil, or unhappiness to the party whose interest is considered: if that party be the community in general, then the happiness of the community: if a particular individual, then the happiness of that individual.[24]

Some note should be taken of the ease with which Bentham transposes from the individual to the community in this definition. On the surface it looks as if he is following both Rousseau and Burke in identifying the best interests of each citizen with that of the general welfare. However, this is the exact opposite of Bentham's meaning.

For utilitarianism is the ultimate expression of the individualist doctrine. To Bentham's thinking, the only things to be considered in the political world are the discrete and autonomous individuals who, taken together, comprise a society. His view of society is, in fact, far more atomistic than that of

[23] *Fragment*, p. 24.
[24] *Principles*, p. 126.

either Hobbes or Locke, for Bentham refuses to employ even the hypothetical device of a social contract to tie citizens in a common social or political endeavor. And utilitarianism stands at an opposite pole from the communitarian theories of Burke and Rousseau: Bentham's society is precisely equal to the sum of the individuals who reside within it. "The community is a fictitious body, composed of the individual persons who are considered as constituting as it were its member," he says. "The interest of the community then is . . . the sum of the interests of the several members who compose it." [25]

While it is often necessary to speak of a "community" or a "society" in the interests of clarity, a theory should avoid investing such aggregates with metaphysical properties. Organic doctrines have an annoying habit of imparting a "life" and a "purpose" to states and societies, and these mystical qualities tend to gain a force and momentum of their own which is quite independent of the lives and purposes of the individuals involved. If Bentham is compelled to talk of a community, then, it is with none of the organic overtones observed in the cases of Rousseau and Burke. Bentham is primarily a political psychologist: his interest is the individual personality. Societies and governments are no more than arithmetic aggregates of citizens who have personal interests and the desire for personal pleasure.

Because this is so, utilitarianism sets up a single standard which applies equally to the act of an individual and the act of a government. "A thing is said to promote the interest . . . of an individual, when it tends to add to the sum total of his pleasures . . ." Bentham says. "A measure of government . . . may be said to be conformable to or dictated by the principle of utility, when in like manner the tendency which it has to augment the happiness of the community is greater than any which it has to diminish it." [26] The interest or happiness of the community is actually a convenient fiction: the reality is the sum of the pleasures of the individual citizens who pursue their own interests and to whom the infliction of legal sanctions may be a source of pain.

[25] *Ibid.* Bentham is worried about placing too great a reliance on fictional constructs in political theory. A hypothetical social contract is a weak base for propounding human rights. "The indestructible prerogatives of mankind," he says, "have no need to be supported upon the sandy foundations of a fiction." *Fragment*, p. 50. Not only the social contract, but all fictions impede rather than aid the political understanding. "With respect to this, and other fictions, there was once a time, perhaps, when they had their use. With instruments of this temper, I will not deny that some political work may have been done, and that useful work, which, under the then circumstances of things, could hardly have been done with any other. But the season of fiction is now over." *Ibid.*, p. 51. The political scientist cannot rely on the subjective and imprecise language of the poet or novelist; he must develop an objective vocabulary and methodology of his own. Whether or not Bentham is successful in this endeavor, he has at least issued a warning against allowing fictions to assume the proportions of political realities.

[26] *Principles*, p. 127.

Out of this atomistic assumption emerges the famous axiom of Bentham's theory: "It is the greatest happiness of the greatest number that is the measure of right and wrong." [27] A good government provides for the pursuit of happiness in the context of human equality. For Bentham the contentment of any one citizen, no matter how humble, is as important as that of any other. The quantitative approach carries with it this democratic postulate. There are no superior or inferior men: all are equally capable of experiencing pleasure and pain.

But what of that attractive rubric, "the greatest happiness of the greatest number"? The difficulty lies in its logic: is it impossible to attain two supreme goals simultaneously and have both retain the status of supremacy. Suppose a community consisting of 100 individuals, and that the greatest possible amount of pleasure which that community might enjoy would be expressed as 1,000 "units" of happiness. It may furthermore be assumed that there are two groups or classes in the community: Group A with 25 members and Group B with 75 members. Whether these groups are distinguished on economic, religious, or regional lines is for present purposes immaterial. Three cases will illustrate some of the actual possibilities:

		Number of Citizens	Units of Happiness	Total Pleasure for Community
1.	Group A	25	20	500
	Group B	75	4	300
		100		800
2.	Group A	25	3	75
	Group B	75	8	600
		100		675
3.	Group A	25	5	125
	Group B	75	5	375
		100		500

The first case satisfies the condition of the greatest total happiness, but it is not the greatest happiness of the greatest number. The second gives greater happiness to the greatest number, but the sum total is lower than the previous case. The last instance equalizes the amount of happiness for all, but at a lower level for the community. Of the three, which would Bentham prefer? In the first case one-quarter of the community gets over half the total happiness, and

[27] *Fragment*, p. 3.

it is highly doubtful if Bentham would approve of such an inequitable distribution. In the second the minority is now an underprivileged group, and there is the danger that the greater number is pleasing itself at the expense of the smaller. Bentham's espousal of human equality would lead him to select the second case rather than the first, although he would be concerned about the possibility of majority tyranny here. The third case presents the most troublesome problems: neither minority or majority has greater happiness, but the community is experiencing only half of its full potential for pleasure. This situation might be called one of "leveling," and it puts a premium on equality rather than quality.

Bentham would prefer this third case to the oligarchical first one, but he would probably choose the second over the third. Ideally, of course, every person would receive ten units of happiness, and no one no more or less than ten. But Bentham would admit that in no society short of a Utopia could public policy secure this end: diversity of tastes and interests lead to "zero-sum" situations where one man's gain is another's deprivation. In societies which are both free and democratic there is no permanent division between a Group A and a Group B. Individuals shift back and forth from minority to majority status as various issues arise over time, and as old alliances are dissolved and new coalitions take their place. Thus, for example, a man may be in the minority in terms of his religion but in the majority camp when it comes to his economic interests. Thus the disadvantages he suffers at one time will be compensated for at another. Bentham would say that so long as this holds true, then in the final analysis the sum of the first and second cases will lead to the third.

However, there is no guarantee of such mobility from minority to majority: in many societies there are individuals who are in a minority status in terms of virtually all of their significant interests. In this event, Bentham suggests, the government must intervene in an active way by making laws which will redress the balance and increase the happiness of those minorities.

Finally, while Bentham does not acknowledge the existence of superior individuals with superior pleasures, he does grant that there can be differentials in intensity of feeling. Hence he refuses to say that classical music is better than popular music, but he does allow that one listener may have a stronger interest in music than another. The question of intensity will be discussed next. At this point it will suffice to note that Bentham's concern is with the quantitative factor rather than the qualitative. Indeed, he indicates that the former can be reduced to such dimensions that it can be discussed whole in quantitative terms.

Rational laws must take account of pleasures and pains in a precise and objective way. Earlier Bentham pointed out that "the various systems that have been formed concerning the standards of right and wrong . . . consist all of them in so many contrivances for avoiding the obligation of appealing to any external standard." When subjective standards are used, there can be no meaningful discussion between those who say yea and those who say nay. If an objective standard such as the utilitarian calculus is used, then all men can be persuaded to the validity of its findings if they are given the facts and are shown the proceeds by which conclusions are arrived at. Public policy can be left neither to subjective sentiments nor to trial and error. Legislators must be engineers with a scientific education.

The policy-making process may now be outlined. First, a survey must be made of the community. "To take an exact account then of the general tendency of any act, by which the interests of a community are affected . . ." Bentham says, "take an account of the number of persons whose interests appear to be concerned." [28] The public must be analyzed to discover its probable reaction to a piece of legislation. With some laws virtually everyone will be affected in a direct way: with others only a small group will have an interest at stake. Needless to say, all citizens sooner or later are indirectly subject to the influence of every law, but for purposes of analysis that universal calculation will be ignored for the time being. Next, the legislator must give positive units to the public pleasure and negative units to the public pain which will result from the enactment of a given law.

Sum up the numbers expressive of the degrees of good tendency, which the act has, with respect to each individual, in regard to whom the tendency of it is good upon the whole; do this again with respect to each individual, in regard to whom the tendency of it is bad upon the whole. Take the balance; which, if on the side of pleasure, will give the general good tendency of the act, with respect to the total number or community of individuals concerned; if on the side of pain, the general evil tendency, with respect to the same community.[29]

Again it would be well to give a specific example to show how legislation should be framed. Suppose that lawmakers are considering a bill which will make it mandatory for all school children to salute the country's flag at patriotic exercises. Of a community of 10,000 people, they first discover, as the result of a pilot survey, that only 2,000 are really interested in the passage or defeat of such a law.[30] For the remaining 8,000 such a requirement will not

[28] *Principles*, pp. 152–153.

[29] *Ibid.*, p. 153.

[30] How can we tell what concerns people? In the summer of 1954 a nationwide cross section of Americans were asked the question, "What kinds of things do you worry about most?" The answers dealt with family and personal economic matters. Less than 1 per cent volunteered that they were concerned greatly about the threat of Communist subversion

disturb their sensibilities or customary expectations. Of the 2,000 who are affected, 1,500 want the law passed and 500 would prefer to see it defeated:

Those Affected Beneficially

Category	Number of People	Units of Pleasure	Sum
Members of Veterans and Patriotic Groups	400	2	800
Flag Manufacturers	50	5	250
General Citizens	1050	1	1050
	1500		2100

Those Affected Adversely

Category	Number of People	Units of Pain	Sum
Jehovah's Witnesses	25	40	1000
Members of Other Minority Religions	150	5	750
General Citizens	325	2	650
	500		2400

It is not difficult to understand how the decision to reject this law was arrived at. While fewer "general citizens" are concerned about protecting minority interests, they generally feel more intensely about the matter than do those who would enforce the majority view on the minority. And the Jehovah's Witnesses have other allies in the form of religious groups which, although they are prepared to salute the flag, are fearful that the law will open the door to legislation adversely affecting their own interests. But the key problem, obviously, is determining the intensity of the pain which will be suffered by the 25 members of the sect. The finding of the lawmakers was that they would suffer 40 units of pain each, or a total of 1000. But why 40? Had they arrived at a figure of 20, then the total for those adversely affected would have been 1900—or not enough to keep the law from being passed.

The calculus is not a one-dimensional formula. As has been shown, both numbers and degree of intensity have to be taken into account. In fact, Bentham suggests that seven variables be introduced into the reckoning so that no mistakes will be made:

To a number of persons, with reference to each of whom the value of a pleasure or a pain is considered, it will be greater or less, according to seven circumstances:

---

or the state of civil liberties. And this was a time when these were supposed to be over-riding national issues. Yet when the interviewers specifically asked if the respondents were bothered about Communism as an internal threat, then most replied that they were. See Samuel A. Stouffer, *Communism, Conformity, and Civil Liberties* (New York: Double-day, 1955), pp. 58–69.

(1) Its intensity. (2) Its duration. (3) Its certainty or uncertainty. (4) Its propinquity or remoteness. (5) Its fecundity. (6) Its purity. And one other: to wit: (7) Its extent; that is, the number of persons to whom it extends; or, (in other words) who are affected by it.[31]

The example which was given deals only with the first and last of these variables. For the other five to be included it is clear that more elaborate mathematical calculations would be needed.

The controversial question, of course, remains: how does a legislator reduce his observations to precise and objective figures? The answer is that he must act as a scientist: he must follow the precepts of the quantitative method which were laid down at the opening of this chapter. The methods of survey research should be used to discover which people will be affected by laws, how they will react to them, and with what intensity. After the first tentative findings are in, legislators should act as the community of scientists does: they must discuss the value of various research methods and the validity of the different data which have been obtained. The decision to give 40 "units" of pain to the Jehovah's Witnesses rather than 30 can only be arrived at after full consideration, criticism, and a review of all available information. It will be argued, for example, that the religious sensibilities in question are far more intensely felt than those of Baptists or Methodists. It will be replied that the Mormon faith did not suffer when polygamy was banned, and the Witnesses will adjust themselves to saluting the flag. So long as this interplay is conducted on the basis of evidence and not sentiment, there is the likelihood that scientific truth will emerge in the form of legislation. The standard which Bentham sets is a high one. If he is not asking for philosopher-kings, he is nevertheless requiring that legislators be both social scientists and mathematicians.[32]

It might be suggested that a legislature actually employs Bentham's calculus all the time without knowing it. Without using the apparatus of scientific research and mathematical calculations, each lawmaker has in his mental filing cabinet a fairly good idea of how he has given pleasure and pain to his constituents by his legislative voting record. And, assuming he wants to get re-

[31] *Principles*, p. 152. There is a good discussion of measuring intensity of feeling in Robert A. Dahl's *A Preface to Democratic Theory* (Chicago: University of Chicago Press, 1956), pp. 90–123. For a more general consideration of this and related questions, see Anthony Downs, *An Economic Theory of Democracy* (New York: Harper, 1957). On techniques see Louis Guttman, "A Basis for Scaling Qualitative Data," *American Sociological Review* (April, 1944) pp. 139–150.

[32] Bentham is not dogmatic: "It is not to be expected that this process should be strictly pursued previously to every moral judgment, or to every legislative or judicial operation. It may, however, be always kept in view: and as near as the process actually pursued on these occasions approaches to it, so near will such process approach to the character of an exact one." *Principles*, p. 153.

elected, he will make sure that the pleasures outweigh the pains so far as his folks back home are concerned. Lawmakers, then, can be said to have the public's happiness always in mind: they strive to give more pleasure than pain, and that after all is the definition of utilitarianism.

Without involved sample surveys or slide rules, the average legislator would appear to be achieving the end that Bentham had in mind. What is more, if his intuitive calculations are correct he is rewarded with re-election. Indeed, the test of his accuracy is found at the polls; if the voters on the whole feel pained, then that demonstrates the invalidity of the lawmaker's formula. Social science and democratic government seem to be not only compatible but necessary to each other.

Would Bentham agree with such a proposition? There is good reason for believing that he would not. And the grounds for his objections would be not far different from those offered by Rousseau. First of all, an elected legislator tends to pay more attention to the happiness of organized and articulate constituents than he does to those who remain silent. Citizens with coherent interests at stake in the political arena are more apt to reward or punish a representative on the basis of his record as it affects them. This may mean that the happiness of the greater number of residents of a district will go unpromoted, and this unorganized majority will have no effective way of influencing legislation. Second, and more important, the expressed wants of voters may not be the same as the laws they really need for their genuine and long-term happiness. Citizens may wish selective service ended and not realize that its continuance is for their own good; they may desire to have the local harbor dredged and not understand that only a comprehensive water-resources program will solve their underlying needs. In brief, if rational lawmakers are to satisfy the real needs of the public, then it is not always valid to rely on what the public says it wants. If surveys are taken preliminary to the framing of legislation, such polls should not only elicit what the citizens think they require to be happy but also plumb deeper into the problem to discover the unconscious needs and social conditions which have to be provided for.

Bentham is more attached to rational policy than he is to the democratic process. While he puts the happiness of all men on an equal footing, his theory does not call for the popular election of those who will protect and promote that happiness. The master of a scientific legislature must, first and foremost, be the facts. Public opinion, expressed by voting, is not the instrument for discovering the truth.

One brief comment is in order concerning the approach to the individual in Bentham's theory. He is no less a creature of self-interest than he is in

Hobbes' writings. Nevertheless, there is a difference between the pursuit of self-interest, on the one hand, and the display of selfishness, on the other. For men to be full individuals they must, as Hobbes and Locke pointed out, have interests which are peculiarly their own and have the will to promote them. The whole discussion of property in its relation to personality was along these lines, and Bentham would accept its basic assumptions. To reduce self-interest to selfishness is to oversimplify: the first is a precondition of the individualist life; the second has to do with the way in which a person approaches the obligations of social intercourse. Bentham's catalogue of pleasures puts self-interest at its head, but closely following this is the pleasure of sympathy—the happiness an individual experiences when the well-being of himself and those around him can be shared by all together.

First comes the self-regarding pleasure: then comes the idea of the pleasure of sympathy, which you suppose that pleasure of yours will give birth to in the bosoms of your friends: and this idea excites again in yours a new pleasure issuing from your own bosom, as it were from a radiant point, illuminates the bosom of your friend: reverberates from thence, it is reflected with augmented warmth of the point from whence it first proceeded: and so it is with pains.[33]

There is no metaphysical speculation here about whether man is "naturally good" or "naturally evil." Men are self-interested, but they are also able to share in the pleasure when their neighbors encounter good fortune. Citizens must at all times, however, be regarded as individuals, and the happiness of every man is distinct from those around him. Individuality of interests renders the science of legislation all the more difficult. But if it is successful, then its rewards are all the greater.

THE POSITIVE STATE

The proposal to apply the methods of quantitative science to the making of public policy is a radical one. And there is much that is radical in Bentham's theory. Like all innovators, he also sets himself up as a critic of existing institutions. If political engineering has as its aim the improvement of life, then the prelude to reform must be the demolition of the attitude proposed by men like Burke.

Thus much is certain; that a system that is never to be censured, will never be improved: that if nothing is ever to be found fault with, nothing will ever be mended: and that a resolution to justify everything at any rate, and to disapprove of nothing, is a resolution which, pursued in future, must stand as an effectual bar to all the additional happiness we can ever hope for.[34]

The status quo, Bentham suggests, must be put on the defensive. It is ra-

[33] *Ibid.*, p. 174.
[34] *Fragment*, p. 10.

tional to assume that any institution which has remained much the same over a long period is badly in need of repairs. Men's needs change over time, and it is usually safe to say that the ancient formulas are incapable of satisfying these new needs.

This institutional lag is a perennial problem of politics: today's governments seem prepared to provide the conditions for yesterday's happiness. A state is seldom ready to confront the present in an effective way, and it is never fortified for the future. It is not the duty of political theory to celebrate things as they are. The job of the theorist is to throw off the venerated wraps and expose the inadequacies of the status quo. This, of course, is the scientific method in practice: criticism is part of the testing and experimentation which lead to true knowledge. "Censure," Bentham says, ". . . has no other effect upon an institution than to bring it to that test, by which the value of those, indeed, on which prejudice alone has stamped a currency, is cried down, but by which the credit of those of sterling utility is confirmed." [35] Whereas Burke's prescriptive theory stated that the passage of time and the play of prejudice rendered institutions legitimate, Bentham's utilitarianism calls for continual skepticism and a proclivity for reform.

And the great object of reform should be the general happiness. Most lawmakers take too narrow-minded a view: either they think only of their own interests and those of their class, or they look at the public welfare in a piecemeal and fragmented way. Bentham is saying that the science of legislation should be construed in a grand manner. "The happiness of the individuals of whom a community is composed . . ." he says, "is the end and the sole end which the legislator ought to have in view." [36] The complicated design of the felicific calculus was not created for the resolution of small problems. Legislators must scan all of society and plan for the contentment of all citizens.

The trouble with traditional governments is that they leave too much to chance, and as a result problems grow worse instead of better. Locke's limited state and Burke's prescriptive society seem to assume that some sort of invisible hand will provide social order and individual happiness. But the lesson of history is that invisible hands are not sufficient: on the contrary, the visible hands of legislators must shape behavior in ways conducive to a maximum of pleasure and a minimum of pain. "The art of legislation," Bentham says, "teaches how a multitude of men, composing a community, may be disposed to pursue that course which upon the whole is the most conducive to the happiness of the whole community, by means of motives to be applied by the

[35] *Ibid.*
[36] *Principles*, p. 147.

legislator." [37] The resemblance here to Machiavelli is striking, except that the goal is the happiness of the community rather than the secure tenure of the ruler.

The phrasing is not that of self-government: rather, the multitude of men are to be moved one way and another by a manipulation of their motives. The lawmakers know an individual's happiness better than he does himself; and, what is more, they know how to impell him in the appropriate directions so that he will find this happiness. Bentham's legislators are not so much the holders of power as they are manipulators of motives. Through a sophisticated calculation of rewards and punishments they create a setting in which men are moved in the direction of pleasure and away from the path of pain. Law, then, is an educational instrument and legislators are the teachers.

> The government a man lives under . . . operates principally through the medium of education: the magistrate operating in the character of a tutor upon all the members of the state, by the direction he gives to their hopes and fears. Indeed, under a solicitous and attentive government, the ordinary preceptor, nay even the parent himself, is but a deputy, as it were, to the magistrate: whose controlling influence, different in the respect from that of the ordinary preceptor, dwells with a man to his life's end. [38]

Power there is, as there is behind all governments; but, unlike the political power of Hobbes, it is power disguised as science and education. The reformed state will have a broad and positive charter: institutions such as the school and family will mesh into the larger scheme of political education and control. For only if there is one authority to coordinate and plan will it be possible to secure the greatest happiness for all in the community.

If there is a logical conclusion to the argument Bentham is setting forth, it cannot be said that he reaches it himself in any unequivocal way. "The business of government is to promote the happiness of the society, by punishing and rewarding," he says. [39] However, Bentham is enough of a liberal, enough a follower of Locke's kind of thinking, that he shows a partiality for limited government. The Principles of Morals and Legislation, for example, devotes a chapter of almost 100 pages to a list of various offenses ("wife-stealing" and numberless others) which ought to be punished by the state. The business of government, as Bentham sees it, is far more to punish than to reward. This means that the general happiness is attained by preventing antisocial behavior on the part of fractious individuals. But is punishment enough? The whole logic of Bentham's thinking is that it is not. If government is to apply motives, then they must be positive as well as negative in character.

[37] Ibid., p. 423.
[38] Ibid., p. 182.
[39] Ibid., p. 189.

This side of politics, the positive state, is a departure from liberal doctrine, for it calls on the government to enter society and the economy in an active way. Bentham is tempted to call such activity supererogatory, not really required by traditional definitions of the legitimate sphere of political operation. And he is at a loss for words to describe this department of state.

> This branch of the business of government, a sort of work of supererogation, as it may be called, in the calendar of political duty, is comparatively but of recent date. It is not for this that the untutored many could have originally submitted themselves to the domination of the few. It was the dread of evil, not the hope of good, that first cemented societies together. Necessaries come always before luxuries. The state of language marks the progress of ideas. Time out of mind the military department has had a name: so has that of justice: the power which occupies itself in preventing mischief, not till lately, and that but a loose one, the police: for the power which takes for its object the introduction of positive good, no peculiar name, however inadequate, seems yet to have been devised.[40]

The function to which Bentham refers is, of course, the welfare function.

The states of Hobbes and Locke were formed to counter the fear of tyranny: the tyranny of a state of war or that of an arbitrary ruler. This necessity having been taken care of, government must now move on to providing the luxuries which turn an embryonic contentment into the full-fledged pursuit of happiness. Activities which earlier liberal theorists might have regarded as optional are now acknowledged to be required. Public education, public health, and public housing must be provided if private agencies cannot do the job sufficiently to give citizens these accouterments of the good life. The state must guarantee minimum wages for those who work, pensions for those who are retired, and a measure of security for all citizens regardless of their status or contribution. Bentham, of course, does not prescribe these as specific policies, but his utilitarian principles lead us to them in a straightforward way.

The welfare state is the consequence of scientific legislation and political engineering. The research which underlies the creation of public policy is bound to bring to light new facts and hence new needs. As individuals are analyzed and society is subjected to constant investigation, the result will be that the status quo will be found wanting. Only a rational government has the resources and the authority to assume the responsibilities unmet by individuals or voluntary associations. A science of legislation, like all sciences, is tireless in its discovery of new fields to conquer. From public education and the minimum wage, it moves on to child welfare and mental health. From agricultural subsidies and protective tariffs, it presses forward to recreational facilities and cultural opportunities. To the post office is added atomic energy; to the national parks are added—perhaps—nationalized industries.

[40] *Ibid.*, p. 323.

Some of these functions are undertaken because of the articulated demands of interested citizens: agricultural subsidies would be a case in point. But others are added to the calendar of government activity because disinterested study shows that a job has to be done: the construction and constant improvement of state hospitals for the mentally ill are illustrative of this. Indeed, these examples show that functions undertaken as a result of specific pressures are usually less rational in their development as policies than are those which the government inaugurates independent of such pressures. The Tennessee Valley Authority, for instance, is a rational plan for utilizing a region's water resources to maximize the happiness of the citizens of that area. Yet the TVA, while filling many needs for the inhabitants of the valley, did not spring from the minds of those individuals. It was the brainchild of a Nebraska legislator who understood the problems of the area better than its own people did. For a government to build dams, to enter the fields of navigation and flood control, to manufacture and sell electricity—these previously unheard of activities are applications of the doctrine of utility.[41]

Where will it end? Can Bentham's theory lead to government planning and a welfare state that will ensure total happiness? The answer is dependent on the facts of the matter. If maximized pleasure can be secured at times by a minimum of government activity, then the utilitarian judgment would be that the state should stand aside. But if the greatest happiness for the greatest number is not being provided by private agencies, then the government must assume new responsibilities. The decision cannot be a dogmatic one: only research on legislative needs and sophistication in policy-making will tell how far the hand of the state should extend.

There is no theory of socialism implicit in Bentham, any more than there is a theory of capitalism: his concern is with legislation, and each new activity that a government is to undertake must be considered on its own merits. Will the general happiness be augmented if the government goes into the business of manufacturing electricity? Some say it will, and others say it will not.

The question is now manifestly a question of conjecture concerning so many future contingent matters of fact: to solve it, both parties are naturally directed to support their respective persuasions by the only evidence the nature of the case admits of;—the evidence of such past matters of fact as appear to be analogous to those contingent future ones. Now these past facts are almost always numerous: so numerous, that till brought into view for the purpose of the debate, a great proportion of them are what may very fairly have escaped the observation of one

[41] For a fine discussion of purposeful government activity to promote the general welfare, see Mario Einaudi, *The Roosevelt Revolution* (New York: Harcourt, Brace, 1959). The analysis of the TVA is especially good, pp. 158–196.

of the parties: and it is owing, perhaps, to this and nothing else, that the party is of the persuasion which sets it at variance with the other.[42]

With rational legislators, disagreements will be over facts and not sentiments. Once research has uncovered all available information and placed it before all concerned, the differences of opinion will disappear. Lawmakers are scientists and engineers, not philosophers or ideologues. They do not ask irrelevant questions about the "socialist" or "capitalist" label on any given policy. They only want to know if it will bring greater happiness to the community.

UTILITY AND FREEDOM

Individualism and liberalism, the scientific method and elite rule—all of these are blended together in Bentham's theory. There is, however, no democratic content in utilitarianism: at no point does Bentham call for elections or popular participation in the making of policy. Happiness is to be provided for the multitude: they have neither the information nor the skills to secure it for themselves. Indeed, a legislator must be willing to ignore public opinion and run the risk of incurring the displeasure of those whose happiness he has at heart. "The people are a set of masters whom it is not in a man's power in every instance fully to please, and at the same time faithfully to serve," Bentham says. "He that is resolved to preserve without deviation in the line of truth and utility, must have learnt to prefer the still whisper of enduring approbation, to the short-lived bustle of tumultuous applause." [43]

For Bentham to say this and at the same time to fail to discuss questions of political power is itself revealing. Unlike Machiavelli, he does not indicate how the legislators will shore up their positions so as to keep public discontent from erupting into revolt. In many cases the greatest happiness for the community will have to be the result of a long-term plan. But Bentham does not show how the average man is to be kept patient during the seven lean years which perforce precede the era of prosperity. He does not, like Rousseau, call for the use of myths or other irrational devices to maintain social order. There is, then, a faith in Bentham in the willingness of the average man to be ruled by rational legislators. Furthermore, Bentham does not state who the lawmakers are to be or where they come from. Because a premium is placed on intelligence, it may be assumed that they are an elite rather than a ruling class. However, there is no discussion, such as Plato provided, of the recruitment and education of this governing minority.

[42] *Fragment*, pp. 102–103.
[43] *Ibid.*, p. 30.

These silences on Bentham's part show that he is more interested in science and engineering than he is in the scientists and engineers. It will remain for John Stuart Mill, who carries on the utilitarian doctrine, to fill in these political questions which Bentham leaves open.

If there is no democracy in Bentham's theory, there is ample room for a consideration of freedom. It has already been seen that he was unwilling to set limits on the sphere of state action: there is no philosophy of Natural Rights, and the citizen cannot appeal to the Natural Law. A limited state would thwart the onward progress of the scientific method: to draw fixed boundary lines would be like telling an astronomer that the lens in his telescope must be no larger than twenty inches in diameter. Bentham wishes governments to be both scientific and free, and for this reason he is unwilling to equate freedom with limitations on political power. The difference between a free government and an oppressive one does not lie in the amount of power in the hands of rulers. To suppose this is to use a standard of judgment which is both abstract and artificial.

In regard to a government that is free, and one that is despotic, wherein is it that the difference consists? Is it that those persons in whose hands that power is lodged which is acknowledged to be supreme, have less power in the one than in the other, when it is from custom that they derive it? By no means. It is not that the power of one any more than that of the other has any bounds to it. The distinction turns upon circumstances of a very different complexion.[44]

If a free government can have lodged in it as much, or even more, power than an oppressive one, then it is legitimate to ask what guarantees there are that a free government will use its power justly. Locke curbed the rightful sphere of political activity because he was not prepared to trust any group of rulers, but then Locke had none of Bentham's scientific pretensions.

There are two utilitarian answers to the problem of freedom. The first is embedded in the scientific method itself. If the goal of a legislative science is the greatest happiness, then it is clear that oppressive acts are not conducive to that end. Legislators who adhere to the scientific method will continually test and criticize the consequences of their policies. The method itself will be a constant reminder that laws are the servants of the public welfare.

To the legislator it is a kind of perpetual lesson: serving at once as a corrective to his prejudices, and as a check upon his passions. Is there a mischief which escaped him? In a natural arrangement, if at the same time an exhaustive one, he cannot fail to find it. Is he tempted ever to force innocence within the pale of guilt? The difficulty of finding a place for it advertises him of his error. Such are the uses of . . . the principle of utility: such the advantages, which the legislator as well as the subject may derive from it. Abide by it, and everything that is

44 *Ibid.*, p. 94.

arbitrary in legislation vanishes. An evil-intentioned or prejudiced legislator durst not look it in the face. He would proscribe it, and with reason: it would be a satire on his laws.[45]

Utilitarianism has within it a feedback and self-correcting mechanism. Political power is to be used for a specific purpose, and uses of power which fail to serve that purpose are abusive in character. No scientist vivisects more laboratory animals than his experiments call for: no scientific legislator exercises power which does not promote the public good. The scientific method immediately shows whether a state has stepped outside its proper bounds.

Bentham readily admits that there are important areas of life where happiness is best secured if individuals are left to find it for themselves without the intervention of the state.

There are cases in which the legislator ought not to attempt to direct the conduct of the several other members of the community. Every act which promises to be beneficial upon the whole to the community, each individual ought to perform of himself; but it is not every such act that the legislator ought to compel him to perform. Every act which promises to be pernicious upon the whole to the community, each individual ought to abstain from of himself: but it is not every such act that the legislator ought to compel him to abstain from.[46]

Any government which tries too hard to compel good behavior will eventually discover that it is defeating its own ends. The welter of regulations, the paramountcy of the police, and the whole atmosphere of state power would soon destroy more happiness than it created. Bentham does not employ abstract arguments from Natural Rights or Natural Law to make this point. Rather, he simply points out that if a government is to succeed in its promotion of happiness, it must have a good idea of that conduct which can be regulated by law and that which cannot. "With what chance of success, for example, would a legislator go about to extirpate drunkenness and fornication by dint of legal punishment?" Bentham asks. And he then replies to his own question: "Not all the tortures which ingenuity could invent would compass it, . . . and before he had made any progress worth regarding, such a mass of evil would be produced by the punishments, as would exceed, a thousandfold, the utmost possible mischief of the offense." [47] Law and even punishment can be educational devices: but there are limits to the curriculum. A rational legislator will not add courses if he knows that all his students will fail the examination.

Few governments are able to regulate the roles of alcohol and sex in the lives of their citizens; and, what is more important, no free governments can ac-

[45] *Principles*, p. 403.
[46] *Ibid.*, p. 414.
[47] *Ibid.*, p. 420.

complish this and remain free. A free government must establish its authority in the eyes of those who will have to obey the laws. If power is used too extensively and to no good purpose, then citizens will withhold the grant of legitimacy. Authority comes in part from the scientific method, but it also rests on the public's understanding of why power must be exercised over them. "A body of proposed law, how complete soever, would be comparatively useless and uninstructive, unless explained and justified, and that in every title, by a continual accompaniment, a perpetual commentary of reasons," Bentham says. "There must be therefore, not one system only, but two parallel and connected systems, running on together, the one of legislative provisions, the other of political reasons, each affording to the other correction and support." [48] If legislation is scientific, then lawmakers must have convincing reasons for each of their acts; if power is to be authoritative, then the legislators must give persuasive reasons for all of their acts. Short-range pains must be made comprehensible in terms of long-range pleasures: the public must be treated with respect, for governments exist only to serve their happiness. Freedom will be ensured so long as all of these features of the utilitarian system are pursued with diligence and devotion.

The second answer to the question of what distinguishes a free government from an oppressive one turns in a wholly different direction. Now Bentham speaks not as a scientist, but as a liberal—indeed, as a liberal with democratic overtones. The difference between freedom and oppression rests on the institutional provisions which permit the governed to criticize and check their rulers.

The distinction turns upon . . . the manner in which that whole mass of power, which, taken together, is supreme, is in a free state, distributed among the several ranks of persons that are sharers in it:—on the source from whence their titles to it are successively derived:—on the frequent and easy changes of condition between governors and governed; whereby the interests of the one class are more or less indistinguishably blended with those of the other:—on the responsibility of the governors; or the right which a subject has of having the reasons publicly assigned and canvassed of every act of power that is exerted over him:—on the liberty of the press; or the security with which every man, be he of one class or the other, may make known his complaints and remonstrances to the whole community:—on the liberty of public association; or the security with which malcontents may communicate their sentiments, concert their plans, and practice every mode of opposition short of actual revolt, before the executive power can be legally justified in disturbing them.[49]

[48] *Ibid.*, pp. 123–124. Carl Friedrich's essay on "Authority, Reason, and Discretion" elaborates on the theme that the ability to give reasons for the exercise of power can be used as a test of legitimacy. *Authority* (Cambridge: Harvard University Press, 1958), edited by C. J. Friedrich, pp. 28–48.

[49] *Fragment*, pp. 94–95.

Here Bentham is presupposing a whole complex of institutions—both political and social—which provide countervailing power against the state. Even Locke did not emphasize a free press and voluntary associations in the way that Bentham does. Power is to be distributed throughout all of society, and rulers and ruled are to rotate in office. Can this liberal and democratic prescription be reconciled with the call for rational legislation? If the man-in-the-street can communicate his sentiments so as to influence the making of public policy, then it is difficult to see how legislators will have a free hand to pursue their scientific tasks. Utilitarianism, with its complex calcuus, calls for an intelligent and sophisticated elite. Freedom, it would now appear, calls for popular participation in the exercise of that legislative power.

It is nevertheless clear from Bentham's emphasis in his writing that his concern is with happiness and the scientific method rather than democracy and political freedom. If people are made happy, he assumes, there will be no need for democracy; if the scientific method is employed, then freedom will be a logical consequence. Yet for all this he is haunted by the thought that even the most rational of legislators may abuse their power—power which is potentially unlimited in its scope and quality. While neither of the other liberal theorists who are to follow, Tocqueville and Mill, have the affinity for science which Bentham displays, they are no less concerned with questions of freedom, rationality, and democracy. And Marx and Engels will create a science of their own and put it to work for wholly different ends.

11.
Georg Wilhelm
Friedrich Hegel

THE MAN AND HIS TIMES

Hegel was born in Stuttgart, Germany, in 1770. His father was a civil servant, and the family's early expectation was that the son would become a Lutheran minister. However, Hegel's interests veered towards the study of philosophy and an academic career. He taught at several universities in Switzerland and Germany, and in 1818 he was appointed to a chair at the University of Berlin, where he remained until his death in 1831. Hegel's life was different from the conventional one of a teacher and scholar in an important respect. During his tenure at Berlin his reputation was not only in the academic world but in the eyes of the nation as well. His lectures and books provided a philosophical justification for the growing power of the German state. Despite—or even because of—the metaphysical overtones to his ideas, Hegel's theory was accorded a circulation far wider than that usually gained by professorial efforts. Hegel himself was not unaware of the role he was playing and he was flattered to be the foremost ideologue of the Prussian regime. His Philosophy of Right and Philosophy of History, the first of which appeared in 1821 and the second posthumously in 1838, leave little doubt that Hegel's generalized propositions about "The State" refer in the first instance to the German state. Yet Hegel would not have survived as a political theorist had he confined himself to rationalizing a specific regime. It was his sincerely held philosophical position that the nation-state was the actualization of eternal reason. His theory gains stature because his imagination and insight transcended the ideological purposes that his writings may have been made to serve.

While the democratic forces unleashed by the French Revolution made their impact throughout Europe, there were at the same time strong centers of power both unsympathetic and resistant to this tendency. The reaction against democracy, however, could not be a complete return to a preindustrial order. The focus shifted to the idea of national power. While Burke's and Rousseau's generation spoke only marginally of the nation-state, the succeeding period brought nationalism to the center of its thinking. The individual was once again relegated to a subordinate status, and doctrines of equality and personal liberty were swept aside. In order that nation and state be given the emphasis they deserved, citizens were to be looked on as servants of the imperatives of history as they were expressed in prevailing political institutions. The states of Europe were beginning to define political obligation in the context of national boundaries. The rising nationalist spirit meant that patriotism would become the central motive force for obedience and participation in the political life.

At the same time, two social forces, one old and one new, were being synthesized with the hegemony of the nation-state. An important component of European society was still the landed economy, and the aristocracy was to continue to play an important political role for some time to come. Hegel's analysis makes provision for the agricultural estates and the corporate guilds, and in this respect his theory occasionally has a distinctly medieval flavor. However he was no less aware of the rising commercial and industrial classes, and he understood that they required for their existence the conditions of constitutionalism. The residents of the growing cities were no longer bound by the traditional social controls, and if their loyalty was to be transferred to the nation, it had to be a nation founded on rule of law. For all his attempts to minimize the importance of the individual, it is revealing that Hegel was prepared to acknowledge the need for constitutional government. That the idea of constitutionalism has always had but a tenuous hold in the major countries of Europe is one of the tragic facts of modern history. Not the least reason for its insecure existence is the great emphasis placed on national power—an emphasis which, in the final analysis, characterizes Hegel's theory throughout.

11.
Georg Wilhelm
Friedrich Hegel

ITALICS AND CAPITALIZATIONS ARE FOUND ON EVERY PAGE OF
Hegel's writings. His theory of politics is an unrestrained and unapologetic
metaphysical theory: his books bristle with abstract words and phrases which
describe a reality unperceived by the human eye and impervious to inductive
study. To talk of "Reason," "Essence," and "Spirit" is to talk of general ideas
which claim to comprehend the myriad events of the political life. A metaphysical theory can offer much in the way of political understanding, but for
this to happen, the reader must approach it with a tolerance for what often
appears to be high-sounding nonsense. Hegel would not have resorted to metaphysics had he not a good reason, had he found other approaches inadequate
to his purpose. The kind of questions and criticisms which are addressed to
Bentham, for example, are simply not relevant for Hegel. He is, rather, in the
tradition of Plato and Rousseau and Burke. What emerges is an attitude or a
mood; or, to use Hegel's own term, a *Weltanschauung*—a sweeping survey of
the entire world of politics. There is, in Hegel's theory, a sense of certainty
and a range of interpretation which generates a power of its own. If some of
the language seems eccentric, if the uses to which words are put appear alien
to the Anglo-Saxon tradition of political theory, the reader should reserve his
initial judgment. For behind the metaphysics there is represented a theoretical attitude of mind which is often dominant in politics and which is one of
the most difficult to understand. At the very opening of The Philosophy of
History we are lifted to the height of abstract thought.

If the clear idea of reason is not already developed in our minds, in beginning
the study of Universal History, we should have the firm, unconquerable faith that
Reason does exist there; and that the world of intelligence and conscious volition
is not abandoned to chance, but must show itself in the light of the self-cognizant
Idea. . . . It is only an inference from the history of the world, that its develop-

423

ment has been a rational process; that the history in question has constituted the rational necessary course of the World-Spirit—the Spirit whose nature is always one and the same, but which unfolds this its one nature in the phenomena of the World's existence.[1]

A number of comments are in order here on the metaphysical method. First, the tendency to capitalize is not solely a result of the fact that Hegel wrote originally in German, where all nouns are capitalized. The words "Reason," "World," and "Spirit" are singled out for such emphasis, whereas "development," "process," and "nature" are not. This is because Hegel wishes to stress that the things he calls Reason and Spirit are real: they are forces which actually exist and which play a vital role in politics. Second, Hegel asks us to begin our study with an act of faith: we should, at least for the time being, accept his assumptions about the existence of these capitalized forces. He is prepared to admit that he has deduced his knowledge of these facts from his study of history. And if he is to have an opportunity to make a convincing case for his theory as a whole, then the reader must go along with the method and the major ordering ideas at the beginning. Third, the subject matter is sweeping in scope and vague in content. It is too early to ask for precise definitions or explicit explanations. Is there a difference between the Idea and the World-Spirit? If so, we might wonder what it is; and if not, we might want to know why two different terms are used. Questions like these have no easy answers at this stage: it is better to try to understand the general drift of Hegel's analysis and to pick up the component pieces later on.

What Hegel is saying is that the history of the world is not an accidental series of events over time: it is, on the contrary, a rational and comprehensible plan. This pattern is in evidence at all times and places: an understanding of politics is possible only if institutions and personalities are studied in the framework of purposeful historical development. The name Hegel gives to this pattern is the *Idea*. The term itself is not the first which might come to mind, and there are doubtless others which might have been used. But the *Idea* is appropriate because Hegel is concerned to underline the importance of thought in the political process. His major interest is not so much the material world of men and institutions: rather, his focus is on the *Idea*, a coherent and rational spirit which gives direction and purpose to the material world. The *Idea* is not the Natural Law of St. Thomas, nor is it the General Will of Rousseau: it shares attributes of both, however, and it comes closer to the latter than the former. The nearest approximation is Plato's theory of Forms: the *Idea* is the One Big Form which encompasses all of the ideal qualities of Freedom, Justice,

[1] G. W. F. Hegel, *Philosophy of History* (New York: Dover, 1956), translated by J. Sibree, p. 10.

and whatever other political abstractions may happen to be relevant to society at a given time.

That the *Idea* does exist is Hegel's first principle. This, he says, is not a hasty or premature deduction: rather, it emerges from a careful and systematic study of history. "We must proceed historically—empirically," he says.[2] Hegel's empiricism is much like Burke's science of politics: it is a deductive theory of history and society. His appraisal of the facts of history has led him to the conclusions that there is an *Idea* which both directs and embodies the destiny of the world. This is Hegel's reading of history, and he suggests that if other reasonable men engage in the same study, they will also come to appreciate the substance and process of the *Idea*. The effort is not dissimilar to Plato's injunction to proceed from the specific to the general conceptions which explain the ultimate character of objects and relationships. But Hegel does not reserve such knowledge for philosophers: he believes that all who will may understand history in terms of the *Idea*. And such an understanding is not a vocation which individuals may take up or put down as their fancy strikes them. To experience the good life they must seek to apprehend the history of which they are a part. The *Idea* pushes onward in a relentless and frequently bloody procession. Men must march in this parade, and at the same time they ought to perceive the direction in which they are moving.

Freedom, for Hegel, lies in human understanding rather than in human action. The plans made by individual men, by groups of men, bear no causal relation to the larger plan which is inherent in the *Idea*. Men, taken one by one, simply do not count. What appears to be inventive and organized activity is actually blind impulse. To understand politics we must not look at what men do but rather at the force which moves them to act.

The history of mankind does not begin with a *conscious* aim of any kind, as it is the case with the particular circles into which men form themselves of set purposes. The mere social instinct implies a conscious purpose of security for life and property; and when society has been constituted, this purpose becomes more comprehensive. The History of the World begins with its general aim—the realization of the Idea of Spirit—only in an *implicit* form that is, as Nature; a hidden, most profoundly hidden, conscious instinct; and the whole process of History (as already observed), is directed to rendering this unconscious impulse a conscious one.[3]

At the center of the historical stage is the movement from the unconscious to the conscious state. And this is progress towards the philosophical goal of freedom. "The essential nature of freedom . . ." Hegel says, "is to be displayed as coming to a consciousness of itself . . . and thereby realizing its

[2] *Ibid.*
[3] *Ibid.*, p. 25.

existence." [4] The suggestion, then, is that we must learn to live with the *Idea*: men cannot escape it, nor can they ever be exempted from its imperatives.

This means that if men and their institutions are to know freedom, an attempt must be made to understand how and where they fit into the over-all pattern of history. What Hegel calls the "mere social instinct" may bring institutions into being, but they take on a political importance as they undergo a process of development and adjustment over time. If an institution is to be free, it must attune itself to the commands of the *Idea*: only by such obedience can it become conscious of the process it is called upon to serve. History, according to Hegel, is institutional change in the direction of freedom. For men to partake of this freedom they must lift themselves to such a level of awareness that they may know their very reason for existence. Freedom, therefore, cannot be seen apart from consciousness: the free man is characterized not by his uninhibited behavior, but by his realization of his unique role in history. Only the *Idea* can tell him this; only the *Idea* can make him free. "The History of the world," Hegel says, "is none other than the progress of the consciousness of Freedom." [5]

THE DIALECTIC OF HISTORY

Men are both spectators and participants. But Hegel does not emphasize the second role: he does not, like the social-contract theorists, stress the willful decisions of individuals. Human action is, for the most part, waste motion: it can, furthermore, be harmful insofar as it deflects men from the responsibility of understanding. Most men live out their lives as helpless and uncomprehending victims of history's juggernaut. They would be better advised if they understood that they are actors with specific parts to play. The world is the stage, God is the author, and the *Idea* is the plot. No lines in the script may be altered by those called upon to speak them. The most an ordinary player can aspire to is that he may follow the subtle theme of the performance. The most the featured actors may hope for is that they will speak their parts as the Author has intended they be spoken. And the dramatic device which develops the plot, the technique which builds each scene and which rings the curtain on each act, is the dialectic.

The *Idea* is in perpetual development and at constant war with itself. Hegel's history is not a straight-line progression: it is, on the contrary, a never-ending battlefield of ideas. At heart the theory of the dialectic is a simple one. At any given point in time the *Idea* may be called a "thesis": the established expres-

[4] *Ibid.*, p. 19.
[5] *Ibid.*

sion of the historical pattern for the current moment. But a thesis will not remain in a unified or self-consistent state for long. It will sooner or later give birth, phylogenetically, to an idea which stands in direct contradiction to that represented by its parent. The offspring, the "antithesis," will for a time seek to live with the thesis. For a period thesis and antithesis may manage to coexist despite the tensions and animosities that occur. But it is most likely that civil war will be the eventual result. Yet, as in all wars, it will be impossible to call one side the unarguable victor and the other the vanquished. While the antithesis will win in an academic sense, it will not have destroyed the thesis in its entirety. Furthermore, the struggle itself will have transformed the antithesis so it is no longer the purely antagonistic spirit that it once was. The surviving remnants of the thesis and the battleworn antithesis are no longer in such stark contradiction, for in their collision they have had each to take on some of the characteristics of the other. The surviving idea, the "synthesis," rises from the ashes of conflict. This synthesis, once it consolidates itself, may be regarded as a new thesis. And it will soon conceive within itself its own antithesis; and the dialectic, which was only momentarily in abeyance, will begin to work again.

All history may be expressed in terms of the movement of the dialectic. It is not a difficult matter for a student of politics to have an idea of the established thesis of his own time. Nor is it hard to know when a war of ideas is actually raging in a society's midst. What calls for sophistication is the ability to detect the antithesis which is almost imperceptibly emerging from what appears to most to be a unified thesis. Men act, and they believe they act purposefully. But—and here Hegel is at one with Burke—their reason is so limited that they are unable to foresee the consequences of all that they plan and do. The aims they pursue are, they believe, in support of the conventional ideas of society. But, unknown to themselves, this pursuit is bound to contain the means to its own destruction.

Thus the passions of men are gratified; they develop themselves and their aims in accordance with their natural tendencies, and build up the edifice of human society; thus fortifying a position for Right and Order *against themselves.* . . . In history an additional result is commonly produced by human actions beyond that which they aim at and obtain—that which they immediately recognize and desire. They gratify their own interests; but something further is thereby accomplished, latent in the actions in question, though not present to their consciousness, and not included in their design.[6]

If men set about to accomplish X, Hegel is saying, they will also—without realizing it—put in motion forces which will lead to Y. And, more often than not, the second condition will be in direct conflict with the first.

[6] *Ibid.,* p. 27.

Legislators may try, as rationally as they know how, to make their country secure and protect it from subversion. They can immediately recognize and desire the need for national security. But the steps they take to promote both security and loyalty may have the actual consequence of weakening the nation. For latent in the actions in question can well be restrictions which hamper scientific development or demoralize the individuals who have a contribution to make to national strength. Something more than the original intention is thereby accomplished: effects which were not included in the original design are brought about. This is, of course, a minor example of the dialectic at work. But it serves to show how purposeful efforts to pursue a thesis will carry with them an unintended antithesis—and how, in time, the antithesis may actually defeat the original thesis. This, Hegel would say, is the rule rather than the exception, and it operates on all levels of political endeavor, large and small. Plans for peace will foment war; programs for prosperity will induce depression; the pursuit of stability will lead to change. Hegel does not say that an awareness of antithetical forces can lead to their removal. There is no such linkage of knowledge and political action in his theory. He is simply saying that it is not enough to be conscious of the prevailing thesis: those who would understand politics must know how and where to read between the lines, how to detect the shape of things to come, and where to be as the future emerges from within the present.

The dialectic is a law: it cannot be mastered and it cannot be evaded. "It is not of such a nature as to be tossed to and fro amid the superficial play of accidents," Hegel says, "but is rather the absolute arbiter of things, entirely unmoved by contingencies, which, indeed, it applies and manages for its own purposes." [7] The chief quality of the dialectic is that it is creative. Out of its ceaseless struggle, out of the unending war between its component parts, comes not destruction but creation. Indeed, any original condition, no matter how decadent or tyrannical its major outlines may appear to be, carries in itself the seeds of its own reform. For this reason, no society or social institution should be condemned out of hand: the changes which will eventually be wrought on it are already invisibly beginning in its own framework. "Progress appears as an advancing from the imperfect to the more perfect," Hegel says. "But the former must not be understood abstractly as *only* the imperfect, but as something which involves the very opposite of itself—the so-called perfect —as a *germ* or impulse." [8]

This analysis, of course, can be turned two ways. On the one hand, an institution may be so structured that it is capable of adapting itself to new con-

[7] *Ibid.*, p. 54.
[8] *Ibid.*, p. 57.

ditions. In this case it will be able to meet demands for reform in a flexible and appropriate manner. It may be said that its mode of construction permits it to resolve conflicts and yet continue to survive. The American Constitution would be a case in point here. On the other hand, an institution may be so rigid that the more it is called upon to change the more it digs in and persists in its habitual ways. In that case the indictment of the critics will be a clear one for all to see, and opposition to the institution itself—not merely its practices—will gain strength in society. The rigidity and persistence which are displayed have within them the inducement to progress. Absolute monarchies are a case in point here.

Hegel's philosophy of history refers largely to violent change: reform motivated by the inflexibility of traditional practices and institutions. His discussion of political institutions, which comes later on, shows a preference for change which is orderly and which can be channeled in predictable ways. But, in either event, the dialectic is always present. Conflict is the abiding characteristic of politics. If there seem to be occasional periods which are tranquil, we may be sure that a new antithesis is mustering its strength for a new surge. Students of politics are warned not to be deceived by apparent unity. In the aftermath of a struggle it may look as if the defeated party has been made to submit, that it can retain no aspect of the way of life it tried unsuccessfully to champion. The dialectic, however, is merely recuperating from its exertions.

There are many considerable periods in History in which this development seems to have been intermitted; in which, we rather might say, the whole enormous gain of previous culture appears to have been entirely lost; after which, unhappily, a new commencement has been necessary, made in the hope of recovering—by the assistance of some remains saved from the wreck of a former civilization, and by dint of a renewed incalculable expenditure of strength and time—one of the regions which had been an ancient possession of that civilization.[9]

To anyone who visited Germany in 1945 the appearance would be of a country which had lost its national and cultural identity. Factories, fields, homes—not to mention the Germans themselves—had been reduced to rubble. Yet in this wreck of a former civilization, although it might not then have been perceptible to a visitor's eye, a new commencement was being made. That Hitler's regime had been toppled at the cost of so much destruction was nevertheless a creative act. What remained in the waste and starvation, unnoticed by the traveler, was the energy and pride of the German people. That it existed and had to exist must be assumed. For the dialectic presupposes that total destruction is an impossibility.

The Idea, whether it is expressed in war or any other political process, never

[9] Ibid., p. 56.

makes a clean break with the past. "It assumes successive forms which it successively transcends," Hegel says. "And by this very process of transcending its earlier stages, gains an affirmative, and, in fact, a richer and more concrete shape." [10] Hegel's regret over the bombings and the human slaughter would not be unqualified. The dialectic of history makes no distinction between death and birth: the two are successive stages in a continuous process. "Change, while it imports dissolution, involves at the same time the rise of a new life— that while death is the issue of life, life is also the issue of death." [11] If Hegel takes the morbid view, if he cites with grim pleasure the destruction attending social and political change, he is only driving home an oft-forgotten rule: that progress is not had save at a price.

REASON, FREEDOM, AND THE HERO IN HISTORY

The *Idea* develops relentlessly and at a tremendous human cost. Political history is an endless tragedy, and neither the nobility of nations nor the virtue of individuals grant exemption from its toll.

Without rhetorical exaggeration, a simply truthful combination of the miseries that have overwhelmed the noblest of nations, and the finest exemplars of private virtue—forms a picture of most fearful aspect, and excites emotions of the profoundest and most hopeless sadness, counterbalanced by no consolatory result.[12]

If this is the price levied by the dialectic, it is in order to ask what is being purchased. "But even regarding History as the slaughter-bench at which the happiness of peoples, the wisdom of states, and the virtue of individuals have been victimized," Hegel says, "the question involuntarily arises—to what principle, to what final aim these enormous sacrifices have been offered." [13] The first answer, and it is the answer of Burke, is that our compassion is misplaced if we occupy ourselves with individual happiness. A political theory which gives primacy to the individual is intellectually arrogant and historically superficial. Mankind has walked the earth for but a fraction of the planet's life, and the span of years known by any single man is only a split second on the cosmic clock. On what ground do men complain if history treats them cavalierly? "The History of the world is not the theatre of happiness," Hegel says.[14] And there is no reason to expect that it should be. Men do not constitute an exceptional case, and they have no legitimate claim for preferred treatment. Just as

10 *Ibid.,* p. 63.
11 *Ibid.,* pp. 72-73.
12 *Ibid.,* p. 21.
13 *Ibid.*
14 *Ibid.,* p. 26.

a farmer can decimate a society of ants with a sweep of his hoe, so ought men to anticipate a similar fate on the slaughter-bench of history. The burden of proof, Hegel would say, is not on the theory of the dialectic: it is, rather, on those who would like to believe that the homo sapiens has privileges and immunities from the laws of history.

Yet if the Idea is a stern master, it is also a rational one: the slaughter-bench is not an end in itself, but a means necessary for attaining a greater goal. The reason which suffuses the Idea has ways of guiding the actions of men so that its purpose is fulfilled. This external direction, the link between objective reason and subjective passion, is no unpremeditated stratagem. "The cunning of reason," Hegel says, ". . . sets the passions to work for itself, while that which develops its existence through such impulsion pays the penalty and suffers loss." [15] The Idea sets flame to men's passions, and they are the ones who suffer and die; but in this noble holocaust society is recreated and history moves onward. This, then, is all that men are good for and it is what they are placed on earth to accomplish. "Individuals, their desires and the gratification of them, are thus sacrificed, and their happiness given up to the empire of chance, to which it belongs," Hegel says. ". . . As a general rule, individuals come under the category of means to an ulterior end." [16]

Yet if individuals are means, they are also connected to the end at which the Idea aims. Like Plato and Aristotle, and Rousseau and Burke, Hegel identifies social and individual happiness and makes the second dependent on the achievement of the first. Men, if left to define and pursue their own happiness, will most surely bring destruction to themselves. But the chances are good that it is precisely this that they are going to do and it is what they have always done. Rather than exhort men to change their irrational ways, Hegel sees beyond the sound and fury of human behavior: he sees that even the vain pursuits of men aid in the fulfillment of the larger pattern.

And the end result is close to Rousseau's conception of the General Will: the self-interested and irrational acts of individuals "cancel out" so as to produce an end which is rational and which men could not achieve for themselves if they set out consciously to do so. The cunning of reason is possible because irrational men are participants in the Idea. The Idea then, is made real through human activity. "Not only do they in the very act of realizing it, make it the occasion of satisfying personal desires, whose purpose is diverse from that aim," Hegel says, "but they share in that ideal aim itself, and are for that very reason objects of their own existence." [17] Men are never independent of the Idea:

---

[15] Ibid., p. 33.
[16] Ibid.
[17] Ibid.

they can have no life apart from its direction. Even when being led to the slaughter-bench, they march in the van of a higher reason; even when they gratify their selfish and shortsighted impulses, they will be cunningly turned to a higher purpose.

The tragedy is not that the happiness of individuals is given up to sacrifice: that is made inevitable by the laws of history. The cause for concern is that so many never realize that there is a pattern emerging and that they are part of it. Most men live and die without understanding that they contribute to the development of the *Idea*. Without this realization, men suffer and are slaves. With it, their physical suffering and material deprivation are not lessened, but consciousness of the role they play makes them free.

For Hegel reason is social and historical. This postulate is based on certain assumptions about man and society, and from it flows a political theory with small place for the discrete individual. Starting with other assumptions about man and society, Locke and Bentham conceived of reason as individual, and their political theories saw the community as no more than an aggregate of the men who comprised it. These opposing conceptions of reason—what it is and where it is to be found—generate contrasting ideas of human freedom. For Bentham and the other liberal writers, freedom is seen in terms of action: the ability to do. For Hegel and the organic theorists, freedom is consciousness: the capacity to know.

If Hegel's law of the dialectic is inexorable, it nevertheless is a law of progress. Despite the ravages of history, men have become increasingly aware of the forces which direct their destinies. "The essential nature of freedom—which involves it in absolute necessity—is to be displayed as coming to a consciousness of itself . . ." Hegel says. "The question also assumes the form of the union of *freedom* and *necessity*; the latent abstract process of Spirit being regarded as *necessity*, while that which exhibits itself in the conscious will of men, as their interest, belongs to the domain of *freedom*." [18] Freedom and necessity, the free will and determined behavior, are part of the identical process. Freedom is not freedom from the *Idea*, nor is it freedom to do as one pleases. Rather, it is an awareness of what it is possible to do and of what ought to be done in any historical epoch. There is an area in which men may make choices from among alternatives: this is the area of freedom. And men will serve themselves well if they come to know the metes and bounds of that area and exercise their potentialities within it. The experience of history has two lessons: the first is that freedom may become the province of not simply some but all men; the second is that political institutions best facilitate a true realization of the free life.

[18] *Ibid.*, pp. 19, 26.

Unlike other theorists, Hegel does not celebrate civilizations of the past. Through the workings of the dialectic, modern societies have a legacy from their predecessors, and the test of history has ensured that only the best has survived. But while freedom may have begun with the Greeks and Romans as an idea, those societies themselves could not be considered free.

The consciousness of Freedom first arose among the Greeks, and therefore they were free; but they, and the Romans likewise, knew only that some are free—not man as such. Even Plato and Aristotle did not know this. The Greeks, therefore, had slaves; and their whole life and the maintenance of their splendid liberty, was implicated with the institution of slavery: a fact, moreover, which made that liberty on the one hand only an accidental, transient and limited growth; on the other hand, constituted it a rigorous thraldom of our common nature—of the Human.[19]

The splendid liberty of classical antiquity was liberty for a restricted class. A fortunate few could pursue the good life because they had the privileges of leisure, education, and wealth. Glaucon, Thrasymachus, and Adeimantus could sit together and discuss truth and justice for days on end because they had slaves to hew wood and draw water for them. A society in which only some are free is, for Hegel, no shining exemplar—even if it produces a Plato and an Aristotle. For the few ride on the backs of the many, and those who labor for their living are no less human and no less capable of enjoying freedom than the leisured and literate.

Hegel's theory is thus equalitarian: freedom is a meaningful goal only if it is shared by all men. For every citizen shares in the Idea, and if institutions of slavery and oppression deny such participation, then a society itself cannot claim a title to freedom. The modern world is beginning to show signs of progress. What Hegel calls the "German nations"—the countries of the Western World—have infused human equality into their conception of freedom. The Christian idea that all men stand as equals in the sight of God has had its political consequences.

The German nations, under the influence of Christianity, were the first to attain the consciousness that man, as man, is free: that it is the freedom of spirit which constitutes its essence. This consciousness arose first in religion, the inmost region of spirit; but to introduce the principle into the various relations of the actual world, involves a more extensive problem than its simple implanation; a problem whose solution and application require a severe and lengthened process of culture.[20]

The focus is on the idea of freedom more than its institutional expression. Christianity and slavery coexisted in the Western World for almost 2,000 years. But, Hegel is suggesting, they were in dialectical conflict, and the Chris-

[19] Ibid., p. 18.
[20] Ibid.

tian idea of equality was at war with the inequality inherent in human slavery. The Christian conjunction of freedom and equality—the idea that freedom is the birthright of all men—has developed among Western nations. Theories of privilege, of caste and of class, are no longer defensible at the current stage of history. And this is progress toward the idea of perfect freedom.

The problem of implementing this idea in actual politics will be a prolonged one: men must learn to live by new principles and to adjust their behavior to new conditions. "That application of the principle to political relations; the thorough molding and interpenetration of the constitution of society by it, is a process identical with history itself," Hegel says.[21] It is impossible ever to return to a limited conception of freedom: that it must henceforward be universal is the dictate of the dialectic. This evolutionary movement is implicit in the Idea: Greece and Rome were not ready for full freedom—the Western World now is. In time other nations will share if not Christianity—for it, too, can be transformed by the dialectic—then the Christian idea of equality. This commitment to progress, to raising all men to the stage where they can be conscious of the liberty which is their desert, softens the blows of the slaughterbench and makes bearable the determinism of the Idea.

At the same time, Hegel singles out for attention the man of action. To be sure, the plans of men are again and again doomed to frustration. Even so, these futile endeavors are the stuff of politics and they deserve close attention. And if at one time the vainglorious passions we see are destined to failure, at the same time the cunning of reason builds for the future on the ill-starred ventures of the present. The student of politics must examine what men do because their actions are intertwined with the master plan of history. "Two elements, therefore, enter into the object of our investigation," Hegel says. "The first the Idea, the second the complex of human passions: the one the warp, the other the woof of the vast arras-web of Universal History." [22]

Most men are passive: in the sphere of politics they neither act nor do they understand. They are the pawns of history, and they accept their fate without rebellion or protest. These men are slaughtered by war, starved by famine, enslaved by tyranny. The movements of history are not of their making, and they can imagine no alternative to the life they must bear. However, there are in all eras a few extraordinary individuals who are active and even revolutionary. They are not members of a particular class, either privileged or otherwise. These men, who emerge at random from the population, are men of political action. They have aspirations and interests, and they pursue these singlemindedly.

[21] Ibid.
[22] Ibid., p. 23.

I mean here nothing more than the human activity as resulting from private interests—special, or if you will, self-seeking designs—with this qualification, that the whole energy of will and character is devoted to their attainment; that other interests (which would in themselves constitute attractive aims) or rather all things else, are sacrificed to them.[23]

Such men, it is to be expected, are self-interested and relentless. As individuals, they will probably be ruthless and impervious to the well-being of their fellow men. Yet these men are the chief instruments of the dialectic, and hence the agency whereby human freedom is enlarged. They sustain the old institutions of society and, more important, create the new ones. They are, usually unknowingly, the authors of the antithesis which challenges the prevailing orthodoxy. By fomenting conflict and contradiction they open the way for progress. "This principle is an essential phase in the development of the creating Idea, of Truth striving and urging towards consciousness of itself," Hegel says. "Historical men—World-Historical Individuals—are those in whose aims such a general principle lies." [24] These men give the dialectic a substance to work with: while the Idea is the only lasting reality, its expression in human politics is given by the few who have the courage and the arrogance to attempt to impose their will on history. They build the edifices which are the shape of things to come.

These men are clearly Hegel's favorites. He finds them awesome as personalities, and he recognizes their contribution to the progress of mankind.

They may be called Heroes, inasmuch as they have derived their purposes and their vocation, not from the calm, regular course of things, sanctioned by the existing order; but from a concealed fount—one which has not attained to phenomenal, present existence—from that inner spirit still hidden beneath the surface, which, impinging on the outer world as on a shell, bursts it in pieces, because it is another kernel than that which belonged to the shell in question. They are men, therefore, who appear to draw the impulse of their life from themselves; and whose deeds have produced a condition of things and a complex of historical relations which appear to be only their interests, and their work.

A World-historical individual is not so unwise as to indulge a variety of wishes to divide his regards. He is devoted to the One Aim, regardless of all else. It is even possible that such men may treat other great, even sacred interests, inconsiderately; conduct which is indeed obnoxious to moral reprehension. But so mighty a form must trample down many an innocent flower—crush to pieces many an object in its path.[25]

Moral judgment cannot be passed on the Heroes as it might on lesser men. They are exempted from censure because their acts of destruction, regardless of the motives which impel them, are acts of creation. Such titans among men

[23] *Ibid.*, pp. 23–24.
[24] *Ibid.*, p. 29.
[25] *Ibid.*, pp. 30, 32.

are to be welcomed and applauded: even the flowers crushed under their feet should rejoice at being trampled by so mighty a force.

The Hero is a builder: of a nation, a political movement, an industrial empire, a new religion. He rises to do battle with the established order, a status quo already living on borrowed time. He defies conventional standards and seeks to impose his own morality on society. Chaos may result, but that is just what is needed at this moment in history. The Hero is no philosopher: indeed, if he were he could not adhere so steadfastly to his practical goal. Nor should it be thought that he is conscious of the dialectic which he serves. "Such individuals had no consciousness of the general *Idea* they were unfolding, while prosecuting those aims of theirs; on the contrary, they were practical political men," Hegel says. "But at the same time they were thinking men who had an insight into the requirements of the time—*what was ripe for development*. This was the very Truth for their age, for their world." [26]

The established thesis, over the passage of time, ceases to have relevance for the emerging needs of society. Its claim to continued existence is ready to be challenged, and it is Hegel's "World-historical individual" who throws down the gauntlet. Such a man is not of a philosophical bent, and he is not aware that his radical behavior is an expression of the dialectical antithesis. The Hero pursues his single-minded goal, and if he thinks of himself as an agent of history, it is purely coincidental. The characteristic of these extraordinary men is that they have an insight—perhaps better called an intuition—into what changes the world is ready to accept. Political history tells of many would-be trailblazers whose misfortune was that they broached their plans too soon. And it relates of just as many capable men who lived at times propitious for change and yet who misjudged the direction to be taken. The mark of Hegel's Hero is not only that he is a man of action, but that he understands when the time and place are ripe for a new departure. If he is not a philosopher, he must at least have the intelligence to assess the needs of his time. By blending his passion for action, his strength of character, and his political insight he is the one who gives the *Idea* its realization in the actual world. Heroes, then, are to be known not by their motives but by their deeds. "They are *great* men," Hegel says, "because they willed and accomplished something great." [27]

Despite the fact that Hegel's theory of politics is a monument in metaphysical speculation, it leads to the deepest approbation for the practical man of action. Hegel's applause is not, as was Plato's, for the philosopher: indeed, the concern of the Hero is a self-interested one and hence irrational. Furthermore, such men are more often than not tragic figures. Like all mortal men

[26] *Ibid.*, p. 30.
[27] *Ibid.*, p. 31.

on the political stage, their reach exceeds their grasp. If they make grandiose plans for themselves and society, their fate is that they will never taste the fruit of their labors.

If we go on to cast a look at the fate of these World-historical persons, whose vocation it was to be the agents of the World-Spirit—we shall find it to have been no happy one. They attained no calm enjoyment; their whole life was labor and trouble; their whole nature was nought else but their master-passion. When their object is attained they fall off like empty hulls from the kernel. They die early, like Alexander; they are murdered, like Caesar; transported to St. Helena, like Napoleon. This fearful consolation—that historical men have not enjoyed what is called happiness, and of which only private life (and this may be passed under very various external circumstances) is capable—this consolation those may draw from history, who stand in need of it. . . .[28]

Heroes, too, are instruments of the cunning of reason which turns the irrational and self-interested acts of men to a higher purpose. Hegel does not suggest that an Alexander the Great, a Caesar, a Napoleon is a more rational creature than the humble citizen who lives and dies in poverty and ignorance. On the contrary, Hegel would agree with Burke that human reason is so frail a quality that the difference between Hero and helot is not a significant one. All men, regardless of rank and status, look much the same when their reasoning powers are compared with the reason inherent in the *Idea*. The Hero stands out because of his conceit, his will to power, and his ability to sense that the time is ripe. And he pays for his fame: his career becomes his whole life, and that life is to be ended in assassination or exile. Lesser men, if they so desire, may console themselves by reflecting on the unhappiness of the Hero. Yet such consolation is a small-minded act: the Hero serves the *Idea* and hence serves his fellow men by ushering in a new and better age. If the process is perforce a violent one, if innocent flowers are trampled underfoot, men would do well to understand that their unhappiness is a means to a greater end. And if a grim smile comes hard at such times, it ought not to be forgotten that the Hero at the center of the stage is the unhappiest actor in the tragedy of history.

There are interesting similarities, but also crucial differences, in the theories of Machiavelli and Hegel. Where the one speaks of Dame Fortune, the other relies on the *Idea*. Where Machiavelli discusses Lions and Foxes, Hegel talks of the Hero. Both agree that political success hinges on the moment of time when society is ready to be led in a new direction. Machiavelli's Lions and Foxes are prisoners of their peculiar personalities, and they must hope that history favors their ascendancy. Hegel does not deign to introduce this psychological element, but it is quite clear that his concern is largely with Lions and not Foxes. If he endows his Lions with the intelligence to assess the paths

[28] *Ibid.*

open to them, he also indicates that their successes are bound to be failures. The Hero who seeks personal power and glory will have but a short moment of fame before his doom is sounded. But the chief contrast between the two theories is at a deeper level. Machiavelli's Dame Fortune is a metaphor for the unknown and ununderstood caprice of historical change: she is endowed with no sense of purpose and no master plan of universal progress. The *Idea* is of quite a different order: it is both plan and purpose, and it relates these abstractions to the seemingly irrational actions of men. While Lions and Foxes and Heroes will pursue their self-defined and narrow quests for personal power, Hegel shows that the Hero is part of history and not simply its pawn. Machiavelli was no metaphysician, and his interest was more with power than it was with purpose. Hegel's concern is with men as means: the *Idea* is the end. If men of action, if great deeds and heroic failures are to command our attention, they should be seen in a broader perspective.

It will fall to Marx and Engels to take Hegel's dialectic of history and pull it down from the realm of spirit to the material world of politics. For them the dialectic deals not with a metaphysical *Idea*, but with the realities of human society. There is, to be sure, a metaphysical basis to the Marxian dialectic; but it is also conjoined with men's consciousness in such a way that political action may be purposeful and, what is more important, successful. Marx and Engels give the dialectic a coherence which is lacking in Hegel's broad theory of history. But they also put it to work for a specific and extremely controversial purpose. If Hegel leaves the future in doubt, Marx and Engels purport to know what it is.

THE POLITICS OF NATIONALISM

In Hegel's political theory the state is seen not only as an instrument of legal power, but also as the embodiment of a national heritage. Interestingly, theorists like Hobbes, Locke, and Bentham were able to talk of states and governments as if they bore no relation to particular countries. A citizen's loyalty is, in fact, seldom to the state as an institution. Most people pledge and give their allegiance to the country of their birth or adoption regardless of the political system that country might have. It is only the exceptional person who will quit his native land because he finds its exercise of political power unbearable: the vast majority would find the severing of national roots even more unbearable. A theory of politics, therefore, must acknowledge that in most cases state and nation are conjoined. It is the state which ultimately acts in the nation's name, and it draws on national sentiment as its primary source of power. All states, no matter what institutional or ideological colors they may wear, are obliged to pay deference to national traditions and national aspirations. Even purportedly universal ideologies like fascism and communism must make concessions to the peculiar national sentiments they encounter throughout the world. On the other side of the coin, if a political movement makes a point of demonstrating its patriotic motives, it may gain freedom of action to bring about important institutional changes under the guise of enhancing the national interest.

Hegel emphasizes the power of national loyalty by talking of the nation as if it were an individual. It is, he suggests, an organism with an explicit life of its own:

> Each particular National genius is to be treated as only one individual in the process of Universal History. For that history is the exhibition of the divine, absolute development of spirit in its highest forms—that gradation by which it attains its truth and consciousness of itself. The forms which these grades of progress assume are the characteristic "National Spirits" of History; the peculiar tenor of their moral life of their Government, their Art, Religion, and Science.[29]

The idea of a "national spirit" is a controversial one. As a figure of speech, one can say that America is generous, Germany is industrious, and France is amorous. But Hegel means a great deal more than this. First of all, he intends to say that "national spirit," as it is found in each country, is real. It is not a metaphor, nor is it just a shorthand device for making a complicated point in a simple way. The spirit or genius of a nation is no less real than the *Idea* of which it is an expression. Furthermore, the national spirit is the best place to observe the unfolding of the *Idea* in the actual world: the stages of development attained by a nation's art, religion, and science are the clearest manifestations of its progress through history. To speak of a nation as if it were a person is to show that it has a capacity for self-consciousness and growth: men and nations both stand in integral relation to the *Idea*, and they participate in its workings through the dialectic.

A nation, then, is an institutional complex and it is also an idea. "It is a Spirit having strictly defined characteristics, which erects itself into an objective world, that exists and persists in a particular religious form of worship, customs, constitution, and political laws—in the whole complex of its institutions—in the events and transactions that make up its history," Hegel says. "That is its work—that is what this particular Nation is. Nations are what their deeds are."[30] Nations and national sentiment are real. At the current stage of historical development the nation-state is the political expression of the *Idea*. Some may argue that nationalism is outmoded: that it may once have

---

[29] *Ibid.*, p. 53.
[30] *Ibid.*, p. 74.

served its purpose, but that an international spirit is now needed if the world is to survive in peace. Hegel does not anticipate such an argument, nor does he offer a direct reply to it. What he does try to do is to show how a sense of nationhood has a rational basis in the political life.

Men are forever in search of identity. The problem concerned both Rousseau and Burke: one offered for an answer the democratic community; the other's solution was a stratified society. In each of these every citizen would have an acknowledged place, and all could feel themselves to be integral parts of an organic whole. Rousseau called for active participation in a small and homogeneous community setting. Burke asked that the classes and orders of society be fixed by tradition and preserved by custom. Both of these prescriptions, however, are ill suited to the real world that Hegel sees. Men cannot maintain the aristocratic social pattern in the face of historical progress. The trend, on the contrary, is for greater social mobility and a breakdown of the ancient institutions on which Burke relied. Identity can no longer be found in the traditional class memberships of an earlier age: men move too rapidly and develop aspirations which transcend the stations they once accepted without question. Nor is Rousseau's image of sturdy peasants under an oak a viable solution in an age when great nation-states are the principal political units. There is no returning to government by town meeting and direct democracy. While Hegel is prepared to use, in the Idea, a conception similar to the General Will, he finds Rousseau's institutional arrangements inadequate.

Our era is the era of the large nation-state, and it is best to make the most of this situation. Personal identity, Hegel says, can be found by accepting the nation as a fact. Once this is done, then national citizenship can impart to men the feeling of identification they continually seek.

The State, its laws, its arrangements, constitute the rights of its members; its natural features, its mountains, air, and water, are their country, their fatherland, their outward material property; the history of this state, their deeds; what their ancestors have produced, belongs to them and lives in their memory. All is their possession, just as they are possessed by it; for it constitutes their existence, their being. . . . It is this matured totality which constitutes One Being, the spirit of One People. To it the individual members belong; each unit is the Son of his Nation. . . .

The relation of the individual to that spirit is that he appropriates to himself this substantial existence; that it becomes his character and capability, enabling him to have a definite place in the world—to be something. For he finds the being of the people to which he belongs an already established, firm world—objectively present to him—with which he has to incorporate himself.[31]

The identification of a citizen with his country takes various forms. If the German wears his love of Fatherland on his sleeve, the Dane or the Nor-

[31] *Ibid.*, pp. 52, 74.

wegian tends to display his affection in a manner which is more subdued. But all men need such a feeling of identity. And because other loyalties are inadequate to this task, participation in the national spirit comes to play an indispensable role in men's lives. The desire to be something can be filled if a man can say, "I am an American," or "I am a Canadian." To be sure, men have other allegiances: religious, regional, economic, and so forth. But these are again and again seen to be subordinate in character. Men are born into a nation: "an already established, firm world." That so many will fight and die for it, their country right or wrong, is overpowering evidence that this is their ultimate loyalty. Pleas that international attachments—to religious or political movements—be given higher priority in the final analysis fall on deaf ears. Men may be Roman Catholics or Communists, but they are also Frenchmen or Chinese. They will subordinate and transform their religion and politics so as to be consonant with their national sentiments. International movements which are successful understand these imperatives, and they allow such adjustments to be made. There are always some exceptional individuals who can live as men without countries. But for all who claim such independence, when a genuine test of loyalty comes, only a few are willing to act on it. Hegel's theory applies to the vast majority: the ordinary citizens who derive a sense of kinship, self-esteem, and belonging from their national citizenship.

The politics of nationalism, Hegel would agree, are irrational. But history has placed us in the age of nationalism, and the cunning of reason turns national sentiment in progressive directions. It may even impel war and destruction, and so bring in a new era of international peace and global loyalty; but Hegel does not venture such a speculation, and he contents himself with analyzing what he sees. However, the very idea of nationalism is a curious one even on Hegel's own terms. Loyalty to a small and homogeneous community, as expressed by Plato and Rousseau, is understandable and plausible. Each member knows his fellow citizens, and each can understand the workings of the political process at first hand. And if Burke's society is larger, each individual nevertheless lives in a fixed class or order where he too understands his role in the political life. The modern nation-state is not only large, but the experience of its growth weakens the loyalties to lesser associations. A society which was once comprised of a plurality of traditional groups is gradually transformed into a mass of individuals. This was Burke's great fear, and it underlay his critique of liberalism. Hegel seeks to avoid the damage which a mass society inflicts on the individual personality by encouraging a sense of national loyalty in all who reside inside the territorial boundaries. This will give the feeling of identity and belonging which the nation-state itself was so instrumental in breaking down. Loyalty is not to a class or a locality, because these ties are no longer meaningful, but is now to the nation as a whole. The problem is that many millions of men do not constitute a community in the traditional sense: Plato and Rousseau knew this and they purposely imposed conditions having to do with size. A modern nation-state is simply too large for its members to know one another on a personal basis. And, what is more important, it is impossible for citizens to participate in—or even understand—the making of laws and the administration of justice. The larger a society is, the more individuals must gain their image of political reality at second or third hand: leaders must arise to inform them about the needs of the nation and to instruct the ordinary citizens on their roles in securing national goals. The spirit of nationalism can result in strong loyalties to the state, but these loyalties are rendered to an institution which the citizen sees at a distance and which he knows only through the reports of others. For this reason the perception of political reality can be a distorted one: the average man must rely on the information which is given him, and these communications may be manipulated in order that particular ends will be achieved. And if each citizen's loyalty is primarily to the nation or state, rather than to lesser associations in society, then the population becomes all the more dependent on strong and centralized leadership. In short, the national tie is the only one which remains: if it is not exploited, then the body of citizens will form a fragmented and aimless mass.

Yet if the spirit of nationalism is invoked and used as a solidifying instrument, there is the possibility that an easily led population will be mobilized for purposes of war and aggression. Most political theorists have no small fears of a mass society and leadership which plays on irrational sentiments. Yet the solutions offered are clearly impracticable: Rousseau's small community of sturdy peasant and Burke's stratified society of orders and classes both lie in the past rather than the future. The large nation-state to which other social institutions are subordinated is the pattern of the present. Hegel realizes that the exploitation of nationalist sentiment carries risks: he is not unaware of the fact that nationalism can be a destructive as well as a constructive force in men's lives. In his discussion of political institutions he searches for ways and means of curbing the excesses of political irrationality. The problem is to accept the existence of the national spirit, to channel it, and to harness its energy. Whether this tremendous ferment, once unleashed, can be kept under control is one of the great political challenges of our times. Modern man must possess a sense of national identity if he is to have that minimum security which makes life bearable. Yet to rely on the spirit of nationalism is to play with fire: at one moment it gives a comfortable warmth; at another it destroys all it touches.

The rise and fall of nations is the pattern of political history. A state is fulfilling its appointed role when it displays a sense of direction and mission. All nations are born in war or revolution: they all emerge from the struggle between thesis and antithesis. As the turmoil and shouting dies, as the emerging synthesis consolidates its gains into a new thesis, the state may begin to rest on its laurels.

The contradiction between its potential, subjective being—its inner aim and life—and its *actual* being is removed; it has attained full reality, has itself objectively present to it. But this having been attained, the activity displayed by the spirit of the people in question is no longer needed; it has its desire. The Nation can still accomplish much in war and peace at home and abroad; but the living substantial soul itself may be said to have ceased its activity. The essential, supreme interest has consequently vanished from its life, for interest is present only where there is opposition.[32]

Just as Hegel showed a preference for the tempestuous Hero, so he shows a partiality for the tumultuous nation. The revolutionary epoch, when the national potential blossoms into actuality, is when the spirit of the people is at its finest hour. At that moment citizens are infused with their national character and they are at one with the spirit which embraces themselves and their fellow countrymen. Once the revolution has been consolidated, however, decay begins almost imperceptibly to set in. New habits and customs mingle with those which survived the struggle, and a quietude settles over the land. Men become content with what they have, and they begin to take their national identity for granted. They may still be militarily strong and materially prosperous, but they look backward to their heritage rather than forward to their destiny. Generations may go by without challenge to the prevailing order: if an antithesis is growing, it is developing slowly and unnoticed by a somnolent population.

The great enemy of national progress, Hegel says, is custom. While St. Thomas and Burke welcomed settled patterns of social intercourse, Hegel sees them as signs that a society is played out. Men and nations who live by custom are, although they do not realize it, already relics of the past.

Custom is activity without opposition, for which there remains only a formal duration; in which the fulness and zest which originally characterized the aim of life are out of the question—a merely external sensuous existence which has ceased to throw itself enthusiastically into its object. Thus perish individuals, thus perish peoples by a natural death; and though the latter may continue in being, it is an existence without intellect or vitality; having no need of its institutions, because the need for them is satisfied—a political nullity and tedium.[33]

[32] *Ibid.*, p. 74.
[33] *Ibid.*, pp. 74-75.

Tedium and death are the eventual fate of all nations. Some, by their vigor and good fortune, will have a longer life than others, but all are subject to the laws of the dialectic. Custom does not challenge itself: it is opposed by forces outside the consensus. Internal revolutionary movements or external aggressors will bring down a state which no longer has the will to survive. The people and the territory are consumed in the dialectical onrush of a new political force. There may be death, but there will never be total destruction. The vanquished will transmit a portion of their civilization and customs to the victors, and in so doing plant the seeds of a new decay. Ideas and institutions carry on from epoch to epoch: nations live and die, but the dialectic counts its losses and moves on.

The death of nations can be a mortal blow to the citizens who depend on the vitality of the national spirit. If a nation ceases to act with passion and vigor, if its enthusiasm for a national mission wanes over time, then it is robbing its countrymen of the will to exist which they so stand in need of. If a nation is dispirited, then men will fail to rise to the common defense; or they may even emigrate to another soil. In either case, the toll will be a heavy one for the dejected and uprooted. The only solution, Hegel says, is that a new national spirit must rise from the decayed ruins of the old.

In order that a truly universal interest may arise, the spirit of a People must advance to the adoption of some new purpose; but whence can this new purpose originate? It would be a higher, more comprehensive conception of itself—a transcending of its principle—but this very act would involve a principle of a new order, a new National Spirit.[34]

This, of course, is easier said than done. It is clear that nations such as Sweden and Spain will never again rise to the heights of national grandeur they once knew. Yet a country like Germany, after ignominious defeat in 1918 and a harrowing inflation in the 1920's, was able to adopt a new sense of purpose and a new conception of order under a new regime in the 1930's. The rebirth of national spirit may take not a decade but many centuries. Both Egypt and China, after more than a thousand years on the sidelines of history, have become national forces to be reckoned with: the one seeks leadership of the Middle East and perhaps all Africa; the other cherishes hegemony over Asia and perhaps the world. In the case of China a new mission—the Marxist ideology—has conjoined with emerging national power. Hegel, who opens his *Philosophy of History* with a description of the past glories of the Oriental world, would probably applaud the new spirit of the Chinese people as their nation advances to the adoption of a new sense of purpose.

[34] *Ibid.*, p. 75.

Hegel's theory is a radical one: it welcomes change and it sees struggle as the necessary condition of progress. The Hero and the nation-state, both instruments of energy and activity, are the central actors on his stage. So long as they are in motion and not at rest, they are bringing to human politics the principles inherent in the *Idea*. At the same time, the theory has the appearance of a conservative statement: it endows with moral authority the political conditions which exist at any given point in time. Men and nations are not called upon to choose between alternative paths of action, because it is assumed that they will pursue their irrational and self-interested ways despite the exhortations addressed to them.

Yet if Hegel is a conservative, he is a conservative with a difference. While he applauds power and authority, they may inhere in a revolutionary movement no less than in an established state. There is no celebration of custom and habit, and the Heroes who are extolled are not noted for their wisdom or virtue. Furthermore, the dialectic itself defies the premise that there can be such a thing as a status quo: there is only ceaseless change, although it may be at work deep beneath the surface.

In the final analysis, Hegel's theory is radical or conservative depending on the uses to which it is put: on the time and place at which it is applied, and on the situation of the men who are wont to invoke it. In this case, however, it is ideology rather than political theory: a rationalization for national power which seeks to grow more powerful or for incipient power which claims to represent a new political order.

THE CONSTITUTIONAL STATE

"The State is the Divine *Idea* as it exists on Earth . . ." Hegel says. "It is the moral Whole, the *State*, which is that form of reality in which the individual has and enjoys his freedom." [35] The individual who wishes to live the free life must therefore find his freedom in his role as citizen. The state is the embodiment of morality, and this may only be known and shared by obedience to political authority. Freedom is consciousness of the *Idea*, and the *Idea* is expressed by the state.

The similarity to Rousseau is a striking one, and if the "General Will" is substituted for the "*Idea*" at this point the differences between the two theories all but vanish. Both Hegel and Rousseau acknowledge that life under political authority limits the citizen's sphere of action. But obedience to the state, in return for the restrictions it imposes, offers a new freedom which is quantitatively and qualitatively superior to any other.

[35] *Ibid.*, pp. 39, 38.

Limitation is certainly produced by Society and the State, but it is a limitation of the mere brute emotions and rude instincts; as also, in a more advanced stage of culture, of the premeditated self-will of caprice and passion. This kind of constraint is part of the instrumentality by which only the consciousness of Freedom and the desire for its attainment, in its true—that is Rational and Ideal form— can be obtained.[36]

The freedom offered to the citizens is freedom from themselves. Men are, as Burke emphasized, passionate and irrational creatures. If they are to experience true freedom—that is, freedom to develop their higher potentialities— then they must allow the state to constrain their baser emotions and instincts. Consciousness of the dictates of the *Idea* is impossible if men are content with the primitive liberty which is no more than license and caprice. Such liberty is, if not a state of war, an environment uncongenial to the exercise of man's finer faculties. For this reason Hegel sees freedom and authority—freedom under authority—as a single process. "Freedom is nothing but the recognition and adoption of such universal substantial objects as Right and Law," he says, "and the production of a reality that is accordant with them—the State." [37]

The distinction between freedom under authority and freedom from authority has already been elaborated. The latter theory is found in Hobbes and Locke and also in Bentham; Hegel follows Rousseau and Burke in proposing the former theory. In the one case the individual is considered rational enough to define and pursue his own freedom; in the other his reason is so limited that he must depend on the state to curb his passions and thereby experience a more genuine freedom than he could achieve by his own efforts. "Society and the State," Hegel says, "are the very conditions in which Freedom is realized." [38] And for this reason he turns his attention to the institutions through which men become aware of their finer potentialities.

But if the state is the earthly expression of the *Idea*, then it is legitimate to ask if this description applies to all states. Is Hegel saying that every political system provides the conditions for realizing freedom, or are only some states

---

[36] *Ibid.*, p. 41. However, Hegel denies any essential similarity between himself and Rousseau. The trouble with Rousseau's theory, Hegel says, is that it gives too central a role to the consent of the governed. If the state is founded on a voluntary contract and if it gains its legitimacy through majority rule, then such a state can easily contradict in its behavior the objective dictates of the *Idea*. "Rousseau," Hegel says, "reduces the union of individuals in the state to a contract and therefore to something based on their arbitrary wills, their opinion, and their capriciously given express consent; and abstract reasoning proceeds to draw the logical inferences which destroy the absolutely divine principle of the state, together with its majesty and absolute authority." *Philosophy of Right* (Oxford: Oxford University Press, 1942), translated by T. M. Knox, p. 157.

[37] *Philosophy of History*, p. 59.

[38] *Ibid.*, p. 41.

worthy of this distinction? The answer to this question is never given in a clear-cut manner. One precondition which has been set down is that a state must be energetic and its citizens infused with national sentiment. Another is that at some time in the present or recent past a Hero should have made his imprint on the society. But the chief factor is that all states are but stages in the development of the Idea, and even a state which seems tyrannical has within it the capacity for an eventual burst of freedom. The cunning of reason is always at work, and it represents the temper and tempo of the Idea. Apparent tyrannies may be unconscionably long lived, but to ask for their premature overthrow is to ask that the dialectic obey a law other than that of its own design. "The constitution of any given nation depends in general on the character and development of its self-consciousness . . ." Hegel says. "Hence every nation has the constitution appropriate to it and suitable for it." [39] A remark like this can, of course, be construed as evidence of Hegel's conservative bias. There is an implicit warning not to press for political or constitutional change because to do so would be to saddle a country with institutions she is ill prepared to live under. There is also the assumption that whatever constitution a nation has is the only alternative open to it at any given moment in history: the dialectic allows no choices, and it moves at its own pace and consults no wisdom other than its own. Finally, in the case of theories like those of Hegel and Burke, if freedom is defined in terms of obedience to authority, then the label of tyranny is not so apt to be affixed to an autocratic state if it exhibits strength and direction. In sum, a political system must be suited to the level of development at which a population has arrived. A people may possess sufficient political sophistication to govern themselves, or they may require a strong ruler who can give firm leadership. They may be at a stage in history where the national regime is energetic and therefore deserves the loyalty of its citizens, or the regime may be a relic of the past and hence ready for overthrow from within or without. Once again, the ascription of conservatism or radicalism to Hegel is not as simple a matter as might at first appear.

Like all theorists who postulate general laws of political development, Hegel has his own preferences when it comes to available political systems. He claims that his judgment is not so much a personal one as it is an objective analysis of the dialectic at work. The most recent institutional stage attained by the most advanced society is, by definition, the goal which all other societies will in time have to pursue. "The development of the state to constitutional monarchy is the achievement of the modern world," he says.[40] Like St. Thomas and Machiavelli, Hegel proposes that national strength and political

[39] *Philosophy of Right,* p. 179.
[40] *Ibid.,* p. 176.

power can only become effective if authority is concentrated in unitary leadership.

> Taken without its monarch and the articulation of the whole which is the indispensable and direct concomitant of monarchy, the people is a formless mass and no longer a state. It lacks every one of those determinate characteristics—sovereignty, government, judges, magistrates, class-divisions, etc.,—which are to be found only in a whole which is inwardly organized.[41]

Just as nationalism gives to each citizen a sense of personal identity, so the institution of monarchy gives a whole people a political identity. The nation needs a unifying symbol if the individuals who comprise it are to be other than an aimless crowd. But Hegel is less concerned with the idea of monarchy than he is with its constitutional underpinning. Insofar as a royal family is hereditary, it gives a sense of permanence to the state. However, Hegel is aware that kings and emperors can lose touch with the emerging needs of their subjects. Unlike St. Thomas and Machiavelli, he does not demand that kings or princes be wise or virtuous or clever. Indeed, there is no discussion of personal character or aptitude, and Hegel shows no great concern about the particular man who ascends to the throne.

Monarchy has its importance because it is a symbol of unity. Were other symbols of equal authority available, there is no doubt that Hegel would give them his approval. The important question has to do with effective political organization: if the state is well organized then the monarch's personality is irrelevant and his power is purely formal.

> It is often alleged against monarchy that it makes the welfare of the state dependent on chance, for, it is urged, the monarch may be ill-educated, he may perhaps be unworthy of the highest position in the state, and it is senseless that such a state of affairs should exist because it is supposed to be rational. But all this rests on a presupposition which is nugatory, namely that everything depends on the monarch's *particular* character. In a completely organized state, it is only a question of the culminating point of formal decision (and a natural bulwark against passion). It is wrong, therefore, to demand objective qualifications in a monarch; he has only to say "yes" and dot the "i," because the throne should be such that the significant thing in its holder is not his particular make-up. . . . In a well-organized monarchy, the objective aspect belongs to law alone, and the monarch's part is merely to set to the law the subjective "I will." [42]

The emphasis, therefore, is on constitutional government. Politics and society must be so organized that rule of law obtains at all times. If the monarch has only to nod his head and give official sanction to the laws, discussion must turn to the legislative process itself. Hegel suggests institutional arrangements which will secure the rule of law and at the same time take account of the

[41] *Ibid.*, p. 183.
[42] *Ibid.*, pp. 188–189.

public's interests. To do this he relates social structure to the exercise of political power, and he raises again some of the traditional questions concerning the role of public opinion in the good society.

PLURALISM AND PUBLIC OPINION

As is already quite clear, Hegel's political analysis has much in common with Rousseau's. And the *Philosophy of Right* shares much of the economic emphasis of the *Discourse on the Origin of Inequality*. Social and political development, Hegel says, follows economic development. As technology becomes more complex and as the principle of division of labor becomes a fact, the self-sustaining family is weakened and individuals are turned loose in society. "Civil society tears the individual from his family ties, estranges the members of the family from one another, and recognizes them as self-subsistent persons," Hegel says.[43] To rip an individual from his family, to push him into an anonymous and forbidding society, and to give legal recognition to a self-sufficiency which he does not in fact have—this is one of the overpowering problems of modern politics. While such individuals may be contented enough in time of economic prosperity, they become a social danger in times of depression.

> When the standard of living of a large mass of people falls below a certain subsistence level . . . and when there is a consequent loss of the sense of right and wrong, of honesty and the self-respect which makes a man insist on maintaining himself by his own work and effort, the result is the creation of a rabble of paupers. At the same time this brings with it, at the other end of the social scale, conditions which greatly facilitate the concentration of disproportionate wealth in a few hands.[44]

As the industrial basis of society increases, people are more and more thrown into an insecure labor market. Bereft of their traditional ties to the family and the land, men find their only dignity in meaningful and rewarding work. Yet an industrial economy is so unstable that periods of unemployment are inevitable: not only do men starve, but they lose their self-respect as individuals. The political consequence is that upstanding citizens degenerate into a discontented rabble, and their plight is exaggerated when contrasted with the wealth of a minority in society.

An industrial economy, therefore, poses the problem of clashing interests and class struggle. This, to Hegel's mind, is a political problem, and it calls for a strong state which can mediate among these disaffected groups. "The differing interests of producers and consumers may come into collision with

---

[43] *Ibid.*, p. 148.
[44] *Ibid.*, p. 150.

each other; and although a fair balance between them on the whole may be brought about automatically, still their adjustment also requires a control which stands above both and is consciously undertaken . . ." Hegel says. "Control is also necessary to diminish the danger of upheavals arising from clashing interests and to abbreviate the period in which their tension should be eased through the working of a necessity of which they themselves know nothing." [45] Government, then, must be a positive force in economy and society: if adjustments among interests do not come about automatically, then there must be conscious and premeditated public policy to secure the general welfare. Furthermore, government must not take sides in the class struggle, but must strive to promote conditions of social unity: contending parties see only their own side of a question, and it is up to public authority to settle differences on the basis of a consensus which the particular interests are unable to perceive by themselves. Finally, there is the ever-present danger of revolution resulting from unemployment and moral disintegration: here the government is obliged to prevent as best it can the rise of such conditions as well as to use its force to put down their consequences.

The society which Hegel describes is a complex one, and the problem of political order does not admit of an easy solution. Burke's proposal that orders and classes be arranged in a fixed hierachy has little relevance for a society where the technological revolution sunders traditional loyalties. The modern state must be prepared to intervene in an active way: interests in society must be regulated, and state power must at all times stand superior to the various groups which make up the social order.

One way for the government to bring political order out of what otherwise might be social chaos is to enlist the contending groups in the legislative process itself. These groups—Hegel calls them "corporations"—are the private associations which men form to better pursue their particular interests. Examples of these would be an association of manufacturers, a society of professional men, a trade union, and a religious or fraternal organization. In each of these associations the members share a common interest and they select certain officials to speak in their name.

Particular interests which are common to everyone fall within civil society and lie outside the absolutely universal interest of the state proper. The administration of these is in the hands of corporations, commercial and professional as well as municipal, and their officials, directors, managers and the like. It is the business of these officials to manage the private property and interests of those particular spheres and, from that point of view, their authority rests on the confidence of their commonalties and professional equals.[46]

[45] *Ibid.*, pp. 147–148.
[46] *Ibid.*, p. 189.

Rousseau, it will be recalled, deplored the existence of such associations, for he thought that their existence would blind their members' perception of their general interests as citizens. Hegel, however, not only tolerates but welcomes these private bodies. If the economic growth of society breaks down traditional ties and reduces men to an aimless rabble, then the rise of voluntary associations based on common endeavors can give individuals a tie to replace the ones that modern society has severed. While Hegel proposed the inculcation of national sentiment as one solution, it is now clear that he is augmenting this with institutions which are more rationally related to the everyday needs of citizens. The excesses of nationalism can be avoided if an individual's loyalties are also to one or more organizations which serve his interests and in which he participates. Clearly this division of allegiance between one's nation and one's organized interest can weaken the former sentiment, but this is a chance that Hegel seems willing to take.

And this is not the only chance that Hegel is willing to take. If a strong state is needed to regulate conflicting interests, it must not be so strong as to be oppressive. While private groups may stand in need of regulation, they are also entitled to protect themselves from capricious and intrusive exercise of state power. Private organizations, therefore, stand as a barrier between the commands of government officials and the coercion of their members. "The security of the state and its subjects against the misuse of power by ministers and their officials," Hegel says, "lies . . . in the authorities given to societies and corporations, because in itself this is a barrier against the intrusion of subjective caprice into the power entrusted to a civil servant. . . ." [47]

Groups in society, then, play a vital role in ensuring that government is by rule of law. The power of ministers and civil servants is not immutable: it may at all times be questioned and tempered by associations which stand between the state and the citizen. Hegel accepts the pluralist idea that state and society are not identical, and that associations other than the state have legitimate power. To be sure, he would say that whatever authority such groups have they have received from the state: he would deny that the state exists only by the consent of private organizations. Yet, despite the legal primacy given to the state, Hegel wishes private groups to use their power to protect their members from laws and regulations which reflect only the whims of officious politicians or civil servants. The relation between public authority and private groups is a two-way one in Hegel's theory. The state is required to intervene so as to ameliorate the conflicts of private interests, but these interests are expected to act as barriers against excessive state action. In legal fact the state is always sovereign, but in political practice power is shared by many institu-

[47] *Ibid.*, p. 192.

tions in society, of which the state is only one. In this way law becomes a reflection of social needs and not simply the determination of those who hold state power.

And the state itself ought not to be a monolithic institution. If it contains a symbolic monarch and a civil service, it must make law by means of a representative assembly. The legislature—which Hegel calls "the Estates"—is yet another barrier to capricious power. A legislature can be both representative and public-spirited without professing to have the wisdom of professional political philosophers. "The Estates are a guarantee of the general welfare and public freedom," Hegel says. "A little reflection will show that this guarantee does not lie in their particular power of insight, because the highest civil servants necessarily have a deeper and more comprehensive insight into the nature of the state's organization and requirements." [48] A legislature is rational not because its members either individually or as a whole are men of superior wisdom, but because it serves a rational political function. It secures the general welfare and the public freedom because it serves as a center of power in the way of arbitrary authority and as a mechanism of communication between the state and citizens.

Here Hegel seems to be invoking the cunning of reason in institutional terms: legislators may be self-interested and unaware of the larger role they play. But as a branch of government they are essential to the protection of important political values.

> The Estates stand between the government in general on the one hand and the nation broken up into particulars (people and associations) on the other. . . . They are a middle term preventing both the extreme isolation of the power of the crown, which otherwise might seem a mere arbitrary tyranny, and also the isolation of the particular interests of persons, societies, and Corporations. Further, and more important they prevent individuals from having the appearance of a mass or an aggregate and so from acquiring an unorganized opinion and volition and from crystallizing into a powerful *bloc* in opposition to the organized state.[49]

The important function of the legislature is an educational one. If executive power has the popular appearance of a tyrant, it is the task of the assembly to demonstrate that the state is in fact representative and that its laws are in the public interest.

Power, when filtered through a legislature, is less naked in its exercise and relates more readily to the lives of those who will have to obey it. At the same time, a representative assembly is based on constituencies—either functional or territorial—and thus a political institution may serve to give a structure to

[48] *Ibid.*, p. 196.
[49] *Ibid.*, p. 197.

an otherwise fragmented society. Representatives become leaders of localities or occupational groups, and they help these sectional interests to take on a form and coherence of their own. In this way, too, society is prevented from becoming a mass of unaffiliated citizens. The danger is that an aimless discontented mob may be given direction by unprincipled leaders who desire exclusive political power. An effective legislature can thwart such a development, and hence promote the security of the state, by speaking for particular interests and thereby giving citizens an incentive to think of themselves as group members.

The public, to Hegel's mind, is to be praised or censured according to the qualities it displays and the social environment in which it operates. This ambiguity of approach is recurrent in political theory. Aristotle and Machiavelli, for example, were prepared to put power in the hands of the average man if certain institutional conditions were met. Rousseau was wary of the public if it was guided by the "will of all," but he had full faith in it if it governed according to the General Will. Similarly, Hegel distinguishes between the public in its rational and irrational roles. When it displays the latter form of behavior, it is not a public at all but a mass. "The Many, as units—a congenial interpretation of 'people' are of course something connected," he says, "but they are connected only as an aggregate, a formless mass, whose commotion and activity could therefore only be elementary, irrational, barbarous, and frightful." [50] Such an aggregate of individuals, although it may have the appropriate external forms, is not a true state or nation. The citizens have not yet reached the level of consciousness which makes them aware of the Idea as it is expressed in a common purpose. On the contrary, such men are impressed by the value of their own thinking, and they tend to be not a little arrogant in their estimation of their own political capabilities.

One of the consequences of this state of affairs is that the citizens view their world in terms of ideology instead of rational thought. They are prey, in particular, to Utopian fantasies which bear small relation to the political reality which confronts them. "These Ideals—which in the voyage of life founder on the rocks of hard reality—may be in the first instance only subjective, and belong to the idiosyncrasy of the individual, imagining himself the highest and wisest . . ." Hegel says. "For the fancies which the individual in his isolation indulges, cannot be the model for universal reality." [51]

A mass, then, is actually an aggregate of isolated individuals even though they may appear to be connected. Unable to attune themselves to a unified mission, they subsist on Utopias which are bound to end in rude awakenings. At the worst such grandiose schemes will bring not the liberty and equality

[50] *Ibid.*, p. 198.
[51] *Philosophy of History*, p. 35.

they promise, but further enslavement. Only if individuals divest themselves of their arrogant pretensions, only if they subdue the impulse to ideology and idiosyncrasy, can they begin to apprehend the objective realities of the political life open to them.

The people must be protected from themselves: it is the responsibility of the state to ensure that its citizens are a temperate public and not a formless mass. Only if this is done may the people be looked upon with respect and sympathy. Hegel has already specified the conditions under which such a transformation may take place: under a constitutional state, buttressed by social pluralism, the public can begin to take on the stature which it is capable of attaining. In this case public opinion is seen in an altogether different light. "Public opinion, therefore, is a repository not only of the genuine needs and correct tendencies of common life," Hegel says, "but also, in the form of common sense (i.e. all-pervasive fundamental ethical principles disguised as prejudices), of the eternal, substantive principles of justice, the true content and result of legislation, the whole constitution, and the general position of the state." [52] Thus constituted, public opinion is not an aggregate of individual opinions, but an objective public philosophy.

Clearly, also, it is but another rendering of Rousseau's General Will. But whereas Rousseau intended that the General Will would be the exclusive governing principle for a democratic community, Hegel feels unable to rely on it in so unqualified a way. While a well-governed nation-state can avoid degenerating into a mass society by promoting suitable institutional arrangements, it cannot hope that the public will at all times rise to its better self. Hegel's final judgment on public opinion has two sides.

> Public opinion therefore deserves to be as much respected as despised—despised for its concrete expression and for the concrete consciousness it expresses, respected for its essential basis, a basis which only glimmers more or less dimly in that concrete expression. But in itself it has no criterion of discrimination, nor has it the ability to extract the substantive element it contains and raise it to precise knowledge. Thus to be independent of public opinion is the first formal condition of achieving anything great or rational whether in life or in science.[53]

From the philosophical standpoint the public and public opinion are deserving of respect because they contain the potentiality for expressing the eternal principles of justice. As the course of history progresses, societies will advance further towards the goal of self-realization and an awareness of the part they play in the unfolding of the *Idea*. The movement from irrational mass to rational public cannot be hurried, yet it must never be forgotten that within

[52] *Philosophy of Right,* p. 204.
[53] *Ibid.,* p. 205.

today's barbarism lie the seeds of tomorrow's civilization. On the other hand, at this still imperfect stage of historical development Hegel advises rulers to stand independent of public sentiment. While a constitutional state, pluralist institutions, and a sense of nationhood can go far in training political maturity, the time is not yet at hand to defer to the expressed will of the public.

The *Philosophy of History* and the *Philosophy of Right* can seem at times to be strange bedfellows. The first emphasizes the spirit of nationalism as a unifying sentiment; the second calls for a stable hierarchy of settled institutions to give the public its coherence. The first stresses the role of the Hero and his impulse to revolutionary change; the second relies on the rule of law and an interventionist state to prevent the excesses of political radicalism. The first calls on men to adjust themselves to the historical laws of the dialectic; the second suggests that men have the ability to shape institutions which will render their politics orderly and predictable.

That there is little place for the Hero in the constitutional state is understandable: the rule of law cannot sit easily with the caprices of a man of destiny. Nevertheless, Hegel says that the test of greatness is to transcend the subjectivity of public opinion. In the *Philosophy of Right* he does not tell us who the rulers are, what qualifications they have, or how they are selected. Like Hobbes, Burke, and Bentham, he assumes that a rational political system will throw to the top rational men. They need not be philosopher-kings: what is required is that they have a sense of national purpose and an intimation of the state's role in history. They must, above all, realize the limitations which their historical epoch places on what politics can achieve; a feeling for the possible is the prime requisite of those who hold power.

In the final analysis, however, Hegel's two books serve two different purposes. If the *Philosophy of History* talks of heroic exploits and human slaughter, this is to set politics in the broad context of divine purpose and eternal progress. If the *Philosophy of Right* speaks of stable institutions and an ordered society, this is to describe the historical epoch which is at hand and within which men may realize freedom. Hegel's two theories do not stand opposed to each other. The determinism in his theory of history sets limits on human action, but it also tells men what is in their power to accomplish in their moment of time. His institutional prescriptions apply to the age the world is now entering. How long this phase of history will last is a question that Hegel does not attempt to answer. But political freedom and the constitutional state are products of the dialectic, and they are also its potential victims. The social and political arrangements which Hegel proposes for today's world will surely crumble beneath the tread of some Hero of tomorrow. Freedom itself will continue, for the dialectic destroys men and states but not ideas. Freedom will express itself in new ways and through new institutions. The responsibility of men is to be aware of the limits within which they must work, to do the best they can with the resources at their disposal. The key lies in a knowledge and understanding of history: an appreciation of the *Idea* as a never-ending drama, of the scene which is now at the center of the stage, and of the roles which we have been called upon to play to the utmost of our ability.

IDEAS AND MEN

Reality, for Hegel, lies in the realm of the spirit rather than in the material world. This assumption, first made by Plato, is an important one in political theory. Plato's conception of the Forms, Rousseau's General Will, and now Hegel's *Idea* are instances of theories which give to ideas the dominant political role.[54] The roles played by ideas in both practical politics and political theory are subject to constant debate and endless disagreement. Men differ on the form taken by ideas and the manner in which they affect men's behavior. At this juncture it would be well to at least distinguish some of the uses to which the idealist approach has been put.

(1) Hegel would certainly claim that ideas, more than any other stimulus, influence men to action. A man may be hungry; but unless the idea is put in his head that it is wrong to be hungry, he will do nothing about it. Millions of men have lived and died on the brink of starvation, never thinking that they might be entitled to a better life. A man may live under tyrannical rule; but until he is confronted with the idea that what he has been experiencing is tyranny, he will accept power without protest. As many millions have lived and died under oppression, never realizing that they had been denied freedom. Ideas, first of all, define a situation: they give a name to a political condition. And, second, they either endow that condition with legitimacy, or they deny its right to continue. Men are roused to maintain or change their situations by the arguments they hear: without words action is impossible. Yet several questions arise. It may be said that the so-called ideas are no more than rallying cries for affected interests, that they are propagandistic devices for preserving or overthrowing a political structure which benefits some men and puts others at a disadvantage. This argument contends that all ideas are

[54] Students of political philosophy usually make a sharp distinction between Idealist and Natural Law theories. "The Idealist ethics of self-realization," one writer says, "is easily confused with the ethics of Natural Law. As a matter of fact, they are sharply opposed." John Wild, *Plato's Modern Enemies and the Theory of Natural Law* (Chicago: University of Chicago Press, 1953), p. 70. "The doctrine of the Ethical State is a complete substitute for the doctrine of Natural Law," another says. "It entirely reverses the relationship between the ideal and the real, which was the necessary proposition of Natural Law thinking." A. P. D'Entreves, *Natural Law* (London: Hutchinson, 1951), p. 73.

ideology and that they should be seen as reflections of material interests. Marx and Engels will elaborate this point of view.

Another question has to do with the origins of ideas. Machiavelli, for example, would say that ideas are fashioned by men and that their effective use depends on the skills of those who devise and employ them. Here again ideas are seen as ideology, but, in addition, the words and phrases which stir men to action are put together by a talented minority in society. These rulers are able not only to control man's behavior, but also the way in which they think. For the thoughts which comprise public opinion are implanted by those who have the power to do so.

(2) Plato, Rousseau, and Hegel would disagree with Machiavelli on this last point: that the significant political ideas are man-made. On the contrary, the idealist approach assumes that ideas have an existence of their own which stands independent of the men who voice or heed them. Thus, if we live in an age of democracy, it cannot be claimed that the democratic idea is the invention of any man or group of men. It is, rather, the product of the historical process and a social consensus. Men may use the rhetoric of democracy to help in securing their political ends, but none of them can claim that they created the idea itself as a premeditated means for achieving their self-appointed goals. To say that major ideas—democracy, freedom, justice—are not man-made is to assume that there exists a higher power which is capable of thought at a higher level. This may, of course, be God. But if Rousseau's General Will is found in the organic community, Plato's Forms and Hegel's *Idea* are able to have a life of their own apart from mortal men and societies.

The invariable question is a straightforward one. Why, it may be asked, should it be assumed that these supernatural ideas exist at all? It may well be argued that they are no more than figments—or literary devices—of men like Plato, Rousseau, and Hegel. There is no evidence that the Form of Justice has any reality at all, and none that the *Idea* looms over men and nations. The answer to this objection is, very simply, that ideas of this sort must exist if the world in which we live is to be comprehensible at all. The problem is one of achieving intellectual order. The material world we see is a chaotic conglomeration of individuals, institutions, and events. It is preferable to assume that the universe has an order, and this pattern must be found in abstract ideas. The order can only exist in ideas because the material world is unequipped to explain its own behavior. The abstractions on which Plato, Rousseau, and Hegel rely have two sides, one descriptive and the other prescriptive. Man's understanding of the world in which he lives is an imperfect one, but in the Forms or the *Idea*, for example, there exists a perfect science of politics. If men wish to know reality, they must attune themselves to the political knowledge inherent in the major ordering ideas. This use of the deductive method was employed by St. Augustine and St. Thomas: men use their reason to grasp the theories which are created for them by a higher power than themselves. On the prescriptive side, similarly, moral knowledge is created by and to be found in the same ideas. The order, both scientific and philosophical, is not made by men: the best men can do is to come to an understanding of this higher kind of theory.

The inevitable question, of course, is who in society are the political scientists and political philosophers capable of apprehending these abstract ideas. Plato asked for philosopher-kings, Rousseau called for a rational community in which the discovery would be a common effort, and Hegel felt that all men eventually would be able to reach this stage of realization. These answers are only partially satisfactory. The history of politics is filled with men who have claimed that they were expressing the truth inherent in abstract ideas.

How, it may be asked, can the claims of these individuals be tested? What distinguishes a Platonic philosopher from a Machiavellian pretender? The problem is aggravated all the more by the fact that some of the most oppressive and aggressive tyrants the world has known have used the language of idealist philosophy as vehicles for their ascent to power. In most cases it is clear that such men are ideologues and not philosophers, that their supposed perception of the abstract ideas is a spurious one. Indeed, it may be argued—as Plato did—that men of power are unable to know the Forms in the real world. Hegel admitted that his Heroes were too involved with their personal ambitions to perceive the workings of the Idea. The answer may be that such abstractions are meant only to aid the understanding of academic scientists and philosophers, that they will never be known to those who exercise political power. But even if ideas are perverted again and again by self-seeking individuals, this does not mean that they do not exist in their true forms. So long as men feel the need for objective standards, so long as they wish to believe that there is an order to the material world and a source of moral knowledge, they will assume that abstract ideas exist and that they have a life of their own.

(3) If abstract ideas exist apart from men, then it may be said that they have a power of their own. Hegel departs from Plato at this point, and he asserts that the political life which men experience is but an expression of the path laid out for them by the Idea. An idea, therefore, is not only an intellectual order, but also a historical plan which is imposed on the material world. The thoughts in men's minds, the thoughts which lead to action, are given to them by this abstract force which they cannot escape. If the Idea states that this is to be an age of democracy, for example, then men will act democratically. The diffi-

culty, of course, is that men frequently do not understand the roles they have been chosen to play, and their pursuit of ideal goals can lead to their own destruction. This imperfect perception of history leads to human unhappiness, but it also brings human progress. If an idea can have such power as to make men act in ways not of their own choosing, then freedom takes on a special meaning. The emphasis is on reflection rather than on action, on understanding what is possible rather than on pursuing goals of one's own choosing. The idea, of course, may state that the time is ripe for revolutionary change, and in this case men are free to move in new and expanded directions. But even here they are creatures of historical circumstances and not their makers. Therefore, Hegel calls on men to become students of history rather than practical participants in the political process. Freedom is first and foremost a matter of understanding: of knowing the present as an outgrowth of the past and the future as the product of the present. Once it is assumed that the *Idea* exists and that the destiny of the world lies in its unfolding, then the obligation of men is not to act but to be aware of the abstract forces which drive them.

Idealist political theories clearly lower the status of the individual in a way which is bound to be unsettling to many. The thoughts and deeds of men become pale reflections of an order which they do not make and can but dimly understand. Yet, despite all this, the thinking of men like Plato, Rousseau, and Hegel has had and continues to have an important influence in political theory. One reason is that some men do not mind a subordinate status so long as they derive in exchange the security which comes of believing that they are part of a higher order of things. Another reason is that the material world and the ideas which men create for their own use do not together produce a satisfactory understanding of the political life. Ideas like the Forms, the General Will, and the *Idea* are necessary because without them there is doubt and contention. With them, there is certainty.

12.
Alexis de Tocqueville

THE MAN AND HIS TIMES

Tocqueville was born in 1805, the son of a Norman family of noble origin. One of his grandparents died under the guillotine during the French Revolution, and members of the family had an almost uninterrupted record of public service. Tocqueville studied law and at the age of twenty-one he embarked on a career as a judicial officer under the restored Bourbon regime. With the July Revolution of 1830, Louis Philippe came to power, and Tocqueville was less than enthusiastic about serving this government. He was granted an eighteen-month leave of absence from his job to go to America to study and report on penal systems. This project had only indifferent sanction from the authorities, and Tocqueville ended up paying his own expenses for the journey and submitting a report which was shelved almost as soon as it was turned in. The expedition across the Atlantic was hardly a waste of time, for out of it came a full-length study of politics and society in the New World. He wrote Democracy in America on his return to France, the first volume appearing in 1835 and the second in 1840. The books enjoyed a successful reception in both Europe and America, and they immediately took on the stature of standard works of reference. Tocqueville served in the Chamber of Deputies from 1839 to 1848, but without any notable distinction. He died in 1859.

The France which produced Tocqueville had become the meeting ground of two great social systems and two great ideologies. The aristocratic structure of French society had been successfully challenged by the forces of democracy represented by the Revolution of 1789. However that upheaval was far from total, and the nobility retained enough of their wealth and popular deference to remain an important influence in the nation. At the same time, the ideologies of conservatism and liberalism were struggling for pre-eminence on the political scene. The idea of an organic society based on fixed classes

461

and ingrained tradition was confronted with the idea of an open society based on personal achievement and social progress. Neither of the two systems or ideologies had a secure footing at the time, and the currents of the age pulled men back and forth between—or among—them. In Tocqueville himself might be seen the tensions and conflicts of his day. He was of aristocratic origin, and he valued the freedoms and privileges his class had enjoyed; yet he saw that democracy was inevitable and that it would liberate new millions who had hitherto been relegated to a submerged status in society. His political sympathies were liberal, and he accorded highest priority to the goal of human freedom; yet he was a conservative in that he acknowledged that the old order had nurtured and maintained the values of culture and civility. Democracy in America had the virtues of exuberance, but it had also the tendencies to excessiveness which threatened liberty. Tocqueville was alternatively attracted and repelled by the new social order and the new political outlook. In this he was typical of much of the thought and sentiment of his time—and of our own.

Tocqueville was writing, too, at the dawn of another new age: the age of sociology. The democracy he describes is a social system. His book has comparatively little discussion of the institutions of government, and when he draws these in, it is usually to illustrate broader sociological themes. His interests were wide-ranging and they cover such topics as language and literature, race and religion, education and economics, women and war. His intention, in short, was to paint on the widest possible canvas and to explain a society in its totality. What emerges is a political theory in a social setting: democracy, freedom, and equality are seen as arising from a social system and not as abstract ideas divorced from reality. There is another dimension to the sociological approach. Tocqueville sat down to write only after he had conducted personal interviews with literally thousands of Americans, from Boston brahmins to convicts in solitary confinement, from as far west as Wisconsin to as far south as Louisiana. He may have arrived in America with aristocratic preconceptions, but his willingness to study the facts at first hand is testimony to his respect for the empirical method. Since Tocqueville's time all serious students of politics have incurred the obligation to be at least one part sociologist. On the whole, they have assumed this wider responsibility and in so doing have broadened the foundations of our political understanding.

12.
Alexis de Tocqueville

Not the least of Hegel's concerns was to emphasize the connection between national character and political behavior. While it goes without saying that a whole people cannot be "characterized" in any simple way, it is nevertheless true that citizens with differing temperaments will put their political institutions to differing uses. As the title itself indicates, Alexis de Tocqueville's *Democracy in America* concentrates its attention on a single country. This nation, furthermore, is a new one: its experience of the political life is comparatively short when set against the full span of the Western political tradition. While American politics do not constitute a sharp break with the European heritage, the new country necessarily had to accommodate both its institutions and its principles to a population of diverse origins and transplanted loyalties. The weight of tradition lies less heavily on the American people, and the structure of American society has yet to take a settled form. In addition, a student of political theory who lands on the shores of a new land soon discovers that the classical doctrines he has learned from books have only partial application to the political forms he sees. American democracy cannot be equated with the democracy found in the ancient texts. For this reason, Tocqueville finds himself compelled to discard much of what he thought he knew about politics and to adjust his thinking to a new reality.

This is not to say that traditional theories are entirely irrelevant: on the contrary, the ideas of Aristotle, Locke, Rousseau, Burke, and Hegel are recurrent in *Democracy in America*. What is interesting is that Tocqueville can draw on only portions of those theories in his effort to explain the American experience; and even those parts must be rewritten if their principles are to be appropriate for the political life of a new nation. The result is a subtle blend of political theory and high-level journalism: ideas which have been debated in academies since Plato's time are deftly conjoined with a reporter's view of an emerging political world—a world which defies the political theorist to make sense out of it.

463

Yet if Tocqueville's subject were only democracy in America, it would have no claim to universal recognition. His book is also a treatise on democracy for all countries which are beginning to accept and implement the principles of human equality and majority rule. The analysis of democracy which is put forward has meaning for a larger and larger part of the world we are coming to know. For if Tocqueville talks of democracy in an American context, it is a context that other nations are beginning to share. On the one hand, the globe is now populated with many new countries which are trying to build democratic political systems literally from the ground up. The trials and triumphs of these countries have frequent similarities to the political experience of the American nation. On the other hand, most emerging states are avid to accelerate their rate of economic development. Tocqueville takes pains to describe the impact of technological progress and material prosperity on the political and social condition of a people. Here too the world is seeing American experience repeated in important particulars. For these reasons and others which will emerge, it is proper to say that Tocqueville's is a general theory of democracy. It is a theory for the young, the experimental, the ambitious. If America has now reached the years of maturity, there is no lack of new nations who are just beginning their political lives. For them Tocqueville's words can have meaning and foreboding.

THE ARISTOCRATIC YARDSTICK

Like all political theorists of stature, Tocqueville combines the role of political scientist with that of political philosopher. He is not content simply to describe the workings of the democratic process; for that process must be evaluated, and Tocqueville is prepared to pass the necessary judgments.

There are, as Aristotle suggested, two ways for a theorist to approach a political system. The first is to take the goals which the system itself professes and to inquire whether it is actually living up to those self-imposed standards. Thus, if a society prides itself on its material prosperity, the critic may judge that society by its own terms. He may possibly conclude that it is not prosperous at all, that there is a great gulf between its professions and its actual performance. The second approach suggested by Aristotle is to take the political system being studied and to hold it up against an external—and presumably objective—standard. In this case a society's own claim that it is materially prosperous is less important than whether it is a good society. No one would say that prosperity and goodness cannot go hand in hand: a high standard of living may be a factor which will help in the attainment of objective political ends. Nevertheless, the theorist will not be so quick to accept a society's own definition of its goals. Rather, he will bring with him a set of principles against which he will evaluate any and all political systems he encounters.

Tocqueville relies primarily on the second approach. He has in his own mind a firm conviction of what constitutes the good life and the good society. Where and how he derived these principles is, of course, a question that can only be speculated upon. If we say that the yardstick he employs is that of aristocracy, then it might be said that he got his ideas from reading Plato or Burke. But this cannot be proved. If it is said that his measure of the good society is the France that he and his ancestors knew so well, then it might be said that he equated the good life with the comfortable life led by his family under aristocratic conditions. But this, too, is not susceptible of proof. It is better therefore simply to accept Tocqueville's values as given and not to inquire too deeply into their origins. So long as it is recognized that an aristocrat is passing judgment on democracy throughout the pages of his writing, what Tocqueville has to say can be seen in its intended perspective.

This is not to suggest that he is an unsympathetic critic of democracy. Like Burke, he places high values on the qualities of freedom and civility. But, unlike Burke, he believes that these aristocratic values can at least in part be infused into a society which is equalitarian and democratic. Burke deplored the tenor of democratic thought, and he wished for a return to a political system founded on social inequality. Tocqueville obviously shares this uneasiness about democracy, but he sees that its advent is inevitable. He understands, further, that it is impossible to impose the aristocratic class structure and the ingrained habits of deference on a new democracy. Democracy is the wave of the future, and for this reason it is futile to talk of returning to the past. The responsibility of the political theorist is twofold: first, to understand democracy and, second, to suggest ways and means of civilizing this unruly child so that it may enjoy—and not destroy—the objective values of freedom and civility.

The tone of Democracy in America is set on its opening pages. "The whole book that is here offered to the public," Tocqueville says, "has been written under the influence of a kind of religious awe produced in the author's mind by the view of that irresistible revolution which has advanced for centuries in spite of every obstacle and which is still advancing in the midst of the ruins it has caused." [1] Democracy is revolutionary, democracy is inevitable, and democracy is rising out of a past which it itself has destroyed. As has been indicated, Tocqueville does not wring his hands as did Burke. Rather, like Hegel,

[1] Alexis de Tocqueville, Democracy in America (New York: Vintage Books, 1956), translated by Henry Reeve and edited by Phillips Bradley, Vol. I, p. 7.

he chooses to regard democracy as an antithesis rising to challenge the decaying aristocratic thesis. That the new order has conquered the old does not mean, however, that the values of aristocracy are never again to be seen. It is possible that a synthesis of democratic and aristocratic values will be the ultimate consequence. This endeavor cannot be left to chance, for aristocracy is the repository of many values, some worth preserving and some not. For this reason men must act consciously if the new synthesis is to preserve the best that the old order had to offer.

"The first of the duties that are at this time imposed upon those who direct our affairs," Tocqueville says, "is to educate democracy, to reawaken, if possible, its religious beliefs; to purify its morals; to mold its actions; to substitute a knowledge of statecraft for its inexperience, and an awareness of its true interest for its blind instincts, to adapt its government to time and place, and to modify it according to men and to conditions. A new science of politics is needed for a new world." [2] This science of politics must operate within the limits that historical conditions place upon it. The scientific fact is that democracy is ascendant: it will take all the skill of men to ensure that the dialectic runs in an orderly way and that the new society carries with it the heritage of freedom. "The question is not how to reconstruct aristocratic society," he says, "but how to make liberty proceed out of that democratic state of society in which God has placed us." [3]

The aristocratic assumption, as advanced by Burke, is that freedom can exist only in a society founded on the principle of inequality. Tocqueville accepts this assumption, at least as an explanation for the historic foundations of liberty. The basis of aristocracy is an established system of social classes in an ordered hierarchy:

An aristocratic body is composed of a certain number of citizens who, without being very far removed from the mass of the people, are nevertheless permanently stationed above them; a body which it is easy to touch, and difficult to strike, with which the people are in daily contact, but with which they can never combine. . . . Aristocratic institutions cannot exist without laying down the inequality of men as a fundamental principle, legalizing it beforehand and introducing it into the family as well as into society. . . .

Among aristocratic nations, . . . a man . . . will frequently sacrifice his personal gratifications to those who went before and to those who will come after him. Aristocratic institutions, moreover, have the effect of closely binding every man to several of his fellow citizens. As the classes of an aristocratic people are strongly marked and permanent, each of them is regarded by its own members as a sort of lesser country, more tangible and more cherished than the country at large. . . .

[2] *Ibid.*
[3] Vol. II, p. 340.

In aristocratic countries the great possess immense privileges, upon which their pride rests without seeking to rely upon the lesser advantages that accrue to them. As these privileges came to them by inheritance, they regard them in some sort as a portion of themselves, or at least as a natural right inherent in their own persons.[4]

Theorists who talk of aristocracy invariably concentrate their attention on the small minority in positions of privilege. The vast majority of the population is usually taken for granted. They, it is assumed, have been taught to think of themselves as natural inferiors: they defer to authority, they accept their station in life, they are ignorant and bound by superstition and prejudice. On the other hand, this humble life is not without its compensations: those who partake of it have the peace of mind that comes of knowing one's place in society, they are well-governed by a responsible and experienced ruling class, they are part of a traditional system of mutual obligations between man and man. To talk of aristocratic freedom is not to say that all men in such a society are free. On the contrary, only the privileged minority enjoy this blessing. What is more important, however, is that the freedom of the aristocratic class itself is what makes the whole society free. For if this small group is able to develop and maintain the values which only it is capable of preserving, then these will become the dominant values of the entire social system.

A privileged and secure class, therefore, serves a social function. What are these values which an aristocracy promotes? Tocqueville answers this question by asking what are your assumptions about the qualities of the good life. "Do you wish to give a certain elevation to the human mind . . . ?" he asks. "Is it your object to refine the habits, embellish the manners, and cultivate the arts, to promote the love of poetry, beauty, and glory?" [5] It is not in order, given the aristocratic assumptions, to protest that only a few minds are elevated and that most are drugged by superstition and prejudice. It is irrelevant to point out that refined habits, embellished manners, and aesthetic cultivation are denied to all but a fortunate minority. The important fact is that intellectual and aesthetic values are kept alive not only for those who live in the present but for future generations in society. The significance of an aristocratic class is not that it lives well itself but that it feels responsibility for the quality of life which characterizes the social whole. Aristocratic theories are generally organic theories: they postulate that all members of society stand in integral relation to each other and that all share the common purposes of the community. These purposes cannot be left to perpetuate themselves of their own power: they must be lived and preserved by a dominant section of society.

[4] Vol. I, p. 438; Vol. II, pp. 104–105, 237.
[5] Vol. I, p. 262.

That is why a privileged class exists and that is why it enjoys the life of freedom.

The difference between aristocracy and democracy has not simply to do with
the distribution of power. Power is only a means to other ends. It is because
power is denied, in an aristocratic society, to the great majority of citizens that
prescriptive social and political institutions are able to flourish. Tocqueville
compares the two types of systems, and here it is made clear that he is holding
democracy up against the aristocratic yardstick.

Among aristocratic nations social institutions recognize, in truth, no one in the
family but the father; children are received by society at his hands; society governs
him, he governs them. Thus, the parent not only has a natural right but acquires
a political right to command them; he is the author and the support of his family,
but he is also its constituted ruler. In democracies, where the government picks
out every individual singly from the mass to make him subservient to the general
laws of the community, no such intermediate person is required. . . .

Among democratic nations new families are constantly springing up, others are
constantly falling away, and all that remain change their condition; the woof of
time is every instant broken and the track of generations effaced. Those who went
before are soon forgotten; of those who will come after, no one has any idea: the
interest of man is confined to those in close propinquity to himself. As each class
gradually approaches others and mingles with them, its members become undifferentiated and lose their class identity for each other. Aristocracy had made a
chain of all the members of the community, from the peasant to the king; democracy breaks that chain and severs every link of it.

The notion of secondary powers placed between the sovereign and his subjects
occurred naturally to the imagination of aristocratic nations, because those communities contained individuals or families raised above the common level and
apparently destined to command by their birth, their education, and their wealth.
This same notion is naturally wanting in the minds of men in democratic ages,
for converse reasons; it can only be introduced artificially, it can only be kept
there with difficulty, whereas they conceive, as it were without thinking about the
subject, the notion of a single and central power which governs the whole community by its direct influence.

Aristocracies are infinitely more expert in the science of legislation than democracies ever can be. They are possessed of a self-control that protects them from the
errors of temporary excitement; and they form far-reaching designs, which they
know how to mature till a favorable opportunity arrives.[6]

While an aristocratic system may not bestow the free life on all citizens, it
goes a long way toward ensuring that all will live in a good society. The institutions of the family and social class, of decentralized government and temperate leadership—all of these establish conditions of life which enhance the
quality of a society and hence the life known by its individual members. The
assumption is that if men are given the opportunity to weaken the ties of
family or to destroy class patterns by their own accelerated mobility, they will

[6] Vol. II, pp. 203–204, 105, 306; Vol. I, p. 247.

be unknowingly harming themselves. A rigidly stratified condition may work individual hardships; the lack of self-government may produce annoyances. But men must be kept from questioning the workings of a system they are incapable of understanding. Ordinary citizens are unable to appreciate the blessings which accrue to them from the institutions of inequality. These benefits are subtle, remote, and more often than not intangible. If men do succeed in their quest for democracy, they are apt to get both more and less than they bargained for. They may, on the one hand, achieve a largess of freedom which is so vast and bewildering that they are unable to make a comfortable adjustment to it. And, at the same time, they are likely to lose the security of mind and being they had once taken for granted and their need for which they never fully realized.

The aristocratic yardstick is a graphic measuring device for evaluating democracy, and Tocqueville relies on it throughout his writings. A question worth raising is whether the aristocratic society he cites so frequently ever in fact existed anywhere in the world. Tocqueville suggests that indeed it did, and he paints its portrait in the most sympathetic of colors. Even so, there is reason to doubt such a claim. The values and institutions of aristocracy which Tocqueville depicts are more an ideal than an account of historical reality. There is no need to point out here that ruling classes often failed to display the social responsibility that was expected of them, that all too frequently security and stability were secured at the price of much human unhappiness. The aristocratic yardstick can be a deceptive one: it abstracts out of history certain qualities, and it conveniently overlooks others. Indeed, one is tempted to conclude that the evidence of history is what the historian chooses to make it.

Any citation of a political tradition or of historical values seems to depend on the tradition or the values which the theorist is predisposed to find in the past. Writers of a conservative bent have a tendency to glorify the experience of history, yet it is clear that the events and institutions they applaud form only a partial picture. Such theorists, in sum, use the past as a kind of reversed Utopia. Unlike liberal and radical thinkers, they do not advise men to press forward to an unknown but idealized future. Rather, they hold up the values of a presumably known but no less idealized past. That there is much for men to be nostalgic about in aristocratic societies is undoubtedly true, but they also had their seamier sides; and it is not simply forgetfulness which leads some writers to minimize these features. The aristocratic yardstick, therefore, is less a description of the way things actually once were than it is a statement of a theorist's own principles for the good society. A Utopia disguised as history is no less a Utopia. And, like all Utopias, it has the virtue of making values explicit and easy to comprehend. It is no criticism of Tocqueville to say that his account of aristocracy is a distorted one: he is, after all, a political philosopher and not a historian. The Utopian device he uses gives him a philosophical vantage point from which to pass judgment on the new phenomenon of democracy: without such a yardstick his comments would be incoherent and his criticisms purposeless.

THE SOVEREIGN MAJORITY

The principle of equality finds its political expression in the principle of majority rule. If all men stand on an equal footing, then all should be counted as equals in the making of public policy. To talk of government by the people in a meaningful sense, it is necessary to talk of government by and with the consent of a majority of the people. Yet, despite the apparent arithmetic simplicity of this principle, it is one of the most difficult to pin down and apply.[7] Majority rule refers to many things at once, and unless its various meanings are sorted out, confusion is apt to result.

(1) *Majority Rule as a Procedure.* Any group which has to come to a decision will usually adopt majority rule as the most effective procedure. This applies to the Supreme Court of the United States, and it also applies to the Program Committee of the Women's Club of Butte, Montana. While this procedure may be ultimately based on the assumption that all members are equals, it is usually employed simply because no other system has been found as a satisfactory alternative. Some groups, like a meeting of the Society of Friends, are so agreed on their common purposes that they can rely on the attainment of a "sense of the meeting" without ever having to take a vote. But not all bodies can hope for such a spirit of unanimity to prevail. Other groups, like the Board of Estimate of New York City, will give each of the members a "weighted" vote so that the representative of a more populous constituency can cast more votes than his colleagues from smaller districts. If this is done, such procedures must be settled in an orderly way and they must be accepted beforehand by all members of the group. Still other groups, like the President's Cabinet, may find that the minority's decision—or even one man's, the chairman's—will prevail over the majority. In these cases the body is not so much a decision-making group as it is an advisory council. At all events, the procedure of majority rule is a common one, and it may be found to operate in political contexts which themselves may either accept or reject the philosophical principles of equality. The Supreme Court in America

[7] See Willmoore Kendall, "Prolegomena to Any Future Work on Majority Rule," *The Journal of Politics,* November 1950, pp. 694–713.

and the House of Lords in Great Britain are not democratic institutions, but each abides by the procedure in its own internal workings.

(2) *Majority Rule as a Political Institution.* Majority rule, according to Rousseau, is operative only at such times as questions of political policy are put to all citizens gathered together at an open meeting. If a majority of the community casts its votes for a measure, then it becomes the law that all must obey. The institution of majority rule is best seen at work in a setting where it is possible for all to gather together for discussion and voting in a single place. Even so, as Rousseau himself admitted, a minority within the majority will have to have greater power and responsibilities. A measure dealing with zoning regulations or tax assessments, for example, may have 46 sections and 391 subsections: not all of these can be put to a popular vote. Therefore, committees become necessary if policy alternatives are to be defined in a clear-cut manner, and such bodies may become centers of minority power. Despite qualifications such as this, however, majority rule can be the central institution for making policy if the average citizen participates actively and vigilantly. But the real problems begin to arise when the community grows too large for all to meet regularly and simultaneously. Then a society is forced to rely on the institutions of representative government. Rousseau felt that representatives would inevitably distort the sentiments of their constituents, and he hoped that communities would not grow so large that such intermediaries would be necessary. Modern states, however, have no option but to try to secure majority rule by means of the representative process. This is no easy thing to achieve. Even if it is assumed that all citizens can and do vote, and even if there are only two nation-wide parties and each of these runs a candidate in each district, the factors which intercede between the voting and the electoral outcome can have a crucial effect.[8]

Rather than expand on this rather obvious point, it would be well to mention a more subtle phenomenon. Suppose for a moment that the Senate did not exist at all. But each voter casts two ballots, one for the President and one for his Congressman. In most cases a voter supports the same party in each contest; and it may even be assumed that, say, a Republican President is elected along with a Republican Congress. Yet it is not at all uncommon for President and Congress, despite their bearing the same party label, to find themselves in disagreement on matters of legislative policy. Both were elected by popular majorities, and both claim to be representing the majority's will. Which branch of government is right in its claim? The answer is that both of them

---

[8] In the 1951 General Election the Labour Party received 48.8 per cent of the votes cast in the country at large, the Conservatives received 48.0 per cent, and the other parties 3.2 per cent. The composition of the House of Commons, however, was 321 seats for the Conservatives, 295 for Labour, and 9 for other parties.

are. For the average voter usually casts his Presidential and Congressional ballots for two different sets of reasons, and these reasons are often in inherent conflict with each other. The voter, in short, is two voters: one role may be that of a citizen with local interests, the other that of a citizen with a national interest. The split personality which characterizes the voter manifests itself in the behavior of the President and the Congress: if the two branches appear to be at odds, it is only a reflection of the internal conflicts in the men and women who put them in office. The majority, then, is actually two majorities at once. If the question is raised as to which is the "real" majority, we are of course back to the age-old questions of political theory. Needless to say, different observers find the "true" will of the majority expressed in different institutions.[9]

These illustrations on British and American institutions are simply intended to show that majority rule in its institutional sense is a very rough instrument. Rousseau was a perfectionist, and he therefore rejected the idea of representation in its entirety. Other theorists and practitioners are not impervious to the fact that representative institutions distort majority rule. But they continue to experiment with these mechanisms on the assumption that, if not perfection, at least improvement is possible.

(3) *Majority Rule as a Social Force.* The institutions of representative government make a number of assumptions about the citizen's participation in the political process. While it need not be postulated that the voter gives rational consideration to policy issues, it is still assumed that he has a general idea of the way in which he would like to be governed and whom he would like to govern him. For if there is to be talk of majority rule in a political context, then there must exist a majority sentiment in one form or another. The difficulty, as has been pointed out, is that often there is no majority which knows what it wants; or the majority may have aspirations which are in essential conflict. It does not take a professional logician to show that political applications of majority rule are often formal exercises without a meaningful content. Nevertheless, most political theorists are persuaded that the idea of majority rule is an important one and that its consequences are real.

In many societies there is, in fact, a majority will even if the individuals who comprise the greater number are unable to articulate their wants in terms of public policy measures or candidates for office. There is, as Rousseau and Hegel pointed out, a consensus in society: and this general body of shared sentiments, while sometimes dormant, is often active and powerful. This will

---

[9] Clinton Rossiter, for example, finds the genuine will of the majority expressed by the President. See his *The American Presidency* (New York: Harcourt, Brace, 1956). James Burnham, on the other hand, discovers it in the Congress. See his *Congress and the American Tradition* (Chicago: Regnery, 1959).

of the majority is a generalized social force, and it is not easily susceptible to representation through political institutions. The majority, acting as a social force, can be the arbiter of taste and agency of enforcement for values. Its impact on the thinking and behavior of individuals can never be minimized, whether those individuals happen themselves to be in the majority camp or outside it. A majority can rule, therefore, in the sense that its members taken together define approved conduct for a society and penalize those who deviate from the conventional norms. This form of majority rule is social and psychological, and yet it can also make its sentiments felt in the political world. Such a majority, as Tocqueville will point out, is often likely to grant to government the power to enforce behavior which has the social sanction of the larger part of society. No more need be said about this now, as the subject will receive further discussion later on.

(4) *Majority Rule as Tyranny.* The debate over majority rule may be put in one of two forms. The argument, first of all, is phrased in terms of majority rule vs. minority rule. Here it is said, quite logically, that if the majority is not to be allowed to rule then power must be given to some minority in society. There are, however, many minority groups in society which would like to rule, and all of them profess to be eligible for this responsibility. Some stake their claim to power on their wisdom and virtue, others on their wealth and breeding, and still others on their talent and experience. The question then becomes one of deciding which minority is to have political power. The theories of Plato, Machiavelli, and Burke have much to say toward the resolution of this problem. But the difficulty, of course, is that there has never yet been found a minority group which can long persuade the majority that power should be handed over to it. Minority rule in the final analysis always ends up being unsatisfactory to the majority, and they, after all, are the ones who are being governed.

The case for majority rule is that it is the only alternative: it is impossible to find a class or a coherent group in society which will not use power to promote its own interests and serve to oppress the majority. Indeed, it may be said that if there is to be oppression, it is preferable to let the majority oppress itself. By making its own mistakes and learning to correct them, it will develop the ability to handle power responsibly. On the other hand, the argument is no less often put in terms of majority tyranny vs. minority rights. Here it is said that if majority rule is allowed to operate without limitation, then there is the ever-present danger that the majority will enact policies which are oppressive to the outvoted minority.

This problem has, of course, been discussed time and again since Plato's day. Indeed, the threat of majority tyranny looms larger in political theory than the threat of minority rule. It is in order now to examine some of the features of this recurrent idea. For the whole tenor of any argument on this subject can depend on which people happen to be in the majority and which in the minority at any given time.

If the minority are the rich and well-born, for example, then the kind of tyranny they are liable to suffer at the hands of a ruling majority is of one kind. If the minority, however, are members of an unorthodox religious sect, then majority tyranny will express itself in a different form. The rights claimed by a minority, therefore, must be spelled out and then evaluated. Is the right of one man to do as he pleases with his inherited wealth to be viewed in the same way as the right of another man to worship God as his conscience dictates? If discussion of majority tyranny is to be meaningful, then the deprivations visited on the minority must be known, and a convincing case must be made that they have actually been subjected to oppressive rule. A related question deals with the extent to which members of a minority are themselves responsible for the treatment accorded to them by the majority.

As a rough rule of thumb, it may be asked if a minority group suffers oppression because of who its members are or because of what its members do. In the former category might come such groups as Negroes, Jews, and women. There are schools which will admit no Negro, no matter how intelligent; there are neighborhoods which will sell homes to no Jew, no matter how personable; there are jobs which are open to no woman, no matter how talented. People who suffer such disabilities cannot do very much to change their race, religion, or sex: they cannot be blamed for having *done* something which merits punitive treatment. Other minority groups consist of individuals who *act* in ways which are felt to be injurious to society. The businessman who uses his economic power irresponsibly can presumably change his ways and therefore escape future prosecutions; the member of a subversive organization has the option of resigning and thereby exempting himself from oppression by the government. The businessman and the subversive are both responsible for what they do, and they at least understand that their behavior can have consequences for them. While the oppression they may suffer may or may not be justified, it is at least more rational than the penalties inflicted on members of racial or religious minorities.

It is necessary also to inquire into the setting in which majority tyranny is believed to be at work. Problems arise, for example, when it is claimed that national political authority is used to oppress those who live in a particular locality. The federal government may require that states carry out a policy of racial integration. It will insist that national laws, and not those of the individual states, must apply when it comes to educational and other public facilities. The problem of majority and minority, however, is not such a simple one. Who, it may be asked, are the majority?

	The Majority	The Minority
The United States	Northerners	Southerners
State of Alabama	White Men	Negroes
Macon County, Alabama	Negroes	White Men

Citizens who reside in the northern states clearly constitute a majority of the total population, and their representatives in the legislative and executive branches of the national government are in a position to make policy which the southern minority finds oppressive. Yet this is obviously not the whole story. For in all southern states there is a white majority, and it is white men who make state laws concerning racial facilities. Here, then, the Negro minority —say, in a state like Alabama—believe that they are being oppressed. Indeed, it may be argued that the northern majority, which is predominantly white, is using its power to redress the condition of the Alabama Negroes. At the same time, there are many counties in southern states where there happens to be a Negro majority. If political and social arrangements are equalized in Macon County, for instance, then the Negroes in that area will, it is said, be able to oppress the whites in the county. Hence the white majority of Alabama is using its power to protect the white minority of Macon County from a situation in which they would be placed at a disadvantage. All three of these constituencies are real, and in all three the question of majority tyranny—real or supposed— takes a different form.

Yet just because political policy is responsive to majority sentiment, it need not be assumed that the consequences will be tyranny. The oppressive character of majority rule depends on the composition of the ruling majority. In some cases there will be a group which seems always to be outvoted: if a particular religious sect, say, is a small minority which stands little chance of recruiting enough members so as to attain majority status, then it may have always to bow to the policies made by the greater number. It can only hope that the majority will restrain itself and will not take advantage of its opportunity to be tyrannical. However, in many political settings religion is not the only policy issue at stake: rather, there are many issues, and they cut across many social lines. And the groups in most societies are not divided solely on the grounds of religious affiliations, but on the basis of various economic and regional and ethnic interests.

If, then, there are many issues and many groups, there is a good chance that "the" majority will be transitory in its composition. That is, the ruling majority at any given time will be a temporary coalition: an alliance tied together to support a particular policy. But as that alliance will not agree among itself on all policies, a new majority will have to form as new issues arise. In a case like this the society is not divided into two fixed camps: a permanent majority and a permanent minority. Rather, the society is actually composed of many minorities, no single one of which has lasting majority status. Insofar as this social condition prevails, majority tyranny is not an abiding problem. If it is a problem, then the pain inflicted on the minority is momentary, for the losing group stands a good chance of being on the winning side when the next issue is presented.

Each citizen, therefore, has several roles, and he identifies himself with different groups in accord with his varying interests. While he may one day be oppressed in his religious role, the next day he may be benefitted in his role as a wage earner. Each individual and each group, in sum, alternates between being oppressed and being an oppressor of someone else.[10] If all groups are minorities, then all groups will have a vested interest in preserving a political system in which no minority can be permanently oppressed.

The quest for minority rights grows not out of a respect for freedom or an attitude of tolerance: on the contrary, it is a technique of self-defense in a society where all groups are aware of the fact that they stand in an exposed position until safeguards are set up.[11] Majority rule therefore need not be tyrannical so long as a society is fragmented into groups and interests, and so long as these groups and interests are prepared to abide by certain ground rules. Whether this favored condition can be attained by all societies is an open question. One requirement is that a certain level of political maturity has been reached: minorities which are outvoted, for instance, must have the patience and foresight to wait on the sidelines for the next vote—and perhaps the next and the next after that. Another prerequisite is that there are no political cleavages which put one group permanently on the losing side: citizens who find themselves with minority status in all their significant roles are, for all intents and purposes, effectively outside the system. To say that a ruling majority can be a transitory coalition is not to say that it has always to take this form. To say that minorities can escape tyranny by allying together to form a majority is not to say that every minority group will find an opportunity to join in this defensive effort.

Finally, it is not always possible to look at minorities in group terms. Many significant instances where rights are at stake turn out to be "minorities of

[10] See David Truman, *The Governmental Process* (New York: Knopf, 1951), especially the discussion of "overlapping memberships" on pp. 508–516.

[11] See John Roche's essay "American Liberty: An Examination of the 'Tradition' of Freedom," in Milton R. Konvitz and Clinton Rossiter, eds., *Aspects of Liberty: Essays Presented to Robert E. Cushman* (Ithaca: Cornell University Press, 1958), pp. 129–162.

one." For again and again there appear unorthodox individuals whose behavior is frowned upon by the general community. These heretics may wish to make speeches, publish books, educate their children, or worship God according to principles of their own choosing. Rebels like this as often as not do not have a like-minded group of fellow thinkers to shield them: they stand —or fall—alone. In terms of strict logic, of course, there must be at least a dozen sets of parents throughout the country who refuse to send their children to existing schools and who want to educate them at home. But it is to torture logic to call these individuals a "group": they are separated by long distances, they act as they do for different reasons, and they probably do not even know or know of one another. In these instances the opposition is not between majority tyranny and minority rights, but rather between majority tyranny and individual rights. The idea of a majority made up of a shifting coalition is not much of a defense here, for the isolated individual has little or no weight to throw into even the transitory alliances which make policy. He is fair game for oppressive treatment unless there are constitutional protections for unconventional people such as himself. This problem of individual freedom will concern John Stuart Mill. While the liberty of minority groups and that of single persons often overlaps, real life presents these distinct cases often enough to make the two worthy of separate analysis.

(5) **Majority Rule as a Principle.** Despite the facts that majority rule as a political institution is an unrealized goal and majority rule as a political or social force can be tyrannical, the idea itself remains as an important political principle. The notion that all men are equals and the view that legitimacy is founded on the consent of the governed lead to the conclusion that the majority ought to rule. This assumption can be seen in its rudimentary stages in the writings of Aristotle and St. Thomas, and it builds up in the theories of Locke, Rousseau, and Bentham. As a principle it may be Utopian. Machiavelli, for example, gives persuasive reasons for believing that in realistic terms the majority will always be ruled by a well-organized minority. Even Rousseau believed that the principle would only have meaning in a small and homogeneous setting. Nevertheless, majority rule, like all political principles, is a goal toward which men and states are asked to strive. The point is not that it is achieved in any perfected form but that the effort to attain it is a praiseworthy one. Tocqueville was struck by the fact that citizens of a new democracy not only live by and believe in this principle, but they bend their every effort to make it a reality in their political and social behavior.

SOCIAL AND PSYCHOLOGICAL EQUALITY

A new society—one which begins from the ground up or which experiences an abrupt break from the past—is apt to stress the principle of human equality. If it is a nation the population of which is comprised mainly of recent immigrants, then there is unlikely to be an established class with a claim to a preferred position. If it is a nation rising in the aftermath of revolution, the chances are good that it will have swept away many of the old institutions of privilege. However, to either or both of these features must be added the environmental conditions conducive to equality. There should, preferably, be a scarcity of labor: in this event each individual has a modicum of bargaining power. There should also be enough material prosperity and opportunity so that traditional social classes are not replaced by new economic classes. Tocqueville sees in America not simply the idea of equality but also an equality of condition which is very real.

Among the novel objects that attracted my attention during my stay in the United States, nothing struck me more forcibly than the general equality of condition among the people. . . . I soon perceived that the influence of this fact extends far beyond the political character and the laws of the country, and that it has no less effect on civil society than on the government; it creates opinions, gives birth to new sentiments, founds novel customs, and modifies whatever it does not produce. The more I advanced in the study of American society, the more I perceived that this equality of condition is the fundamental fact from which all others seem to be derived and the central point at which all my observations constantly terminated.[12]

For this reason, Tocqueville's analysis is always a combination of politics and sociology. He is interested in political institutions and behavior, but he at all times places his observations in their over-all social setting.

Majority rule, which concerns him again and again, is viewed primarily as a social force with political manifestations. If popular sovereignty is expressed in a legal form, it is no less embedded in the habits and customs of the population. The two aspects, in short, are part of a single phenomenon.

In America the principle of the sovereignty of the people is neither barren nor concealed, as it is with some other nations; it is recognized by the customs and proclaimed by the laws; it spreads freely, and arrives without impediment at its most remote consequences.

There is no more invariable rule in the history of society: the further electoral rights are extended, the greater is the need of extending them; for after each concession the strength of the democracy increases, and its demands increase with its strength.

The people reign in the American political world as the Deity does in the uni-

[12] *Democracy in America*, Vol. I, p. 3.

verse. They are the cause and the aim of all things; everything comes from them, and everything is absorbed in them.[13]

Tocqueville speaks of the vast majority of citizens. And this majority seems to have taken Rousseau's advice to heart: they are avid participants in the political process. At the local level they take part in town meetings and they hold offices of responsibility; at the national level they form themselves into a galaxy of associations in order better to pursue their interests; and at all levels they act and talk politically. "No sooner do you set foot upon American ground than you are stunned by a kind of tumult," Tocqueville says. "A confused clamor is heard on every side, and a thousand simultaneous voices demand the satisfaction of their social wants." [14]

While these wants may be social, Tocqueville is enough of a student of politics to stress the fact that government is the chief agency for satisfying their desires. Citizens participate in government and politics because they have interests of their own to protect. Yet at the same time this participation reveals to them that their interests are part of a larger design. Whatever the motives for entering politics, the experience itself gives men a sense of responsibility for the public welfare as well as their own. If Tocqueville occasionally displays an amused irony in his account of democratic politics, he is no less ready to salute its serious side. "I maintain that the most powerful and perhaps the only means that we still possess of interesting men in the welfare of their country is to make them partakers in the government . . ." he says. "How does it happen that everyone takes as zealous an interest in the affairs of his township, his county, and the whole state as if they were his own? It is because everyone, in his sphere, takes an active part in the government of society." [15]

There is, however, another side to this matter, and it can run counter to the salutary consequences of universal participation in politics. Democracy in a large and growing nation cannot be viewed wholly in terms of self-governing town meetings. Policy must be made on a national level as well, and it must be made by agencies removed from the people. Rousseau's simple idea of direct democracy is a statement of principle rather than practice. Tocqueville seems at times to be caught between Rousseau and reality. "The very essence of democratic government consists in the absolute sovereignty of the majority . . ." he says. "Wherever universal suffrage has been established, the majority unquestionably exercises the legislative authority." [16] There is no

[13] Vol. I, pp. 57, 59, 60.
[14] Vol. I, p. 259.
[15] Vol. I, pp. 264, 222.
[16] Vol. I, pp. 264, 222.

need at this point to ask whether majority will is better expressed by an elected legislature or an elected executive: actually both carry out such a will, but in different ways; and each tends to stress a different aspect of the majority's wishes. What is important is that the instruments of government reflect the sentiments of those who have the power to elect the officeholders. This means that politicians must be prepared to respond to the demands of their constituents: to do otherwise is to court defeat. "Democratic republics extend the practice of currying favor with the many and introduce it into all classes at once," Tocqueville says. "This is the most serious reproach that can be addressed to them." [17]

Elected representatives, in short, allow their masters to do their thinking for them. And, what is worse, the public is so flattered that it sees little reason for attempting to elevate its conception of its political role. The conclusion— measured by the aristocratic yardstick—would seem to be that democracy produces not statesmen but vapid politicians. Yet while such a conclusion might proceed from the assumption that the majority is the political sovereign, this is not the last word. Tocqueville is attempting to describe a complex system, and there are conflicting forces at work. A society based on equality also means that all men are equally insignificant when set up against the power of the society itself. Insofar as equal citizens share common interests, they are prone to believe that what is good for one is good for all. When this tendency takes on national proportions, there is a strong likelihood that the institutions of a centralized government will be permitted to make uniform policy for the nation as a whole. Men who have similar needs and aspirations are not restive under laws which impose common conditions on everyone.

This process is accelerated if the majority is mistrustful of legislation which favors a privileged section of the community. "This never dying, ever kindling hatred which sets a democratic people against the smallest privileges," Tocqueville says, "is peculiarly favorable to the gradual concentration of all political rights in the hands of the representatives of the state alone." [18] What may occur, then, is that the government can become a powerful force which is actually independent in many ways from the citizens who elect its personnel. As democracy leads to political centralization, so may it lead to the concentration of power in the state. Indeed, so long as it is popularly believed that the power of government is based on the majority will, then that government may increase the scope and penetration of its activities.

Yet experience has shown that active governments develop, as it were, wills of their own, and they consequently educate the citizens to an acceptance of

[17] Vol. I, p. 277.
[18] Vol. II, p. 312.

new measures and new powers. "Men who live in the ages of equality are naturally fond of central power and are willing to extend its privileges," Tocqueville said. "If it happens that this same power faithfully represents their own interests and exactly copies their own inclinations, the confidence they place in it knows no bounds, and they think that whatever they bestow upon it is bestowed upon themselves." [19]

If there is a concentration of political power, what troubles Tocqueville even more is the power which comes to inhere in society as a whole. In a democratic society more so than others men are apt to become lost in the crowd. Realizing this in a half-conscious way, they therefore identify themselves and their interests with that of the social totality. Rather than fighting society, they exalt its power. Rather than wandering aimlessly in an anonymous aggregate, they submit themselves to its wisdom and authority as a defense mechanism.

As the conditions of men become equal among a people, individuals seem of less and society of greater importance; or rather every citizen, being assimilated to all the rest, is lost in the crowd, and nothing stands conspicuous but the great and imposing image of the people at large. This naturally gives the men of democratic periods a lofty opinion of the privileges of society and a very humble notion of the rights of individuals; they are ready to admit that the interests of the former are everything and those of the latter nothing. They are willing to acknowledge that the power which represents the community has far more information and wisdom than any of the members of the community; and that it is the duty, as well as the right, of that power to guide as well as govern each private citizen.[20]

Tocqueville is not an organic theorist in the sense of either Burke or Hegel. When he speaks of "society" as having a power and a wisdom somehow apart from these qualities as they belong to individuals, he is simply describing a sociological fact as best he can. There is no denying that the interaction of individuals produces social forces which are best explained as forces in their own right rather than as the sum total of the discrete contributions of each individual.

What Tocqueville is saying, then, is that an equalitarian condition has two sides in its impact on those who partake of it. On the one hand, it leads each individual to think highly of himself and to demand a share in the process of government. On the other, it impels that same individual to defer to social opinion and political power. The two forces are not contradictory: the beliefs may be held simultaneously even though actual behavior shows that men submit in a democracy more than they will admit that they do. One reason for this is that the pressures of society are often unperceived by those who

---

[19] Vol. II, pp. 318–319.
[20] Vol. II, p. 307.

bow to them. "The public, therefore, among a democratic people, has a singular power . . ." Tocqueville says. "It does not persuade others to its beliefs, but it imposes them and makes them permeate the thinking of everyone by a sort of enormous pressure of the mind of all upon the individual intelligence." [21] It will have to suffice to call this power of society a "sort" of pressure which operates on the minds of all men: if Tocqueville is vague in his description, it is because he is unwilling to become involved with an idea having metaphysical overtones like the General Will.

This force, therefore, is both social and psychological. The public mind has a pervasive influence on the private mind. And here too questions about freedom of the will are bound to arise. Each citizen holds certain attitudes, and he believes that he has come by them rationally and personally. Most individuals, for example, are prepared to take up arms when their nation issues the call; most are willing to testify before public authority concerning their political beliefs. And these citizens will doubtless claim that they think as they do for good and sufficient reasons. Yet it may also be argued that they are victims of the "enormous pressure" of which Tocqueville speaks and that they are not aware that this force is at work on them. The majority in this sense is behaving as a tyrant, but it is a psychological tyranny which is being exercised over the individuals who constitute the majority itself. Tyranny over the mind is invisible, and its victims feel no pain. The traditional defenses against oppression break down when the enemy is not only elusive but also the collective power of the individuals who are, in effect, oppressing themselves. "The authority of a king is physical and controls the actions of men without subduing their will. But the majority possesses a power that is physical and moral at the same time, which acts upon the will as much as upon the actions . . ." Tocqueville says. "In democratic republics, . . . the body is left free, and the soul is enslaved." [22]

This is a new problem, and it calls for new approaches. The old forms of tyranny enchained a man's body, but at least he knew that he was being oppressed, and he protested as best he could. In the new tyranny there are no identifiable tyrants: psychological restraint is possible without the conscious intervention of a particular ruling group. Tocqueville uses the language of Rousseau and Bentham to describe what can occur. "I perceive how, under the dominion of certain laws, democracy would extinguish that liberty of the mind to which a democratic condition is favorable," he says, "so that, after having broken all the bondage once imposed on it by ranks or by men, the human mind would be closely fettered to the general will of the greatest num-

[21] Vol. II, p. 11.
[22] Vol. I, pp. 273–274.

ber." [23] And the most disheartening feature of this oppression is that it is sufficiently painless not to evoke protest from those subjected to it. It is hard to criticize a despot who cannot be seen: it is difficult to revolt against a condition which is comfortable no less than it is enervating. And even if the vast majority of citizens find no objection to this consequence of the democratic condition, they and their society are being harmed in ways they cannot perceive.

The pressures Tocqueville describes put a premium on mediocrity: in an equalitarian society the lowest common denominator becomes the norm, because that is the level of performance most men can attain and understand. "I confess that I apprehend much less for democratic society from the boldness than from the mediocrity of desires," he says. "What appears to me most to be dreaded is that in the midst of the small, incessant occupations of private life, ambition should lose its vigor and its greatness; that the passions of man should abate, but at the same time be lowered; so that the march of society should every day become more tranquil and less aspiring." [24] These are, although slightly muted, the tones of Hegel: a nation is a grand enterprise, and its citizens should be men of great passion and high aspirations.

Tocqueville is now speaking less as an aristocrat and more as a friendly critic of democracy: he is meeting the idea of equality on its own ground and is asking if it can raise men to their finest potentialities. A democratic society, he is saying, has undoubted talents among its citizens. But can such a society encourage these talents rather than repress them? The answer to this question is the answer to the question whether liberty and equality can grow on the same soil. And Tocqueville is not yet ready to speak of solutions.

THE PRICE OF PROSPERITY

Some new democracies are prosperous enough to give to all their inhabitants a high and rising standard of life. But all new democracies, whether or not they are so fortunate, implant in all their citizens the expectation that they will secure new and greater material comforts. For if democracy is a revolt against privilege, its corollary is that not only power but the other fine things of life will be distributed with greater equality.

In addition, the principle of equality encourages the materialist impulses of men. If Locke emphasized the role of property it was because he realized that the security it gives to its holders compensates for what is lost when the class foundations of traditional societies are weakened. Democracy and materialism

[23] Vol. II, pp. 12–13.
[24] Vol. II, p. 261.

are therefore in close relation: the condition of equality puts each man on his own and forces him to find his identity through the institutions of ownership. "It tends to isolate them from one another, to concentrate every man's attention upon himself, and it lays open the soul to an inordinate love of material gratification," Tocqueville says.[25] This is one of the costs of freedom. In an aristocratic society, as Burke pointed out, the majority of men did not need property: their prescriptive status gave them the security they needed. A new democracy must accept the fact that the mundane pursuits of its citizens are necessary substitutes for patterns of behavior which have been shattered.

> When . . . the distinctions of ranks are obliterated and privileges are destroyed, when hereditary property is subdivided and education and freedom are widely diffused, the desire of acquiring the comforts of the world haunts the imagination of the poor. . . . If one were to inquire what passion is most natural to men who are stimulated and circumstanced by the obscurity of their birth or the mediocrity of their fortune, I could discover none more peculiarly appropriate to their condition than this love of physical prosperity.[26]

Yet it is not simply the ungentlemanly displays of the acquisitive impulse which concern Tocqueville. He is more interested in how the materialist orientation affects the lives of individuals. An equalitarian society encourages rapid mobility: social, geographic, and occupational. Men are not prone to devote their lives to a single craft, and they are impatient with time-honored methods or practices. This attitude is conducive to productive efficiency, but it has its impact in human terms. "The inhabitants of the United States are never fettered by the axioms of their profession," Tocqueville says. "They escape from all the prejudices of their present station; they are not more attached to one line of operation than to another; they are not more prone to employ an old method than a new one; they have no rooted habits, and they easily shake off the influence that the habits of other nations might exercise upon them." [27] To sever the roots of tradition, even in the economic sphere, takes its toll. The craftsman may have a narrow range of skills, but they are true skills, and they give meaning to his life. The accelerated mobility which characterizes a democracy means that men experience many trades, but at no time do they have the satisfactions which come of creative work. Work, indeed, becomes a fragmented and inchoate process through which men are compelled to pass but which adds little to their character.

If men of an equalitarian age cannot know creativity in their work, then it is left to them to acquire. The acquisition of wealth soon becomes the com-

---

[25] Vol. II, p. 23.
[26] Vol. II, p. 137.
[27] Vol. I, p. 443.

mon aspiration in a society where alternative symbols of status are destroyed. But this pursuit, too, leaves its mark on the human personality. If access to opportunity is equal, then a large section of the community will in fact be able to satisfy their material aspirations. The difficulty, however, is that this satisfaction is invariably short-lived. Expectation always outruns attainment, and today's success looks paltry when contrasted with the prizes that are as yet unwon.

Among democratic nations, men easily attain a certain equality of condition, but they can never attain as much as they desire. It perpetually retires from before them, yet without hiding itself from their sight, and in retiring draws them on. At every moment they think they are about to grasp it; it escapes at every moment from their hold. They are near enough to see its charms, but too far off to enjoy them; and before they have fully tasted its delights, they die. To these causes must be attributed that strange melancholy which often haunts the inhabitants of democratic countries in the midst of their abundance, and that disgust at life which sometimes seizes upon them in the midst of calm and easy circumstances.

He who has set his heart exclusively upon the pursuit of worldly welfare is always in a hurry, for he has but a limited time at his disposal to reach, to grasp, and to enjoy it. The recollection of the shortness of life is a constant spur to him. Besides the good things that he possesses, he every instant fancies a thousand others that death will prevent him from trying if he does not try them soon. This thought fills him with anxiety, fear, and regret and keeps his mind in ceaseless trepidation, which leads him perpetually to change his plans and his abode.[28]

This is, indeed, the somber side of democracy. Melancholy and disgust at life are heavy prices to pay for the blessings of equality. Anxiety, fear, and regret dilute the pleasures of material prosperity. Tocqueville is prepared to grant that equality of condition is a liberating experience. But he also takes pains to point out the unforeseen and undiscussed accompaniments of this achievement of the modern world.

It should be noted, in addition, that the symptoms he cites are couched more in the language of mental health than in the language of morality. The anxieties which haunt men's minds are dismal to behold, yet those who suffer from them are more to be pitied than censured. If the condition of equality is also a neurotic one, it is inappropriate to assign blame to individuals. Tocqueville may evaluate the institutions of democracy in moral terms, but he is less quick to judge the behavior of individuals according to the same standards. His dispassionate stance is seen again as he points out that envy and depravity of taste are democratic characteristics.

It cannot be denied that democratic institutions strongly tend to promote the feeling of envy in the human heart; not so much because they afford to everyone

[28] Vol. II, pp. 147, 145.

the means of rising to the same level with the others as because those means perpetually disappoint the persons who employ them. Democratic institutions awaken and foster a passion for equality which they can never entirely satisfy.

There is, in fact, a manly and lawful passion for equality that incites men to wish to be all powerful and honored. This passion tends to elevate the humble to the rank of the great; but there exists also in the human heart a depraved taste for equality, which impels the weak to attempt to lower the powerful to their own level and reduces men to prefer equality in slavery to inequality with freedom.[29]

It has already been observed that the equalitarian temper can take two opposed forms. On the one hand, there is the "downward-looking" view: men may extend a helping hand to their less privileged fellows, telling them "you're as good as we are." On the other hand, there is the "upward-looking" view: men cast envious eyes at those standing above them and, saying "we're as good as you are," try to pull them down to a common level. The second trait is what Tocqueville sees at work in a new democracy: envy of the rich and well-born, a yearning to have privileged classes stripped of their unequal status in society. Indeed, there is a tendency to make a political scapegoat out of the symbols of wealth and breeding. Traditional financial and educational institutions, for example, are often represented as being enemies of the people. This is, of course, populist democracy at work, and the target can be economic royalism or intellectual subversion.[30]

Such an expression of the equalitarian spirit comes into being when the society sets standards of attainment which are applied to all individuals and then does not permit the achievement of these goals. The result is that a scapegoat must be found, and the undemocratic elements in society serve this function well. This is not to say that all citizens of a new democracy are constantly gnawed at by the canker of envy, nor should it be suggested that their most fervent wish is to see their betters dashed to the ground. All that Tocqueville is pointing out is that there are psychological ramifications to democracy which are often unperceived by those who celebrate the ideal of equality. Such an ideal is a noble one, and Tocqueville has nothing but respect for its lawful and temperate expression. But if the system as a whole works so as to frustrate the equalitarian aspirations of individuals, then they will give vent to their frustrations: outwardly on the symbols of inequality in their midst, and inwardly on themselves.

What makes Tocqueville a modern theorist is the fact that he discusses democracy in the setting of an emerging industrial society. The industrial mode of production, as was indicated, undermines the traditional role of the craftsman. At the same time, the productive process begins to make demands of its

[29] Vol. I, pp. 208, 56.

[30] See the essays in Daniel Bell, ed., *The New American Right* (New York: Criterion, 1955), especially those by Richard Hofstadter, Peter Viereck, and Seymour Lipset.

own, and they are demands which those who would earn a living are compelled to heed. The first of these is the division of labor: each individual does a specialized and repetitive task, for only in this way can a high level of manufacturing efficiency be achieved. Yet if efficiency is the highroad to prosperity, it also has its effects on a man in his role as producer. "Nothing tends to materialize man and to deprive his work of the faintest trace of mind than the extreme division of labor," Tocqueville says.[31] This view, which will be elaborated by Marx and Engels, is bound to have political consequences. In an industrial society men work with machines, but in an important sense they also work *for* machines. The tools themselves come to govern the thinking of the individuals who are little more than human extensions of a technological system. And not only do men work with and for machines: they also work with and for other men. When technology calls forth a division of labor and legal authority sanctions private ownership, then the conditions are set for economic classes.

Tocqueville is not a radical, but rather a conservative aristocrat. If his words have a Marxist ring, this is good evidence that the institutions of the free market are open to criticism from the right as well as the left. What concerns Tocqueville most is not economic exploitation—for he admits that material prosperity can be distributed equitably—but the impact of industrial technology on the human mind.

It is worth quoting a famous passage of his in its entirety.

In proportion as the principle of the division of labor is more extensively applied, the workman becomes more weak, more narrow-minded, and more dependent. The art advances, the artisan recedes. On the other hand, in proportion as it becomes more manifest that the productions of manufactures are by so much the cheaper and better as the manufacture is larger and the amount of capital employed more considerable, wealthy and educated men come forward to embark on manufactures, which were heretofore abandoned to poor or ignorant handicraftsmen. The magnitude of the efforts required and the importance of the results to be obtained attract them. Thus at the very time at which the science of manufactures lowers the class of workmen, it raises the class of masters.

While the workman concentrates his faculties more and more upon the study of a single detail, the master surveys an extensive whole, and the mind of the latter is enlarged in proportion as that of the former is narrowed. In a short time the one will require nothing but physical strength without intelligence; the other stands in need of science, and almost of genius, to ensure success. This man resembles more and more the administrator of a vast empire; that man a brute.

The master and the workman have then here no similarity, and their differences increase every day. They are connected only like the two rings at the extremities of a long chain. Each of them fills the station which is made for him, and which he does not leave; the one is continually closely, and necessarily dependent upon the other and seems as much born to obey as that other is to command.[32]

[31] *Democracy in America*, Vol. 1, p. 443.
[32] Vol. II, p. 169.

At no point does Tocqueville say that the master exploits the workman: it is the industrial system, rather, which turns the worker into an appendage of the machine he runs. It is the machine, in a word, which degrades the man who operates it. To use Marx's terms, Tocqueville is concerned with the "modes of production" rather than with the "relations of production"; he is interested in the pattern of technology rather than in the pattern of ownership. This emphasis has much to be said for it, and it will be explored in the next chapter.

If the advent of industrialization degrades the average worker, it also throws up a new class—or, more properly, a new elite—which reaps the benefits of the system. When labor must be divided, there must always be a few who are charged with planning, coordinating, and managing. These men Tocqueville is prepared to celebrate. The industrial manager must see a whole economic process at work, and those who ascend high in executive ranks will have a broadened understanding of the whole economic and social order. Whether this industrial elite can mature into a national aristocracy is a problem which Tocqueville attempts to conjure with later on. They are responsible for only one aspect of the community's total activities, and it may be wondered whether their economic power can lead them to the assumption of wider social obligations. A democracy cannot hope to impose an aristocratic social structure on itself and remain democratic: it must develop its leaders within the setting of equality and social mobility. If modern technology has unfavorable consequences for the ordinary worker, it may also compensate for this by producing men capable of responsible leadership.

And what of the worker who fares so poorly in an industrial setting? Not only Marx, but many theorists would prophesy that class antagonism and revolution might well be the political consequence of such a bifurcation in society. Tocqueville certainly sees that tensions can build up. "The workman conceives a more lofty opinion of his rights, of his future, of himself," he says, "he is filled with new ambitions and new desires, he is harrassed by new wants. Every instant he views with longing eye the profits of his employer; and in order to share them he strives to dispose of his labor at a higher rate, and he generally succeeds in the attempt." [33] It is one thing to admit of antagonism: it is quite another to predict that the result will be revolution. For if Tocqueville is describing a state of perennial economic dissatisfaction, he is also not forgetful that this state of affairs exists in the over-all circumstance of social equality. Workers may envy the comforts of the well-to-do, but the abiding aspiration is to ascend to that favored status. The average man may in one breath wish to tear down the privileged orders he sees above him, but in the next he will

[33] Vol. II, p. 199.

voice his ambition to climb to the top of the economic ladder. While there is bound to be a measure of antagonism between economic classes, there is also a consensus on the basic institution of private property. In sum, the ordinary citizen does not wish to destroy private property, for it is his hope that he will partake of its benefits in his own or his children's lifetime. "In no other country in the world is the love of property more active or more anxious than in the United States," Tocqueville says. "Nowhere does the majority display less inclination for those principles which threaten to alter, in whatever manner, the laws of property." [34]

A society can put up with economic tensions so long as there is a social consensus on important institutions and values. There can be class conflict in the economic sphere without its having to express itself in any profound way in the political or social spheres. If men of democratic societies display opposing tendencies in their thought and behavior, this is because democracy itself seeks to attain disparate goals. It is altogether possible for economic inequality and political equality to co-exist in a society: antagonisms arising out of an unequal distribution of property can be subordinated to a larger social consensus. But for this to occur, most men—the propertyless as well as the propertied—must identify their welfare with the welfare of this system. They will make such an identification so long as the promise is held out to them that they can ascend on the economic ladder. As that promise becomes less real, however, in that proportion will the institution of private property lose its basis of popular consent. To be sure, the dream of equality of opportunity may cease to have a factual foundation, and it may nevertheless remain a powerful myth in men's minds. But in this case it is living on borrowed time: men eventually discover that their dreams are illusions, and when they do, their behavior will soon take a new turn. In what direction this will be, however, is no easy matter to predict.

For all its economic and psychological aggravations, the democracy Tocqueville sees is not fallow ground for the seed of revolution. While masters and workmen, rich and poor, may constitute antagonistic economic classes, they do not describe the whole of society. On the contrary, there are many levels and gradations of both economic and social classes, and these are important buffers against extreme political tendencies.

I am aware that among a great democratic people there will always be some members of the community in great poverty and others in great opulence; but the poor, instead of forming the immense majority of the nation, as is always the case in aristocratic communities, are comparatively few in number, and the laws do not bind them together by the ties of irremediable and hereditary penury.

[34] Vol. II, p. 270.

The wealthy, on their side, are few and powerless; they have no privileges that attract public observation; even their wealth, as it is no longer incorporated and bound up with the soil, is impalpable and, as it were, invisible. As there is no longer a race of poor men; so there is no longer a race of rich men; the latter spring up daily from the multitude and relapse into it again. Hence they do not form a distant class which may be easily marked out and plundered; and, moreover, as they are connected with the mass of their fellow citizens by a thousand secret ties, the people cannot assail them without inflicting an injury upon themselves.

Between these two extremes of democratic communities stands an innumerable multitude of men almost alike, who, without being exactly either rich or poor, possess sufficient property to desire the maintenance of order, yet not enough to excite envy. Such men are the violent enemies of violent commotions; their lack of agitation keeps all beneath them and above them still and secures the balance of the fabric of society.[35]

This prescription is, of course, as old as Aristotle: a strong middle class is the best bulwark against revolution. And if that class is large enough to absorb most citizens, then there will not be enough malcontents to mount a significant barricade. If either the fact or the aspiration of property ownership is widely spread, then most people will have a vested interest in maintaining the laws of ownership and political order.

Yet even here there is a danger. Once the middle class grows large, it inevitably begins to include individuals who may own small amounts of property but who only qualify for middle-class status in the most marginal of ways. Such people are never secure in their status, and they are apt to display an overzealous affection for the status quo. The lower-middle class, in short, has much to lose and nothing to gain by radical change. They are so situated that they stand little chance of gaining more property, and they regard any advances made by those beneath them as endangering their own tenuous status. Tocqueville wonders if the fear of revolution on the part of small property-owners is not as dangerous as the urge to revolution by the propertyless.

Not only are the men of democracies not naturally desirous of revolutions, but they are afraid of them. All revolutions more or less threaten the tenure of property; but most of those who live in democratic countries are possessed of property; not only do they possess property, but they live in the condition where men set the greatest store upon property.

Now, these eager and apprehensive men of small property constitute the class that is constantly increased by the equality of conditions. Hence in democratic communities the majority of the people do not clearly see what they have to gain by a revolution, but they continually and in a thousand ways feel that they might lose by one.[36]

[35] Vol. II, p. 266.
[36] Vol. II, p. 267.

If men fear revolution too much then they will fear more than revolution: they will tremble at any suggestion of change, and they will imagine threats in all proposals for reform.

The "apprehensive men of small property" concern Tocqueville for good reason. Traditionally speaking a middle class is a fairly small group in society, and its members are possessed of fairly substantial wealth. The social processes of democracy have the effect of enlarging the middle class and admitting to it people who in an earlier day would not be considered qualified for such status. These new entrants, the lower-middle class, are not secure: and their insecurity governs their political attitudes and behavior. Having little property, their apprehensions over its safety become exaggerated. While they must defer to those wealthier than themselves, they are often contemptuous of the poorer classes who in fact are separated from them by the slenderest of margins.

If Tocqueville hopes that the middle class is a preventive of revolution, he sees in that same class tendencies no less harmful than the ones to be prevented. "The men of democratic times require to be free in order to procure more readily those physical enjoyments for which they are always longing," he says. "It sometimes happens, however, that the excessive taste they conceive for the same enjoyments makes them surrender to the first master who appears." [37] If the desire for material betterment can have this political consequence, then the desire to preserve what one already possesses can have an even more serious result. Men may surrender themselves in the hope of a modicum of prosperity: they will prostrate themselves even more ignobly to keep that which they have managed to attain. For to lose one's property is to lose one's cherished status as a member of the middle class. And men will abandon their sense of political responsibility if they feel their status is threatened. Tocqueville clearly dislikes the thought of a proletarian revolution: but the prospect of a middle-class counterrevolution is no less unsettling. If the former is carried out in the name of equality, the latter is perpetrated by men who are anxious lest equality has gone too far. Men may need freedom to gain property; but they can lose their freedom in their attempt to hold it. "It is not necessary to do violence to such a people in order to strip them of the rights they enjoy," Tocqueville says. "They themselves willingly loosen their hold." [38]

Tocqueville has much to say on the relation between economic and political life. Yet, in the final analysis, his comments are illuminating fragments. He

---

[37] Vol. II, pp. 148–149.

[38] *Ibid.* See also Robert Lane, "The Fear of Equality," *American Political Science Review*, March 1959, pp. 35–51.

sees in democracy many forces at work, and he describes what he sees. Unlike Hegel, he has no overarching philosophical design which provides a comprehensive order. The advance of industrial technology, for example, is an inescapable material fact; and it is a fact which clearly conditions the attitudes and behavior of men. Social equality, on the other hand, is an idea; yet that idea in the minds of men is also a fact and it too governs the actions of individuals and groups. Tocqueville's theory makes no real attempt to relate the material world and the world of ideas in any coherent way. He shows how the equalitarian condition of a new democracy fosters the materialist impulse. If this drive leads to advances in industry and technology, then the development of the factory system will have consequences for the equalitarian ideal.

Whether the creation of disparate economic and intellectual classes will act so as to defeat democratic aspirations is something Tocqueville is silent upon. Indeed, his conception of class is itself a nebulous one: sometimes he talks of workmen, masters, and the property-owning middle class; sometimes he talks of the existence of social equality in such a way as to suggest that class distinctions are insignificant. Clearly he sees opposing tendencies in democracy, and to impose a neat logical or metaphysical scheme would be to do violence to reality. Only time can tell which tendencies are important and which are peripheral.

Yet on one thing Tocqueville is clear: the ideals and experience of men cannot be separated by too wide a gulf. The equalitarian ideal tells all men that they are equal and that opportunity to succeed is a universal birthright. The citizens of a democracy, so far as Tocqueville can see, believe this premise and its accompanying promise. But can a democratic society make good on its word? The development of industry opens new vistas to some men, but it degrades others. The materialist spirit induces fears and anxieties no less than it brings prosperity to the community. While class struggle and revolution need not be the consequence, the price of equality is a heavy one. Tocqueville understands full well why men quest for democracy. What he is trying to do is to analyze some of the unanticipated concomitants of this new way of life.

LEADERSHIP IN A FREE SOCIETY

If Tocqueville acknowledges that democracy is inevitable, he also affirms the eternal value of human freedom. He is not slow to express his concern over those features of a democratic society which are inimical to individual liberty. And if Tocqueville speaks on occasion in the conservative accents of a Burke, he is no less committed to the liberalism of a John Stuart Mill.

While he may judge democracy by the aristocratic yardstick, he is no less aware that aristocratic institutions are things of the past. "I am persuaded that all who attempt in the ages upon which we are entering, to base freedom upon aristocratic privilege will fail," he says; "that all who attempt to draw and retain authority within a single class will fail." [39]

Furthermore, Burke's conception of freedom was freedom for a class: it was assumed that the creative and responsible actions of this limited group would be of such a high quality as to infuse the air of liberty into the whole society. Tocqueville, however, accepts Locke's assumption that freedom is the desert of all men: that a society can only be called free if all its inhabitants have the fullest opportunity to express themselves to the limits of their potentialities. This is why he is troubled by the tyranny of the majority. While earlier theorists were concerned lest the untutored mob oppress the wealthy and cultured minority, Tocqueville's fear is over what the public will do to itself. The individual's own worst enemy is his social self as it is expressed when he acts along with his fellow members of the majority.

It is on this basis that Tocqueville makes his own view quite plain. "I hold it to be an impious and detestable maxim that, politically speaking, the people have a right to do anything . . ." he says. "A majority taken collectively is only an individual, whose opinions, and frequently whose interests, are opposed to those of another individual, who is styled a minority. If it be admitted that a man possessing absolute power may misuse that power by wronging his adversaries, why should not a majority be liable to the same reproach?" [40] The majority may believe that its will is sovereign; it may even be politically and legally sovereign; but this does not make it morally sovereign. Insofar as acts of the majority violate the freedom of individuals—either members of minority groups or its own members—such acts are devoid of moral sanction. The answer is not to try to withhold the power of self-government from the people: in the modern age such an endeavor would be abortive. Rather, ways and means must be found to lead and mold majority sentiment so that it acts with temperance and tolerance.

Democratic societies harbor conflicting aspirations, and for this reason both analysis and prescription are bound to be complex rather than simple matters. Tocqueville is persuaded that freedom is a democratic goal no less than equality.

I think that democratic communities have a natural taste for freedom; left to themselves, they will seek it, cherish it, and view any privation of it with regret. But for equality their passion is ardent, insatiable, incessant, invincible; they

[39] Vol. II, p. 340.
[40] Vol. I, p. 269.

call for equality in freedom; and if they cannot obtain that, they still call for equality in slavery.[41]

Democracies, after all, are born in freedom. It is liberation from the oppressive rule of an alien or home-grown minority which impels men to strive for social equality and political self-government. The problem is how to preserve this natural taste once the initial institutional reforms have been made. The important task is to keep the society's conception of freedom at a high qualitative level. A majority of men may be willing to define freedom in terms of shallow materialistic goals or simply as freedom from physical harm. Leadership is required if they are to elevate their sights so as to see freedom as a uniquely individual possession. If liberty is to encompass the intellect and the conscience, the mind and the spirit, then the public must be encouraged to tolerate expressions of freedom which they themselves will often have no desire to exercise. This is a difficult assignment, and it is legitimate to ask who is to be charged with it.

In an aristocratic society the answer was an easy one: a prescriptive ruling class is the defender of a society's liberty. In a democratic society the answer is not so clear-cut. Tocqueville's method is to search for a group which may fulfill this aristocratic function in the social and political setting of a democracy. This is not an impossible task, for, despite the spirit of equality which reigns in a society, there still remains a residue from an earlier age. "The picture of an American society has, if I may so speak, a surface covering of democracy, beneath which the old aristocratic colors sometimes peep out," Tocqueville says.[42] There is, to be sure, a deference to traditional symbols of authority even in the most equalitarian societies. While they may be subject to occasional attack by populist leaders, the institutions of justice and higher education are usually accorded respect by the man in the street. Yet while courts and universities may be defenders of freedom, they must rely on the shifting sands of public consent for their power. The deference paid to such traditional institutions may vary as political currents run in first one direction and then another. For this reason, Tocqueville is unwilling to depend on such remnants of the old aristocracy as continue to subsist.

A democracy must produce its own guardians of freedom, and here the process of industrialization may be of advantage. "In proportion as the mass of the nation turns to democracy," he says, "that particular class which is engaged in manufactures becomes more aristocratic." [43] These men, it was suggested earlier, are talented individuals, and their assumption of responsibilities has contributed to their breadth of outlook. Perhaps they may be enlisted to

[41] Vol. II, p. 102.
[42] Vol. I, p. 47.
[43] Vol. II, p. 170.

replace the old ruling class of an aristocratic society. Perhaps they may be induced to take on political obligations as well as the economic ones they have already shouldered. This calls for an industrial statesmanship which will transcend a limited view of freedom and extend it to political as well as economic rights. The new industrial elite have the power and the prestige, the resources and the freedom of action, to be conservators of liberty for all of society. While it is not being suggested that business executives run for political office or dominate the parties, it is nevertheless clear that there are many ways in which they can commit themselves to the preservation of freedom.

After making this suggestion, Tocqueville then proceeds to show that its implementation is easier said than done. For businessmen are men of special talents, and there are essential differences between them and the aristocrats who preceded them. The industrial elite, first of all, is not a coherent class. "To tell the truth, though there are rich men, the class of rich men does not exist," Tocqueville says. "For these rich individuals have no feelings or purposes, no traditions or hopes, in common; there are individuals, therefore, but no definite class." [44] Men of economic power in a democracy, then, are an elite group. As individuals, they are recruited on the basis of their aptitudes for enterprise and management, and, taken together, they form a business community in only the most loose sense. While industrial executives may have much in common with each other, what binds them together is the jobs they happen to be doing and not similar backgrounds or family ties. Such a group cannot easily be enlisted as an entity, especially for purposes which transcend their immediate business responsibilities.

The difference between an elite and a ruling class has already been discussed: at this stage the importance of the distinction becomes apparent. In addition to this, the industrial elite have neither the temperament nor the training for far-reaching social and political undertakings. They have not been born into families of rank and in this way conditioned to the stations they will in time attain. Indeed insofar as they are self-made men, they have had to make a long and strenuous climb to achieve the positions they hold. This struggle takes its toll, and it tends to constrict the outlook of those who have had to make it. "A man who raises himself by degrees to wealth and power contracts, in the course of this protracted labor, habits of prudence and restraint he cannot afterwards shake off," Tocqueville says. "A man cannot gradually enlarge his mind as he does his house." [45] While there are notable exceptions to this rule, it may be generalized that members of an elite in one

---

[44] *Ibid.*

[45] Vol. II, p. 258. See also Andrew Hacker, "Liberal Democracy and Social Control," *American Political Science Review*, December 1957, pp. 1009–1026.

field are unlikely to have an aptitude for effective work in another area. The aptitudes required for successful business careers are ones quite different from those needed for statesmen who will defend a society's freedom. The industrial elite are products of an equalitarian society, and their rise is one of the fruits of equality of opportunity. But they may not for this reason be expected to assume the mantle of an aristocracy. Furthermore, men of wealth and power in a democratic society are not tied in an organic way to those who subsist beneath them in society. There are no mutual obligations between classes, for the classes themselves are economic and impermanent rather than social and fixed. The rapid development of industry prevents the relationship between employer and employee from taking on a full significance in the lives of both parties. The elite have few of the characteristics of a ruling class, and they are not joined to the rest of the community in a settled way.

Not only are the rich not compactly united among themselves, but there is no real bond between them and the poor. Their relative position is not a permanent one; they are constantly drawn together or separated by their interests. The workman is generally dependent on the master, but not on any particular master; these two men meet in the factory, but do not know each other elsewhere; and while they come into contact on one point, they stand far apart on all others. The manufacturer asks nothing of the workman but his labor; the workman expects nothing from him but his wages. The one contracts no obligation to protect nor the other to defend, and they are not permanently connected either by habit or by duty. The aristocracy created by business rarely settles in the midst of the manufacturing population which it directs; the object is not to govern that population, but to use it.[46]

Men who become rich in their own lifetimes do on occasion enter politics, but this act in itself is not a sufficient one by Tocqueville's standards. They must not only take on political leadership, but they must exercise it in responsible ways. And responsibility is not to be construed as simple responsiveness to the expressed desires of the man in the street, but responsibility to the enduring values of freedom. Businessmen may be characteristic leaders in a democracy, but they have not been brought up with the leisure and security which gives them an appreciation of human liberty in its political applications. Perhaps their sons and grandsons will develop the qualities which Tocqueville demands. The problem here is that an elite has its power by virtue of the positions its individual members attain, and they cannot pass on their status to their children. Thus an industrial elite is renewed by recruiting among the new generation of talent and, unlike a ruling class, it has not the property in its own right to establish family dynasties.[47]

[46] Vol. II, pp. 170–171.

[47] While businessmen of exceptional wealth can pass on fortunes which enable their children and grandchildren to lead independent lives, very few of the second or third gen-

In sum, Tocqueville has strong doubts as to whether the industrial aristocrats are aristocrats at all. If leadership is needed so that freedom will be preserved, then he is not prepared to depend on the business elite's assuming that responsibility. Both the structure of a democratic society and the character of the business mind offer little hope that a class of leaders will emerge.

The aristocratic solution to the problem of freedom is therefore inapplicable: a democratic society, so long as it adheres to the principle of freedom of opportunity, cannot produce a class of leaders capable of preserving political liberty. For this reason, Tocqueville turns away from superior individuals and to the society itself. In a democratic society men are taught to respect themselves and to comport themselves by standards of their own making. While such egotism may have its less pleasing side, it also tends to make the average citizen suspicious of the voice of political authority. "The principle of equality, which makes men independent of each other, gives them a habit and a taste for following in their private actions no other guide than their own will," Tocqueville says. "This complete independence . . . tends to make them look upon all authority with a jealous eye and speedily suggests to them the notion and the love of political freedom." [48]

It will be recalled, however, that Tocqueville also saw the tendency for citizens of a democracy to submit to political authority when they believed that the government was expressing the common will. If freedom is to be preserved, then, each individual should think of himself as an autonomous being with interests of his own: indeed, he should be wary of identifying his interests too much with those of society as a whole. Tocqueville, therefore, is calling for the liberal individualism of Locke and Bentham. The principle of self-interest can be turned to the defense of traditional political values. If citizens of a democracy are materialists, then their material stakes should be promoted and put to good use.

The phrase which Tocqueville employs is "self-interest rightly understood," and by this he means that it should be a rational pursuit. Men should think not only of their immediate benefits, but of the conditions they will require if they are to enjoy long-term prosperity. They must not forget their own interests, but they must always understand them to exist in a society where others are pursuing the same goal. Whether men are acting in their political, economic, or religious roles in society, they are advised to think of themselves as individuals with legitimate claims to the satisfaction of their own wants.

---

eration enter the political life. And if they do, it is almost invariably as individuals and not as representatives of their class. Indeed, politicians of upper-class background seem more often to be liberal than conservative in their outlook.

[48] Vol. II, p. 304.

While self-interest is perhaps not the noblest of virtues, it can at the same time bring out admirable qualities in men and produce healthy consequences for society's freedom.

The principle of self-interest rightly understood produces no great acts of self-sacrifice, but it suggests daily small acts of self-denial. By itself it cannot suffice to make a man virtuous; but it disciplines a number of persons in habits of regularity, temperance, moderation, foresight, self-command; and if it does not lead them straight to virtue by the will, it gradually draws them in that direction by their habits. If the principle of interest rightly understood were to sway the whole moral world, extraordinary virtues would doubtless be more rare; but I think that gross depravity would then also be less common. The principle of interest rightly understood perhaps prevents men from rising far above the level of mankind, but a greater number of other men, who were falling far below it, are caught and restrained by it. Observe some few individuals, they are lowerd by it; survey mankind, they are raised. I am not afraid to say that the principle of self-interest rightly understood appears to me the best suited of all philosophical theories to the wants of the men of our time, and that I regard it as their chief remaining security against themselves.[49]

Men like this will not humble themselves before an oppressive society or an officious state. Tocqueville does not accept the proposition that either a democratic society or a democratic state, because it claims to represent the majority, can order the thoughts and actions of all in the community. Even those in the consenting majority—not to mention the dissenting minority—have lives as individuals and pursuits which should be followed independently. In proportion as men develop coherent interests of their own, that far will they develop a vested interest in a free society. The point is not to quest after liberty as an abstract goal: it is rather to encourage behavior and institutions which will lead men to desire freedom as a means to ends of their own choosing. If enough citizens act in this way, then the result can be a free society for all.

THE GROUP BASIS OF FREEDOM

The problem of power is to be solved not by abolishing power, but by diffusing it. Tyranny in a democracy draws its power from the consent of the majority: indeed, it is the alacrity with which this consent can be granted that concerns Tocqueville. The tendency in a democracy, especially as industrialization takes root, is for men to take note of the features they share with their fellow citizens. If this is carried to too extreme a point, there will emerge the mass society which Burke took such pains to warn against. Men acting and thinking as a mass have little tolerance for political behavior which deviates from conventional norms: a mass society distrusts and fears the critic, the

[49] Vol. II, p. 131.

rebel, the individual. The principle of equality inherent in democracy, coupled with the facts of industrial life, can serve to weaken the personal identity of each citizen and strengthen the power of society. If this tendency is to be combatted, then steps must be taken to encourage the individual to think of himself and for himself. Suggestions, such as those of Rousseau and Hegel, that the citizen subsume his interests to the general interest must be given a reply.

As a beginning, a theory of democratic freedom must not start with a preconceived idea about perfect governmental forms. If government is to be a reflection of a free society, and if that society is comprised of free men, then it is best to be pragmatic. The interplay of personal and group interests will, if allowed free rein, demand that the state accommodate itself to men's wants— and not the other way around. "The course of time always gives birth to different interests, and sanctions different principles, among the same people," Tocqueville says; "and when a general constitution is to be established, these interests and principles are so many natural obstacles to the rigorous application of any political system with all its consequences." [50] The stronger and more widely diffused the various interests and political principles in a society, the less chance will there be that power will be concentrated in the state. The political system which Tocqueville wishes to see tempered is equalitarian democracy, especially that taking the form of mass democracy. The way to do this is to persuade citizens, who might submerge themselves in an anonymous majority, that they have interests as individuals. But this persuasion takes more than words: institutions are needed if the opportunity to discover these interests is to be provided.

The idea of pluralism has, of course, been discussed by many theorists. What is interesting, however, is that the pluralism of Aristotle, Burke, and Hegel is woven into the fabric of an organic society: the variety of groups, orders, and classes takes a settled form in a settled hierarchy. Locke, who talks the language of democracy at least part of the time, makes no mention of groups or associations. And Rousseau, an avowed democrat, finds such bodies to be dangers and asks that they be banned altogether.

Tocqueville realizes that a democracy is too loosely structured to have an organic pluralism: at the same time, he regards the principle of association worth pursuing despite the lack of a stratified social order. Associations play a role inside the sphere of government and outside it.

In no country in the world has the principle of association been more successfully used or applied to a greater multitude of objects than in America. Besides the permanent associations which are established by law under the names of

[50] Vol. I, p. 123.

townships, cities, and counties, a vast number of others are formed and maintained by the agency of private individuals.

In the United States associations are established to promote the public safety, commerce, industry, morality, and religion. There is no end which the human will despairs of attaining through the combined power of individuals united into a society.[51]

The emphasis is placed equally on what may be called public and private associations. The former are the institutions of local government: these repositories of local power may be boards of selectmen, municipal courts, town meetings, and even volunteer fire departments. "The townships, municipal bodies, and counties form so many concealed breakwaters, which check or part the tide of popular determination," Tocqueville says.[52] The assumption here is that there is a given quantum of power in society: that in proportion as power is diffused among local political agencies, that far will the power of the central government be weakened. This is, of course, one of the major underpinnings of the federal idea: if the states and the national government share power, then the former will have the capacity to ward off inroads of the latter. A second assumption is that citizens have two political roles: they are members of a locality and members of a nation. If they think too much of themselves in their national role, then they will subvert the interests they have on the local level. In a democracy the tendency is for men to increasingly forget their local loyalties and to sanction the growth of national power. Yet such an expansion can be against the interests of the very men who consent to it.

"I believe that provincial institutions are useful to all nations, but nowhere do they appear to me to be more necessary than among a democratic people . . ." Tocqueville says. "An aristocracy protects the people from the excesses of despotism, because it always possesses an organized power ready to resist a despot. But a democracy without provincial institutions has no security against these evils." [53] An aristocratic society is so organized that power is traditionally given to such intermediate groups as the church, guilds, and the land-owning classes. This power is not based on consent, but rather on prescriptive authority. Men participate in local institutions more out of habit and custom than because their personal interests so motivate them. A democracy, however, frees men so that they take part in self-government only if they find it to be to their advantage. There is a marked tendency for local institutions to lose their appeal and their power. In many cases localities will veritably barter away their authority for a price: they will abdicate their power to a central government in return for the provision of services.[54]

[51] Vol. I, pp. 198, 199.
[52] Vol. I, p. 282.
[53] Vol. I, p. 99.
[54] See Arthur J. Vidich and Joseph Bensman, *Small Town in Mass Society* (Princeton: Princeton University Press, 1958).

To maintain a diffusion of power is an uphill struggle in a society where equalitarianism brings rapid mobility and industrialization creates higher material expectations. The rhetoric of local autonomy dies hard, and it is clear that many men acknowledge the advantages of power shared among various political levels. But in a democracy power is founded on consent, and it is apparent that citizens do not feel strongly enough about lesser agencies of government to participate in their operations. If the central government augments its power year by year, it is because citizens want it this way.

Tocqueville does not discuss the decline of local government in an explicit way. However, he does see fit to examine the role of private associations in democratic politics. These groups take on a new importance because they tend to be national in their constituencies. The interests which they represent cross local and state boundaries; this means that even if power has less meaning in terms of local public associations, it can still find a significance in private associations which do not respect geographic boundaries. Power can therefore be diffused in a "functional" sense rather than along territorial lines. "The most natural privilege of man, next to the right of acting for himself," Tocqueville says, "is that of combining his exertions with those of his fellow creatures and of acting in common with them." [55] This is the right of association, and it is a necessary condition for a free society. If the interests of individuals are to be safeguarded, then they must buttress them with power. Only if like-minded men can pool their resources and present a common front will they secure the freedom to pursue their self-chosen goals.

However, the principle of association is more than a right: in a democracy it is necessity. The principle of equality makes all men equally powerless; the abandonment of the aristocratic order severs the ties of mutual help and obligation. "Among democratic nations, . . . all the citizens are independent and feeble; they can hardly do anything by themselves, and none of them can oblige his fellowmen to lend him their assistance," Tocqueville says. "They all, therefore, become powerless if they do not learn voluntarily to help one another." [56] Voluntary associations are a necessary mechanism of self-defense. If men are to be powerful enough to turn back the inroads which the state may make on their lives, they must be encouraged to join with others who share their interests. There is strength in numbers, and men must come to learn that in the fact of organization lies the key to power.

Yet men will not organize themselves into groups simply because a theory of freedom says that they ought to. They must have an inducement to associate, and this means that they must have an interest to defend. Not all citizens have interests which can be sustained through organized activity, however:

[55] *Democracy in America,* Vol. I, p. 203.
[56] Vol. II, p. 115.

for many people their interests are so vague or generalized that it is virtually impossible for them to join together with others to pursue a particular program; for others there is not a sufficient perception of a personal interest to lead them to establish or join an association.

A few examples will make this clear:

(1) A doctor or a dentist or a real-estate man, for instance, has a fairly clear-cut idea of the kind of social and political conditions which are needed if his interests are to be safeguarded. Such a man, furthermore, has the money to support an organization which will look out for his profession's welfare. Thus out of 227,000 doctors in America, 173,000 belong to the American Medical Association; out of 101,000 dentists, 91,000 belong to the American Dental Association.[57] This is a high degree of involvement, and clearly Tocqueville would approve this awareness of interest and willingness to support it. Yet the question remains whether most citizens have such well-defined interests or whether they can associate to defend those they have.

(2) Veterans and Negroes have interests even though they are less coherent than those of the doctors and dentists. If the veteran's interest is partly economic and partly one of status, it is not clear what measures are required to bulwark his position in society and the economy. And because the Negro's interest is tied to even subtler questions of status, it is that much harder to pinpoint in policy terms. Nevertheless, both the veteran and the Negro are free to join groups which will press for government action to ameliorate their condition. The problem, however, is that most Negroes and veterans are too poor or too preoccupied to have arrived at the level of consciousness where they can think about taking organized steps. Many will be well aware of their special problems, but they do not think of them as ones which can be solved through political action.

Of the 15,045,000 Negroes in the United States, only 312,000 belong to the National Association for the Advancement of Colored People; of the 22,727,-000 veterans, only 4,040,000 belong to the American Legion or to the Veterans of Foreign Wars.[58] While over 15,000,000 Americans know that they are Negroes and that they suffer disabilities because of their race, only 2 per cent of them have a sufficient interest in bettering their condition to join an association which works to this end. If every Negro joined the N.A.A.C.P., there is little doubt that that group would be a powerful force and that its members would not receive the treatment they currently do from state and society.

[57] Figures from U.S. Bureau of the Census, *Statistical Abstract of the United States 1959* (Washington, D.C.: 1959), 80th edition, p. 74; and *Encyclopedia of American Associations* (Detroit: Gale, 1959), 2nd edition, pp. 326, 318.

[58] Figures from *Statistical Abstract, op. cit.*, pp. 29, 254; and *Encyclopedia of American Associations, op. cit.*, pp. 292, 416, 422.

Certainly Tocqueville would wish that Negroes, veterans and similar individuals augment their power by means of associations. That they do not means not only that they will suffer but that power will be concentrated elsewhere in society.

(3) There are millions of white-collar workers whose interest is that inflationary tendencies be slowed down or brought to a halt. There are millions of mothers of draft-age sons whose interest is that there be no war. There are millions of citizens of recent immigrant ancestry whose interest is that social and economic opportunities be opened regardless of national origin or parental background. While these interests are general, they are nevertheless real. It seems out of the question that such individuals come together to form a Sound Dollar Association, an Anti-War League, or a Recent Americans Society. If the government is to work against inflation or for peace, it will not be because of organized pressure by associations constituted for purposes such as that.

What happens, then, is that first priority is given to measures backed by organized interests.[59] Those who are unwilling or unable to associate together are frequently ignored: furthermore, they may end up footing the bill for the benefits accorded to their fellow citizens with specific and articulated interests. Indeed, the white-collar employees have all the characteristics of the powerless mass of which Tocqueville is fearful. Yet there is no easy answer to how they are to fit into the associational pattern.

(4) Finally, not all groups or associations are politically relevant. By stretching the imagination, it can be found that all individuals in a society belong to some organization or another: a trade-union branch, a church, a parent-teachers association, or even a bowling league.[60] Those groups, however, seldom deal with the commodity of power: their purpose is social and not political. Even a totalitarian society, where power is centralized in the state, will have bowling leagues.

The basis of associations, therefore, is the existence of interests. The most durable source of personal interest is private property: this was postulated by Locke, and it is assumed by Tocqueville. "Most of those who live in democratic countries are possessed of property," he says. "Not only do they possess property, but they live in the condition where men set the greatest store upon their property." [61] Yet the rise of industrial technology and organization can create a propertyless class and transform traditional property holdings into

[59] See Earl Latham, "The Group Basis of Politics: Notes for a Theory," *American Political Science Review*, June 1952, pp. 376–397.

[60] Actually America is not so much a "nation of joiners" as the folklore makes out. See Charles R. Wright and Herbert H. Hyman, "Voluntary Association Memberships of American Adults," *American Sociological Review*, June 1958, pp. 284–294.

[61] *Democracy in America*, Vol. II, p. 267.

legal forms rather than instruments of power. Despite this tendency, the principle of association is an important one: even if interests are no longer based on property as they once were, men should be encouraged to define their needs and articulate their wants. Only in this way will they be able to set up the associational barriers which will protect them from both the state and their fellow citizens.

Tocqueville's emphasis is on creating a theory of a free society. For this reason, he does not prescribe political institutions which, in his view, are best suited to promote the general welfare. In fact, unlike most theorists who precede him, he doubts whether there is a specific arrangement which will secure the welfare of all citizens. "No political form has hitherto been discovered," he says, "that is equally favorable to the prosperity and the development of all the classes into which society is divided." [62]

With those words the schemes of Aristotle and St. Thomas, Hobbes and Rousseau, Burke and Hegel are all rejected. All governmental forms in one way or another are bound to favor one section of society or another. Tocqueville accepts this as a fact of political life. His next step, however, is to encourage all individuals to develop and become aware of their interests, and to organize themselves so as to be armed for the political struggle. No one class or elite in a free society has exclusive title to preferred status: every citizen is entitled to use his power so as either to gain control of the government or to ensure that the government does not oppress him.

The group struggle, therefore, is a sign of political health: it shows that many interests are interacting and that men are looking out for themselves. Yet it need not be pointed out that the combatants must observe certain constitutional rules of the game. Citizens must learn to take defeat patiently and to wear their victories with humility. "It cannot be denied that the unrestrained liberty of association for political purposes is the privilege which a people is longest in learning how to exercise," Tocqueville says. "If it does not throw the nation into anarchy, it perpetually augments the chances of that calamity." [63] This is a serious warning. The group struggle—or class struggle—in many countries leads to revolution or civil war. This is because the stakes are high and the contending parties fear that if they lose an engagement they will be banished from the political scene. A tradition of temperate behavior must be built on a consensus: conflict must take place within an arena bounded by shared values and common aspirations.

Tocqueville sees that this condition is satisfied in America: "In a country like the United States, in which the differences of opinion are mere differences

[62] Vol. I, p. 248.
[63] Vol. I, p. 202.

of hue, the right of association may remain unrestrained without evil consequences." [64] Despite all the epithets which one group hurls at its antagonists, there is good evidence that this is a grandstand play (or, just as likely, an effort to rally one's own members) rather than a deep-seated animosity. How many of the new democracies of the world will have the time or the conditions to develop a consensus within which group conflicts may be peacefully resolved is a vital question. It is at this point, perhaps more than all others, that it may be wondered how far the lessons of American democracy may be taught elsewhere.

If the group struggle is to be related to the governmental process, then there must be institutions which channel conflict and evaluate the claims of the interested parties. The chief of these institutions is a system of free and periodic elections, based on universal suffrage. Suppose, for example, that an association spokesman comes into a legislator's office and claims that the members of his group who live in that legislator's district favor a particular bill. There are two forces at work here: on the one hand, the individuals who are in the group are using their vote as a means of influencing legislation; on the other hand, the legislator can test the group's claim or at least wonder whether its members would vote against his re-election if he did not support their measure.

In these ways, then, the vote can serve as a touchstone of group power. One group may have many members, but few of them are sufficiently concerned over their special interests to use their vote as their associational tie might dictate. Another group may have few members, but virtually all of them cast their ballot as the organization directs. And yet another group may also have few members, but possess sufficient resources so as to be able to enlist public support for its cause.

This last factor is crucial, for all associations are minorities: no single one has a majority of the community's population on its membership roles. Indeed, the only group in society which can claim to represent the majority is the political party which last elected a President and a majority of the House of Representatives. This party majority—however devoid it may be of a concrete political program—is evidence that private associations speak only for minorities.

Perhaps the most powerful of the causes that tend to mitigate the violence of political associations in the United States is universal suffrage. In countries in which universal suffrage exists, the majority is never doubtful, because neither party can reasonably pretend to represent that portion of the community which has not voted. The associations know as well as the nation at large that they do

[64] Vol. I, p. 204.

not represent the majority. This results, indeed, from the very fact of their existence; for if they did represent the preponderating power, they would change the
law instead of soliciting its reform.[65]

Every association, therefore, must address itself not only to the policy-
making branches of the government but also to the general public. A group
cannot rely on the votes of its own members alone—for they are not sufficient
—and it must gain at least the tacit support of voters who do not share the
group's immediate interests. In this activity a private association works much
as a political party does: while it does not run candidates for office, it seeks a
broad basis of consent to its program. To achieve this goal it must persuade the
public that what is good for doctors, for example, is good for them.[66]

This appeal for consent is, after all, the basis of majority rule. Associations
accept the principle of majority rule, then, because they see that they may put
it to their own use at some future time. "All parties are willing to recognize
the rights of the majority, because they all hope at some time to be able to
exercise them to their own advantage," Tocqueville says.[67] This majority, however, is unorganized and shifting in its composition: it is sovereign, but it is
also capable of being persuaded by minority interests. Indeed, it may be asked
whether this drowsy giant is a tyrant at all if organized groups are able to secure
its consent so readily. While Tocqueville never says as much, it may well be
that power gravitates to purposeful minorities and that majority tyranny is more
fiction than fact.

So long as the citizens of a democracy develop personal interests and establish voluntary associations, they may be said to remove themselves from the
mass condition. If individuals see their roles as belonging to one or several
minorities in society, then the majority becomes a residual role which all share
but none take too seriously. These groups which are formed become the real
breakwaters against the power of the state. For while the state in a democracy
is backed by majority consent, the same people who give their public consent
to the state are also giving their private consent to the associations they join.
Indeed, the same individual may with one hand urge his government to expanded activity and with the other seek to prevent further inroads on his own
interests. In this seeming irrational process Tocqueville sees in democracy the
application of one of the key principles of aristocratic society:

I firmly believe that an aristocracy cannot be founded in the world, but I think
that private citizens, by combining together, may constitute bodies of great wealth,

[65] *Ibid.*

[66] For a description of the way in which the American Medical Association made its
case, see Stanley Kelley, *Professional Public Relations and Political Power* (Baltimore: Johns
Hopkins Press, 1956).

[67] *Democracy in America*, Vol. II, p. 204.

influence, and strength, corresponding to the persons of an aristocracy. By this means many of the greatest political advantages of aristocracy would be obtained without its injustice or its dangers. An association for political, commercial, or manufacturing purposes, or even for those of science and literature, is a powerful and enlightened member of the community, which cannot be disposed of at pleasure or oppressed without remonstrance, and which, by defending its own rights against the encroachments of government, saves the common liberties of the country.[68]

Yet the transplantation of principles is not an easy one. The rise of the associational life in a democratic society is more often than not a matter of chance, and the interplay of interests is not controlled by a traditional class structure. There are no guarantees that individuals will develop interests, nor is there any assurance that the struggle will proceed within a consensus. The democratic conception of freedom demands that men be released from rigid class ties and that they be allowed to pursue their interests as they see fit. Such a society has little in common with the organic community that Tocqueville uses as his yardstick. He realizes this, and he speculates on whether the atomistic groups of the democratic process will result in a viable barrier to state power. For these groups form not a chain, as did the aristocratic orders and classes, but rather a series of disconnected group interests which may or may not be inclined to thwart the state as occasions for tyranny arise. "The notion of secondary powers placed between the sovereign and his subjects occurred naturally to the imagination of aristocratic nations . . ." Tocqueville says. "This same notion is naturally wanting in the minds of men in democratic ages . . . ; it can only be induced artificially, it can only be kept there with difficulty." [69]

This is, of course, the key difference between the liberal and the conservative approaches to politics and society. Tocqueville is clearly caught between the two vantage points, and he can only point out what a democracy will have to do if it is to preserve freedom for its citizens. Voluntary associations will have to be induced artificially, and this means that men must be taught to know their interests as individuals. Furthermore, ways will have to be found to restrain state power even in those areas where organized groups do not have an interest in turning back the inroads of the government. In short, not simply minority rights as expressed by groups, but also individual rights which have no organized support will have to be protected. Tocqueville does not explore this question at any length, and it will remain for John Stuart Mill to pose the problem of individual freedom in explicit terms. Nor does Tocqueville suggest that the associational barriers against power in the political sphere will

[68] Vol. II, p. 342.
[69] Vol. II, p. 306.

protect men from the tyranny over the mind which society exercises over its members. It may well be possible to have a free government and free citizens and yet to discover that at the same time there exists an oppressive society and subjugated individuals. Mill, too, will take up the question of freedom as it relates to both politics and society.

The complex and contradictory picture presented by a new democracy reflects itself in Tocqueville's theory. If he is vague or uncertain or ambiguous at times, this is only because democracy itself displays these characteristics. Despite his aristocratic standards of judgment, he sees that democracy is the wave of the future. And despite his nostalgia for the past, he bends his efforts to show how freedom and equality can live side by side. The equalitarian temper can lead to intellectual mediocrity and oppressive rule. The suspicion of excellence can deprive a nation of a responsible class of leaders, and the fear of freedom can drive men into an anonymous mass. Yet for all this there are in democracy attitudes and institutions which can, if properly understood and guided, lead to a realization of individual freedom. It remains for democrats themselves to become free men: no one else can perform this task for them. "Let us then," Tocqueville concludes, "look forward to the future with that salutary fear which makes men keep watch and ward for freedom, not with that faint and idle terror which depresses and enervates the heart." [70]

[70] Vol. II, p. 348.

13.
Karl Marx and
Friedrich Engels

THE MEN AND THEIR TIMES

Marx was born in the Rhineland region of Germany in 1818. He studied philosophy and history at several German universities, including Berlin, where Hegelian ideas were in full flower. He came to his radical outlook early in life, and this prevented him from securing an academic position. Consequently, he turned to journalism, but his activities in this field caused him to be expelled from the country by the Prussian government. From there he went to France, and here again he was forced to leave by official request. After a period in a more tolerant Belgium, he moved to England in 1849, where he remained until his death in 1883. Marx is buried not in Moscow's Red Square, but at the Highgate Cemetery in North London. His years of travel and exile were active ones. In France he met Engels, a young man two years his junior and of far different social origins but almost identical political persuasion.

Engels was the son of a wealthy German manufacturing family and had been put in charge of their English interests. At the age of twenty-five he had published a study of the abysmal conditions of English working-class life, and it was clear that he was no friend to the class which produced him. He did not, however, turn his back on his inherited fortune, and his possession of a private income was to underwrite much of Marxist theory.

Marx and Engels collaborated on The Communist Manifesto in 1848, and it soon became the most notorious political document of the century. This succinct analysis of capitalist society is coupled with a stirring call to arms, and it clearly grew out of the practical activities in which its authors were wrapped up. Despite the fact that the Communist movement would never become the dominant force in Western Europe, Marx and Engels devoted much of their time and energy to an attempt to create an international

509

working-class party. They served with the First and Second Internationals, although in retrospect most of their activity seems to have centered on sectarian controversy rather than in mobilizing a mass movement. Nevertheless, the pamphlets and speeches engendered by these involvements have all made an important contribution to the substance of Marxist theory.

In England Marx lived off the largess of Engels, and this enabled him to write Capital, the first volume of which appeared in 1867. Though The Communist Manifesto is less than fifty pages in length, Capital runs to almost a thousand. It is a painstaking study of the economic and social foundations of capitalism, and much of its impressiveness derives from the work that went into it. Marx sat day after day at a table in the British Museum pouring over the reports of Parliamentary commissions and analyzing the statistical data which was just beginning to be collected. He died before he could complete the last two volumes, and Engels, who outlived him by twelve years, put them together from the rough drafts and notes.

Marx and Engels, along with Tocqueville, wrote in a revolutionary age. There are interesting expressions of both democratic and liberal thought in Marxist theory, despite the fact that both of these outlooks are derided as bourgeois ideology. Marx and Engels saw that industrialization would bring to the great mass of the population a heightened awareness of their exploited status in society. This class consciousness, they predicted, would lead to the formation of a working-class party and a violent bid for political power. While this form of democracy is neither peaceful nor constitutional, it is a variety of democracy nevertheless. The liberal component of Marxist theory can be seen in its goal of a society where the finest potentialities of human life would be released and encouraged. Marx's humanitarian instincts emerged most clearly in the poignant passages of Capital where he describes the subhuman level of existence of urban industrial workers.

Marx and Engels wrote as they did because, unlike Tocqueville, they could not help but take notice of the fantastic disparities between the conditions of rich and poor in Nineteenth Century Europe. The capitalism they knew was exploitative, and to them violent revolution seemed the only way out. For the affluent and relatively classless society Tocqueville observed in America, democracy might run to excesses, but it could be made to function in a peaceful and constitutional manner.

If both America and Western Europe have shown that they can solve their economic problem by legislative and voluntary means, it is by no means certain that the new nations of the twentieth century have the time or inclination to follow their example. Without material resources or the experience of self-government, Marxist precepts frequently are made to appear relevant to countries which have known exploitation at first hand. Yet their problems are not those of industrial capitalism: they involve the conflicts of race and national pride, and they are aggravated by pressures of population. For purposes of theoretical understanding, Marx and Engels—despite the ideological uses to which they may have been put—may be a beginning, but they are far from being the final answer.

13.
Karl Marx and
Friedrich Engels

THE CONVENTIONAL APPROACH TO THE WRITINGS OF MARX AND
Engels is to juxtapose them against the reality of the Communist world. The
Soviet Union, Communist China, and a host of lesser states are facts of political life. And these nations themselves profess to be guided by Marxist principles. In these countries the works of Marx and Engels are studied in the
schools, the phrases of Marx and Engels are engraved on public buildings, and
the precepts of Marx and Engels are openly affirmed by political leaders at all
levels. Never before in the history of political thought has a single body of
literature been so closely embraced by national systems of power. To be sure,
it may be claimed that the principles of John Locke gave inspiration to the
American Revolution or that the ideas of Jean Jacques Rousseau influenced
the course of the French Revolution. Yet these links between political theories
and actual events seem tenuous indeed when they are contrasted with the impact of Marx and Engels' writings on the behavior of Communist nations. Only
rarely does an American or a Frenchman invoke the words of Locke or Rousseau when he discourses in the political arena. It is true that the texts of Locke
and Rousseau continue to be read in American and French classrooms, but
American and French politicians look on the *Second Treatise of Civil Government* and *The Social Contract* as less than adequate authorities for justifying
national goals. The reasons for this are not hard to find, and no one is surprised that these historical texts are not parts of a national political rhetoric.

Yet Communist leaders have constant recourse to the writings of Marx and
Engels. It is not as if Russia and China had no national traditions of their
own and therefore adopted the principles laid down by two nineteenth-century
Germans. Russia and China both have historical traditions and aspirations,
and the behavior of these two countries can often be explained on this basis

512

alone. The curious fact is that Communist leaders have elected to embrace the books and pamphlets, the letters and speeches of Marx and Engels as their official doctrine. The doctrine is official enough, but it is not a straitjacket: it has sufficient elasticity so that all acts of state up to this time have been unblushingly reconciled with it.

Communist spokesmen, whatever others may say, insist that their nations have yet to break faith with the basic tenets of the works they profess to live by. These men of power have been so imbued with the words of Marx and Engels that they roll off their tongues at every public occasion. When Mr. Khrushchev visited the United States in 1959, he held a press conference at the National Press Club in Washington. This was, let it be recalled, a gathering of practicing journalists—not a meeting of professors of political theory. Yet in the course of answering a question posed by a newspaperman, the Soviet ruler felt moved to add:

At one time the most wide-spread system of society in the world was feudalism. Then capitalism took its place. Why was that? Because capitalism was a more progressive kind of system than was feudalism.

As compared to feudalism, capitalism provided better opportunities to develop the productive forces of society. We believe that now capitalism has developed so far that it gave birth to certain fundamental differences within itself, and each society gives birth to the kind of society that will follow it. We believe that Karl Marx, Engels and Lenin gave scientific proof of the fact that the system, the social system of socialism, would take the place of capitalism.

We believe in that.[1]

That these propositions are the sincere belief of Communist leaders is most likely the case. Whether Mr. Khrushchev's affirmation is the consequence of his own attempt to understand history or whether it is a political catechism he long ago learned by rote is, of course, a more difficult question to answer. What is significant for present purposes is that even before an audience of journalists a practising politician saw fit to expound the tenets of a complex political theory. For in the Soviet leader's brief summary is contained the outline of Marx and Engels' dialectical materialism. This theory of history, as will be seen on the pages to come, is an academic exercise which is as subtle and intricate as it is sweeping. That a man whose job it is to rule a huge nation claims to adhere to such a theory is not an ordinary occurrence in the world of politics. And this raises the further question of whether his commitment to the science of Marxism has an influence on the way he and his fellow leaders govern their nation.

There is no denying that ideas do influence action. Indeed, it was pointed out in the chapter on Hegel that political conditions only assume meaning

[1] *New York Times*, Sept. 17, 1959.

when they are interpreted and political action can have direction only if goals are proposed. What must be decided by the student of politics, however, is what kinds of ideas are the ones which move men to act politically. Ideas may be entertained by anyone with a mind, and all men have minds. Some ideas are simple, and some are complex; some are the stereotyped ruminations of men in the street, and others are the considered reflections of men of superior intellect. In dealing with political ideas, it is always best to ask if they are in the realm of theory or of ideology. When dealing with Marxism, it is especially important to ask if the ideas under discussion are Marxist theory or Marxist ideology.

Since the time of Plato it has been insisted that political theory is the province of the scholar. Only individuals who are unencumbered by interests, who are not obliged to exercise power over their fellow men, are in a position to perceive and analyze political reality. The possession of interests and the exposure to power distorts a man's image of the world: only if an individual removes himself from these blocks to understanding may he begin to discourse as a theorist. For the responsibility of the theorist is to pursue knowledge: to comprehend what is and to realize what ought to be. Men of knowledge must give the highest priority to the truth. If the goal is to be approached at all, intensive study, disinterested reflection, and an unprejudiced mind are required. Political truth is never simple: it is always a complicated system of abstract relationships. From Plato through Tocqueville, it has already been seen that political reality can only be analyzed if recondite models are utilized. The writings of political theory are not intended for an audience of average men. If only one or two men in a generation can create a political theory, it is possible that at any point in time only one person in a hundred is capable of understanding such a theory in all its fullness.

All this needs to be said because Karl Marx and Friedrich Engels are political theorists of the first rank. Their writings range from short pamphlets to multivolumed texts: but all that they have to say is based on a theoretical system, an understanding of which is not likely to be within the intellectual reach of the average reader. Even the polemical *Communist Manifesto* requires for its full interpretation a knowledge of history, economics, and sociology. Indeed, the hortatory phrases of the *Manifesto* only take their place as political theory if the reader is acquainted with the less popular writings of Marx and Engels in which their system is spelled out in its entirety. Political theory, in sum, serves but a small constituency. In fact, if political theories were simplified so as to draw a larger audience for themselves, they would cease to be theories at all.

There is always the temptation to assume that theories and theorists have an influence on the events of the political world. Such an assumption is believed to demonstrate that ideas are important, that books leave their mark on the lives of men and nations. There is much truth in this belief, but it is often not thought through with sufficient care. For it is generally the case that books in political theory—regarded as political theory—have virtually no influence on political affairs. The influence of theoretical ideas is usually confined to the small company of theorists themselves. Thus it can be shown that Plato had an influence on Rousseau, and Rousseau on Hegel, and Hegel on Marx and Engels. Or Locke's intellectual debts to Hobbes can be traced, or Mill's to Bentham. But to say all this is to speak of the influence of book writer on book writer. It may be argued that while the development of political theory runs along lines parallel to the development of political institutions, nevertheless the two realms are usually separate and distinct. The authors of political theories, insofar as they are playing the role of theorist, seldom have an impact on the course of political history.

Rather, what does occur is that men who have or who would obtain power often abstract out of books of political theory certain *slogans* and catch phrases, certain very simplified explanations and rationalizations of reality. These words and phrases, lifted from the complexities of their original context, are then used in the defense of an actual set of political arrangements or to justify a call for political change. As this process takes place, however, the original theory ceases to be a theory. The abstracted portions are now an ideology which has been put to work for some practical purpose. This ideology will in most cases preserve the underlying spirit which suffused the theory on which it draws. But the intention no longer is to impart to a limited audience a scholarly interpretation of reality: the new motive is to stir large numbers of men to act in particular ways.

The words and phrases drawn from Marx and Engels' writings clearly constitute the ideological framework of Communist power in the present century. And it is equally plain that Marx and Engels themselves hoped that their ideas would be put to ideological use. In their own lifetimes they condensed their theory into popular pamphlets with the expectation that these simplified messages would move men to revolutionary activity.

Nevertheless, Marx and Engels were not successful in their role as ideologues: Communism never took hold in the Western Europe to which they addressed themselves. The success of Marxist ideology must be attributed not to Marx and Engels, but to the men of power who elected to use these ideas as political doctrines. Marx and Engels have had their influence in modern ideology because Lenin, Stalin, Khrushchev, Mao, and Tito decided to put the Marxist writings to work in their countries. It would be wrong to say that two nineteenth-century political theorists are responsible for the course of Communist behavior in the twentieth century. The truth is that it is the Communist leaders of the twentieth century who are responsible for keeping alive the Marxist ideology.

The conclusion must be that political power is the master and ideology plays the role of servant. Leaders in Communist states use the precepts of Marxism as an aid in mobilizing citizens for the pursuit of political objectives. Just how far this ideology contributes to national success in these countries is an unanswerable question. Had a Marx and an Engels never lived and written the books they did, would the Russia and the China of today be conducting themselves any differently than they do now? Certainly it should be clear that throughout history there may have been many political systems which have come into existence and have prospered without the benefit of a book-based ideology such as Marxism. The strands of a national ideology are of diverse origins, and the formal writings of political theorists constitute but one minor source of ideas. Both Soviet Communism and American democracy, for example, have their ideologies. If the former's is conveniently found in the books of Marx and Engels, the latter's is strewn over a wide area and virtually defies any attempt to put it together in a coherent way.

At all events, it is probably best to suppose that Communist leaders are much like any other political leaders: that they are not bound to run their states according to the rules laid down in a shelf of books. While they may voice the words of Marx and Engels from day to day, it is probable that they make and carry out their plans just as other men of power do. It is, in short, highly unlikely that they have pursued a particular line of policy simply because Marx and Engels' writings seem to demand it. While it is true that the Marxist ideology may be construed so broadly as to permit all manner of political acts, the main point is that Communist leaders are the official interpreters of that ideology in their countries: if they say that their behavior is sanctioned by the theory of Marx and Engels, then their word is the last one.

It would be less than fair to say that the words of Marx and Engels are no more than convenient slogans which have been put to use by men who find it to their advantage so to use them. This is only part of the total picture. For the strength of an ideology lies not so much in the content of its ideas as in the spirit which moves it. And the real success of the Marxist ideology must be attributed to its messianic quality. Socialism and Communism, Marx and Engels assert, are undoubtedly the wave of the future: capitalism and democracy are doomed, and the rise of a new collective order is inevitable. This strident self-confidence gives Marxism its appeal. To the emerging millions of people who desire to be liberated from what they now look on as oppressive rule, here is a message of hope. The Marxist spirit, which underlies the theory as well as the ideology, is the major reason why contemporary movements continue to utilize a body of historical writings as the basis for their rhetoric. Marx and Engels' views of man and society have found their uses, albeit in a simplified form, in the politics of the present. Yet it must not be forgotten that it is an ideology which is observed at work. It is not a theory.

Marxist theory is infused with a spirit of optimism and inevitability, but this pervasive mood does not prevent it from being at the same time a sophisticated analysis of social reality. While men of power may draw on Marxism as an ideology, men of knowledge find in the theory of Marx and Engels an explanation of politics and society which is brilliant in conception and rewarding in intellectual application. If Marxist writings are to be approached as political theory, then the student must attempt an act of will: he must try to put on the shelf his personal feelings concerning the ideological uses to which Marxism has been put by Communist leaders. This is not an easy task and no one can ever carry it out with completeness. Yet it is the responsibility of all who seek to understand Marxist theory, and this dictum applies no less to those who are sympathetic to Communist objectives than it does to those who are hostile to them.

A political theory must be evaluated on the basis of what it says on its pages: its descriptions are true or they are not; its prescriptions are good or they are not. If men of power decide to use a body of writings for their own purposes, if they elect to transform a theory into an ideology, that ought not to affect a student's judgment on the original books. There is enough to criticize in Marxist theory, taken as a theory, so as not to have to bring in additional criticisms based on its ideological impact. There is much in Marxist theory which illuminates the politics of the world we now know. The student who does not make every effort to understand what Marx and Engels have to say is harming no one but himself. And this understanding will only be attained if Marx and Engels are regarded as men of intellectual stature rather than as the inspirers of Communist ideology. Had Soviet power never emerged on this planet, their contribution to political theory would still be a major one.

DIALECTICAL MATERIALISM

At the heart of Marxist theory is a theory of history: past, present, and future seen in a continuous ordering perspective. This theory, furthermore, draws on Hegel's dialectic in an explicit way, and Marx and Engels acknowledge their profound debt to their predecessor. Yet they are not satisfied with the major philosophical assumption which underlies Hegel's use of this scheme.

They are prepared to employ the dialectic, but only after altering its central characteristic. Engels summarizes his understanding of the Hegelian view, and he suggests what he sees as its major inadequacy.

According to Hegel, dialectics is the self-development of the concept. The absolute concept does not only exist—where unknown—from eternity, it is also the actual living soul of the whole existing world. It develops into itself through all the preliminary stages. . . . Then it "alienates" itself by changing into nature, where, without consciousness of itself, disguised as the necessity of nature, it goes through a new development and finally comes again to self-consciousness in man. This self-consciousness then elaborates itself in history from the crude form until finally the absolute concept again comes to itself completely in the Hegelian philosophy. According to Hegel, therefore, the dialectical development apparent in nature and history, i.e., the causal inter-connection of the progressive movement from the lower to the higher, which asserts itself through all zigzag movements and temporary setbacks, is only a miserable copy of the self-movement of the concept going on from eternity, no one knows where, but at all events independently of any thinking brain.[2]

Hegel postulated the existence of an overarching *Idea*. This absolute spirit not only directed its own movement through time, but also reached down and imposed its pattern on the actions of men and nations. As the *Idea* changed, so did the institutions which were its earthly reflections. Men might achieve an understanding of these movements and the role they were destined to play in them, but they could in no way hinder or divert the onward march of the *Idea*. Yet if history followed an inexorable pattern, there was an order to its motion. This order was the dialectic—the zigzag movements and temporary setbacks of which Engels speaks. New ideas would be unwittingly sired by their aging progenitors; the perverse offspring would then struggle with their parents; and youth would conquer age, but not without carrying on as scars of battle some of the heritage out of which it was born.

Marx and Engels are more than happy to accept the conceptions of thesis, antithesis, and synthesis. They are prepared to answer to the name of dialectician, and they are particularly attracted by the revolutionary cataclysms which are periodic in the Hegelian scheme. What is unacceptable, however, is the idealist framework in which Hegel sets his theory. For Marx the important movements are not in the realm of ideas but those found in the material world.

My dialectic method is not only different from the Hegelian, but is its direct opposite. To Hegel, the life-process of the human brain, i.e., the process of thinking, which, under the name of "the Idea," he even transforms into an independent subject, is the *demiurgos* of the real world, and the real world is only

---

[2] Engels, *Ludwig Feuerbach*, in *Marx and Engels: Selected Works* (Moscow: Foreign Languages Publishing House, 1951 and 1958), Vol. II, p. 350. This selection will henceforward be referred to as *Selected Works*.

the external, phenomenal form of "the Idea." With me, on the contrary, the ideal is nothing else than the material world reflected by the human mind, and translated into forms of thought. . . .

The mystification which dialectic suffers in Hegel's hands, by no means prevents him from being the first to present its general form of working in a comprehensive and conscious manner. With him it is standing on its head. It must be turned right side up again, if you would discover the rational kernel within the mystical shell.[3]

Hegel's idealism led him to see earthly politics as pale reflections of the rational and transcendental *Idea*. Marx and Engels regard the very conception of such an abstraction as mysticism. The *Idea* cannot be seen or touched: its impact on the minds and behavior of men can never be verified. In short, there is no one's word but Hegel's that the *Idea* even exists, let alone that it determines the course of human history.

Marx and Engels are willing to use the dialectic so long as it is stripped of its idealist foundation. Their strategy is to stand Hegel's theory, which they believe to be standing head-downward, back on its feet. This must be done if the dialectic is to do service with a materialist base. "We comprehended the concepts in our heads once more materialistically—as images of real things instead of regarding the real things as images of this or that stage of development as the absolute concept," Engels says. "Thus dialectics reduced itself to the science of the general laws of motion—both of the external world and of human thought—two sets of laws which are identical in substance, but differ in their expression in so far as the human mind can apply them consciously." [4] What Engels is saying here is that there are undoubtedly ideas in men's minds, but these abstractions take the form that they do because of the material conditions in which men live. The ideas of men change through history, and these transformations may best be understood—as Hegel suggested—in terms of the dialectical unfolding. However, the source of power of the dialectic itself is found in the material world: matter, in short, governs mind. This assumption, this reversal of Hegel, is a first principle of the science of society which Marx and Engels are to propose.

This controversy is clearly a metaphysical one: Hegel, on the one hand, and Marx and Engels, on the other, differ on a basic interpretation of reality. Whereas the one theorist saw the universe existing as a single *Idea* with concrete institutions as only reflections of that abstraction, the other two are only prepared to assign reality to the material world. While this difference in approach cannot be resolved in philosophical terms, the alternative theories are important for the consequences which flow from them.

[3] Marx, *Capital* (New York: Modern Library, n.d.), p. 25.
[4] Engels, *Ludwig Feuerbach*, p. 350.

Marx and Engels claim, as did Bentham, that a scientific study of society is possible. If this method is to be applied to the political world, they argue, then it is necessary that the mysticism surrounding idealist philosophy be discarded. The only reality which a scientist can recognize is that of material phenomena. Natural and physical scientists have as their objects of study things which can be seen, touched, or heard. Even in instances where the objects are invisible to the eye—as in the case of genes and atoms—physicists and geneticists are able to agree that these phenomena exist, and they can predict their behavior with the aid of standardized instruments. None of this can be said for an invisible abstraction like the *Idea*: that exists only in the mind of a theorist and he is unable to demonstrate to his fellow scholars that it has a reality at all. It is not possible to build a science on an abstraction which cannot be seen or studied and whose future behavior can in no way be predicted.

For this reason, Marx and Engels admit for consideration only those aspects of human and social life which can be observed and whose operations can be agreed upon by a community of social scientists. Social scientists, if they are to claim title to the mantle of science, must confine their studies to the material world. "Dialectics," Engels says, "is nothing more than the science of the general laws of motion and development of nature, human society, and thought." [5] The universe is dynamic, and laws must be evolved which trace these movements. Natural forces, social institutions, and the ideas in men's minds must be accounted for in a single theory which relates all three and assigns each to its appropriate causative level.

By the material basis of life Marx and Engels mean any and all physical objects. But their chief concern is a more specific one. They focus their attention on two particular phenomena: men and machines. The raw materials of the dialectic are human beings and the tools which these individuals use to maintain life. This emphasis is a new departure in political theory. Hobbes was a materialist, but his materialism was more philosophical than technological. Locke gave a central role to property, but he stressed legal ownership rather than the productive process. Hegel and Tocqueville took note of the impact of industrial organization on human psychology, but they did not put this factor at the center of their theories. Marx and Engels are the first to insist on the determinative role of the machines themselves, the physical objects which constitute property in the modern world. "The first premise of all human history is of course the existence of living human individuals," they say. "The first fact to be established is therefore the physical organization of these individuals and their consequent relation to the rest of nature." [6]

[5] Engels, *Anti-Duhring* (Moscow: Foreign Languages Publishing House, 1954), p. 195.
[6] Marx and Engels, *The German Ideology* (New York: International Publishers, 1947), edited by R. Pascal, p. 7.

The important variable is what Marx and Engels call the "physical organization" of men. It is not enough to say that man is a social animal. He is social because the single most important feature of his existence is the matter of keeping alive: the getting of food, clothing, shelter. No theory can take this elemental process for granted: it is, on the contrary, the foundation stone on which all theories must build. The organization of society and politics takes form as a result of the way men interact with each other in their efforts to keep alive and comfortable.

Social organization throughout time and place takes a variety of forms: the nomadic tribe, the agricultural village, the industrial city. These various forms of social life are constituted as they are because men have developed a certain relationship to the resources of nature which they draw on to make their livings. Different societies will draw in different ways on the things which grow in the soil, the animals which roam the forests, the resources which lie buried in the ground. Some societies, in addition, will find electric power in their rivers, energy in the atom, and perhaps even a source of potency in the sun. All men in all societies exploit nature: this is the constant fact. But men and societies vary in the ways they use the material resources they encounter.

The key variables Marx and Engels abstract out for a study are the tools men use to harness nature at any given point in time. These tools are called the "mode of production." The representative productive instrument may be a stone axe, a metal plow, or a spinning wheel. In more advanced eras it will be an automatic factory or an atomic reactor. If the iron plow is the typical mode of production, then a society will be organized in one way and its citizens will be of one character. If the automated assembly line is the prevailing mode, then there will be a different form of social organization and men will take on a different personality structure. Marx and Engels spell this theory out in language which makes plain the certainty with which they adhere to it.

The way in which men produce their means of subsistence depends first of all on the nature of the actual means they find in existence and have to reproduce. This mode of production . . . is a definite form of activity of these individuals, a definite form of expressing their life, a definite mode of life on their part. As individuals express their life, so they are. What they are, therefore, coincides with their production, both with what they produce and with how they produce. The nature of individuals thus depends on the material conditions determining their production.[7]

This is, to use the familiar phrase, an economic determinism. Human personality and social structure are the products of the prevailing organization of the economy at any stage in history. How far this is a thoroughgoing economic orientation is a matter of some controversy. What may be said, first of all, is that it is probably better to call Marxist theory a technological approach rather

[7] *Ibid.*

than simply an economic one. For Marx and Engels' basic interest begins with the machines which men use: it is the development of these tools to higher and higher levels of efficiency which brings forth new economic systems. The focus, therefore, should be on the factory rather than the bank—on Detroit or Pittsburgh rather than Wall Street. It is the machines which act on men and society: the economic setting is but one part of the over-all technological context. Second, the stress on material production may be construed less as a determinism and more as an order of priority. Marx and Engels are not blind to the noneconomic features of social life, and they are not so foolish as to deny that such forces have an influence. "Political, juridical, philosophical, religious, literary, artistic, etc. developments . . ." Engels says, "react upon one another and also upon the economic basis. It is not that the economic condition is the cause and alone active, while everything else only has a passive effect. There is, rather, interaction on the basis of economic necessity, which ultimately always asserts itself." [8]

Only a blind man would focus on a society's technology and ignore everything else. The point which is being made is that when social causation is being discussed it is necessary to assign priorities to various factors. Marx and Engels give first priority to economic forces and choose to regard others as secondary. All social change may in the long run be attributed to technological advance: on that Marxist theory is certain. However, there are periods, perhaps when the invention and exploitation of new machines are not proceeding at a rapid rate, when noneconomic forces can make their weight felt. And at these times political, religious, and other developments may serve to shape the society. However, if the long view is taken, then man's relation to the machine must take precedence over his relation to other authorities. "The mode of production of material life conditions the social, political, and intellectual life process in general," Marx says. "It is not the consciousness of men that determines their being, but, on the contrary, their social being that determines their consciousness." [9] Perhaps it takes an uncompromising materialist assertion such as this to lay the ghost of Hegelian idealism. Yet both Marx and Engels are careful to hedge their remarks: economic necessity is seen to operate as an ultimate principle, and the mode of production conditions other features of life as a general rule. Allowance is made for interim periods and for exceptions to a pattern. In the final analysis, the economic outlook is not a monolithic one. It is, rather, an approach to the study of history and society which is believed to be more fruitful than alternative methods. Marx

[8] Engels, Letter to Starkenburg, in *Selected Works*, Vol. II, p. 457.

[9] Marx, *Preface to "A Contribution to the Critique of Political Economy,"* in *Selected Works*, Vol. I, p. 363.

and Engels will emphasize technology and economic organization because they regard these as the underlying forces of social and human life. If they appear to caricature reality, it is because they are constructing a theory which seeks to analyze social causation in a coherent way. To stress one factor to the neglect of others is to engage in oversimplification; yet it may be assumed that Marx and Engels know what they are doing, that there is a method in their model.

THE TRIUMPH OF THE BOURGEOISIE

If the Hegelian dialectic and Marxist materialism are to be joined together, then the connecting link is the conception of class. Men's relations to productive instruments through history are best seen in terms of their class memberships. The study of class in political theory is as old as Plato and Aristotle, and it is indispensable for an understanding of politics and society. Nevertheless, it is an ambiguous idea, and it is to the credit of Marx and Engels that they used it in a fairly explicit way. Edmund Burke, for example, spoke of the classes and orders which make up a society: these various ranks and strata, defined by birth and function, were arrayed in hierarchical form. This is one of the more popular views of class, and it is currently employed by many sociologists. The Marxist conception, however, is less broad: "In so far as millions of families live under economic conditions of existence that separate their mode of life, their interests, and their culture from those of other classes, and put them in hostile opposition to the latter, they form a class." [10]

Classes are, first of all, large: or there is at least one class in society which is very large—probably comprising a majority of the population. What Marx and Engels will not allow is an analytic proliferation of classes: they would object to sociological studies which discover six or eight or ten "classes" in society. Second, the determinant of class is economic condition. By this is meant either role an individual plays in the productive process: his ownership or lack of ownership of property, but probably both. Class is based almost entirely on wealth. The Marxist view has no room for something called "social class," which presumably takes into account such factors as education, religion, or parentage when assigning individuals to ranks in the social structure. Third, groups of individuals only take on the character of classes when hostility and conflict mark their relations with one another. Classes are not categories which a sociologist sets up in order to better understand society so much as they are groupings which develop when real people find their interests opposed to those of others. Marx and Engels would say that the hostile op-

---

[10] Marx, *The Eighteenth Brumaire of Louis Bonaparte,* in *Selected Works,* Vol. I, p. 334.

position between classes always exists and that it may always be found by a theorist willing to look for it.

The problem, as will be seen, is that members of classes do not always realize that their interests are at odds to those of others. It is possible to have classes, therefore, without class consciousness on the part of individuals. This, however, does not make those classes any the less real. With the conception of class in mind, Marx and Engels open *The Communist Manifesto* with their now-familiar analysis:

> The history of all hitherto existing society is the history of class struggles.
> Freeman and slave, patrician and plebean, lord and serf, guild-master and journeyman, in a word, oppressor and oppressed, stood in constant opposition to one another, carried on an uninterrupted, now hidden, now open fight, a fight that each time ended, either in a revolutionary reconstruction of society at large, or in the common ruin of the contending classes.[11]

The struggles between classes are sometimes hidden and sometimes open; but they are always in process even if the battle itself is not apparent to the combatants. What transforms one section of a society into a class of oppressors and another into a class of oppressed is the distribution and organization of productive property. What causes the struggle to break into open revolution is the eventual realization that technological progress has rendered obsolete the prevailing system of ownership.

Marx and Engels illustrate their theory of history by analyzing the transition from feudal to capitalist society. Production in the feudal economy was based on home manufactures and local crafts. The typical form of economic organization was the guild: a self-elected group of skilled workers who set prices, controlled quality, and generally governed the condition of their trade. The guild was, in short, a means of establishing legal relations between men and the tools they use to earn their living. Yet, despite the inherent efficiency of the system, external forces—over which the guildsmen had no control—produced a demand for manufactured goods which soon outran the supply. Populations had grown, tastes had developed, consumption patterns were accelerated. "The feudal system of industry, under which industrial production was monopolized by closed guilds, now no longer sufficed for the growing wants of the new markets," Marx and Engels write.[12] The result was that the factory system began to develop alongside the guild structure; but the primitive factory, where one man hired a dozen or so helpers and worked alongside them on his own premises, was only a beginning. "The markets kept ever growing, the demand, ever rising. Even manufactures no longer sufficed.

[11] Marx and Engels, *Communist Manifesto* in *Selected Works*, Vol. I, p. 34.
[12] *Ibid.*, p. 35.

Thereupon, steam and machinery revolutionized industrial production. The place of manufacture was taken by the giant, modern industry: the place of the industrial middle-class, by the industrial millionaires." [13]

The movement from feudalism is best seen as a technological revolution: the important transition is from hand tools to steam-powered machinery. It is this change which impels into being a new form of economic organization. The guild craftsman owned his own tools, and he used them to turn raw materials into a finished product. But a machine which operates on steam power, while it can be owned by a single individual, can only be used effectively in a factory setting. This means that the owner must hire employees, that they must come to work at his establishment, and that they must adhere to the discipline of the workplace if a manufactured product is to result. The social consequence is that two classes of people are created: property-owners and wage-workers.

The dialectical character of this process may now be suggested: "Modern bourgeois society," Marx and Engels say, "has sprouted from the ruins of feudal society. . . ."

The means of production and of exchange, on whose foundation the bourgeoisie built itself up, were generated in feudal society. At a certain stage in the development of these means of production and of exchange, the conditions under which feudal society produced and exchanged, the feudal organization of agriculture and manufacturing industry, in one word, the feudal relations of property became no longer compatible with the already developed productive forces; they became so many fetters. They had to be burst asunder; they were burst asunder.[14]

The two essential social facts are the mode (or means) of production and the relations of production (or property). The first, which has already been discussed, is the stage of technological development: the juxtaposition of men and the machines with which they work. The relations of production are the stage of social and legal development: the juxtaposition of men and men in the respective roles they play in the productive process. Thus, in the feudal economy the mode of production might be represented by a craftsman's dependence on his tools of his trade; the relations of production would be typified by the authority of the guild-master over the apprentice.

It is the interplay of mode and relations of production which gives the Marxist dialectic its motive force: the question is whether those two facts are compatible with each other in any given historical epoch. Throughout the feudal period, Marx and Engels assume, mode of production and relations of production were in essential harmony: the handicraft technology and the

[13] *Ibid.*
[14] *Ibid.*, pp. 34, 39.

guild form of economic organization were agreeable systems. However, it soon developed that technological developments had run well ahead of the guild basis of property: indeed, it is a basic Marxist premise that modes of production will advance more rapidly than the relations of production. Nevertheless, the guilds attempted to retain control over the productive processes even though they were no longer equipped to do this job. This marks the end of the harmonious feudal era. That the guilds would not relinquish their authority and permit a new organization of property relations to come into being was a sign that society now had warring within it two incompatible systems. To the men who owned the burgeoning factories and who wished to supply the opening markets, the guild organizations looked like so many fetters. These chains, Marx and Engels say, had to be burst asunder because no society can longer put up with an internal contradiction of this magnitude. The restraints imposed by the guilds and the laws which sanctioned these regulations had to be thrown off: "into their place stepped free competition, accompanied by a social and political constitution adapted to it, and by the economical and political sway of the bourgeois class." [15]

Capitalism, then, is the child of feudalism as well as its conqueror: it is an antithesis growing up amidst the old order. The internal contradiction of feudal economy—the incompatibility of a mode of production which outstrips the traditional relations of production—gives capitalism its opportunity to overthrow the old system of property and to replace it with one in harmony with the new technology. This contradiction can only be resolved by revolutionary means: at this stage of history the bourgeoisie must assert itself in an unmistakable way. In almost all cases force and violence is required if state and society are to be refashioned so as to be in accord with the emerging productive process. The capitalist class, then, begins its life on the barricades: born in revolution, it will see yet another revolution before it expires.

The victorious capitalist class is no small object of admiration in Marx and Engels' eyes. It is made up of men who are admired because they have found new ways of exploiting the forces of nature and have shaped society so as to encourage this exploitation. They are successful revolutionaries, and this stamps them as being in the mainstream of history. "The bourgeoisie . . ." Marx and Engels write, "has been the first to show what man's activity can bring about. It has accomplished wonders far surpassing Egyptian pyramids, Roman aqueducts, and Gothic cathedrals; it has conducted expeditions that put in the shade all former Exoduses of nations and crusades." [16] No one who has studied the writings of Marx and Engels can say that their theory is "anti-

[15] *Ibid.*, p. 39.
[16] *Ibid.*, p. 37.

capitalist": on the contrary, their recital of capitalism's accomplishments is fulsome and ungrudging.

Subjection of nature's forces to man, machinery, application of chemistry to industry and agriculture, steam-navigation, railways, electric telegraphs, clearing of whole continents for cultivation, canalization of rivers, whole populations conjured out of the ground—what earlier century had even a presentiment that such productive forces slumbered in the lap of social labor? [17]

The capitalist class consists of men who understand the potentialities inherent in technology and who can make these potentialities actual. Simply by acting as entrepreneurs they serve the role of revolutionaries: their pursuit of wealth has the consequence of remaking the entire social order. "The bourgeoisie cannot exist without constantly revolutionizing the instruments of production, and with them the whole relations of society . . ." Marx and Engels write. "All fixed, fast-frozen relations, with their train of ancient and venerable prejudices and opinions, are swept away, all newly formed ones become antiquated before they ossify." [18] The liberalism which Locke espoused and Burke deplored, the democracy which Tocqueville welcomed and feared, the nationalism which Hegel championed—all of these are seen by Marx and Engels as new social relations brought into being by the triumph of the bourgeoisie. The capitalists are neither ideologues nor theorists: they are vigorous and imaginative individuals who pursue their own interests unremittingly. Indeed, they are Hegel's Heroes placed in an economic setting. At no time do Marx and Engels hold these entrepreneurs morally responsible for their acts. If they exploit their employees, if they cheat the consumers, if they degrade the level of culture, as individuals they cannot be praised or blamed for what they do. The bourgeoisie is fulfilling the historic role in which the dialectic has cast it.

Because the impact of the bourgeoisie is economic, it becomes more than economic. That is to say, if a class ascends to dominant economic power in a society, then it will cast its influence over all the other aspects of social life. A capitalist economy, therefore, produces a capitalist culture. The entrepreneurial class does not set itself up as the conscious arbiter of taste or style: nevertheless, it unwittingly shapes the values of society so that the general pattern of life is a reflection of the economic system. This theory of Marx and Engels' can be illustrated by what Marx calls the "Fetishism" of commodities. A capitalist society is concerned with physical objects only insofar as a monetary value can be imparted to them.

---

[17] *Ibid.*, pp. 38–39.
[18] *Ibid.*, p. 37.

There is a physical relation between physical things. But it is different with commodities. There, the existence of the things qua commodities, have absolutely no connection with their physical properties and with the material relations arising therefrom. There it is a definite social relation between men, that assumes, in their eyes, the fantastic form of a relation between things. . . . This I call the Fetishism which attaches itself to the products of labor, so soon as they are produced as commodities, and which is therefore inseparable from the production of commodities.[19]

The problem is one of rationality. Do men, Marx asks, exploit the resources of nature in a rational way? His answer is that capitalism, by giving a price to all it produces, channels human behavior into directions which are essentially irrational. Men live by producing commodities: all of their actions are guided by the expectation of price. They exist to create objects of value, not objects for use. Because the price tag continually hangs over the productive process, men begin to evaluate themselves in the same terms. The medieval craftsman might be concerned with the quality and the usefulness of his product; the capitalist is concerned with the market value of the commodity he sells, and he compels both workers and consumers to accept this evaluation.

Furthermore, the relationships between man and man—between employer and employee, between buyer and seller—are governed by price considerations. Each individual comes to have a monetary value in the eyes of others because each is used by the other for the purposes of making money. Men become oriented to looking at the world—the world of men and things—as a bundle of commodities. Health, education, art, and even human affections are all touched by market standards. Men calculate their actions and make the decisions in economic terms rather than any other.[20] The final consequence of this pervasive fetishism is that individuals are forced to sell themselves. Personalities are turned into saleable commodities, lives are turned into careers.

One of Marx and Engels' chief contributions is to stress the psychological ramifications of a free-market economy. While they obviously present their case in extreme form, they do show how the values of an economic system can infuse the personalities of those who live and work within it. The bourgeois class sets the values for society even though their only concern is the narrow one of making money. Society and personality, Marx and Engels suggest, are best understood by studying the level of technology and the patterns of ownership and distribution. Men are reflections of the productive tools they use, on the one hand, and of the ways in which productive property is socially organized, on the other. And human history, it should now be clear, is best understood as economic history.

[19] Marx, *Capital*, p. 83.
[20] For an expanded discussion of this theme, see Erich Fromm, *Man for Himself* (New York: Rinehart, 1947).

The capitalist class is powerful because it owns the means of production: in particular, the factories in which commodities are created by hired workers. Marx and Engels attribute the power of the bourgeoisie to the fact of ownership: if a man owns a factory, then he is able to compel other men to do as he pleases. Each member of the capitalist class is therefore presumed to possess productive property, and this class taken as a whole is presumed to have dominant social power. Yet it has become increasingly clear that the power of which Marx and Engels speak is based not so much on ownership as on the *control* of the productive process. When a man owns his own enterprise, it is likely to be fairly small, and the owner usually serves in the role of manager as well. When Marx and Engels speak of the capitalist class, they are assuming that this group also carries out the managerial function. That is, they have the power to make decisions about employment, production, investment, prices, and so forth.

There is no need to point out that modern capitalist economies are now characterized by large corporate institutions. Giant corporations are not owned by any discrete class, and only a handful of the significant enterprises can be said to be the personal property of a single man. In short, the functions of ownership and management have become divorced. The corporate shareholders are a widely scattered group, and they exercise little or no control over the operations of the companies which in theory they own. At the same time, there has emerged an elite of salaried managers who run these private enterprises and who are largely accountable to themselves alone.[21] The corporation is a powerful institution, and the largest corporations taken together have every bit as much power as Marx and Engels ascribed to capitalist property. The owners, on the other hand, may share in corporate earnings, but they have no substantial economic power. Nor is it possible to call the managerial elite a social class: its members are well paid but not so well paid that they can amass fortunes sufficiently great to become owners of the enterprises they control. In addition, most managers serve fairly short terms of office and they retire as they are replaced by younger men.

The distinction between class and elite is well illustrated here. Marx and Engels understand that economic power in a capitalist society is not the power of ownership taken by itself. The significant role is that of management. Marx is well aware of the importance of the corporate form—which he calls the "joint-stock company"—and the power it gives to the elite which manages it. Corporations, he says, have a number of important consequences:

[21] On the power of the managers, see A. A. Berle's two books, *The Twentieth Century Capitalist Revolution* (New York: Harcourt, Brace, 1954) and *Power Without Property* (New York: Harcourt, Brace, 1959). On the impotence of the stockholders, see Joseph Livingston, *The American Stockholder* (Philadelphia: Lippincott, 1958).

(1) An enormous expansion of the scale of production and enterprises, which were impossible for individual capitals. . . .

(2) Capital, which rests on a socialized mode of production and presupposes a social concentration of means of production and labor-powers, is here directly endowed with the form of social capital . . . as distinguished from private capital, and its enterprises assume the form of social enterprises as distinguished from individual enterprises. It is the abolition of capital as private property within the boundaries of capitalist production itself.

(3) Transformation of the actually functioning capitalist into a mere manager, an administrator of other peoples' capital, and of the owners of capital into mere owners. . . .

. . . This result of the highest development of capitalist production is a necessary transition to the reconversion of capital into the property of the producers, no longer as the private property of individual producers, but as the common property of associates, as social property outright.[22]

Capital is abolished, but not capitalism. The owner sits at home and receives his dividend checks, and a manager does the work and exercises the power. Engels makes the same point in no less straightforward terms. "The conversion of the great organizations for production and communication into joint-stock companies," he says, "shows that . . . the bourgeoisie can be dispensed with. All the social functions of the capitalists are now carried out by salaried employees. The capitalist has no longer any social activity save the pocketing of revenues, the clipping of coupons, and gambling on the Stock Exchange, where the different capitalists fleece each other of their capital." [23] And as the owning class gives up its social functions and activities, so it abdicates its economic power. A new elite is now at the controls, and it rules society no less than did the entrepreneurs it has replaced.

Does the emergence of the corporation and the managerial elite obviate the theory of bourgeois dominance? Marx and Engels, through their remarks on joint-stock companies, demonstrate that in the final analysis they are not concerned with the bourgeoisie as a class. Rather their main focus is on capitalist institutions: the privately owned enterprises which characterize an economy. Even if corporations are operated by salaried managers, they still employ profit as the standard of performance. These managers also hire employees for wages and salaries, and they judge their work by its profitability for the organization. Finally, the great corporations have a profound influence on the lives of all in society even if the managerial elite makes no attempt to impose social values in a conscious way.

The shift in control from the entrepreneur to the manager, Marx and Engels would say, should not be overexaggerated. Property is still private

---

[22] Marx, *Capital: The Process of Capitalist Production as a Whole* (Chicago: Charles H. Kerr, 1909), Vol. III, pp. 516–517.

[23] Engels, *Anti-Duhring*, pp. 385–386.

property and hence put to private uses. Society is still dominated by the profit motive, and personality is still a commodity. And the class struggle continues to be a reality even though the class of owners is now on the sidelines. The conflict between employer and employee is less clear-cut when the employer is not a person but an impersonal institution. Nevertheless, the system is still a capitalist one, and for this reason its life span is governed by the dialectic of history.

THE AWAKENING OF THE PROLETARIAT

A class struggle requires at least two classes to play the role of antagonists. In the eras prior to the advent of industrialization, it was possible to speak of many orders and gradations in society. Burke, for example, saw the social structure as a pyramid with many horizontal layers, and each stratum was linked to the one above and beneath it through a network of mutual obligations. Marx and Engels agree that this was the case in preindustrial societies. "In the early epochs of history, we find almost everywhere a complicated arrangement of society into various orders, a manifold gradation of social rank," they write. "In ancient Rome we have patricians, knights, plebeans, slaves: in the middle ages, feudal lords, vassals, guildmasters, journeymen, apprentices, serfs; in almost all of these classes, again, subordinate gradations." [24] This complexity of the social fabric was made possible by the leisurely tempo of the economic life: the arrangements of property and the processes of production were matters of settled tradition, and it was therefore possible for a prescriptive class structure to take root.

Yet, just as the triumph of the capitalist class shattered the feudal economy, so did it destroy the social order which surrounded it. Industrial technology became the great machine which ripped men from their traditional places in society and threw them into the new world of the factory and the city. The delicate arrangements among a hierarchy of classes were broken, and, as a result, class took on a simpler and harsher meaning. "The epoch of the bourgeoisie, possesses, however, this distinctive feature: it has simplified the class antagonisms," Marx and Engels write. "Society as a whole is more and more splitting up into two great hostile camps, into two great classes directly facing each other: Bourgeoisie and Proletariat." [25] The bourgeoisie has already been considered: it is now time to turn to the proletariat.

The proletariat is the industrial working class. Engels gives this definition: "the class of modern wage-laborers who, having no means of production of

[24] Marx and Engels, *Communist Manifesto*, p. 34.
[25] *Ibid.*, pp. 34–35.

their own, are reduced to selling their labor-power in order to live." [26] There are, then, two chief characteristics of this class. First of all, the proletarian does not own productive property. The machine at which he works and the factory in which he is employed belong not to him but to someone else: to a member of the bourgeois class. Second, the proletarian is compelled to throw himself on the labor market: he must sell his talents for an hourly payment if he and his family are to survive. It follows from both of these propositions that the proletarian is at the mercy of his bourgeois employer: he must take the wages which are offered, and he will more likely than not be exploited by an economic system based on profits.[27] What is most important is that the proletariat constitutes a class. It is large: as industrialization progresses, the majority of the working population is forced to join the ranks of wage-labor. It is economic: the social status of workers is defined by their relation to the productive process and to the system of property in which they earn their livelihood. And the proletariat's interests stand in fundamental conflict with those of the bourgeoisie: the owners of property make their profits by driving down the wages of the working class.

Marx and Engels are prepared to say that the industrial workers in all technologically advanced societies form such a proletariat. In other words, the existence of this class is proposed as an objective social fact. The political theorist, Marx and Engels suggest, ought to acknowledge that exploitation and the class struggle are the inevitable accompaniments of the private ownership of the modes of production. The problem with this theory is that the conception of class resides in the theorist's mind, and it may not have its counterpart in reality. That is, it is proper to ask if the proletarian himself knows he is being exploited, if he realizes that he is engaged in a struggle with his bourgeois employer.

It is quite possible that the proletarians are not aware of their social and economic situation. While as a matter of political theory they may be a class with all the necessary attributes, as a matter of political fact they may not be conscious of their condition. Marx and Engels are well aware of the gulf between the objective definition and the subjective image. Class-consciousness is not a Marxist requisite for the existence of a class: men need not think of themselves as working-class in order to be working-class. In the early stages of industrial development in particular, workers will be forming themselves into a class without comprehending what is happening to them. "At this

[26] *Ibid.*, p. 34n.

[27] Unfortunately, for reasons of space, it will not be possible to discuss Marx's economic theory in this chapter. A good summary may be found in Robert Heilbroner, *The Worldly Philosophers* (New York: Simon and Schuster, 1953), pp. 127–160.

stage the laborers still form an incoherent mass scattered over the whole country, and broken up by their mutual competition . . ." Marx and Engels write. "Therefore, the proletarians did not fight their enemies, but the enemies of their enemies." [28]

Because men exist in an incoherent mass, because they are unable to see themselves as a unified class with a common interest, they are susceptible to fragmentation and manipulation. Worker is turned against worker, and every effort is made to exaggerate small antagonisms and obscure the overriding identity.[29] The proletariat, Marx and Engels contend, should be unified and class-conscious. Only in this way will they come to an understanding of their own best interest: a head-on struggle with the bourgeoisie. If exploitation is to be ended, then workers must awaken to their condition and raise the class struggle to an open and political level.

Marx and Engels want the objective fact of class to become a subjective image in the proletarians' minds. And this, they believe, is bound to occur in time. The dialectic unfolds in such a way that class-consciousness will inevitably develop on the part of industrial workers. "With the development of industry . . . it becomes concentrated in great masses, its strength grows, and it feels that strength more . . ." Marx and Engels write. "The unceasing improvement of machinery, ever more rapidly developing, makes their livelihood more and more precarious, the collisions between individual workmen and individual bourgeois take more and more the character of collisions between two classes." [30] This process is an example of dialectical materialism at work. It is a material condition—the disciplined life encountered in the factory— which determines the ideas in men's heads. The environment, Marx says, creates human consciousness of its status and interests.

Large-scale industry concentrates in one place a crowd of people unknown to one another. Competition divides their interests. But the maintenance of wages, this common interest which they have against their boss, unites them in a common thought of resistance. . . .

[28] Marx and Engels, *Communist Manifesto*, p. 42.

[29] V. O. Key writes in his *Southern Politics*: "Sustained effort to improve the Negro's economic and political status costs money, and upper-class southerners, dislike to part with cash. . . . The almost overwhelming temptation, especially in areas with many Negroes, is to take advantage of the short-run opportunity to maintain the status-quo by using, or tolerating the use of, the race issue to blot up the discontent of the lesser whites. By this means the governing classes can kill off or minimize pressures for improved governmental services from whites and find support for low public outlays for the benefit of the Negro. It is naive, of course, to interpret southern politics as a deliberate conspiracy among the better-off whites to divide the mass of people by tolerating Negro-baiting. Nevertheless, with a high degree of regularity those of the top economic group—particularly the new industrialists— are to be found in communion with the strident advocates of white supremacy." (New York: Knopf, 1949), p. 662.

[30] Marx and Engels, *Communist Manifesto*, p. 42.

Economic conditions had first transformed the mass of the people of the country into workers. The combination of capital has created for this mass a common situation, common interests. This mass is thus already a class as against capital, but not yet for itself. In the struggle, of which we have noted only a few phases, this mass becomes united, and constitutes itself as a class for itself. The interests it defends become class interests. But the struggle of class against class is a political struggle.[31]

It is interesting to note that while theorists like Plato, Burke, Hegel, and Tocqueville view with alarm the emergence of a mass society, Marx and Engels show no such concern. The earlier writers regard such a social mass as a threat to stability and to traditional values. Marx and Engels, on the other hand, see the mass condition as a necessary historical stage which precedes the emergence of proletarian class-consciousness. If a mass of men is fragmented, isolated, and prey to irresponsible leadership, this is thought of as a difficult period which must be experienced by society before men come to know the truth about themselves. Poverty, exploitation, and oppression may be the lot of the working class, but the severity of this life accelerates the demand for serious reform.

How long the transition from mass to class will take, Marx and Engels do not say. This transformation is essentially a psychological one, and if men are left to themselves they may take their own time in awakening. Yet if the process is a prolonged and painful one, then this is simply a sign that the dialectic cannot be hurried. Historical circumstances themselves will decree when the time is ripe for political change based on class-consciousness. Marx is particularly harsh with the theorists who wish to embark on radical social change before the proletariat is ready to play its role. He brands as Utopian those writers who believe that society can be transformed before the working class has come to realize its true identity in the capitalist system.

So long as the proletariat is not yet sufficiently developed to constitute itself as a class, and consequently so long as the struggle itself of the proletariat with the bourgeoisie has not yet assumed a political character, and the productive forces are not yet sufficiently developed in the bosom of the bourgeoisie itself to enable us to catch a glimpse of the material conditions necessary for the emancipation of the proletariat and for the formation of a new society, these theoreticians are mere Utopians who, to meet the wants of the oppressed classes, improvise systems and go in search of a regenerating science.[32]

Under this indictment would fall thinkers like Rousseau and Bentham who, while not socialists in any economic sense, sought to create a rational social

[31] Marx, *The Poverty of Philosophy* (Moscow: Foreign Languages Publishing House, n.d.), pp. 194, 195.

[32] *Ibid.*, p. 140.

order without waiting for material conditions to liberate the working class from its psychological fetters. Marx and Engels, therefore, depend on the proletariat to find freedom for itself. The exhortations of reformers will fall on deaf ears if the working class is not historically prepared to rise to the occasion. Class-consciousness and class action will dawn when the internal contradictions of an industrial technology and a capitalist economic system rise to the surface in an unmistakable way. Until that day comes the proletariat will remain unaware of its role in history: until that day it will have yet to know that it is a proletariat at all.

Marx and Engels display a monumental patience on this matter. They are able to do this because they believe that when the working class comes to a realization of its identity it will be invincible. "All previous historical movements were movements of minorities, or in the interests of minorities," they write. "The proletarian movement is the self-conscious, independent movement of the immense majority, in the interests of the immense majority." [33] In one sense this is an affirmation of the legitimacy of majority rule: that change should only come when the majority has made up its mind about what it wants. This approach is limited, however, in the ways that Rousseau's and Hegel's conceptions were limited. The majority decision, for Marx and Engels, is rightful only if it is a scientific one—if it accords with the materialist dialectic. They certainly say that throughout history the majority has been deceived and misguided about its true interests, and that it has been coerced and manipulated by ruling minorities. Only with the advent of industrial technology can the majority finally come to act in a rational and purposeful way. If the moment of truth has not yet come to all workers of the world, Marx and Engels wish to warn us of its historical inevitability and its impending arrival.

To divide society into two major classes—a property-owning bourgeoisie and a propertyless proletariat—is to engage in a great simplification. For many centuries the Western world has known a middle class, and from Aristotle's time to the present it has played an important role in politics. The question is not whether Marx and Engels overlook the middle class—for they do not— but rather why they see it as having no substantial future. Marx certainly is aware of the part played by the middle class in capitalist society: one of his criticisms of classical economists, Ricardo in particular, is that they neglect this class. "What [Ricardo] forgets to mention is the continual increase in numbers of the middle-classes, . . . situated midway between the workers on one side and the capitalists and landowners on the other," Marx says. "These

[33] Marx and Engels, *Communist Manifesto*, p. 44.

middle-classes rest with all their weight upon the working class and at the same time increase the social security and power of the upper class." [34]

Many theorists have suggested that the function of a strong middle class is to act as a buffer between the classes at either extreme of the social structure. Marx and Engels, however, regard the middle class as an ally of the property-owning bourgeoisie. For this middle stratum shares the values of the capitalist class, and it tends to be antagonistic to the aspirations of the proletariat. At the same time, it is observed that the middle class is increasing in proportion to the whole working population. The advance of technology calls for more clerical and supervisory employees, more technicians and professional people, more workers engaged in service trades rather than productive labor—more people, in short, who will wear white collars rather than blue, who will draw salaries instead of wages. Indeed, as automatic machinery is introduced, it would appear that the proletariat will actually shrink in size.

The answer which Marx and Engels give to this is that the so-called middle class must be subjected to careful examination. Several basic questions must be asked of it, and the chief of these has to do with its economic position. For as the middle class grows larger, it admits to its ranks individuals who in fact own no property. These people may wear white collars, but they are nevertheless employees: they are totally dependent for their livelihood on the jobs which they manage to secure. The vast majority of the middle class, because it is propertyless, is insecure and powerless. They have not the economic resources to live lives of their own choosing, and if they are protected from the fluctuations of the labor market, they nevertheless stand or fall in their role as employees. A few members of this middle class may have salaries which are so high or talents which are so much in demand that they can achieve an independence similar to that known by the property-owning bourgeoisie. But most of the middle class are not in this favored position. They, like the proletariat they look down on, are reduced to selling their labor—and their personalities—in order to live.[35]

Marx and Engels' answer is that the middle class is, as a matter of objective fact, becoming a white-collar proletariat. Even though its members receive monthly or annual salaries and do not dirty their hands with manual labor, they share the essential characteristics of the working class. "The lower strata of the middle-class . . ." Marx and Engels write, "sink gradually into the proletariat, partly because their diminutive capital does not suffice for the

---

[34] *Theorien über den Mehrwert*, in *Karl Marx: Selected Writings in Sociology and Social Philosophy* (London: Watts, 1956), edited and translated by T. B. Bottomore and Maximilien Rubel, pp. 190–191.

[35] See C. Wright Mills, *White Collar* (New York: Oxford University Press, 1951).

scale on which modern industry is carried on, . . . and partly because their specialized skill is rendered worthless by new methods of production." [36] It is certainly true that small businessmen can find that they have not the resources to compete with economic giants; and even the entrepreneurs who stay in business find themselves increasingly dependent on their large suppliers and customers. It is not true that the skills of middle-class technicians and professional men are rendered worthless as technology advances: nevertheless, they are only able to sell their skills by gaining employment in an enterprise they do not themselves own.

The important point Marx and Engels are suggesting is the essential similarity between the white-collar proletariat and the blue-collar proletariat. The chief problem is that white-collar workers are even further removed from having a sense of proletarian class-consciousness than are the members of the working class. Salaried employees identify their interests with those of their employers, and they seek to adopt the same values and style of life as those above them on the social scale. While they may in fact be proletarians, they show little or no sign of awakening to this condition. In psychological terms, then, the middle class has yet to identify itself with its true class status. Marx and Engels granted that even production workers would have to gain an awareness of their class interests in their own time: they would be forced to admit that a far longer span will have to pass before even the lower-middle class reverses its traditional view of its role in society. And even here, as Tocqueville pointed out, the middle class might well turn not to alliance with the proletariat but would rather become its most severe enemy.

The prospects for the middle class are, in the final analysis, dim ones in Marxist theory. Either its members join the working class, both economically and psychologically; or they rally against the proletariat, in which case they will go to defeat along with the property-owning bourgeoisie they so admire. When this will occur is in the hands of the dialectic: and until the moment of revolution arrives, Marx and Engels find it appropriate to analyze the politics of capitalist society.

THE POLITICS OF CAPITALISM

So long as productive property is privately owned, Marx and Engels argue, political power will gravitate to the hands of those who hold economic power. Institutions of government in a capitalist society exist to support and impart authority to the property-owning class. The state, they write, must be viewed as part of the economic system:

[36] Marx and Engels, *Communist Manifesto*, p. 41.

Each step in the development of the bourgeoisie was accomplished by a corresponding political advance of that class. . . . The bourgeoisie has at last, since the establishment of modern industry and of the world-market, conquered for itself, in the modern representative state, exclusive political sway. The executive of the modern state is but a committee for managing the common affairs of the whole bourgeoisie.[37]

This classic Marxist dictum—that the state is the executive committee of the bourgeoisie—must not be construed as a conspiracy theory. There is no assumption that men of wealth organize together for the purpose of using political power to aggrandize their own interests. Such an interpretation is not only an oversimplification: it also vulgarizes the main outlines of a complex theory. What Marx and Engels are suggesting, on the contrary, is that because the substructure of any society is economic, it is inevitable that political institutions will form a derivative and contingent superstructure. Governments take the shape that they do because they arise in particular economic and technological settings: a society which is principally agrarian will give rise to a state which is quite unlike that produced by a society which is urban and industrialized.

For this reason, it is idle to start any debates over what is the best form of government. The kind of argument which theorists like Hobbes, Locke, and Rousseau engaged in is a false controversy, for governmental forms are settled once the economic foundation has been laid. There may, of course, be discussions on matters of detail—such as the respective virtues of cabinet government as opposed to the separation of powers—and this is appropriate so long as it is acknowledged that these are only details. If the study of politics is to be scientific, Marx and Engels write, then both social and political institutions must be regarded as outgrowths of the material conditions which direct the major paths of human behavior.

> In every single instance empirical observation must show the connection of the social and political structure with production—empirically and without any mystification and speculation. The social structure and the state always arise from the life-process of definite individuals, but of these individuals, not as they may appear in their own or other people's ideas, but as they really are, that is, as they act, produce in a material way, and therefore as they produce under definite limitations, presuppositions and conditions which are material and independent of their will.[38]

There is no point, then, in making political plans. The theories which talk of a social contract or those which propound a utilitarian calculus are essentially Utopian. The ideas which men originate, whether they concern political re-

[37] *Ibid.*, pp. 35–36.
[38] Marx and Engels, *German Ideology*, p. 18.

form or political stability, are based on an ignorance of social reality. Citizens tend to believe that they make the governments they live under and that they have a choice of political systems. Marx and Engels are trying to demonstrate that political action by itself is of no avail. Political change only follows on economic change: if men wish to alter their form of government, they must first come to realize that economic power must be transmuted. The trouble with political discourse as it has been traditionally approached is that it confuses cause and effect. States and citizens operate under limitations imposed by the material realities which underlie a society: if those limits are to be transcended, then political action must start as economic action.

The chief function of the capitalist state is to protect the interests of property from depredations consequent on the class struggle. The bourgeoisie requires power and authority which will keep the workers in line. While the state may appear to stand independent of the class struggle, in fact the order it maintains is the order desired by the capitalist class. Engels describes the origin and function of the state:

It is a product of society at a certain stage of development; it is the admission that this society has become entangled in an insoluble contradiction within itself, that it is cleft into irreconcilable antagonisms which it is powerless to dispel. But in order that these antagonisms, classes with conflicting economic interests, may not consume themselves and society in sterile struggle, a power apparently standing above society becomes necessary, whose purpose is to moderate the conflict and keep it within the bounds of "order"; and this power arising out of society, but placing itself above it, and increasingly separating itself from it, is the state.

As the state arose out of the need to hold class antagonisms in check, but as it, at the same time, arose in the midst of the conflict of these classes, it is, as a rule, the state of the most powerful, economically dominant class, which by virtue thereof becomes also the dominant class politically, and thus acquires new means of holding down and exploiting the oppressed class.[39]

The class which is economically dominant, then, will be the class with dominant political power. In a society where property is in private ownership the state's chief function is to encourage the basic conditions necessary for the security of the capitalist system. To be sure, such a state may enact welfare legislation; it may also use its taxing and regulatory powers to redistribute income and control economic excesses. But these activities, Marx and Engels would say, are on the margin: they do not tamper with the fundamental principles of private property.[40] The state, for example, will continue to assume

---

[39] Engels, *The Origin of the Family, Private Property, and the State*, in *Selected Works*, Vol. II, pp. 289, 290.

[40] The Marxist contention is that if a substantial portion of society's economic power remains in private hands, then governmental efforts at regulating industry will be frustrated or even turned to the advantage of the enterprises which are supposed to be regulated. On the experience of the British Labour Government in this connection, see Arnold Rogow,

that profits are legitimate, and the law will assume that ownership of the means of production is an unquestioned axiom. Major economic decisions will be left in the hands of private individuals. Thus, the realm of management prerogative will encompass matters of wages, prices, profits, and plant location; this sphere will also include the making of plans for capital investment and the exercise of authority within the place of work. While trade unions may have a voice on matters of wages and discipline, they do not intrude into the more significant areas. The capitalist state, then, underwrites the sanctity of private economic power. It may go even further and pass laws which give positive encouragement to the propertied interests: facilities which businessmen need for their profitable operation may be supplied by the state on the assumption that what is good for business is good for the country.

All this, Marx and Engels argue, is bound to occur. The state acts as it does not because capitalists conspire to secure this end, but because there is no other alternative. If property is in private hands, and if goods are to be produced and services to be supplied, then the class capable of performing these tasks must be given political support. Both the government and the whole population must rely on the men who control the material means of production. So long as productive property is so managed, the entire society will have to provide an environment favorable to the operations of the business community. Of course, the businessman will complain, as a matter of habit, about such injustices as high taxes, government spending, and public regulation of his enterprise. At the same time, he will prosper because the state protects and encourages him at every significant juncture. Indeed, he complains about details because that is all there is to complain about: small governmental incursions are called socialism or tyranny because, ironically, the state refrains from real acts of socialism or tyranny. In short, Marx and Engels are saying that the owners and managers of property control the state even if they are not themselves aware of this fact.

How does this class which is a small minority in society, commandeer political power? Throughout the course of political theory it has been shown that minority rule is no less possible than majority rule. The question which arises is how a numerically smaller group is able to assume such disproportionate power. The answers given have varied: Machiavelli, for example, said that a clever elite could dupe the mass of men into consenting to their

The Labour Government and British Industry (Ithaca: Cornell University Press, 1955). And even if a socialist government nationalizes some of a country's basic industries, there may be enough economic power remaining in the private sector of the economy so that the state-owned enterprises are effectively controlled by men sympathetic to nonsocialist objectives. On the British experience with nationalization, see Clive Jenkins, *Power at the Top* (London: MacGibbon and Kee, 1959).

rule; Burke suggested that a ruling class might exploit the habits, customs, and prejudices of a society and thereby have political authority ascribed to it. The approach taken by Marx and Engels attempts to get behind the traditional—and presumably superficial—explanations.

Engels first of all tries to show that the majority, just because it is large in numbers, usually does not have the power to rule society in its interests. The social-contract theorists postulated that there was force in numbers: Engels answers this "force theory":

> Then there arises the problem of explaining the origin of classes and relations of political rule. . . . The simple fact that the ruled and exploited have been at all times far more numerous than the rulers and exploiters, and that therefore the preponderance of actual force has rested with the former, is by itself sufficient to make clear the absurdity of the whole force theory. The problem of explaining relations of mastery and servitude still remains.

> Force is no mere act of will, but requires very real preliminary conditions for its exercise, in particular, instruments, of which the more developed prevail over the less developed, and which, moreover, must be produced. To recognize this is to admit that the producer of more highly developed instruments of force, commonly called weapons, defeats the producer of less highly developed instruments, that, in a single word, the triumph of force is based on production of weapons and this in turn on production in general—on "economic power," on the "economic situation," on the material means force has at its disposal.[41]

Power is based not on numbers but on the possession of superior weapons. The owners and managers of property have, through their access to the means of production, the ability to shape the general attitudes of the political public. This is why there is no incompatibility between free enterprise and free elections.

Even if citizens are at liberty to form political parties and vote for the men who will govern them, so long as economic power is in private hands, then none of the parties or candidates will present a serious challenge to the prevailing system. For standing above the electoral process is a class which, by its very existence and activities, is able to define the political battlelines and ensure that they do not invade the economic order. The average citizen accepts this limited role, and he happily believes that the political power he shares with his fellow voters is a substantial one. However, he has been conditioned to this belief since the day he was born into a capitalist economy. His political values, expectations, and aspirations are all products of a society which itself derives from an economic substructure. The bourgeoisie has not consciously set out to indoctrinate the public to accept without question capitalist political standards. The point is that the economic power of this minority also becomes power over the minds of men.

[41] Engels, *Anti-Duhring*, pp. 247–248, 230–231.

Control over the instruments of production is ultimately power over the way men will think and act. This is why it is so difficult for the proletariat to become class-conscious. Every feature of a capitalist society is so conceived that the citizen is led to identify his interests and his welfare with those of the owners and managers of property. To break down this sense of identification is a task for no less an agency than the dialectic. But until that historic moment comes, capitalism will have little to fear from a political system based on majority rule. For so long as a minority has economic power, it can control what the majority will do with its political power.

Marxist political theory is therefore an extension of Marxist materialism. Political power is to be had by controlling the instruments of production. "The most powerful, economically dominant class . . ." Engels says, "becomes also the politically dominant class, and thus acquires new means of holding down and exploiting the oppressed class." [42] Yet, despite the certainty with which they express their view, Marx and Engels are aware that power is not always so unequally distributed. The political pluralism advanced by Aristotle and carried on by Hegel and Tocqueville has some basis in historical fact. There are occasions when the state cannot be described as the executive committee of one class or another. There are times when the various interests in society contend among themselves for political power, and the state becomes an arbiter which sets the rules and basis for compromise.

The idea of struggle among political interest groups without the absolute domination of any single one is, of course, an ingredient of liberal and democratic theory. Marx and Engels, however, regard such a situation as an exceptional circumstance. "By way of exception," Engels says, "periods occur in which the warring classes balance each other so nearly that the state power, as ostensible mediator, acquires, for the moment, a certain degree of independence of both." [43]

The trouble with liberalism and democracy is that they generalize from a momentary condition in human history. The long-term trend is for one class—the class which owns or controls productive property—to be in the ascendant over all other classes. A pluralist theory of balance requires that power be distributed among the many groups which comprise a society. The facts of economic life show that in most cases power will be concentrated in a few hands and that it is not possible for the majority of men to engage in meaningful political participation. The state ceases to be an independent institution at the moment that one of the contending classes gains control of the economic substructure. Marx and Engels' evaluation of democratic pluralism

[42] Engels, *Origin of the Family*, p. 290.
[43] *Ibid.*

would be that it characterizes one short and transitional epoch in the history of politics. A balance of interests and an impartial state have been operative for little more than a hundred years and in a handful of countries. As the dialectic unfolds and class lines become sharper, the era of democratic politics will be seen as an interim period of brief duration.

THE ALIENATION OF LABOR

As the capitalist economy, sustained by a state of its own shaping, is consolidating itself, capitalist technology is proceeding according to its own laws of development. For if the bourgeoisie has been able to control the social and political institutions of its time, it is not able to hold the reins over the material forces which bring it its power. The modes of production grow more technical and more efficient as each day passes. Efficiency means higher profits, and new machines and methods are introduced without thought for their social and psychological consequences.

The first effect of this is on the individuals who must live and work in closest proximity to the machines themselves. "Owing to the extensive use of machinery and to division of labor, the work of the proletarians has lost all individual character, and, consequently, all charm for the workman," Marx and Engels write. "He becomes an appendage of the machine, and it is only the most simple, most monstrous, and most easily acquired knack that is required of him." [44]

This is the beginning of the Marxist theory of alienation, and it is worth quoting Marx at some length so that his emphasis will be clear.

While simple cooperation leaves the mode of working by the individual for the most part unchanged, manufacture thoroughly revolutionizes it, and seizes labour-power by its very roots. It converts the labourer into a crippled monstrosity, by forcing his detail dexterity at the expense of a world of productive capabilities and instincts; just as in the states of La Plata they butcher a whole beast for the sake of his hide or his tallow. Not only is the detail work distributed to the different individuals, but the individual himself is made the automatic motor of a fractional operation. . . . By nature unfitted to make anything independently, the manufacturing labourer develops productive activity as a mere appendage of the capitalist's workshop.

Within the capitalist system all methods for raising the social productiveness of labour are brought about at the cost of the individual labourer; all means for the development of production transform themselves into means of domination over, and exploitation of, the producers; they mutilate the labourer into a fragment of a man, degrade him to the level of an appendage of a machine, destroy every remnant of charm in his work and turn it into hated toil; they estrange from him the intellectual potentialities of the labour-process in the same proportion as science

[44] Marx and Engels, *Communist Manifesto*, p. 40.

is incorporated in it as an independent power; they distort the conditions under which he works, subject him during the labour-process to a despotism the more hateful for its meannness. . . .[45]

Marx and Engels are not liberals in the sense of Locke or Bentham. But they are humanitarians, and they are concerned over the human toll inflicted by the onward march of industrialization. They see the improvement of technology as inevitable and irreversible. Men cannot forsake the life of the machine and return to the hand loom and the spinning wheel. The question is how to make men masters of the instruments they tend and not robot-like appendages of these powerful engines. For Marx and Engels believe, no less than Rousseau, that men are rational and creative. They see in mankind the potentiality for the intelligent pursuit of the good life. The problem must therefore be defined in Hegelian terms: men must come to realize their true condition and liberate themselves in accord with their historic destiny.

Technological progress fragments work and degrades the individual. This process will be a social fact so long as goods are scarce and men must toil for their living. The mode of production, Marx and Engels say, is a constant: if men are to improve their condition, it cannot be by the reactionary device of halting or retarding the course of technology. The capitalist class will not cease its efforts to improve the productive instruments they own, and the proletariat ought not to impede those endeavors. If the economic life is to be humanized, then the focus must be not on the mode, but on the relations of production. To toil in a factory is perhaps unavoidable in our modern age, but to toil at a machine so that another man may reap a profit is an injustice that can be redressed. The alienation of man, then, is not so much a consequence of technology as it is of capitalist technology. Our industrial economy may fragment work and render it meaningless. But it is the fact that he is an employee of someone else that saps work of all human purpose.

Marx tries to show how a man's labor becomes something altogether apart from his existence.

In what does this alienation of labour consist? First, that the work is external to the worker, that it is not a part of his nature, that consequently he does not fulfill himself in his work but denies himself, has a feeling of misery, not of well-being, does not develop freely a physical and mental energy, but is physically exhausted and mentally debased. The worker therefore feels himself at home only during his leisure, whereas at work he feels homeless. His work is not voluntary but imposed, forced labour. It is not the satisfaction of a need, but only a means for satisfying other needs. Its alien character is clearly shown by the fact that as soon as there is no physical or other compulsion it is avoided like the plague. Finally, the alienated character of work for the worker appears in the fact that it is

[45] Marx, *Capital*, pp. 396, 708.

not his work but work for someone else, that in work he does not belong to himself but to another person.[46]

Central to Marxist theory is the idea that the work an individual does is the single most important facet of his life. If a man's work is mechanical and monotonous, his existence will be mechanical and monotonous. If his work is alienated from creativity and meaning, then his life will take on the same character. Finally, if a worker spends the major part of his waking life in the employ of another man, then he is not his own master but a means that someone else uses to achieve an end.

It may be protested that work is not this important a phase of the human condition. There are people who argue that individuals may develop their creative powers in their leisure time, that their family and social roles in life are amply fulfilling. Others will say that as automation proceeds and working hours shorten men will not be governed by the jobs they do.[47] To all this Marx and Engels would reply that the disciplined eight hours an individual must put in at a job are bound to form the character he takes home with him. Furthermore, the values which characterize work, especially the view that profit is the ultimate objective, will inevitably infuse the total personality. Leisure time and family life cannot be compartments separated from the work experience. The consequence of trying to live two lives can only be a neurosis, and the majority of men have not the will even to try to segment their personalities in this way.

Capitalist employment has the end result that the individual cannot call his life his own: his mind and spirit are scarred by the fact that the largest portion of his existence is rendered a means to an end selected by someone else. That the human personality must be fragmented by the division of labor and then sold as a commodity can only be seen as an act of human destruction. The theory of alienation starts as an economic theory: a contractual relationship wherein one man sells a part of his life to another for a cash payment. But the theory finishes as a theory of personality: man in capitalist society is unable to secure an identity for himself because his role is that of a thing to

---

[46] Marx, *Economic and Philosophical Manuscripts*, in *Selected Writings in Sociology and Social Philosophy*, pp. 169–170. Of the extensive literature dealing with the impact of work on the total life of the individual, two books may be singled out: Erich Fromm, *The Sane Society* (New York: Rinehart, 1955) and Hannah Arendt, *The Human Condition* (Chicago: University of Chicago Press, 1958).

[47] See Ralf Dahrendorf: "While there can be no doubt that income and prestige are in all industrial societies to a definable extent functions of occupation, . . . that sector of social behavior which is not immediately determined by occupation is extending steadily. . . . The worker, when he passes the factory gate, increasingly leaves his occupational role behind him with the machines and his work clothes; outside, he plays new roles defined by factors other than his occupation." *Class and Class Conflict in Industrial Society* (Stanford: Stanford University Press, 1959), p. 273.

be manipulated by an irrational system rather than that of a creative individual whose aim is to find himself for himself.

Over this spectacle of human degradation, however, there presides the dialectic. Through long exposure to the life of the factory, the worker eventually begins to sense that there is an inherent rationality in the productive instruments at which he labors. And there are, indeed, few things more rational than the organization of modern technology. Anyone who has observed the flow of materials, the synchronization of operations, and the discipline of a work force will grant that the factory has a logic of its own. Marx finds in the productive process an organic rationality which is strikingly similar to the reason which Hegel discovered in the realm of the *Idea*:

> The knowledge, the judgment, and the will, which, though in ever so small a degree, are practiced by the independent peasant or handicraftsman, in the same way as the savage makes the whole art of war consist in the exercise of his personal cunning—these faculties are now required only for the workshop as a whole. Intelligence in production expands in one direction, because it vanishes in many others. What is lost by the detail laborers, is concentrated in the capital that employs them. It is a result of the division of labor in manufactures, that the laborer is brought face to face with the intellectual potencies of the material process of production, as the property of another, and as a ruling power.[48]

This cannot escape the worker for long. He is brought face to face with the fact that the productive process as a whole displays a rationality and an intelligence even as his own personal contribution to it is an alienated fragment. He is bound to wonder why his own status is so degraded in the midst of a material environment which exists on such an elevated plane. Sooner or later he is bound to see the contradiction in capitalist technology.

The moment of truth will come when the worker perceives that while the modes of production are rational, the relations of production are irrational. That is, the association between men and machines, taken as a whole, displays a logic and a coherence which cannot be denied. But the association between men and men, between employees and employers, is founded on the exploitation of the many so that the few may enrich themselves. A rational technology is incompatible with an irrational economic system. The worker who is exposed all day to the logic of the factory cannot help but call into question a system of property-ownership which alienates him from the product of his labor and the possibility of creative work. As these two aspects of industrial capitalism come more and more sharply in conflict, it is less and less likely that the worker will remain impervious to the contradictions which stare him in the face. Mutilated and alienated though his body and mind may be, he will still be enough of an individual to see what is increasingly obvious.

[48] Marx, *Capital*, pp. 396–397.

And equally obvious to him will be the fact that economy and technology are thesis and antithesis: capitalism as an economic system can no longer contain the fruits of industrial progress. For one of these fruits has been the awakening of the proletariat to its true status and to a realization of the untenable character of the status quo. "It follows, from the relation between alienated labour and private property, that the emancipation of society from private property, from servitude, takes the political form of the emancipation of the working class," Marx says.[49]

This emancipation is psychological: the proletariat is at last able to think for itself. And it now realizes that political action, to be meaningful, must address itself to the economic foundations of society. The worker is no longer willing to play politics as a children's game: no longer can he be conditioned to take as important all the maxims that an alien system has taught him. "Law, morality, religion," Marx and Engels write, "are to him so many bourgeois prejudices, behind which lurk in ambush just as many bourgeois interests."[50] He now realizes that he has interests of his own and that they are in deep conflict with those of the men who own and control property. The stage is now set for revolution.

THE INEVITABLE REVOLUTION

And the curtain now opens on the act for which all that has gone before is but an overture. The theories of history, of class struggle, of capitalist exploitation, of human alienation—all come together as latent antagonisms rise to the surface. The dialectical contradictions can no longer be contained within the framework of bourgeois society. Only by revolution, Marx says, can these conflicts be resolved.

> At a certain stage of their development, the material productive forces of society come in conflict with the existing relations of production, or—what is but a legal expression for the same thing—with the property relations within which they have been at work hitherto. From forms of development of the productive forces these relations turn into their fetters. Then begins an epoch of social revolution.[51]

Private ownership of the instruments of production was, in its time, the rational economic system for promoting industrial progress. But it has now outlived its usefulness: once a positive force, it now constitutes so many fetters. The proletariat, which has slowly become more and more conscious of itself as a class, now realizes that to labor for someone else is to be exploited and

[49] Marx, *Economic and Philosophical Manuscripts*, p. 177.
[50] Marx and Engels, *Communist Manifesto*, p. 44.
[51] Marx, *Preface to "A Contribution to the Critique of Political Economy,"* p. 363.

degraded. What brings this awareness to a head is the stark material fact that every day things are getting worse instead of better. "The modern laborer," Marx and Engels write, "instead of rising with the progress of industry, sinks deeper and deeper below the conditions of existence of his own class." [52] This prediction of increased pauperization assumes not only that depressions will recur in a capitalist society, but that they will get more and more severe as one follows another. The assumption of Marxist theory is that so long as economic decisions are in private hands there will be overproduction and consequent unemployment.

Whether the problem is more one of underconsumption rather than over-production is a question which has been raised by economists since Marx and Engels' time. Whether a society which leaves economic planning to private enterprise can guarantee full employment at all times is a matter which capitalist countries have yet to resolve. Certainly it has been shown that it is possible for the average worker to share in the over-all prosperity of the economy, although here, too, there is no certainty about the forces which bring this about. What is left is that the working class under capitalism is in no position to assume that depressions and unemployment will never again occur. The Marxist revolution must wait for such a time as jobs are scarce and poverty is widespread. It is the Marxist assumption that this time will come again.

The revolutionary awakening of the proletariat has been hastened, further-more, by the pattern of industrial life. Factory employment has taught men to work together under discipline; the concentration of productive processes has created great urban centers where the working class develops social and associational ties. The bourgeoisie, in pursuing their profits, have unwittingly been planting the seeds of their own destruction.

> The advance of industry, whose involuntary promoter is the bourgeoisie, replaces the isolation of the laborers, due to competition, by their revolutionary combination, due to association. The development of modern industry, therefore, cuts from under its feet the very foundation on which the bourgeoisie produces and appropriates products. What the bourgeoisie therefore produces, above all, are its own grave-diggers. Its fall and the victory of the proletariat are equally inevitable.[53]

Thus capitalist society creates an environment which is conducive to revolutionary activity. Once the working class senses that the time is ripe for a change it is able to organize to effect that change. Factories and cities throw men together and give them a common experience.

In addition to this, the capitalist class has also through the years been giving the proletariat some practical lessons in how to make a revolution.

[52] Marx and Engels, *Communist Manifesto*, p. 45.
[53] *Ibid.*

Altogether collisions between the classes of the old society further, in many ways, the course of development of the proletariat. The bourgeoisie finds itself involved in a constant battle. At first with the aristocracy; later on, with those portions of the bourgeoisie itself, whose interests have become antagonistic to the progress of industry; at all times with the bourgeoisie of foreign countries. In all these battles it sees itself compelled to appeal to the proletariat, to ask its help, and thus, to drag it into the political arena. The bourgeoisie itself, therefore, supplies the proletariat with its own elements of political and general education, in other words, it furnishes the proletariat with weapons for fighting the bourgeoisie.[54]

Not only has the working class been exploited economically for many years; it has also been exploited politically. Every revolution until this time, Marx and Engels suggest, has used the proletariat as an ally but has never rewarded it once victory has been secured.

This is, of course, Machiavelli's explanation of political change. In order to secure or maintain its power, an elite would stir up the mass of men and with their support it would be able to put down the bids for power of rival elites. But in the end the slogans and promises held out to the man-in-the-street prove to be hollow: the new men of power govern in their own interests as did their predecessors. Century after century the working class shed its blood that others might profit. The talk of liberty and equality held out to induce their participation was a snare and a delusion. The time has come, Marx and Engels now say, when the proletariat can no longer be deluded. After centuries of broken promises and generations of unbroken elite rule, the working class will have learned some of the lessons of political life. Having again and again been manipulated so as to fight for the interests of the bourgeoisie, they will eventually come to see that they have interests of their own. "The proletarian movement is the self-conscious, independent movement of the immense majority, in the interest of the immense majority," Marx and Engels write.[55] And here, too, they break company with Machiavelli's realism. Once the proletariat becomes class-conscious and organizes as a class it will be possible to base a revolution on majority will and build a government on majority rule. With the proletarian revolution, the epoch of minority rule is forever over. No longer will there be self-interested elites; no longer will power gravitate to the hands of the few.

The aim of the revolution is to expropriate the expropriators. Marx and Engels are frank with the bourgeoisie: "You reproach us with intending to do away with your property," they write. "Precisely so; that is just what we intend." [56] The revolution is to be social and economic: the citadels of capital-

---

[54] *Ibid.*, p. 43.
[55] *Ibid.*, p. 44.
[56] *Ibid.*, p. 49.

ism are to be attacked. And they are to be attacked at their foundation: the time is past when forays at the political superstructure can be deemed sufficient.

If society is to be reconstructed from the bottom up, then private ownership of the productive processes must be done away with. If the proletariat is to create a society where the majority will truly rule, then the inordinate power of the bourgeoisie must be toppled. That power is essentially economic power: a minority rules because it owns and controls the instruments of production in society. By having this means of control, the bourgeoisie is able to make its influence felt on every aspect of social life. Bourgeois property is the underpinning of a bourgeois society: if a new society is to be brought into being, then the dominant class must be stripped of the weapons which gives it its power. Only by revolution can this be accomplished: lesser political means are useless for an endeavor this sweeping.

Marx and Engels do not elaborate on the strategy of revolution, but it is clear that force and violence are the order of the day. "Every real revolution is a social one, in that it brings a new class to power and allows it to remodel society in its own image," Engels says.[57] The old ruling class will not give up its power peacefully or voluntarily, especially when it knows that it will have no privileged status in the new society. If change is to be significant, then bloodshed will be the rule rather than the exception. "Force is the midwife of every old society pregnant with a new one," Marx says.[58] Only by civil war will the proletariat be able to wrest control over the instruments from the bourgeoisie.

Nor ought this transformation be looked at in terms which are too narrowly economic. Marx and Engels are saying that a whole social class must be destroyed. It is necessary to strip the bourgeoisie of its property: for so long as it controls the productive process, it remains the ruling class. Those capitalists who put up a struggle must be killed, imprisoned, or exiled; those who surrender must be forced to join the proletariat. "With the change of the economic foundation the entire immense superstructure is more or less rapidly transformed," Marx says.[59] Only if private property is abolished at the root can law and politics, religion and philosophy, art and literature—indeed, the whole pattern of capitalist culture—be changed. This is to be a revolution to end all revolutions.

With the success of the proletarian revolution, a new era is ushered in. In the wake of the destruction of bourgeois property there follows the abolition of

[57] Engels, *Social Relations in Russia*, in *Selected Works*, Vol. II, p. 49.
[58] Marx, *Capital*, p. 824.
[59] Marx, *Preface to "A Contribution to the Critique of Political Economy,"* p. 363.

all classes and class antagonisms. There is no longer the need for organized force, for the tensions of capitalism have been for once and all obviated. And, as the capstone of Marxist political theory, the state disappears from the social scene. Engels describes this process, and in doing so he draws together the many strands of the Marxist analysis.

The proletariat seizes the state power, and transforms the means of production in the first instance into state property. But in doing this, it puts an end to all class differences and antagonisms, it puts an end also to the state as the state. Former society, moving in class antagonisms, had need of the state, that is, an organization of the exploiting class at each period for the maintenance of its external conditions of production; that is, therefore, for the forcible holding down of the exploited class in the conditions of oppression (slavery, villeinage or serfdom, wage labor) determined by the existing mode of production. The state was the official representative of society as a whole, its embodiment in a visible corporation; but it was this only in so far as it was the state of that class which itself, in its epoch, represented society as a whole; in ancient times, the state of the slave-owning citizens; in the Middle Ages, of the feudal nobility; in our own epoch, of the bourgeoisie. When ultimately it becomes really representative of society as a whole, it makes itself superfluous. As soon as there is no longer any class of society to be held in subjection; as soon as, along with class domination and the struggle for individual existence based on the former anarchy of production, the collisions and excesses arising from these have been abolished, there is nothing more to be repressed which would make a special repressive force, or state, necessary. The first act in which the state really comes forward as the representative of society as a whole—the taking possession of the means of production in the name of society— is at the same time its last independent act as a state. The interference of the state power in social relations becomes superfluous in one sphere after another, and then ceases of itself. The government of persons is replaced by the administration of things and the direction of the process of production. The state is not "abolished," it withers away.[60]

For once the state has met its match: the organized proletariat is able to confront force with force, and in this case the side with overwhelming numbers is victorious. Once productive property has been nationalized, classes disappear. Society is now one large, unified class, and it is unnecessary to speak of it as a class at all. Under capitalism the only rationale for the state was to keep order among conflicting classes, but now the state has lost its reason for being. Power politics are replaced by the science of administration. There is no need for a state, and, sensing this, the apparatus withers away.

Is violent revolution a necessary condition of Marxist theory? The stakes are so high and the objectives so sweeping that it would appear that only by this means can such radical reforms be secured. Furthermore the Marxist dialectic, no less than the Hegelian, calls for cataclysmic change when thesis and antithesis face each other on the battlefield of history. New societies are only

[60] Engels, Anti-Duhring, pp. 388–389.

built on the ruins of those that precede them, and for the new foundation to be a strong one, the existing structure must be leveled to the ground. Yet, for all this, the theory is not so dogmatic as not to admit of exceptions. The admission that violent means are not the only ones for transferring power is made at least once by Marx. The goal of proletarian supremacy remains always the same; however, there is more than one way to achieve this end. "We do not assert that the way to reach this goal is the same everywhere," he says. "We know that the institutions, manners, and customs of the various countries must be considered, and we do not deny that there are countries like England and America . . . where the worker may attain his object by peaceful means." [61] It will take all the imagination of the student of political theory to reconcile this statement with all that has gone previously. After Marx and Engels have shown that the contradictions of capitalism are bound to erupt in violence, after they have demonstrated that a new society can only rise out of the ashes of the old, it is no small reversal to say that a peaceful path to socialism does exist. Furthermore, the capitalist state was always characterized as an institution whose sole purpose is to support the interests of private property. To suggest that the working class can achieve its ends by working through that state is, again, an avowal that democratic politics can be supreme over capitalist economics.

If Marx is prepared to grant that Britain and America and perhaps a few other countries will tolerate peaceful social reform, it must be acknowledged that these countries are exceptional instances. Marx allows the possibility of peaceful change for societies where democratic institutions are mature. For the majority of nations, however, Marxist theory would insist that peaceful means are neither available nor possible. The reason for this is that if the proletariat formed itself into a constitutional political party and tried to get its representatives elected to office, there is a good chance that the bourgeoisie itself would abandon its commitment to constitutional methods of change and would marshal its resources to put down the working class by violent means. This would be all the more likely if the proletarian party openly stated that its intention, on gaining control of the state, would be to abolish private property and the capitalist class.

A revolutionary program, even if it professes an adherence to a peaceful transition, may well be met by counterrevolution. Marx and Engels would anticipate such a reaction by the bourgeoisie, and therefore the working class is advised to take the offensive. In addition to this, it must be recalled that Marxist theory speaks of social change which reaches to the very foundations

[61] Quoted in Hans Kelsen, *The Political Theory of Bolshevism* (Berkeley and Los Angeles: University of California Press, 1948), p. 41.

of society. An entire culture must be replaced by a radically new way of life. If the proletariat tries to work through the constituted political institutions, it will discover the severe limitations which are imposed on the legislative process. For the working class is a majority, and its acts would clearly be regarded as majority tyranny by groups whose interests would suffer by social reforms. All the constitutional forces designed to protect the rights of minorities would be ranged against the enactments of a proletarian legislature. And if the objective is to create a new society, then statute law will be found to be a less than adequate instrument for changing the attitudes and practices of those who have little sympathy with the aims of the new regime.

The general rule, then, is that violent revolution is the only means for bringing the dialectic to its next stage. The exceptions to this rule are only possibilities, and hazardous possibilities at that. That Marx and Engels feel compelled to prescribe force is made all the more evident when they discuss the infancy of the new society.

SOCIALIST DICTATORSHIP

The socialist society, in theory at least, is a society without power. The proletariat organizes and fights as a unified class; and when victory is won, it puts down its weapons, never to pick them up again. Marx and Engels describe what will happen when property is socialized and classes are no more:

When, in the course of development, class distinctions have disappeared, and all production has been concentrated in the hands of a vast association of the whole nation, the public power will lose its political character. Political power, properly so called, is merely the organized power of one class for oppressing another. If the proletariat during its contest with the bourgeoisie is compelled, by the force of circumstances, to organize itself as a class, if, by means of a revolution, it makes itself the ruling class, and, as such, sweeps away by force the old conditions of production, then it will, along with these conditions, have swept away the conditions for the existence of class antagonisms and of classes generally, and will thereby have abolished its own supremacy as a class.

In place of the old bourgeois society, with its classes and class antagonisms, we shall have an association, in which the free development of each is the condition for the free development of all.[62]

What is being observed is the passing of politics. Political processes—those involving interests and power—are replaced by social processes. Productive property now belongs to all of society and not to a single class: men are no longer employers and employees, exploiters and exploited, but equal human beings in a free society. "The society that will organize production on the basis of a free and equal association of the producers will put the whole machinery

[62] Marx and Engels, *Communist Manifesto*, p. 54.

of the state where it will then belong: into the Museum of Antiquities, by the side of the spinning wheel and the bronze axe," Engels says.[63] Cooperation replaces conflict, agreement replaces antagonism, a common purpose replaces coercive power. With the end of the old order the dialectic enters a new era: socialism marks a new epoch in the life of man. "This social formation brings, therefore, the prehistory of human society to a close," Marx says.[64] The history of mankind has really been prehistory: a world of class struggle and human enslavement. Now men may begin for the first time as free individuals: a history worthy of that name has been born.

Yet history and prehistory have between them a tremendous gulf. The proletarian revolution may be consummated in several earth-shaking days, yet the two ways of life are separated by values which are centuries apart. The morning after the revolution will not unveil the new society even if the night before every capitalist has been drowned in his own blood. Bourgeois habits and attitudes are the products of centuries, and they cannot be abolished in a day. Marx and Engels therefore postulate that there will have to be a transition period during which the last vestiges of capitalist culture are removed. "Between capitalist and communist society lies a period of revolutionary transformation from one to the other," Marx says. "There corresponds also to this a political transition period during which the state can be nothing else than the revolutionary dictatorship of the proletariat." [65]

This period may be called socialism, and it should be distinguished from communism, which will emerge as the new society reaches its full stage of development. The socialist dictatorship keeps the revolution alive: it uses the power of the bourgeois state it has captured to consolidate its revolutionary gains. Talk of a free association must be postponed until there is certainty that the bourgeoisic has been completely destroyed. Dictatorial methods are necessary because the capitalist remnants will fight back if given the slightest opportunity: owners of property have the resources with which to fight many a delaying skirmish. There can be no thought that the deposed ruling class will hand over its wealth voluntarily. The armed working class will use the power of the state to expropriate the means of production.

"The proletariat will use its political supremacy to wrest, by degrees, all capital from the bourgeoisie, to centralize all instruments of production in the hands of the state, i.e., of the proletariat organized as the ruling class," Marx and Engels write.[66] And they have no illusions that this will be a short or sim-

[63] Engels, *The Origin of the Family*, p. 292.
[64] Marx, *Preface to "A Contribution to the Critique of Political Economy,"* p. 364.
[65] Marx, *Critique of the Gotha Programme,* in *Selected Works*, Vol. II, p. 30.
[66] Marx and Engels, *Communist Manifesto*, p. 53.

ple matter: the danger of counterrevolutionary outbreaks is great, and force must be on hand to suppress such tendencies. The socialist dictatorship will use the state's power of coercion so long as there are enemies lurking in the proletarian camp. Marx and Engels do not say how long this transitional period is to be, how long oppressive measures are necessary. It is not unlikely that society will be an armed camp for at least a generation, and probably more than that. For the danger to be repressed is not so much bourgeois gunfire as it is bourgeois sentiments in the minds and hearts of men.

Socialist dictatorship and political repression are made necessary by the fact that the proletarian revolution has, like all important historical transformations, been part of the dialectical process. "What we have to deal with here is a . . . society," Marx says, "not as if it had developed on a basis of its own, but on the contrary as it emerges from capitalist society, which is thus in every respect tainted economically, morally, and intellectually with the hereditary diseases of the old society from whose womb it is emerging." [67] If bourgeois society is the thesis and the proletarian movement is the antithesis, then the synthesis which emerges will inevitably contain some elements of the old order. Bourgeois society had two features of importance, an industrial technology and a system of private ownership. The socialist society destroys private ownership and places all the productive processes under public control; but at the same time it retains the high level of technology developed under capitalism and, indeed, will carry it to further heights. Yet the dialectical movement is not this simple; even though the institution of private property is abolished by the revolutionary act, there linger on in individuals the attitudes and habits which centuries of capitalist culture have inculcated.

Perhaps the chief task of the socialist dictatorship, then, is not coercion but rather education. While it is important to render powerless the bourgeois dissidents who remain alive, it is even more important to condition the minds of the coming generations who are yet to be born. The proletarian state, for example, will probably want to take children from their parents and teach them the principles of communism. For if youngsters are left too much with their fathers and mothers—who knew capitalist society at first-hand—then they might be contaminated with the values of the old regime.

The socialist transition, in short, will not be an easy one. If the new society is to make the best use of the human resources available to it, it may even have to make temporary compromises. While Marxist theory is Utopian in many respects, it is very much aware of the practical problems which arise when a new social order is abuilding. A good illustration of this is the material question of wages and incentives. Under capitalism men were taught to believe

[67] Marx, Critique of the Gotha Programme, p. 21.

that their labor was a commodity and that they were justified in selling it to the highest bidder. This attitude will linger on in many minds even after the revolution, and the chances are that it will be retained especially by the men who will be needed for the vital jobs in the socialist society. That is, the industrial managers and technicians, the professional men and the civil servants cannot be dispensed with if there is to be material progress. Individuals such as these cannot be impressed into service: their talents must be bought at what is actually a market rate. And the socialist society must pay this rate. Therefore, socialism will still have the inequalities of income known under capitalism. Bourgeois incentives will have to be employed by the state if the society is to advance. "These deficiencies are unavoidable in the first phase . . . when it is just emerging after prolonged birthpangs from capitalist society," Marx says. "Right can never be higher than the economic structure and the cultural development of society conditioned by it." [68] The conception that economic equality is just and right will take time to become established. Coming generations of managers and technicians will be taught to work for noneconomic incentives; but until these individuals are trained—both technically and ideologically—society will have to retain the existing economic values.

At least one force militates in this direction: while the first generation of managers and technicians may have to be highly paid, they will not be allowed to possess private property. This means that they will not have wealth, in the form of stocks or similar securities, which they can pass on to their children. They may have fine houses and fancy cars, but these are the property of the state: they are, in effect, loaned to men of talent so long as they perform needed services. Therefore, this group comprises an elite rather than a ruling class: it will not be able to give its private property over to its children, nor will these offspring receive any competitive advantages. Presumably inheritance taxes will be confiscatory, and the sons and daughters of the elite will be educated and employed along with everyone else in their generation. This will have the consequence that the emerging socialist elite, recruited and trained in the new social order, will not need the high salaries or the material comforts that their bourgeois predecessors required as an incentive.

If all of this sounds familiar, it is so simply because it is a revival of Plato's problem: how does a society create an elite which is dedicated to furthering explicit social values? For Marx and Engels, however, the problem is more acute because their Utopia must grow out of existing society through the tortuous dialectic. Rather than painting a picture with words alone, they seek to discover the means by which the transformation may actually be achieved. And Marxist communism differs from its Platonic counterpart in

[68] *Ibid.*, p. 23.

that Marx and Engels sought to secure a society in which all men would stand as equals in economic and noneconomic terms.

The communist elite is not a group set apart, but rather stands on an equal footing with its fellow citizens. And all individuals in the communist Utopia, not simply the elite, are expected to abide by the high principles of human conduct called for by the new stage of history. The socialist transition, therefore, will exhibit mixed tendencies. First, it will be dictatorial toward the remaining bourgeois elements. Second, it will compromise its principles and meet the economic demands of the personnel it needs for vital jobs. Third, it will educate the oncoming generations for their new life in the communist epoch.

Will the dictatorship of the proletariat be able to carry out these three tasks simultaneously? No small effort will be required if it is to be ensured that the first and second functions are means to a higher end and not ends in themselves. Repression of reactionary elements must cease when the property-owners are under control: coercion must never be visited upon members of the proletariat unless there is conclusive proof that they are secret agents of the old order. Compromise to bourgeois values must be a temporary policy and cease as new elites are recruited: material rewards must not be held out as a permanent incentive, as this will prolong the evil of economic inequality. And education for communist life must at all times be the sovereign obligation of the socialist state. Marx and Engels realize that this transition stage will be a difficult one; they also believe that it will in time come to an end.

THE COMMUNIST UTOPIA

When the last vestiges of bourgeois culture have faded away, it will be possible for the socialist dictatorship to bow from the scene as well. The communism which has been developing slowly in the years succeeding the revolution now comes into full flower. The communist society has most of the attributes of the Utopias known to political theory; however, there are sufficient differences of emphasis and direction so that it is worth spelling out the major outlines of the community Marx and Engels have in mind.

(1) A communist society is, first of all, an equalitarian society. All men stand on an equal plane, and all are respected simply for being individuals. There is no ruling class: this is necessarily so because private property has been abolished and classes are based on property. There are elites, but these are individuals of talent who are freshly recruited each generation to do specific jobs that society requires to be done. There will be administrators and artists, scientists and sculptors, managers and musicians. But these talented

men and women will have no greater social status than the farmer or the factory worker. For all are employed in useful labor, and no function is qualitatively superior to any other.

The best evidence of this is that men and women will be paid not on the basis of what they could command in an open market but according to a far more rational standard. "In a higher phase of communist society . . ." Marx says, "only then can the narrow horizon of bourgeois rights be crossed in its entirety and society inscribe on its banners: From each according to his ability, to each according to his needs!" [69] The plumber with five children will receive a higher salary than the poet with two. But another poet who requires a special diet because of a physical infirmity will be paid more than a plumber in an otherwise similar condition of life. Presumably a Benthamite calculus of pleasures will be drawn up, and all in society will share the public resources so that each will receive the same intensity of happiness. Thus, one man whose pleasure requires that he have a grand piano will be given one, whereas another who gets equal happiness out of pinochle will be pleased to settle for a deck of cards. The point is that all men give their labor gladly and to the best of their ability, and their reward is the knowledge that they have made a worthwhile contribution to society. Material incentives are rendered superfluous, for the needs of men are satisfied on an equitable and scientific basis.

(2) The state, as Engels points out, will wither away. Coercion and power will cease to exist. Indeed, the communist society will be a society without politics. Men will cease to be citizens and will become free individuals who gather together in a voluntary association. "The working class, in the course of its development, will substitute for the old civil society an association which will exclude classes and their antagonism," Marx says. "There will be no more political power properly so-called, since political power is precisely the official expression of antagonism in civil society." [70] Everyone is now a worker, either of hand or brain, and society constitutes a single class—which is to say no class at all. There are no longer clashes of interests, because interests are based on property ownership and that has been abolished. With the demise of political conflict, a state is no longer needed. Engels suggests that once counterrevolutionary elements have been destroyed the state will divest itself of its power to coerce the individual. Communist society will not have a free government or political freedom, for it will have no government and politics at all.

As, therefore, the state is only a transitional institution which is used in the struggle in the revolution, in order to hold down one's adversaries by force, it is

[69] Ibid.
[70] Marx, The Poverty of Philosophy, p. 197.

pure nonsense to talk of a free people's state: so long as the proletariat still uses the state, it does not use it in the interests of freedom but in order to hold down its adversaries, and as soon as it becomes possible to speak of freedom the state as such ceases to exist. We would therefore propose to replace "state" everywhere by "community." [71]

Marx and Engels do not concern themselves, as Rousseau did, with the problem of public participation in the political process. Questions of democracy and self-government are no longer relevant, because power will no longer be exercised by man over man. Life becomes associational rather than political. There need be no guarantee of individual rights, because there is no state to trespass on rights and society has no coercive power over its members. Indeed, the whole conception of individual freedom and the rights of man is questioned by Marx and Engels. To a man like Locke they say, "You must therefore confess that by 'individual' you mean no other person than the bourgeois, than the middle-class owner of property." [72] And rights, in actual practice, turn out to be property rights. As these can only be exercised meaningfully by the capitalist class, the so-called rights of life, liberty, and the pursuit of happiness which are guaranteed to all men are actually hollow promises for most men. "Capitalist production takes care to ensure that the great majority of those with equal rights shall get only what is essential for bare existence," Engels says. "Capitalist production has, therefore, little more respect, if indeed any more, for the equal right to the pursuit of happiness of the majority than had slavery or serfdom." [73] The communist answer is that every one of the traditional political goals is made irrelevant by the emergence of a community with no need of state or citizens. Men have perfect freedom, and, what is more, they do not have to secure it by a constant and vigilant pursuit of their inherent rights.

(3) The government of persons, Engels also predicts, will be replaced by the administration of things. In communist society industrial management will be science: if discipline must be exercised, it will be in the form of control over not men but machines. The communist world will be highly industrialized, and probably few areas will remain untouched by technological progress. Here again Marx and Engels depart from Rousseau as they reject the idea of a small and pastoral Utopia. Communism takes over the industrial technology of capitalism and improves on it. But the old inequities of exploitation and profit-making will be gone: workers will acknowledge that the mode of production and the new relations of production are now in harmony. Public

[71] Engels, Letter to Bebel, in *Selected Works*, Vol. II, p. 39.
[72] Marx and Engels, *Communist Manifesto*, p. 49.
[73] Engels, *Ludwig Feuerbach*, p. 347.

ownership and public service will endow the productive process with a self-evident rationality, and for this reason the industrial scene will be harmonious. Any changes made will presumably be made on scientific grounds, and workers will understand and accept the reasons which are advanced for them.[74]

In fact Marx and Engels are so optimistic in their forecast about industrial progress that they see what can only be called the automated factory. Working hours will become shorter and shorter as fewer and fewer human hands are needed to do particular jobs. The result will be that the division of labor, the process whereby a man devotes his working life to a single monotonous and repetitive task, will no longer be required. "In time to come there will no longer be any professional porters or architects," Engels says. "The man who for half an hour gives instructions as an architect will also act as a porter for a period, until his activity as an architect is once again required." [75] Whereas the capitalist technology fragmented the worker's labor, and thus mutilated his life, the communist technology will be so far advanced and so automatic that each man will be able to employ his full talents in a wide variety of pursuits.

> In communist society, where nobody has one exclusive sphere of activity but each can become accomplished in any branch he wishes, society regulates the general production and thus makes it possible for me to do one thing to-day and another to-morrow, to hunt in the morning, fish in the afternoon, rear cattle in the evening, criticize after dinner, just as I have a mind, without ever becoming hunter, fisherman, shepherd or critic.[76]

Men are no longer to be bound by their occupational roles, but they become integrated human beings: the individual leads a life, not a career. Thus a rational social plan makes men ends in themselves rather than means to an end. And with these developments ends the alienation of human beings. The concurrent abolition of private property and fragmented labor brings men to a true compatibility with their fellow men and the forces of nature. Marx defines communism in these terms:

> Communism is the positive abolition of private property, of human self alienation, and thus, the real appropriation of human nature, through and for man. It is therefore the return of man himself as a social, that is really human, being, a complete and conscious return which assimilates all the wealth of previous development. Communism as a complete naturalism is humanism, and as a complete humanism is naturalism. It is the definitive resolution of the antagonism between man and Nature, and between man and man. It is the true solution of the conflict

[74] For an expansion of this theme on lines which parallel those of Marxist theory, see Elton Mayo, *The Social Problems of an Industrial Civilization* (Boston: Harvard University, Graduate School of Business Administration, 1945).

[75] Engels, *Anti-Duhring*, p. 278.

[76] Marx and Engels, *German Ideology*, p. 22.

between existence and essence, between objectification and self-affirmation, between freedom and necessity, between individual and species. It is the solution of the riddle of history and knows itself to be this solution.[77]

The communist conception of freedom is not totally dissimilar from that advanced by Plato and Aristotle and Rousseau and Burke. It rejects, first of all, the liberal idea of freedom because that theory can only benefit a small minority in society. Furthermore, it regards genuine freedom as a product of life in an integrated community. Man reaches his highest liberty as a social being. "Only in community with others has each individual the means of cultivating his gifts in all directions; only in the community, therefore, is personal freedom possible," Marx and Engels write.[78] The communist world is not held together by a Guardian class, as Plato's community was; nor is it made cohesive by constant political participation, as was Rousseau's; nor is it built on class and custom, as was Burke's. Marx and Engels predict a rational society, but they make no provision for an elite of planners; they forecast a harmony of interests, and they see no need for institutions to ameliorate conflict. But they are writing a Utopian scheme, and their image of the way things will be cannot be criticized because it is not something else.

And what of the dialectic? Does it, with the end of prehistory and the commencement of history, grind slowly to a halt? It may be too much to ask a theorist that comes *after* his Utopia: he has taken one gigantic step into the future and he ought not to be made to create another such leap. Marx and Engels believe that the dialectic is an eternal and undying process: in this they are in agreement with Hegel. "Communism is the necessary form and the active principle of the immediate future," Marx says, "but communism is not the aim of human development or the final form of human society." [79] One hint has been given: men turn their attention from exploiting each other and bend their efforts to a conquest of the forces in nature. Yet this does not answer the big question. We do not know what antithesis is building up in the womb of communist society. Perhaps Nature herself will rebel at the uses men have made of her and will destroy the human race with a revolutionary explosion. But this speculation is one that Marx and Engels are themselves unwilling to make.

IDEAS AND IDEOLOGY

Marx and Engels, like many of their predecessors, take time to theorize about the role of ideas in human history. At the very beginning they make

[77] Marx, *Economic and Philosophical Manuscripts*, pp. 243–244.
[78] Marx and Engels, *German Ideology*, p. 74.
[79] Marx, *Economic and Philosophical Manuscripts*, p. 246.

clear their rejection of Hegel's idealism: for them only the material world is real; ideas are not independent forces but are expressions of material conditions. The Marxist dialectic gains its motion from the clash between technological and property relationships: indeed, it could be suggested that men need not think at all and historical development would nevertheless proceed in its determined course.

At the same time, Marx and Engels themselves are theorists, men of ideas, and they feel obliged to explain how the thoughts of men fit into their political system.

The production of ideas, of conceptions, of consciousness, is at first directly interwoven with the material activity and the material intercourse of men, the language of real life. Conceiving, thinking, the mental intercourse of men, appear at this stage as the direct efflux of their material behavior. The same applies to mental production as expressed in the language of the politics, laws, morality, religion, metaphysics of a people. Men are the producers of their conceptions, ideas, etc.—real, active men, as they are conditioned by a definite development of their productive forces and of the intercourse corresponding to these, up to its furthest forms. Consciousness can never be anything else than conscious existence, and the existence of men is their actual life-process.[80]

This is, of course, a direct reply to Hegel. Marx and Engels deny that there exists any such thing as the *Idea:* men, they say, create their own ideas—their mental expressions are not simply pale reflections of some overlooming essence which pervades the universe. However, the ideas which men develop rise out of the material conditions they have experienced. The intellect is shaped by the technological environment more than by any other force. If ideas change over time, as they do, this is because the material world is in a process of dialectical change as well. "Does it require deep intuition to comprehend that man's ideas, views, and conceptions, in one word, man's consciousness, changes with every change in the condition of his material existence, in his social relations and in his social life?" Marx and Engels ask.[81] There is little point, they would go on, in studying the history of political thought, for these ideas are but the surface manifestations of more profound material forces.

True history, according to Marxist theory, is the history of technology and economic and social history. Ideas only show their meaning if the material substructure which produces them is understood. Furthermore, the important men are neither the theorists nor the politicians. If any individuals are to be singled out, they are the entrepreneurs: the industrial pioneers who develop new processes of production and who have the will to establish them in the

---

[80] Marx and Engels, *German Ideology*, pp. 13–14.
[81] Marx and Engels, *Communist Manifesto*, p. 52.

social framework. These are Marx and Engels' equivalents of the Hegelian Heroes. For the most part they are names which will be forgotten after a generation or two, but they more than anyone else are the men who help to make history.

What usually passes for political theory, therefore, is ideology. Theoretical schemes are but rationalizations of the material status quo, and theorists write as they do because their thinking is shaped by the society they know. Actually, these rationalizations can take two forms. There are, first of all, theories which serve to justify things as they are: these may be said to be verbal defenses of the dialectical thesis. A writer such as Burke, for example, serves as an ideologue for the prevailing order—or the order which is about to be challenged by rising forces in society. Other theories, Marx and Engels would say, give expression to the dialectical antithesis: they explain and defend new classes which are making a bid for power. Locke, for example, provides an ideology for emerging men of property who seek to break down the prevailing economic system.

But whether we are dealing with ideologies of the status quo or ideologies of social change, we are still dealing with ideologies. Ideas are always bound up with interests, and for this reason theories distort reality so as to make a particular case. Each theorist does not describe or analyze the world as it actually is. On the contrary, even the man of ideas has a stake in the material world, and his generalizations will depict not politics as they are but politics as he would like to have them be. The great problem is that the theorist usually does not realize that he is bound by such interests: he is blind to the fact that what he sees is a partial and distorted reality. For this reason, Engels prefers to speak of ideology rather than of theory when it comes to political thought.

> Ideology is a process accomplished by the so-called thinker consciously, it is true, but with a false consciousness. The real motive forces impelling him remain unknown to him: otherwise it simply would not be an ideological process. Hence he imagines false or seeming motive forces. Because it is a process of thought he derives its form as well as its content from pure thought, either his own or that of his predecessors. He works with mere thought material, which he accepts without examination as the product of thought, and does not investigate further for a more remote source independent of thought; indeed, this is a matter of course to him, because, as all action is mediated by thought, it appears to him to be ultimately based upon thought.[82]

It is the responsibility of the theorist to show that he is in touch with the material world. He must understand that even his own ideas are a product of his

---

[82] Engels, Letter to Mehring, *Selected Works*, Vol. II, p. 451. For the classic analysis of ideology, see Karl Mannheim, *Ideology and Utopia* (New York: Harcourt, Brace, 1936).

environment. Many thinkers tend to live in a world of abstract ideas, and this leads them to believe that ideas develop out of other ideas. What they fail to realize, Marx and Engels suggest, is that they also live in the real world, and they may be blinding themselves to the fact that material conditions shape the outlines of their theories.

All men are members of one class or another, and each class tends to take a particular view of social and economic arrangements. The material world, therefore, presents a different image to individuals who are located at different points on the social structure. The average member of the bourgeoisie sees politics in one way; the average proletarian sees the identical process in quite another. Marx and Engels address their *Communist Manifesto*, for example, to the working class. They do not expect that their bourgeois readers will find any meaning in it that is relevant to their experience. "Don't wrangle with us . . ." they write. "Your very ideas are but the outgrowth of the conditions of your bourgeois production and bourgeois property." [83] Only a proletarian who has attained to the level of class-consciousness is able to perceive the truth in Marxist theory. For this theory challenges the bourgeois ideology which prevails in capitalist societies. Those who have a vested interest in capitalism are incapable of understanding the antithesis which is rising in their midst. On this basis, of course, all critics of Marxist theory are immediately disarmed. Anyone who finds objections may be labeled a prisoner of capitalist ideology and someone with a vested interested in the prevailing order.

It is conventional to ask at this juncture how two intellectuals like Marx and Engels can free themselves from the psychological chains which bind most men of ideas. They have anticipated this question, and they provide an answer. On the eve of the revolution, they say, a few members of the bourgeoisie will attach themselves to the proletarian movement.

> When the class struggle nears the decisive hour, . . . a small section of the ruling class cuts itself adrift, and joins the revolutionary class, the class that holds the future in its hands. Just as, therefore, at an earlier period, a section of the nobility went over to the bourgeoisie, now a portion of the bourgeoisie goes over to the proletariat, and in particular, a portion of the bourgeois ideologists, who have raised themselves to the level of comprehending theoretically the historical movement as a whole.[84]

The minority of bourgeois intellectuals who can detect the course of the dialectic cease to be prisoners of ideology and now become true theorists. These individuals rise above their class ties, and their minds are liberated from the distorted image of capitalist reality. Only a few members of the

[83] Marx and Engels, *Communist Manifesto*, p. 49.
[84] *Ibid.*, p. 43.

capitalist class will experience this moment of truth: most are too involved with the status quo to adjust their perceptions of the world. It is not possible to predict who will make this shift, which is both intellectual and political. Marx and Engels clearly believe that they are among the favored few. And that such a minority must exist, they say, is borne out by the evidence of history. The proletariat, like all revolutionary groups before it, needs its intellectuals—and Marx and Engels are prepared to fill this role.

The determinist element in Marxist theory is a powerful one. There are constant allusions to the inexorable character of the dialectic and the inevitability of revolutionary change. Marx and Engels claim to have discovered the central forces which shape the structure of society and give direction to its development. These material forces set the limits within which men may and must act. It is idle, they say, to talk of pure freedom. With Hegel, they agree that men must first know what is necessary and what is not. If a man is to be free, he must be aware of the forces external to him which draw the boundaries inside of which he can make choices. "Freedom does not consist in the dream of independence from natural laws, but in the knowledge of these laws, and in the possibility this gives of systematically making them work toward definite ends," Engels says. "Freedom therefore consists in the control over ourselves and over external nature, a control founded on knowledge of natural necessity." [85]

The student of the dialectic will understand the laws of historical materialism: he will come to realize how far he may make decisions as a free agent and how far he must bow to the inevitable march of events. The individual who supposes that he has perfect freedom will experience continual frustration: he will be constantly thwarted by circumstances he neither understands nor can control. The most obvious example of a force which cannot be controlled is technological progress. Men may destroy machines or enact laws to restrict their efficient operating, but in the final analysis the machine will have its way and men will be forced to submit to the mode of life it imposes.

Yet, despite all the talk of inevitability and determinism, Marx and Engels allow to men far more freedom than did Hegel. For Hegel's conclusion was that the individual should strive to understand the workings of the *Idea*: any serious attempt to act contrary to it would come to no good end. Marxist theory embodies a call to action, and it tries to balance its determinist strand with a measure of human choice. "Men make their own history, but they do not make it just as they please," Marx says. "They do not make it under circumstances chosen by themselves, but under circumstances directly en-

[85] Engels, *Anti-Duhring*, p. 158.

countered, given and transmitted from the past." [86] Engels elaborates on this theme:

> Men make their history themselves, but not as yet with a collective will according to a collective plan. . . . Their aspirations clash, and for that very reason all such societies are governed by necessity, which is complemented by and appears under the form of accident. The necessity which here asserts itself athwart all accident is again ultimately economic necessity.
> This is where the so-called great men come in for treatment. That such and such a man and precisely that man arises at a particular time in a particular country is, of course, pure chance. But cut him out and there will be a demand for a substitute, and this substitute will be found, good or bad, but in the long run he will be found. That Napoleon, just that particular Corsican, should have been the military dictator whom the French Republic, exhausted by its own warfare, had rendered necessary, was chance; but that, if a Napoleon had been lacking, another would have filled the place, is proved by the fact that the man was always found as soon as he became necessary: Caesar, Augustus, Cromwell, etc.[87]

And it is on this ground that Marx and Engels would explain whatever role in history might be theirs. The conditions of their time called them into being and caused them to write as they did. Had they never been born or had they exercised their talents in other directions, two other writers would have emerged to say much the same things. There is little room for great men—men of thought or of action—in Marxist theory. If Marx and Engels are thought of by some as having made history, they would be bound to reply that their times called out for theorists to explain the proletarian revolution, and it was pure chance that they and not someone else happened to undertake this task.

If men make their own history, as Marx and Engels say, then it is men as classes or as movements. Even the Napoleon or the Caesar or the Cromwell is what the sociologists call a role-player: not a personality so much as the individual who emerges into a position of leadership. Such a man stands not by himself, but at the head of a significant social group: he exerts the powers of leadership, but he is also carried along on the shoulders of those who both follow and impel him. The men who make their history, then, are those sections of society who make a break with the past and who forge ahead into the future. At one time the bourgeoisie had this role: now it is the proletariat. In part men move themselves, in part they are moved by forces they but dimly comprehend.

On one thing, however, Marx and Engels are clear: ideas play little or no part in the making of history. "The ultimate causes of all social changes and political revolutions," Engels says, "are to be sought, not in the minds of men, but in

---

[86] Marx, *Eighteenth Brumaire*, p. 247.
[87] Engels, Letter to Starkenburgh, *Selected Works*, Vol. II, p. 458.

the changes in the mode of production and exchange." [88] To be sure, if men are to act politically, they must use words to exhort and mobilize; and this political rhetoric may lead the observer to believe that ideas are what are leading men to move in new directions. This, Marx and Engels say, is a superficial analysis. "When people speak of ideas that revolutionize society," they write, "they do but express the fact, that within the old society, the elements of a new one have been created, and that the dissolution of the old ideas keeps even pace with the dissolution of the old conditions of existence." [89]

Revolutionary ideas are but words and phrases put in the mouths of ideologues by social movements which proceed in their historically determined course. The minds of both intellectuals and practical men are given their shape by the social and technological conditions they know. New ideas replace old ideas as new modes and relations of production replace old modes and relations of production. Men's minds cannot be too far behind or too far ahead of the machines at which they work. The area of freedom is found in the opportunity for emerging classes to grasp the new ideas which express the new social order. Marx and Engels close their *Communist Manifesto* with the plea: "Working men of all countries unite!" The proletarian is free to realize that he is a proletarian; he is free to join with his fellow workers in the revolution which will overturn capitalism and open the way for communism. There is much that is frankly hortatory in the writings of Marx and Engels. Yet here, too, they would not say that their ideas were what would impel men to political action. The working class, they would suggest, is now historically ready to play its revolutionary role, and history calls forth a few intellectuals to express in words the tendencies which material conditions have brought into being. In calling on working men of all countries to unite, Marx and Engels are presuming that this mobilization will inevitably occur, and they are not originating a battle-cry so much as they are expressing a sentiment which is already latent in society. Even without a Marx or an Engels to give intellectual shape to the proletarian revolution, that momentous event would come to pass all the same.

There is no escaping the fact that the Marxism which is here at work is ideology. Its system of ideas is based on a special view of society: a view as seen through the eyes of the proletariat. Marxism, no less than other writings, has a vested interest in a particular set of social conditions—in this case, conditions which will come into existence once the prevailing structure of society is destroyed. Marx and Engels have a stake in the future, and they therefore perceive the past and present as prelude to the world which is to come. Their

[88] Engels, *Anti-Duhring*, p. 369.
[89] Marx and Engels, *Communist Manifesto*, p. 52.

eagerness to see the future ushered in is bound to distort their image of reality. "The philosophers have only interpreted the world in various ways," Marx says. "The point, however, is to change it." [90] The goal of theory is to understand the world: the goal of ideology is to influence the course of events. If the two goals are combined, there is little doubt that theory will become transformed into ideology: the writer's perception of what the world is like will be beclouded by his vision of what it ought to be. Marx and Engels are perceptive enough to see that ideology takes its toll on all who would aspire to the role of theorist. They stop short, however, when it comes to acknowledging that they themselves might become ensnared in the ideological trap.

The claim of Marxist theory to the status of a science is often reiterated. This contention, like that of Bentham's, rests on the method of analysis which the theory employs. Bentham's utilitarianism called for the painstaking and systematic measurement of the pleasures and pains which varying policies would give to individuals in a community. Marx and Engels' science does not rely on measurement: rather, it focuses on the material, and therefore the observable, world. Scholars ought to be able to agree on what are the dominant modes of production in society, and it is hoped that they will agree that these productive processes give shape to the entire social structure. A machine, be it a bronze axe or a mass-production assembly line, can be seen and its operations can be analyzed in an objective way. Furthermore, most people will acknowledge that technology is in a constant process of change and that these changes have an impact on the life of the whole society. This, then, is the positive side of the scientific claim: Marx and Engels propose to discuss a world which can be seen and touched. It is also supposed that their hypotheses may be verified by any student who undertakes to study technological development and economic organization over the course of history.

On the negative side, Marx and Engels are explicit in their rejection of an idealist approach. The ideas discussed by Plato, Rousseau, and Hegel cannot be seen or touched, and therefore their very existence may be questioned. If these essences cannot be observed, then the theories which embody them are based on airy fictions. Similarly, the theories of Natural Law and Natural Rights are founded on empty phrases which are used by interested parties to secure goals of their own choosing. One by one, Marx and Engels would find that all theories but their own are unscientific because they utilize preconceived and unverifiable ideas. Even Bentham's utilitarianism would be rejected because it takes insufficient account of the material forces which set the conditions within which pleasures and pains are experienced.

What of the Marxist dialectic? The dialectic itself might appear to be an

[90] Marx, *Theses on Feuerbach*, in *Selected Works*, Vol. II, p. 367.

idea even though it operates on the material world. It may be granted that the technological element in the dialectic, the mode of production, is material in character. However, it is less easy to talk in scientific terms about the social strand, the relations of production. While scholars may agree on the role of the machine in society, they are less willing to concur on the parts played by property ownership and economic control. Marx and Engels assume that the relations of production have no less an objective existence than the modes of production. They look on capitalist ownership and control as a material reality in the same way that they regard industrial technology. It is at this point that the scientific claim may be most strenuously contested. For the Marxist dialectic assumes that two material forces will come into contradiction and that revolutionary upheaval will be the inevitable result. Yet it can in no way be verified that capitalism as an economic system is "incompatible" with the advanced stages of machine production. Certainly the hypothesis that modern technology is rational and private ownership is irrational is more an opinion than it is an established scientific fact. This means that one coequal part of the dialectic is incapable of being verified by the methods of science: and this is a fatal blow to the status of the historical process as described by Marx and Engels. Nevertheless, many students of politics share their opinion on the objective contradiction between these two features of contemporary society. However, a shared opinion is not a scientific truth: many theorists, after all, share Hegel's views about the role of ideas but this does not prove that these essences exist or that they have an influence in politics. In the final analysis, it is difficult to demonstrate that Marxist theory is a science in any rigorous meaning of that term. The claim to scientific status is an ideological one: it expresses the certainty in the minds of two writers that they are right and that they have the key to the future. If their claim seems an unfounded one, then the appropriate alternative is not to take it too seriously.

For the stature of Marxist theory does not depend on whether or not it is a science. It is an attempt to describe the condition of man and society in the industrial age. While both Hegel and Tocqueville gave attention to the impact of industrialization on the social and political life, it was left for Marx and Engels to make it the basis of a theory. No modern analysis of politics, whether conservative or revolutionary, can safely ignore the role of technology and economic organization. Marxist theory is not without shortcomings, and most of these stem from the fact that its authors embarked on an enterprise of sweeping magnitude. Their predictions of an inevitable future are uncompromising, and many of them clearly have not come to pass. Their materialist methodology is resolute, and the subsequent exceptions and qualification which have to be made destroy the over-all integrity of the theory. Their scientific pretensions are inadequately supported, and they serve to conceal philosophical assumptions about the good life and a rational society. And their perceptions of contemporary reality are distorted by a strong ideological bias and an interest in one class in society.

Theorists who undertake grand theoretical projects are bound to fall into greater errors than their less daring colleagues who stick to safer and surer ground; yet there will also be greater successes. There is in the writings of Marx and Engels a power of imagination and a brilliance of conception which both friends and critics are willing to acknowledge. Marxist theory will rouse emotions in the minds and hearts of men so long as it provides the basis for communist ideology. If half the world clasps the writings of Marx and Engels to its bosom and if half abhors their very existence, it is an obligation of both at least to understand what these theorists were trying to say.

14.
John Stuart Mill

THE MAN AND HIS TIMES

Mill was born in 1806 into an environment which would leave its mark on him for the rest of his life. His father was a friend of Bentham's, and the boy was early introduced into the sophisticated discourse of the Utilitarian circle. The elder Mill had strong ideas about education and saw to it that his son was learning Greek at the age of three and higher mathematics not much later. As a result, John Stuart Mill's entire life was destined to be a disciplined one: the stern regimen he followed was a product of early conditioning coupled with his own strength of character. Testimony to this is the fact that from 1823 to 1856 he was able to hold a well-paid and responsible position at the East India Company (a modern equivalent would be Standard Oil of New Jersey) and at the same time engage in extensive economic and political writing. He sat in the House of Commons for three years following his retirement from the East India Company, but his record there was not distinguished. He died in 1873, knowing that the England of his time looked on him as her foremost political theorist.

That Mill is direct heir to the Benthamite tradition is evidenced throughout his writing. But, whereas Bentham could confine his attention to the subjects of law and administration in a less hectic day, Mill lived in an age when democracy was in the ascent. Indeed, he was familiar with Tocqueville's work and had published a long and sympathetic review of Democracy in America. If he was aware of Marxist theory, however, there is no evidence that he was prepared to give it serious consideration. Mill's concern was to conjoin Bentham's principles of rational government with the emerging demands for political equality. He was a sincere democrat, and in his thinking there is very little nostalgia for aristocratic rule. At the same time, Mill understood that the business of government is complex and that qualified men must be permitted a relatively free hand if they are to be effective

571

administrators. The problem, which he spelled out in his Representative Government in 1861, is to establish a political system which will be responsive to the expressed wants of those who are governed and which will at the same time allow public officials to provide for the needs of society. Mill was a serious student of political institutions, and his prescriptions for a representative democracy were based on a close examination of parliamentary practice. The England of his time was not in a revolutionary ferment, and the established class structure of that nation checked any radical demands for sweeping democratic reform. This meant that the moderate solutions proposed by Mill were conservative enough to keep from upsetting the ruling classes and sufficiently progressive to satisfy the urge for change. That he was writing for a stable society with a constitutional tradition lends focus to his theory and occasionally gives it something of an insular cast.

The essay On Liberty, which appeared in 1859, is Mill's greatest contribution to political theory. The quest for human freedom has a long history, and it takes a wide variety of forms. What Mill argued for was not so much freedom from oppressive rule as the more positive freedom to pursue one's own thoughts and to give expression to them. The English middle class had won its battle in the economic arena and it subsequently gained political power. But after these initial conquests have been won, a middle class tends to develop interests in other aspects of what life has to offer. As its members gain the wealth and leisure to educate themselves and their children, they frequently find that their minds turn to new and unexplored avenues of thought. Some of these new ideas concern the solution of social or economic problems, but others center on art and literature and religion and the general style of life. A middle class, particularly a professional upper-middle class, contains individuals who feel the need to think freely, to criticize conventional standards, and to express themselves. Such a group was growing in Mill's time, and it provided a loyal audience for his defense of liberty. The succeeding century has become more and more an age of the middle class in the Western world, and it is not difficult to see the relevance of Mill's theory to contemporary conceptions of the good life.

14.
John Stuart Mill

IN THE WRITINGS OF JOHN STUART MILL ARE SET DOWN THE
major dilemmas of modern democracy. Here are found no metaphysical leaps
as in Hegel, no allusions to historical inevitably as in Marx and Engels, no
Utopian formulas as in Rousseau. Mill's approach is at all times a careful and
painstaking one. When he speaks of democracy, he gives close attention to
the concrete political institutions which may hopefully make that form of
government a reality. When he discusses human freedom, he lists the explicit
consequences which may be expected if men are allowed to express themselves
without hindrance.

There is much in Mill's theory that parallels Tocqueville's: in particular,
the two men share an abiding fear of tyranny by the majority. But Mill is not
nearly so prone to employ the aristocratic yardstick for evaluating democracy's
performance. On the contrary, he sees democratic government as a positive
good to be pursued and not a mixed blessing which must be tolerated because its advent is inevitable. Tocqueville's conception of liberty, furthermore,
was also an aristocratic one: he was chiefly concerned to protect the freedom
of the class in society which maintained the values and tradition of civility.
While Mill is frequently inclined to share this concern, he is no less interested
in the liberty of the individual citizen—any citizen—whose thought and action
run counter to those entertained by the majority.

Mill, then, assigns equal weight to two political values. On the one hand,
he believes that the greater number in society should be free to elect and
control their governors. In this he accepts the principle of political equality
laid down by Rousseau. On the other hand, he believes that the autonomous
individual, whether he stands alone or is part of a social minority, should be
free to think and act as his conscience dictates. Whether these two values can
thrive together in the same political framework is the problem which haunts
all of Mill's writing. His theory may best be examined by turning first to his
essay on *Representative Government* and then to his essay entitled *On Liberty*.

573

REPRESENTATIVE DEMOCRACY

Government is a purposeful enterprise. Its objective, reduced to simplest terms, is to educate its citizens. Those who hold public office must use their power to develop human potentialities and to elevate the quality of life of all who reside in society. "The most important point of excellence which any form of government can possess," Mill says, "is to promote the virtue and intelligence of the people themselves." [1] This is by no means a new idea: it is found in Plato and Aristotle, and many subsequent theorists have suggested that those in political authority have this educational responsibility. But most of these writers believed that a specific elite or class were the true custodians of wisdom and virtue. Only these favored few could distinguish truth from error, and it was only from their lips the public might learn the lessons of the good life. Even Rousseau, an avowed democrat, was moved to speak of the public as a "common herd," and he assumed that its members required authoritative guidance if they were to come to know their higher interests. Mill, however, is wary of any explicit conjunction between the educational process and political authority. If virtue is taught by those who wear the robes of office, then their teachings may be accepted not because they are true, but because they emanate from high places. It was Burke's suggestion, for example, that citizens should learn the lessons of obedience without questioning the authority of those who rule over them. This, Mill would say, is not education at all: political education can only be meaningful if every citizen is encouraged to participate in the process of self-government. An individual learns best in the course of making and correcting his own mistakes. Virtue and intelligence should become genuine attributes of character in a citizen and not simply a catalogue of catch phrases he has memorized. The teachers, in short, must respect their pupils as equals. This respect will only be achieved in a democratic government or, as Mill sometimes calls it, by a representative constitution. The political world is a classroom, and citizens should have the opportunity to go through the trials and errors by means of which they will come to know their potentialities as individuals.

Mill professes an unqualified esteem for all citizens regardless of their station in life. He insists that political power should belong to those who will be subject to it: only popular sovereignty can impart legitimacy to a government. "There is no difficulty in showing that the ideally best form of government is that in which the sovereignty, or supreme controlling power in the last resort,

[1] John Stuart Mill, *Representative Government*, in *Utilitarianism, Liberty, and Representative Government* (London: Dent, 1910), p. 193.

is vested in the entire aggregate of the comunity," he says.² It has been observed more than once that any discussion in terms of sovereignty is bound to be troublesome.

There are theorists who are willing to admit that *de jure* sovereignty rests with the people as a whole, but who at the same time are unwilling to allow the people a free hand in selecting their rulers. It is frequently claimed that the public is competent to exercise its legal sovereignty only when it acts in a reasonable way, and it usually develops that the custodians of the knowledge of reason are some group which stands apart from the public. There are other theorists who grant that the people may well have *de facto* sovereignty but are unable to use it effectively because political power inevitably gravitates to the hands of a small minority. In this case democracy is said to be no different from other political systems as only a few people make the key decisions.

Mill is aware of these objections but he believes they can be overcome. He affirms that citizens should choose their own rulers and bring their influence to bear on the character and direction of public policy. And he suggests that ways and means can be found so that popular participation will play a genuine role in the political process. His position is supported by two lines of argument.

The first one is negative in that Mill denies that an exclusive class or elite is capable of promoting political interests other than its own. Unlike Plato or Burke, Mill cannot conceive of rulers so steeped in virtue and wisdom that they may always be counted on to understand the problems of those they govern. He is not contending that rule by an exclusive minority will necessarily be oppressive. What he does claim is that such a class or elite will be composed of human beings, and they will tend to assume—often in good conscience— that what is good for themselves is what is good for everyone else. When the public does not elect its rulers it has no assurance that its interests will be either understood or looked out for.

We need not suppose that when power resides in an exclusive class, that class will knowingly and deliberately sacrifice the other classes to themselves: it suffices that, in the absence of its natural defenders, the interest of the excluded is always in danger of being overlooked; and, when looked at, is seen with very different eyes from those of the persons whom it directly concerns.³

The problem Mill is describing here is a psychological one no less than it is political. Even the wisest of rulers are men with interests of their own, and experience has demonstrated that they will show greater sympathy for the in-

² *Ibid.*, p. 207.
³ *Ibid.*, p. 209.

terests of those in society who have backgrounds similar to their own. And even when such rulers make an honest attempt to provide for the needs of the average man, they will tend to project their own images of reality onto the situations which confront others.

It is a rare individual who can understand the style of life and attitude of mind of people who live at the other end of the social scale. Plato tried to solve the problem by divesting his Guardians of all personal interests so that their vision of the general welfare would not be obscured by their own preferences. Bentham sought to cope with it by suggesting that policy be decided according to the scientific method in the hope that rulers would engage in a systematic study to determine what were the public's needs. As philosophical ideals both of these proposals are attractive, but Mill clearly regards them as impractical for use by actual governments. Each and every individual in society must be given the opportunity to defend his own interests. No man should count on having this done for him by someone else. "The rights and interests of every or any person," he says, "are only secure from being disregarded when the person interested is himself able, and habitually disposed, to stand up for them." [4] Like Tocqueville, Mill looks on the possession of personal interests and the consequent pursuit of self-interest as laudable qualities in a citizen. And when political power is held by an exclusive minority, then the excluded majority has no motivation to develop individual interests of their own. "They themselves have less scope and encouragement than they might otherwise have to that exertion of their energies for the good of themselves and of the community, to which the general prosperity is always proportioned." [5]

This, then, is the positive argument for popular sovereignty. Only if men are allowed to govern themselves will they begin to think of themselves and for themselves as individuals. Democracy is not only a system of government whereby the interests of all in a community may be protected; it is also an educational process in which men will develop interests of their own and in this way extend the horizons of their personalities.

If all citizens are encouraged to participate in the exercise of political power, then the entire community will profit. In a democracy political education is universal; in other systems the benefits of such schooling are bestowed only on a privileged few. When participation is widespread, each individual has the chance to take part in the life of society. While he will not give up his personal interests, he will learn that he must live with other men and join with them in determining policies which apply to all.

---

[4] *Ibid.*, p. 208.
[5] *Ibid.*, p. 211.

More salutary is the moral part of the instruction afforded by the participation of the private citizen, if even rarely, in public functions. He is called upon, while so engaged, to weigh interests not his own; to be guided, in case of conflicting claims, by another rule than his private partialities; to apply, at every turn, principles and maxims which have for their reasons of existence the common good: and he usually finds associated with him in the same work minds more familiarized than his own with these ideas and operations, whose study it will be to supply reasons to his understanding, and stimulation to his feeling for the general interest. He is made to feel himself one of the public, and whatever is for their benefit to be for his benefit. . . .

From these accumulated considerations it is evident that the only government which can fully satisfy all the exigencies of the social state is one in which the whole people participate; that any participation, even in the smallest public function, is useful; that the participation should everywhere be as great as the general degree of improvement of the community will allow; and that nothing less can be ultimately desirable than the admission of all to a share in the sovereign power of the state.[6]

Like Rousseau, Mill looks on political participation as a continuing lesson in the moral life. If men are creatures of self-interest, the give and take of politics broadens their understanding and they begin to perceive the interests they share with their fellow citizens. But Mill does not go so far as Rousseau: he does not insist that individuals forego their personal interests and think only of the common good. There is no allusion to a General Will in Mill's theory, and there is never the suggestion that a dissenter is obliged to admit his error if he finds that the majority opposes him. Rousseau's democracy develops in the framework of a homogeneous community; therefore, the individual's real interest lies in his identification with a shared consensus called the General Will. Mill's democracy must be seen in the context of a loose society made up of autonomous individuals; hence, the general welfare must not be promoted at the sacrifice of the discrete citizens who have rights and interests of their own.

The value of participation is not simply as a means for uncovering the consensus latent in society. Rather, the discussion of issues, the compromises among interests, and the explorations of common goals are all experiences which serve to mature the individual. The aim of political education is not to specify what is the good life; the purpose of political authority is not to teach a particular conception of virtue. The subjects to be taught are more important than any of these: the subjects of instruction are the men and women who make up a society.

Institutions of government must be created if democratic theory is to be transformed into democratic practice. Rousseau evaded this problem by confining his discussion to a small community where it was possible for citizens

[6] *Ibid.*, p. 217.

to govern themselves while standing underneath an oak. This recourse is not open to Mill. The modern world he has undertaken to discuss is large and complex, and the model of the town meeting cannot be applied to a nation with a population running into tens of millions. Indeed, the discussion and debate which characterize an open meeting become impossible if more than two or three hundred are in attendance. Past that point a meeting is transformed into a rally where those present cheer their leaders and ratify the programs presented to them. While a large convention can maintain the forms of democratic procedures, in reality decisions must be made by acclaim rather than by deliberation. And it is even more of a distortion to speak of direct democracy on a national scale. An undifferentiated mass of citizens, whether or not they are gathered together in one place, are apt to throw their collective power behind a man or a mass movement which will claim to act in the public's name.

Burke, Hegel, and Tocqueville all saw the dangers inherent in mass participation on a national scale. For this reason, they suggested that there be maintained in society a hierarchy of intermediate institutions so that citizens could participate at levels where they knew political conditions at first hand. Mill's solution to the problem of mass politics is representative government. Rousseau could perhaps afford the luxury of denigrating the very idea of representation: he was certainly right in saying that an individual's will is something unique and that it does not admit of being represented by someone else. But some compromise with his position is needed if a theory is to be applicable to societies now in existence. Men must put up with representative government as a second-best alternative to direct democracy if they are to have any form of democracy at all. "The meaning of representative government," Mill says, "is that the whole people or some numerous portion of them exercise through deputies periodically elected by themselves the ultimate controlling power." [7] The introduction of representatives to mediate between citizens and their government cannot be avoided. On the local level, if the jurisdiction is small enough, it may still be possible for individuals to participate directly in the making of political decisions or to rotate public offices among themselves. But at the national level these powers must be delegated: an elected officeholder is given the authority to act for his constituents.

It may be hoped that the voters will give careful scrutiny to the political ideas and legislative record of the man they have chosen to represent them. It may be hoped further that they will replace him with someone else if they find he is not representing their interests. Mill has faith that the average voter will cast a responsible ballot. If elections are honest and if the voter has

[7] *Ibid.*, p. 228.

an opportunity to become acquainted with the candidates, then there is no reason why the franchise should not be given to all adults. "The multitude have often a true instinct for distinguishing an able man, when he has the means of displaying his ability in a fair field before them," Mill says.[8]

Yet for all his astuteness on Election Day, the modern citizen has personal concerns to look after and little time to familiarize himself with the problems of government. Public affairs grow increasingly complex, and elected representatives are as often as not left to legislate as they think best. At the very most, only one or two interested groups will have a strong opinion on any given bill that comes before the legislature. This means that the representatives will not know the electorate's sentiments and will consequently have to pass their own judgments. In short, an important step has been taken, and it is one in a direction away from the democratic process. Political participation for the average citizen now means little more than casting a vote in periodic elections: he is no longer obliged to hold office or to decide on issues himself. Just how far this step weakens the integrity of democratic government depends on several factors, and these will be considered momentarily. Mill allows that "in the last resort" political power should be vested in the whole people. If this is so, then it is important to know how many stages separate the man-in-the-street from the men who make the nation's crucial decisions. For as each stage is added, the government loses some of its claim to being government by the people.

If Mill is inclined to think of the electorate as a multitude, it may also be claimed that the typical legislature is not far different. The average voter is an amateur in politics, but the average legislator is usually no better than a semiprofessional. A parliamentary body consists of several hundred men and women, and the majority of these have no more than a passing acquaintance with the bills they consider. If some elected representatives have expert knowledge, they often use it to promote particular interests. While Mill trusts the voters to pass on the merits of their representatives, he is not equally trusting that these representatives are competent to pass on the merits of legislation. "There is hardly any kind of intellectual work which so much needs to be done, not only by experienced and exercised minds, but by minds trained to the task through long and laborious study, as the business of making laws," he says.[9]

Here, of course, Mill is very close to Bentham's view. If public policy is to be rational, then it can be left neither to amateurs nor to semiprofessionals. The drafting of effective legislation is a complicated business, and it calls for

[8] *Ibid.*, p. 267.
[9] *Ibid.*, p. 235.

superior intellect, broad experience, and disciplined study. Bentham assumed that this was the case, and he never suggested that policy-makers should be elected to office: he desired government for the people but not government by the people. It is clear that the democratic ideal is about to suffer another blow, for Mill desires rational legislation no less than did Bentham, and for this reason he must rely on the professionals who are equipped to draft and administer laws.

The actual government, then, consists of party leaders and heads of executive departments who have both the training and resources to make and carry out public policy. The elected legislators, Mill suggests, should acknowledge the limits of their competence: the semiprofessionals should delegate the responsibility of governing to the professionals. A representative assembly must be content to check, to criticize, and on occasion to remove from office the men who actually govern the country.

> Instead of the function of governing, for which it is radically unfit, the proper office of a representative assembly is to watch and control the government: to throw the light of publicity on its acts: to compel a full exposition and justification of all of them which any one considers questionable; to censure them if found condemnable, and, if the men who compose the government abuse their trust, or fulfill it in a manner which conflicts with the deliberate sense of the nation, to expel them from office, and either expressly or virtually appoint their successors. This is surely ample power, and security enough for the liberty of the nation.[10]

The effective lawmaking agency, then, is a cabinet or a council of party leaders or the heads of executive departments or some combination of these.

This is the government in a positive sense, and whether it is either democratic or representative is a troublesome question. The government is now not one but two stages removed from the electorate. This is bound to occur once it is granted that the members of modern legislatures are unfit to carry out the business they were, in theory, elected to do. Indeed, it is possible to suggest that the more legislators represent the people who make up their constituencies, the less likely will they be competent when it comes to making effective policy. Conversely, the more competent they are on this score, the less apt are they to be representative of the voters who elected them. Mill is once more pursuing two values simultaneously: both democracy and rationality should be evidenced in the governmental process. His compromise is to have elected representatives oversee in a general way the men who have the actual power to govern. It is obvious that the party leaders and department heads cannot be controlled in any systematic way, and it is inevitable that many of their acts will be unquestioned and even unnoticed. But while de-

[10] *Ibid.*, p. 239.

tails of policy and administration may escape legislative scrutiny, it is hoped that the major outlines of the government's program will be subject to constant review.

The legislature does not draft the laws, nor does it decide the order of priority for the bills it considers. Its task of control and criticism is essentially a negative one, but for this reason it should not be minimized. Mill is concerned that the government listen to the voice of the people and that this voice be expressed by their elected representatives. A legislature is not obliged to give unanimous consent to the bills which are submitted to it, and, even if certain laws are favored, its members should feel free to debate the merits of particular provisions. Having been elected to office, representatives are only one stage removed from the voters, and they are therefore entitled to pass judgment on leaders and administrators who may not have been elected at all. The chief weapons of the legislature are words: talk, especially representative talk, is a vital component of self-government.

I know not how a representative assembly can more usefully employ itself than in talk, when the subject of talk is the great public interests of the country, and every sentence of it represents the opinion either of some important body of persons in the nation, or of an individual in whom some such body have reposed their confidence. A place where every interest and shade of opinion in the country can have its cause even passionately pleaded, in the face of the government and of all other interests and opinions, can compel them to listen, and either comply, or state clearly why they do not, is in itself, if it answered no other purpose, one of the most important political institutions that can exist anywhere, and one of the foremost benefits of free government.[11]

The words of elected representatives are apt to be heeded; for these men speak for the voters, and it is the electorate which ultimately decides which party leaders and department heads are to remain in office. Criticism of legislative assemblies for being talk-shops is misplaced criticism: talk is necessary and effective. These are the channels through which public sentiment is communicated upward so it is made known to those who make policy.

In representative government there are institutional means for knowing if the people approve of the ways political power is being exercised over them. There is at work, then, a subtle chain of controls. The citizen uses his vote to control and inform his representative, and the representative acts as the spokesman for a constituency when he criticizes those who make and administer policy. If either of these links breaks or is significantly weakened, then the government's claim to being democratic is less persuasive. But it is also apparent that Mill does not want government to be too democratic. The representative process allows an area of freedom to both legislators and administrators, and

[11] *Ibid.*, p. 240.

it is assumed that they will use this freedom to do things that the public might not approve of were they allowed to make a direct decision. Representation is not only a channel for democracy but also a check on it.

THE CONFLICT OF INTERESTS

"A representative constitution," Mill says, "is a means of bringing . . . the individual intellect and virtue of its wisest members more directly to bear upon the government." [12] Men of wisdom and virtue are seldom chosen for political office in popular elections. The average voter for the most part wants as his representative someone pretty much like himself. If individuals of superior talent are to be recruited to public life, then they must be protected from a public which neither understands nor appreciates them. This is why Mill makes ample provision for appointive positions in the government: while such officials may be criticized or even removed by the legislative assembly, that body still stands as a shield between the extraordinary man and the ordinary man.

For all his faith in the voters, Mill nevertheless harbors doubts as to their ability to know and pursue their own best interests. In a democracy, as Tocqueville pointed out, citizens tend to a habit of egotism. They have been told that they are fit to govern themselves, and they are happy to believe this. It follows naturally that they will feel qualified to define their best interests and to act in ways they feel will secure that end. There is little point in saying that the public is misguided on this score, for they are going to be their own judges on this. "It is not what their interest is, but what they suppose it to be, that is the important consideration with respect to their conduct," Mill says.[13] Democracy gives power to average men, and once this is done it is difficult for superior men to persuade them to take a loftier view of their political roles.

When we talk of the interest of a body of men, or even of an individual man, as a principle determining their actions, the question what would be considered their interest by an unprejudiced observer is one of the least important parts of the whole matter. As Coleridge observes, the man makes the motive, not the motive the man. What it is the man's interest to do or refrain from depends less on any outward circumstances than upon what sort of man he is.

On the average, a person who cares for other people, for his country, or for mankind, is a happier man than one who does not; but of what use is it to preach this doctrine to a man who cares for nothing but his own ease, or his own pocket? He cannot care for other people if he would. It is like preaching to the worm who crawls on the ground how much better it would be for him if he were an eagle.[14]

[12] Ibid., p. 195.
[13] Ibid., p. 250.
[14] Ibid., pp. 251–252.

Mill's tone here is not a pessimistic one. He has surveyed the existing forms of government and has decided that, on balance, representative democracy is the best system. But he has no illusions about the problems that will have to be faced. Democracy teaches men to think of themselves as individuals and to look out for their own interests. The consequence of this may not be pleasing to thoughtful people. For the majority of men set personal and short-term goals. "The interests by which they will be led, when they are thinking only of self-interest," Mill says, "will be almost exclusively those which are obvious at first sight, and which operate on their present condition." [15] There is no attempt here to exalt the average man or to endow him with a wisdom he does not have. Yet this awareness of the public's shortcomings does not lead Mill to search for an elite of philosopher-kings who will rule firmly and justly. This alternative has already been rejected, and there is no returning to it.

The democratic strand in Mill's theory postulates that only affected individuals can know and protect their own interests. The Benthamite strand in Mill's theory postulates that trained and experienced specialists know what conditions are required for an individual's well-being. In very simple terms, it is possible to talk of "wants" on the one hand and "needs" on the other. Wants are the conscious desires of citizens: they rise from a person's own definition of his interest, and he is able to articulate these in the form of demands made on his representative. It is the responsibility of a representative to keep these wants in mind and to check the government whenever it appears to be ignoring them. Needs are the unconscious or only dimly perceived desires of citizens. They are perceived not so much by the person himself as by men of superior insight who are able to define an individual's best interests better than he can himself. A citizen is not able to articulate his needs to his representative, because he is not usually aware of them. But government officials frequently perceive these needs, and they attempt to persuade the elected representatives that they exist and ought to be satisfied by means of particular legislation. It is then the job of the representatives to convince their constituents that the proposed policies are actually in their best interest.

The representative, then, is the middle-man in this two-way cross current of wants and needs. If legislation is framed solely on the basis of wants, then the short-term view will predominate and long-run problems will become more aggravated as time runs on. The public itself will grow restive over this, for these problems are its problems. It may grow so frustrated as to abdicate its power completely and follow a strong leader who promises easy solutions. If matters are allowed to go this far, then democracy has ceased to exist. On the other hand, Mill does not want to have legislation framed solely on the basis

[15] *Ibid.*, p. 253.

of the public's needs. For while he admires the professional, he knows that appointed officials are fallible and that they can tend to confuse their own wants with the public's needs. While such men may take the long-term view, they may forget the immediate interests and personal sensibilities of the average citizen. The point is that both wants and needs are important, and one should not be allowed to obscure the other. "Governments must be made for human beings as they are, or as they are capable of speedily becoming," Mill says.[16] And this means that if an individual sets great store on a short-term interest which he perceives for himself, then government officials must be wary about telling him that his view is wrong. Yet if that individual is to be well served over a long period his government must rely on the intelligence of trained men. A compromise is clearly called for, and Mill hopes that representative government will achieve the best of the two goals.

> It is, at the same time, one of the most important ends of political institutions . . . to secure, as far as can be made compatible, the great advantage of the conduct of affairs by skilled persons, bred to it as an intellectual profession, along with that of a general control vested in, and seriously exercised by, bodies representative of the entire people.[17]

One of the great problems of democracy, as mentioned earlier, is the frustration experienced by the electorate because they do not understand the conditions which confront them. In theory, voters support or oppose a candidate for office on the basis of his legislative or administrative record. In practice, however, votes are cast either out of habit or because of an important shift in social conditions. Very frequently legislators are turned out of office not because of the policies they have enacted, but because of events over which the government had no control. The electorate punishes the incumbents, even though they were not responsible, and hopes that their successors in office will provide a solution. This divorce of punishment and responsibility is far from rational, and it opens the doors for political opportunism. The answer is for governments to strive, as best they can, to anticipate and deal with the major problems of society. If this is to be done, then men of superior training and talent must be allowed entry to positions of power. They will not remedy all of society's ills, but it is likely that they will do a better job than those who are not professionals. The stakes are high, and Mill believes that a political elite such as this is necessary if the democratic process is to function at all.

Representative government calls for a certain quality of citizen. He is not required to defer to his self-styled betters, but he must be temperate enough to acknowledge that the knowledge of specialists may operate in his favor.

---

[16] Ibid.
[17] Ibid., p. 247.

There is a danger that democratic institutions will create a citizen who will not only adopt an arrogant pose, but will take his position not as an individual but as a member of a crowd. Both Tocqueville and Mill observe this tendency, and both hope that citizens will develop personal interests so they are not forced to submerge themselves in a mass. The problem of majority tyranny arises because the larger portion of the population is unable to think of themselves as autonomous beings. There is a qualitative difference between an individual interest and a group interest. The former is the extension of a person's ego, and it is his unique possession. The latter actually destroys the ego and compels the individual to identify his personality with others in a similar condition. There may be similarity, but there is not identity—and the forcing of the two together crushes the integrity of those who join such groups. This process has political consequences, for there can develop in a democracy a majority interest of great power. Such an interest is clearly capable of dominating first a legislature and then a government.

Looking at democracy in the way in which it is commonly conceived, as the rule of the numerical majority, it is surely possible that the ruling power may be under the dominion of sectional or class interests, pointing to conduct different from that which would be dictated by impartial regard for the interest of all.

Suppose the majority to be whites, the minority Negroes, or vice versa: is it likely that the majority would allow equal justice to the minority? Suppose the majority Catholics, the minority Protestants, or the reverse; will there not be the same danger? Or let the majority be English, the minority Irish, or the contrary: is there not a great probability of similar evil?

In all countries there is a majority of poor, a minority who, in contradistinction, may be called rich. Between these two classes, on many questions, there is complete opposition of apparent interest. We will suppose the majority sufficiently intelligent to be aware that it is not for their advantage to weaken the security of property, and that it would be weakened by any act of arbitrary spoliation. But is there not a considerable danger lest they should throw upon the possessors of . . . the larger incomes, an unfair share, or even the whole, of the burden of taxation; and having done so, add to the amount without scruple, expending the proceeds in modes supposed to conduce to the profit and advantage of the laboring class? [18]

The majority about which Mill is concerned is, in the final analysis, the proletarian class in which Marx and Engels placed their hopes. While he is fearful of tyranny at the hands of racial, religious, and national majorities, his chief apprehension is of a mass movement on economic lines. Once all citizens are given the vote, once the franchise is extended beyond the rich and well-born, then the fate of democracy lies in the hands of the majority. If interests are individual in character, then the majority will be a transient and shifting coalition, and its composition will change from day to day as different issues are considered. A social pluralism, based upon a multiplicity of interests and

[18] *Ibid.*, pp. 249–250.

a variety of roles for each citizen, will prevent a majority from taking on a permament form.

But the average man tends not to look on his interests as individual: he identifies himself with groups and finds his interests in the common goals they set for their members. The danger in this tendency is that as time moves on the majority of ordinary citizens may come together in a single group, that they may become an active and class-conscious proletariat. Even if this mass party does not pursue communist objectives, it may still inflict damage on the remaining interests in society. "One of the greatest dangers, therefore, of democracy . . ." Mill says, "is the danger of class legislation; of government intended for (whether really effecting it or not) the immediate benefit of the dominant class to the lasting detriment of the whole." [19] In democracy numerical strength is the key to political dominance. The class legislation to be feared is not so much that of minority interests, because there are a variety of these and they tend to cancel each other out, but that of a monolithic majority. Democracy encourages the growth of mass movements, Mill is saying, and these movements can destroy the system which brought them to life.

If there is a solution to this problem, it must be found in the institutions of government. Both Tocqueville and Mill understand that majority tyranny is a social force, but Mill sees that it can be ameliorated in its political forms. His proposal cannot be guaranteed to work at all times and all places, but it does have wide application. "The desirable object," he says, "would be that no class, and no combination of classes likely to combine, should be able to exercise a preponderant influence on the government." [20] How is class government to be avoided under conditions of representative democracy? It has already been seen that the party leadership and administrative officials will have an area of relative freedom of action in which they can make policy. If this freedom is used rationally, then there may result legislation which takes the national interest and the long-term view into consideration. Nevertheless, the legislature has the power to check such laws if it sees fit, and this power may be used to sabotage these worthwhile endeavors. For this reason, Mill hopes that the legislature itself will be so constituted that it will not be able to ride roughshod over considered proposals.

By way of illustration, it may be supposed that a parliamentary body has 200 members. Of this group, 90 belong to the Blue Collar Party and 90 to the White Collar Party. If either of these two parties had a firm majority, it would enact a program of legislation aimed at promoting the interests of a particular class. Fortunately, Mill would say, neither of them has sufficient strength for

[19] *Ibid.*, p. 254.
[20] *Ibid.*, p. 255.

this, for there is also an Independent Party with 20 members. These representatives not only hold the balance of power, but they are able to use their strategic position to enhance the national interest. The Independents, Mill suggests, form a group "who are governed by higher considerations, though too few and weak to prevail against the whole of the others, usually after sufficient discussion and agitation become strong enough to turn the balance in favor of the body of private interests which is on the same side with them." [21] By supporting first the White Collar and then the Blue Collar Party, by making temporary bargains with each, and by demanding that both of these class parties take account of the public good, the Independents may have a disproportionate influence on national legislation. There is no guarantee, of course, that this 90-90-20 distribution will come into being. But at least, Mill suggests, steps may be taken to introduce Independents into the legislature on the chance that they will have an opportunity to play their role. Extra seats may be given to university or functional constituencies, a system of proportional representation may be used, or one house of a bicameral legislature may give added weight to certain important minorities in society.

All of these devices, in one way or another, run counter to the principle of majority rule. But Mill's trust of the majority is not unqualified: clearly he doubts whether the average voter will select as his representative a person who puts the national interest ahead of more specialized interests. And his fear of mass behavior is so great that he is willing to give power to the elements in society which might curb the extreme tendencies of class parties.

Even if conditions prevail in which a majority party is dominant and hence has its way all of the time, it may be questioned whether this right should be exercised without limitation. For a majority, even if it is based on a mass party and seems able to win election after election, cannot and should not last forever. While Mill's theory does not invoke the dialectic of either Hegel or Marx and Engels, it still assumes that political power is dynamic in its operation. Today's majority may seem to be firmly entrenched, but there is also within one of today's minorities—we do not know which one—the seeds of tomorrow's majority. In order that the transition from party to party be an orderly one, Mill asks that minorities be allowed the right to criticize and to voice their views.

In a representative body actually deliberating, the minority must of course be overruled; and in an equal democracy the majority of the people, through their representatives, will outvote and prevail over the minority and their representatives. But does it follow that the minority should have no representation at all? Because the majority ought to prevail over the minority, must the majority have all the

[21] *Ibid.*, pp. 255-256.

votes [i.e. win all the rollcalls], the minority none? Is it necessary that the minority should not even be heard? [22]

There must be constitutional guarantees which allow minorities to be heard, and these guarantees should be so established that even a legislative majority may not withdraw them. While minorities may not, under the democratic principle, have great political power, they must still have the opportunity to speak freely.

Mill's theory, as has been already noted, places great emphasis on the role of talk and discussion in the political process. Of the citizens who lend their support to today's majority, an appreciable number may in time be won over to another point of view or another conception of their interests. But they can only be won over if other viewpoints are expressed and allowed to be made known. If a minority party talks well, if its criticisms of the majority party are persuasive, then it may augment its numbers by gaining the defectors from the dominant group. Through discussion and debate, the loyalties of individuals will be transformed, and democratic politics will remain both fluid and free. Talk is an instrument of persuasion in proportion to an individual's degree of commitment to a particular position or interest. The man who has a vital stake in a certain set of conditions cannot usually be persuaded to change his stand by means of talk. But most men, Mill assumes, are not heavily committed on all matters. They may have vested interests in several areas, and no amount of discussion will cause them to change; however, they will have potentially open minds on many other subjects. Furthermore, it is likely that on any given issue only a minority of the population will resist all attempts at persuasion. This means that the uncommitted or only lightly committed majority may be brought to change their outlook and hence support new departures in policy.

Talk, then, brings into the political arena new facts, new symbols, and new ideas. It is probably too much to expect that this talk will always be rational in substance or even relevant to the problems at hand. What is important is that it be free. For in a democracy talk is the best means for effecting political change and for enlisting citizens in the governmental process. Mill sees the legislature as the great forum for the never-ending political conversation. And through the right of free speech the best chance of reconciling the principles of majority rule and individual liberty.

SOCIETY VERSUS THE INDIVIDUAL

On Liberty describes the social setting in which representative democracy must operate. In this essay Mill lays down certain political principles and then

[22] Ibid., p. 257.

contrasts them with the practices of existing societies. At the same time, he advances a theory of human nature on which he hopes to build the political and social institutions of a good society.

The subject of his essay is stated in its opening paragraph: "the nature and limits of the power which can be legitimately exercised by society over the individual." [23] To juxtapose society and the individual this way calls for some explanation. Most theorists would insist that every individual is an integral part of a society and that it is impossible to conceive of anyone living the political life outside of society. There are at least two ways of dealing with this question. The first, which was employed by Tocqueville, is to suggest that each person has two roles: on the one hand, he thinks and acts as an autonomous individual; on the other, he participates with others as a social being. Different people will devote varying amounts of time to each role; and in some areas some will think of themselves as individuals while others will emphasize their social selves.[24] Each person, then, will have a social self, but not all will play this role under the same circumstances.

The tension between the individual and society arises when one person chooses to think of himself as an individual whereas the majority of his fellow citizens are prone to regard themselves as social beings. In this instance the individual is isolated, and he stands alone because he refuses to play the social role as the others around him are doing. It may well be that to be in a state of such isolation is a rare occurrence for most people, and they find themselves at one with society at virtually all critical junctures. On the other hand, there are some who seem always to be wearing their individual roles just when everyone else is thinking in social terms. Perhaps it would be ideal if every person took his turn at being isolated once in a while but for the most part was able to know the security which comes of being in agreement with the majority. Were individual and social roles to be so allocated over time, then no one person or group would endure permanent suffering because of his perpetual minority status.

Because this is not the case in most societies, Mill carries Tocqueville's approach one step further. When a tension between society and the individual is described, what is really being assumed is that there exist two classes of people in a single community. The first group consists of the vast majority: they are people who think of themselves in their social role almost all of the time, and for this reason it is appropriate enough to call them "society" in a collective sense. The second group consists of a small minority: they are

---

[23] John Stuart Mill, *On Liberty*, in *Utilitarianism, Liberty, and Representative Government, op. cit.*, p. 65.

[24] The question of roles is explored fully in George Herbert Mead's classic *Mind, Self, and Society* (Chicago: University of Chicago Press, 1934).

people who think of themselves in their individual role almost all of the time, and they may legitimately be called "individuals." This latter class is not a social group at all, but is more likely to be a scattered number of persons who constantly find themselves out of step. The conflict at work, then, is not so much a class conflict—although it may on occasion be that—as a tension between a group and individuals who stand apart from that group. These individuals are, of course, members of society in many important respects: they do not challenge every social convention they encounter. But when political questions arise, they are often on the outside looking in. Mill's concern is twofold: he wishes to see the isolated individual protected from the penalties which a smug or fearful society is apt to inflict on dissenters; and he wants to demonstrate that the members of the majority would experience a fuller life if they thought of themselves more frequently as individuals.

For all men are capable of individuality. It is only if this capacity is exercised with courage and imagination that one may know the best that life has to offer. Only by engaging in independent thought, by unleashing one's creative powers, by pursuing truth as best one is able, can a man achieve his promise as a human being.

> If it be any part of religion to believe that man was made by a good Being, it is more consistent with that faith to believe that this Being gave all human faculties that they might be cultivated and unfolded, not rooted out and consumed, and that He takes delight in every nearer approach made by His creatures to the ideal conception embodied in them, every increase in any of their capabilities of comprehension, of action, or of enjoyment.
> Why is it that there is on the whole a preponderance among mankind of rational opinions and rational conduct? If there really is this preponderance—which there must be unless human affairs are, and have always been, in an almost desperate state—it is owing to a quality of the human mind, the source of everything respectable in man either as an intellectual or as a moral being, namely, that his errors are corrigible.[25]

The greatest of human faculties is the capacity for rational thought and action. Mill bases this assertion not on religious grounds, but on his observation of human affairs over the course of history. Men have shown that they can secure order and progress for themselves; they have proved that they can learn by experience. Mill is prepared to assume that reason is the property of all individuals, and this explains his faith in democratic government. While certain individuals may have had greater opportunity to develop and put to use their intellectual qualities, the potentiality for such development is distributed throughout the entire population. This explains, too, Mill's concern with education as an integral part of the political process. The point is not that all

[25] *On Liberty*, pp. 120, 80.

men think and act rationally, but rather that they are able to do so if they are properly encouraged. In this Mill takes a position similar to Rousseau's: he assumes that if politics and society are so organized that individual potentialities are liberated rather than frustrated, then men will show their true character. And for this reason, he attempts to show how and why public policy should be oriented so as to bring out the best in every citizen.

The great obstacle to individual expression is the opposition of society. Whenever there appear men who wish to live their lives in unconventional ways, there invariably rise up social forces which attempt to thwart such nonconformism. Mill's concern is to remove the barriers to free expression whether it be in words or deeds. The burden of proof is put squarely on those who would place limitations on the conduct of their fellow citizens. Anyone who objects to the way another man acts must give compelling reasons why that behavior deserves to be interfered with.

The sole end of which mankind are warranted, individually or collectively, in interfering with the liberty of action of any of their number, is self-protection. That the only purpose for which power can be rightfully exercised over any member of a civilized community, against his will, is to prevent harm to others. His own good, either physical or moral, is not a sufficient warrant. He cannot rightfully be compelled to do or forbear because it will be better for him to do so, because it would make him happier, because, in the opinion of others, to do so would be wise or even right. These are good reasons for remonstrating with him, or reasoning with him, or persuading, or entreating him, but not for compelling him, or visiting him with any evil in case he do otherwise. To justify that, the conduct from which it is desired to deter him must be calculated to produce evil to some one else. The only part of the conduct of any one, for which he is amenable to society, is that which concerns himself, his independence is, of right, absolute. Over himself, over his body and mind, the individual is sovereign.[26]

Mill makes it quite clear that this is not simply a case of one person objecting to the acts of another: on the contrary, the objecting party is society at large, which is likely to use its collective power to frustrate an individual's freedom. This statement is as much exhortation as analysis: Mill is saying that it is not right for the social majority to set limits on personal liberty. His essay, indeed, is an essay in moral persuasion: he first explains his own position and then tries to show that society will itself benefit if his prescriptions are heeded.

But it may be argued that Mill weakens his whole argument by granting that the acts of an individual may be interfered with if it can be shown that such intervention will prevent harm to others. It is at this point that it must be asked in what ways freedom of expression on the part of individuals can be a danger to society. To exercise the right of free speech is a political act, and

[26] *Ibid.*, pp. 72–73.

it is likely that the words which are uttered will not please all who hear them. But it is one thing for a speech to be displeasing and another for it to be dangerous. Mill offers an illustration to show where a line may be drawn. "An opinion that corn-dealers are starvers of the poor . . ." he says, "ought to be unmolested when simply circulated through the press, but may justly incur punishment when delivered orally to an excited mob assembled before the house of a corn-dealer." [27] An inflamed speech to a mob obviously presents a clear and present danger to the life of the corn-dealer cowering inside. Society, through the agency of the police, is entitled here to arrest the speechmaker even before he completes his first sentence. But the number of instances where words can be observed stirring a mob to immediate action are relatively few. And in these cases society usually punishes the speechmaker after the damage has been done. In the final analysis, the "clear and present danger" rule can seldom be invoked with any vigor.

This raises the question of whether the exercise of speech, in oral or printed form, can be a danger to society even if it is not addressed to a mob primed for action. Mill says that if someone writes radical articles or editorials, these ought to be tolerated because their aim is primarily to change men's minds. They may even have the objective of inducing people to behave in new ways: to vote for a certain party, to attend meetings, to put pressure on the legislature. It is clear that many citizens of conservative leanings will regard the circulation of these ideas as a subversive activity. The argument will be advanced that such radical speech will weaken the community's faith in its established institutions and may even convince large numbers of people to seek the overthrow of existing social values. In short, it will be said that even if the danger is not clear and present, it may be subtle and indirect. Radical ideas can take advantage of whatever dissatisfactions men may have with their social condition and lead them in the course of time to use violent means. Even if violence is not the eventual result, the gradual erosion of traditional values will sooner or later undermine the foundations of society. Mill is not unaware of this argument, and his answer to it is straightforward and unqualified. Speech, whether it be radical or conservative, must be met with speech. To use the power of the state or the pressure of society to close a man's mouth is to admit that there is no rational answer to what he has to say.

Mill's analysis will be presented in more detail later on. At this point it will suffice to say that he rejects the contention that the exercise of free speech may be a subtle and indirect danger to society, for to say this is to show lack of faith in the intelligence and common sense of the listening public. Most people who would ban dangerous ideas are quick to say that they *themselves*

[27] *Ibid.*, p. 114.

would not be convinced by them: they profess to worry about the harm which may be done to their fellow citizens who are easy prey for irresponsible talk. That one group in society is able to distinguish truth from error, whereas another is not, is to Mill's mind a suggestion which is not only arrogant but also untrue.

In addition to this, Mill proposes that it is entirely proper to draw a line between a person's private and public life. While no hard and fast boundary can be made, it is necessary for state and society to acknowledge that each individual has a part of his existence which is his private property and in which he may do so as he pleases. Here, too, Mill is acquainted with the objections which may be raised.

> The distinction here pointed out between the part of a person's life which concerns himself only, and that which concerns others, many persons will refuse to admit. How (it may be asked) can any part of the conduct of a member of society be a matter of indifference to the other members? No person is an entirely isolated being; it is impossible for a person to do anything seriously or permanently hurtful to himself, without mischief reaching at least to his near connections, and often far beyond them. . . . Finally, if by his vices or follies a person does no direct harm to others, he is nevertheless (it may be said) injurious by his example; and ought to be compelled to control himself, for the sake of those whom the sight or knowledge of his conduct might corrupt or mislead.[28]

The difficulty with this logic is that it has a tendency to run wild. If no dividing line is seen between private and public life, then the pressures are in the direction of making the public sector an increasingly larger one. First it is said that a man has not the right to practice nudism if he so desires; the argument is that his example will corrupt others. Then it is said that he may not purchase and consume liquor; the argument is that he affronts the sensibilities of his abstemious neighbors. It is later said that he may not educate his children at home, the argument being that he denies them their right to an approved level of schooling. At the next juncture he is told that he must mow his lawn and rake his leaves; the argument is that the shoddiness of his home lowers the value of surrounding property. Each of these arguments for interference is plausible on its own merits. The problem is that once each one is accepted, the door is open for another plausible limitation of individual freedom. As these restrictions pile up, the area of personal liberty is constricted to a smaller and smaller province.

Mill's answer must be expressed in Benthamite terms: the sensibilities of society which are injured by nonconformist behavior do not, in reality, give the majority as much pain as the restrictions on this behavior will cause unhappiness to the affected minority. It is Mill's judgment that, in terms of in-

---

[28] *Ibid.*, pp. 136–137.

tensity of feeling, the desires of individuals carry more weight than the pains society claims to suffer. "With regard to the merely contingent . . . injury which a person causes to society, by conduct which neither violates any specific duty to the public, nor occasions perceptible hurt to any assignable individual except himself," he says; "the inconvenience is one which society can afford to bear, for the sake of the greater good of human freedom." [29]

While Mill gives no examples here, his position is clear. First of all, he looks on nonconformist behavior as an inconvenience to society and not as a threat. The sight of saloons and empty liquor bottles in garbage cans may be displeasing to some people, but this is no reason to enact laws prohibiting drinking. A free society must tolerate inconveniences if it is to remain free. Second, Mill asks for a demonstration that the conduct of one person will cause perceptible hurt to another assignable individual. When a Negro moves into a suburban community, he threatens the social status of his white neighbors by his very presence. But this intrusion on his part affronts their sense of psychological security and does them no physical injury which can be perceived. Furthermore, the Negro's freedom to move out of an urban slum should be given a higher value than the loss of status suffered by any single one of the people who must now live next to him. There is a danger that the majority in any community will come to feel that they have collective rights and that these rights outweigh an individual's claim to free action. Householders may, for example, invoke a right to privacy and therefore get passed an ordinance forbidding individuals to use sound-trucks in the street. Mill's suggestion would be that the individual's right to free speech, even with a sound-truck, outweighs society's right to peace and quiet. The majority must learn that they can afford to bear such inconveniences. There is a natural tendency to take the easy way out, to curb the distasteful behavior of one's fellow citizens in the name of the public good. Mill is asking that the more difficult path be taken, and he is prepared to show why it will be rewarding to those who tread it.

THE PURSUIT OF TRUTH

The quality of a society may be judged by the amount and kind of encouragement it gives to the pursuit of truth. While most societies give lip service to this goal, there is a strong tendency for them to prejudge what is true and to silence those who would question the dominant myths. The most important liberty of the individual is the ability to criticize his society and to persuade others that his criticisms are justified. Yet society itself, despite all its professions to the contrary, does all that it can to silence such talk. "It is not

[29] *Ibid.*, p. 138.

difficult to show, by abundant instances, that to extend the bounds of what may be called moral police, until it encroaches on the most unquestionably legitimate liberty of the individual, is one of the most universal of all human propensities," Mill says.[30] Whether or not it is possible to reform this propensity is a difficult matter to decide. Mill believes that it is at least worth the effort. His approach is to appeal to men's reason: to use rational arguments for free speech in the hope that society will acknowledge the value of this right.

His line of attack is to suggest that to grant free speech is not to gratify personal idiosyncrasies but to provide society with the means of discovering the truth. It is worth quoting Mill at some length on this point.

> If all mankind minus one were of one opinion, and only one person were of the contrary opinion, mankind would be no more justified in silencing that one person, than he, if he had the power, would be justified in silencing mankind. . . . The peculiar evil of silencing the expression of an opinion is, that it is robbing the human race; posterity as well as the existing generation; those who dissent from the opinion, still more than those who hold it. If the opinion is right, they are deprived of the opportunity of exchanging error for truth: if wrong, they lose, what is almost as great a benefit, the clearer perception and livelier impression of truth produced by its collision with error.
>
> We can never be sure that the opinion we are endeavouring to stifle is a false opinion; and if we were sure, stifling it would be an evil still.
>
> The opinion which it is attempted to suppress by authority may possibly be true. Those who desire to suppress it, of course deny its truth; but they are not infallible. They have no authority to decide the question for all mankind, and exclude every other person from the means of judging. To refuse a hearing to an opinion, because they are sure that it is false, is to assume that *their* certainty is the same thing as *absolute* certainty. All silencing of discussion is an assumption of infallibility.[31]

Few individuals, when the question is put this way, will claim that the entire truth on all matters has been determined. There are always subjects which are still open, always problems which continue to stand in need of solution. The answers, or at least the best answers which are currently available, may lie in the minds of people society regards as crackpots or radicals. It may well be that only one out of a thousand of those who clamor for a hearing will have something constructive to say. But all one thousand must be heard if the grain of truth is to emerge out of all that chaff. Anyone who decides in advance who may express his ideas and who may not is presuming that he knows the direction from which right knowledge will come. Perhaps such a presumption is necessary. The editor of a scientific journal must have a basis for deciding which of the many manuscripts submitted to him he

[30] *Ibid.*, p. 141.
[31] *Ibid.*, p. 79.

will publish. The members of a legislative committee must decide which of the various petitioners they will allow to testify on questions of public policy. What Mill is saying is that those in power should be humble when the truth is involved. They should have the courage and the imagination to give a hearing to the unorthodox as well as the conventional. For no man knows where the next departures in our knowledge will come from.

Why is society so unwilling to give an open hearing to all ideas? The answer, as Mill noted earlier, is that strange opinions are regarded as dangerous. They are thought to constitute a threat to traditional values and established institutions. "There is the greatest difference between presuming an opinion to be true, because, with every opportunity for contesting it, it has not been refuted, and assuming its truth for the purpose of not permitting its refutation," he says.[32] There is a conflict, then, between men's desire for the truth and men's desire to secure their interests. Were they only concerned with truth, they would allow all opinions to be contested, and they would make their judgments on the basis of whether or not they thought the attacks were sufficiently damaging. But men are also creatures of interest. They are prone to assume that the truth of certain propositions ought not to be challenged, because they give support to certain interests they would prefer not to see disturbed. The truths which men seek to have maintained are frequently the dominant myths that a society lives by. Or, to use the word employed by Marx and Engels, ideology takes the center of the stage and crowds out the truth. Men of power tend to think it in their interest that certain myths be given currency so that the public will consent to things as they are. They do not conspire to prevent the truth from coming to light: indeed, there is evidence that such men themselves believe the ideology they are having disseminated.

It is Mill's hope that interested individuals will rise above what is really a very narrow conception of their personal welfare. To rely on the dominant myths is to rely on a depiction of reality which is only partially true. In the long run those who promote ideology and discourage the truth will be harming the very interests they seek to protect. For the world is in a constant state of change, and institutions must adjust to emerging conditions if they are to survive. If men are led to live in a world of myths, then they will be unable to see the rising forces which challenge them. In preventing the expression of new ideas, a society may be denying itself the new facts and new interpretations which it needs if it is to cope successfully with what the future holds. There is already some sign that intellectual decay has set in.

The dominant myths of a society may not be as dominant as it is thought. The reason for this weakened hold on the minds of men is that the ideology,

[32] *Ibid.*, p. 81.

by not having to defend itself against criticism, is living on capital. While men of power may be persuaded by their own rhetoric, they may soon discover that they are talking to no one but themselves.

> Instead of being, as at first, constantly on the alert either to defend themselves against the world, or to bring the world over to them, they have subsided into acquiescence, and neither listen, when they can help it, to arguments against their creed, nor trouble dissentients (if there be such) with arguments in its favour. From this time may usually be dated the decline in the living power of doctrine. We often hear the teachers of all creeds lamenting the difficulty of keeping up in the minds of believers a lively apprehension of the truth which they nominally recognise, so that it may penetrate the feelings, and acquire a real mastery over the conduct. No such difficulty is complained of while the creed is still fighting for its existence.[33]

There is a great deal of lamenting about the lack of public enthusiasm for the dominant myths. There is a renewed call for efforts at education, but what is meant is that the outdated ideology will be repeated once more.

The point is that the public has a good sense of social reality, and it is unimpressed with arguments which have small applicability to the world they know. The dominant myths may once have described society, but that society is now history. They may once have offered persuasive justifications for social practices, but those practices can no longer be defended by the old rhetoric. All this occurs because men of power have been more concerned to circulate ideology than they have to know the truth. They have found it expedient that only their interpretation of reality be given, but in preventing the free competition of ideas they have weakened the force of their own case. "The loss of so important an aid to the intelligent and living apprehension of a truth, as is afforded by the necessity of explaining it to, or defending it against opponents," Mill says, "though not sufficient to outweigh, is no trifling drawback from, the benefit of its universal recognition." [34] Indeed, universal recognition of a truth will last only so long as it is shown to be true. If speech is free, then all viewpoints will have to be explained and defended, and myths will not gain an easy acceptance. But this is all to the good, for a myth is a frail support on which to base the institutions of society. Mill advises men of power to look after their long-term interests and to see that the truth is their best weapon.

The argument for the social utility of free speech is an appealing one. The pursuit of truth is made to coincide with the enlightened pursuit of self-interest. Mill is making a number of assumptions here, and it would be well

[33] *Ibid.*, p. 100. For an example of what Mill is talking about, see William H. Whyte's analysis of American businessmen's abortive attempt to "sell" free enterprise to an uninterested public. *Is Anybody Listening?* (New York: Simon and Schuster, 1952).

[34] *On Liberty*, p. 103.

to bring them to light. First, he is saying that men can master the dialectic of history. He rejects the contention of Marx and Engels that ideas arise from interests and are bound to be half-truths so long as men have the stakes in society that they do. He believes that even individuals who have the ability to impose their ideology on their fellow men have the choice to refrain from doing this. Mill suggests further that institutions can adjust to new conditions in an orderly way and that a knowledge of the truth will facilitate this accommodation. The problem is that many individuals have done exceedingly well by encouraging ideology rather than truth. They have found that free speech is inconvenient for their purposes, and they prefer an open field in which to spread the facts and interpretations they would like known. Men such as this are not impressed with the argument that the long-term good of the whole society depends on the free expression of dangerous ideas. In fact, all that they can see are the short-term threats to themselves which would be unleashed by such talk. The obduracy of men of power has even greater consequences for the pursuit of truth when control over education and mass media is concentrated in a few hands. "Wrong opinions and practices gradually yield to fact and argument," Mill says. "But facts and arguments, to produce any effect on the mind, must be brought before it." [35] Recent history has amply shown that through the skillful use of propaganda and conditioning men may be brought to believe what they are taught to believe. And, rather than weakening a society, this can instill a loyalty and patriotism which imparts new strength. If certain facts and arguments are not permitted to be circulated, then a whole population can be given an image of reality which is consonant with the attainment of certain national goals. To be sure, there are limits to the use of mass media and propaganda.[36] There is no use, even if you have a monopoly of the communications facilities, in telling people that they are prosperous if unemployment and hunger exist before their eyes. Even myths may not violate reality to that great an extent. And it is best to play on sentiments which are already latent in individuals: national pride, social status, or the need for authority.

In the final analysis, Mill is trying to sell the idea of free speech by arguing on society's own terms. It may well be that men of power and members of the majority feel they are doing quite well by curbing unorthodox ideas. Whether they can be talked out of this conviction is problematical. And Mill seems to know this.

[35] *Ibid.*, p. 82.

[36] On the limits on persuasion by means of mass media, see Elihu Katz and Paul Lazarsfeld, *Personal Influence* (Glencoe: Free Press, 1955). On the techniques of propaganda and public relations, see Edward L. Bernays, ed., *The Engineering of Consent* (Norman: University of Oklahoma Press, 1955).

COMMON MEN AND UNCOMMON MEN

The impact of industrialization and the tendencies toward a mass society have been acknowledged by political theorists since the time of Rousseau. The fragmentation of labor, the unequal distribution of economic power, and the breakdown of the aristocratic order all impinge on political behavior in the modern world. And all recent theorists, with the exception of Marx and Engels, are of mixed feelings as to this development. While many features of traditional society are well got rid of, there remains the conviction that the stratified systems of the past were able to preserve political values which raised the quality of life for the entire community. Mill expresses this ambiguity of outlook in his dual loyalty to democratic government and individual liberty. And, like most of his predecessors, he sees very well the conditions which are effecting grave changes in the social structure and the human personality.

The circumstances which surround different classes and individuals, and shape their characters, are daily becoming more assimilated. Formerly, different ranks, different neighborhoods, different trades and professions, lived in what might be called different worlds; at present to a great degree in the same. Comparatively speaking, they now read the same things, listen to the same things, see the same things, go to the same places, have their hopes and fears directed to the same objects, have the same rights and liberties, and the same means of asserting them. Great as are the differences of position which remain, they are nothing to those which have ceased. And the assimilation is still proceeding.

All the political changes of the age promote it, since they all tend to raise the low and to lower the high. Every extension of education promotes it, because education brings people under common influences, and gives them access to the general stock of facts and sentiments. Improvement in the means of communication promotes it, by bringing the inhabitants of distant places into personal contact, and keeping up a rapid flow of changes of residence between one place and another. The increase of commerce and manufacturers promotes it, by diffusing more widely the advantages of easy circumstances, and opening all objects of ambition, even the highest, to general competition, whereby the desire of rising becomes no longer the character of a particular class, but of all classes.[37]

These changes affect everyone: no person and no class is immune to them. Yet they affect different people in different ways. Rousseau and Marx and Engels are concerned over the increasing alienation and powerlessness of the common man: as property-ownership becomes more centralized, the ordinary individual is compelled to submit to forces beyond his control and which he only dimly understands. His life becomes a commodity which he sells on a competitive market, and he has no choice but to do the bidding of an economic and political elite which monopolizes the effective power in society. If there is oppression, it is the oppression of a minority over the majority. Yet,

[37] *On Liberty*, pp. 130–131.

in viewing the same turn of events, Burke and Tocqueville come to quite different conclusions. To their minds the aristocratic order has lost its sources of power, and effective control is now in the hands of the majority. Their concern is with what is happening to the cultured minority, for these uncommon men can no longer command the deference of the man-in-the-street. The majority has become arrogant: it talks unceasingly of its rights and thinks nothing of its obligations. The age belongs to the common man, and his chief aim seems to be to draw those of superior taste and intellect down to his own level.

Mill accepts both the radical and the conservative critiques of mass society. For, rather than standing in contradiction to each other, both can be true.[38] The emerging conditions of society render each common man all the more powerless, and they give all the more power to the majority as an aggregate; these conditions threaten the status of certain minorities, and they give enhanced power to a new elite of uncommon men. And talk of majority tyranny must not be too facile. For if there is a tyranny at work, it is exercised not only over various nonconformists, but also over the members of the majority itself.

Indeed, Mill prefers to speak of society, and not simply the majority, as the tyrant.

When society is itself the tyrant—society collectively over the separate individuals who compose it—its means of tyrannizing are not restricted to the acts which it may do by the hands of its political functionaries. Society can and does execute its own mandates: and if it issues wrong mandates instead of right, or any mandates at all in things with which it ought not to meddle, it practices a social tyranny more formidable than many kinds of political oppression, since, though not usually upheld by such extreme penalties, it leaves far fewer means of escape, penetrating much more deeply into the details of life, and enslaving the soul itself.[39]

The souls which are enslaved are both common and uncommon. The common man devotes his efforts to evoking the approval of society: his social self comes to predominate over his individual self, and his potentialities for creativity and self-expression are never allowed to emerge. The uncommon man finds himself isolated and besieged by society: every pressure is exerted on him to conform to the thoughts and behavior sanctioned by society. "A large portion of the most active and inquiring intellects find it advisable to keep the general principles and grounds of their convictions within their own breasts," Mill says, "and attempt, in what they address to the public, to fit as much as they can of their conclusions to premises which they have internally renounced." [40]

[38] See William Kornhauser, *The Politics of Mass Society* (Glencoe: Free Press, 1959), pp. 21–38.
[39] *On Liberty*, p. 68.
[40] *Ibid.*, p. 93.

But how long can the uncommon man lead this secret life? Sooner or later many of them will, whether they realize it or not, give up their principles and convictions and will accept the values endorsed by society. For the uncommon man no longer has the power to withstand the subtle tyranny which is being inflicted on him by his neighbors.

Perhaps the best way to draw Mill's theory together is to distinguish the various sorts of uncommon men who can be observed in modern society:

There are first what may be called the "isolated rebels." These individuals are found throughout the length and breadth of society, and sometimes in the most unusual places. They are not confined to any single class, and at best it may be said that they appear at random. Some are perceptive thinkers, and others are neurotic crackpots. Some possess a shrewd but untutored wisdom, and others are people of learning and erudition. These individuals are the ones for whom Mill would guarantee freedom of speech and freedom from interference by society. Most frequently the isolated rebel is without protection: he may be the village atheist, the suburban nonjoiner, the organization radical. He is inwardly moved to think and act as he does, and yet society will not leave him alone. He is cajoled and tempted, threatened and even punished in an attempt to smooth his rough edges.

This uncommon man, more likely than not, lives in the midst of a society of common men, and for this reason the pressures at work on him are all the more apparent. Very frequently he has all the outward appearances of a common man, yet within his own heart and home he is quite different from those he seems at first glance to resemble. His problem is that his life is a constant battle against forces which greatly outnumber him. He is powerless, as all modern men are when taken singly, and yet he is unable to reap the advantages won by the collective power of the majority. For he prefers to stand alone, and he does not seek fellow-thinking allies, for usually there are none close to him. Indeed, the isolated rebel, if he is to be thought of as uncommon, is apt to be found standing by himself.[41] There are members of unconventional religious sects or political associations who live and work together, but these people rebel against society less out of convictions they develop for themselves and more because they were raised in a particular environment or are seeking fellowship—or even punishment—for its own sake. Society will not have many genuine rebels. But it is Mill's contention that every society needs them and that they ought to be tolerated, and even encouraged to think and act in their

---

[41] David Riesman discusses this sort of person in his analysis of the "inner-directed" man and the "self-directed" man. On the former, see *The Lonely Crowd* (New Haven: Yale University Press, 1950); on the latter, see "The Saving Remnant" in *Individualism Reconsidered* (Glencoe: Free Press, 1954), pp. 99–120.

unorthodox ways. That society is lacking in such tolerance and encouragement is one of the great problems of our time.

If the isolated rebel should be looked at as an autonomous individual, the
next type of uncommon man must be regarded in a somewhat different light.
For this person, who may be called a "tradition-bearer," is actually the member of the group which seeks to live by and preserve the values of civility.
These are individuals who are raised and educated in a certain tradition and
who have disciplined themselves to an understanding of the literary and
aesthetic heritage of their society. These bearers of a tradition are not, however, found at random throughout the social structure. On the contrary, they
are discovered in the upper and upper-middle classes: they have been raised
in homes sympathetic to civil values, they have gone to schools and universities where liberal learning is emphasized, and they live in an environment
where the life of culture is appreciated.

At one time these uncommon men were shielded by family wealth and
public deference. They could devote their formative years to the study of their
tradition because their economic position afforded them the opportunity to
do this. This class could support exclusive institutions of learning where the
values of civility were transmitted, and it could mark off an area of society
where these values might be preserved without depredations from those who
feared or failed to appreciate them. Out of the class structure grew deference:
uncommon men held an unquestioned authority in the eyes of the common
man. While the ordinary person might not understand what his betters were
doing, he nevertheless refrained from criticizing their way of life.

That such deference is necessary if the tradition is to be carried on is acknowledged by Mill. This is as true in the political sphere as it is in the cultural.
"No government," he says, ". . . ever did or could rise above mediocrity, except in so far as the sovereign Many have let themselves be guided (which in
their best times they have always done) by the counsels and influence of a
more highly gifted and instructed One or Few." [42] The gifts of which Mill
speaks are those of discipline and social responsibility, and these emerge only
from that class which knows and bears the tradition of the entire community.
It troubles Mill that this class no longer has the security that it once did: its
inherited wealth has ceased to have the power it once carried, and the public
has ceased to accord deference to its guidance. In short, these uncommon men
have lost not only their power but also the freedom which went with it. The
assumption is that this class had power and freedom not for their own sakes,
but because they were able to use these gifts to carry on traditional values and
hence improve all of society.

[42] *On Liberty*, p. 124.

It is by no means easy to be a tradition-bearer without wealth of one's own. This is especially so when the majority of society is uninterested in what the tradition has to offer. For the power of the common man can be seen in sharpest focus as it is used to deny to uncommon men the cultural sustenance they so sorely need. "The evil is, that individual spontaneity is hardly recognized by the common modes of thinking as on its own account . . ." Mill says. "Originality is the one thing which unoriginal minds cannot feel the use of. . . . In sober truth, whatever homage may be professed, or even paid, to real or supposed mental superiority, the general tendency of things throughout the world is to render mediocrity the ascendant power among mankind." [43]

Majority rule is operative in culture and politics: each man has one vote, and a television comedy outvotes *Titus Andronicus*. If the common man ceases to be humble, then the only shield for uncommon men is wealth. If the uncommon man is not rich, then he will be denied the cultural food he needs to survive. Indeed, he will be forced to pander to society's whims to earn his own livelihood, and it is likely that he will sooner or later discard the values he cherished and will accept those of the majority. The most crushing blow of all will be that he will devote his talents to celebrating mediocrity and to persuading others—and himself—that the taste exhibited by society is really not so bad after all.

There are, finally, uncommon men who do well out of the growth of democratic politics and mass society. These are neither isolated rebels nor tradition-bearers, although some of them may be suppressing the impulse to rebellion or the fondness for tradition which resides in their breasts. This group of men, and they may be approached either as individuals or as a group, are Hegel's heroes or Machiavelli's elite. They are uncommon because they have the qualities which make for success in the modern world. On the whole, their origins and education are comparatively humble, or at least they are compared to those of the exclusive class which hitherto ruled. This new elite has the ability to give the majority the kind of leadership they want. If political power must rest on popular elections, then a political elite will present such an appearance that voters will give them their confidence.

"The mass do not now take their opinions from dignitaries in Church or State, from ostensible leaders, or from books," Mill says. "Their thinking is done for them by men much like themselves, addressing them or speaking in their name, on the spur of the moment." [44] It would be better, however, to say that while the elite leader looks much like his followers, in reality he is a

---

[43] *Ibid.*, pp. 115, 123.
[44] *Ibid.*, p. 124.

superior man. Whether he is a Lion or a Fox, he senses the political needs of a society and bends his efforts toward satisfying them. If the majority calls for a leader who has a touch of the common man about him, then someone will emerge to play that role for them. If they want a leader of patrician mien or a figure of charismatic authority, then he too will present himself. The point is that the uncommon men who rise to power do so because they know how to please a democratic constituency. They can take the latent sentiments of a society and channel them into political programs; they can sense when the public wants to be told what to do and are willing to issue commands. No democratic leader can be far ahead of his following, but the best are always a few steps in front of it. This political elite, furthermore, has an area of discretion in which to act, for the majority will often give it a free hand to govern as it sees fit. That these men have uncommon talents should be obvious. Earlier leaders, depending on the deference of the common man, could secure obedience fairly effortlessly. The new men of power must work at their job, for they can never be sure that the consent they obtain one day will be accorded to them the next.

As economic power becomes more concentrated, there emerges an elite, a group of uncommon men who administer the giant organizations which produce wealth and provide employment. These individuals gain their power not from the consent of the majority, but by rising through the managerial hierarchies. Their talents are directed to the task of making and executing decisions, and only seldom are these men known to the general public. Yet they are men of uncommon power—power to decide how the common man will live his life and what directions the society itself will move. By and large the political and economic elites are different in composition, the members of each possessing varying backgrounds and aptitudes. If democratic political leaders tend to be Lions, the economic leaders in more advanced stages of industrialization tend to be Foxes. For the uncommon administrator gets where he does by being coopted by his superiors, not by popular election.

But these new men of power have one attribute in common, and it is one that disturbs a theorist like Mill. Both the political and economic elites in modern society feel little sense of responsibility toward the tradition of civility which was borne by the class they are replacing. They see no obligation on their part to promote culture or to safeguard freedom. It is no job of theirs to protect the isolated rebel or to encourage tolerance in the majority. Indeed, the orientation of the new elites is to their personal careers and to the organizations which give them their power. They have not been brought up to think in terms of social responsibility or political liberty, and as individuals they can ill afford to risk their positions by undertaking such an outlook. This new approach to the role of leadership concerned Tocqueville, and it dismays Mill as well. There is not much point in exhorting these men of power to define their responsibilities more broadly, for they are not shielded from public disapproval by any veil of deference. These uncommon men have done well out of the present, but they have succeeded because they have played the game of power on society's own terms.

The problem of freedom is too often viewed as a metaphysical abstraction. If freedom is to be considered politically, then it must always be discussed in the context of power. Men can only be free if they possess the power to ensure this condition for themselves. Men without power have invariably been vulnerable to tyranny and oppression.

And the key questions having to do with power deal with its distribution in society. Is power to be in the hands of the few or of the many? If the former, which of the various and competing minorities in a community will win out in the struggle for dominance? If the latter, how is majority power to be expressed and through which agencies will its sentiment be crystallized? These matters have concerned every serious writer from Plato through Mill, and the substantive problems they wrestled with are still among us. For it follows that if power is distributed in one way, then some men will be free while others are not. If it is distributed in another way, then the blessings of a free life will be known by quite different groups in society.

Mill's abiding concern is with the isolated rebel in society: the lonely person who stands by himself in the face of society's opposition. "If all mankind minus one were of one opinion, and only one person were of the contrary opinion, mankind would be no more justified in silencing that one person, than he, if he had the power, would be justified in silencing mankind . . ." This heretic is entitled to his freedom of expression, but his difficulty lies in the fact that his isolation renders him virtually powerless. Consequently he can only enjoy the free life as he seeks to define it if the rest of society agrees to tolerate him and to regard his heresies as an annoyance they are willing to put up with. There are, Mill sadly acknowledges, no effective ways of endowing the isolated rebels with the political power to protect themselves. They are a scattered minority and consequently vulnerable to majority sanctions. He can only plead with the majority to be tolerant and try to demonstrate that all of society will benefit in the course of time if the heretic is given a hearing. Constitutional protections—if they are written into the basic law of a state—will often place the power of the government behind the isolated rebel. This is why documents like a Bill of Rights are considered as being vital to the maintenance of a free society. Yet such legal bulwarks cannot prevent the social and economic victimization of heretics, and the experience has been that protections of this character are more effective for minority groups than they are for isolated rebels. Indeed, in the final analysis, even the strength of constitutional guarantees lies in the majority's willingness to endure the inconvenience of putting up with heretics of various shades.

Edmund Burke could not find it in himself to shed many tears over the oppressive treatment meted out to isolated rebels. But he was concerned to protect that class in society which assumes the obligation of transmitting the tradition of civility. What interested Burke were "our manners, our civilization, and all the good things which are connected with manners and civilization." What needs to be encouraged, he went on, is "the spirit of a gentleman." And it was Burke's feeling that only if dominant political power was actually in the hands of a hereditary ruling class would this spirit be maintained. For society to possess and transmit the tradition of civility, then, there is no other solution than to give power to the minority which bears this tradition. This class is quite candidly aristocratic, and Tocqueville joined Burke in saying that only an aristocracy could provide the environment in which these higher values would flourish. "Do you wish to give a certain elevation to the human mind . . . ?" Tocqueville asked. "Is it your object to refine the habits, embellish the manners, and cultivate the arts; to promote the love of poetry, beauty, and glory?" If these are important goals for a society, then power must be bestowed on the few who are capable of sustaining these values. But such a class can only maintain power if it is accorded unquestioning deference by the vast majority of men. Burke suggested that the bearers of the tradition of civility would have to employ certain controls if they were to carry on the heritage of freedom with any degree of effectiveness. These controls included the unequal distribution of property, a stress on religion with its prospect of an afterlife, and the promotion of prejudice and popular ignorance. Tocqueville wondered whether even these controls would be sufficient in an age of equalitarian sentiment and material affluence. (Marx and Engels clearly thought they would be inadequate in the face of industrialization and the rise of class consciousness.) And Mill was none too sympathetic towards the premeditated promotion of ignorance and prejudice as a means of holding the majority in check.

At all events, the tradition-bearers of a society can only maintain the free life as they elect to conceive of it if they have a source of power. Like the isolated rebels they are vulnerable to majority oppression, for the majority cares about as much for the heritage of civility as it does for the nuisances of heresy. The basis of power of the bearers of the civil tradition is weaker in our time than it has ever before been, and in consequence the freedom of those who would live according to the spirit of a gentleman grows increasingly constricted. Whether the majority can be brought once again to defer to a class they cannot easily identify with, whether they will continue to tolerate a conception of freedom they but dimly appreciate—these are open questions which only the future can answer. Tocqueville began his book on America by saying that "the first of the duties that are at this time imposed upon those who direct our affairs is to educate democracy . . ."; and he closed by asking that we "look forward to the future with that salutary fear which makes men keep watch and ward for freedom." This, certainly, must be the outlook for all who cherish both the tradition of civility and the freedom of those who would sustain it.

Ours is increasingly an age of majority power and this means that the majority will secure to itself the freedom it wants. Perhaps Machiavelli was oversimplifying when he said that the people ask "nothing more than not to be oppressed." It may well be that this is what freedom means to the vast majority of men. However, Hegel was surely right in pointing out that freedom for the common man also entails his expression of national pride; and Rousseau was no less correct in saying that most men desire the sense of participating in the process of self-government. Yet it must never be forgotten that throughout history tyranny and oppression have been the lot of most men in most times. The ruling minorities may have been political autocrats or economic exploiters or colonial overlords or some combination of these. The fact remains, nevertheless, that the majority is mistrustful of minority power. This is one reason why the class which has carried the tradition of civility is so subjected to attack. To the majority, this class is identified with minority privilege and irresponsible power. It also gives some indication of why the majority is intolerant of the isolated rebels in society. Deviations from popular orthodoxy are seen as subverting the principle of majority rule. If the voice of the people is to direct political policy, then the odds are high that the freedoms enjoyed by privileged minorities will be curtailed. Indeed, it may be said that the majority feels less secure, and consequently less free, if these minorities are allowed to pursue their inclinations unfettered. This is not to say, of course, that all instances of majority rule bring in their wake majority tyranny. Especially in more mature nations the people have frequently displayed an admirable self-restraint even though they had the power to oppress minorities. But in new democracies—and in times of crisis in old ones—the fear of such oppression is not altogether unwarranted. The power of the majority is, in sum, the power of organized numbers. And no minority class in our day can challenge this power for long.

But if the majority is organized, then someone must do the organizing. What Mill preferred was that the common man would be "guided by the counsels and influence" of those uncommon men among him who are "more highly gifted and instructed." If there was to be democracy at all he wanted it to be a deferential democracy, with the majority according deference to the superior individuals in their midst. (There is even some indication of this way of thinking in Marx and Engels when they speak of the role of the "bourgeois ideologists" who defect to the proletarian movement. Presumably these intellectuals were to assume leadership of the working-class revolution and would subsequently be the architects of the socialist dictatorship.) But the majority disappointed Mill by stolidly ignoring the counsels of the men who are prepared to maintain the tradition of civility and who would encourage the toleration of heretics. The leaders selected by the majority, Mill said, were "men much like themselves", and the members of these elites are prepared to accommodate themselves to majority sentiment. "The leaders choose to make themselves bidders at an auction of popularity," Burke had said. "They . . . become flatterers instead of legislators; and instruments, not the guides of the people." Yet this analysis of democratic leadership is too simple. We are dealing, as Burke acknowledged, with "new power in new persons", and the elites in question are indeed men of substantial power. In return for flattering the majority and for providing it with its material and psychic gratification, these political and economic elites gain for themselves great areas of freedom. And these elites are, as Machiavelli was prepared to grant, uncommon men—even if, in the eyes of writers like Burke and Tocqueville and Mill, they were the wrong kind of uncommon men.

There is increasing evidence, furthermore, that majority power and majority freedom are meaningful only when the majority of men is considered as an undifferentiated mass. The majority, when it is viewed as a number of individuals, is composed of isolated men and women—although few of them are rebels in the traditional sense—and they are compelled to emphasize their social selves at the expense of whatever individuality they may have. Majority power and elite rule, therefore, do not stand in contradiction to each other. A majority may be powerful when it is considered as an aggregate, but its constituent members can simultaneously be alienated and powerless. A majority can threaten the freedom of minorities, but the freedom its own members experience can apply to their collective interests rather than to them as individuals. The new elites, as Machiavelli again and again warned, must respond to the expressed wants and the unexpressed needs of the people they lead. But in so doing they acquire substantial freedom of action for themselves. And this freedom brings with it the power to direct the lives of ordinary men and women.

There is, then, much unfinished business in political theory. A theory of freedom must be constructed which will harmonize with the facts of power.

A theory of equality must be developed which will accord with the realities of elite rule. And a theory of democracy must be written which will accommodate the aspirations of autonomous individuals. The theorists of the Western tradition have given us the beginnings we need. But political science and political philosophy have a long road to travel before we fully comprehend human behavior and reach agreement on the principles of the good society. This further quest for scientific and philosophical knowledge is the task which confronts all those who would add to our understanding of the political life.

List of Authors
Cited in Footnotes

611